A JUDICIAL BIOGRAPHY

William Wayne Justice

Photo by John Katz, Dallas

WILLIAM WAYNE
JUSTICE

A Judicial Biography

By Frank R. Kemerer

UNIVERSITY OF TEXAS PRESS, AUSTIN

First edition, 1991

Requests for permission to reproduce material from this work should be
sent to Permissions, University of Texas Press, Box 7819, Austin, TX
78713-7819.

∞ The paper used in this publication meets the minimum requirements
of American National Standard for Information Sciences—Permanence of
Paper for Printed Library Materials, ANSI Z39.48-1984.

Library of Congress Cataloging-in-Publication Data

Kemerer, Frank R.
    William Wayne Justice : a judicial biography / by Frank R.
Kemerer. — 1st ed.
        p.   cm.
    Includes bibliographical references and indexes.
    ISBN 0-292-79066-X
    1. Justice, William Wayne, 1920–   .   2. Judges—Texas—
Biography.   3. Judges—United States—Biography.   4. Political
questions and judicial power—Texas.   5. Political questions and
judicial power—United States.   I. Title.
KF373.J87K46   1991
347.73'14'092—dc20
[B]
[347.30714092]
[B]   91-11743
                                                            CIP

For Barbie, whose support and encouragement were instrumental to the completion of this book.

Contents

Maps

Photographs following page 111

Preface

"Now about this proposed biography," Judge Justice said, looking intently at me from behind his big desk, "I have some reservations." I knew that my luck had been too good to last. I had been surprised when he accepted my invitation to be the featured luncheon speaker several weeks before at an education law conference I had arranged in Dallas. I had heard that he rarely ventured outside of Tyler, and, indeed, he had declined an earlier invitation. I was even more surprised when he agreed to think about the idea of a biography which I proposed to him following his speech. "I would like to leave a legacy," he had mused.

I had arranged to meet him on Saturday, January 4, 1986, in his Tyler chambers. I sent some of my previous publications for him to look over before the visit. His secretary, Marcelle Simmons, assured me on the telephone that the Judge would not at all mind meeting me on a Saturday. That was about the only time he had available. "I don't want to interrupt his weekend," I told her. "Oh, you won't be," she said. "He often comes to the courthouse on week-ends." So it had been arranged. I would park behind the post office and call him from a pay phone. He would come down from his office to unlock the courthouse doors.

I found the courthouse and parked my car where I was told. I called him at the appointed time from the dingy downtown bus station. After several rings, he answered. He met me at the courthouse doors. From there, we walked up three flights of stairs to his chambers. He made coffee in the small study adjacent to his office, chatting amiably. He asked about my drive over from Denton. Did I have a family? I told him I had a wife and two children. He wanted to know their ages, where they were in school. I answered his questions quickly, gaining confidence and becoming more at ease as we talked. I had met him only once before, at the Dallas conference, and was nervous about being in his company.

Like everyone else in Texas, I had read and heard much about William Wayne Justice, Chief Judge, U.S. District Court for the Eastern District of Texas. While studying and teaching constitutional law and civil liberties in other states, I had encountered some of his rulings and knew him to be one of a handful of liberal activist federal judges enmeshed in institutional reform litigation. But it wasn't until I moved to Texas in 1978 to teach education law that I began to realize the full impact of his work. By the mid-1980s, he had issued comprehensive reform orders on statewide school desegregation, incarceration of juvenile delinquents in state institutions, the teaching of bilingual education in public schools, the operation of state prisons, and the care of institutionalized mentally retarded persons. In addition, he had been involved in landmark voter discrimination litigation and had ordered a tuition-free public education for undocumented alien children. The landmark decisions had generated considerable publicity. Feature articles about them and about him were appearing in such publications as *Texas Monthly, Newsweek, Life,* the *Washington Post,* and the *New York Times.*

Not surprisingly, a great many Texans viewed William Wayne Justice negatively. It was said that he was the most hated man in Texas, the Antichrist of Smith County, an egomaniac caught up in the power of the federal district court judge. When Attorney General Edwin Meese and other Reagan administration officials railed against excesses of activist judges, they were obviously talking about judges of his genre. But others regarded Judge Justice as a giant in the civil liberties field. One journalist noted that he was a sort of "dashboard Jesus" to liberals and minorities in a state which cared little for either. Given the controversy swirling about his court and the obvious impact of his decisions on Texas and national life, I concluded that writing his biography would be a very interesting and worthwhile project.

Here I was, alone in the presence of one of the most powerful persons in Texas. As he puttered about the small kitchenette, he seemed innocuous enough. I began to relax. He gave me a lengthy tour around his offices, carefully explaining how the court was laid out. We saw the lockup area where prisoners were stationed before appearing in court for their trials. He showed the security office, with its bank of television monitors and electronic gadgetry. We toured the spacious courtroom and the adjacent jury room. As he moved through the complex of offices and rooms, it was obvious that he had given this tour many times. He clearly was enjoying showing off the seat of his power.

Now back in his spacious office, with Justice in the big leather chair behind his desk and myself seated in one of the blue captain's chairs in front of it, I realized that I might have to be content with an hour of conversation and a tour of the court. I asked him about his reservations. "While I don't want to appear overly modest," he replied, "I really don't think my somewhat colorless background and lifestyle would be sufficiently interesting to be worthy of a biography."

I was incredulous. But then I realized that he was missing the main purpose of the study. I explained to him that I planned to focus as much or more on his decisions as on his personal life. In effect, I said, I was proposing a *judicial* biography. "Most people don't know much about the decisions you have rendered," I explained. "They only know you are a person they are supposed to dislike." I told him that, whether he wished it or not, he had become an important figure in Texas contemporary affairs and that I thought his decisions and the jurisprudence behind them were important for people to understand. Additionally, while there were biographies on federal appellate judges including various members of the U.S. Supreme Court, there were hardly any on federal district court judges. Consequently, few outside of the legal profession know what a federal district court judge does.

The idea of a judicial biography caught his attention. I could see that he was intrigued. He leaned back in his chair, a smile coming to his lips. "Well, now, that sheds a different light on things," he said slowly. "If the book will focus on my decisions, then I have no reservations other than the amount of time I will have available to work with you." He added, "I'm not worried about my decisions. They will stand on their own merits." I had cleared the first of two major hurdles before I could begin what I thought would be a two-year project. It turned out to take five.

The second came when we met in his chambers again several weeks later, this time on a Sunday. As before, he made coffee in the study and talked informally as he opened the mail that had come in over the weekend. Once we had taken our accustomed places in his office, I talked over how I planned to go about researching the book. I wanted a list of his law clerks and his major decisions. No problem on either count. Marcelle Simmons could supply the list of clerks, and he would loan me his set of bound volumes, courtesy of the West Publishing Company, containing most of his published decisions. For unpublished material, I planned to review the civil and criminal order books in the clerks' offices at the various divisions of the Eastern District. I asked for access to his private correspondence. "Outside of the business of the court, I don't really have any," he observed. "I'm not much of a writer." This made the next question I was about to raise all the more important.

"Judge," I said, "I know how reluctant you are to be quoted directly. But you are the only source for much of the information I want to include in the biography." I explained that I anticipated many hours of interviews and—this was the sensitive part—that it would be of great help to me if he would consent to let me tape-record them. Justice turned his high-back chair nearly all the way around and looked out the windows behind his desk. He said nothing. I knew this would not be an easy decision for him to make. But I desperately needed to be freed from the arduous task of notetaking and wanted to enrich the biography with direct quotations. It seemed like minutes before he responded. Without looking directly at me, he nodded ever so slightly. The second hurdle had been crossed.

The book is divided into two sections, the first focusing on William Wayne Justice as a person and the second on the decisions he has rendered. The first three chapters in the first section examine Justice's life before he became a federal judge. I have opted to include numerous quotations from our interviews in these chapters, thus giving them a conversational tone. Letting the Judge describe events in his own words enlivens the discussion and provides insight into his personality. Like everyone who is directly quoted in the book, the Judge has executed an authorization agreement allowing use of these statements, a requirement of the University of Texas Press. Other than his direct quotations, he has not had access to the manuscript. The fourth and final chapter in the first section describes Justice's activities as a judge, his early falling-out with Tyler society, and his judicial philosophy. It is a transitional chapter between the first and second sections of the book.

The much longer second section is devoted to the decisions he has handed down in over twenty years on the federal bench. In most of the chapters in this section, the focus is on a single major decision per chapter. The background of each case is presented, followed by Justice's decision, reactions to it, and some assessment of the decision's impact. Four chapters focus on groups of cases to illustrate the Judge's noteworthy decisions in the areas of voter discrimination, First Amendment rights, rights of the accused, and employment. In addition to extensive commentary from the Judge, all the chapters in this section also contain commentary from selected key figures associated with the litigation. I have interviewed well over a hundred people in preparing the manuscript, including nearly all of Justice's law clerks, and have intensively reviewed court records associated with the cases. Only the threat of making each chapter a book in its own right has forced curtailment of additional research. A complete list of all the cases referenced in the book is contained in an index. A list of all Judge Justice's law clerks is included in an appendix.

My goal in this second section is to describe the important rulings and the jurisprudence behind them. Judgment about the wisdom of Justice's decisions is, for the most part, left to the reader. The final chapter presents a reconsideration of the Judge's judicial approach. Throughout, I have tried to present the material objectively, keeping my own commentary to a minimum. To grasp the full significance of the complexity of judging, I suggest readers put themselves in the position of Judge Justice. What would they have done had they been faced with these cases and the duty to decide them? How would their decisions fit within an overall judicial philosophy? Assuming the position of the Judge will assist readers to comprehend the complex nature of judicial decision-making at the trial court level and gain insight into the continuing debate about the proper role of the federal judiciary.

Numerous individuals have assisted in the preparation of this book. I am indebted to Justice's former law clerks Richard Mithoff, Marianne Wesson, Fritz Byers, Robert McDuff, Susan Stefan, James L. Sultan, Audrey Selden, Roger Parloff, and David Brown for reading early chapter drafts. Other reviewers of early drafts include Austin attorneys Creekmore Fath and Eric Schulze; University of Chicago Professor Gary Orfield; Lehigh University Professor Perry Zirkel; University of Texas Professors Michael Churgin of the School of Law and Richard Schott of the LBJ School of Public Affairs; and my colleagues Gerald Ponder, Clovis Morrisson, Roosevelt Washington, Ruskin Teeter, and Judy Adkison. A number of persons involved in the cases themselves also contributed valuable suggestions with regard to early drafts. Included among them are Steve Martin, Gilbert Conoley, Alexandra Buek, David Richards, Richard Arnett, Gail Littlefield, and William Bennett Turner.

Two individuals deserve special recognition for reading through all of the chapters in the interest of providing the perspective of the educated layperson. My University of North Texas colleague Richard Simms and my father-in-law Hack Kellner were asked to be candid in their appraisal, and they willingly provided invaluable commentary on how the material might be better presented so that the general reader could understand it.

My research assistants rendered much welcomed help in the preparation of portions of the manuscript. Ann Gill worked on chapters on incarcerated juveniles, care of mentally retarded persons, and segregated public housing while a student at the University of Texas School of Law. Allan Cook, who later enrolled in Northeastern School of Law in Boston, spent over a year researching and drafting material on prison reform. Pat Peters spent many hours transcribing taped interviews, reading early chapter drafts, and engaging in library research. My secretary, Sandy Behrens, also spent hours running off countless updated drafts on the word processor, as well as sorting through the mass of newspaper clippings we received from cooperative editors and publishers from across the state. I am especially indebted to Nelson Clyde of the *Tyler Courier-Times* and *Morning Telegraph* for assembling a mass of materials going back over thirty years.

Judge Justice's court staff made me feel welcome from the first time I met them. Secretaries Marcelle Simmons, Debra Magee, and Evelyn Armstrong rendered help in many ways. Judge Justice's long-time deputy court clerk

Joyce Almaraz and courtroom reporter Dorothy Daugherty readily recalled the names and dates of long past cases and litigants. I am also indebted to Doris Stanley and Sandi Sutherland, federal district court clerks in Tyler and Sherman, respectively, who provided access to unpublished orders and opinions over the duration of this project. Officials at the Federal Record Center in Fort Worth also were helpful in providing access to court records of closed cases, as were those at various courthouses and law libraries throughout the state.

The University of North Texas graciously provided me with a sabbatical to launch the project in 1986 and has assisted me ever since. Additional financial support was provided by individual donors and by an anonymous Texas foundation. I am especially indebted to Judge Joe Tunnell of the District Court of Smith County, 241st Judicial District of Texas, for his assistance in securing financial support.

Finally, I want to thank all of the persons who consented to meet with me and share their thoughts about Judge Justice and about the litigation coming before him. While only those persons who have been directly cited are listed in the reference section, the comments of many others have been instrumental in the preparation of this manuscript. Among those interviewed but not quoted directly are family members and friends; former associates and law clerks; and lawyers, judges, and public officials across the state. The vast majority I sought to talk with cooperated willingly and graciously. I had anticipated considerable difficulty in this direction and found very little. A few agreed to speak on condition of anonymity. Only a handful refused to cooperate under any circumstances.

Special thanks must go to the Judge himself. Over the duration of this project, he willingly accommodated my requests for extensive interview time and documentary material. True to his character, he has been open and candid in his comments, rarely asking that some matters be kept off the record. His commentary infinitely enriches the manuscript.

William Wayne Justice is an extremely controversial judge. As a result, this book cannot avoid being controversial as well. Some will regard it as overly supportive of the Judge, while others will find it not supportive enough. Some will charge that too much space has been devoted to the cases, while others will assert that the case discussions leave out important details. I fully shoulder the responsibility for the book's shortcomings. My hope is that readers will find this book not only enlightening regarding Judge Justice and his judicial career, but also helpful in pondering contentions regarding the proper role of the federal judiciary in contemporary American affairs.

PART ONE

The Judge and His Court

CHAPTER 1

The Early Years

In 1927, when William Wayne Justice was seven years old, Will Justice, his father, put his son's name on the law office door. From that day on, Wayne Justice knew he was going to be a lawyer. "I never seriously questioned the idea," he asserts without hesitation. Other boys went hunting and fishing with their fathers. Wayne Justice went to the law office and the court. There he watched his father, a tough, flamboyant criminal lawyer, practice his profession. The values and lessons he learned from his father were later reflected in the son's work as an attorney and as a judge on the federal bench. Without question, the single most significant influence on William Wayne Justice was Will Justice.

Jackie May Justice, Wayne's mother, tended to her son's early upbringing. A sweet and gentle person, she offered him companionship, nursed him through a series of childhood illnesses, and encouraged his early interest in reading. Her legacy to her son was a shy, somewhat formal personality and a strong humanitarian instinct.

The product of two significantly different people, the only son of Will and Jackie Justice would one day as a federal judge become perhaps the single most influential agent for change in twentieth-century Texas history. Through a series of momentous judicial decisions, his influence would sweep across the Texas landscape far beyond the geographic boundaries of his court and out into the nation.

William Wayne Justice—Wayne to old friends and acquaintances—comes from a family whose roots lie deep in the Confederacy on his father's side and in Norway on his mother's side. Three great-uncles served in the Confederate Army during the Civil War, one receiving a posthumous decoration for bravery. After the ruin effected by the war, his paternal family moved to Texas from

Alabama, where the family had owned considerable land. His father, William Davis Justice, was born on August 18, 1882, in Wills Point, Van Zandt County, Texas, one of six children. Though of slight build, Will was combative from the start. A nose made crooked by an early break made him the target of childhood teasing. As a consequence, he had many fistfights in his youth. Will had black hair and eyes a penetrating deep brown from his mother's Cherokee ancestry. Years later as a trial attorney, he used those eyes to full effect in the courtroom.

After brief attendance at the University of Texas at Austin, Will held a number of jobs ranging from dynamite blaster to California ranch hand. Eventually, he settled into the teaching profession. He taught in several towns before becoming principal of the high school in Chandler, a small East Texas town in Henderson County. While there, he boarded at the home of the school board president, a prominent member of the community named Charles Richard Yarborough. One of his children was Ralph Yarborough, who became a close friend of the Justice family and later as U.S. Senator was instrumental in placing Will's son on the bench.

After serving as principal of Chandler High School, Will Justice became a school principal in the town of Cushing in Nacogdoches County, where he met Wayne's mother, Jackie May Hanson, also a teacher. Jackie May's family had originated in Norway. Blonde, blue-eyed, and reserved, she provided a striking contrast to Will. The Hansons had emigrated to Brownsboro, Texas, then called Normandy, in 1854. Wayne's maternal grandfather, Theodore Webster (Ed) Hanson, married Wilce Idella (Della) Rogers, and they had ten children. One of the nine who survived was Jackie May, born on January 7, 1891. The Hansons operated a cotton gin in the Pine Grove Community about four miles south of Athens. Jackie May was closely tied to her sisters and her parents, who would serve as her primary social contacts all her life.

She and Will Justice were married in November 1910 in Fort Worth. After working a short time in the Quitaque school district in West Texas, the couple moved to Athens, thirty-five miles west of Tyler and the county seat of Henderson County, where Will became principal of the Athens High School. There, Jackie May gave birth in 1912 to their first child, a girl named Ava Inez. Later, they moved to Poyner, another East Texas town about twenty miles away, to teach. There the baby contracted diphtheria and died before the doctor could arrive. Years later, Wayne recalls that his father, by then a hard-bitten trial lawyer, would weep when recalling how he walked back and forth on the porch outside the little girl's bedroom, listening to her choking for breath.

During his time as principal in Chandler, Will had developed an interest in the law. When school was not in session, he worked at the Johnson and

Edwards law firm in Tyler. He was attracted to the courtroom, where he often watched the lawyers in action. Eventually, he received his law degree through a LaSalle extension course. Wayne still prizes some of his father's old lawbooks.

After passing the bar exam in 1913, Will moved back to Athens from Poyner and ran for Henderson County attorney. Drawing on his unique ability to sway an audience, Justice beat his well-heeled opponent. Despite his lack of legal experience, Will was a very successful county attorney, with a long record of convictions during the two-year term.

In 1924, Will ran a successful race for district attorney of the Third Judicial District, encompassing Henderson, Anderson, and Houston counties. A deadly prosecutor, Will Justice sent a number of men to the electric chair. He later said he had tried 155 jury cases during his two years as district attorney and had won convictions in 147 of them. Finding the job stressful and not very lucrative, Will did not seek reelection. Instead, he settled into private law practice in Athens, where he quickly established a reputation throughout East Texas as an outstanding trial lawyer, especially in criminal cases. Occasionally he was hired as a special prosecutor, with equal success. It was said that in East Texas there was no justice but Will Justice.

It was into this world that William Wayne Justice was born on February 25, 1920. Because of the death of their first child, the Justices were overly protective of their son during his early years. "If I showed signs of any kind of illness, they'd get a doctor," Wayne points out. "They were frightened to death, I guess, that they might lose their other offspring. They were very, very kind to me. Throughout my whole life, I was blessed with parents who were extraordinarily kind."

Wayne Justice lived most of his early years in the company of his mother. Will Justice, like a great many other men of that generation, was almost completely involved in his work, spending many evenings and even whole nights—as well as days—in his office or out interviewing clients and witnesses. Jackie May Justice, as was to be expected in this very traditional household, cared for her one remaining child diligently. At age four, Wayne came down with whooping cough, first diagnosed as malaria, and spent six weeks in Baylor Hospital in Dallas. "In those days, if you were sent to a hospital, that meant you were in extremis," he observes. He attributes his slight stoop to that illness. From that time on, he had a number of childhood illnesses, including three bouts of pneumonia. Jackie May was determined that her second child would not suffer the fate of her first, and nursed him through illness after illness. "She was always trying to get me to eat," Wayne recalls. "She would even let me eat sweets if I wouldn't eat anything else."

Jackie May Justice often elicited the help of Elvin Lamb, who lived across the street and was two years older than Wayne, to watch out for him. Among other things, Elvin was to help "Billy Wayne," as he was known then, keep his shoes on. Wayne remembers the Lambs well, especially Elvin's brother Donald, who once shot him in the buttocks with an air rifle over a brief childhood feud. Since the Lamb family had six children, Wayne, an only child, gravitated toward their yard, where there was always a lot of activity. Elvin Lamb jokingly says that he has to take some of the credit for teaching Wayne how to read. Mrs. Justice used to give a dime to each of the three boys—Elvin, Donald, and her son Wayne—and send them to the picture show on Saturday afternoon. As the oldest, Elvin read the subtitles of the silent movies to his brother and Wayne. The young boys often went out to the Hanson farm on weekends to play in the cotton gin and to ride bareback on several antiquated mules. Mr. Lamb was employed to pump water from a pond for steam locomotives operated by the Cotton Belt Railway. One day Donald and Wayne went to the pond to fish. They caught several small perch, which they cleaned and fried in an old iron skillet. "Billy Wayne told his parents that we had cooked and ate those fish 'without any salt or soder'—he meant soda," Donald says.

Sickly though he was, Wayne was not sick enough to avoid school. He enrolled in first grade in the Athens Grammar School in September 1926 and progressed normally through the elementary grades. But the illnesses persisted. In fourth grade, he missed eight weeks of school. It was recommended that his tonsils be removed. Worried at the possibility of losing his second child, Will Justice resisted. But finally Wayne was taken to Baylor Hospital for the operation. After that, he rarely missed any school.

The effect of his childhood illnesses compounded by an often absent father and a protective mother resulted in a shy boy who was physically underdeveloped. He sought to overcome his physical deficiency by riding a bicycle his father had given him when he was eight or nine years old. Bicycle riding not only improved his health; it also expanded his world. He used it to explore all of Athens and to range far and wide through the surrounding countryside. The terrain he saw was just outside the piney woods of East Texas. It was mostly farmland dotted with clumps of oak, some bois d'arc, cottonwood, and pine. Cotton was still king, though no longer profitable. Athens itself was then a town of five thousand residents, 25 percent black. People of means lived on Tyler Street. But aside from bankers and a few professional people, most of the citizens of Athens, both black and white, were of moderate means or poor.

Athens has not grown much over the years; the population today is about ten thousand. In the middle of the square the county courthouse, built in 1913, is still standing. In the 1920s the streets leading off the square were paved with brick for about a block in each direction. Tyler Street, which ran through the silk-stocking district, was paved all the way to the city limits. When Wayne was born, water was the only public utility. Since no city sewer system existed until the mid-1920s, people had outhouses. Pages of old Sears catalogues sufficed as toilet paper in many of these facilities. For the Justices, discarded advance sheets of the *Southwestern Reporter,* a legal publication, served the purpose.

Like other southern towns, Athens was rigidly segregated by law and custom. Black residents lived in the north section of town, attended their own schools, and ventured into white neighborhoods only to work as laborers or domestics. Like other white families of some means in Athens, the Justices employed blacks as domestics.

Early influences outside his home were beginning to shape Wayne Justice's outlook on the world. Included among them were his teachers. He remembers with particular fondness Mrs. Tillman Owen, who taught him fifth- and sixth-grade history. "She made it so real, her eyes glistened when she talked about the American Revolution. That's probably where I first got interested in the concept of tyranny when we studied about King George and Lord North." Mrs. Owen told a reporter some years ago that she remembered Wayne as a keen student with an encyclopedic knowledge of Texas history.[1] Later, Miss Lillian Barber, who taught high school civics, augmented the teachings of Mrs. Owen by having students memorize parts of the U.S. Constitution and engage in class debates and mock trials.

Wayne's knowledge of history also resulted in part from another early influence: books. Almost as soon as he learned to read, he became a bibliophile. "I met the full definition of a bookworm," he says. His initial forays into the world of literature centered around an eight-volume set of *Compton's Pictured Encyclopedia.* "I think I got as much education out of that set of books as I did school. I still have little obscure bits of information in my head that I picked up from reading them."

In addition to bicycling and reading, Wayne became interested in tennis starting at age thirteen. Former classmate Ed Blythe remembers that after the school got a clay tennis court, he, Wayne, and several others began playing regularly. "Racquets of any quality were expensive, so our equipment and our dress left something to be desired. Wayne read books [on tennis] and got pictures of Tilden and other greats to pattern his game after."[2] During his last two years in high school, Justice represented Athens in local meets, reaching the finals of the county meet in his junior year.

By this time, Wayne's father had superseded his mother as the dominant influence in their son's life. Wayne deeply admired Will Justice and the power he wielded in the courtroom, and wanted to learn as much as he could from him. The senior Justice reciprocated by having his son work in the law office during the summers and occasionally after school. "He treated me as a kind of junior league associate," Wayne says. Both father and mother assumed their son would eventually become a member of the firm. Ed Blythe recalls that later in high school Wayne and his friends often dropped by the law office to see what was going on. "We could listen to Mr. Justice dictate some legal paper to his secretary who was so fast on the typewriter that she typed directly rather than take shorthand to be transcribed later. Her rapid typing sounded like a machine gun to me. If Mr. Justice was dictating a will or something personal, we were not allowed to listen, but if it was some of his pleadings of fact for a trial, we listened. Sometimes Wayne said, 'Come on over to the courthouse—Dad has a real interesting case.'"

Whether his father suggested it or Wayne thought it might be a good idea, he learned shorthand his senior year so as to be of greater assistance in the office. Wayne and his cousin, John Neal Justice, were the only boys to enroll in the high school shorthand class. Neither did well at first. John remembers that one day, one of the girls brought her two-year-old nephew to the class. The teacher, Miss Eula Nagle, was moved to remark, "Well, it appears that John and Wayne will have some competition today." That convinced John to drop out. Wayne, however, buckled down and mastered the subject. "I'd come home every night and I'd work on those damned brief forms and copy down all the exercises in those shorthand books."

Wayne's hard work paid off. He and Leona May Cope were the top students in the class and represented Athens High School in the district meet. Wayne also represented the school in the tennis competition. Miss Nagle urged him to practice his shorthand, but his mind was more on tennis. He was eliminated early on in the shorthand competition at the district meet but won in tennis. He also won in the regional meet but lost at the finals.

Wayne was frequently elected to class office, wrote sports articles for the school newspaper, the *Athenian,* and was elected its editor during his senior year. His classmates remember him as quiet, studious, and unassuming. Romantic interests were in the future. "I'd get along with girls fine as friends, but I was too scared of them to attempt romance," he admits. "I was so timid it was pathetic. I got over that, I'm glad to say." Fortunately, serious dating was not a social prerequisite in Athens at the time. One of his classmates, Lelia May Garner, observes that "all of the young people 'ran around' together and had great get-togethers and parties, seldom attended as couples." [3] Wayne Justice's main loves in high school were tennis and books—and working in his father's law office. It was here that he was introduced to the world of politics.

A die-hard progressive Democrat, Will Justice talked politics incessantly. "I heard my dad talking to people who were running for office. I participated in the low-level jobs in politics like tacking up posters, handing out leaflets, watching my dad make speeches, listening to other politicians speak." Stimulated by his successful race for county and then district attorney, Will ran for

Congress in 1933 on a decidedly New Deal platform. Wayne worked in that campaign, handing out leaflets and tacking up posters. When Will's uncle Jeff Justice, who was financing the campaign, died unexpectedly, the money dried up and the primary was lost. Later, when Ralph Yarborough ran for state attorney general in 1938, Will Justice traveled the countryside speaking for him, with Wayne again attending to the poster-tacking.

"Dad was an economic liberal for those days, a populist in the sense that he was for the underdog. He felt the bankers, the corporations, and those on Wall Street were swallowing up the people, and he was utterly outraged that Texas went for Herbert Hoover instead of Al Smith in 1928. When the Depression came along, I heard Hoover denounced on a day-to-day basis. I suspect that had a lot to do with the formation of my thoughts about politics." John Neal Justice well recalls the fervor with which his Uncle Will lashed out at the Republicans. One time, John criticized one of President Roosevelt's policies in front of Mr. Will. "He sat me down and lectured me for two hours about the New Deal."

Wayne was sheltered from the effects of the Depression. It was said that while Mr. Justice was not wealthy, Wayne was reared like a rich boy. And to the extent that Wayne never suffered for lack of anything, it is a true statement. "If I expressed a wish for something, my dad would do his best to get it for me. Sometimes, of course, he didn't, but I grew up in perfect comfort." Still, intellectually and socially, the Depression years had their impact. His father's strong support for Franklin Roosevelt was reinforced by some of his teachers at school. He saw his father's clients paying with watermelons and peas. And frequently he would ride his bicycle down to the railroad station and watch the trains go by with people hanging onto the boxcars. "That would really bring it home to me." Wayne wonders if the unfortunates riding the boxcars had an "underground railway system," for strangers from the railway station would show up daily at the Justice household asking for food and work. "I never did see my mother turn down a single one of them. About the only thing that it cost them was that she liked to hear their stories. She always was very interested in where they were from, if they had a family they'd left behind." Jackie May's kindness toward unfortunates was part of her legacy to her son, as is evident in the humaneness which underlies many of his judicial decisions.

Religion played a limited role in Wayne's early life. His parents were members of the mainline First Baptist Church in Athens, where his father was at one time on the board of deacons. Will Justice's activities as a criminal lawyer did not endear him to church officials, and as a result, by the late 1920s he had ceased going to church regularly. His mother, however, remained a regular churchgoer and for many years was a member of a church circle, meeting weekly. Wayne started going to Sunday school as a boy and was baptized at the age of eleven. But when he became a teenager, other interests beckoned. Then, too, old-fashioned Bible-thumping preaching did not appeal to him. He began going to church less and less. His mother disapproved but allowed her son to go his own way. Religion was never to be very important to Wayne Justice.

Not quite making the honor roll, Wayne graduated from high school in 1937. While he maintains that he studied little in the formal sense, his cousin John remembers that Wayne "always had his head in a book." His high school English teacher, Helen Carroll Bever, remembers Wayne Justice as "studious and cooperative." "Wayne was always a gentleman," she maintains.[4] Other former classmates remember him as a good conversationalist, well read, and interested in the affairs of the day. It was taken for granted that Will Justice's son would go to college and then law school. But Wayne did harbor some thoughts about journalism as a career. He thinks he might have enjoyed being a combination lawyer and journalist. "I've always wanted to be a journalist who covers the U.S. Supreme Court." But he never had a choice. Except for the war, his career path was clearly marked: first college, then law school, then his father's law firm. Since Will had briefly attended the University of Texas at Austin, Wayne was destined to matriculate there. Fearing her son would be swallowed up at the big state university, his mother preferred that he go to a smaller school closer to home. But it was not to be.

Father and son traveled to Austin in the late summer of 1937 to locate rooming facilities for Wayne. "Dad wanted me to be well accommodated. We finally found a place at 2511 Nueces Street, a boarding house. Everyone spoke highly of the cuisine there. It turned out to be a very fine place to live. It was run by Mrs. George M. Hopson of Vernon, Texas. The price was pretty high for those days—$35 a month." Wayne never joined a social fraternity, partly because of the cost and partly because "my father thought they were not egalitarian enough."

The plan had been for Wayne to secure a combination business and law degree by majoring as an undergraduate in business administration and then enrolling in law school—a five-year program. But the looming threat of a world war resulted in his taking academic courses for two years, then enrolling in the law school, a common route in those years. During his first year at college, Wayne did not do much studying. "But I was very good at cramming. I'd wait till the night before, stay up all night and read everything that I was supposed to have read during the preceding period. I'd go in the next morning and disgorge it onto my exam paper. Strangely, I remember a whole lot of what I studied by that system." It was also effective enough to keep him on the honor roll all four semesters.

Aside from academics, Wayne continued his interest in tennis by trying out for the freshman tennis team. He lettered in the sport, playing in some inter-collegiate competitions. He tried out for varsity tennis his second year but decided to preserve his eligibility for law school and did not letter. Later, he drifted away from the sport. He also had begun dating and became more active socially, though he was still very shy. He remembers the weekly dances held at Gregory Gymnasium on the UT campus. "There were several hundred people out there on the dance floor at one time, and it was a case of catch-as-catch-can. You'd meet a lot of girls that way."

But there were no serious romances. Wayne does remember a brief infatua-tion with a girl in his second-year accounting class. Though she was engaged to another student, the two studied together in a subject he found difficult. But the relationship did not mature. He completely lost touch with her until several years ago. "I got a letter from her in which she was condemning my decisions. She wrote, 'Now you were such a fine fellow, why are you doing these radical things?' She's apparently really over on the right wing now."

When Justice began law school, he was under the mistaken assumption that he knew a good bit about law, since he had worked part time with his father for several years. Knowing that he would return to the law office and having mastered the art of cramming as an undergraduate, he did not apply himself during his first year. He had become a member of the Young Demo-crats and was more interested in the political affairs of the day than in law. He became close friends with James W. Dibrell, who had been actively involved in student government at the University of Texas on a decidedly leftist platform. Dibrell was the son of an attorney from Coleman, Texas, and had graduated Phi Beta Kappa from the university with a major in physics. Besides deepen-ing Justice's interest in politics, Dibrell introduced him to economics, philos-ophy, and classical music. Though Dibrell was not interested in law and stayed in law school only a short time, he was able to do creditable work without studying. It was not that easy for Justice. He read his case assignments regu-larly but did not do any extra reading. Nor did he outline his courses like the rest of the students. "I passed everything, but God Almighty, I made poor grades that first year. My father was disappointed." So Wayne tried harder his second year. While he was no scholar, his friends recall that he applied himself diligently. As a result, his grades improved.

In the third year he realized that time was growing short. "On December 7, 1941, Pearl Harbor occurred. And everybody had the idea that we've got to pass the bar before we go. This was December and finals of the first-semester courses were going to be right after Christmas. They were conducting the bar exam in February, so I started out studying for the bar and studying for the finals at the same time. And by some miracle I passed both of them."

Wayne had met some interesting and later prominent people in law school.

Included among the members of his class were Lloyd Bentsen, later U.S. Senator and vice presidential candidate; William Junnell, whose last name placed him in the chair next to Justice and who later became a member of the Texas Court of Appeals for the Fourteenth District in Houston; Baine T. Kerr, later president of Pennzoil, and Eldon Mahon, who was appointed U.S. district court judge in Fort Worth. Another member of the class was Tom Law, who became a prominent Fort Worth attorney. Members of the class used to say that they knew their class was destined for greatness with both Law and Justice in their ranks.

Justice's closest friends in law school were Grover C. "Cleve" Spillers, Jr., and George T. Reynolds. The three shared an apartment with another student. Justice recalls that he and Reynolds studied hard for the bar exam. Reynolds had the annoying habit of constantly scratching his head while studying, while Wayne rocked back and forth in a squeaky swivel chair from his father's law office. Spillers, however, spent a good part of his time with his girlfriend, Mary. "Spillers would come in and sit down for awhile, with ol' Reynolds scratching his head and me squeaking around in that chair. And we'd just be knocking ourselves out studying. Before long, Spillers would go off with Mary. Reynolds and I would shake our heads—no way he could make it." Spillers agrees that his infatuation with Mary, whom he subsequently married, kept him from doing any studying at all.

The three took the bar exam in February. When the results were available in May, they drove to the clerk's office of the Texas Supreme Court to find out how they had done. The first one in line was Spillers, then Justice, and then Reynolds. Spillers got his results and found that he had passed, ranking near the top of those taking the test. Justice, who came up next, had passed too, but he had not done as well as Spillers. Reynolds, who was the acknowledged "brain" of the trio, also had passed but had not done as well as the other two. "We've never figured that out," Justice notes.

During the summers and before he left for the army after graduating from law school in 1942, Wayne worked in his father's law firm. With his legal training, he could now do some briefing in addition to secretarial and "go-fer" work. Will Justice was a facts lawyer; he was not skilled in legal research. Thus, his son's skills added a new dimension to the practice. At the same time, Wayne learned a good deal about trial preparation and strategy. And he learned it from a master.

Will Justice, known about town as "Mr. Will," exhaustively prepared his witnesses. "He would examine them as if they were on the witness stand," his son recalls. "Then he would cross-examine them. And then he would critique their performance. As a result, they were not at all intimidated by the opposing lawyer because they had already been subjected to much worse by what my dad had done to them in the privacy of his office."

Mr. Will claimed that witnesses have a tendency to be much too verbose. One favorite way of getting them to focus on the question being asked was through the use of an old brown hat. "Dad was a cigar smoker; he'd get cigar ashes over everything. And he had this old brown hat that he'd smeared with cigar ash up there on the hat stand in his office. He'd tell the witness that he was on the witness stand and was placed under oath. He'd point to that ol' brown hat and say, 'That hat's yellow, isn't it?' Most of them would look at the hat and say, 'No it's not yellow. It's brown.' He'd say, 'I didn't ask you whether or not it was brown. Your only answer to that question is, "No, it's not yellow." If I want to know what color it is, I'll ask.' That got the idea across."

A great many of the people Will dealt with had little formal education and were generally afraid of lawyers. With his meticulous preparations, he would compensate for the former and play upon the latter. He would explain to witnesses that the lawyer on the other side was going to try to get them mixed up, often by using legal terms that they might not understand. Mr. Will would tell witnesses, "If he asks you something using some of these words you don't understand, you tell him you don't understand. The juries will sympathize with you because most of them won't know what he means either." Witnesses were told to hold their temper when provoked, lest they blurt out something they would regret once off the stand. All they were to do was to answer the question asked and nothing more. Wayne notes that since his father was considered the best in the business, they would listen to what he had to say as if it were gospel. And they knew better than to lie to Will Justice.

Mr. Will was a master at cross-examination. "He'd study the case so much that he knew more about it than anyone in the courtroom. If a witness varied one iota from what he knew to be the facts, he would note it down in his mind. He didn't need a pencil. And when it came time for him to cross-examine, he'd hit the witness with every one of those things he had noted. If the witness wouldn't admit that he had been mistaken or had lied, my dad would tie him down to the story. 'Now let me see if I understand what you're testifying to. Are you saying that that car was black? Is that your testimony? I don't want there to be any mistake about this. You're testifying that that car was black?' And the witness would reply, 'Yeah, that car was black.' Then he'd bring in three or four witnesses, you know, to say that, hell no, that car wasn't black; it was white. And whether the witness admitted his error or dad proved it later to be an error, why, the jury got the idea that the whole case against my dad's client was a tissue of lies."

Mr. Will was also a master at jury preparation. "Dad knew the genealogy of nearly every juror in Henderson County. He knew just who to take and who not to take." In the 1920s the senior Justice had run-ins with the Ku Klux Klan, which he openly opposed. As a result, he began to notice that he was getting hung juries. He approached some local Klansmen who owed him favors and was able to learn the identity of the secretary of the Klan in Henderson County, who turned out to be an elderly Baptist preacher. Mr. Will went to him in the dead of night with a financial transaction. The deal consummated, Justice received a list of all the Klansmen in the county and an agreement to be supplied with a new list periodically thereafter. From then on he was able to strike the Klansmen off the jury panels, and everything returned to normal.

Will Justice's reputation as the consummate trial lawyer became legendary. "Some of my dad's best clients were those whom he had taken to court and just whipped the hell out of them on the stand. And when they had legal troubles later on, they didn't want to have to be facing him. They wanted him on their side." Will Justice developed a big following throughout Henderson County and much of East Texas, though not among Chamber of Commerce members. "They hated him," his son observes, "because he could always whip them." So did the law-and-order members of the community who believed Justice aided criminals by taking their cases.

Wayne attributes his father's success to the fact that he was a perfectionist and a workaholic, traits which carried over to his son. "Dad never stopped," his son maintains. "His work was his play. He thoroughly enjoyed everything that he was doing. He had endless energy; he wanted to know every little detail about a case he was working with. He had gone out and talked to every witness, maybe two or three times. He had been to the scene where it happened, not just once but two or three times. If he was worried about something, the way something happened, he'd take the witness out there: 'Now point it out to me; where did it happen? Where is this stump that you were telling me about?' In a land title suit, he'd get out there with the surveyors and follow their footsteps. He was the best person for getting prepared in a case that I have ever come in contact with." Often, Will Justice would get up in the middle of the night and head for the law office, a few blocks away, to take care of some minor detail. Weekends meant little to him. Jackie May never objected. She was proud of her husband and his standing in the community, though she did not concern herself with the law practice or Will Justice's political activities. Her life revolved around her home, her sisters, and her son.

Wayne's remarkable education in the tricks of the trade of a trial lawyer was temporarily interrupted with the outbreak of World War II. As a senior in law school, he had tried to enlist in a program that provided a direct commission as an officer in the navy. But he was rejected, primarily because of intermittent high blood pressure, a problem which manifested itself only during the physical examination. Knowing that he was likely to be drafted at any time, Wayne announced to his parents shortly after he returned to Athens from law school that he was enlisting in the army. It was June 26, 1942. This time, as luck would have it, his blood pressure was normal. Later that same day, he was on a bus for Camp Wolters in Mineral Wells.

Wayne Justice spent about four years in the U.S. Army, where various experiences provided him with insights he might otherwise never have had. Probably the most important of these was the discrimination he, along with millions of others, endured as a private. Long accustomed to a more or less privileged position in his hometown and the generally privileged state of being an undergraduate and law student at a major state university, he had never been treated as a second-class citizen.

Awareness of his lowly status came early. Justice's first order was to shepherd several young enlistees from nearby towns to Camp Wolters. This posed a challenge, since one of the men was drunk and got drunker as the trip progressed. But Justice completed the mission successfully and expected a word of commendation. The only reward was a curt "Get in line over there." The authority he would eventually exercise as a federal judge was far in the future.

After a few days' orientation at Camp Wolters, Justice was sent for basic training in the army—air force to Sheppard Field in Wichita Falls, Texas. Given his college and law school background coupled with his typing and shorthand abilities, he had expected an office job. "They must have analyzed those tests they gave us carefully because they ended up putting me in airplane mechanics school." Even now Justice has trouble changing a tire on his car.

While he hated the regimentation as a new enlistee and did not take kindly to constant verbal abuse, he complied. "Oh, Lord, I complied. I was the most meek fellow you ever saw when an officer or a non-com came around. I was ready to do what they wanted because I wanted to get out of that mess."

Army life added another new dimension to the education of the young Athens attorney. He found himself in the company of worldly-wise young men from upstate New York and South Boston. At first, their use of lurid epithets shocked him. "The vocabulary those people employed was so gross and so extraordinary that I was simply shocked out of my mind. They would say things to each other that would have caused an immediate breach of the peace in Athens, Texas." But by the end of five months at the base, Justice himself became proficient in "talking army."

At one point before being assigned to a new B-17 squadron, Justice was routinely placed on KP duty. His job was washing dishes without the aid of a dishwasher. He considered it one of the lowest points of his army experience. "I will put that beside anything as being something that will not inspire you to the lofts of heaven," he says emphatically. But just as he was deep in a sink of dirty dishwater, along came a lucky break.

"I was sitting there washing those damn forks and spoons. I just hated it. About that time along came a sergeant and he says, 'Anybody here named Justice?' And I thought to myself, 'O my God, what next?' I identified myself. He said, 'Can you type?' I said, 'I sure can.' I saw some glimmering of hope there, you know. He said, 'Come with me.'" It turned out that, with the formation of the new outfit, someone had forgotten to requisition clerks. Because of Justice's ability to type and take shorthand, he was sent to the orderly room and later reclassified from airplane mechanic to clerk. All of the months of training had gone for naught, though with his admitted limited mechanical ability, "I would have been a severe hazard to the pilots."

Though he had no intention of becoming an officer when he enlisted, Justice quickly realized that was the only way out of the dreary existence of a private. "I quickly came to feel very uncomfortable about the condition of life of an enlisted person. It came as a shock to me that I was a second-class individual. I didn't like not being able to speak directly to those who were my superiors without going through all of the formalities that military protocol requires. So I decided that, if I could, I would get into an environment where I could live the life that I'd led as a civilian. For that reason, I started thinking about Officer Candidate School."

His time as a private was not completely wasted. Years later when he began trying desegregation cases, he remembered how he had reacted to his experiences. "We had lived a rigidly segregated existence from the officers. When we went to the orderly room, we were required to use a separate entrance. When we went to the latrines, there was a separate latrine for enlisted men. When we went to the mess hall, the officers either were in a separate mess or were segregated from us. The officers had their own clubs. Later on in life when I was confronted with racial cases, it was very easy for me to empathize with blacks and other subordinate groups because I had a little insight into what a segregated existence must be like to them. In the days when I was growing up, everything was segregated. I had never thought about what it must be like until I got into the army."

So Justice applied to Officer Candidate School. Again the rise in blood pressure initially presented an obstacle, but he eventually passed the physical and was assigned his third choice, army field artillery. He had put this option down because while in law school he had gotten to know a girl whose father was a colonel in field artillery. "I thought vaguely that maybe the fact that I knew his daughter would give me some advantage somewhere down the line." It didn't.

Before being sent to Fort Sill, Oklahoma, for officer candidate training, he was assigned as a clerk to the Courts and Boards Office at base headquarters. His job was to transcribe, then type up, the hearings associated with the general discharge of undesirable individuals from the army. It was as close to the work of a court as he would get while in the service.

Fort Sill was real army, military in the extreme. For a time, it looked as if the officer candidates from the air force would be washed out because they had not had basic training in field artillery. This became apparent about halfway through the six-week gunnery course. But fortunately, they were allowed to interrupt their training for a month of specialized work on gunnery. This provided the necessary ingredient for Justice to complete the training successfully and become a second lieutenant.

He stayed in Texas and Oklahoma at various army camps working mostly as a motor officer—"this was another interesting thing, the army's persistence in trying to make me into a mechanic"—until the summer of 1945. At that time, with a provisional company under his command, he boarded a troop ship in New York bound for the China-Burma-India theatre. During the slow voyage, they learned of the atomic bombing of Hiroshima and Nagasaki.

"From a purely personal, subjective point of view, I have never had any quarrel with President Truman's decision to drop those atom bombs because I figured that he saved my life," Justice asserts. Had the atom bomb not brought an end to the war, he would have been sent into Burma as part of a mule pack artillery group, which carried small French .75 howitzers. As a second lieutenant, Justice would have been assigned as a forward observer, which was extremely hazardous duty. In those days forward observers worked alongside the infantry and with their hand radio sets sent back fire commands. Since the hand radios carried antennas, the Japanese snipers could zero in on the forward observers as their primary targets.

After the ship docked at Calcutta, the men were sent to Camp Kanchrapara, about forty-five miles to the north. It was at an officers' club briefing that Justice learned he would be assigned to an evacuation unit to send the troops home. While in India, he was promoted to first lieutenant. By February 1946, after six months in Calcutta, he had accumulated sufficient points in longevity and overseas service to be ordered home. His father met him in San Antonio, and together they returned to Athens, where the very next day Wayne entered the practice of law.

The Justice law firm at the time was located over the Hairston Book Store on the south side of the Athens town square. A long flight of stairs led to the suite of offices. Clients entered a large reception room with offices opening off it.

R. Homer Moore's office lay to the left of the entrance. A self-taught lawyer from Frankston, Texas, Moore had joined the law firm some years earlier after soliciting the services of Will Justice to help him in a land title case against the highly regarded J. D. Pickett of Palestine. Moore was so impressed with the skill Mr. Will demonstrated in defeating Pickett that he asked if he could join the firm as an associate and handle routine cases. Moore knew he could learn a lot from an association with Mr. Will. By the time Wayne joined the firm, Moore had developed into a fine attorney and had become a one-third partner in the firm.

Next to Moore's office was the library and conference room, and beyond it the secretary's desk, then occupied by Marcelle Pinkerton, who later as Marcelle Simmons would commute to Tyler to serve as Judge Justice's secretary for his first nineteen years on the bench. At the back of the reception room was Mr. Will's large office and next to it, the small office assigned to his son. Its small window faced west, and in the late afternoons of summer the heat nearly became unbearable. There was no air conditioning. Fans stirred the air so vigorously that Wayne had to anchor the papers on his desk to keep them from flying around the office.

When Homer Moore had been made a partner, Mr. Will had retained a two-thirds interest in the firm. He now gave one-third to his son, and in 1946 the firm became known as Justice, Moore & Justice—locally called "Justice and More Justice."

Will Justice, of course, was the heavyweight. For the first several years, Wayne helped him with briefing and handled minor justice of the peace and county court cases. "But the main thing I did was to go to court with him and sit at his elbow and watch him try cases," Justice says. "He liked for me to whisper in his ear if I thought of something that ought to be asked of a witness." If they were representing a plaintiff, Mr. Will would have Homer or his son make an opening statement to the jury to lay out the facts. He reserved to himself the final argument to the jury. "Dad was a stemwinder; he made the damnedest speeches you ever heard. They were brilliant. He used a lot of oratorical flourishes and would let his voice go high and then get down to a conspiratorial whisper to the jury. He'd start talking to those old farmers, who looked like they hadn't expressed an emotion in fifty years, in that tremulous voice that he could affect when he wanted to, and they'd be pulling out their handkerchiefs and wiping their eyes."

In a story he has often told, Wayne recalls the time his father and Homer Moore represented a junk dealer by the name of Ike Hart who had been accused of receiving stolen property. The prosecutor was John Dowdy, later congressman from the Seventh Congressional District. Wayne was seated next to his father in his role as observer. Dowdy had brought out the facts well. Wayne thought the case was open and shut against their client, and was startled when his father asked him if he wanted to make the closing argument. "I told him, 'What in the hell would I talk about? I don't see any defense.'" Homer and Will just laughed. Slapping his son on the back, Will Justice got up and made his usual dramatic closing speech. "He just talked about moonshine as far as I was concerned. He never did touch topside nor bottom of the case—just talked in generalities about presumption of innocence and made light of some of the state's witnesses." The jury was out ten minutes and returned with a verdict of not guilty. "I shook my head and reached the conclusion then and there that there's always something that can be said in any kind of case."

Wayne knew that he could never hope to equal his father as a spellbinding trial attorney. Nor could he assume the same folksy, down-home style. "I realized that if I was going to emulate him, I was going to fall flat on my face. So I adopted a style more in keeping with my personality and talents." Mr. Will appealed to people's emotions; his son sought to appeal more to their intellect. They complemented each other's talents, and with the added contributions of Homer Moore, the firm prospered.

Some of the cases the firm handled during these years were highly publicized and difficult. Soon after his return to Athens, Wayne was introduced to public disfavor in a murder case his father handled. The case involved an Athens deputy sheriff named Willie Chapman. Chapman had a background in law enforcement, including a stint as constable and justice of the peace in his hometown of Malakoff, about eight miles from Athens. When Dean L. Holiman was elected sheriff in Athens in 1946, he appointed Willie Chapman to serve as one of his deputies. Holiman had been warned of Chapman's reputation for being "trigger happy," but he ignored it.

On August 15, 1947, the American Legion held a reunion on the outskirts of Athens. A good deal of beer was consumed. Several of the participants were later jailed for disturbing the peace. Willie Chapman, a man in his early fifties and slight of build, was the jailer. J. D. Robertson, a popular young Athens family man and vice-commander of the Legion, learned that some of his comrades were in jail and decided to get them out. Here the facts get muddy, for Chapman was the only surviving witness. Chapman testified that Robertson, who Chapman said had been drinking, walked into the lobby of the jail. Chapman, who had been resting in a room adjoining the lobby, heard the door open. When he walked into the lobby to investigate, he testified, he saw Robertson going through the drawers of the desk. Chapman asked him what he was doing. According to Chapman, Robertson said he was looking for the keys, that he was going to let his comrades out of jail. Chapman told him, no, he couldn't do that. Robertson told him that he could and would. Then, according to Chapman, Robertson advanced on him. When Robertson wouldn't stop, Chapman pulled out his revolver and fatally shot him.

The news of the killing quickly spread through the small town. Chapman made his way to Will Justice's home, where he asked the senior Justice to represent him. Justice agreed to do so and told him to get the sheriff's permission to leave town for awhile till things cooled down.

The town was in an uproar. By daybreak a mob had formed and advanced on the jail. Holiman convinced them that Chapman was not present. According to stories in the town newspaper, the *Athens Daily Review,* the Robertson funeral held in the Methodist Church was packed; resentment against Chapman ran high. Resentment was also expressed toward the Justices when it was learned they were representing him. Will Justice had long dealt with occasional community opprobrium. He shrugged it off. But it was new to Wayne. "That's the first time that I'd ever encountered community hostility. Some of my friends wouldn't speak to me. It was damned uncomfortable for awhile."

Chapman was indicted for murder with malice, and District Attorney John Dowdy said he would seek the death penalty. Bond was set at $12,500. Dowdy had asked that Chapman be held without bond pending trial. The case of *Texas v. Chapman* was set for October 13. Meanwhile, on advice of Will Justice, Chapman left town. After a lengthy change-of-venue hearing, the case was transferred to Cherokee County. Working with two law firms in that county, Will Justice carefully screened prospective jurors. He was able to secure several continuances. Finally, trial was set for May 3, 1948, in Rusk, before Judge H. T. Brown of the Second Judicial District. On that first day of the trial, several hundred people from Athens showed up. A special venire of two hundred persons was called for jury selection; everyone was searched upon entering the courtroom. Mr. Will knew it would be a tough case, even though the evidence against Chapman was circumstantial. He conducted his usual sterling defense, but at the conclusion of the six-day trial, the jury was deadlocked eleven to one for a guilty verdict. A mistrial had to be declared. Chapman's attorneys concluded that the people from Athens had biased the panel from which the jury had been selected.

Mr. Will often said that time is the best lawyer in a criminal case. When the Chapman case was again called for trial, he filed three successive motions for continuance. All were granted. The case finally came to trial a second time some two years later. By then, interest had died down. The second jury took about twenty minutes to reach a verdict of not guilty. But among many in Athens, the view persisted that Will Justice, now aided by his son, had succeeded in freeing another guilty person. As a lawyer, Wayne Justice quickly learned to put his own personal feelings and beliefs aside. "You presented your client's case in the best possible light consistent with truth and the law," he observes. "I never tried to make any judgment about guilt or innocence. That wasn't my role. That was the role of the jury and the judge."

Not all of the activities at the office involved conflict. Justice recalls one hot summer day when the front door to the law firm opened and an extremely attractive and well-dressed woman in her early twenties asked for Mr. Will Justice. She was ushered into his office. Since in the absence of air conditioning all the doors were open, Wayne could overhear part of the conversation from his office. They were discussing how to secure the release of a young man from the service. "I decided at that point that my dad could use my assistance, so I went in and was introduced to Sue Rowan. She flipped her eyes over at me and I was hopelessly harpooned from that point on. My Lord, was she pretty!"

Sue Rowan was one of five children of Sam and Stella Rowan. Rowan was a farmer and country schoolteacher who had overcome polio and other adversities to make money buying oil leases when the East Texas oil field opened up in the 1930s. Although the Rowans were by then financially successful, they continued to live on a farm out in the country near the little community of Ben Wheeler. Sue's father stressed the importance of formal education for all his children. He wanted them to be independent and self-reliant. Sue started school at age eight when her parents judged her strong enough to walk the two miles to the schoolhouse. She completed high school in the nearby town of Van and continued on to college at her father's insistence. She graduated from Texas State College for Women (now Texas Woman's University) in Denton in 1944, majoring in costume and textile design. She had ambitions of becoming a fashion designer and worked for a short time following graduation for the U.S. Navy Department as a materials quality control inspector.

After a number of dates, Wayne and Sue became engaged and were married on March 16, 1947, in Denton. Following a week's honeymoon in New Orleans, the couple settled down in Athens. After renting first an apartment and then a house, they built a two-bedroom house at 1015 Crestway Drive in Athens and lived there until 1968, when Wayne was appointed to the bench. It was there that they raised their only child, a daughter, Ellen, born on Christmas Eve in 1949.

An attractive woman with the same reserve and formality as her parents, Ellen Justice, who has retained her maiden name, lives with her husband, Eric W. Leibrock, and daughter, Jane, in Houston. She recalls that early on she perceived that her family was different from others in Athens. The Justices were not regular churchgoers. They did not take vacations. Her father was always busy with his work, something that Ellen found hard to understand. "I have to admit that I resented his profession mainly because I couldn't understand what he did. It's just a little difficult for a child to understand exactly what it is that a lawyer does." He never took her hunting and fishing like the fathers of some of her friends. Her father's only hobbies were reading and going to the movies.

Though Wayne Justice had a different parenting style from other fathers, he did involve himself in his daughter's life. "I remember he taught me to sing songs. He taught me how to spell my name. I remember him taking me to the movies. I remember him teaching me how to count with pennies. My mother says he used to take me down to meet the train at night when I was an infant. I had a horse that my grandfather gave me, and I remember him catching the horse once for me, which he hated because he is afraid of horses."

Together with a number of other couples, the Justices took dancing lessons. They learned how to do modern dances like the rhumba and the samba, and have enjoyed dancing ever since. On many Saturday nights, Wayne and Sue went dancing at the Athens country club. "We were charter members of the country club," Sue notes. "We were very involved in town life in the 1940s except for religion. Neither of us was involved in religious activity." Sunday was usually a day to visit family. Ellen recalls, "We would go out into the country and visit with his aunt who lived out there. We would join family gatherings at the Homeplace, which is what we called the house that his mother grew up in. We would frequently go to my mother's family home." Wayne and Sue spent considerable time with Will and Jackie May, and Ellen remembers that her grandparents were with her a great deal.

In 1951, Homer Moore died, and for awhile, father and son practiced alone. "It was pretty damn hard; we had more business than we could attend to," Wayne maintains. "And I was always on the run." In these days he smoked heavily—mostly cigars like his father's—and was overweight. "Smoking gave me a headache and every morning, first thing I did when I arrived at the office was to take a couple of aspirin." Appointments were seldom scheduled. People were handled on a first-come, first-served basis. The place was a frenzy of activity. Cases included personal injury, criminal, worker's compensation, land titles, divorce, deeds—whatever came in the door. "Marcelle was our staff. She was as busy as a one-armed paper hanger."

About mid-morning, Wayne would say that he had something to take care of and would be gone for a few minutes. He'd pick up Willis D. Moore, a rival attorney and friend. The pair would join the usual roundtable for coffee at Stirman's Drug Store on the north side of the town square. There they would ordinarily find Tom Sharpe, a butane dealer; dentist Robert Fisher; the owner, Winfield "Doc" Stirman; newspaper editor and later banker R. T. Craig; savings and loan operator J. P. Pickens; and others. "There was always a crowd there. And we'd sit and drink coffee and discuss the affairs of the day for about thirty minutes." Then it was back to the office, where the intense activities would continue until suppertime. At night, Wayne would often catch up on briefing and other unfinished work.

The frantic pace Wayne maintained in his sixteen years as a practicing attorney was no different from the pace he would set as U.S. attorney and, later, judge. But the disorganization in the office was atypical. How could he tolerate such a disorganized law practice? "You understand that that was not of my doing; it was not my law practice. This was my father's law practice. I had just joined him, so we did things the way that he had always done them."

Despite all the activity, however, the law firm never prospered as much as it could have. "Dad wasn't really interested in money," Wayne observes. "Our debt collection practices were a joke. I imagine that upwards of half of our fees were never collected. Looking back on it now, I can see what we ought to have done is to have gotten a bookkeeper, send out notices, get after them if they didn't pay. If we had done so, we'd have been on easy street." Marcelle Pinkerton Simmons, their longtime secretary, remembers that just before Christmas nearly every year, Mr. Will would announce that he was going out to collect fees. It became a joke around the office. "He'd grab his hat and be gone the better part of a day. When he returned, he had less money than when he set out!" The hard-luck stories from delinquent clients had just been too much for him.

A year and a half after Homer Moore's death, Wayne concluded that another lawyer had to be brought into the practice. He suggested his brother-in-law, Justin Michael Rowan. Mike Rowan had graduated from the University of Texas after World War II and had worked in the Texas General Land Office, where he had been in charge of the Veteran's Land Program. Though his conservative political views were at odds with those of the Justices, Rowan had good organizational abilities and wanted to practice law. Wayne believed that he would bring in a new kind of client. Rowan was invited to join the firm in 1952. He was a good attorney and was well liked in Athens.

Rowan became particularly fond of the senior Justice. During the time he spent at the firm, Rowan says that they tried a case nearly every week and lost only two. "And we would have won one of those if we had found the witness in time." He remembers Mr. Will telling of the time he was trying a murder case in Houston in the early thirties. A young lawyer who was observing the trial would come to see him during recesses and ask him about certain strategies he had employed. Why had he taken this particular tack? Why had he not employed that line of questioning? Mr. Will would patiently explain. The young attorney was Percy Foreman, who was to become one of the outstanding criminal trial attorneys in the nation.

With a special interest in oil and gas work, and a conservative political philosophy, Rowan left in 1955 to practice law in Tyler. He and Wayne did not get along well. Rowan found Wayne impersonal and inflexible, quick to make political differences an issue. Continuing political and family differences have resulted in strained relations between the Justices and the Rowans over the years. Litigants opposed to having their cases heard in Justice's court have at times sought out Mike Rowan to be their attorney, thus forcing Justice to take himself out of the case. Rowan maintains that he routinely refused employment when he perceived it was for such purpose.[5]

As the years went by, Wayne began playing a more prominent role in the work of the firm. In 1955, Will Justice was operated on for cancer. While he gained sufficient strength to rejoin the law firm and practice law for another five years, his son began to do a great deal more of the trial work. One of the more notable cases he handled involved the charge of criminal libel leveled against the former mayor of Corsicana, a town about forty-five miles south of Dallas. It was alleged that C. C. Sapp had written, printed, and circulated a scurrilous pamphlet entitled "A Short History of the Men Backing the Big Bond Issue." The pamphlet charged that the then mayor had manipulated sugar stamps during World War II and "managed to lie himself out of prison." It accused a former mayor of being homosexual. A former city commissioner was said to have made a career out of "renting low, shabby shacks to gamblers, bootleggers and prostitutes at exorbitant rates." Another was said to have "sired more illegitimate children than the inventor of the sewing machine." And on it went.[6]

Sapp was indicted on July 30, 1955, on the charge of criminal libel, carrying a penalty of a fine of not less than $100 nor more than $2,000 or imprisonment for up to two years. Sapp first tried to hire local attorney R. Matt Dawson, who had already agreed to represent the state as special prosecutor. Sapp then turned to the Justice law firm and local attorney Joe Anderson. Because of his father's illness, Wayne took over preparation of the case for trial and conducted much of the trial itself. The evidence against Sapp was nearly overwhelming. At the trial on March 6, 1956, the printer of the pamphlets, W. T. Stokes, testified that Sapp had asked him to print five hundred copies. He described the transaction, how he had sent the pamphlet to Dallas for typesetting and delivered the printed material to Sapp.

On cross-examination, Wayne tried to undermine the weight of Stokes' testimony by asking "the standard stuff of a turncoat witness: Didn't you receive a grant of immunity? Wasn't your story different before you received immunity?" Stokes admitted that he had been given a grant of immunity and that he had told several persons before the grant that Sapp had not been involved. The prosecution presented other witnesses to link Sapp with the pamphlets. Retired postmaster G. C. (Jake) Hudson testified that shortly after the post office opened, he had found a bunch of pamphlets in the lobby and had read the contents of one to Elmer Pryor, the blind operator of the post office newsstand. Pryor then testified that Sapp had been in the post office a short time before, because he recognized Sapp's voice. Other witnesses, including some of those libeled, testified that Sapp had made inflammatory statements to them on other occasions. Altogether, the prosecution put on thirteen witnesses.

Wayne Justice knew his defense was thin. The only witness he could put on the stand was Sapp, and he was afraid to do so, for Sapp would not stop talking. Wayne and his father, who had recuperated sufficiently to join the trial, decided they had no choice but to put Sapp on the stand. But they sternly instructed him not to stray beyond a direct answer to any question put to him. The advice was not heeded. Sapp proceeded to ramble during cross-examination by special prosecutor Dawson. But, surprisingly, Sapp weathered Dawson's intense cross-examination. "Sapp would make an exculpatory speech to every question Dawson asked. Finally, Dawson gave up," Wayne recalls. Dawson agrees that he could not make any headway against Sapp. Dawson remembers that the courtroom was packed. "That was in the days before television, and local trials would draw a host of spectators," he points out. Tension ran high. At one point, Dawson learned that both those libeled and Sapp were armed. He asked that he and the defense attorneys be allowed to approach the bench, where County Judge Jim Sewell was presiding. Sewell, who was blind, was a close personal friend and political associate of Wayne Justice. Dawson told the judge and the defense attorneys what he had learned and asked Sewell to disarm the courtroom. Dawson says that Will Justice quickly agreed. "Mr. Will said, 'Oh my God, yes, Judge, I've had two clients shot down by my side and I don't want it to happen again!'" The elder Justice said that one of the times he had to get down on the floor and crawl around under the benches to keep from being shot.

With testimony in, time came for final arguments. Using the detailed notes he had taken during the trial, Wayne proceeded to examine the state's case systematically, pointing out the weak points. Will Justice made the final argument. "It was one of Dad's stemwinders." As Dawson readily acknowledges, Will Justice's spread-eagle style of oratory could dominate a courtroom—and, if the windows were open, the streets outside. On this occasion, he talked to the jury in emotional terms about the "green-eyed devil" of envy and greed. The jury returned a verdict of not guilty the next day. Wayne attributes the victory to careful selection of the jury—"people from out in the country who didn't much like these Corsicana bigwigs, anyway, you know"—and to his father's final summation. "After the trial, no one remembered what I said, but they all remembered Dad's speech about the 'green-eyed devil.'"

With his father's illness and Rowan's departure, Wayne looked around for a third partner. William H. Kugle, Jr., had come to East Texas as a Democratic organizer after five years of law practice in Galveston. The Democratic Party was in shambles after Eisenhower's 1952 landslide, and Kugle was trying to reorganize the party in thirty East Texas counties. "Somewhere I had gotten the name of Wayne Justice, and so the first thing I did when I got to Athens was to look him up and that began an acquaintanceship," Kugle says. "After the elections were over in November 1955, he asked me to come practice law with him." Kugle had intended to practice law in Tyler rather than return to Galveston, but he took a liking to the Justices and moved to Athens instead. "Our common denominator was a pretty liberal philosophy and certainly our zeal for the Democratic Party."

Kugle and Mr. Will seemed to gravitate to one another. Both were out-going and enjoyed being with people. Mr. Will's reputation continued to bring business to the firm from all over East Texas. Kugle remembers traveling with Wayne's father to places like Muleshoe in far West Texas, Carthage in far East Texas, and numerous towns in between. Though in his late seventies and in ill health, Mr. Will was "an incredibly flamboyant, brilliant courtroom lawyer. He would always make an electrifying speech in court, right up to his last illness." Will Justice was posthumously selected as one of the first lawyers to be inducted into the Texas Criminal Defense Lawyers Association's Hall of Fame. It is said that he tried over two hundred murder cases in his career. The vast majority of his clients were acquitted outright. The few convicted received relatively mild sentences. None was sentenced to life imprisonment or death.

Though Mr. Will continued to bring in the business, his son and Bill Kugle did most of the work. Though different in their personalities, the pair became close friends during the five years they practiced together. Kugle recalls that while Wayne venerated his father, there was no demonstration of affection between them. "Wayne was so formal, even formal with his father."

Practicing law was Wayne's main occupation during the 1940s and 1950s. But he also harbored a strong interest in politics. Early on, he became involved in political activities, first locally and then on a statewide basis. It was this interest in politics and the ensuing personal contacts that eventually led to his appointment as U.S. attorney and then judge.

CHAPTER 2

Political Activity: Outside the Mainstream

Ever since his election to class office as a schoolboy, Wayne Justice had been interested in politics. Though his mother didn't favor political discussion at home, it flourished at his father's office. Will Justice was always talking politics, and politics at the Justice law firm in those days meant the populist wing of the Democratic Party. While Wayne engaged in considerable discussion about political events during college, his involvement was limited largely to membership in the Young Democrats. Campus politics did not interest him. About his only political involvement in these years was tacking up posters in Henderson County for Lyndon Johnson, who ran for Senate in the special election of 1941. Johnson narrowly lost the race—under suspicious circumstances—to Governor W. Lee "Pass the Biscuits, Pappy" O'Daniel.[1] It was not until after the war that Wayne took an active part in Democratic political affairs.

From the very beginning Wayne Justice's political views were decidedly liberal, liberal at least in everything but race relations. That would come later. Justice thinks of himself as a populist, in the sense of being "for the little 'un against the big 'un." In fact, his coffee cup at the courthouse bears the designation "WWJ Populist."

In Texas, the populist movement began with the establishment of the Southern Farmers Alliance in Lampasas County in the fall of 1877. Its primary concern was the falling price of cotton.[2] The economic strategies pursued by the alliance to improve the condition of members through local trade agreements and the organization of cooperatives gave way to political action in 1890. Two years later the alliance endorsed the new People's Party. The Populists died out as a political force in Texas around the turn of the century when the Democratic Party co-opted their platform. Many of the progressive reforms introduced in the 1890s by Texas Governor James Stephen Hogg and his successor, Charles Culberson, addressed populist concerns.

Nevertheless, in many poor rural communities, populist sentiment lingered, even enjoying something of a renaissance—though not under the name of populism—during the 1920s and 1930s. Such was the case in Henderson County, where farmers continued to protest the exploitive practices of the railroad, banking, and utility companies. When the town of Athens went bankrupt in the late 1930s under the crushing weight of the Depression, Democrats with Populist sentiments took over. From then on, taxes were low and city services limited.

Populists asserted that government should work for the people, not for the interests of the large corporations. Justice expressed the same view in a 1986 television interview: "I don't believe in Social Darwinism—the sink or swim philosophy. I think that part of our Christian heritage is that we should help other people if they are in trouble. And if that means the government helping them some, why, that's fine."[3]

This political orientation kept Justice outside the mainstream of Texas postwar politics. Governor James V. Allred (1935–1939) is generally regarded as the last of the "people's governors" in Texas. He championed public assistance programs for the needy, a state income tax, higher taxes on the oil and gas industry, a public utility commissioner, lower utility rates, and the registration and regulation of corporate lobbyists. Though largely unsuccessful, the Allred progressive program prompted a strong counterreaction by monied interests in Texas. The growth of the oil and gas industry during and after World War II added considerable political muscle to the old-line southern conservative wing of the Democratic Party—as did increasing corporate concentration in Texas urban centers. When Allred retired from politics in 1939, the conservatives took over political control of the state. Surface appearances to the contrary, what has been called "the Establishment"—a loosely knit plutocracy of white businessmen, oilmen, bankers, and lawyers—assured that, for the most part, conservative political leaders would remain in office through the 1940s and 1950s.[4]

While still overseas, Justice had read about the dismissal of University of Texas President Homer Price Rainey. Rainey had been named president during the Allred administration and, since the governor appoints the regents, had enjoyed a supportive board of regents. But with the election of conservative Democratic governors W. Lee O'Daniel (1939–1941) and Coke Stevenson (1941–1947), conservative regents dominated the board. Influenced by the rising tide of anticommunist fervor stirred up by Congressman Martin Dies from Southeast Texas, chairman of the House Un-American Activities Committee, the regents began placing pressure on Rainey to dismiss professors with allegedly leftist leanings. The struggle for control of the university came to a head over the issue of academic freedom. The board questioned the use in an English class of John Dos Passos' classic trilogy *U.S.A.,* a work they considered obscene, perverted, and un-American. The book was banned by board action. Rainey condemned the censorship and, after announcing a long list of grievances with the board of regents, was fired on November 1, 1944. The university was in turmoil. With thousands conducting a funeral march to the capitol and governor's mansion, students went on strike over the proclaimed death of academic freedom.

Meanwhile, Homer Rainey began giving speeches on public issues and in the spring of 1946 announced that he planned to run for governor. Opposed in the primary by four conservative Democrats, Rainey defended academic freedom and supported the nascent civil rights movement. In 1944 the U.S. Supreme Court had ruled in *Smith v. Allwright* that blacks could not be restricted from voting in primary elections.[5] A New Dealer, Rainey spoke of the need for increased corporate taxes, including a tax on oil at the wellhead, and stronger antitrust laws. He endorsed the work of the Fair Employment Practices Commission, which President Roosevelt had established in 1940 to assure racial equality in employment practices. When Rainey announced his candidacy, Wayne Justice, just back from the war, traveled to Rainey's home town in Denison, Texas, to hear his opening speech. Justice was impressed and volunteered to serve as Rainey's campaign manager in Henderson County.

While Rainey was pounding home his campaign themes, the voters were also hearing about the evils of communism, big labor, and racial strife. The latter was of particular concern to many in East Texas, given its large black population. Justice remembers it as an extremely bitter campaign. Rainey's opponents made John Dos Passos' book a central campaign issue. For example, one of the candidates, state Attorney General Grover Sellers, ended his campaign speeches by dramatically asking the ladies present to leave. Then he would don white gloves, pick up the "filthy" Dos Passos book, and read selected "obscene" passages from it.[6] When it was discovered that Justice had a copy of the book, several Athenians came by to borrow it. "I think they thought that they were getting some classic piece of erotic literature," Justice says with a smile. "They'd come back with this disappointed look, you know. They hadn't found anything and didn't want to have to read every page of that long book."

Aided by newspaper support in small and medium-sized towns, and by his image as the victim of overzealous reactionaries on the University of Texas Board of Regents, Rainey outpolled all Democratic candidates but Beauford Jester, a corporate attorney and member of the powerful state Railroad Commission, which nominally regulated the oil industry. With the bulk of corporate big money interests and big city newspaper endorsements behind him, Jester had achieved wide recognition as the moderate candidate in the campaign.

Mudslinging was particularly vicious during the Jester-Rainey runoff campaign. So much prejudice had been built up against Rainey in Athens that he could not rent a hotel room. He changed clothes and readied himself for a campaign speech at the Justice household. Wayne had his father introduce Rainey at the speech. But this may have been a mistake, for Will Justice was an extraordinarily good speaker and Rainey paled in comparison.

Rainey lost the runoff election by a two-to-one margin. His loss in Henderson County was a keen disappointment to his campaign manager. Election results, however, showed the emergence of an embryonic liberal-labor-minority Democratic coalition. It was that coalition which would finally realize success with the election of Ralph Yarborough to the U.S. Senate in 1957.

The Rainey campaign over, Wayne Justice turned his attention to his law practice in Athens and to thoughts of holding office himself. Initially, he wasn't interested in becoming involved in community activities. "When I came back from the army, I'll confess that I felt fairly aloof from the community. I had read a lot of Sinclair Lewis. I'd read *Babbitt* and *Arrowsmith* and *Elmer Gantry,* and so I had ambivalent feelings about the Rotary Club and Kiwanis and the Chamber of Commerce. I couldn't see any common feelings I had with local boosters." But in 1948 Justice became friends with Farris Block, who convinced him otherwise. Block, who had just become editor of the *Athens Daily Review,* would stay in Athens only seven months. But during that short time, he came to know Wayne and Sue well, often meeting them socially. Block convinced Justice that if he wanted to seek political office, he would have to think like a politician. "I asked him how he could expect to influence those people if he didn't associate with them."

"Well, I hadn't really thought about it in that light," Justice recalls. "After I got to thinking about it, I decided that he was probably right. So from that point on, I began to participate in community activities." With the encouragement and assistance of his law partner, Homer Moore, Justice made application and was accepted as a member of the Masonic Lodge. He found that, contrary to his earlier assumptions, fraternal life in a small town did have much to offer. In 1954 he headed the Taylor Commandry of Knights Templars and later became master of the Athens Masonic ("Blue") Lodge. He also joined the Rotary Club and later became its president, as well as serving as commander of the local VFW Post from 1952 to 1954.

Among the most fruitful and rewarding public service duties that Justice performed was serving as the Athens city attorney. He served twice— 1948–1950 and 1952–1958. It was a part-time job requiring that he attend city commission meetings, draft ordinances, and advise council members on legal matters. The salary was $75 a month. Court appearances earned extra pay. He was initially appointed to the position when Earnest Landman was mayor. Landman, a local attorney, and Will Justice were rivals. The latter, who had himself served many years as city attorney, suggested to the other two members of the city commission that his son might provide a good check on Landman's legal advice if he were to serve as city attorney. Wayne was appointed. Not only did Wayne never find Landman wrong on legal matters, but the two also became friends. Landman was heard to say that while he couldn't understand it, Will Justice's son was a pretty good boy.

In his role as city attorney, Wayne Justice was always interested in saving the city money. In true populist fashion, he took particular interest in holding down the cost of public utilities. During his second term, he advised the city commissioners against routinely approving utility company rate increases. Drawing on his study of administrative law in law school, he drafted an ordinance that required utility companies to give public notice and hold a public hearing on proposed rate increases. The commission passed the ordinance. Shortly thereafter, the telephone company applied for a rate increase. Athenians had long complained about the quality of telephone service, and when several hundred people showed up, the hearing had to be moved to the state district courtroom.

Justice and his father questioned the telephone company officials about the rate increase. Then the citizens were given a chance. "They weren't interested in all that abstract information the telephone company had presented," Justice observes. "They wanted to express their opinion about the quality of telephone service. And it got worse and worse and worse. It went on for a couple of hours. You could tell the backbones of the commission members were getting stiffer and stiffer as they saw all of this public outrage. So they just outright flat denied any rate increase!" The next time around, the commission allowed Justice to call on rate experts to counter the claims of the company. Again, the rate increase was denied. When the matter came up for a third time, Justice could see that the telephone company was getting ready to take the city to court. So he advised the commission to grant a small increase.

Wayne Justice has been portrayed in the *Washington Post* as the small town stereotype of the 1940s and 1950s—an overweight, cigar-smoking fraternal club president.[7] It is a characterization which fits, with one notable exception: Most such men were *not* members of the liberal wing of the Democratic Party, nor were they interested in statewide politics. In spite of his membership in basically conservative organizations, Justice was still a populist, and he was very active politically, first locally and then statewide. In 1947 he involved himself in the Young Democrats of Texas. In 1948 he attended the state Democratic convention in Fort Worth as a delegate from Henderson County, where the contest between the regular Democrats and the ultraconservative Dixiecrats was intense. Rather than support the Truman-Barkley ticket, the

Dixiecrats walked out. Justice joined the loyalists in lustily cheering their departure. "I was standing beside the delegation from Anderson County. We'd been talking together in moderate tones, and I, of course, realized that they were Dixiecrats. But it's always been my style to try to get along with people on the other side as best you can. When all this Dixiecrat thing started, I began yowling just as loud as the rest of them. And they looked at me as if to say, 'Why, you reptile.'" These events captivated him, and he began to consider politics as a career. "I was going to run for Congress like my dad and perhaps governor on down the line." The two personalities that most influenced him were Lyndon Johnson and Ralph Yarborough.

Although Justice did not realize it at the time, the 1948 Democratic primary that resulted in the nomination and subsequent election of Lyndon Johnson to the U.S. Senate was of monumental importance to him and the nation. From the Senate, Johnson was chosen as John Kennedy's running mate in 1960, and when Johnson became president following Kennedy's assassination, he appointed Wayne Justice to the federal bench at the insistence of Ralph Yarborough. Of possibly equal importance to Justice was the distaste he came to feel for behind-the-scenes political work as a result of his association with Johnson.

Justice and Johnson met for the first time during the 1948 primary campaign. Congressman Johnson had amassed a New Deal record of voting for countryside liberalism—rural electrification, river development, farm-to-market roads. He had also voted for the poll tax, had opposed Truman's civil rights program, and had voted for the pro-business Taft-Hartley Act in 1947. Powerful Texas business leaders, particularly those at Brown and Root Construction Company in Houston, were impressed and poured money into his campaign. His chief opponent was former governor Coke Stevenson (1941–1947). A conservative, "Calculatin' Coke" had chosen not to seek reelection in 1946. Colonel George Peddy, a wealthy conservative corporate lawyer, was also in the race.

Like others of the progressive faction within the Democratic Party, Justice preferred Johnson to Stevenson. He called Johnson headquarters and volunteered to serve as Johnson's campaign manager in Henderson County. He was readily accepted, since Johnson then had little following in East Texas, the result of his New Deal past.

Justice first met the man who would name him to the federal bench when Johnson held a political rally in Palestine, some thirty-five miles from Athens in Anderson County. The candidate was scheduled to speak in Athens the following morning. Johnson had attracted considerable publicity by being the first candidate to use a helicopter to travel around the state. With the use of the helicopter, which generated as much interest as the candidate, and advance men, he was able to address up to sixty thousand people a week. Justice traveled to Palestine to hear Johnson speak and to meet him.

Johnson was staying at the O'Neal Hotel in Palestine. His campaign manager for that county had assembled a makeshift platform and four rows of seats from old boards and bricks in a vacant lot next to the hotel. A string of naked light bulbs was strung across the lot. It was an inelegant arrangement. But if it bothered Johnson, he did not give any sign. Justice remembers that Lyndon in shirt sleeves spoke to the few people who came to hear him as though he were addressing a multitude. It was a good speech. Justice came away impressed.

After the speech, several campaign officials including Justice were invited to join the candidate for coffee at the hotel. Johnson, he recalls, was in a jovial mood and told a number of good stories. He made an effort to become acquainted with everyone at the table. What impressed Justice was that Johnson remembered their names long after the event. The candidate then adjourned to his hotel quarters.

About fifteen minutes later, Johnson sent word that he wanted to see his Henderson County campaign manager. "Boy, I was impressed. I would get a chance to meet my hero." When Justice entered Johnson's room, he was in for a surprise. "Lyndon was sprawled out on the bed," he recalls, "one of these old iron bedsteads, in his BVDs. He still had his socks on. And he was talking over the telephone with somebody. My God, he was really excoriating someone. He was using a lot of profanity, calling the guy a son of a bitch. I gathered from what I was hearing that this was his helicopter pilot, who had failed to meet him at a certain place. From the conversation, I learned that Lyndon was going to rendezvous with him in Athens. He planned to leave Palestine by car and arrive in Athens at the landing place at the exact same time that the helicopter landed."

Meanwhile, members of Johnson's campaign staff were going back and forth like a bunch of ants. Included among them were several women. "They were extremely busy and didn't pay any attention to him lying out there in his BVDs." It was an eye-opening experience for a small-town politician. "I'd never seen anything like this. This was high-powered campaigning." When Johnson got off the phone, he turned to Justice and asked to know all the details for the next day's stop in Athens.

When Justice had first learned that Johnson would be making a campaign swing through Athens and expected a big crowd, he had pondered where to mark a place for the helicopter to land and how to guarantee a crowd. The latter was particularly challenging, since Johnson planned to be there at 8 A.M. Justice hit upon the idea of having the helicopter land on the grounds of the Henderson County Junior College. As it turned out, the president of the college, Orval Pirtle, was a Johnson supporter and was delighted with the idea. So, in accordance with directions from Johnson's staff, Justice planned to anchor crepe paper to the ground so that it could be seen from the air.

He explained all of this to Johnson after the congressman had hung up the telephone. Johnson was courteous but insistent on knowing all the details. Justice remembers that every once in a while, Johnson would interrupt the conversation if someone came into the room. "He was very unpleasant to them. He didn't have a single commendatory word to say to anybody passing through that room. All he said was, 'What are you doing about this?' or 'Why didn't you do that?'"

Justice says emphatically, "From that point on, I never did like Lyndon Johnson very much. I greatly respected his abilities. But I didn't like him as a person. I formed the opinion that I wouldn't be around this disagreeable guy on any extended basis if I could avoid it. I just don't like to be around people who are that unpleasant." Justice returned to the coffee shop. About ten minutes later, Johnson joined the group. "He was his old mild-mannered self, good ol' Lyndon again. But I had been behind the scenes, and I knew what lay back of all that."

Early the next morning, Johnson's helicopter began making passes around the Athens downtown square to drum up interest. When the helicopter began circling, Sue Justice and four friends were the only ones assembled at the landing site. But by the time the helicopter landed, President Pirtle had dismissed classes, and the students rushed to the site, more interested in the helicopter than the candidate. It was precisely 8 A.M., and Johnson's car pulled up at the same time. In the general hubbub, the crowd assumed Johnson had arrived in the helicopter. Justice was on hand to witness the scene. "He shook hands with everybody. I could tell that he was really delighted with that crowd. He didn't identify them all as students. He knew they were young, but it didn't really sink in on him that these were all just a bunch of damn students who probably couldn't vote. There must have been a hundred people from Athens itself who had been excited by that helicopter. They were all mixed in. Lyndon got up and made a speech, and it went over well. He was enthusiastic and exhilarated by that big crowd I had for him. I was so excited about the whole thing that I got in my car and drove over to his next stop, Frankston, at about eighty-five to ninety miles an hour. I arrived there shortly after the helicopter landed and he'd just started his speech. Lyndon made his speech for about fifteen minutes and he took off again, but he noted me out there in the audience."

The runoff with Stevenson, who had amassed the most votes in the primary, was one of the closest and most disputed elections in American history. Johnson won by a handful of votes and thereby earned the title "Landslide

Lyndon." But it wasn't until Supreme Court Justice Hugo Black stayed the hand of Federal Judge T. Whitfield Davidson, who had launched an investigation into election irregularities, that Johnson's nomination was secure. Johnson had no trouble beating his Republican opponent, Jack Porter, by a comfortable margin in the fall election. But charges and countercharges over Johnson's nomination have continued to this day.

While a number of counties were targets of investigations over alleged fraudulent voting tallies, Henderson County was not one of them. Justice knew that in order to win in Henderson County, Johnson would have to get the votes that had gone to the third candidate, Peddy, in the first round. Justice therefore arranged a meeting with Peddy's county campaign manager, R. T. Craig, former publisher of *Athens Daily Review*. Craig was a conservative Democrat with little liking for Johnson's New Deal activities. But Justice knew that Craig was also not happy with Stevenson. Learning that Craig was leaning toward Johnson, Justice prevailed upon him to help arrange Lyndon's next county campaign speech. When Johnson and Craig met, Craig was won over. Johnson was delighted. He was particularly pleased to have an establishment Democrat endorse his campaign.

Shortly after the runoff election, and just before the official canvass of votes at the state convention, Johnson called all his county campaign managers, including Wayne Justice. This time, it was the "other" Johnson that Justice had seen in the hotel room. Justice remembers the event vividly. "You could tell that he was in a high state of irritability. He asked me how things were going. I told him, well, he'd won by such and such a vote. He said, 'Hell, I know that, but are they going to be able to challenge any of it?' I said no. He said, 'How do you know about this total? How did you get it?' I told him that I was there at the election board when the returns came in. He said, 'Is that all you've done? You haven't checked with the precinct chairmen?' I said no, I hadn't found it necessary. He said, 'Well, damn it, go out and check those precinct chairmen, make sure those totals are right.' He was just mean about it. I didn't do that because I was pretty confident that it was a square deal. If there'd been any crooked boxes, I would have known about it." A canvass of the votes revealed that the preliminary tallies were correct. Justice called Johnson headquarters and relayed the message that nothing had changed in Henderson County.

Though Johnson and Justice were never close and though Justice later joined the Yarborough forces against Johnson in unsuccessful attempts to control the Texas Democratic Party, Johnson would remember years later that Justice had come through for him in his hour of need.

With growing interest in state politics, Wayne Justice began expanding his political contacts around the state. One of the persons he decided to meet was

Jim Wright, then a liberal legislator in the Texas House of Representatives who was generating considerable newspaper coverage, much of it negative. "Wright turned out to be a charming fellow, red-headed, athletic-appearing, just exuded charm," Justice remembers. "He was one of the most affable and likeable persons I've ever met. I just couldn't understand how the people in the House could scorn him like they did."

During the 1950 Democratic primary election for governor, Justice modified his views about Jim Wright. Justice was supporting Caso March, a young Baylor law professor with a populist platform, although March's defeat was a foregone conclusion. Governor Allan Shivers, who was then perceived as a moderate but later became an archconservative, was favored. At the Democratic convention, Justice chanced upon Wright in an elevator. "There were only the two of us on the elevator," he remembers. "I told Wright that I was for Caso March, and he gasped in horror as if I were out of my mind and looked around to be sure no one was listening. He gave me the understanding that this was a very dangerous thing to do. I decided right then and there that Jim Wright had retreated from his progressive positions."

Why would Wayne Justice support a candidate like Caso March, who was so obviously a loser? "Well, it's been characteristic of me throughout the whole time I was in politics that I was ready to go down with a sinking ship," Justice asserts. "If they were somebody I liked, by God, I'd stay with them. I didn't give a damn whether they were going to win or not." It is a revealing statement, and perhaps explains why Wayne Justice would never be successful as a politician. It is also indicative of Justice's unswerving devotion to his principles. It helps explain as well his unalterable support for the progressive wing of the Democratic Party and for Ralph Yarborough despite repeated defeats.

Ralph W. Yarborough graduated *cum laude* from the University of Texas School of Law. He quickly became an expert in land and water rights law, and was appointed assistant attorney general by Attorney General James V. Allred in 1931. Yarborough was responsible for the Permanent School Fund, an investment fund of over $40 million. He won several important lawsuits against the oil companies, including a judgment against the Magnolia Petroleum Company for the oil and gas and bonus rental income from 3.9 million acres of land. When the progressive Allred became governor, he rewarded Yarborough for his work with an appointment to the judgeship of the Fifty-third District Court in 1936 to fill a vacancy. Yarborough then won election to the post. He campaigned for attorney general in 1938 but was beaten. Later he volunteered for the army in World War II and requested combat service. He emerged a lieutenant colonel. After the war, Yarborough quickly established himself as one of the state's leading land and personal injury lawyers.

A native of Chandler, Texas, in Henderson County, Yarborough was for many years a Justice family intimate. Yarborough's political views coincided with those of the Justices, and father and son greatly respected Yarborough's abilities both as a lawyer and as a politician. Shortly after Wayne began practicing with his father, he called on Yarborough to see if he could help the firm with a difficult case. "I shall never forget seeing him in his office," Justice says. "He had a very nice suite of offices, reflecting that he had a good income. Very spacious, secretary out there, everything very neat. When I got in his office, there he was with a barricade of paper in front of him. His desk was literally stacked at least three feet high in all directions. When we were talking, every once in a while if he needed to make reference to something, he'd reach into that stack of papers and pull out something and then carefully put it back. He apparently knew where everything was, but all of his filing system was on top of his desk."

In 1952 Yarborough planned to run for attorney general. But he changed his mind at the last moment and decided to run for governor against conservative incumbent Allan Shivers instead. "Now that was about as impractical a decision as was ever made by any living person," Justice observes. "There was absolutely no way that he could have won that race, but he nevertheless decided he was going to run for governor and so he made the announcement."[8] The Justices immediately rallied to their friend's cause. They liked his progressive platform, which, as he phrased it in a later campaign, was designed to put the jam on the lower shelf where the little people could reach it. "It was a populist-type platform, which I certainly did like," Justice says. "So I immediately began to ask for his literature and campaign materials. It ended up that I just assumed the job of working for Ralph Yarborough in that campaign."

Yarborough had no organization and no money. "I was almost alone," the Senator admits.[9] His family and a close circle of friends in and around Chandler were his only base of support. "I immediately thought that Henderson County, my home county, was the only place I could go and expect to get any crowd for an opening speech, which a candidate generally had if he had any kind of campaign." Athens, the county seat, would be the site of the speech, which was to be broadcast statewide on the radio. Yarborough asked Wayne Justice to organize it for him. R. T. Craig, then president of the First National Bank of Athens, resigned from the State Democratic Executive Committee to lend his support. While a conservative Democrat, Craig had given Yarborough his first job in Chandler, and a strong bond of friendship had developed between the two.

A major problem was the lack of money. Few were willing or able to make contributions. So most of the local arrangements were financed by a few young professional people in town and by the Justice law firm. With little money to work with, arrangements had to be kept simple. A platform, of course, was necessary. Justice decided to use the back of a cattle truck. He had used one before when Homer Rainey spoke in Athens, and it had served the purpose. He borrowed one from a political opponent, Leon Barron, who ran a pea threshing plant in Athens. Though they were diametrically opposed politically, Barron and Justice were friends. "Ol' Leon had done real well by me. He'd had all of the cow manure washed off of that flatbed." Justice had the trailer placed next to the front steps of the courthouse on the square. He located a sign painter and at a bargain rate had him paint a large sign which could be attached to the side of the flatbed trailer to disguise it.

Yarborough drew a big crowd. Justice remembers that the entire east side of the courthouse square was covered, with people spilling out onto the streets. He had had the sign painter assemble a number of small cardboard signs with the names of Texas counties painted on them. "I and several of my compatriots went out and started handing these signs around. I told the people, 'I don't give a damn where you're from, just hold up the sign. This is just for the benefit of the press.' They were all Yarborough supporters, so they didn't object. The newspaper people could look out there and see that forest of signs, you know. 'My God, look, there's some from Lubbock and other counties way out in West Texas.'"

As soon as the radio hookup was established, Justice introduced the candidate, who proceeded to give a rousing speech to an enthusiastic East Texas crowd. Several young speechwriters who had worked for Lyndon Johnson in the 1948 campaign volunteered to help Yarborough polish his delivery. "They knew their business," Yarborough says. "We practiced that speech. They had been radio advisers for Lyndon Johnson and knew the cadence of speech, emphasis to put on certain words, the tone, and how to deliver. I practiced, and it was probably the best or one of the best radio speeches I ever made."

R. T. Craig cut big strips of cloth the shape of men's overalls and hung them on wires between the trees on the courthouse lawn. Craig told the reporters that the big inverted "Y's" blowing in the breeze signified Yarborough's plan to clean up the governor's office. The newspapers reported a good send-off. But Yarborough's campaign was doomed from the start. Buried by conservative Democrats in the primary, he did manage to win a half-million votes, and in so doing helped consolidate liberal forces in the party. From 1952 on, politics in Texas was a three-arena affair: the liberal and conservative Democratic factions and the struggling Republicans.

It was also in 1952 that Justice briefly considered running for Congress. To obtain needed financial backing, he consulted Frank C. "Posh" Oltorf, a Washington, D.C., representative for Brown and Root Construction Company and intimate of Lyndon Johnson and Sam Rayburn. Justice had met Oltorf on the troopship returning from India in 1946. During the long voyage, the pair spent many hours discussing politics. Oltorf, who had also served two terms as state representative from Falls County, explained the hazards of undertaking a campaign. One of the biggest was recognizing just how much money was needed and finding out where to get it. Oltorf told Justice that while a liberal could get money from the business community, "he would have to show them that he doesn't have horns, that he was not out to punish business. There would have to be compromise." Oltorf indicated that Lyndon Johnson had been able to secure financial backing from business interests—which Justice took to mean the Brown and Root Construction Company—even though the company was antiunion. While Oltorf was talking, Justice was thinking to himself, "You reckon I could do that?" Oltorf doubted that a purist like Wayne Justice could.

While Justice was pondering his next move, John Dowdy, an attorney in Henderson County, announced his candidacy. Dowdy was serving as a state district attorney and had built up a strong base of support among conservative Democrats. "When he announced, that doomed me right there on the spot because I knew that he was a formidable politician and would split the home county vote with me," Justice says.

In May 1952, Justice was a delegate to the state convention in San Antonio, where delegates would be selected to the national convention. While Governor Shivers had control of the party machinery, he refused to pledge that he would support the national ticket. Led by fiery Maury Maverick, Sr., former New Deal congressman and San Antonio mayor, the liberal-loyalist faction walked out. Justice was among those who bolted the party. "It was raining outside, but we went over to La Villita, a restored Spanish village close by the convention hall. They got very romantic about it later in the *Texas Observer,* calling it 'The Walk in the Rain.' When we got over there, it was a madhouse. Very little organization. You can imagine what it would be like to establish a convention just right there on the spot. But we managed to do it."

The liberal-loyalists selected a slate of delegates to send to the national convention in Chicago. Justice was selected as the delegate from the Seventh Congressional District. When the delegates got to Chicago, there was a fight before the credentials committee. After Shivers made assurances that he would support the Democratic nominee in the fall, the Shivers delegation was seated. The rejected liberal delegation was given favored seating in the balcony. "We were right up there against the rail where we could see and hear everything that was going on," Justice remembers. "It was pretty disheartening when they seated the Shivers group." When the nomination went to Adlai Stevenson, who not only favored civil rights legislation but also was opposed to state ownership of the supposedly oil-rich tidelands off the coast of Texas, Shivers became one of three southern governors to endorse Republican nominee

Dwight Eisenhower. From that point onward, Justice could not abide Allan Shivers. At the fall convention, the State Democratic Executive Committee, for the first time in history, endorsed a Republican for the presidency.

In an effort to placate the liberal faction of the Texas Democratic Party, the Democratic National Committee established a committee called the "Texas Advisory Council of the Democratic National Committee." It was purported to be the prototype of similar committees in other states. Wayne Justice's name was among its fifty-five members. He notes with a laugh that though committee membership is listed on his résumé, "The advisory committee never did meet so far as I know, and our advice was never sought." According to long-time Texas liberal Democrat Creekmore Fath, "Sam Rayburn organized the committee as a lever against Shivers." The committee was disbanded in 1956.

Sue Justice had accompanied her husband to the 1952 Democratic convention and became so caught up in political life that she began devoting much of her time to state politics when she returned to Athens. Before 1952, Sue's political activities had been limited. Politics played no role in her upbringing. Her parents rarely even voted, though her father admitted to her that he had slipped away to vote for Harry Truman in 1948. But Sue shared her father's compassion for those less fortunate than she. "My father never wanted us children to ignore anyone's plea for help. He was a very compassionate man. If we drove the seven miles from our house to town, he would give a ride to any person along the road. He would never dream of not using what we had to help someone in need."

With these humanitarian instincts, Sue Justice readily embraced the liberal political philosophy of her husband. He was, she maintains, her political Pygmalion. Soon after their marriage in 1947, she began working alongside him in Henderson County Democratic politics. As his law practice grew, Wayne left more and more of the mechanics of politics to Sue and to Marcelle Simmons, the law firm secretary. "I liked it. It was very stimulating to me," Sue says. In 1962, she was elected a member of the State Democratic Executive Committee and served one two-year term. After Wayne became a federal judge, ethical considerations precluded her from further high-profile political activities. However, she has never wavered in her support for Democratic candidates and liberal causes.

Yarborough tried again in 1954. It was Allan Shivers' bid for a third term. Despite scandals arising in the Shivers administration, Yarborough's chances were doomed by successful conservative exploitation of union threats and fear of communism. However, his loss by only twenty-three thousand votes in the primary convinced the conservative Democratic establishment that the liberals were a real threat. In the 1956 presidential election year, Sam Rayburn and

Lyndon Johnson wanted to keep both "Shivercrats"—those who had supported Eisenhower in 1952—and liberals from controlling the state Democratic machinery. To do so, Rayburn proposed that Johnson run for president as a favorite son at the national convention and also serve as chairman of the delegation. At the state convention in May, John Connally orchestrated a successful move to have delegates back LBJ at the national convention for as long as he remained a candidate.[10] This move upset an uneasy alliance the Johnson forces had made with the liberals, who had agreed only to back Johnson on the first ballot. The Johnson forces also rejected a liberal move to oust the Shivers-controlled State Democratic Executive Committee.

Up to this time, Wayne Justice had considered himself a member of the Johnson team. Since the 1948 senatorial campaign, he had continued to support Johnson, including making nominal political contributions. "When we had political conventions, I could always go around if Lyndon was in any way involved and be greeted by the upper ranks of his organization. They were glad to see me, you know, and they'd ask me things about Henderson County and that section of the state. I was one of his men. Of course, I worked for Ralph Yarborough, but I was still on the Lyndon Johnson team."

But all that came to an end at the May convention when Justice had occasion to visit the Johnson headquarters. What transpired provides a clear contrast between the political styles of the two men. "There he was, same ol' Lyndon," Justice says. "But he was in a very mellow mood, very mellow. He was surrounded by his advisers. It became obvious to me that he was siding with the Shivers group. I'd heard what might be in the offing, but I didn't really know that until that time. I couldn't stomach it. And I was sitting there, thinking, well, I ought not to be here, for gosh sakes. I can't take this. But I stayed around anyway just out of curiosity to see what the hell was happening. And this lawyer was advising him about the various maneuvers that could be made to thwart a liberal takeover of the executive committee. And Lyndon would say, 'Now, counselor,' in a very patronizing way, 'Now, counselor, what about the legalities of this?' You know, Lyndon wasn't a lawyer. And so this lawyer would tell him. I left that suite and I never again approached any Lyndon Johnson functions. That was the end. By Johnson's siding with the Shivers group, we didn't throw out that damned executive committee. If we'd done it, why, the political history of Texas might have been different. Lyndon never did understand political unregenerates." Indeed, in the second volume of his Lyndon Johnson biography, Robert Caro notes that Johnson "ridiculed—intensely and harshly—politicians who fought for ideals and principles." He quotes Helen Gahagan Douglas, who became part of the Johnson crowd after she was elected to Congress in 1944, to the effect that "He [Johnson] made fun of those who refused to bend."[11]

At the national convention, the delegation voted as planned for Johnson. Justice served as an alternate to principal delegate Lloyd Bentsen, Jr. Bentsen left early, thus giving Justice his first and only opportunity to serve as a delegate to a national convention. Adlai Stevenson was renominated on the first ballot. After getting nowhere at the national convention, Johnson faced a chaotic situation at home. The liberals were poised to take over the party machinery at the fall convention, when a new executive committee would be selected. Faced with a choice between working with the liberals or siding with the conservatives, Johnson chose the latter. The conservatives were tied in with the business establishment and money. The liberals were once again stymied in their desire to control the party.

Meanwhile, scandals prevented Shivers from running again for governor. In his place, conservatives had U.S. Senator Price Daniel run against Yarborough, who was trying a third time. This time there was real fear about Yarborough's chances. Conservatives rallied to keep what they considered to be an uncontrollable liberal out of the governor's mansion. Daniel had no trouble winning the first primary. Yarborough placed second, followed by former governor and U.S. Senator W. Lee "Pappy" O'Daniel and West Texas rancher and writer J. Evetts Haley. In the runoff between the top two contenders, Daniel won, but just barely. The Yarborough campaign as usual had run out of money and press support. But now a fortuitous opportunity presented itself. In order to serve as governor, Daniel had to resign his Senate seat. A special election was called. It was to be a plurality election in which the person securing the highest number of votes would win. When Yarborough announced his candidacy, it was generally assumed that he would win. And he did.

It was a time for celebration by Texas liberals. After working all of these years for Yarborough, Justice was particularly gratified. "It's impossible for a person now to think back and realize the odds against which he labored. They were just enormous. He had no money, just next to no money at all. He was superhuman. I can't tell you how much respect and admiration I have for that man and the fact that he made it."

The feelings were mutual. On February 17, 1960, Yarborough wrote a letter to Wayne Justice, requesting an autographed photo to hang on the wall of his Senate office "as a permanent reminder of your aid to me and your service to all the people of Texas on behalf of good government in our time in that State." Yarborough noted that "As we lost race after race, some of the faint-hearted dropped away, but you grew bolder and more influential in each race."

Yarborough asked Justice to manage his statewide campaign in the regular election for a six-year term in 1958. "Wayne Justice had managed my campaigns in the past in Henderson County, either three or four times, carrying the county every time," Yarborough notes.[12] "I asked him to manage my statewide campaign for reelection because of his unimpeachable integrity, honesty, fairness, and good judgment. I knew it would be a terrible drain for him, because we had so little money. But I had had some very sad experiences with other campaign managers, some of them doublecrossing me, supporting the opposition in the middle of the campaign, etc." Justice pondered the matter for several weeks before telling Yarborough that he would do it. But in the meantime, R. C. Slagle, Sr., a lawyer in Sherman and Sam Rayburn's campaign manager, offered to undertake the job. Yarborough jumped at the chance. "Since Slagle had one congressional district organized and ties with the Rayburn and former Tom Connally campaign managers in other districts, I thought I would let Wayne Justice off the hook." Justice was relieved. "I immediately applauded the decision. In the first place, I didn't want the job. It would have been a great sacrifice. And second, I thought Slagle would make an excellent campaign manager, as he indeed did." Yarborough won decisively over conservative Democrat William "Dollar Bill" Blakley and went on to serve in the U.S. Senate until 1970, when he was beaten in the primary election by conservative Democrat Lloyd Bentsen, Jr.

After their 1956 loss, the liberals had established a statewide organization called the Democrats of Texas (DOT). The goal of the organization was to fuse together diverse groups to form a liberal coalition that could exert influence over the candidates and platform of the state Democratic Party. They held their first convention in Austin on May 18, 1957. Wayne Justice was a charter member and later served in a variety of roles for the organization.

The DOT tried to get control of the state Democratic Party machinery in 1958. Blind Navarro County Judge Jim Sewell was DOT's choice to serve as temporary chairman of the fall Democratic state convention. Justice had the highest respect for Sewell, who overcame his handicap to become one of the perennial leaders of Texas liberal Democrats. Democratic National Committeewoman for Texas Mrs. R. D. "Frankie" Randolph, who headed the DOT, and Yarborough hoped to take control of the convention from the Johnson forces. Justice gave the seconding speech for Sewell. "I started off by telling that I was from Henderson County, which I called the birthplace of a person well-known in Texas politics (Yarborough)," Justice says. "Of course, they knew who I was talking about, and so I got a huge round of applause to start it off. The applause continued. I turned around to see the reaction of the chairman of the executive committee. He was trying to rap the convention to order because he didn't want all this going on. He looked very concerned and didn't like this a damn bit." The DOT lost, but not by nearly as big a margin as expected.

Justice's last major political involvement took place in 1960. In February at the fourth annual statewide meeting of the renamed Democrats of Texas

Clubs, Justice, who then was DOTC statewide meeting chairman, gave the keynote address. He began by noting that he was a "brass collar Democrat." "I can truthfully assert, and I frequently do, that I have never scratched the Democratic ticket, . . . and that I have always voted for the Democratic nominees from constable to president." [13] He took issue with independents and those who participate in party affairs but, when the chosen candidates do not suit them, sit out the race or bolt the party. He was referring both to Johnson supporters who threatened not to support the ticket if Johnson was not on it and to liberals who said they would do likewise if he was on it. "We need thinking Democrats," he continued, "who will vigorously fight for the course they think best. But let the conflicts be within the party." And when the election arrives, "we must call a truce among ourselves and fight the common enemy."

His words were prophetic. For at the 1960 Democratic state convention in June, DOTC leaders realized that they did not have the votes to control the convention. Some thought was given to bolting, holding a rump convention, and then hoping to be seated as the official Texas delegation at the national convention in Los Angeles. [14] The bolt failed to materialize, and the DOTC collapsed. It was once again Johnson's convention. Justice describes his faction's decisive loss in pure East Texas terms: "Johnson cleaned our plow."

Though Johnson told reporters that he was not a candidate, he had the backing of most of the delegates. While Justice did not want to be a delegate to the national convention and have to cast a vote for Johnson, he was interested in being selected as a presidential elector and agreed to vote for the Democratic nominee regardless of who it might be if the Democrats won the national election.

"About that time, we got word that Senator Johnson wanted to see all of the delegates to the national convention and the presidential electors," Justice recalls. "So we lined up and walked down the aisle to the stage, and then back of the stage. I felt like a slave with a metal ring around my neck being led by a chain through the jungle. They took us into the women's lounge, which was large and elaborately furnished with divans and the like. Cliff Carter, one of Johnson's factotums, got everybody over in a corner of the room. There weren't enough chairs; I remember that I stood. Johnson got up and told us that when we got out there to California at the national convention, he wanted to be sure that every one of us would be working hard for Johnson for president. You understand this guy was at the same time telling the papers he wasn't even a candidate. But there he was, just telling us, by God, that you had to be a Johnson delegate or he didn't want you on the delegation."

"When Lyndon got through making his presentation, Cliff Carter took over. He pointed to the guy to my immediate left, who was a delegate. He said, 'Well, what about you, Mr. So-and-so?' Hell, I thought the fellow was going to get down on his knees and kiss the ground. He said he thought Lyndon Johnson was the greatest man that had ever lived, and of course, he wanted him for president. It was just sickening. So once Carter was assured that this guy was all right, he moved on to the next one. And each of them tried to outdo the other. A good number of them were the damnedest bunch of phonies I ever saw in my life. It really turned my stomach watching these folks."

"When he finished with the delegates, he turned to me as presidential elector and asked, 'What about you, Mr. Justice?' I said, 'Well, I've just got two things to say. When Lyndon Johnson ran for senator in 1948, I was one of his campaign managers over in East Texas.' When I said that, Lyndon broke in and said, 'Yes, he was for me when some of these other sons of bitches around here wouldn't have spit on me.' I then said that I as presidential elector would vote for the nominee of the convention whoever he might be. Apparently, that took care of it. I wasn't called upon to say anything else, nor would I have done so."

The entire Justice law firm worked hard for the successful Kennedy-Johnson ticket in the 1960 campaign. By this time, Justice was looking around for other opportunities. Fellow Athens attorney Willis Moore believed that "Wayne was a small-town person, but he couldn't be satisfied in a small town." Unlike other attorneys in town who were interested in the mechanics of the law, Moore found Wayne Justice to be equally interested in its philosophy.

After briefly considering running for state district judge, Justice decided on seeking a little patronage for himself. He'd try to secure appointment as U.S. Attorney for the Eastern District of Texas. It was a fortuitous decision, for it set him upon the road to the federal bench.

CHAPTER 3

U.S. Attorney:
The Road to the Bench

In 1956 Justice had gone to Tyler to seek a settlement in a civil case with the Office of U.S. Attorney for the Eastern District of Texas. In talking with James T. Burke, one of the assistant U.S. attorneys, he learned about the work of the office. Having served as part-time city attorney in Athens, Justice had developed a liking for government work. A term as U.S. attorney would give him experience in federal court and thus add prestige to his law practice. He decided to seek the appointment.

Sue Justice was opposed to the idea. "I'm much more materialistic than Wayne. I wanted him to make a lot of money." Neither Wayne nor his father, she maintains, was very much interested in money. "They would just as soon live in a world where money isn't important." She did not see much future in the job of U.S. attorney. Besides, by this time Will Justice was up in years and in ill health. She worried that if Wayne were to go to Tyler, the law practice would atrophy. On the other hand, she recognized that Wayne was becoming bored with his work and needed a new interest. She was confident that if he wanted the job, he would get it, given all his years in state Democratic politics and his position as chairman of the Henderson County Democratic Executive Committee.

Though he did not talk much about it, Wayne's father was also ambivalent about the idea. If Wayne secured the post, he would have to leave the firm. But the senior Justice did not stand in the way of his son's ambition. He died just seven months after Wayne became U.S. attorney.

When Kennedy was elected in 1960, Republican appointee Paul Brown resigned as U.S. Attorney for the Eastern District of Texas. Wayne Justice told Senator Ralph Yarborough that he was interested in the job. Yarborough was somewhat taken aback. "He looked at me so explicitly," Justice recalls. "I think I really surprised him. He said he would take my application under consideration. He didn't pledge himself to me at all." Yarborough was indeed surprised that Wayne Justice wanted to become a criminal prosecutor after years of civil practice in Athens. Furthermore, he could not commit himself to Justice since he had pledged to other candidates that the selection would be wide open.[1]

One of the other contenders was Joe Tunnell, who had been hired as assistant U.S. attorney by William M. Steger in 1958 and who had taken over as interim U.S. attorney after Brown's resignation. Tunnell had also secured the appointment of Yarborough's nephew, Richard Brooks Hardee, as assistant U.S. attorney. Tunnell, a longtime friend and occasional courtroom opponent of Wayne Justice, had served as county attorney in Van Zandt County and, like Justice, had managed Yarborough's campaigns in that county. In his first courtroom skirmish with Tunnell, Justice had lost.[2]

The appointment of a new U.S. attorney was held up, pending resolution of an impasse between Yarborough and Lyndon Johnson over Democratic political patronage in Texas. Yarborough insisted that Johnson, as vice president, was not entitled to any. Johnson maintained that even though he had won election as vice president, he had also won reelection to the U.S. Senate under a special provision in state law. While he could not serve, he was entitled to the patronage of that office. His claim was reinforced when a Republican, John Tower, won the seat in the special election. Eventually, the impasse was broken when President Kennedy told Johnson and Yarborough to split state Democratic patronage between them. "We had a gentleman's agreement," says Yarborough. "We agreed that we wouldn't submit someone personally obnoxious to the other."

The impasse broken, appointments began to be made for a number of important federal offices, including the four U.S. attorneys in Texas. Since Yarborough's home is in the eastern section of the state, he asserted a strong claim for patronage in that section. But he had a hard time making his selection. "Eventually I settled on Wayne Justice, given the strong ties between our two families that go back three generations." Yarborough maintains that it was the most difficult patronage decision he had to make as U.S. Senator.

Since Justice had campaigned for Johnson, the latter had no valid objection to his being considered for the position. On June 6, 1961, President John F. Kennedy nominated Justice to the post for a four-year term. The appointment was readily confirmed by the U.S. Senate, and on July 1, 1961, William Wayne Justice took office as U.S. Attorney for the Eastern District of Texas.

A branch of the Justice Department, the Office of U.S. Attorney functions as the federal government's trial lawyer. Government agencies such as the Department of Agriculture and the Internal Revenue Service forward case files with all the necessary documentation for use in civil and criminal prosecutions. Lawyers from the U.S. attorney's office argue the cases in federal court. The variety of case work is extensive—everything from unpaid crop loans to lands condemnation to counterfeiting.

When Justice took office as U.S. attorney for the forty-one county Eastern District, the office was divided into civil, criminal, and lands divisions. The professional staff consisted of seven assistant U.S. attorneys—"ridiculously small," Justice maintains, "considering our responsibilities." Except for an attorney in Texarkana doing lands condemnation work and another in Beaumont, all the attorneys were located in Tyler. Criminal prosecution work had been handled by the interim U.S. attorney, Joe Tunnell. Since Justice had had little federal court experience, he asked Tunnell to stay on as first assistant. Tunnell declined, because he had already decided to enter private practice in Tyler. But he did agree to remain for two months to help Justice during the transition period.

Justice found a suitable replacement in the person of Leighton Cornett from Paris, Texas. Cornett, whose rustic appearance belies a liberal political philosophy and keen legal mind, had just concluded a stint as county attorney in Lamar County. Justice and Cornett knew each other casually from law school—Cornett had been a year ahead of Justice—and from their involvement in the Yarborough campaigns, which they had managed in their respective counties. "I never had seen Leighton in action, but everybody told me that he was a fierce prosecutor," Justice says. "He convicted nearly everybody. And I knew him through politics, not real well, but we were both on the same side of the fence. I knew that I wouldn't have any problems getting him confirmed."

Cornett initially expressed reluctance to take the job. "I had just finished eleven years as a prosecutor in Lamar County, and I wanted to get out and practice." But he eventually accepted the job of first assistant U.S. attorney, with responsibility for criminal prosecutions, and agreed to stay two years in that role.

Brooks Hardee, a native of Chandler, Texas, and nephew of Senator Yarborough, also remained on the staff. Justice initially was concerned that Hardee's appointment might have been based primarily on political patronage. "But I was pleasantly surprised. He turned out to be a top grade assistant to whom I entrusted a great deal of my administrative matters." Hardee eventually headed the lands division, which at the time Justice was appointed had the largest caseload of any U.S. attorney's office in the country. Later he became first assistant U.S. attorney and was appointed U.S. attorney when Justice was elevated to the bench.

Justice found the position of U.S. attorney "utterly fascinating, the best job in terms of enjoyment that I have ever had." His only regret was that supervisory responsibilities prevented his being in court as much as he would have liked. He took pride in his administration of the office. "I'd get there at 7 o'clock in the morning and by the time 8 had rolled around I had read every speck of mail that had come into the office, including the case files, so it was ready to be parceled out to the various attorneys and discussed with them. I usually left around 5:30 in the afternoon and by that time had read every bit of mail that had gone from that office during the day. I knew exactly what was happening." Cornett considers Justice one of the most dedicated, hardworking lawyers he has ever known, a view echoed by others who worked with him. "He drove back and forth from Athens and was in that office seven days a week. I'd say, 'Wayne, you don't have to come over here on Sunday morning.' But he did. I had my farm over in Paris, and I told him that if we weren't absolutely tied up on the weekends, I would be hitting the trail for Paris. Wayne said that was okay; that was part of our working relationship."

As U.S. attorney, Justice gave his legal staff considerable discretion to do their work. At the same time, he was cautious about the use of the power of his office. Carl Roth, who served for a time as law clerk to Judge Joe W. Sheehy, Tyler's only federal judge, before becoming an assistant U.S. attorney under Justice in the civil division, recalls that "no matter how persuasive your logic, you had to support your position with clear-cut authority or he would be reluctant to follow your recommendation. Philosophically, he was concerned about the abuse of government power." In Roth's case, Justice wanted to be sure the law and the facts were on the government's side before prosecuting oil companies in the Beaumont area for oil and chemical spills under a seldom-used 1899 federal statute.

Justice did not move to Tyler because he assumed that when the four-year term was up, he would return to his law practice in Athens. The fifty-minute morning and evening commute, coupled with his extensive traveling throughout East Texas, meant that he had little time for family and social life. Sue Justice, who refused to go to most evening social events without him, found their lifestyle changing. She did make one concession. She kept their box at the high school football field and regularly went to football games during the years Wayne was away.

Sue's loneliness was accentuated by the decision to place their daughter, Ellen, in a private boarding school. By the time Ellen was thirteen, her parents had become ambitious for her future. This reflects in part their own bootstrap experiences at achieving success and in part their contact with others who were reaping the benefits of formal education at prestigious eastern colleges. As U.S. attorney, Wayne Justice perceived that most of the top positions in the Department of Justice went to those who were graduates of such institutions.

Believing that their daughter's chances for gaining admission to an eastern college would be enhanced by a college-preparatory education, the Justices set about finding a suitable eastern boarding school. But friends alerted them to St. Stephen's Episcopal School in Austin. After visiting the campus, they decided to enroll Ellen, who developed a strong attachment to the institution and thrived there.

Wayne Justice acknowledges that placing his daughter in an elite private school is inconsistent with his populist philosophy. "All I can say is that I was ambitious for my daughter. If either my dad or I had had an inkling that it would be of benefit to me in my later career to have gone to one of those eastern schools, he wouldn't have hesitated a minute. He'd have sent me up there. But neither one of us had that realization." One thing Justice wants there to be no mistake about: he did not send his child away to school to avoid integration in the Athens public schools. "At the time that Ellen was taken out of the Athens schools, there was no integration. None whatever. They had at least nominal integration at St. Stephen's when she enrolled."

The Slant-Hole Oil Drilling Case

The biggest case Justice was involved with during his tenure as U.S. attorney was the prosecution of directional or "slant-hole" oil drillers. The slant-hole scandal arose from investigations into the siphoning of oil by directional drilling techniques in the huge East Texas oil field. Most of the illegal drilling was done by independent oil producers who sought to siphon oil from nearby leases owned by major oil companies.

When Justice took office, the slant-hole oil scandal had just been brought to light. Criminal indictments had been returned in state court, but with little success. By 1964, approximately three hundred indictments against some fifty individuals had been brought in Gregg County, and another twenty indictments against a like number in Rusk County. Only a single case went to a jury for a verdict. In that instance, the jury acquitted the defendants. The presiding judge reproached the jury. Leighton Cornett speculates the reason was that "The East Texas oil field had become a law unto itself. They were doing what had become perfectly acceptable. In other words, it's all right for you to drill a slant hole and draw some oil out from under my neighbor's land because he's going to do me the same way." Justice has his doubts. "I don't think companies like Humble Oil and Refining Company, Texaco, and Magnolia would have stood by and let that happen if it had been general knowledge." It has been estimated that over $100 million worth of oil was stolen via slant-hole drilling.[3]

The fact that little was being done about it in state court did not surprise Justice. "These slant-holers had made millions of dollars. They were big political contributors, mostly to right-wing Republican organizations, but they also had made big contributions to county officeholders. It seemed obvious that district attorneys weren't going to do a damn thing." And there was insufficient popular opinion to sustain vigorous prosecution or to hold the violators accountable.

In 1962, when it became clear that nothing was likely to be done at the state level, Justice contacted the Department of Justice about prosecuting the slant-holers in federal court. The 1935 Connolly Hot Oil Act made it illegal to ship oil produced in violation of state law in interstate commerce. The Justice Department gave its approval, and Wayne Justice made plans to seek indictments before the federal grand jury.

When Justice requested that the grand jury be summoned, Federal Judge Joe Sheehy questioned why he wanted to prosecute. Justice responded that it did not appear that the state was going to do anything. Sheehy was not enamored with the idea of the federal government jumping into the breach. "He told me that this was the state's mess and that the state ought to be the one to clean it up. I told him that the Justice Department agreed with the position of my office and the likelihood was that we would proceed. I could tell that that didn't please him one damned bit." It was rumored around the courthouse that a number of wealthy Tyler oil people with whom Sheehy socialized had been involved in slant oil activities and were prevailing upon him to discourage the prosecution.

Justice and Cornett secured criminal indictments from the federal grand jury against separate groups of slant-holers under the statute making filing false reports with a federal agency a felony and also under the Connolly Hot Oil Act, which made interstate shipment of oil and gas produced in violation of a state rule or regulation a misdemeanor. In December 1962, they began preparations to try the first case, *United States v. Gaumer*. Daryl Gaumer, E. B. Hearn, Sr., and E. B. Hearn, Jr., along with Associates Drilling Company, were to be tried on a twenty-nine-count indictment. The case would be the first brought to trial in a Texas federal court and would be carefully watched by the oil industry.

Cornett assumed the responsibility of chief prosecutor. Justice's role was to prove the existence of slant-hole drilling. "Leighton and I decided that because I had had a one-year course in geology when I was at the University of Texas during my freshman year, that made me the 'expert.' I would undertake the technical aspects of an underground survey to show not only where the well was plugged in at the top but where it ended up. And to do that I had to understand the extremely technical methods used to survey the bore hole." A third attorney from the Criminal Division of the Justice Department, Jacob F. Bumstead, traced the oil produced from the illegal wells to show that it had been transported in interstate commerce—no easy task, in that the hot oil was usually commingled with other oil, and the shipment lines went everywhere. It took the prosecutors six months to prepare for the trial. Their difficulties were increased by the fact that, as a result of the state lawsuits, nearly all the witnesses had secured lawyers and were reluctant to cooperate. Preparing for the defense was no easier. All the attorneys had to become schooled in the basics of petroleum engineering.

Trial began on June 3, 1963. Judge Sheehy, who ran his courtroom with an iron hand and had a ferocious temper, gave the federal prosecutors little quarter. The trial lasted nearly a month, and was carefully chronicled in the Tyler newspapers. It had been expected to last a week. Cornett recalls that during the entire four weeks, "We were in court by one question. If this old boy we were questioning had answered the question differently, the judge would have thrown us out of court." In addition, the defendants' lawyers, Tyler attorney John Glass and his son, "were tenacious as hell. I think they were as thorough as any I have ever run across in the courtroom."

The case which the prosecutors had carefully constructed nearly came undone two weeks after it began. The defense challenged them to prove the scientific validity of one of the underground survey methods they were using to show that directional drilling had occurred. Justice had concluded that they could not rely just on the commonly used Eastman survey because it was by no means certain that it was considered reliable throughout the oil industry. A second method was needed to demonstrate the existence of slant holes. The Sperry-Sun method was employed for this purpose. It involved the use of gyroscopes. Here Justice found his army training of some value, for he had studied their use in connection with the automatic pilot system used in airplanes. The prosecutors also needed a third method in case there was a discrepancy between the first two methods. They seized upon a new technique called sonic triangulation, which through a device lowered into the well measured the movement of sound waves produced by touching off small explosives at three surface locations near the wellhead. "We didn't realize all the obstacles, of course, when we first got into this," Justice points out. "We were just lawyers used to trying personal injury, land title, and criminal cases in state court; yet here we were going to present all of this complicated material in federal court with a hostile forum."

On the evening of June 14, during testimony about the results of the Sperry-Sun survey, defense attorney John Glass rose to object to the evidence on the grounds that the scientific validity of the technique had not been established. Without the Sperry-Sun testimony, it would have been nearly impossible for the prosecutors to prove that slant-hole drilling had even occurred, and thus the foundation for later questioning about the purpose of the drilling would have been lacking. Justice was caught off guard. "I will freely admit that I should have done some study regarding that point but had not. I made some lame response to the objection, and at that point, Sheehy sustained it. We were dismayed. I immediately took the witness off the stand and then proceeded to just filibuster with some other little ol' inconsequential testimony until he let us go about nine or ten o'clock that night."

The prosecutors feared a fatal setback. A request for a delay was out of the question. The only hope was to establish the scientific validity of the survey method and do so quickly. A member of the Federal Petroleum Board in Kilgore, Texas, noted that the premier authority for the Sperry-Sun method lived in Palo Alto, California. Hurried phone calls revealed that Samuel Williston, executive vice president of the Sperry-Sun Company, was on a flight to the East Coast. Justice entrusted the petroleum board member with locating the expert witness and having him brought to Tyler. In the meantime, the prosecutors hoped to keep the case going until he arrived.

To their surprise, the expert witness was in Tyler the next morning at 6 A.M. Justice was elated. "In about forty-five minutes he taught me enough about the system that I was able to put him on the stand right at 9 o'clock when court convened. Everybody was so goddamned surprised, Sheehy most of all. So I went through the proceedings with Williston, and he laid it out for the jury. I'd just give him a question and he'd run with the ball. In lay terms, he'd explain in full detail just how the thing operated. This fellow was so good that Glass got nowhere on cross-examination. I then said, 'Your Honor, I now ask for a ruling as to whether or not the scientific validity of this instrument has been proved by preponderance of the evidence.' Sheehy was a professional. If you put a matter squarely before him, he would rule the way he had to rule, and so he ruled that we had proved it. I was lucky as hell to get by that obstacle, to be frank about it."

After that, the case moved along quickly, though it was never an easy one to try. Judge Sheehy was often antagonistic toward the prosecutors, at one point dressing Justice down so thoroughly in open court that the defense attorneys worried about undue sympathy by the jurors for the prosecuting attorneys. Before final arguments, the defendants moved for judgment of acquittal. Much to the surprise of the U.S. attorneys, Judge Sheehy granted the motion with respect to one of the defendants and dismissed the felony counts for the other defendants. Justice was incredulous. "There wasn't any question that we had made a case. The proof was virtually the same to establish both felonies and misdemeanors. You can imagine that ruling was pretty crushing. We thought he was entirely wrong. But since the government has no right of appeal in a criminal case, there wasn't anything we could do about it." The jury was left with seventeen misdemeanor counts against two of the defendants and the oil drilling company and two counts of misdemeanor conspiracy to commit offenses against the United States. Final arguments were made, and after being charged by Judge Sheehy, the jury began deliberations.

Late in the morning of the next day, Justice and Cornett left the courthouse for lunch. They were met on the way back by Bumstead, who excitedly told them that the jury had returned and had rendered a guilty verdict. The trio of government attorneys was elated. Justice considered the speed at which the jury reached a verdict as clearly indicative of the effectiveness of the government's prosecution. "They would have done the same thing with all those felony counts if they could have gotten them," he asserts.

The guilty verdict was a surprise in many quarters. Given the decisiveness of the jury's action, the U.S. attorneys hoped that the maximum penalty under the Connolly Act would be meted out. Gaumer had been found guilty on seventeen counts, his firm on fourteen counts, and E. B. Hearn, Jr., on one count. The maximum penalty was six months in jail and/or a fine of $2,000 per count. But Sheehy would have the final word. Three months later he fined Gaumer $250 on each of seventeen misdemeanor counts and gave him a suspended sentence. His firm, likewise, received a fine of $250 per count, payable only upon execution, meaning that the government could only obtain the money by seizing and selling property belonging to the company—an impossibility, since the holdings had been liquidated. Hearn, Jr., was found guilty on one count and fined $2,000. He, too, was given a suspended sentence.[4] For the government attorneys, it was the ultimate irony. "We had spent what was in those days an enormous sum on the prosecution of that case," Justice says. "And despite all our efforts, the judge had just slapped them on the wrist." After reviewing the case, Justice Department officials advised Justice to forego prosecuting the second indictment. The defense attorneys were elated. "Judge Sheehy had to set some punishment in light of the jury verdict," John Glass, Jr., notes, "but it was as light as any judge could have come up with."

While it may have been a Pyrrhic victory for the U.S. attorneys, they could take gratification that the jury verdict against the slant-holers served as a catalyst to the filing of civil actions in federal district court by leaseholders who sought damages for the oil illegally drained from their land. Justice notes, "To the best of my knowledge, there wasn't a single verdict returned in favor of defendants. They were utterly wiped out. And what was bad about it for Judge Sheehy is that he had to sit up there and preside in those civil trials where the people he was thought to have such sympathy for were systematically found liable."

The case helped establish Justice's reputation as a law-and-order U.S. attorney. He likes to tell of the time he and an FBI official got to talking over beers about U.S. attorneys. The official told him that it was customary for FBI agents to separate U.S. attorneys into two groups: those who are "aggressive" and those who are "non-aggressive," the difference being the desire to take cases, even those where the chances of winning are slim, and fight to obtain convictions. Wayne asked how he was regarded. "You're in the aggressive category." Justice considers it "the best compliment I have ever had." Years later, when serving by invitation as an appellate judge on the U.S. Court of Appeals for the District of Columbia Circuit, he was surprised to find that Judge Malcolm Richard Wilkey, a Nixon appointee who also had served as a U.S. attorney in Texas, initially mistook him for a law-and-order judge— which he is, to a point. As a judge, Justice enjoys a reputation as tough on criminals, whether white or blue collar. But, as Chapter 11 makes clear, he also strongly supports constitutional rights for the accused.

Civil Rights

Several days before the end of testimony in the 1963 slant-hole case, Justice received a call from Ramsey Clark, then assistant U.S. attorney general in the Department of Justice. Clark told him about a recent incident at Lake Texarkana (now Lake Wright Patman) involving the attempt of several blacks to go swimming on the Cass County side of the lake. A riot had ensued. The blacks were again going to try to desegregate the beaches, this time on the Bowie County side. Clark wanted Justice at the scene. "I said, 'Ramsey, I'm in the middle of this slant-hole case, which is the most important case that I've got on my docket. Is there any other way that we can arrange this?' He said, 'No, I think you need to be up there.'" So Justice left the case to Cornett and Bumstead, and headed for far Northeast Texas.

When he arrived in Texarkana, Justice sought out the publisher of the *Texarkana Gazette*. Pointing out that a riot would do no good for the image of the town or Bowie County, Justice hoped to secure his cooperation in an effort to accommodate desegregation of the beach. The publisher agreed. Justice later met with local law enforcement personnel, who also concurred that a peaceful approach was preferable. Hoping to get the state behind the effort as well, Justice telephoned Governor John Connally and secured assurances from his chief assistant that the Texas Highway Patrol would lend its support.

At a joint meeting, the federal and state law enforcement personnel agreed that they would stay in the background and would intervene only if circumstances warranted. The plan was that two young blacks would arrive at the public beach at a particular time on Monday, June 24. Law enforcement personnel would station themselves and their vehicles behind a clump of trees about 100 yards away and on nearby roads. They would be in radio contact with each other at all times.

After plans had been made, the leaders of the blacks insisted on integrating the beaches on the Cass County side where the riot had previously occurred, not on the Bowie County side. Justice told them that, as American citizens, they had a right to go swimming wherever they wished. But he cautioned them that should they choose to return to the Cass County side of the lake, a riot could break out. He noted that the Cass County law enforcement officers were not sympathetic to civil rights and would in all likelihood not support the blacks if trouble broke out. He pointed out that the federal and state authorities would do what they could to take care of a riot, but their numbers were small. "The blacks all kind of took a deep breath, and finally the two young men who were going to do the integrating spoke up and said, 'We want to go in on the Bowie County side,' which I thought evidenced damn good sense. There was some grumbling among the old-timers, who were the leaders. But, of course, they weren't the ones who were going to take the brunt of it."

At the appointed time, the two blacks drove up to the beach in their pickup. Justice recalls that it was a beautiful, peaceful day. A number of white women, together with their children, were at the beach, along with a few white men. The blacks made their way quickly to the water's edge, where they spread out their towels and waded into the lake.

"I was very curious as to the reaction of the whites. A few mothers got up, took their children, and left. A white man jumped up when he saw the blacks, and he looked around, you know, as if he was calling upon others for assistance. He walked around in an agitated fashion. If you've ever seen a fly that's been disturbed and just flies here and there and everywhere, that's the way he acted. Finally, he jumped in his pickup truck. I don't know what he had in mind. He drove around the perimeter of the beach, and he got close to the edge of that clump of trees. Then he spotted the whip antennas and all the law enforcement officers. All of us were looking at him; I can imagine he felt the glare of those eyes. When he saw us, he suddenly became very deliberate. He drove off peacefully and that was the last we saw of him." The next day, the *Texarkana Gazette* carried a low-keyed front page story on the integration of the beach, noting that it had occurred peacefully.

The other significant civil rights activity Justice was involved in during his first term as U.S. attorney involved prodding East Texas school districts to begin integrating their schools at the behest of the Justice Department. When Justice, Leighton Cornett, and Lloyd W. Perkins, who was the head of the civil division within the U.S. attorney's office, visited small towns to talk with school board members about integration, they made sure that the board members knew that they were East Texans talking with East Texans. With their small-town backgrounds and East Texas accents, the trio had little trouble convincing their audience that they were not part of the Washington, D.C., establishment. They then described the need to begin integrating the school system to comply with the law or face loss of federal funds and possible injunctive action in federal district court.

On one of these visits to a small rural district just west of Texarkana on the Red River, the attorneys found the school parking lot filled. The attorneys had previously talked with the superintendent, who was concerned that precipitous action might undermine the cause of integration. A meeting had been set up with the school board to explore these concerns. After much driving around, the three attorneys found a parking place on the fringe of the parking lot. Many of the parked vehicles were pickups, indicating a large rural turnout. As they proceeded toward the building and up the first flight of steps, they heard the roar of the crowd as the band struck up "Dixie." Lloyd Perkins remembers the tension and fear he felt. "I said to Wayne and Cornett, 'Now let's wait a minute, we're not here to start another Oxford, Mississippi,'" referring to the race rioting triggered by James Meredith's attempt to enroll at the University of Mississippi. Wayne Justice, who was in the lead, paused and took a tighter bite on the cigar he was chewing. He thought a moment, then told Cornett and Perkins that they would tell the crowd they were there to listen, not to talk. With that, the three attorneys entered the building. Directly ahead lay the gymnasium, filled to the rafters with people. The band continued to play. Just as they started in that direction, the superintendent appeared from a side door. He told them the school board was meeting in another part of the building, since a band concert was in progress in the gym. "You talk about relieved," Justice smiles at the recollection.

As U.S. attorney, William Wayne Justice was not the ardent integrationist he would become as a federal judge. The monumental 1964 Civil Rights Act was not enacted until well into his first term. Even after its enactment, it would take federal officials several years to begin enforcing it vigorously across the South. When enforcement began, federal agencies did the investigating, and attorneys from the Civil Rights Division of the Justice Department did the litigating. It was not until Justice became a federal judge that he pursued integration with a vengeance.

Playing Cops and Robbers

Administrative responsibilities kept Justice from trying many cases as U.S. attorney. But he did like "playing cops and robbers" from time to time, and the difficult criminal conspiracy cases afforded the best opportunity. The several he tried helped establish his reputation as a law-and-order U.S. attorney and added to his criminal law experience. The first involved a bank robbery in Mount Enterprise, Texas.

On the night of July 27, 1963, thieves broke into the Merchants and Planters State Bank in Mount Enterprise, a small town located at the junction of State Highway 259 and U.S. Highway 84 about fifty miles southeast of Tyler. Highway 84 was then known as the "thieves' highway" because it was less heavily patrolled than Interstate Highway 20.

When FBI agent Robert J. Stevens got to the bank, he found the contents of the vault in disarray. Like many small banks at the time, the bank did not have lockboxes for its customers. Personal items were stored in whatever containers the customers brought in—cigar boxes, fishing tackle boxes, and the like. These were all strewn about. Eventually, it was estimated that several thousand dollars' worth of cash was missing, along with savings bonds, blank cashier's checks, and other items of value.

A few days after the burglary, several of the cashier's checks showed up in the Dallas area. At one store, a photograph had been taken of the check and the person cashing it. The person turned out to be a prostitute living with a former convict named Leroy "Donkey" Duncan. Duncan had a close friend named James Berry, who also had a record. Berry was arrested and confessed in state court to his part in the burglary. But Duncan, whom Justice was to prosecute in federal court for bank larceny, refused to admit any part in the robbery. Berry, along with several others involved in passing the stolen money, refused to testify against him. Thus, Justice had to convince the jury that Duncan was part of the conspiracy and was in on the robbery.

In a conspiracy case, the rules of evidence allow one coconspirator to testify to the acts and statements made by other coconspirators during the course of the conspiracy. In effect, once the elements of a conspiracy have been shown, the rules of evidence allow the prosecutor to introduce into trial what otherwise would be considered excludable hearsay evidence. Thus, the investigatory phase of a criminal case is of key importance in determining the individuals who were involved in the conspiracy and the extent of their complicity.

United States v. Duncan was Justice's first conspiracy case. He credits investigator Stevens with helping him learn how to establish the elements of a conspiracy involving multiple defendants. Justice interviewed the coconspirators so that he would know exactly what they would say on the witness stand. He also hoped that through these encounters he might persuade some of them to testify against their partners in crime.

At the trial, Justice established that Berry and Duncan were friends and that they had traveled to Mount Enterprise four days before the robbery. On that trip, they had had car trouble. While the car was being repaired, the pair cashed traveler's checks in the Merchants and Planters Bank. At the trial, Berry testified that he might have burglarized the bank on that occasion if he had not had car trouble, but that Duncan was not aware of his intention. Though Justice thought he could count on Berry's testimony regarding the role Duncan had played in the robbery, Berry became very evasive on the stand. Justice recalls that finally in exasperation, he looked sternly at Berry and demanded to know if Duncan was there. "And he looked at me and said, 'Yes, he was there.'" But he then volunteered that Duncan had been drunk and remained in the car. Justice was not overly concerned; enough had been established through other testimony to convince the jury that Duncan had, indeed, robbed the bank with Berry. Duncan was convicted and sentenced to ten years. On appeal, the U.S. Court of Appeals for the Fifth Circuit affirmed the conviction.[5]

In another conspiracy case a year later, Justice and Stevens were not so successful. *United States v. Fisher et al.* involved the transportation in interstate commerce of counterfeited American Express money orders. Following a six-month investigation, Stevens traced the forgery conspiracy to the office of a Marshall, Texas, attorney. Justice and Stevens were convinced they had a solid case.

The trial involved four defendants. The federal courtroom in Marshall was filled with attorneys. Two prominent Dallas attorneys and the leading law firm in Marshall represented the Marshall attorney, Paul W. Anderson. The trial lasted a week and included fifty witnesses for the government, fifteen for the defense.[6] Testimony was introduced regarding the purchase of paper for the forgery, the printing of the documents, and the role of Anderson as the alleged mastermind of the operation. When the verdict was read, all were found guilty except Anderson. It was a bitter disappointment for Justice and Stevens. But it illustrates Justice's determination to treat white-collar crime no differently than blue-collar crime.

Second Term as U.S. Attorney

In 1966, Justice was reappointed as U.S. attorney, though for awhile he believed that his vigorous prosecution of the slant-hole oil drilling case might doom the possibility. Some of Lyndon Johnson's financial supporters were implicated in the scandal. His wife did not oppose a second term. "I didn't oppose it because it improved Wayne to be U.S. attorney. He grew from being his father's son to his own man. And he loved it so much. He was so happy." Sue herself found the position had its benefits. She recalls with pleasure the trips the couple made to Washington and the social events they attended, "especially when Kennedy was president."

During the second term, which lasted only until July 1968, when Justice was appointed to the bench, there were no sensational cases like the slant-hole litigation. However, one of the criminal cases prosecuted by Justice's office in 1965 did reach the Supreme Court, which used it to establish an important new constitutional right for those accused of crimes.

The case, *United States v. Wade,* was prosecuted by H. D. Nicholson, Jr., who had assisted in the earlier conspiracy cases. Justice had hired Nicholson in 1963 to replace Leighton Cornett, who left as he had intended after two years as first assistant U.S. attorney and criminal prosecutor. Nicholson had been a prosecutor in Dallas County and had been strongly recommended for Cornett's position.

The *Wade* case involved a robbery of the Eustace, Texas, bank on September 21, 1964. A man with strips of tape on his face entered the bank and pointed a pistol at the cashier and the vice president, the only persons in the bank at the time. Saying something like "Put the money in the bag," the man forced the bank employees to fill a pillowcase with the bank's money. On March 25, 1965, an indictment was returned against Billie Joe Wade and two others. Wade was arrested. Federal Judge Joe Sheehy appointed Weldon Holcomb of Tyler to represent Wade. Holcomb is a colorful defense attorney, whose trademarks are a snow-white cowboy hat, boots, and sticks of striped candy, which he hands out in the course of conversation. Justice calls Holcomb "a civil rights lawyer specializing in the Fifth and Sixth Amendments. He doesn't much like that designation."

Fifteen days after Wade's arrest, he was placed in a lineup without notice to his attorney. Prosecutor Nicholson was unaware that this had occurred and in fact had intended to forego a lineup since he believed he had ample evidence establishing Wade as the robber. All those in the lineup had strips of tape on their faces, and each was instructed to say "Put the money in the bag." Both bank employees identified Wade in the lineup. At trial, both employees again identified Wade. Nicholson hoped to avoid the lineup issue by never mentioning it in establishing the case against Wade. But Holcomb was able to elicit testimony about it during cross-examination. At the close of testimony, Holcomb moved for judgment of acquittal or, alternatively, to strike the bank officials' identification of Wade on the grounds that Wade had been denied his Fifth Amendment privilege against self-incrimination and his Sixth Amendment right to assistance of counsel during the lineup. The motion was denied, and Wade was convicted. The prosecutors didn't worry about an appeal, for they had not relied on the lineup identification to obtain the conviction.

Several days after the trial, Justice encountered Holcomb, a personal friend and political rival for years, in front of the Tyler post office. "I stopped him, and he promptly handed me a piece of stick candy. I said, 'Weldon, are you going to appeal that *Wade* case?' He said, 'Yeah, I am.' I said, 'What's going to be the basis for your appeal?' He said, 'I'm going to appeal because the defendant didn't have a lawyer present at the lineup.' I laughed and laughed; I thought that was the funniest thing that I'd ever heard. And I continued to laugh every time I thought about it—until the Supreme Court came down with its decision in favor of Wade. That was the most notable failure that my office encountered in my term as U.S. attorney."

The high court agreed with the Fifth Circuit, which had reversed the trial court, that Wade was entitled to an attorney at the lineup because that stage is such an important part of the prosecutorial process. The way the lineup is structured, together with the manner in which the accused is portrayed, could significantly influence witness identification. Writing for the Court, Justice William Brennan, Jr., pointed out, "The trial which might determine the accused's fate may well not be that in the courtroom but that at the pretrial confrontation, with the State aligned against the accused, the witness the sole jury, and the accused unprotected against the overreaching, intentional or unintentional, and with little or no effective appeal from the judgment there rendered by the witness—'that's the man.'"[7] The Court sent the case back to the trial court for further proceedings.

Justice regards the last case that he tried as U.S. attorney as one of his most successful. *United States v. Hawkins* was a complicated criminal conspiracy case involving the forgery and coast-to-coast passing of money orders stolen from a Texas post office. Assisting Justice was William Louis White, a former Harris County prosecutor who had taken over as criminal prosecutor in February 1967, but had not tried a conspiracy case. Before White was hired, Justice had spent months meticulously preparing the case for trial with the assistance of federal investigators.

The case developed from events in Gregg County. With the oil boom, the county had become a mecca for criminal activity. It was the only county in East Texas where liquor could be purchased, and nightclubs and prostitution flourished. "A good part of my criminal docket," Justice says, "had to do with matters that either occurred in Gregg County or elsewhere instituted, planned, or plotted in Gregg County."

James C. Hawkins, known as "Hawkshaw Hawkins," operated a nightclub in Gladewater. It was he who allegedly had masterminded the conspiracy. On January 22, 1966, the Frankston, Texas, post office was robbed of a number of U.S. postal money orders. According to evidence introduced at the trial, Hawkins arranged to have two persons, Raymond M. Shelby and Marvin E. Key, purchase the money orders from the thief and cash them, with the provision that he, Hawkins, would get a percentage of the proceeds. It was Key, an ex-convict, who passed the bulk of the orders, going first to the West Coast and then to the East Coast. He and Shelby were arrested in Tennessee and later convicted for possessing and passing stolen government money orders.

Key agreed to testify in the June 1967 conspiracy trial against Hawkins and Shelby in Tyler federal court on the condition that he not be prosecuted for his role in the conspiracy. Since Judge Sheehy had died several months earlier, the case was tried before visiting Judge Joe E. Estes, Chief Judge of the U.S. District Court for the Northern District of Texas. Justice remembers that Key was not a very trustworthy-looking witness, speaking in the lingo of the underworld, eyes darting from side to side. But he was the one who could tie the conspiracy together. "I realized that if we were going to get a conviction, he would have to be the first witness," Justice says. "By having him outline the conspiracy, from that point on I would be able to employ the rule of evidence which says one coconspirator can testify to statements made by the other coconspirators during the course of the conspiracy." In response to questions from Justice, Key described in detail how he had purchased the money orders from Hawkins, giving Hawkins jewelry to fence in lieu of cash. Key also testified that he had obtained false credit cards from Hawkins and had wired money back to Hawkins from proceeds obtained by passing the stolen money orders.

Justice knew that the jury would not be likely to believe Key unless his testimony was corroborated by other witnesses. Helping him with this phase of the case was a postal inspector, who had the job of tracing Key's route as he passed out the stolen money orders. The postal inspector did his work well. "Everywhere that these things had been passed, we had the person there to whom the instrument was passed. And he would identify the convict as the person who passed it," Justice says.

In addition, Justice produced Key's female companion, who testified that she had been present during a meeting between Hawkins, Shelby, and Key at which the matter of obtaining and passing stolen money orders was discussed. She also testified about contacts with Hawkins while she and Key were passing the stolen money orders around the country. Justice introduced testimony from another woman along the same lines. This woman also testified that Hawkins had beaten her severely.

Watching Justice try the case, White was impressed. Justice had made thorough preparations for trial—so thorough that at one point just before trial, he castigated White in front of other key players for not actually taking possession of a particular piece of evidence, though White had made arrangements to do so. Later, Justice apologized. White regarded Justice's courtroom presence as impressive and his legal research as flawless. "Generally, you don't find a fellow who is good in the courtroom and also good in the books. Justice was the exception."

Justice's old friend and colleague, Joe Tunnell, was one of the attorneys representing Hawkins and Shelby. Throughout the trial, Tunnell tried to undermine the credibility of the government's witnesses and to emphasize the tenuous relationship of the prosecution's case to his clients. He put Shelby on the stand. Shelby denied passing any money orders and stated that his only relationship with Hawkins was one of friendship.

But the government's case had been well prepared. The evidence supporting the conspiracy was substantial. Justice says with a smile, "Opposing counsel didn't have a chance. We had Hawkins sacked up from the word 'go' and the jury had no difficulty in finding him guilty." Shelby was sentenced to five years in prison and Hawkins to ten. Tunnell filed an appeal, but to no avail. The Fifth Circuit found sufficient evidence to support the convictions of both Hawkins and Shelby.[8]

As Justice approached the end of his tenure as U.S. attorney, he participated in more civil rights matters. At that stage of federal civil rights enforcement, the U.S. attorney's office was involved mostly in familiarizing the owners of places of public accommodation such as restaurants and motels with the terms of the 1964 Civil Rights Act. The law required that these facilities be integrated. Justice was well aware of the sensitivity of these discussions and concerned that conflict with both Washington officials and East Texas owners be minimized. During William White's first day on the job in 1967 as assistant U.S. attorney, Justice called him into his office to talk about pronouncing a word. Puzzled, White followed him into the office. Seated behind his desk, Justice pointed to his kneecap, telling White that he should think of the word "knee" when using the term "Negro" in conversations with Washington civil rights officials. Apparently, White's East Texas pronunciation was uncomfortably close to "nigra."

Justice recalls talking with a Nacogdoches motel owner who had run off several blacks when they tried to register. Justice explained that it was against the law to discriminate on the basis of race and that if it happened again, prosecution would result. The owner tried to be very cordial; he invited Justice into his restaurant and club for a drink. Justice accepted a soft drink. "As I sipped the soda, I looked out and saw that he had a pool. I said, 'Now you realize, of course, that these persons are entitled to go swimming, too.' His eyes wide, the owner replied, 'They are?' Apparently that had never occurred to him." No trouble was afterward encountered with the owner regarding desegregation.

If integration were to occur peacefully, the cooperation of local police officers was essential. Justice was invited to speak to an East Texas law enforcement group in Longview about the 1964 law. "One of them said, 'Well, now I know we're going to have to let these guys come in and sit down at the restaurant, but, how long do we have to let them stay?' I said, 'You let them stay just as long as you'd let a white person stay.' That didn't go down well at all there. They just couldn't believe it. Apparently, they figured that if blacks did come in, they were supposed to stay five minutes and leave."

Personal Decisions

During his years as U.S. attorney, William Wayne Justice made some important personal decisions. First, he decided to quit smoking. Before switching to pipes and cigars, he had been a two-pack-a-day cigarette smoker. At the insistence of his wife and daughter, he had tried to quit without success. But in October 1962, he read an article in *Time Magazine* about the hazards of smoking. The article, plus pressure from his wife and daughter, caused him to quit. He has not smoked since.

About the same time, he decided to lose weight. Since returning from the military in 1946, he had gradually gained weight until he tipped the scales at nearly two hundred pounds. Even spread over his six-foot frame, the weight is clearly evident in photographs from this period (see the photographic section). When he was first appointed to the U.S. attorney position, Justice began complaining of stomach pains. It turned out that his pants were too tight. Brooks Hardee recalls that soon after this, the U.S. attorneys from Texas were invited to Washington for a meeting with Attorney General Robert F. Kennedy. The meeting continued into the weekend, and the attorneys were invited to Kennedy's home. When they arrived, Kennedy was swimming in his pool and invited the attorneys to join him. Justice protested that he did not have a swimsuit. Kennedy assured him that one could be found. Noting how slim and trim Kennedy was, Justice admitted to Hardee he was just too embarrassed to get into a swimsuit.

What convinced Justice of the need to slim down was watching Supreme Court Justice Hugo Black, then in his late seventies, play tennis in the hot sun in St. Augustine, Florida, at a meeting of the Fifth Circuit Judicial Conference in the early 1960s. "I was in a second-floor room overlooking the tennis courts. I saw this old geezer out there playing. He looked pretty old. I thought, could that be Justice Black? I went down there and, sure enough, it was the great Justice. He wasn't all that agile but there he was, in his late seventies running around the court playing tennis. I was scared to death to play tennis because I was afraid that I would have a heart attack and die. I hadn't had any exercise in a long time. It just hit me that here I was, in my early forties, and I hadn't been doing any exercises since I left the army."

When he got home, he started taking off weight. Justice continued his weight reduction program until by the time he was appointed to the federal bench in 1968, he weighed 154 pounds, the same as when he was in the army. Since then, he hasn't varied more than a pound. At the same time, he began a program of exercise. At first, he walked. Then he began to jog. By the end of his tenure as U.S. attorney, he was jogging five miles four or five times a week. Later, he added weight lifting to his regimen. He continues to do both jogging and weight lifting religiously. And for a while in the 1970s, when antagonism toward his decisions was particularly pronounced, he studied karate. "I was in excellent physical shape, and it was fun to get out there and spar with those sixteen, seventeen-year-old kids. They could care less that they were dealing with some judge. To them I was just some old guy out there trying to do the same things they were, and they'd kick the hell out of me. And I'd kick back, of course, and get in a few kicks of my own. The stress must have made the adrenalin flow by the gallons because sometimes I wouldn't even feel the kicks. When I'd get home, I'd discover these big bruises where I'd been kicked. But it was a very good way to remove tension."

Now in his early seventies, Wayne Justice has a craggy and lean, almost gaunt, appearance. From a distance, he might be mistaken for California Senator Alan Cranston, who is also an inveterate jogger. Justice is compulsive about his exercise program, and credits it for his stamina and lack of tension.

While politics had played a big role in Wayne Justice's life prior to appointment as U.S. attorney, the federal Hatch Act precluded continued involvement. As U.S. attorney, he devoted most of his time to his work. But he did develop one new interest. He discovered sports cars. When he became U.S. attorney, he continued to live in Athens rather than move to Tyler. He assumed that he would return to his law practice when his term as U.S. attorney was over. Daily travel back and forth between Athens and Tyler, coupled with driving throughout East Texas in his role as U.S. attorney, resulted in growing concern about the gap between his expenses and the government's per diem allowance. He also complained to his assistant U.S. attorneys that the tires on his gas-guzzling Oldsmobile sedan were always blowing out. The reason may have had something to do with his fast driving. One of the assistants, William M.

Williams, Jr., suggested that he ought to sell the Olds and buy a sports car. Justice was skeptical. "I wasn't even sure what a sports car was. From time to time, I'd seen two or three of these odd-looking cars go around the square in Athens and wondered what they were, but I didn't really have time to investigate."

Williams told Justice that only a few blocks away a good, used Jaguar was for sale. "A Jaguar didn't mean any more to me, you know, than any other kind of car." Williams described the car, and the two went to look it over. It was an XK-150 rag-top Jaguar, one of the hottest cars on the road. "To me, it was a strange-looking vehicle. They opened up the hood, and there was that huge nickel-plated engine. I was intrigued at that point, so we took it out on the road. Since Bill was familiar with sports cars, he did the driving. We were making these corners pretty fast at practically ninety degrees, and the car wasn't even swaying. That intrigued me even further. Then he drove out on the highway and flipped it into electric overdrive, and whoosh! We took off like a rocket. By this time I was really interested."

Over his wife's opposition, Justice purchased the car for $3,000, a suspiciously low price. The car had only 4,000 miles on the odometer. "It didn't take me very long to find out what was wrong with it. It was using a quart of oil every hundred miles." He took it to Fort Worth, the closest place that had adequate repair facilities, and found out that it had five scored pistons. Fortunately, although it was a used car, the car agency agreed to furnish the parts free. Justice paid only for the labor. The result was a practically new car.

The love affair between Justice and the Jaguar lasted nearly three years. During that time, he literally drove the wheels off it. "Like an airplane, I rushed back and forth over the Eastern District of Texas." But, as every owner of an expensive, finely tuned car eventually finds out, little things go wrong. "There was always something that was malfunctioning. The windshield wipers would go out, and there wasn't anybody in town who could fix them. It had these electric fuel pumps with sumps on them, and I would never think to drain the sumps, of course. So, the consequence was that during cold weather, the sumps would freeze up and I couldn't use the car."

Justice eventually sold the Jaguar. He wanted to purchase a new XKE Jaguar but did not have the money. Instead he bought the first model of the Ford Mustang. "I shall never forget. I went into a filling station with that thing. It was the first one the filling station attendant had ever seen. He looked it over, and said, 'You know, that car looks like it's been kicked in the ass.'" Justice continued to buy small cars, including a Camaro, which he liked, and an Oldsmobile Starfire, which he hated. Eventually he returned to foreign sports cars, first a Datsun 280 Z and then a Mitsubishi Starion. Cars, along with going to the movies, remain one of his few indulgences.

Appointment to the Federal Bench

In February 1967, Justice was at home recuperating from gall-bladder surgery when he heard on the radio that Judge Sheehy had died suddenly. Though Sheehy called Justice "that damned liberal," the two were cordial to one another. Justice recalls that toward the end of his life, Sheehy seemed to mellow. "I'd go down and talk to him from time to time about problems within the district, and he was genuinely friendly for the first time. Before that, he always seemed to have a chip on his shoulder."

Sheehy's passing left only one judge in the district, Joe Fisher, who replaced him as chief judge. With the vacancy, a number of contenders began jockeying for the position. The incumbent U.S. attorney is normally considered a contender for a vacant federal judgeship, so Justice's name was included as being under consideration among those listed in the Tyler newspaper. Justice discussed the matter with his wife, who never doubted he would get the appointment. Her husband had been a political intimate of Senator Yarborough for years and had actively campaigned for President Lyndon Johnson in the critical 1948 senatorial election. Few had straddled the Yarborough-Johnson fence as successfully as Wayne Justice. Sue was so supportive of the idea that she encouraged Wayne to go to Washington to meet with Senator Yarborough.

So, after Judge Sheehy's funeral, Justice met with the senator. "He was surprised to see me. I told him that I would like to be considered for the vacancy that Sheehy's death had brought about. He said, 'Wayne, I'll consider you.' He didn't promise the job to me at all, just said he'd consider me. He added, 'One thing about it: you've had the decency to wait until after the funeral to come up here and ask for the job.'" Yarborough explained that he had had fifteen or sixteen calls from Texas lawyers, some of them before the funeral. Yarborough also advised Justice that it would be best if he were a quiet candidate for the office instead of seeking public endorsement from newspapers, law firms, and bar associations. Justice talked to close friends in Athens and Tyler about his application and asked for their support. A review of White House records from that period reveals that over twenty personal letters, some from local attorneys, were sent to President Johnson or to his special assistant, W. Marvin Watson, in support of Justice's candidacy. There were no endorsements from major law firms or professional associations.

Yarborough also advised Justice that, as a matter of protocol, he should contact President Johnson's office about his interest in the position. "So I called Marvin Watson, who was then kind of the chief of staff, and talked very briefly about it," Wayne recalls. Justice had not forgotten his wounds from past political battles with Johnson forces. "He kept making these little openings for me to say that I wanted the job. I never did do it. Hell, no. There are some things you just don't do. I wasn't going to put myself under obligation to that guy. I kind of liked Marvin Watson, so don't get me wrong. But I'd been fighting that group all these years, and I didn't want to be beholden to them."

Justice also paid a call on Attorney General Ramsey Clark, who was noticeably cool. "I was shocked. I'd thought that Ramsey'd be for me because he knew I'd been doing good work as U.S. attorney. I'd worked very hard at that job and, I think, was an efficient U.S. attorney. I never did get any encouragement from Ramsey Clark." When honored at a Texas Civil Liberties Union awards banquet in 1988, Justice reminded Clark, who was seated on the dais, of his lack of encouragement, but noted that "Senator Yarborough can be an obstinate person, and he refused to waiver in his support for me." The aged former senator, who was also present, beamed.

Justice returned to Texas. It was not long before he learned that part of the reason for the coolness he had received in Washington was that President Johnson was seriously considering Phillip B. Baldwin, a lawyer in Marshall and nephew of Yarborough loyalist Franklin Jones, Sr., for the position. Baldwin had long been a Johnson supporter, as well as a supporter of Yarborough, and was also a personal friend of Lady Bird Johnson and her family. "When I first heard that, I pretty much discounted my chances," Justice says. "But, what the hell. I knew that Lyndon Johnson was going to be influenced by his wife, but if he thought there was some political advantage to be gained, why, he'd forget about that. So I just bided my time."

Another factor causing Justice some concern was a vacancy in the Federal District Court for the Northern District of Texas. Yarborough and Johnson had agreed when Johnson was vice president to split the patronage in Texas. Assuming the agreement would continue to be honored, the question was who was going to get to appoint his candidate to the Eastern District. After some posturing over the issue, Johnson and Yarborough once again agreed to split the patronage. Meanwhile, Baldwin withdrew from consideration. "When it appeared that the appointment was a hopeless deadlock between myself and Wayne Justice, I contacted President Johnson and asked to be released from his commitment to my nomination," Baldwin maintains. "I felt that Wayne Justice, who is a personal friend of mine, would be an outstanding District Judge, which he has, in fact, proven to be." [9] With these developments, Yarborough nominated Justice for the Eastern District, and Johnson advanced Halbert O. Woodward for the Northern District. A short time later, President Johnson nominated Baldwin for an associate justice position on the Court of Customs and Patent Appeals in Washington, D.C. (now the U.S. Court of Appeals for the Federal Circuit).

Justice learned of his nomination when he was in Washington at a U.S. attorneys' conference. President Johnson had invited the government lawyers over to the East Room of the White House. Justice believes that, like almost everything Johnson did, the invitation was politically motivated. "Lyndon Johnson seemed to think he ought to make himself available to U.S. attorneys because he felt that they were a group that in the near future would have a great deal of impact on the political processes of the nation." At the session, Johnson briefly addressed the group, pointing out their importance to the nation and noting that some were going to be rewarded for their efforts. Justice recalls, "When he said that, he looked at me as if he was trying to tell me something." Two days later while he was still in Washington, Justice got the word that he had been nominated. "That was the biggest thrill of my life. I was just floating on air. And what made it so good is that I was right there among all my peers, all of whom would have given their eye teeth for an appointment like that. And they gloried with me."

There was still the matter of confirmation by the Senate. In May 1968 Justice returned to Washington in the company of Halbert O. Woodward, Johnson's nominee for the Northern District judgeship. While the two were waiting for their plane, Woodward's brother, Warren, strode up. After congratulating the two men, Warren, who then was a vice president of American Airlines, asked to see their tickets. He made some cryptic notations. When they boarded the plane, they were ushered to new seats in first class. "That's the only first class flight I've ever had in my life," Justice exclaims. "I remember we had champagne for breakfast. God Almighty, I just couldn't conceive of such things!"

At the Justice Department, an official told Justice and Woodward that their FBI reports had been favorable. He told them that a subcommittee of the Senate Judiciary Committee would be convened to pass on their nominations. He said that the only person representing the subcommittee would be Senator James O. Eastland, the Democratic senator from Mississippi who chaired the full Judiciary Committee. This news came as a disappointment, for the two appointees had assumed that a large contingent of the committee would be present, along with a room full of newspaper reporters and onlookers. The official told the men that when Eastland came into the committee room, he would look to the back of the room where the official would be sitting. An affirmative nod meant that everything was all right. A shaking of the head meant that Eastland should review notations in the files before him. In both their cases, the official assured them that he would nod affirmatively. Sure enough, when Eastland entered, he first looked to the back of the committee room and, apparently receiving an affirmative nod, proceeded with the session.

As he introduced the nominees to his senatorial colleague, Senator Yarborough had words of praise for both men. Eastland thanked Yarborough, then asked Justice if he had had any federal court experience. Justice replied that he was serving as U.S. attorney. Satisfied, Eastland turned to Woodward. When he learned that Woodward had worked for Humble Oil and Refinery Company eighteen years before, the two engaged in a friendly chat. Eastland later recommended that the full Judiciary Committee confirm both men. Looking back on it, Woodward laughs, "Of all the Judiciary Committee hearings, this was probably the lowest profile and the quickest ever held." But, he adds, "It wasn't to us."

It is ironic that it was Senator Eastland, an ardent segregationist and foe of liberalism in any guise, who screened the appointment of William Wayne Justice to the federal bench. That he did not inquire further is largely attributable to the power of senatorial patronage. "Senator Eastland respected the right of a senator to use his patronage as he saw fit," Yarborough notes. Even if Eastland had inquired further, Wayne Justice had assembled no legacy of controversy as a lawyer or as U.S. attorney. On the contrary, he was generally regarded by members of the bar as a law-and-order U.S. attorney.

Before the Judiciary Committee could confirm the nominations, Texas Republican Senator John Tower had to give his approval by returning a blue card to the committee. The blue cards on Justice and Woodward had not been returned. So the pair had to pay a courtesy call on Senator Tower. He was cordial, if reserved. Justice recalls that the conversation was pleasant, but rather stiff. For a few moments, Justice thought the nominations might be in jeopardy. "I tried to be just as nice as I could be. But Hal Woodward kind of took the approach, 'Listen, you little pipsqueak, why the hell are you holding up this blue card?' He didn't put it in those terms, but he had a faintly indignant sound to his voice. Scared the hell out of me." But if Woodward was coming across a little too strong, Tower did not seem to notice. A day later the blue card was returned. Apparently, Tower expected both to pay him a courtesy call, something neither had done, and his holding up the blue card was his way of forcing them to act. Shortly thereafter, the two men were confirmed by the Judiciary Committee and the full Senate.

Justice returned to Tyler where he finished up his work as U.S. attorney and prepared for the swearing-in ceremony, which took place on June 29, 1968, in the second-floor courtroom in the old federal courthouse in Tyler. Newspaper accounts of the event report that the aisles and halls were overflowing with dignitaries and guests.[10] Sue Justice attributes the prominence of the ceremony in the Tyler social community to the close ties Judge Sheehy had cultivated with it and to the fact that Tyler then had only one sitting federal judge.

Senator Yarborough introduced Justice and Brooks Hardee, who had been selected to serve the remainder of Justice's second term as U.S. attorney. In his remarks, the senator indicated how pleased he was that two small-town men were being appointed to fill the two positions. He noted the courage it took "to withstand the months, and sometimes years, of waiting for appointments like these." He added, "Thank goodness, neither the president nor senators have to undergo the fine-tooth screening and FBI investigations equal to those nominated for a federal judgeship."[11] After Justice received the oath of office from Chief Judge Joe Fisher, he performed his first official duty by swearing in Brooks Hardee as U.S. attorney.

It was the most memorable of days for the Justices. Yarborough called it "one of the greatest days in East Texas." There would be many in East Texas who soon would not think so.

CHAPTER 4

Life as a Judge

The federal district court to which William Wayne Justice received a lifetime appointment in 1968 is one of ninety-four in the country. Four are in Texas, each responsible for cases arising in a particular geographic section of the state—North, South, East, and West (see Map 1). The U.S. District Court for the Eastern District of Texas sprawls across a forty-three-county area from the Gulf of Mexico to the Oklahoma border. The territory is partitioned into seven divisions, with a federal courthouse in each division, and at least one courtroom in each courthouse. Map 2 shows the configuration of the Eastern District. The number of judges for these seven divisions has steadily grown to handle the burgeoning caseload. When Justice was appointed, there was only one other judge, who spent most of his time in the Beaumont Division. Twenty years later, there were eight, two of whom had taken senior status but continued to hear cases on a full-time basis.

The characteristics and ambiance of the seven divisions of the Eastern District, named after the cities in which the federal courthouses are located, reflect the diversity of Texas. They range from the Sherman Division north of Dallas–Fort Worth, populated with high-tech industries, to the Beaumont Division far to the southeast, a largely blue-collar section of the state dependent on its Gulf shipping and vast petrochemical industries. The Tyler Division, located in the middle of the district, is an agricultural area and home of a growing metropolitan community built largely with railroad and oil money. To the east, the Lufkin Division encompasses a large section of the piney woods of East Texas where forestry is the prime economic endeavor. To the northeast, the Texarkana Division reflects the unique culture engendered by its location adjacent to Oklahoma and Arkansas. For Judge Justice, the Paris Division along the Red River boundary line with Oklahoma retains many of the characteristics of country life in the Old South, populated as it is with many small East Texas towns. "I feel utterly at home in Paris; it's much like Athens. It's very easy for me to understand the attitude of the people," he maintains.

The federal district courts are the trial courts of the federal judiciary. Criminal and civil cases are heard by a single judge, either with or without a jury, depending upon the nature of the case. The jurisdiction of the federal judiciary is limited to two categories of cases: those involving "federal questions" and those that relate to particular characteristics of the parties. The categories are wholly independent of one another. Federal questions pertain to matters involving the U.S. Constitution and to federal laws and treaties. Those depending on certain characteristics of the parties include cases in which the federal government is a party, as well as those in which a state is a party. Citizens of different states may sue in federal court, even for claims arising under state law when no federal statute is involved. These so-called "diversity cases" are so prevalent that Congress, which controls most of the jurisdiction of the federal judiciary, has restricted the federal courts from hearing them unless the amount in controversy is at least $50,000. Short of this figure, cases are confined to state courts. Often, federal and state claims will be involved in the same case. The most prevalent of the diversity cases in Justice's court in recent years have been those involving product liability and negligence.

Since federal district courts are charged with the responsibility of hearing both federal and state cases, the types of disputes coming before them are diverse in the extreme. In his years on the bench, Justice has presided over trials with subjects ranging from interstate cattle rustling to corporate disputes over trademarks and sailors' claims that they were injured due to an unseaworthy boat.

Appeals of federal district court decisions go to U.S. courts of appeals, presently arranged in thirteen judicial circuits. In Texas, appeals from the federal district courts are routed to the U.S. Court of Appeals for the Fifth Circuit, which hears appeals from Louisiana and Mississippi as well. Cases taken to the Fifth Circuit are normally decided by panels of three of the court's twenty judges. Neither the parties nor the lower court judge have a role in selection of the circuit court panel. Beyond the Fifth Circuit lies the U.S. Supreme Court.

The higher the court in the hierarchy, the wider its geographic jurisdiction. Thus a ruling of the U.S. Supreme Court applies to the entire country, while a decision of the U.S. District Court for the Eastern District of Texas ordinarily applies only to disputes arising in that district. But this is not always true, a fact which is crucial to understanding why so many of Judge Justice's rulings have had an impact beyond the confines of the Eastern District. When a matter involving the entire state is heard, the ruling likely will have a statewide impact. Knowing this to be true, plaintiffs' attorneys initiating litigation against a state institution try to find the most favorable court in which to file their lawsuit. This practice, known as forum shopping, is a recognized part of

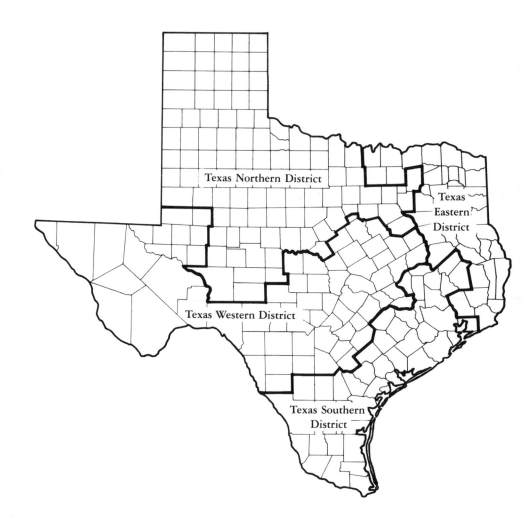

Map 1.   Geographic Jurisdiction of U.S. District Courts in Texas

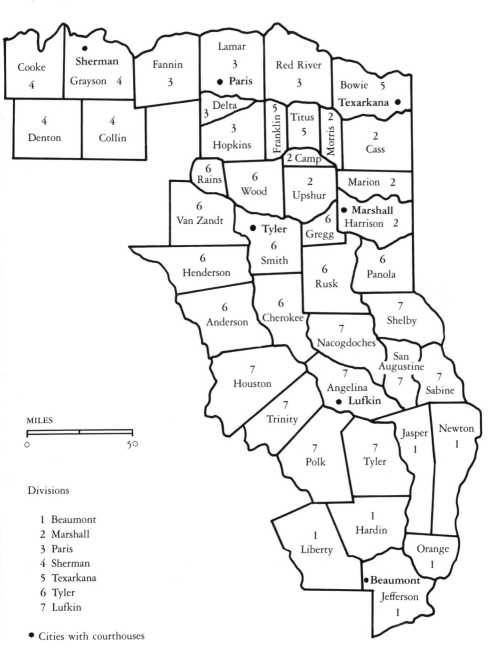

MILES

0   50

Divisions

1 Beaumont
2 Marshall
3 Paris
4 Sherman
5 Texarkana
6 Tyler
7 Lufkin

● Cities with courthouses

Map 2. The Eastern District of Texas

the litigation process—"as American as the Constitution," according to the Fifth Circuit.[1] The first example of forum shopping in Justice's court was *United States v. Texas,* the statewide school desegregation case discussed in Chapter 5.

Getting cases before Judge Justice was easy during the 1970s. When Justice was appointed in 1968, the only other judge assigned to the Eastern District, which at that time had six divisions over a forty-one-county area, was Chief Judge Joe J. Fisher. As the junior judge, Justice was responsible for lawsuits filed in five of the six divisions: Marshall, Paris, Sherman, Tyler, and one-third of the Beaumont docket. Judge Fisher, appointed to the bench in 1959 by President Eisenhower, had two-thirds of the Beaumont caseload and all of the Texarkana docket. As Justice explains it, "I was perceived as being liberal. And I was the only sitting judge in several divisions in the Eastern District. So it was very easy to forum shop. They simply filed a case in that division and it ended up in my courtroom." Justice's willingness to use the remedial powers available to him in cases involving wrongs inflicted by state institutions prompted reform-seeking plaintiffs' attorneys to beat a steady path to his court. In short order, constitutional law cases of major import were being filed in unlikely places like Sherman and Marshall, Texas.

With the appointment of additional judges, it has become harder to forum shop. Judge Justice is now based in the Tyler division and shares the Tyler docket with two other judges. In 1987, together with the other Tyler judges, Justice began to hear cases in a new courtroom in the Lufkin Division. Previously, the Lufkin cases had been handled in Tyler. When a case is filed in the Tyler or Lufkin Division, the Tyler clerk dips into a box and pulls out the name of a judge. Quite literally the luck of the draw determines which judge will hear a case.

During much of the time Justice has been on the bench, the Eastern District has had one of the heaviest case loads per judge of any federal district court in the country. As more and more plaintiffs' attorneys found their way to Justice's court, his case load continued to expand. Yet, during the two years Justice and Fisher were the only judges assigned to the district, the mean disposition time for civil actions was eight months. Both judges worked long, hard hours. Justice was on the road six months of the year. He recalls, "I was in a frenzy of activity in those days. I wanted to make my mark, to demonstrate that I was a competent trial judge. I worked like a Trojan. I would get to the office early and leave late. We had one trial right on top of another. And when I wasn't on the bench, I was as busy as a bee on other matters. Traveling from place to place was very stressful."

While traveling the countryside to hold court has its drawbacks, many federal judges enjoy the prestige associated with being the most powerful government official in town. Often a close social relationship develops between the pillars of the community and the traveling federal judge. Opportunities abound for social gatherings, hunting trips, and the like. Wayne Justice did not fit the pattern. A private person, Justice did not particularly enjoy these activities. Nor did he want to be beholden to anyone who one day might appear before him. From the beginning, he sought to avoid even the hint of impropriety. Consequently, his relationships on the road revolved mostly around his law clerks, his office staff, and his wife, who would occasionally join the small traveling band of court personnel. The one exception was Paris. Given his special fondness for the Paris Division, Justice looked forward to holding court there and to the party the local bar association would throw for him when he came to town.

The Judge's reluctance to follow his predecessor's pattern of social involvement has contributed to his image among many members of the bar, the press, and the general public as aloof and humorless. From the point of view of those who know him, this is unfortunate, for he is quite the contrary. An optimistic and self-confident man, Justice has a quick wit and a good sense of humor. He loves a good story—both in the telling and in the listening. Even many of his critics admit they like him once they get to know him.

One of his early clerks, Robert F. Stein, Jr., recalls that the hours were long on the road and the work hard. "We would go into some of these smaller communities and try cases that most federal judges would not have tried. They would have forced a settlement in order to avoid staying in a place like Paris, Texas." Stein observes that often the attorneys were not skilled at working up proposed directions regarding the law for the judge to give the jury on behalf of their clients. With only a year of judicial experience, Justice did not have a ready-made file to draw upon. Thus, together with his clerks, he would often labor long into the night perfecting jury charges.

But there were good times on the road as well. "In those early years, it was the order of the day for all of us to eat together in the evenings," Stein remembers. "We traveled with a barbecue grill so we could fix our own steaks on the grill outside the motel. We had our own blender to mix up our mixed drinks, though the Judge was not a drinking man. We'd go out to a butcher shop and buy some steaks because we could fix them cheaper than we could buy them. We didn't have much per diem. Invariably, we'd have to cook the Judge's steak to the consistency of shoe leather. He wanted to have all the fat cooked out of it." After dinner, the Judge retired early, usually to read.

Traveling among the divisions of the Eastern District did enable the Judge to indulge his passion for fast sports cars. He admits to occasionally exceeding the speed limit. One incident which has become legend among the law clerks involves a car race Justice had with his first two clerks, Wayne V. R. Smith and

Michael P. O'Reilly. Shortly after Smith arrived in Tyler, he bought a 1969 Mustang Mach 1 car and had the engine modified for fast driving. Justice at the time was driving a yellow Camaro, which he considered superior to the Mustang. On a return trip to Tyler after holding court in Marshall in 1969, Justice in his Camaro caught up to and passed Smith and O'Reilly in the Mustang on a stretch of double-lane highway. Both Smith and O'Reilly agreed that they could not let the Judge get away with that, and pulled up parallel to the Camaro. From there on, the two cars raced along the highway until Smith pulled ahead in a burst of speed. The Camaro disappeared behind them. The next day, Smith learned from Sue Justice that the Camaro had overheated and blown the engine. The Judge had apparently forgotten that the engine in the Mustang had been modified. "But he remembered it then," Smith laughs.

When Wayne Justice was appointed to the bench, he did not have an articulated judicial philosophy. Nor did he have a defined social reform agenda which he intended to implement by judicial fiat, though there are many, including some Fifth Circuit judges, who believe the contrary. When Justice ascended the bench, he knew only what he wanted to avoid as a judge. "I'd made up my mind that I was not going to do some of the things that a few of the state and federal judges I had dealt with in the past had done. I decided I wasn't going to be a tyrant. I was going to play by the rules; I was going to go by the book."

Early on Justice sought an expeditious way of processing cases through his court. He found one method at a seminar for newly appointed federal judges held at the Earl Warren Legal Center on the campus of the University of California in Berkeley. One presenter, Judge Hubert L. Will, U.S. district judge for the Northern District of Illinois, explained his practice of calling the attorneys into his chambers for a preliminary conference after a case was filed to get an understanding of the case. He would then establish a time frame and set of procedures for the attorneys to follow in getting ready for trial. In effect, Will took over the management of the case from the moment it was filed. This contrasted with the prevailing practice of letting the attorneys proceed at their own pace. Under the old system, the attorneys invariably requested more time from the court to prepare their cases. The docket of cases not ready for trial piled up while attorneys enriched themselves at the expense of their clients.

Judge Will also conducted a final pretrial conference on the eve of the trial, requiring all the lawyers to be present and to deliver a jointly prepared final pretrial order. That document would set forth all the uncontested and contested facts, a list of the uncontested and contested issues of law, a list of the witnesses both sides would call, a list of the exhibits to be presented, and so on. The pretrial order imposed a major burden on the attorneys. But it largely eliminated the "Perry Mason" surprise factor, something that Wayne Justice and his father had down to an art. "My father and I were specialists in the pitfall theory," he acknowledges. "My dad just loved to dig a deep pit for the unwary opponent and let him fall in at the proper moment." But, as a judge, Justice's views changed. "I don't think it necessarily leads to a just result because many times, if you are made aware of a hole in your case like that before trial, you could find things that may be comparatively unimportant to shore it up and do so without taking up the time of the judge and the jury. Or you might decide, 'Hell, I don't really have a case here,' and settle."

Upon returning to Tyler, Justice immediately began overhauling court procedures in the interest of better managing his docket. It was an abrupt change from past practice under Judge Sheehy, and initially, the lawyers complained about it, particularly over the tight time frames. Justice told his first two clerks, Michael O'Reilly and Wayne Smith, to direct complaints to him. "Boy, did we get besieged," Smith recalls. But the authority of a federal judge to manage the docket and courtroom is extensive, and no direct challenges were issued. Within a year, Justice had reduced the backlog significantly and had put attorneys on notice that they would be expected to move their cases along in his court in the interest of both efficiency and justice. Today, the major features of the case management system advocated by judicial innovators like those Justice heard at the California seminar are incorporated into Rule 16 of the Federal Rules of Civil Procedure, a set of procedural requirements governing the processing of cases through the federal judiciary.

In designating Judge Justice as the Outstanding Federal Trial Judge in 1982, the Association of Trial Lawyers of America acknowledged his interest in effective trial management by referencing a 1981 ruling which it characterized as "probably the first federal court opinion dealing with ground rules for taking of video-tape depositions." The case involved an elderly woman whose physical condition prevented her from appearing at trial. The Judge set forth guidelines for the videotaped deposition, requiring that a stenographic record be kept as well in case the videotape should not be suitable for playback at the trial.[2] "I'm very interested in innovative procedures, anything that will lead to a more expeditious trial or a trial that is more likely to be just," Justice asserts. "And it's also just a plain matter of interest. If you read depositions to the jury, they have a tendency to fall asleep. If you have a videotape of the witness, you're seeing an actual person, you're seeing his or her facial expressions, reactions to questions, responses, and you can judge the witness very much as if the witness were there in the courtroom."

Despite Justice's early interest in innovative courtroom management, he has not enjoyed a reputation for efficiency. He tries cases the traditional way, according lawyers a lengthy pretrial preparation process and full opportunity to develop their cases in the courtroom. He takes considerable time to prepare his decisions. "Early on, Wayne Justice decided to sacrifice efficiency for substance," notes fellow Federal Judge Robert M. Parker. "He has been less concerned with productivity than the quality of his work. He never succumbed to the pressure for efficiency." The downside is a reputation for clogged dockets, lengthy trials, and delays in disposing of cases. However, it must be noted that Justice has endured a staggering case load during much of his tenure on the bench.

Much of the work of the federal district court is not conducted in the courtroom. The judges, law clerks, and staff function like government bureaucrats as they attend to the flow of paperwork into and through the court. A perusal of the ponderous civil order books in the Tyler Division reveals the grist of a federal trial court. The early volumes contain dispositions of hundreds of employment disability claims under the Social Security Act, an equal number of applications for the writ of habeas corpus from prisoners seeking release on the grounds of unjust imprisonment, and a large number of civil rights cases filed by prisoners. From his first days on the bench, Justice scrutinized these claims carefully to determine if there were any merit to the contentions and granted many. Even when U.S. magistrates began handling the cases in the interest of judicial economy later in the 1970s, Justice did not automatically accept their recommendations for disposition.

The Tyler civil order books also contain numerous judicial orders granting or refusing requests from plaintiffs' attorneys for temporary restraining orders and preliminary injunctions to halt some contested practice pending a trial. There are case settlement reports, orders and judgments in adjudicated cases, orders to correct errors in previous orders and judgments.

And then there is a great profusion of orders relating to the routine processing of cases through the court—responding to petitions for change of attorneys, motions to intervene or withdraw as parties in a lawsuit, motions relating to pretrial discovery of facts in a case, requests for continuance of cases, motions to file an amended complaint or dismiss a complaint, motions for summary judgment, motions for a new trial, motions to transfer a case. Some, such as a motion for summary judgment, require considerable deliberation by the court, since the attorneys submit evidence to the court seeking to have the issues resolved prior to a full trial.

Most judges deal with this endless parade of motions summarily, devoting no more than a line or two per motion. But Judge Justice is known as a writing judge. It is said that he takes three pages to say what other judges say in three sentences. His orders on important motions are accompanied by detailed explanations and legal references. Decisions in cases tried before the Judge without a jury include detailed findings of fact and conclusions of law, followed by a final order and judgment. Decisions in more significant cases include this same information in an often lengthy memorandum opinion which discusses the issues in narrative form.

Little of this detail will ever be published in the Federal Supplement. The Supplement, a series of volumes published by West Publishing Company and found in most libraries and law offices, contains only decisions the judges of the federal district courts wish to have published. Justice has traditionally submitted relatively little. "I have been very selective," he notes. "If it's particularly well done, I'll publish it. If it's not, I don't publish it." Most procedural orders are not important enough to warrant inclusion. Nevertheless, Justice has always been committed to seeing that all parties appearing before him get their day in court. One of his former law clerks, Marianne Wesson, related the story of the tiny hamburger in her tribute to the Judge when New York University Law School dedicated its *Annual Survey of American Law* publication to him in 1986. Wesson was reviewing the daily influx of prisoner civil rights petitions—claims that prisoners' rights had been violated in some way by the Texas Department of Corrections—when she came across a petition alleging that at dinner one night the petitioner had been served a hamburger patty much smaller than those served to the other inmates. Wesson prepared a one-page order dismissing this one-issue petition and presented it to the Judge for his signature.

But Justice did not sign it immediately. Suppose, he pondered, the prisoner had received the tiny hamburger in retaliation for his speaking out on some prison policy or because of his race. Well, said Wesson, he hadn't said so in his petition. No? smiled the Judge. Maybe he didn't know that it was important. Wesson rewrote the order, pointing out that the prisoner's allegation was not actionable under the civil rights laws unless in retaliation for his exercise of First Amendment rights or because of his race. The revised dismissal order was sent. Wesson suspected that the prisoner might treat it as an invitation to change his argument. But the prisoner did not respond.

"I've thought about this episode many times, imagining how it must have felt to that prisoner to open the order and realize the care with which his complaint had been read. This thoroughness, and the refusal to do things the way they had always been done in East Texas, was absolutely characteristic of the Judge."[3]

Robert Stein recalls that the Judge instructed him to avoid the "general's aide" syndrome as a law clerk—the idea that he was there to protect the Judge from the routine of the court. "He said he operated an open court, that he was available to talk to the lawyers, and that his law clerks were there for the benefit of the lawyers and litigants," Stein observes. "The Judge was always interested in the minutiae of the operation of the court. Many, many nights we spent on uninspired, poorly tried, insignificant lawsuits, trying to work it out so that justice would be achieved for both parties." In many federal district courts, it is a difficult feat even to reach the law clerks, much less the presiding judge.

For most of his time on the bench, Justice has used the standard two law clerks, recent law school graduates, to help him with the work of the court. While the prison case was pending, though, he had as many as five. Given a caseload ranging from six hundred to over nine hundred pending cases at any one time through much of the 1970s and early 1980s, the clerks got a work-out. The cases are assigned to the clerks on a random basis. Thus, a clerk's work can be extremely diverse. One may handle cases of considerable moment, while another will deal with minor matters. Procedural motions filed by the parties in a lawsuit are often difficult to resolve and take up much of the clerks' time, as does the determining of plaintiffs' attorneys' fees in civil rights cases.[4] Clerks occasionally consult one another on particularly complex matters.

Conflicts sometimes arise, given the clerks' strong personalities and intellects. And romantic involvement among them has not been unknown, though it is strongly discouraged because of the tensions generated. The Judge has not been particularly attentive to either interclerk conflict or romance, leaving such matters to the clerks themselves or to his personal secretary, first Marcelle Simmons and then Debra Magee. Until her retirement in 1987, Marcelle Simmons handled much of the clerks' orientation to the work of the court and to the style of the Judge. The many clerks who served during her tenure regard her with great esteem. Simmons had served the Justice law firm in Athens for many years and was invited by the Judge to join him in Tyler when he was appointed to the bench. The clerks, particularly those serving two-year clerkships early in the Judge's judicial career, also have great affection for Sue Justice, who took a personal interest in their welfare.

Generally, Justice allows his clerks considerable leeway in drafting orders and opinions. They are there to research and write. Federal district judges depend upon their clerks for most of this work, since they are on the bench trying cases much of the time. Following a hearing in a non-jury case, Justice sets out his understanding of the relevant law and how he prefers to handle such matters, then lets the clerk assigned to the case take it from there. The clerks meet frequently with the Judge to discuss the difficult cases they are working on, and he holds them to high standards. He is particularly concerned to see that his decisions are well cited to points of law, particularly those established by the Fifth Circuit, the court that hears any appeal of his decisions. He goes over and over important opinions that are likely to be appealed to be sure that the facts are clearly set out and the reasoning is sound and amply supported. Amy Johnson, who clerked for Justice in 1985–1986, at times found this frustrating. "It would drive me crazy because sometimes you can say something that is common sense and doesn't need a cite. There are judges on the Fifth Circuit who want to overrule Judge Justice, so he is particularly careful to see that his opinions are well supported." The inevitable result is lengthy, heavily footnoted, and often technical opinions which are difficult for non-lawyers to read.

Justice's early clerks joked about wanting to present him with the "Brown Cow/White Horse Award" for his insistence on thorough legal research. A case is said to be "on all fours" when it is directly on point to the legal issue being researched. Among East Texas lawyers, a brown cow case signifies such a case. To law students, a white horse case does the same. The planned award, which was never actually presented, would have had the front of a horse at one end and the front of a cow at the other, thus signifying Justice's quest for precedent "on all eights."

Since most of his law clerks have graduated at the top of their classes and have had law review editing and writing experience, their skills are highly refined to begin with. Still, Justice scrutinizes everything issued under his signature. He takes pride in his writing and edits the drafts from the clerks carefully. Always at his side are a dictionary and thesaurus. He uses both frequently, given his penchant for working obscure vocabulary into his opinions. The Judge admits to having always been interested in words and their derivation. "Sometimes when I have a hard time getting to sleep or wake up in the middle of the night, I pick up a dictionary and study words," he says. In a 1984 case the Judge had an opportunity to consider the meaning of the word "nerd." He relished the opportunity, going so far as to appoint an *amicus curiae* ("friend of the court") to assist in the task. After considerable study, Justice wrote that the word "nerd" is a "polysemantic neologism" which must be viewed as a kind of "undifferentiated belittlement."[5] He was sufficiently intrigued with the definition to work it into a footnote in a later decision striking down portions of Texas' mass picketing statute.[6]

It is natural that clerks with a particular orientation will gravitate to judges with similar perspectives. And it is apparent that judges will tend to select clerks who support their outlook on life. Thus, the clerks working for Justice have for the most part been politically liberal. Justice's first clerk, Wayne Smith, remembers his interview keenly, for the Judge did not ask him about his activities in law school but focused instead on his political and social philosophy. "It was clear to me that it was important for Judge Justice that the people that worked with him in research had the same philosophy as he had." For those few clerks who have not shared that philosophy, the association with the Judge and his staff coupled with the cases coming before the court has often worked a conversion. Robert Stein labeled himself a Goldwater conservative when he signed on as law clerk. "I went to Tyler as a conservative Republican, church-going Catholic. I came out of Tyler much changed by the experience, to the point where I would feel much more comfortable with the liberal wing of the Democratic Party in politics."

When Justice was first on the bench, he obtained law clerks by visiting the University of Texas School of Law in Austin. As his opinions found their way into law books and law courses, his reputation spread. He no longer had to travel to recruit clerks; prospective clerks came to him. In recent years, he has had over thirty candidates for a clerkship, most at the top of their classes in the nation's best law schools. David Brown, a Harvard Law School graduate who clerked for Justice in the mid-1980s, points out that Justice is part of a network of liberal judges well known to top law students in the Northeast. Students gravitate toward him because "he's one of the best of the group." (A list of all the clerks and the law schools from which they graduated is included at the end of this book.) The Judge likes to be in the company of bright people; his clerks certainly afford him that opportunity. And his orders and opinions reflect their scholarly contributions.

Since most of the prospective law clerks now come from outside the state, Justice has a routine he follows to orient them to the community. "I find out where they are staying and pick them up at 6:15 for breakfast. I drive them to the place that I think would thoroughly acquaint them with Texas 'redneckdom.' It's a coffeeshop that caters to construction workers; it has a jukebox that plays crying-in-your-beer songs. I buy them breakfast and we talk." None has admitted to finding the experience unnerving. The rest of the day is spent visiting with the present clerks and office staff. "We make it a point to treat them all with great courtesy and don't want them to leave the chambers with the feeling that they didn't get a fair evaluation," he says. But he is careful to tell them that they should not wait for him to decide if they get an offer somewhere else. "I remind them that a federal clerkship is a valuable spot. It is the best training I can think of for a lawyer who is going to have a federal court practice. Don't wait for me. If you get an acceptance, take it."

Some have asserted that the law clerks exert a strong eastern, anti-Texas influence on the Judge and his decisions. He takes exception to such accusations, noting, "If you look at my record, you'll see that I have maintained a consistent attitude from my earliest days on the bench. That same attitude was manifested when I had all of my clerks from the University of Texas." At the same time, there is no question that the Judge profits intellectually from the new ideas and insights his clerks bring with them, as the comprehensive and scholarly character of many of his recent opinions attest. "They've been exposed to brilliant college professors in these high-ranking law schools, and it's always interesting to me to hear what they have to say." It is thus a two-way street: the clerks learn the mechanics of the federal court, and the Judge gains new legal insights and theories for use in crafting his decisions. He has gone so far as to say that "my association with the law clerks is the best part of this job."

The chambers of Judge William Wayne Justice in Tyler are located in the modern, unimposing federal courthouse off the downtown square. Justice arrives about 7 A.M. to go through his mail before general office activity begins with coffee at 8 A.M. Until a lounge was constructed across the hall from his courtroom, the Judge would gather with his clerks and staff in the small study adjacent to his office. Conversation among court personnel at these early morning gatherings is informal, often spirited. With the assignment of more judges to the Eastern District in recent years and with a decline in the numbers of pending statewide lawsuits, more time is available for family-like social interaction among the office staff, the law clerks, and the Judge. Justice is relaxed in this setting; he is at home here. The discussion is light, often focusing on stories in the morning newspaper—sometimes about one of his decisions—or on sports. There is considerable humor. By 8:30, the clerks and court staff begin to drift away to their nearby offices or to the court library to begin work.

On days when hearings are not scheduled, the Judge closets himself in his large office with its blue carpet—"picked out by Sue because it matches my eyes"—to spend the balance of the morning reviewing the work of the clerks, signing orders, holding pretrial conferences, and occasionally discussing a pending matter with one of his staff. Surrounded on two sides by glass, the large modern office offers an expansive view of a rather unattractive section of downtown Tyler—mostly buildings and parking lots. At one end of his office stands the Judge's desk, with a half-dozen dark blue upholstered captain's chairs arranged in a semicircle in front of it. A couch, armchairs, and coffee table at the opposite end near the entrance provide a more relaxed setting. Justice occasionally uses a smaller antique standup desk in the office, though most of the time he is ensconced in the high-backed swivel chair behind the large desk flanked by U.S. and Texas flags. To his left is a complex telephone and intercom system. His "all thumbs" mechanical ability often results in frustration in trying to get it to work properly. As a result, he frequently delivers messages to his clerks and staff in person.

On days when hearings are scheduled in the courtroom, Justice emerges from his chambers fully robed and walks through the library to the courtroom door behind the bench. Dorothy Daugherty, his courtroom reporter, and Joyce Almarez, his deputy clerk, are already at their places on the lower part of the massive two-tiered bench. The law clerk assigned the case sits at a small table adjacent to the bench. To conserve space, the bench is set at an angle in the spacious dark-paneled courtroom with its indirect lighting, blue carpeting, and walnut furniture. To let those assembled in the courtroom know that he is about to enter, one of the Judge's staff strikes the heavy brass knocker on the door behind the bench three times. The audience rises. The law clerk intones:

> Hear ye, Hear ye, Hear ye! All persons having business before the honorable, the United States District Court for the Eastern District of Texas, are admonished to draw near and give attention, for the court is now sitting. God save the United States and this Honorable Court!

The clerk's voice carries to the very back of the courtroom, the result of careful practice and several dress rehearsals with the Judge standing at various places in the courtroom. The door opens and Justice emerges to take his place behind the high part of the bench above the courtroom reporter and the deputy clerk. The proceedings begin.

Often after all pretrial motions have been disposed of and with the trial about to begin, a case will be settled. Disappointing as it may be to the law clerk who has been assigned the case and has geared up for the courtroom experience, the purpose of the judicial system is served when disputes are resolved short of a formal trial.

The law clerks, members of the Judge's staff, and an occasional guest meet at noon in the lounge for lunch, usually sandwiches either brought from home or made in the compact kitchenette. A game of dominoes follows. The long-standing champion prior to her retirement was the Judge's personal secretary, Marcelle Simmons. Debra Magee, her successor, is also a master of the game. Justice usually has lunch away from the court. Favorite places include one of several Tyler cafeterias, a nearby sandwich and yogurt shop, or, when entertaining guests, the Petroleum Club across the square. While working at the court over the weekend, the Judge and his clerks often will head for the legendary Pat Gee's barbecue located off a country road a few miles outside of Tyler. "There may be better barbecue food, but if there is, I don't know where it can be found," he says. A black establishment, Pat Gee's place is populated by people of all races. It is little more than a one-room shack out in the country. A potbelly stove provides warmth in winter; open screened windows are its source of air conditioning in the summer. Pat offers a variety of barbecue meat—with or without hot sauce—to be washed down with soft drinks from the old refrigerator near the counter.

Afternoons at the court follow the same pattern as the mornings. Following an occasional fifteen-minute catnap after lunch, Justice continues working at his desk or conducting hearings in the courtroom until 5:30 or 6 P.M., sometimes later. Now and then, he will wander into the library to look up some point of law or will visit the law clerks in their offices. But most of the time he is working behind piles of papers and open lawbooks stacked neatly on his desk. Like that of his father, the Judge's work never stops. Even on weekends and holidays, he spends part of the time at the office.

When the Judge assumes his position on the bench, there is no doubt that he is in full control of the courtroom. He very seldom uses the gavel. "I've always been of the opinion that if a judge can't control the courtroom with his voice, he's lost control," he maintains. He has little tolerance for poorly prepared attorneys or those who seek to employ delaying tactics during the pretrial discovery period and has been known to deal harshly with both. Yet, from experiences trying cases before Judge Justice prior to becoming a judge himself, fellow Federal Judge Howell Cobb observes that "Wayne Justice would not embarrass a lawyer before his client or before the bar. He could show signs of volatility, but he keeps it under control." Formality is the rule in the courtroom. All personnel are to be properly attired, including the litigants. Attorneys are to conduct their questioning from behind a podium, not at the counsel table. Justice also has a reputation as being one of the toughest judges on white-collar crime, though he considers sentencing the worst part of his job. "It leaves me with an emotional bitter aftertaste which lingers for days."

He moves the cases along quickly, but not at the expense of the litigants. He is particularly solicitous of *pro se* litigants—those who are appearing without the benefit of an attorney. He makes sure that they get their day in court. "Judge Justice always kept sight of the people whose cases were before the court," recalls Kathlyn A. Knobloch from her clerkship experience in the 1970s. "The Judge never lost sight of the fact that a system dedicated to the resolution of conflict belongs to the people caught up in it and not to the lawyers, clerks, reporters, and judges."[7] One court staff member has observed that when accused individuals plead guilty as part of plea bargains in criminal cases, Justice makes sure they understand what they are giving up. "He tells them about every right they could possibly have, and then some."

When conducting trials, the Judge allows as much evidence in as possible, though this occasionally undercuts his strong commitment to the pretrial order and invariably lengthens trials. He is a strong believer in the jury system. If there is a choice between his deciding an issue or the jury's deciding it, he will tend to defer to the latter. Justice is clearly at his best as a trial judge. Whatever else they may say, both plaintiff and defense attorneys are almost universal in their praise of his ability to try cases. "Trial in his courtroom was an absolute delight," says Judge Robert M. Parker, who tried cases before Justice before being appointed to the bench himself by President Carter in 1979. "If you were prepared and knew what you were doing, he let you fully develop your case." John Hardy, who has appeared many times before Judge

Justice as the attorney for the Tyler school district, expresses the prevailing view among attorneys: "He wants you to be professional and prepared in his courtroom; he won't accept sloppy work. He runs a business-like courtroom. You're there for legal business."

As a former trial attorney himself, Justice appreciates talented lawyers no matter what side they represent. Through notes passed to his clerks, Justice will point out noteworthy events during trial. Lucas Guttentag, who clerked for the Judge in the late 1970s, remembers that during a medical malpractice case the Judge pointed out to him how the local defense lawyers were playing to the East Texas jury. Many of the clerks plan to be trial lawyers, and the opportunity to watch the best argue cases of some moment in Justice's courtroom is of inestimable value.

The Judge's interest in effective advocacy in the courtroom has an academic side as well. For a number of years, he has participated in the trial advocacy program at Harvard Law School. At Harvard he presides at mock trials and critiques the performances of the students. He looks forward to the opportunity. "I like to go to Cambridge. I'm enchanted by the atmosphere around there," he admits.

The formality Judge Justice exhibits on the bench also is apparent off the bench. He dresses in a dark suit or blazer; he is rarely seen in informal attire. He jokingly calls the suit his conservative camouflage. He has taken great pains to avoid even the hint of impropriety. "I have been under the impression, and I think it is absolutely accurate, that my every action has been under surveillance here in this hostile town. So I have been so strict and so ethical in all of my dealings that my personal life has been, I hope, irreproachable." His sense of propriety came to the attention of former Chief Justice Warren Burger, who appointed him a member of the Judicial Ethics Committee and its successor, the Judicial Review Committee, to investigate possible conflicts of interest among federal judges. He served on this committee for a number of years. The appointment carried with it membership on the Joint Committee on Canons of Judicial Ethics, a sixteen-member body. The Judge feels strongly about ethical issues and holds himself strictly accountable to the rules of propriety governing the federal judiciary. His concern for propriety extends to his clerks. Early on, they are instructed to have no dealings with the press. Occasionally, he has cautioned them about their personal activities away from the court.

Justice became chief judge on April 16, 1980, when Joe Fisher, then chief judge, turned seventy, and served for ten years. With the change of title came the shifting of some court offices to Tyler, the most central city in the Eastern District. The role of chief judge is less significant than it might sound. Justice estimates that for him the responsibilities associated with the office took up about ten hours a month. One of the most important involves periodically adjusting the case load among the judges with their consent. The chief judge also chairs meetings of the judges in the district several times a year and administers a small judges' fund resulting from a tax levied on case filings. Since the Administrative Office of the U.S. Courts in Washington handles budgetary and most administrative affairs for all the federal district courts, the judges are primarily concerned with case load distribution; the approval of new local court rules; communications from the administrative office; and matters of concern expressed by magistrates, the probation department, and the district clerk's office.

During his tenure as chief judge, Justice did not assert a strong leadership role over the affairs of the Eastern District. He made a point of doing as much by consensus as possible. Given the strong personalities and differing political philosophies of his colleagues in the Eastern District (the only other liberal Democrat among eight judges is Judge Robert M. Parker), there was always potential for conflict. Justice recalls a colleague from another Texas federal district telling how the judges in that district would have an argument over who got on the elevator first. The fact that the judges in the Eastern District are not all located in the same building or town helps prevent such petty bickering. Judge William M. Steger, who was appointed the third sitting judge in the Eastern District by President Nixon in 1970, acknowledges the tranquil working relationships among the judges during Justice's tenure as chief judge. "Politics doesn't seem to have become involved," he observes. Steger attributes the lack of conflict among the three judges assigned to Tyler— Steger, Justice, and Parker—to the fact that each is autonomous. "With Wayne, Bob, and me here in Tyler, it takes only one to make a decision." While the judges occasionally see one another, the courtrooms and the chambers operate completely independently.

Judge Justice turned over the title of chief judge to Judge Parker upon reaching the age of seventy on February 25, 1990.[8] Justice continues as a full-time judge.

The Justices had barely settled in Tyler when controversy erupted in his courtroom and permanently altered the couple's position in the community. Historically, Tyler, known chiefly for its rose industry, has been as conservative a community as Athens, thirty-five miles to the west, has been liberal. The only Democratic presidential candidate to prevail in Smith County in recent times was Harry Truman. Ralph Yarborough, who was reared in the little town of Chandler in Henderson County just to the west of Smith County, notes that in his day when you crossed over the Neches River into Smith County, "you were in a different world." Politically, "they were reactionaries." Built largely with railroad and oil money, Tyler became the home of the area's nouveaux riches. Its population in 1980 stood at slightly over 70,000. Palatial homes are spread through its shady south-side neighborhoods. In his 1978 *Texas Monthly* article entitled "The Real Governor of Texas," Paul Burka notes that the business community of Tyler has a deep-dyed conservatism that asks little of government. "They are people who are used to having things their own way and they look upon outsiders like Wayne Justice with suspicion."[9] It was, as Burka observes, a most unlikely location for an activist federal judge with populist roots.

In one of his earliest decisions, Judge Justice shocked the Tyler community when he declared the Tyler Junior College rule against long hair unconstitutional. The local college had adopted a rule prior to the opening of the 1970 fall semester prohibiting "extreme hair styles." The rule directed male students to wear their hair above their eyebrows in front and above the shirt collar. Hair had to be trimmed around the ears. Beards were prohibited; sideburns could not extend below the bottom of the earlobe. Mustaches were allowed but had to be neatly trimmed so as not to extend below or beyond the upper lip.

Several long-haired plaintiffs, including a Vietnam veteran, challenged the rule. One of the plaintiffs had attended the college previously and had earned straight A's. He had not been a disciplinary problem. All of the plaintiffs cited personal preference and contemporary style as the reason for wearing their hair long. Justice's old law partner, Bill Kugle, represented the plaintiffs. Kugle considers *Lansdale v. Tyler Junior College* one of the most significant cases of his career. "The idea that the administrators of a public college that belongs to the people of Texas could arbitrarily tell the students to conform to their personal notions of grooming is just ridiculous," he scoffs. "The administrators had a notion that they were just going to run that place like a military school."

Justice himself found the case fascinating and researched the law on hair length while the case was being argued. As soon as the trial was over, he ruled from the bench that the school policy was unconstitutional. Accustomed to the style of his predecessor, Judge Sheehy, the members of the Tyler establishment were shocked and enraged. Not only had the Justice interfered with the administration of the local college; he had intruded on community standards of propriety. His ruling from the bench was cited as further evidence of his eagerness to thwart the establishment and flaunt his judicial power. To assertions that it would have been more politically astute to have taken the case under advisement, Justice responds, "I wasn't aware that I had to be political in my decision. The reason I ruled from the bench is that I'd gotten very interested in the case and had read every bit of law I could find on the subject even before the hearing. So when I listened to the evidence, I already knew what the law was. I was able to rule from the bench." He adds, "I had already realized that I wasn't going to be a popular fellow in the community. If I'd have taken it under advisement and then come out with a decision later on, I don't see that that would have made any difference. You can't please all the people. That's not what you were put on the bench for."

In his published memorandum opinion, Justice found spurious the college's contention that long-haired students are prone to violence. "In any given era, a society's greatest men and its blackest villains customarily have worn the same hair style affected by most males in their respective circumstances." [10] He noted that thirty-seven of the thirty-nine delegates to the Constitutional Convention would have been ineligible under the rule to enroll in the Tyler college. The college had ample authority to deal with disruptive students however they preferred to wear their hair. The hair-length rule was thus unreasonable and discriminatory under the Fourteenth Amendment equal-protection clause. Justice's decision, which served as precedent only in the Eastern District, was extended two years later to public community colleges throughout the southeastern United States by virtue of its affirmance by the U.S. Court of Appeals for the Fifth Circuit. [11]

In reaching this decision, Judge Justice made clear his willingness to use judicial power to defend individual rights, even beyond the margin of what the Constitution specifically protects. This willingness would become the hallmark of his tenure on the bench. "The paramount objective of our society," he maintained in a 1978 interview, should be "to see that human rights are preserved." [12] Ten years later, his views had not changed. "My general philosophy is that I think the individual is entitled to as much breathing room and as much privacy as can be accorded to him, consistent with civilized society," he asserts. In decision after decision, he has steadily pushed for recognition of, and where possible, expansion of, individual freedom.

Coinciding with the hair-length case was desegregation of the Tyler public schools. After years of inaction following the 1954 *Brown v. Board of Education* Supreme Court decision, the school board permitted voluntary transfers among schools in 1963, and in 1966 approved moving four black teachers from the all-black Emmett Scott High School to all-white Robert E. Lee High School. Faced with continued pressure from the Department of Health, Education, and Welfare (HEW), the district adopted a five-point desegregation plan in January 1969 and submitted it to HEW for approval. HEW was responsible for enforcing Title VI of the Civil Rights Act of 1964, banning discrimination on grounds of race, color, or national origin in programs or activities receiving federal assistance. The Tyler plan essentially continued the past policy of voluntary desegregation through "freedom of choice." Emphasis was also placed on improving educational programs, increasing faculty integration, and continuing the integration of transportation and student activities. No forced integration measures were included.

The pace of integration was slow. School officials liked to point out that under freedom of choice, integration had increased from 6 percent to over 20 percent in the district. Still, during the 1969–1970 school year, seven of the twenty-seven Tyler public schools were all black, three were all white, and eleven had student enrollments over 90 percent white. Seventy-seven percent of black students in the school district were enrolled in the seven all-black schools.

Despite an effort by Texas Republican Senator John Tower to intervene on Tyler's behalf with HEW officials, [13] the 1969 school district plan was rejected. In the fall of 1969 HEW presented the district with four options for achieving a unitary school district, i.e., one in which there were no racially identifiable schools. None was accepted, and HEW referred the matter to the U.S. Department of Justice for prosecution. Some Tylerites assumed that failure to satisfy the federal government would result only in the loss of federal funds, since this was the only penalty HEW could impose. For the Tyler school district this could have meant the loss of $450,000. But much more was at stake once the Justice Department instituted suit. The 1964 Civil Rights Act required integration, and failure to achieve it could result in an integration order imposed by the federal district court—in this case, Judge Justice's court. Furthermore, decisions then being handed down by both the U.S. Supreme Court and the U.S. Court of Appeals for the Fifth Circuit clearly outlawed the very type of gradualism then being pursued by the Tyler school district. [14]

The Justice Department, then under control of the Nixon administration, waited until the summer of 1970 to bring the lawsuit. With the opening of school only weeks away, Justice and Colin J. Carl, the law clerk assigned the case, had insufficient time to design a comprehensive integration plan of their own. There was little choice but to rely on what the parties presented. The Justice Department advanced one of the desegregation plans developed earlier by HEW. That plan had also received the endorsement of the Texas Education Agency. Six members of the Tyler school board, together with the school superintendent, presented a different plan. The seventh board member, Martin L. Edwards, the only black on the board, endorsed the HEW plan with certain modifications.

Before the July 25 hearing, Justice decided to take a few days off. While away on vacation in New York City, he received a call from a friend who was also a Tyler school board member. It didn't take very long for him to realize that the school board was bent on influencing his decision. If the phone call had been designed to "talk reason" with the Judge, it backfired. "That was very bold on their part and that crystallized my feeling more than anything that ever happened to me that I was going to do what the law and the facts required," Justice says angrily. He resolved never again to engage in a conversation in which only one party to a lawsuit pending before him was represented.

On July 27, Justice accepted the HEW plan, which rejected the school district's neighborhood-school approach.[15] Schools were paired and grouped in threes by grade level (all students in the third and fourth grades, for example, would be educated on an integrated basis in two or three schools exclusively), resulting in substantial busing across the district. School board member Edwards remembers leaving the courtroom and coming face to face with angry whites at the elevator. "This white man came up to me, accompanied by others, and said, 'If anything happens to my girl, I'm coming after you.' I'm going to tell you that scared the hell out of me."[16] In early August, the government attorneys supported school district requests for modifications to the plan, eliminating the pairing and grouping, and returning the district to the neighborhood school configuration. Desegregation was to be accomplished largely through altered attendance zones and busing. It was apparent to Judge Justice that word had reached officials in the Justice Department to make the plan more palatable to the school district. "I had ambivalent feelings about the way they had done it, but it did accomplish what I was demanding." Time left him little alternative. He accepted the modifications.

The 1970 order resulted in the closing of the black Emmett Scott High School, with its students to attend the two white high schools, Robert E. Lee and John Tyler. The closing, together with busing, increased racial tension in the school system and in the community. The boiling point was reached in March 1971, when school officials at Tyler High School held a cheerleader election. The ballot listed four black candidates separately from ten white candidates and instructed students to vote for two black students and four white students. The racial split in the school was 62 percent white and 38 percent black. Two hundred black students, unhappy with the separate listing and lack of parity, staged a walkout and were suspended. A lawsuit resulted. Judge Justice ruled that the students had been suspended in violation of their rights to free speech and procedural due process. He ordered their reinstatement without penalty.[17]

In July the Judge issued an order over opposition from the white-dominated school board establishing a biracial committee to investigate the cheerleader dispute and propose an equitable means of resolving the dispute. Biracial committees were then being increasingly used by federal district courts to facilitate integration. In his order he wrote, "The mere fact that a dispute arising out of a cheerleader election has been brought before the federal courts speaks loudly of the need for some mechanism wherein the issues affecting the conversion of the school district to a unitary system can be brought out, discussed, and hopefully, resolved without need for litigation." [18]

Justice subsequently accepted the recommendation advanced by the biracial committee that the cheerleader dispute be resolved by adding one white cheerleader and one black cheerleader to the squad. The composition of the group for the 1971–1972 school year would then reflect the ethnicity of the school's enrollment. The school board had opposed the recommendation. In December 1971, Justice issued an order making the biracial committee an agent of the court to advise and make recommendations regarding the transition of the Tyler school district to unitary status.

Evidence of the depth of antagonism from the white community toward the creation of the committee can be seen in the school district's unsuccessful appeal of the Judge's order, first to the Fifth Circuit and later to the U.S. Supreme Court. White school officials claimed the creation of the committee constituted an abuse of discretion and a usurpation of power.

The Texas Education Agency added to community discontent in Tyler when, pursuant to Justice's order in *United States v. Texas,* the statewide desegregation ruling discussed in Chapter 5, it ordered Robert E. Lee High School to cease using Confederate memorabilia including Confederate uniforms for its marching band and "Dixie" as its fight song. At stake was state accreditation for the school district and $800,000 in state funds. Even though it was the Texas Education Agency which ordered the change, it did so under a statewide desegregation order issued by Justice. People who called TEA in Austin were told to take their complaints to the Judge. Local lawyer and state legislator Bill Clark expressed the view of the majority of white Tylerites: "There's a difference between being proud of your Southern heritage and being racist." [19]

Justice's Tyler desegregation ruling was neither extreme nor unprecedented. Federal judges all over the country were similarly applying the Supreme Court desegregation mandates in their localities. But this did not lessen the sting of community resentment. For most of the early 1970s, the Tyler community was up in arms over school desegregation. One-sixth of the city's population of 65,000 signed a petition calling for Justice's impeachment. Hate mail and obscene phone calls poured in both at home and at the office. He received death threats but joked, "There were lots of people saying, 'Somebody ought to shoot that son-of-a-bitch Justice.' But no one was saying, '*I'm* going to shoot that son-of-a-bitch Justice.'" At one point when the Judge was in Sherman, a caravan of automobiles and pickup trucks bearing Confederate flags and blaring horns circled the Tyler federal courthouse.

Several workers remodeling the Justices' newly purchased two-story red brick house walked off the job. Relations with downtown professional and

business people were strained. The minister of the First Baptist Church, ironically located across the street from the federal courthouse, called Justice a
socialist intent on tearing down the fabric of Tyler society.[20] A neighbor who
was an influential member of the Episcopal Church made it clear when the
Justices sought to attend services there that they were not wanted. Fellow
federal Judge Woodrow Seals from the Southern District remembers the time
he and his wife walked into the prestigious Petroleum Club in downtown Tyler
for dinner with the Justices and several patrons in the club got up and walked
out. Justice's law clerks found it wise to keep their affiliation with the court to
themselves.

Justice accepted the social isolation and denunciation as part of what goes
with being a federal judge in a small community. "You know, I just never have
thought of social acclaim as being one of the important things in life. I'd like
to have it; I like a party just as well as anybody else. And I like the esteem of my
fellow citizens, but it's not nearly as important to me as respect for the law as an
institution. That's the way I was reared." More than anything else, the Tyler
decision indicated that the Judge would not shirk from deciding other controversial cases coming before his court.

Justice was not alone. Other federal district court judges in Texas and across
the country who took to heart the U.S. Supreme Court's mandate to remove
school segregation "root and branch" were likewise being ostracized and vil-
ified within their communities.[21] As Justice sees it, "The public makes an
effort to punish the judge. And if the judge doesn't care to take that kind of
heat, he'll start rendering innocuous orders, knowing that they will be appealed. And in the meantime, he is safe. He's still welcome at the country
club, and still can play golf with his buddies. And they think he's a great
fellow. When he gets reversed, he can make some other innocuous order and
that'll be appealed too. And it'll go on for years. In the meantime, his place in
the scheme of things is safe. Many of the judges opted to do that, unfortunately."

The vilification was particularly hard on Justice's wife. Born and raised out
in the country, Sue Justice had found roots in Athens and enjoyed a very active
social life. The couple continued to live in Athens during Wayne's tenure as
U.S. attorney, though Wayne's preoccupation with his work in Tyler curtailed
most of their social activities. It was a year into Justice's judgeship before the
couple moved into an apartment in Tyler. A gregarious and ambitious person,
Sue had initially been drawn to the glamor and sophistication associated with
being the wife of Tyler's only federal judge. The fact that they would be liberals
in a conservative town did not concern her, because she assumed that politics
would not affect personal relationships. It never had in Athens. She looked
forward to a busy social calendar. At first, the couple were overwhelmed by
social invitations. "During that first year, we could not possibly have re-

sponded to the invitations and kindnesses of the Tyler community," she recalls. She became a member of several women's clubs and, together with her
husband, was involved in a variety of social activities befitting a federal judge
and his wife.

Sue knew that Wayne Justice would not be judge for long before his decisions would generate criticism. But she never anticipated that her husband
would almost overnight become a pariah in the community. "Wayne always
knew what would happen. I didn't. I believed that people would not like what
he did. But I had no idea there would be a whole onslaught of criticism about
it." For a time, the conservative Tyler newspapers, the *Morning Telegraph* and
evening *Courier-Times,* devoted so much space to critical comments concerning
Justice and his decisions that it seemed to her "like they devoted all their time
to us." Sue believes the denunciation had a snowballing effect. "People got the
idea that it was socially right to be mean to us." She speculates that Wayne's
reluctance to ingratiate himself with the community elite was a contributing
factor. She asserts pointedly, "He wouldn't become a lapdog."

The swirl of controversy surrounding Justice in and around Tyler early in
his tenure on the bench led to his being counseled by a member of the U.S.
Supreme Court about becoming "too controversial." At a judicial meeting in
Jackson Hole, Wyoming, in the early 1970s, Justice, an early riser, frequently
would run into Justice Harry Blackmun, also an early riser, in the deserted
hotel coffee shop. Being the only two people in the room, they sat together on
several occasions. At one of these breakfasts, Blackmun gently counseled Justice to assume a more moderate stance as a judge. Justice thanked him for his
advice, which he chose not to follow. "Since then," Justice observes, "I have
thought on many occasions how ironic it was that Justice Blackmun would be
the one who'd advise me not to become controversial when shortly thereafter
he would become the most controversial judge in the judiciary by writing the
1973 *Roe v. Wade* abortion decision."

After the Tyler desegregation decision, the doors to Tyler society closed and
have remained closed over the years. Knowing that Sue's social ostracism is
directly attributable to fallout from his judicial decisions bothers the Judge.
He told reporters in 1987, "The real grief is felt by my wife, a wonderful
person who enjoys the social events and happenings. I work up here in an office
where the people approve of what I do. But my wife has to go out in town and
mix with people. She has had to be very courageous."[22]

The storm of protest and denunciation depressed Sue. "I was very, very sad.
Wayne thought my reactions were very bad. My daughter couldn't understand
it. It wasn't that I wasn't invited to a party. It was the disapproval for something that I thought was right. I think it's right for me to stand for what I
believe in just as it is for them to stand for what they believe in. I would not

dare to say to someone that I don't like you for what you believe. I thought it was an unjust reaction." Sue's circle of friends in Tyler narrowed, and her involvement in social activities largely ceased. She did continue her involvement in the literary club and the garden club, despite an undercurrent of resentment from some of the members, but only at her husband's urging. "I didn't want to do it, not at all," she admits. "But Wayne insisted." She took up sewing and did a lot of reading. By the mid-1970s, one of Sue's sisters prevailed upon her to expand her interest in bridge, and Sue quickly became a life master.

In 1978 the Justices met famed architect Bruce Goff and presented him with a futuristic design for a new home in Tyler. Sue had sketched out on a yellow piece of paper a house whose rooms were all octagons (see the photographic section). The house, which was never built because of high construction costs, was to have been made of a translucent fiberglass material causing it to glow in the dark. Had it been built, the unconventional house would have been an apt symbol of the Justices' presence in the staid Tyler community.

Though the doors of Tyler society may have closed to the Justices, Sue Justice's assertion that all through the years "no one ever doubted that Wayne was *the* judge in Tyler" has the ring of truth about it. The boundaries of social propriety in Tyler may prohibit public acknowledgment, but Justice's reputation as one of the country's leading civil rights trial judges undoubtedly earns respect from many in the community who admire an independent thinker.

As plaintiffs' attorneys involved in class action lawsuits involving state institutions chose his court as their forum, Justice unhesitatingly responded by handing down a steady procession of judicial thunderbolts. Denunciation spread across Texas. The Justices' daughter, Ellen, was shielded from most of the community reproach by attending college at Mount Holyoke in Massachusetts from 1967 to 1971. After leaving for St. Stephen's Episcopal School in Austin when she was thirteen, Ellen was rarely home, even in the summer. She grew apart from Athens and never really knew Tyler at all. Her parents rarely talked to her about the controversy swirling about them, aside from "making some comment like, 'We've been getting a lot of calls in the middle of the night.'" It was not a matter they cared to dwell upon. About the only direct experience Ellen had with controversy stemming from her father's decisions occurred when she was in law school at the University of Houston in the early 1980s. In almost every course she took, she recalls that the professor at one time or another would comment negatively about something "Ol' Willie Wayne" had done. But Ellen did not go out of her way to engage in debate. "I didn't see any reason to bring it on myself," she says simply. "I've always kept a very low profile, just like Father."

Texas metropolitan newspapers, which are by and large conservative, were particularly quick to pick up on Justice's rulings, starting with the school-desegregation decisions in and around Tyler. Former Democratic Senator Ralph Yarborough, whose recommendation had placed Justice on the bench, believes that much of the attack on Justice was really orchestrated by conservative Democrats to keep him out of office. "I would run into people as far west as Del Rio who'd say, 'Oh, you put that Judge Wayne Justice on the bench over there.' Same thing high up in the Panhandle. People would say, 'You put that radical judge on the bench.'" Yarborough lost his senate seat to Lloyd Bentsen, Jr., in the 1970 Democratic primary and was never able to regain political office. The Judge agrees that much of the adverse publicity given his early rulings was politically motivated. But denunciation continued long after Yarborough ceased running for office in 1974. The cries of protest were genuine; Justice's rulings were interfering with what many Texans wanted out of their government—little interference with the status quo.

All during the turmoil, the Judge reacted stoically. He refused to respond to inquiries from the press and ordered his clerks to do the same. As social invitations declined, his world revolved more and more around the court. Still, he refused to compromise his pattern of living. His phone number has always been listed in the telephone book, and he continued to jog regularly on the high school track or park near his home. His car bears prominently displayed federal judge license plates. "I knew exactly what I was getting into. I'd been United States attorney for seven years, and I'd been watching federal judges and reading their decisions all along. I could pretty well foresee what was in store. It's not been the most pleasant thing in the world, but it's something I foresaw," he told the *Texas Observer* on the anniversary of his tenth year on the bench. [23]

If the denunciation heaped upon him has ever bothered the Judge, he has rarely shown it. Some say he is energized by it. "Nerves of iron," says Judge Woodrow Seals. His wife reports that even during the worst fallout over his decisions, he had no trouble turning off the cares of the court when he came home. "He never had trouble going to sleep at night. It was never difficult for him," she says. "It never bothered him a bit. My daughter thought it was funny, and Wayne just didn't care. But it never was funny to me." For a time, even Sue's mother stopped speaking to her. "You can't replace things like that," she declares. While time has softened the harsh edges of bitterness, it has not erased them for Sue Justice. "It's a cruel fate to be for the underdog," she says.

Contrary to popular opinion, Wayne Justice is not outwardly combative outside the courtroom and rarely inside it. He is reserved and dignified, much in the manner of Senator Lloyd Bentsen, a member of his law class at the University of Texas. Away from the court, Sue says that Wayne "is a very pleasant man, very even tempered. He is a good companion, a good friend. I think of him as a very loving person." People who have known him over the years will attest that he has changed little in the face of all the controversy. "He neither hunkered down nor became arrogant after the great outcry against his rulings," comments Fifth Circuit Judge Thomas Reavley. "He kept a perspective on himself and his court. He never lost his sense of humor." Adds fellow Federal District Court Judge Howell Cobb, "Wayne Justice has never been impressed with himself as a person of status and stature. What does impress him is the office he holds."

Strange as it may seem, Justice dislikes controversy. "I'm basically a very shy, retiring person, but fate has put me in a situation where I've been in the midst of controversy. The whole time I was practicing law with my father, we were in the midst of controversy. And when I was United States attorney, of course, there was no way to avoid controversy in that job. And as federal district judge, it's been the worst of all. Now I'm hardened to it, you understand. Controversy is now kind of a way of life with me. But I have never particularly liked it."

The controversy which has greeted many of Justice's judicial decisions is directly attributable to his view of the individual in society and the role of the federal court in interpreting the Constitution. The latter was most clearly delineated in a response to the views of Justice William H. Rehnquist, later to become the Chief Justice of the U.S. Supreme Court. In 1976 Rehnquist delivered the annual Will E. Orgain Lecture at the University of Texas School of Law. Entitled "The Notion of a Living Constitution," the speech was subsequently published in the *Texas Law Review*.[24] "When I read that article," Justice says, "I was deeply offended. I felt he was entirely wrong in his concept of judicial decision-making." Several years later, Justice was invited to speak at the law school, and he used the opportunity to deliver a reply to Rehnquist. That speech, entitled "A Relativistic Constitution," was later reprinted in the *University of Colorado Law Review*.[25] The speeches reveal two fundamentally different approaches to the role of the judiciary and the use of judicial power.

Rehnquist began his speech by pondering the term "living Constitution." He noted that the framers of the Constitution had written in general language, leaving to later generations the task of applying that language to a changing environment. The framers, he asserted, intended the judiciary to play a very limited role in this process. To illustrate what the judiciary should not do, Rehnquist quoted from a legal brief filed with a federal district court:

> We are asking a great deal of the Court because other branches of government have abdicated their responsibility. . . . Prisoners are like other "discrete and

insular" minorities for whom the Court must spread its protective umbrella because no other branch of government will do so. . . . This Court, as the voice and conscience of contemporary society, as the measure of the modern conception of human dignity, must declare that the (name of prison) and all it represents offends the Constitution of the United States and will not be tolerated.

Rehnquist maintained that judicial review—the power of the federal courts to declare laws and administrative acts unconstitutional—is basically anti-democratic and antimajoritarian in a nation which prides itself on being a self-governing representative democracy. It should be used sparingly.

He found repugnant the brief writer's assumption that non-elected members of the federal judiciary should address social problems simply because the other branches of government have failed to do so. "Once we have abandoned the idea that the authority of the courts to declare laws unconstitutional is somehow tied to the language of the Constitution that the people adopted, a judiciary exercising the power of judicial review appears in a quite different light. Judges then are no longer the keepers of the covenant; instead they are a small group of fortunately situated people with a roving commission to second-guess Congress, state legislatures, and state and federal administrative officers concerning what is best for the country."

The Court would be ill advised to adopt the brief writer's views, Rehnquist said, for three reasons. First, the Constitution delegates sufficient grants of power in general terms to both President and Congress so that they have ample means to address changing needs. He noted as well that the Bill of Rights imposes limits on the exercise of these powers. He also noted that the Thirteenth, Fourteenth, and Fifteenth Amendments added after the Civil War impose restraints on the exercise of power by state legislatures, but only in the context of protecting the newly freed slaves.

Second, when the Supreme Court embarked on social problem-solving in the past, the result was disastrous. He cited the infamous 1857 *Dred Scott* decision in which the Court ruled that Congress had no authority to regulate slavery despite efforts to resolve the slavery issue through legislation for thirty years.[26] That decision sent the nation cascading into the Civil War. He also cited the 1905 *Lochner v. New York* decision in which the Court struck down legislation limiting the length of the work day on the ground that it interfered with the right to contract, a right not stated in the Constitution but coinciding with the laissez-faire economic doctrine then endorsed by a majority of the Supreme Court justices.[27]

Third, Rehnquist maintained that the brief writer sought an end-run around popular government, ignoring the development of political values through the process of legislation and constitutional amendment. Once a competing view is written into legislation, it takes on "a form of moral goodness" precisely because the majority has endorsed it. "It should not be easy for any one individual or group of individuals to impose by law their value judgments upon fellow citizens who may disagree with those judgments. Indeed, it should not be easier just because the individual in question is a judge."

In sum, Rehnquist argued for a conservative judiciary with limited powers to adapt the Constitution to changing times. That responsibility, he asserted, is more properly left to the elected branches of government.

In his speech, Judge Justice refuted Rehnquist's arguments point by point. Citing the writings of Alexander Hamilton, he argued for an independent, activist judiciary which must from time to time override the other branches of government in order to enforce the commands of the Constitution. Justice noted that like other noble statements of human liberty, the Bill of Rights was adopted after a time of strife. "At such times, it appears that those involved are so invested with a sense of urgency to memorialize the rights they have so painfully obtained in the form of a 'solemn and authoritative act,' as though they realize that they may later desire to modify the principles and be tempted to retract them in practice."

In fact, this is what often happens. Justice noted public opinion polls revealing that a sizable percentage of Americans do not support the Bill of Rights. He also cited the backsliding of Congress in enforcing the post–Civil War amendments against racial discrimination.

Justice argued that Rehnquist's uncritical deference to the will of the majority goes far toward judicial abdication. The framers of the Constitution did not give evidence of any such deference to legislative action, he argued. If the Rehnquist view accurately reflected that of the framers, reasoned Justice, there would have been no need for any rights to have been written into the Constitution. "After all, those rights are only the preferences or 'value judgments' of one set of men, and there would have been no reason for them to be put on a 'legal basis' which would make them difficult for later men, with differing opinions, to change."

Justice rejected Rehnquist's views that consensus itself is sufficient to add legitimacy to laws. "The plain fact of the matter is that the majority is sometimes wrong."[28] "Certainly the will of a transient majority should not lightly be permitted to overturn hard-won Constitutional rights." The purpose of a Constitution, Justice asserted, is to make certain laws more permanent than others. The responsibility of the judiciary, whose members are appointed for life, is to be assured that those more important laws in the form of the enduring values of the Bill of Rights are not thwarted by legislative action in response to the day's passing fancy. "Judicial review may seem anomalous in the light of a 'democratic theory' which dogmatically insists on popular choice . . . ; it is not anomalous in a Constitution which attempts to reconcile the principle of popular choice with inherent rights." In a 1986 television interview, Justice noted that when he desegregated the Tyler public schools, he read newspaper editorials in the Tyler paper suggesting that no more than a dozen people in Smith County approved of his desegregation order. "I thought to myself, what has that got to do with it? I was enforcing the Constitution as I'm required to do."[29] This view of the Bill of Rights as an antimajoritarian document would later result in a series of controversial decisions supporting individual rights in a variety of contexts, including free expression, employment, and the criminal justice system.

Justice then turned to defend the position of the brief writer. He found nothing startling about the writer's urging the court to find prisoners to constitute a "discrete and insular minority," noting that the "discrete and insular minority" expression was first advanced in a footnote by Justice Harlan Fisk Stone and later became the basis for the Supreme Court's interpretation of the Fourteenth Amendment equal protection clause.[30] Nor did he find startling the writer's assertion that prisoners should be treated with human dignity, a point Justice himself would repeatedly assert in his 1980 prison reform decision. The general wording of the Eighth Amendment's provision against cruel and unusual punishments was intended by the framers to allow the judiciary to determine its meaning over time, he observed. The Supreme Court itself had noted in *Trop v. Dulles* that "the words of the Amendment are not precise, and . . . their scope is not static. The Amendment must draw its meaning from the evolving standards of decency that mark the progress of a maturing society."[31]

Justice emphasized that he much preferred a system in which the elected branches of government are sensitive to constitutional restraints in carrying out their functions. "I infinitely would favor legislative and administrative reform of prisons to attempts at reform by the judiciary." But he cited Justice Benjamin Cardozo's belief that the greater danger is not that the judiciary will suppress legislative initiative but rather that an independent judiciary will not live up to its responsibility of interpreting the Constitution in light of evolving social conditions.

The Rehnquist-Justice views are manifestations of a debate about the legitimate role of the federal judiciary going back to its origin. As a member of the Supreme Court, Justice Rehnquist has considerable authority to "decide what the law is." As a federal district judge, Judge Justice is subject to review by higher courts. His authority is limited; he must follow their legal precedents. And he has scrupulously done so since he was first appointed.[32] But in some areas there are no legal precedents. Where they exist, there often remains considerable room for interpretation. Justice told an interviewer in 1978 that

"The law is full of interstices. If the law is settled—I'm a professional—I'm going to decide the case just exactly the way the law reads. On the other hand, if there is some vacancy or gap, I try to take into consideration what the Supreme Court has said about 'the evolving standards of decency.' I think the law ought to be decent if it's nothing else. It ought to afford justice." [33]

When viewed in combination with his strong support for individual rights, this assertion reveals a great deal about his use of judicial power. In cases ranging from mundane workers' compensation and social security disability claims to those involving novel questions of constitutional law, Justice has never lost sight of individual rights, nor hesitated to extend constitutional protections to situations where he believes "evolving standards of decency" warrant doing so. A prime example is his 1974 order in *Morales v. Turman* extending a right to treatment to juvenile offenders confined in state institutions maintained by the Texas Youth Council. The decision is the focus of Chapter 6. Another is *Watson v. Thompson,* a 1971 public high school student hair-length decision, in which he sought to broaden the protections of the Bill of Rights, using the Ninth Amendment of the Constitution.

The Ninth Amendment states, "The enumeration in the Constitution, of certain rights, shall not be construed to deny or disparage others retained by the people." Its meaning has long been debated, the prevailing view being that it adds no rights but merely states what is implicit in the Bill of Rights— that the people continue to possess rights within their respective states. Some jurists, however, believe that the Ninth Amendment is more than a tautology, that it is an affirmation of additional constitutionally protected rights. Justice is one of them. He stated in the *Watson* case, "Considering the backgrounds of the framers and their personal experience with despotic and autocratic government, I submit that their purpose in adopting the Ninth Amendment was to retain for the people such privileges and immunities, complemental and parallel to the enumerated rights, as might be essential for the preservation and promotion of human dignity and liberty. In various decisions, the Supreme Court has given tacit recognition to this design of the framers, employing the methodology of interpretation, extrapolation, and analogy." [34]

In relying on the Ninth Amendment, Justice referenced with approval the rationale advanced by the Supreme Court majority in *Griswold v. Connecticut* in elucidating a constitutional right of privacy. [35] In this controversial 1965 decision involving a state law against the use of contraceptives by married couples, Justice William O. Douglas located a right of privacy in the penumbras of various Bill of Rights guarantees, including the First, Third, Fourth, Fifth, and Ninth amendments. Dissenting justices, particularly Justice Hugo Black, decried the use of judicial power to read into the Constitution rights which are not explicitly there in an effort to keep the Constitution up to date. He found no difference between the notorious *Lochner* decision defining a liberty of contract in the Constitution and the *Griswold* personal-privacy decision.

Much of Justice's thinking in *Watson v. Thompson* was based on a law review article he had read by Yale Law School Professor Charles L. Black, Jr., which examined the methodology underlying Douglas' reasoning in *Griswold*. Black observed that *Griswold* posed a methodological challenge to constitutional law decision-making. "[A] constitutional law inadequate to deal with such an outrage [state regulation of contraceptives] would be too feeble, in method and doctrine, to deal with a very great amount of equally outrageous material. Virtually all the intimacies, privacies and autonomies of life would be regulable by the legislature . . ."[36] Professor Black pointed out that the Supreme Court justices in the past through interpretation had extended the words of the Constitution to matters not specifically listed in the document. As a case in point, he cited Court recognition of the right of parents to control the upbringing of their children.[37] In the *Griswold* decision, Black wrote, Douglas used the civil law method of reasoning by analogy to extend the protections of the document through the Ninth Amendment. "That methodology must take all the guarantees in the constitution together, work to fill in the arbitrary and irrational blank spaces between them, and listen continually for their harmony and overtones. The ninth amendment, I think, does validate this method— and the method is the means of filling in the content of the ninth amendment." Judicial restraintists like Chief Justice Rehnquist and many currently on the U.S Court of Appeals for the Fifth Circuit find such views abhorrent because they invite judges to stray beyond the written words of the document. But in the opinion of Professor Black and many contemporary commentators, this is a judicial responsibility fully intended by the framers.[38]

Judge Justice was impressed with Black's reasoning. "I thought he was right on the money." In Justice's discussion of the Ninth Amendment in *Watson*, he cited Black's thesis with approval. Personal grooming is one of the rights "complemental and parallel" to those specifically stated in the Bill of Rights. But ultimately Justice chose to rely on the Fourteenth Amendment's liberty provision for the right of public high school students to choose their hair length and style, given the greater support in the case law. A later Fifth Circuit decision to the contrary mooted the decision.[39] Since the *Watson* case, Justice has not further developed his Ninth Amendment jurisprudence because of the lack of support for the concept at the appellate level. But he has not retreated from his view that the Constitution is an organic document whose meaning and application must evolve over time in light of changing social conditions.

Judge Justice's support for individual rights manifests itself most clearly in non-jury class action suits on behalf of those confined in state institutions. He has also consistently opposed racial, ethnic, and sex-based discrimination in a variety of contexts. Given a conservative state with limited support for individual and minority rights by either the legislative or the executive branch and a federal judge with precisely these sympathies, it should not be surprising that such cases would find their way to his court and that his remedies would be extensive.

More than the rights he protects, Justice's orders detailing the steps state officials must follow to correct constitutional wrongs have generated criticism, for it is argued with considerable truth that his remedies interfere with state sovereignty. Yet Justice asserts that the charges of excessive judicial activism often convey the erroneous message that these decisions are not based on accepted legal precedent. In a 1988 speech to students at his alma mater, the University of Texas School of Law, Judge Justice maintained that "It is a mistake to judge the institutional legitimacy of a judicial declaration of constitutional right simply by its remedial implications—the worst judicial excesses often cause the least remedial ferment."[40] He cited as an example the Supreme Court's infamous decision in *Lochner v. New York*. The high court merely announced that the New York maximum-hours law interfered with a constitutional right to make a contract and declared it unconstitutional. No remedial plan was necessary. The decision touched off a furor among legal scholars, since there is no right of contract explicitly set forth in the U.S. Constitution. As previously noted, Justice Rehnquist also regarded this decision as illegitimate.

Conversely, Justice pointed out, "instances of proper enforcement of fundamental rights which raise questions of competency or practicality do not, necessarily, signal some basic transgression of the separation of powers." As examples of the latter, the Judge cited school-desegregation and prison-reform litigation, both of which have come before his court and both of which resulted in detailed remedial orders designed to enforce existing legal precedents. As explained in later chapters, the Judge has never hesitated to employ comprehensive and detailed remedies to correct the constitutional wrongs he perceives. The pattern has been followed again and again in areas such as school desegregation, bilingual education, and reform of state institutions for juvenile and adult offenders.

Can repeated judicial involvement on behalf of individual and especially unpopular minority rights lead to excessive dependency on the judiciary with corresponding atrophy of the other branches of government? Harking back to his University of Colorado law review article, Justice replies, "I certainly think that's possible, in fact I think it's happening far too often that the legislature deliberately remains inactive because they know that if they don't take care of a problem, some judge will take care of it for them. I think that's a terrible indictment of the legislature, but it is true."

Though Justice's detailed remedial orders are legend, he maintains that he has tried to force the state to act on its own before imposing his remedy. "I tried that in all my institutional cases. I've entered an order and have then asked the state to draw up a plan to relieve the unconstitutional conditions. I've done that in every case, and in every case there has been an inadequate response." One reason is that state officials do not accept Justice's premise that conditions are unconstitutional. Rather than accede to his orders, they fight them on appeal. Another is that it is politically more palatable for legislators to wait until Justice mandates changes, then pass the blame on to him when new statutes are imposed or taxes raised.

At the start of the Sixty-ninth Legislative Session in 1985, Speaker Gib Lewis (Democrat, Fort Worth) told the House of Representatives that no federal judge was going to tell Texas how it could spend its money, referring to court-ordered reforms in the prison and mental health and retardation systems. "I am tired of trying to make reasonable deals with unreasonable people!" he asserted.[41] Though he did not mention Justice by name, it was clear to whom he was referring. But the legislature eventually did appropriate funds to be in compliance. Justice has been so successful in motivating the legislature that *Texas Monthly Magazine* included him in its listing of the ten best legislators in its July 1981 issue.

Justice's name has often been invoked by those seeking to advance their own political objectives. Both William P. (Bill) Clements and Mark White repeatedly capitalized on the unpopularity of Justice's 1980 prison ruling in their campaigns for governor. Reform-minded members of a Texas legislative task force studying indigent-health-care reform in 1984 raised the specter of Justice's taking control of county health-care services if the legislature did not act. At the time, a lawsuit had been filed in his court on the issue.[42] "From a purely legal analysis, it wasn't a real risk at that point," observes Austin attorney Steve Bickerstaff, a member of the task force. "But it proved to be a very valuable tool for people who wanted the legislation." They were successful. Legislation requiring Texas counties to provide indigent health care was enacted in 1985.

Justice's reputation for judicial activism has not been limited to the public sector. On numerous occasions, he has applied broad-based remedies in the private sector, especially in employment discrimination cases (see Chapter 12). Law clerk Roger Parloff remembers a securities case he worked on in the early 1980s in which Justice's reputation as a mover and a shaker prompted the parties to settle. At issue was whether Donaldson, Lufkin and Jenrette Securities Corporation could be held liable as a clearing broker for actions taken by a local broker. Justice was prepared to review recent rule changes of the New York Stock Exchange and of the Securities and Exchange Commission to determine whether the new rules themselves were a form of securities fraud, leaving shareholders· unprotected. According to Parloff, "as soon as Judge Justice began talking about reviewing rule changes, the securities industry took notice." The case was settled before the Judge could issue a ruling. "They were justifiably alarmed," Justice maintains, "because the order we had drawn up was going to hold the rule invalid and we were going to publish it [in the Federal Supplement]. We were prepared to enter that order on Monday, and they settled over the weekend." Had the order been entered, "it would have sent shock waves through Wall Street."

For all the power he is said to wield, Judge Justice often points out that as a federal district judge, he is at the bottom of the judicial hierarchy. His power is limited by the actions of higher courts. To a large extent this is true. But the federal district judge does have considerable influence over what is appealed. For example, rather than reverse a U.S. magistrate's decision adverse to the claimant in a social security disability case and thus allow the Social Security Administration to appeal the decision to the Fifth Circuit, Justice often remanded the case to the magistrate for reconsideration. This strategy, which the Social Security Administration unsuccessfully tried to appeal, usually resulted in the claimant's getting the requested benefits.

More significantly, in many of his most significant decisions, Judge Justice has taken particular pains to bolster the validity of his decisions by setting forth the facts exhaustively in the trial record, particularly those which are shocking to a sense of decency. Rule 52 of the Federal Rules of Civil Procedure provides that the findings of fact at the trial court level in a non-jury case are not to be disturbed by the appellate court unless clearly erroneous. Thus, his lengthy memorandum opinion in *Morales v. Turman* contains a litany of horrors incarcerated juvenile delinquents suffered in the facilities operated by the Texas Youth Council, and the opinion in *Ruiz v. Estelle* does the same for prisoners in the units of the Texas Department of Corrections. Rule 52 notwithstanding, appellate court judges sometimes display their independence by downplaying the factual record developed by the trial court. But more often, in reversing lower court decisions, they refuse to accept the trial court judges' conclusions of law.

The federal district court judge can also affect the way a case is argued. In several cases, including the two above, Justice ordered the U.S. Department of Justice to intervene as a party on the side of the plaintiffs. Having been a U.S. attorney, Justice is fully aware of the investigatory and advocacy powers of the Justice Department. The Judge has also routinely allowed powerful public interest groups to intervene as litigants on behalf of plaintiffs. By his actions Justice explains that he is balancing the sides more evenly in the interest of a just outcome. "All through my judicial career I have desired to have the sides equally balanced so that I could get a true perception of what the facts are. In class action lawsuits like *Morales* we had on one side these ill-financed public interest lawyers with little capacity to develop the facts, and on the other the whole state of Texas with the Office of the Attorney General to defend it."

At the same time, Justice acknowledges that the assistant attorney generals representing the state are not always a match for the experienced counsel representing plaintiffs in suits against state institutions. "I have seen some exceptionally poor courtroom representation by assistant attorney generals; on the other hand, I have had some very astute assistant attorney generals before me. You never know what you're going to get." Justice's efforts to enhance the quality of legal representation for plaintiffs in class action lawsuits involving state institutions has had the effect of upgrading the quality of representation by the state. For example, in *Morales v. Turman,* the state secured an experienced trial attorney to head its defense team, and in *Ruiz v. Estelle* the state turned to a prestigious law firm to handle its appeal.

Though Judge Justice was not often reversed in his first years on the bench, by the early 1980s the Fifth Circuit began increasingly to modify his orders or reverse them, particularly in decisions involving state institutions and setting forth detailed remedial orders.[43] Two factors accounted for the acceleration. The first was the appointment to the appellate court of more conservative judges attuned to the judicial philosophy of William Rehnquist, and the second was Justice's refusal to curtail use of his remedial powers to achieve equitable results, particularly when civil rights were at stake, even though a more compromising attitude would likely have improved his chances of being affirmed. Robert McDuff, who clerked for Justice in the early 1980s, observes that Justice never worried about being reversed. "If it was an unresolved question of law, and he felt a particular course was necessary to accord justice, he would follow that course even at the risk of reversal." As an example, McDuff cites that part of Justice's 1981 *Ruiz v. Estelle* prison-reform order requiring the reorganization of the Texas prison system into smaller units as a way of improving prison management and prisoner conditions. There was no precedent saying it could not be done; on the other hand, there was no precedent supporting it. Relying on expert testimony, the Judge seized the opportunity to advance the law of penology. He was not surprised when the Fifth Circuit reversed the action.

However, by the end of the decade, Justice recognized that if he were to avoid outright reversal by conservative Fifth Circuit judges, he would have to curtail his activism. "I have become more cautious, perhaps, about my legal position. Sometimes in the past, I would be willing to take an action if the law was murky to any extent when I thought equity required it. Now, unless I am certain of my step, I am not likely to act." But he has not changed his position with regard to areas where the law is silent. "I think I am as entitled as any judge to decide how to fill in interstices in the law."

Justice wanted to be an appellate judge. On two occasions early in the 1970s he was invited to serve as an appellate judge on the U.S. Court of Appeals, District of Columbia Circuit, a court generally recognized as second only to the U.S. Supreme Court in its importance. Occasionally, federal district court judges are offered this opportunity when the federal appellate judges find themselves overwhelmed with cases. The invitation came from Chief Judge David L. Bazelon, one of the most liberal judges then on the bench. Bazelon was well known for his civil rights decisions, particularly those involving prisoners and the mentally ill. Justice had come to Bazelon's attention through the *Morales v. Turman* decision in which Justice had found that juveniles incarcerated in the facilities of the Texas Youth Council had a constitutional right to treatment. As a result, twice in the early 1970s Justice served several weeks on three-judge appeals panels for the D.C. Circuit and wrote opinions in several significant cases as noted in later chapters. Law clerk Jack T. Friedman, one of those who accompanied him to Washington, notes that Justice strongly admired a number of the judges then on the D.C. Circuit and when given the opportunity to sit on the appellate bench with them "was like a kid in a toyshop."

Justice has not been accorded a similar invitation from the Fifth Circuit, a matter of some bitterness. But given the difficult and controversial issues the Fifth Circuit has had to confront by virtue of appeals from Justice's institutional rulings and the conservative hue of many of the appellate judges, Justice has not been one of their favored federal trial judges. In fact, it is said that several of the conservative appellate judges are so convinced that Justice suffers from judicial arrogance and greed that they relish the opportunity of reversing him. Justice has done little to dispel the image. Both by choice and by temperament, he has not been political in his dealings with the Fifth Circuit. The relationship between Justice and the Fifth Circuit can best be described as formal.

The time spent on the D.C. Circuit court has been Justice's only experience as an appellate court judge. Though brief, it convinced him that the scholarly life of an appellate court judge is to be preferred to the tribulations of a trial judge. "If I had my choices of things to do in the law, it would be to sit in the library and research and write. I love that." He found the life of an appellate judge more genteel than that of a trial judge and possessed of considerable opportunity for intellectual exchange. For both Justice and his clerks, it was an opportunity to interact with some of the greatest legal minds in the country.

Justice also served briefly as a district court judge in New York City. He had been on the bench only two weeks when retired U.S. Supreme Court Justice Tom Clark informed him of the need for judicial assistance to deal with a crushing backlog of cases in that district. Justice said he would be pleased to help. Chief Judge Joseph C. Zavatt of the Federal District Court for the Eastern District of New York assigned him twenty criminal cases during a two-week period in the winter of 1969. As a relatively inexperienced trial judge, Justice was apprehensive about having to face sophisticated big-city lawyers. The lawyers apparently were also leery of the visiting judge, for when he took the bench, he found twenty motions to postpone trial. "That's when I lost all my awe of New York lawyers, for they didn't advance a single ground in their motions for continuance that I myself had not made or heard other lawyers make on numerous occasions beforehand." He rejected all but one.

At one time Justice was a candidate for a federal appellate judgeship himself, a position he deeply coveted but one which would never have afforded him the opportunity to prompt as much change as his federal trial judgeship. In 1979 Justice submitted his name for one of five openings on the Fifth Circuit. President Carter had established judicial nominating commissions for each of the federal circuits. Justice appeared before the commission for the Fifth Circuit and was one of fifteen names they advanced for appointment. It was a foregone conclusion among courthouse associates that he would be appointed. But Justice was not so sure. "It would have been politically unsound for the President to appoint someone to the appellate court who had been hacked up the way I'd been," he says. "That's just not in the nature of good politics."

David R. Richards, long-time Austin civil rights attorney, also was a candidate for one of the Fifth Circuit vacancies. Considerable support from liberal forces in Texas was behind Richards. Justice believes that had the two not been in competition, his—Justice's—chances of being appointed would have been considerably enhanced. But Richards did not think Justice had a prayer of a chance. "I told him, 'the only chance you've got is if Senator Bentsen thinks he'll make more friends getting your ass out of East Texas and into New Orleans where you can't bother so many people.'" The two joked about submitting their names to give the Carter administration a chance of proving its professed interest in seeing that qualified liberals were appointed to the federal appellate bench. Neither was selected.

About the same time, Justice was invited to appear before the judicial nominating commission for the District of Columbia Circuit. He did so and was candid in discussing his lackluster performance in law school. He also was straightforward in discussing his upbringing in a segregated environment. "I could tell that one or two of the black committee members didn't much like that answer." He learned subsequently that the commission members had agreed not to select anyone unless by unanimous choice. His name was not on the list of nine advanced.

Since the American Bar Association will not endorse anyone over the age of sixty-five for appellate appointment, Justice's chances for appointment to the appellate bench are long over. Even if he were not precluded by age, the political climate suggests that he would have no chance of being confirmed. His destiny is to continue to serve as a federal district court judge, a destiny he has accepted. Bereft of ambition and with the security of lifetime tenure, Justice is now more willing to accept speaking invitations and express himself candidly.

William Wayne Justice clearly enjoys his work and the challenge it presents. "Father is the happiest person that I know," reports Ellen Justice. "You know, he seems to me like the sort of person who gets up in the morning and knows that he's going to do good. He does good all day, goes to bed at night feeling that he's done his job and eager for the next day." With no particular interests outside of the court and nowhere to retire to—Sue Justice maintains that her husband neither has nor needs roots—Wayne Justice is emphatic about not retiring or taking senior status. "If you take senior status, you are entitled to a reduced case load if you want it. There are certain restrictions if you do reduce your case load—you can only have one law clerk and you don't have a court reporter assigned to you. If they want to, the other judges can make it hard on you. That's not going to happen to me. I'm not likely to take senior status unless my health fails. I am going to retain my vote. I'm going to retain my chambers, my secretary, my court reporter, and my two law clerks. Circumstances may change, but it is my firm intention right now to go full blast until I just can't do it anymore."

Going "full blast" has been his practice since appointment in 1968. In his wake are a string of controversial decisions, some highly charged, some less so. All have left their mark on life in Texas, many on the nation. It is to Judge Justice's judicial record that we now turn.

Will and Jackie May Justice in 1909.

William Wayne Justice at eighteen months.

Billy Wayne Justice, as he was then known, enjoys his tricycle, April 1923.

Jackie May Justice with her son, December 1925.

Law school graduation photo in the 1942 University of Texas *Cactus*. (Barker Texas History Center, The University of Texas at Austin.)

Mr. Will at his desk in the 1950s. "This is what you saw when you entered Dad's office."

Private William Wayne Justice in 1942.

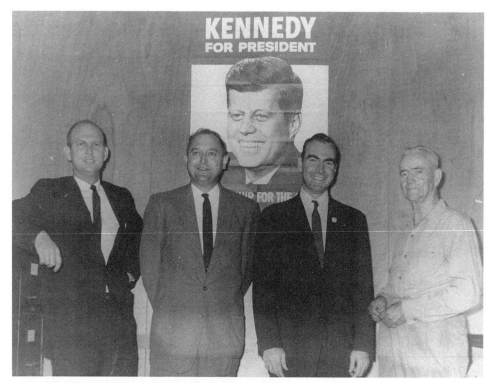

Celebrating John Kennedy's election in 1960. *Left to right:* law partner Bill Kugle, Justice, Congressman Jim Wright, Henderson County Democratic Chairman Henry Meredith.

Delivering the "brass collar Democrat" speech at the statewide convention of the Democrats of Texas Clubs (DOTC), February 1960. This was before Justice started his weight-reduction and exercise program. (Barker Texas History Center, The University of Texas at Austin.)

Senator Ralph Yarborough poses with his nominee at Justice's 1968 swearing-in ceremony as federal district court judge. (*Tyler Morning Telegraph/Courier-Times.*)

Left to right: Senator Ralph Yarborough and Tyler attorneys Joe Tunnell, who served as master of ceremonies, and Tom Pollard, Jr., at the 1968 swearing-in ceremony. (*Tyler Morning Telegraph/Courier-Times.*)

At the 1968 swearing-in ceremony, *left to right:* Ellen Justice, William Wayne Justice, Sue Justice with her niece, Jean Dixon. (*Tyler Morning Telegraph/Courier-Times.*)

Justice performs his first judicial act as federal judge: swearing in Brooks Hardee as U.S. Attorney. (*Tyler Morning Telegraph/Courier-Times.*)

The judges of the Eastern District in 1970: *left to right,* Justice; Joe J. Fisher, who served as chief judge; and William M. Steger. The picture behind the judges is of Joe J. Sheehy, whom Justice had replaced on the bench two years before.

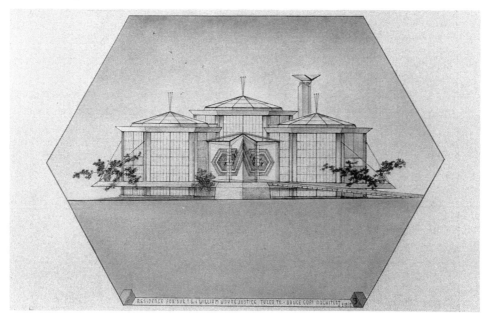

The futuristic "glow-in-the-dark" home designed from Sue Justice's sketch by renowned Oklahoma architect Bruce Goff in 1979. The home was never built.

Emperor of Texas

Austin American-Statesman cartoonist Ben Sargeant's rendition of the 1977 Texas legislative session, which included an unsuccessful effort to place a juvenile halfway house adjacent to the Justice residence in Tyler. (Copyright © *Austin American-Statesman*. Reprinted with permission.)

Cartoon appearing in the *Houston Chronicle* at the height of the prison reform litigation. (Copyright © *Houston Chronicle*. Reprinted with permission.)

Howard A. Specter, president of the Association of Trial Lawyers of America, presents Justice with the 1982 Outstanding Federal Trial Judge award.

William Wayne and Sue Justice in 1990. (Copyright © 1990 by Les Wollam.)

Governor William P. Clements (*at left*), Attorney General Jim Mattox (*at right*), and Justice enjoy some humor during the second in-chambers meeting in the spring of 1988 to discuss settlement of the *Ruiz v. Estelle* prison reform case. Note the photograph of Will Justice on the wall behind William Wayne Justice.

Justice tours a Texas prison in the spring of 1988. *Left to right:* Special Master Vincent M. Nathan, William Bennett Turner, F. Scott McCown, Justice, Eastham Prison Warden George Waldron, U.S. Department of Justice Attorney Daniel S. Jacobs. (Photo by Mike George, courtesy Texas Department of Criminal Justice.)

Justice in chambers with his two long-time secretaries, Debra Magee (*left*) and Marcelle Simmons. (Photo by Dan Santema.)

Justice poses with fellow liberal judges Frank M. Johnson (*at left*) and Irving L. Goldberg in January 1989, at an SMU lecture series honoring Circuit Judge Goldberg. (Photo by Joe Mark Horn.)

Sue Justice, March 1990. (Copyright © 1990 by Les Wollam.)

PART TWO

The Decisions

CHAPTER 5

Statewide School Desegregation

William Wayne Justice grew up in a segregated environment. Blacks were just as discriminated against in Athens as elsewhere in East Texas. When Justice was a boy, blacks were often the target of ridicule. "When they had their Juneteenth celebration," he recalls, "they'd parade on the town square. And everybody'd jibe at them, laugh at them. When their high school football team would play, there'd usually be some white spectators out there to make fun of them. The whites thought it was really funny. The blacks didn't have much coaching, you understand, and some of their plays were crude and ill-executed. It didn't occur to the whites that those people could make really outstanding athletes." Ralph Yarborough maintains that in fact athletics broke segregation faster than lawsuits. "People in deep East Texas have told me, 'Ralph, football's the main thing here that's done more to end friction between whites and blacks, and more to bring about integration of schools than all of the courts put together.'"

Will Justice, Wayne's father, was the son of a Confederate family and believed in separation of the races. Like everyone else in the community, Will Justice routinely referred to blacks as "niggers," or "nigras" if he wanted to be more polite. And like many in Athens, the Justices had black domestics. But Will Justice also had blacks as clients. He wanted to win their cases, just like every other case, whether he got paid or not. Will Justice's reputation as a phenomenally successful trial lawyer was not lost on blacks. "The blacks knew that they could always find themselves a champion, in case they got in trouble," Wayne points out. In cases where Will Justice represented a black in a dispute with a white, Wayne maintains it often worked to the advantage of the black. "When a black was arrayed against a white in a civil case—you understand that you had a white man's jury—a great deal of the time, the whites would think to themselves, 'If this nigger is so convinced that he's right that he'll take on a white man, there must be something to it.'" Will Justice's careful cultivation of the jury, of course, did not hurt. He was looking for white jurors who were fair-minded despite their racial prejudice. Wayne Justice cannot recall any civil cases his father lost when representing blacks.

Though all his classmates were white, Wayne did have opportunities to play with blacks as a child. When he visited his grandfather's farm, he and his cousins would play with the children of black families hired to work the cotton gin. "We'd play with them just like we would with white kids."

Justice remembers one incident from his childhood which probably influenced his thoughts about race relations. When he was about seven years old, he and a white playmate were out playing in a vacant lot adjacent to the latter's house when a little black boy about the same age came along. Several black families lived nearby and used an alleyway through the white neighborhood to reach their homes. The three started playing together. But just then the mother of Justice's playmate rapped on the window, calling her child inside. "After awhile, he came back out and said that he couldn't play with niggers. This little ol' black kid, he just didn't know what to make out of this. I imagine it just crushed him. He just slunk on home. That angered me."

However, Justice remained largely passive about minority rights before becoming a federal judge. He told a television interviewer in 1985 that while he privately supported the *Brown v. Board of Education* school desegregation decision when it was announced in 1954, "I would not have for the life of me let that be known out in the community, because I suppose that my law practice would have practically dissolved at that point. And I don't know of any other lawyers in small towns that adopted a stance in favor of the decision, at least immediately after it happened. It was a question of economic and social preservation. You couldn't have made it if you'd come out publicly in favor of the decision. I know I didn't."[1] According to his former law partner, Bill Kugle, Justice's position on race relations was more philosophical than activist. "I always thought Wayne was entirely too timorous in asserting himself on matters like the race issue. Being for integration about the time I came to practice with Wayne was a damned unpopular idea. But God-dang, when he got on that bench with a lifetime appointment, he turned into a tiger."

A skirmish with school desegregation in Judge Justice's court just after he was appointed to the bench gave some indication of what was to come. Its significance was not lost on U.S. government attorneys who were looking around for a supportive court in which to file a statewide desegregation lawsuit. Tatum Independent School District (ISD), located fifty miles east of Tyler, adopted a desegregation plan in December 1968 to the effect that all students would be educated on its campus in Tatum. The all-black Mayflower campus would be closed. The plan was approved by the U.S. Department of Health, Education, and Welfare (HEW).

In July 1969, following failure of a bond election to finance new construction, the school board amended its plan so that students in grades 1–5 would be assigned to the Tatum and Mayflower schools on a freedom-of-choice basis. In effect, this arrangement perpetuated the prior dual school system, since few students would avail themselves of the option. HEW officials disapproved the change. Despite the objections, Tatum ISD officials opened school on this basis on September 2. Also on this day several black students who had chosen the Tatum school pursuant to the freedom-of-choice option were refused admission and returned to the Mayflower campus.

A week later, HEW gave formal notice to Tatum ISD of its noncompliance with federal law, and the U.S. Justice Department filed suit in Judge Justice's court. Prior to the hearing, the Tatum school board rescinded the freedom-of-choice amendment. In his brief decision, Judge Justice ruled that the district had been out of compliance with Title VI with its freedom-of-choice plan and issued an injunction against it.[2] At the same time, he commended Tatum school officials from the bench for their efforts to desegregate the school system. The new plan establishing a unitary school district for Tatum was approved. The rapidity with which the court acted—the decision was rendered a week after the HEW formal notice of noncompliance to Tatum—indicated that Judge Justice would not hesitate to apply U.S. Supreme Court desegregation precedents.

United States v. Texas, the statewide school desegregation case, has humble beginnings. It started with an investigation by HEW into discriminatory practices by the Daingerfield ISD in East Texas. The district had for years accepted white students transferring from the adjacent, predominantly black and unaccredited Cason ISD. In 1968 the HEW Office for Civil Rights advised Daingerfield officials to stop accepting transfers, and the district did so. White citizens in Cason then sought under state law to detach a portion of land from Cason and annex it to Daingerfield. The respective school districts approved the petition. The Cason school superintendent later testified that he was informed of the deannexation after it occurred. The irregular area annexed to the Daingerfield school district siphoned off all the white students in Cason and cut the black district into two noncontiguous portions. This meant that Cason students had to be bused across school district lines, contrary to Texas law. Through their investigations, HEW officials discovered similar efforts to perpetuate segregation by other Texas school districts, some of which received no federal aid. Since HEW's only weapon was to terminate federal aid under Title VI, the matter was referred to the U.S. Department of Justice with its broad enforcement powers.

Attorneys in the Civil Rights Division of the Justice Department concluded that the Texas Education Agency (TEA) was ignoring the mandates of federal law by permitting boundary changes and by continuing financial assistance to dual school systems based on race. Charged with overseeing the state's public school system, TEA reflected the political culture of the public school community. Many of its staff members had been teachers, coaches, and administrators. By statute and by attitude, TEA was less a regulatory agency than a facilitator of local control.

On-site investigations by government attorneys revealed a number of small all-black school districts contiguous with largely white districts. The investigations also revealed many instances of unequal educational facilities for blacks. Alexandra P. Buek, one of the Justice Department attorneys, recalls that the one-room schoolhouse and two outhouses comprising the all-black Jeddo District in Bastrop County outside Austin was located on a remote dirt crossroad. The average daily attendance was fifteen students, the minimum under state law to receive state financial aid. The school employed one teacher and a teacher's aide. In order for Jeddo to meet the minimum, neighboring white Smithfield ISD bused in three black students. It was apparent that fifteen years after *Brown v. Board of Education,* blatant school segregation was still a fact of life in parts of Texas.

Justice Department attorneys concluded that a case-by-case approach to eliminating the remnants of discrimination in the Texas public school system would take forever. A shorter route would be to seek to have the state as a whole placed under court order. In addition, to implement the proper relief in situations involving the small all-black school districts like Cason and Jeddo, it would be necessary to include adjoining county school boards as well as the Texas Education Agency in any court action. Accordingly, the complaint filed on March 6, 1970, in the Marshall Division of the U.S. District Court for the Eastern District of Texas named the State of Texas, TEA, the nine all-black districts, their neighboring districts, the affected county boards of education, and the appropriate individuals in their official capacities. It had become a very large case.

Aware of Justice's strong support for integration in the *Tatum* case, the government attorneys chose to file their lawsuit in the Marshall Division, since Judge Justice was the only United States district judge presiding there. The complaint alleged denial of equal educational opportunities under Title VI of the 1964 Civil Rights Act and the Fourteenth Amendment to black students in the nine all-black school districts, which were scattered around the state, including Cason and Jeddo. All but three of those districts had enrollments of fewer than one hundred students. All had been created or encouraged by state action. The complaint asserted that the State of Texas through the Texas Education Agency, the adjoining predominantly white school districts, the county boards of education, and county superintendents either directly or indirectly were discriminating against the black districts.

Prior to trial, some of the defendant county boards of education began taking steps to eliminate the all-black districts by consolidating them with neighboring white districts. However, because Judge Justice could not evaluate the extent to which such consolidation would eliminate the discrimination, he allowed the suit to continue. At about the same time, the Nixon administration reined in the Justice Department with respect to seeking school-consolidation remedies from federal courts in desegregation cases. Justice Department attorneys told Judge Justice that they were not sure they could continue the case as they had planned in light of the change in policy. "The Judge would have none of it," attorney Buek observes. "He said that, of course, we would have to represent whatever position the Justice Department approved, but he personally wished to hear the other issues addressed and ordered us to do so." Only a handful of other southern federal judges would likely have taken the same position.

What made *United States v. Texas* an important case was the inclusion of the state as a party in the lawsuit, together with the Texas Education Agency (TEA). This had the effect of giving the case statewide significance. Since the Texas Legislature had established TEA as the general policy-making and directing body for the Texas public school system, the government argued that the agency was responsible for, and contributed to, continued segregation, even though it had filed a statement of compliance with HEW as required under Title VI in order to receive federal funds. Despite assertions by federal officials that TEA had legal authority to desegregate public schools, TEA officials considered desegregation a matter for local school districts and individual plaintiffs.

The trial, which began on September 14, 1970, revealed that the Texas Legislature through legislation had encouraged a reduction in the number of small and uneconomical districts. Indeed, from 1948 to 1969 the number of school districts in Texas had declined from 5,000 to under 1,200. Consolidation had the added effect of eliminating many which were segregated. But at the same time, the funding formula used for disbursing state aid favored small districts. It was also evident that the defendant white school districts and county boards of education had perpetuated all-black districts through an assortment of detachments and annexations of territory and through student transfer and transportation arrangements. The Texas Education Agency had acquiesced in the continued existence of the all-black districts by financing them and by approving inter- and intradistrict student transfer policies.

The trial generated almost no press coverage. In fact, Justice recalls very few spectators in the courtroom. Apparently few—including the Texas Office of the Attorney General, which represented the state—recognized *United States v. Texas* as a significant case. In East Texas much more interest was focused on a lawsuit involving the desegregation of a number of East Texas school districts, including Elysian Fields, Jefferson, Kilgore, Lufkin, and Sulphur Springs. Cited as *United States v. Texas Education Agency,* this case is best known by its civil docket number 5193. Early on, several attorneys involved in this litigation were successful in getting Chief Judge Joe Fisher to transfer their cases to the Beaumont Division, where he presided. One of the attorneys, who requested anonymity, remembers that when Judge Justice learned of the transfer, "he gave me a verbal thrashing like I have never experienced before. He said that he knew exactly what I was up to in trying to get the case transferred out of his court and that he would not forget it. Afterwards, one of the government attorneys told me that he had never seen a federal judge so angry with an attorney. We make a point now of sending another attorney from our firm to Tyler when we have a case before Judge Justice." For the most part, the desegregation of districts remaining under Justice's jurisdiction in this lawsuit has proceeded routinely over the years.

Devoid of the attention it would later receive, the *United States v. Texas* trial ended. Judge Justice issued the first of two orders in November 1970. Relying on evidence introduced by the government, including a series of photographs, maps, and overlays developed by the FBI, Judge Justice found that each of the nine black districts had inferior educational facilities and personnel. Only three of the largest were accredited by TEA. In contrast with the modern and well-equipped neighboring white school districts, the libraries of the black districts contained few volumes, educational equipment was substandard, and sanitary facilities were primitive. Orange crates were often used for chairs, and outhouses were not uncommon. The Judge found that boundary changes prior to the initiation of the lawsuit had resulted in perpetuation of all-black districts by siphoning off white children from the black districts and vice versa. Cited among them was the gerrymandering of the Cason ISD boundaries to place white students in Daingerfield ISD. Justice also noted that the existence of dual school systems within districts had the added effect of "isolating racially homogeneous residential areas into formal political enclaves," thus entrenching segregation and "insur[ing] its continuation after its legal basis was declared unconstitutional."[3]

Citing the mandate from the U.S. Supreme Court in the second *Brown v. Board of Education* ruling *(Brown II)* in 1955 that federal district courts have the primary responsibility of overseeing the desegregation of dual school systems and the further mandate in *Green v. County School Board* in 1968 that racial discrimination be eliminated "root and branch," Justice fashioned a broad remedy designed to bring about integration. The relief was granted in two parts. The first required defendant school districts in collaboration with the U.S. Office of Education and the Texas Education Agency to prepare integration plans. Those districts which had voluntarily integrated subsequent to the filing of the lawsuit were required to undergo a review by TEA and the U.S. Office of Education to assure both faculty and staff desegregation and nondiscriminatory assignment of students to schools and classes.

The second part involved only the Texas Education Agency. Judge Justice followed the recommendation of federal attorneys in placing primary responsibility for carrying out the court's mandates on officials at the agency. TEA was ordered to halt approval of discriminatory interdistrict student transfers and school district boundary changes. The agency was also required to reevaluate its policies and procedures in light of its responsibilities under federal desegregation law and file a detailed report with the court no later than January 1, 1971, outlining actions it would take to desegregate Texas public schools.

The decision to place the Texas Education Agency in a central role to desegregate Texas schools was a dramatic development. State education officials found themselves in the unenviable position of enforcing Judge Justice's order, an order they strongly opposed. They argued that the federal government should be given this responsibility, an argument Judge Justice rejected. "This Court . . . firmly believes," he wrote, "that the time is long past for permitting the States of this Union to enjoy the benefits of Federal assistance while refusing to accept a concurrent obligation with that of the National government to take affirmative action to insure the protection of constitutional rights and the enforcement of Federal statutes."[4] Even more significantly, the decision thrust Justice center stage in supervising the desegregation of public schools statewide, including those within the jurisdiction of the other three federal district courts in Texas. This unprecedented assumption of authority flew in the face of Texas' strong tradition of local control over public education and ran counter to the regional character of the federal district court system. The resulting resistance from school officials and other federal judges was a major factor in explaining why enforcement of the order did not live up to Justice's expectations.

Judge Justice maintains the case was easy to decide because the weight of the evidence was clearly on the side of the federal government. In addition, he found the performance of the state's attorneys lackluster. It was obvious that the Texas attorney general's office had not sent its best representatives. "They just didn't seem to know what they were about," he observes. "They just sat there kind of like a boxer in the ring who doesn't try to fight back. They had virtually no evidence to present in refutation to what was presented by the federal government. The government had some very forceful evidence, most of it documented. It just was not to be gainsaid."

Following the filing of TEA's plan, and with the case now transferred to the Tyler Division and reassigned civil action number 5281, by which it was to become best known, Justice issued a final detailed order in a supplemental memorandum opinion in April 1971. Relying primarily on proposals advanced by the Justice Department, he ordered that each of the nine all-black school districts be annexed to or consolidated with a neighboring school district to eliminate segregation and achieve a more administratively and educationally sound school system. The remainder of the order dealt with requirements imposed on the Texas Education Agency. The proposals TEA advanced in its plan to further desegregation across the state were rejected. The agency sought a racially neutral system. Justice wanted the agency to take affirmative action to promote integration. As noted in the order itself, he regarded the duty of the state as twofold: "First, to act at once to eliminate by positive means all vestiges of the dual school structure throughout the state; and second, to compensate for the abiding scars of past discrimination."[5]

Highlights of Justice's order convey its sweeping character: the Texas Education Agency was ordered to monitor interdistrict student transfers and prohibit those which reduced or impeded desegregation or encouraged discriminatory treatment of students; school districts were to report annexation or consolidation intentions to the Texas commissioner of education, who was required to conduct an investigation as to the likely impact on desegregation; the agency was required to examine bus routes and even individual bus runs of all school districts in the state to determine whether they were being operated in a segregative manner; there was to be no discrimination in extracurricular activities; discriminatory personnel practices were prohibited; assignment of students to schools and individual classrooms or activities on the basis of race, color, or national origin was prohibited except when it furthered integration.

In the case of assignment of students to schools, TEA was required to show why districts with a percentage of minority students greater than 66 percent and an enrollment of fewer than 250 students should not be annexed to or consolidated with neighboring districts. TEA was also required to conduct an annual review of all districts in the state with one or more campuses having a 66 percent or greater minority enrollment to determine their compliance with federal desegregation law. These reports were to be filed with the court and were to identify what steps were being taken to eliminate racially and ethnically identifiable schools and what compensatory activities were being provided the students in these schools. The reports were also to be filed with the

Justice Department and HEW, and were to be open to public inspection at TEA offices.

If TEA found a district to be in noncompliance with any part of the order, the agency was required to levy sanctions including loss of funding and even denial of accreditation. In addition, the agency was ordered to assist school districts in providing equal educational opportunities in all schools. The agency also was required to see that complaint and grievance procedures were posted in all educational institutions. Finally, Judge Justice retained jurisdiction over the case for the purpose of entering any supplementary orders which might be necessary to enforce or modify the decree.

At first, school districts in the state did not know what to make of the decision. Richard Morehouse wrote in the *Dallas Morning News* that there was considerable confusion over whether the order applied to large school districts like Dallas and Houston, which for some time had been operating under desegregation orders of other federal judges.[6] The article also noted that Judge Justice had written of the need to take affirmative action to compensate the victims of discrimination but had set no time limits. Morehouse wrote that the responsibilities imposed on the Texas Education Agency constituted "a large order for the agency." Indeed they did. Governor Preston Smith asserted that the court order "would centralize control of public education in TEA and destroy the traditional system of local control of public schools."[7] He added that TEA did not have the statutory authority to do what Justice demanded. It was soon evident that he was right: the agency was not equipped philosophically or operationally to carry out its new court-ordered responsibilities.

The Texas attorney general's office was initially reluctant to appeal the decision, but did so under pressure from members of the State Board of Education and top TEA officials. The argument was that Justice had abused his authority by undertaking the task of rewriting the school laws of Texas to drastically alter the role of the State Board of Education and likewise change the statutory authority of local school districts.

Some clarification regarding the extent of the order was soon provided by the U.S. Court of Appeals for the Fifth Circuit, which had taken a leading role among the federal courts of appeals in desegregating schools. In a decision handed down on July 9, 1971, that court affirmed the original order in its entirety and most of the April 20 order.[8] But there were several important modifications to the latter. The most significant was the addition of this paragraph: "Nothing herein shall be deemed to affect the jurisdiction of any other district court with respect to any presently pending or future school desegregation suits." This paragraph later caused jurisdictional problems among Texas' federal district courts. It also effectively removed about one-third of the student population in the state from the order's coverage, since most of the large city school districts such as Houston, Austin, and Dallas either were or would become embroiled in their own desegregation lawsuits.

The commissioner of education, Dr. J. W. Edgar, and the Texas Education Agency sought a stay of the Fifth Circuit's ruling before Justice Hugo Black of the U.S. Supreme Court. Justice Black denied the request. In a brief opinion, Black observed that "The District Court's opinion and order are comprehensive and well reasoned. In my judgment the facts found by the District Court, which do not appear to be materially disputed by the applicants, fully justify the order."[9] One of the Justice Department attorneys was in Judge Justice's courtroom when she received notice of Justice Black's decision. She requested and received permission to approach the bench. She presented Justice with the slip of paper and watched as a slow grin spread across his face.

In the interim between Justice's initial decision in November 1970 and the Fifth Circuit ruling eight months later, the Supreme Court had specifically endorsed the affirmative action remedies Justice favored. The Court's 1971 *Swann v. Charlotte-Mecklenburg Board of Education* decision represented the high tide of Supreme Court involvement in sanctioning a variety of remedies to eradicate *de jure* school segregation, such as permitting federal courts to use busing, the altering of attendance zones, and mathematical ratios as a starting place for developing an equitable remedy.[10] The *Swann* decision added considerably to the credibility of Justice's order.

Even as modified by the Fifth Circuit, the statewide desegregation order issued by Judge Justice remained the most comprehensive such order in history, encompassing over one thousand school districts and two-thirds of the Texas student population. By making TEA responsible for implementing the order, Justice was now in the position of supervising desegregation in many school districts across the state outside of his normal jurisdiction. The full meaning of this fact was not long in coming. The San Felipe–Del Rio school-consolidation suit involved two school districts five hundred miles from Judge Justice's court. Del Rio then had a population of slightly over 71,000 and two districts within the city limits, Del Rio ISD, which was predominantly white Anglo-American, and San Felipe ISD, which was mostly Mexican-American. The matter arose when the Del Rio school district, pursuant to the *United States v. Texas* desegregation order, refused to accept transfers of Anglo students from the San Felipe school district. Transfers had been a routine matter between the two school districts, since Laughlin Air Force Base is located in the San Felipe district. The Anglo officers wanted their children to attend the largely Anglo and affluent Del Rio schools, a preference that resulted in children being bused through the San Felipe district to Del Rio schools. The transfer shutdown touched off a furor at the base and in the community of Del Rio.

The solution Del Rio officials came up with was to consolidate the two school districts. But San Felipe school officials opposed the move, fearing that their special interests would be submerged in a district they did not control. A lawsuit was filed. Despite urgings from the Texas attorney general's office not to file the lawsuit in Tyler, Del Rio school officials did so. In August 1971, Judge Justice issued a comprehensive order consolidating the districts. Colin J. Carl, the law clerk who worked on the case for the court, acknowledges that he and the Judge "felt some discomfort" both over extending the jurisdiction of the court outside the Eastern District and over submerging the Mexican-American district in the larger Anglo system. But they could see no other solution. Del Rio ISD officials were pleased with this part of the ruling. But, to their dismay, the order also included comprehensive directives relating to the use of bilingual and bicultural programs for both faculty and staff. These they bitterly opposed. Relying on precedent from both Texas and federal courts, Justice ruled that Mexican-Americans constituted an identifiable minority group and were thus entitled to the same desegregation remedies as blacks. The U.S. Supreme Court later came to the same conclusion in a desegregation case involving the Denver schools.

An appeal of the San Felipe–Del Rio order was taken to the Fifth Circuit, contesting both affirmative action requirements and Judge Justice's right to hear the case. Before the Fifth Circuit heard the appeal, however, the Del Rio school board and the Department of Justice informed the court that they had agreed on a new comprehensive plan. The Fifth Circuit sent the matter back to the Judge.

But at the November 1971 hearing in Tyler, it was revealed that none of the former members of the San Felipe school board had participated in developing the new plan, even though several were members of the newly constituted interim school board for the consolidated district. Nor had there been much progress by either the interim board or HEW in securing federal funds to implement the plan. Judge Justice's patience had worn thin. He wrote in his decision, "This court feels very strongly that the Department of Health, Education, and Welfare and the Department of Justice should not urge the adoption of a plan upon this court, giving assurance of practically unlimited funds to implement it, and then, through neglect, inaction or misdirection, effectively frustrate its implementation." [11]

Finding the school board to have acted in bad faith, Justice handed down a comprehensive new order, which a state assistant attorney general labeled "the goddamnedest cradle-to-grave order in legal history." [12] Drawing from proposals advanced by the Justice Department and TEA officials, the order described affirmative action steps the newly consolidated and integrated district had to take to remedy past discrimination against Mexican-Americans. A key component was the requirement of developing individualized instructional programs for educationally or economically deprived children. The educational program was to "incorporate, affirmatively recognize and value the cultural background of all of its children." This meant including extensive bilingual instruction—English for Mexican-American students, and Spanish for other students—as well as bicultural programs to aid students in developing an understanding of and appreciation for each other's cultural background. The order outlined in considerable detail the step-by-step procedures for doing so, taking up ten single-spaced, double-column pages in the published opinion. It was indeed a bold step in the direction of federal court involvement in the operation of a public institution, possibly the first to include both bilingual and bicultural remedies to eradicate the legacy of discrimination.

The parties appealed again to the Fifth Circuit. This time the appeals court in an unsigned opinion affirmed the judgment, including the necessity of implementing the comprehensive desegregation plan. However, the court, believing the case could be more effectively supervised by the U.S. District Court for the Western District of Texas, transferred it to that court.[13] The transfer was not surprising, in that the Fifth Circuit had indicated in upholding Judge Justice's statewide order that the other Texas federal courts were not precluded from deciding desegregation issues within their respective jurisdictions. Judges in the Western District had made it clear to Justice that they did not take kindly to his intrusion into their affairs. The transfer of the case back to them had the effect of limiting the impact of the statewide order and undercutting uniformity in carrying out statewide school desegregation.

Indeed, as it turned out, only feeble gestures were made to implement the Justice plan in the San Felipe–Del Rio school district. Eventually, Judge John Wood, the conservative judge to whom the case was assigned, dismissed it from his docket. The plaintiffs appealed once again to the Fifth Circuit, which found that Judge Wood had not adhered to then prevailing principles in the Fifth Circuit for closing the case. It was not until 1984 that Judge Edward C. Prado, who took over the case from Judge Wood, declared the district unitary in all aspects except bilingual education.

Meanwhile, enforcement of Justice's 5281 order by the Texas Education Agency was proceeding, but not swiftly. With members of the State Board of Education opposed to the ruling and with the commissioner of education appointed by the board, it is understandable that enthusiasm for reform was lacking. Commissioner Marlan Brockette, who assumed his position in 1974, summed up the stance of top officials: "Our approach was soft touches and smooth operations, so that local officers wouldn't be torn up by the force of a central office." [14] Robert Alexius, a TEA official associated with the enforcement of *United States v. Texas* from the start, acknowledges that "If it was a borderline situation, then the decision would go in favor of the school district." When changes had to be made in the face of flagrant violations, neither the Texas Education Agency nor school districts were reluctant to inform those affected that it was Judge Justice who was responsible, and not they. The result was a steady stream of correspondence to the court, much of it reflecting the bitterness that the writers felt toward a decision-maker they would never meet and had little chance of influencing.

Sometimes community reaction turned violent and ugly. A graphic display of the hostility toward school desegregation in East Texas is evidenced in the criminal trial before Judge Justice of two men who took it upon themselves to stop desegregation in its tracks by bombing the Longview school district bus fleet shortly after Chief Judge Joe Fisher had entered a desegregation order in 1970. The men, Fred Hayes and Ray McMaster, were part of a small group of "super-patriots" in Longview who feared a revolution by black members of the community. The ensuing explosion seriously damaged or destroyed thirty-three vehicles and the parking area, though no one was injured. Hayes and McMaster were indicted and tried in Justice's court. Evidence was introduced to show that Hayes had also dynamited a house purchased by a black woman in a white neighborhood and that the pair had constructed "booby traps" by placing dynamite in flashlight cases, wiring an electric cap to a battery connected to the flashlight switch. These devices were then placed in black neighborhoods. Following a jury verdict of guilty, Justice rejected pleas for clemency and sentenced both men to eleven years in prison and an $11,000 fine. The sentence was subsequently lowered to eight years for Hayes and six for McMaster. At the sentencing, the tense courtroom was filled with armed marshalls. The decision was subsequently upheld on appeal. [15]

Some years later, Justice was startled to look up from his desk and find McMaster standing before him. The secretaries and clerks were out, and Justice had left the door to his chambers open in case someone came into the office. McMaster said he had been sent by the federal parole office to determine whether it would violate his parole for him to possess a gun for hunting purposes. Justice responded that it would. McMaster thanked him and left. Justice lost no time in contacting the parole office and telling them never to send paroled prisoners to see him again.

Actual enforcement of Justice's statewide desegregation order was delegated to a TEA sub-office, the Office of Technical Assistance, later renamed the

Technical Assistance Division (TAD). Its first director, Gilbert Conoley, reported to the assistant commissioner of education, whose attitude toward enforcement was known around the agency as "benign neglect." As a former high school coach, teacher, superintendent, and president of the Texas County Superintendents' Association, Conoley had the confidence of the Texas superintendents and school board members. He maintains that 5281 "was the greatest thing ever written for desegregation," adding that members of the staff went as far as they could without getting fired.

But whatever Conoley's intentions, the fact is that TEA early on adopted procedures that kept his division on a short leash. Districts under desegregation orders from other courts were off limits to TAD unless a specific complaint was received. Random, unannounced visits to school districts were prohibited. Field visits were allowed only in cases involving districts where at least one campus had a minority enrollment of 66 percent or greater, when complaints were received from a district, or when accompanying a TEA accreditation team on a scheduled monitoring visit. This meant that for most school districts in the state, unless a complaint was received, a TAD visit would occur only once every three to five years. To make matters worse, the TAD staff was small. At any one time, fewer than a dozen staffers were available for field visits. Requests for increased funding and staffing were routinely denied, even though there were abundant federal funds available for this purpose. In short, TAD was directed to do what was minimally necessary to fulfill mandates of the order and nothing more.

It must be noted that the Texas Education Agency had not requested the assignment it received from Judge Justice. Established by the Texas Legislature as a support agency, it had become an enforcement agency by court order overnight—against the wishes of most school districts, state government leaders, and the general public. As William Bednar, TEA general counsel from 1976 to 1979, puts it, "The Division of Technical Assistance was light years apart from the U.S. Office of Civil Rights in its regulatory approach." The agency chose to walk a narrow line between offending the judge and alienating its primary constituency. The result was inevitable foot-dragging and lip service, coupled with quiet negotiation. Richard Arnett, TEA general counsel in the early 1980s, maintains that negotiation was more effective than one might assume. "The 5281 order was a powerful tool, and we stepped on districts in transfer situations. Because we were partly on their side, we could be very effective in dealing with them. We would say, 'Look, we've tried to help you on this but we just can't go this far. You've *got* to do something about this under the court order.'" Still, there was little interest in Austin in helping William Wayne Justice desegregate the state's public school system.

The fact that implementation was spotty is also attributable to the order itself. The Technical Assistance Division was required to monitor all districts with one or more campuses having a 66 percent or greater minority enrollment. Through the years, the total number of districts in the 66 percent category has hovered just below 200. The 66 percent figure was selected as a triggering device, a recognition by Justice that requiring a yearly review of all 1,100 school districts would be impractical. However, it resulted in the Technical Assistance Division's wasting considerable staff time carrying out the mandate. A review of figures assembled by researchers at the Lyndon B. Johnson School of Public Affairs in Austin shows why. Of the 196 districts identified in this category in 1981, 95 were in effect unitary districts since all students attended school in the same building at any grade or series of grade levels. Another 45 had such a large minority population that further desegregation could not be achieved other than by consolidation, an option rural isolation ruled out. Still another 30 districts were under separate court order and thus off limits to TAD. This left 26 districts where annual investigatory efforts appeared warranted, based on the disparities between racial composition of individual campuses and overall district minority enrollment. But TAD had to monitor all 196 annually to comply with the order.[16]

Until 1984, TAD officials dutifully conducted on-site visits at all school districts in the 66 percent category. Thereafter, desk audits were substituted. While more efficient, desk audits could not discern the extent to which classroom segregation was occurring in a district whose overall student assignments appeared in compliance with the order. After 1984, annual site visits were routinely conducted through the accreditation process at about thirty of the total districts in the 66 percent category.

More significantly, Justice's "more than 66 percent" figure ignored those districts with a substantial, but less than 66 percent, minority population on any campus, yet showing strong district-wide segregation. The Lyndon B. Johnson School of Public Affairs study identified twenty districts in this category in 1978–1979. Because of limited staffing and restrictions placed on TAD by the agency, little effort was expended to desegregate them.

Aided by hindsight, Judge Justice acknowledges that the 66 percent triggering device posed a problem. Without precedent to rely on, he chose the 66 percent figure as a rule of thumb for beginning an investigation. "I just reasoned that if two out of three students were of one race, it ought to be checked into pretty carefully to see whether or not discrimination was taking place. I should have granted an exemption, however, for the Valley schools [the largely Mexican-American area bordering the Rio Grande and the counties adjoining it to the north], which are largely one-race to begin with."

He also acknowledges that placing TEA in the role of enforcer of the order turned out to be a mistake. "I imposed this burden on the Texas Education

Agency without any form of monitoring because I believed the United States Department of Justice was going to stay very active and would perform the monitoring functions themselves. I anticipated that they would have someone down there most of the time checking TEA activities to see that the order of the court was complied with. However, it was about that same time that the Nixon administration began, and I noticed immediately a significant decline in enforcement activity. The administration and its Department of Justice did not have the same attitude toward school desegregation nor the earnestness that the prior administration had had." As a result, in an exercise of judicial activism, Justice invited the Mexican American Legal Defense and Education Fund (MALDEF), GI Forum, League of United Latin American Citizens (LULAC), and National Association for the Advancement of Colored People (NAACP) to appear as plaintiff-intervenors in the case. All four filed motions to intervene on the side of the original plaintiffs, motions which Judge Justice granted. "It was my expectation that they would be doing the monitoring. I was entirely disappointed. The actions that they have taken through the years have been sporadic; there has been no day-to-day supervision or monitoring of the activities of TEA at all. Apparently, they do not have the funds to do that, or even see the need to do so."

The appointment of a special master with responsibilities similar to those of the special master in the prison case, *Ruiz v. Estelle,* would have resulted in much more effective enforcement. TEA officials dispute this, asserting that a special master might well have produced greater resistance from school districts. In any case, complex institutional litigation was in its infancy at the time, and the option of appointing such an overseer did not occur to the Judge.

Another deterrent to successful implementation was the end run to state and other federal courts by parents and school districts threatened with sanctions imposed by the Texas Education Agency. For example, in the summer of 1972, the Texas commissioner of education denied a request by eighty-seven white students to transfer from the Dallas school district to the all-white Highland Park school district. When the Highland Park superintendent refused to admit the students, a group of parents and students sought an injunction against Highland Park in state district court. Judge Dee Brown Walker granted a temporary restraining order on the novel theory that the commissioner's denial of the transfers violated a contract between the parents and the Highland Park school district.[17] The U.S. Justice Department then sought an injunction against enforcement of the state district court's restraining order in Judge Justice's court. Attorney Arlen D. "Spider" Bynum represented the residents. He knew that Justice would not take kindly to interference with his order. Indeed, former law clerk Richard Mithoff recalls that the Judge was outraged at the idea of a state district judge countermanding the Constitution by assertion of a contract right. When Bynum appeared in court, Justice from long habit was absently clipping his fingernails at the bench. The microphone amplified the clipping sound. Bynum turned to a colleague and said, "There he is up there, sharpening his claws for us!" [18]

Following a clear line of precedent, Justice observed that the state court order interfered with implementation of his 1971 statewide decision and permanently enjoined the court from meddling in matters not its concern. [19]

A more complicated and important example of an end run involved efforts to desegregate the Gregory-Portland Independent School District, whose enrollment in 1973 was about 36 percent minority, almost all Mexican-American. Gregory-Portland, located northeast of Corpus Christi, encompasses two towns four miles apart. Gregory is mostly Mexican-American, while the much larger Portland is mostly Anglo. Portland is to a large extent a bedroom suburb of Corpus Christi. At the time of the lawsuit, the consolidated district, with an enrollment of 4,400 students, operated three elementary schools (a fourth was opened in 1980), one junior high, and one high school.

Noting that one elementary school had an enrollment of 92 percent Mexican-Americans, while the others had minority enrollments of 21 and 9 percent, TEA informed the district in November 1973 that it was operating a segregated system. Two desegregation plans were drawn up for the elementary schools, and the district was ordered to adopt one or face loss of accreditation and state funding after receipt of a formal ten-day notice. Gilbert Conoley, then director of the Technical Assistance Division, acknowledged that the order was controversial and advised Gregory-Portland school officials that if they were dissatisfied, they should go to court. Though the agency never sent the ten-day notice, the school district filed an action in the U.S. District Court for the Southern District of Texas, claiming that it was not segregated and that TEA had not given the district a hearing to prove it, a denial of due process of law. The U.S. Justice Department was unsuccessful before the Fifth Circuit in getting the case transferred to Tyler. After a trial, the district court issued an injunction in January 1976 against TEA's denial of accreditation.

Content to let the matter die, the State Board of Education refused to allow TEA to appeal the decision, whereupon attorneys for the Justice Department did so a second time, challenging the district court's jurisdiction. This time, a different three-judge panel of the Fifth Circuit reversed directions by overturning the lower court order and directing the case to be retried in Judge Justice's court, on the grounds that the matter involved enforcement of the original 5281 order. The U.S. Supreme Court refused to overturn the Fifth Circuit's decision, and the matter came to trial once again in 1980, this time in Judge Justice's court.

Relying on his earlier ruling in the San Felipe–Del Rio case and on precedents from the U.S. Supreme Court and the Fifth Circuit, Justice concluded that the 5281 order encompassed Mexican-Americans as a minority group. Though Texas had never by law discriminated against Mexican-Americans, it had done so against blacks. He relied on the 1973 Supreme Court decision in *Keyes v. School District No. 1* to infer an equally invidious intent to discriminate against Mexican-Americans, both by the state and by Gregory-Portland ISD, based upon prior *de jure* discrimination against blacks. Invocation of the *"Keyes* presumption" has the effect of shifting the burden of justification to the defendants to show that they are not operating a segregated system. Justice was significantly aided in invoking the *Keyes* presumption by stipulations (admitted facts) made by the assistant attorney general representing TEA, Susan Dasher. Gregory-Portland ISD was not a party to the stipulations, but was bound by them. These stipulated facts became the center of a major battle among attorneys and judges in a related case involving bilingual education in Texas as described in Chapter 10. They also figured prominently in the appeal of the Gregory-Portland ruling.

According to Conoley, Dasher, who had inherited the case after the Fifth Circuit decision, quickly assumed full control. "She was more interested in cooperating with the Justice Department than with us." Dasher acknowledges that she found the case enjoyable to work on. "I absolutely loved it because it was the first time Texas had ever been on the side that I would like to be on." It wasn't until after the case was over, she maintains, that "I learned that nobody wanted me to win it."

Among the stipulated facts were eleven which Judge Justice used to support his ruling, including: "Segregation of Mexican-American students is a historical fact in the Texas Public Schools" and "Mexican-American children have historically been provided inferior facilities, often drastically overcrowded, sometimes necessitating one-half day classes." Indeed, the TEA brief acknowledged that the 5281 order was fully applicable to one-race schools for Mexican-American students. Justice was moved to comment that TEA "has shown commendable candor in admitting the existence of unconstitutional statewide discrimination against Mexican-Americans and in joining the battle to eliminate this malign bias from all but the history books."[20]

Why this curious about-face? The stipulations were part of a strategy designed by attorney Dasher for the bilingual offshoot of *United States v. Texas,* which she was also litigating in Judge Justice's court. As described in Chapter 10, fallout from use of the stipulations in both cases led to Dasher's departure from the Texas Office of the Attorney General, as word of their existence reached her superiors.

Judge Justice also observed that state law at one time had prohibited the speaking of Spanish in the public schools. He cited a stipulation to the effect that violators of the "no-Spanish rule" were "corporally punished, shamed, threatened, fined, suspended and expelled from school by Texas school administrators."[21]

With systematic, statewide discrimination admitted by state officials who accredit and supervise public schools in Texas and with these same officials having ordered Gregory-Portland ISD to comply with the 5281 order, the school district was left with the unenviable task of proving that its continued segregation did not result from acts committed by either the district or the state. Justice did not give school officials much wiggle room. "Where the state's intentional acts have contributed to the segregation, yet the school district itself has done nothing intentionally segregative, TEA is, nevertheless, under an obligation to withdraw support for the segregated district, inasmuch as the state agency is responsible for the illegality of conditions in the district."[22]

The Gregory-Portland ISD attorney asserted that TEA had denied the district due process of law by determining that desegregation was in order merely by looking at the numbers and without bothering to give the district a hearing to ascertain whether segregatory intent was evident. Justice countered, "If TEA determines the existence of ethnically identifiable schools, it need show nothing further to implement the sanctions provided in the *U.S. v. Texas* orders." However, he then softened this assertion somewhat, noting that "the school district should have the opportunity to rebut the prima facie case."[23] But since the court proceeding afforded it an opportunity to do so, a remand to the agency for a hearing was not necessary.

Given Justice's perspective on the case, it was not surprising that the school district lost. The facts showed significant segregation, a point that Gregory-Portland officials could not successfully explain away by citing commitment to a policy of neighborhood schools. Since Portland was substantially Anglo and Gregory substantially Mexican-American, all the consolidated district was doing, its officials asserted, was recognizing what had been a fact of life all along. Justice disagreed. Based on the evidence before him, Judge Justice concluded that the consolidation of the districts in 1950 was triggered not by magnanimous efforts to integrate Anglo students in Portland ISD with Mexican-American students in Gregory ISD but rather to increase tax revenues in the former district from a tax base created by the imminent construction of a huge Reynolds Aluminum Company plant in Gregory. Prior to consolidation,

Justice observed that both districts had at one time operated segregated elementary schools for Mexican-American students, called at the time "Mexican schools," or "little Mexican schools." Through classroom assignment, school attendance zones, assignment of teachers, and grade assignments, prior patterns of segregation had been reinforced. No effort to integrate the schools had been made. Justice noted as well a school policy against the speaking of any language but English at the schools, contrary to state law permitting bilingual education. "Indeed, over the years, the rule against speaking Spanish at school was repressively enforced at [the school district], elementary and high school students having received corporal and other punishments for doing so." [24]

Having found willful district-wide discrimination in the Gregory-Portland school district and no effort by school officials to take affirmative action to eliminate it, Justice adopted a plan proposed by the Texas Education Agency whereby all students in each elementary grade would be assigned the same school, e.g., all first-graders in the district assigned to Austin Elementary School. This plan, while instantly converting the district into a unitary system, necessarily involved intercommunity busing of 60 percent of the elementary children. According to Robert Alexius, the TEA consultant who worked on the plans, this was one of two plans proposed by the Technical Assistance Division. It was essentially a mathematical rearrangement of students to achieve integration. TEA preferred the other plan, which was more moderate and had been developed in association with Gregory-Portland officials. But Dasher did not advance it in court. Her reason was simple. "I knew Judge Justice wouldn't accept it."

The Judge also ordered establishment of a biethnic committee composed of an equal number of Anglos and Mexican-Americans to assist the school district to erase the legacy of discrimination and to monitor progress on behalf of the court. An editorial in the *Portland News* lambasted the biracial committee as "repulsive and repugnant," a new tool to strike down local control. "No doubt if the judge fails to get a committee to do his work in a manner pleasing to the court, he will just issue another order doing away with the group and blatantly installing a court appointed lackey to supervise his bidding." [25] The bitterness reflected in the editorial was typical of the depth of resentment school communities around the state felt toward integration in general and Judge Justice in particular.

The school district appealed the decision to the Fifth Circuit. One of the judges assigned to the three-member panel was Adrian Spears, a Kennedy appointee, from the U.S. District Court, Western District of Texas. In 1976 Judge Spears had overturned TEA sanctions imposed under the 5281 order on Northside ISD (in San Antonio), which had elementary schools containing substantially more than 66 percent minority students, though the district itself was predominantly white. Northside's position was that the imbalance stemmed from residential patterns, in part attributable to a federal low-income housing project, and not to district discriminatory practices. As in the Gregory-Portland case, the State Board of Education did not allow the agency to file an appeal.

The other two judges were Charles Clark and Thomas Gibbs Gee, both appointed by President Richard Nixon. Justice was already familiar with Judge Gee, having experienced reversals at his hand in several employment cases (see Chapter 12). Justice had also sat on a three-judge panel with him and fellow Tyler Federal Judge William M. Steger in a case involving an alleged unlawful inspection of a Gibson's Discount Center. In that case, the judges had all agreed that the warrantless inspection by federal Occupational Safety and Health Act (OSHA) investigators was unconstitutional. When Justice and Steger were in Austin trying the Gibson's Discount Center case, they had been Gee's guests for dinner. Justice found Gee personally charming.

But in writing for the appeals court in the Gregory-Portland case, Gee was anything but charming. In an important decision which led to reduced TEA enforcement of 5281 from 1981 onward and talk at the agency about seeking an end to *United States v. Texas,* the Fifth Circuit reversed Judge Justice's ruling. Gee wrote that Justice had misapplied the Supreme Court's *Keyes* decision, which had involved alleged discrimination against Mexican-Americans by school officials in a triethnic school district. The case at hand was substantially different, involving a state agency without authority to run schools and a district which was not triethnic. The inference of intent to discriminate should not have been placed on the school district, Gee wrote, requiring it to prove the converse. Doing so "resulted in a proceeding erroneously and fundamentally skewed against Gregory-Portland ISD." [26] Instead, the state should shoulder the burden of proving Gregory-Portland school officials guilty of segregatory acts.

The appeals court placed little weight on the controversial TEA admissions about statewide discrimination against Mexican-Americans through the stipulations of fact, noting that they did not bind Gregory-Portland ISD. "Clearly, the state lacked power to 'concede' anything about the intent of Gregory-Portland ISD." [27] It also criticized Judge Justice for concluding that TEA could order a desegregation plan merely by looking at numbers. In the absence of state-mandated segregation, the appeals panel viewed the numbers as a starting place, not a conclusion. It ordered Judge Justice not to let TEA levy sanctions against a district where Mexican-American students are involved without first affording the district notice and a hearing.

The panel then reviewed the record of alleged discrimination. It concluded that consolidation was motivated by ethnically neutral purposes and that between the time of consolidation and the trial, the school district had done nothing other than continue the pattern of assigning elementary students to the schools located in their neighborhoods. The construction of new buildings had followed population growth in the Portland community. Hence the disparate racial populations of the elementary schools reflected that of their respective communities.

The appeals court downplayed most of the other evidentiary matter used by Judge Justice in support of his decision. They rejected his assertion that the state had advanced a "no Spanish" policy. The "no Spanish" law was actually a law against German passed at the time of the First World War. The panel noted that the state had for some time had statutes asserting English as the basic language of instruction, but observed that these laws had been amended to allow instruction in other languages and to accommodate bilingual programs. The "little Mexican schools" in Gregory and Portland prior to consolidation had existed so many years earlier that the panel could not ascertain what their purpose was. In any case, the consolidated Gregory-Portland ISD had never operated such a school.

The panel pointed out that the district was a leader in the state in hiring Mexican-American teachers and had made significant efforts to place them in all its schools. The fact that a disproportionate number remained in the elementary school with the largest Mexican-American enrollment appeared to the appeals judges to be for pedagogical reasons.

The appeals court concluded, "It is apparent from the record evidence—indeed it is without significant dispute there—that the existence of an ethnically identifiable student body at Gregory elementary school is the natural consequence of a corresponding Mexican-American population concentration in this somewhat distinct and isolated part of the district. This condition, the record makes clear, was not caused and has not been contributed to by any governmental action whatever, state or local, but is rather the product of indifferent historic and demographic forces." [28]

The Fifth Circuit reversal was a major setback to Judge Justice's efforts at enforcing 5281. He did not take it kindly. "That *Gregory-Portland* ruling was to me an obnoxious decision. They didn't bring out the facts clearly in their decision. Basically, what happened was this: there was a little Mexican district and there was a white district. A big, new manufacturing plant was located in the Mexican district. Well, the white district coveted that plant for their district so they'd have a big increase in their tax base. They engineered the merger of the two districts but then made no effort whatever to see to it that the schools in Gregory were brought up to the standards of those in Portland. You would assume that under these circumstances they'd run schools of similar quality in each district. They didn't. They made no effort to integrate the schools as had been demanded by the *Brown* decision. It had already been decided that Mexicans are a separate, cognizable ethnic group entitled to special protection under the Fourteenth Amendment. They ran old, inferior schools over there in Gregory. It was a situation that demanded relief."

Justice attributes the reversal to judges who "just have a different view of the Constitution from that of their immediate predecessors." In this there may be an element of truth, for judicial appointments by the Nixon administration were giving the Fifth Circuit, a crusading court for integration across the South in the 1960s, a distinctly conservative hue. Conservative judges are more apt to support the view that the court's role should be over when official acts by public officials to separate the races have been terminated. Ardent integrationists support judicial action requiring students to go to school together in integrated schools and the sanctioning of affirmative-action efforts to erase the legacy of prior discrimination.

Justice is in the latter category. In a case involving the Denison ISD in Northeast Texas near the Oklahoma border, Justice demanded that something more must be done than simply ending official separation of the races. The school board had been successful for years in resisting Justice's integration orders through a variety of dilatory practices including repeated appeals to the Fifth Circuit. Though it was a small district with a small black population (11 percent), racial imbalance existed among its elementary schools after the end of *de jure* segregation. After *Gregory-Portland* was decided, the Fifth Circuit sent the district's appeal of Justice's latest desegregation order back to him, with the direction to consider the applicability of the *Gregory-Portland* ruling. Justice distinguished his Denison decision on several grounds, including the fact that the Denison case fell into the *de jure* category, not the *de facto* category the Fifth Circuit found applicable in *Gregory-Portland*.

The school board's attorney had asserted that sprinkling black students throughout the predominantly white district would be less productive than allowing them to attend school together in concentrated numbers. In pointed language, Justice wrote that this argument assumed that black students cannot learn effectively in an integrated environment and that white students do not benefit when they attend school together with black students. "These dual considerations, which are premised on the incontrovertible truth that students benefit from mutual sharing, are fundamental cornerstones of the entire body of desegregation law, and indeed of our current social order. They are certainly not open to question by defendants, who advance their contention in the specious garb of altruism and racial solicitude." [29]

In a television interview, Judge Justice asserted that the victims of discrimination need to be treated differently in order to be treated equally. "If we now just simply say that discrimination is abolished, but we don't go any further, then that leaves these people in that position of subjugation that was originally mandated by the law and they'll continue in that course. It might take centuries for them to be brought back up to the level that they would otherwise be justly entitled to—the equal protection of the laws. What I'm saying is, that if we leave them like they are, then the status quo—where they're in a state of subjugation—is maintained, and that's not equal protection. It's only the status quo that is being given protection."[30]

But even among those who embrace these so-called "affirmative-action" remedies, there are differences of opinion. For example, efforts have been made in the Dallas school district to raise achievement levels of minority students by increasing resources for selected schools in minority neighborhoods in lieu of extensive crosstown busing.[31] These schools have substantially reduced class sizes, longer school days, extra pay for teachers, and similar compensatory features over the regular school to which the students had previously been assigned. Even if the so-called "super-schools" are successful, racial balance across the district is not achieved. To Justice, such efforts constitute a return to the "separate but equal" doctrine repudiated in *Brown v. Board of Education.* Worse, they smack of racism. "What the white establishment is doing is giving the black community some money so that they'll keep their black schools. The black school administrators have gotten places in the school system now, and they're making good salaries. They're ready to go along with this idea that we don't have to have integration. All we've got to do is have separate but equal schools." He adds, "I don't think they're going to get any significant amount of upgrading. I hope I'm wrong, but I don't believe it."[32] Judge Justice cites the integrated Charlotte-Mecklenburg school system involved in the *Swann* decision as the preferred model. "The judge there, James B. McMillan, made an earnest effort to see that schools were integrated. They were integrated, and there has been a significant advancement in black achievement. *Charlotte-Mecklenburg* is a shining example of what can be done if the court will take its role seriously and do what it's supposed to do."

Of course, in a city-wide school system such as Dallas where fewer than 25 percent of the students are white Anglo-Americans, options to achieve integration are limited unless largely white suburban school districts are included in integration plans. The Charlotte-Mecklenburg system is a consolidated metropolitan district involving schools in Charlotte, North Carolina, and surrounding Mecklenburg County. The present political and judicial climate, coupled with massive logistical problems, precludes court-ordered city-suburban desegregation in most urban areas, even though, as in the case of Dallas, this would be the only means to bring about real school integration.

Underlying these issues of remedies to constitutional wrongs is a fundamental question about the purpose of education. Is the school only to instill knowledge and skills, or is it also to perform a socialization function whereby students learn to live and work with each other? If the latter is part of the educational process, then the school can most effectively perform this mission when the student and teaching populations are heterogeneous.

Complicating the matter further are factors outside the educational system which nevertheless have an impact upon it and which may directly or indirectly have resulted from previous *de jure* school segregation. Included among them are neighborhood residency patterns, the location of business and industry, economic resources, and, most important, the attitudes of people. When minorities living in largely one-race neighborhoods prefer neighborhood schools over the cause of integration, further court intervention to bring about integrated schooling is at an end.[33]

Reversal of the Gregory-Portland ISD decision largely halted efforts by both state and federal agencies to utilize the *United States v. Texas* order to desegregate schools with large Mexican-American student concentrations. It also exerted a chilling effect on desegregation of schools with large concentrations of black students, the original purpose of the 5281 order. The decision was also the first significant rebuff to Judge Justice in the long history of *United States v. Texas*.

Another major setback occurred in 1986 when the Fifth Circuit overruled Judge Justice's granting of a temporary injunction on administration of the Pre-Professional Skills Test (PPST), a competency examination in reading, writing, and mathematics designed by the Education Testing Service, a major producer of educational tests, and given to sophomore college students as a condition of admission to a teacher preparation program.

The League of United Latin American Citizens (LULAC), the GI Forum, and the NAACP, intervenors on the side of the government in *United States v. Texas* in 1972, together with a group of students who failed the PPST, sought to challenge its use as a violation of the U.S. Constitution, federal civil rights laws, and the *United States v. Texas* 1971 court order. They based their claims largely on the test's racially discriminatory impact. Since its first administration in March 1984, 77 percent of blacks and 66 percent of Mexican-Americans taking the test had failed. For Anglos, the figure was 27 percent.

While the matter did not directly involve school desegregation, Judge Justice nevertheless asserted jurisdiction to hear the case. His 1971 order forbade discrimination in personnel decision-making, and use of PPST affected the hiring of teachers. The Justice Department, which had so vigorously participated in the original suit, sided with the Texas Education Agency in opposing jurisdiction. As to the merits, Justice concluded that in light of the history of state segregation, the presence of a severe teacher shortage, and the absence of state-sponsored remedial programs, plaintiffs were likely to prove their claim at trial. He took special note of the fact that TEA had recently instituted an alternative certification program to meet the teacher shortage: "The choice to sacrifice the requirement of two years of training specifically directed at being a teacher, including student teaching, rather than change the PPST preclusionary scores or petition the Legislature to allow waiver of the PPST requirement, was one of the strongest indications of racial intent presented at the hearing."[34]

The plaintiffs were granted a preliminary injunction against further administration of the test until a trial on the merits could be held. The reaction across the state was swift and largely negative. The often stridently conservative *Dallas Morning News* gave Judge Justice an "F" for "Effort" in an August 29, 1985, editorial, asking rhetorically, "Would someone please specify how this helps the students—black students, brown students, white students—who sit, metaphorically, at the feet of these teachers? Or don't students matter? Is ideology (viz., teacher-selection-by-racial-quota) the purpose of knocking out the test?" Commissioner of Education William Kirby defended the test as necessary to improve classroom teaching. "The lower passing rates among minorities stems from the fact that the state has fallen short in the past in educating these students, a cycle that must be broken in part by ensuring that future generations are taught by only the most capable teachers."[35] The solution, he argued, lay not in doing away with the test but in providing special assistance to those who fail it. However, failure of the state to do so largely prompted Judge Justice to issue the preliminary injunction.

The Texas Education Agency immediately appealed, with support from the Reagan administration. Assistant Attorney General William Bradford Reynolds, director of the Justice Department's Civil Rights Division, filed a brief on the side of the state, sharply criticizing the ruling as "legally erroneous on all points."[36] Norma Cantu, national director of education for the Mexican American Legal Defense and Education Fund (MALDEF), noted that the filing of the brief constituted a complete reversal of the Justice Department's past position.

Justice had gone out on a limb to bring the dispute under the 5281 umbrella. Thirteen years had passed since the order had been entered. His assertion of jurisdiction and his conclusion about discriminatory intent were both tenuous. The Fifth Circuit reversed the district court decision as an abuse of discretion. Surprisingly, the appeals panel, composed of Johnson appointee Homer Thornberry, Carter appointee Alvin Rubin, and Reagan appointee E. Grady Jolly, did uphold Judge Justice's assertion of jurisdiction, though with some reservations.[37] But the panel did not accept his rationale for granting the preliminary injunction. Under Supreme Court precedents, disproportionate impact on minority groups starts the inquiry, rather than ends it, regarding discriminatory intent.[38] "A state is not obligated to educate or certify teachers who cannot pass a fair and valid test of basic skills necessary for professional training, and the record contains considerable evidence tending to show that the PPST is a valid measurement of such skills. Without assessing this evidence, the district court had no adequate basis to decide the requisites for issuance of a preliminary injunction."[39] In response to Judge Justice's concern about the impact of the PPST on availability of minority teachers in view of the state's high percentage of minority students, the Fifth Circuit wryly observed that, "the 1971 order does not require the State to provide minority-group students with teachers who are not competent."[40]

The Fifth Circuit sent the case back to Judge Justice for trial on the issue of whether or not the test itself was a racially biased measure of competency to undertake education courses. The plaintiffs delayed in pursuing the matter, an indication of the heavy burden of proof they bore. Eventually, the PPST was supplanted by a basic skills test, and the matter became moot.

The PPST reversal contributed to growing sentiment around the Texas Education Agency that the bite had gone out of 5281. Since the early 1980s, agency personnel had become more and more lax about enforcement. For example, the original order required that no student transfers could be approved if the majority or minority percentage of the school population in either the sending or receiving district would be altered by more than 1 percent. Since many Texas school districts are small, the shift of a handful of students could trigger the 1 percent rule. Under this rule, even the most meritorious transfer requests—such as seeking a special curriculum in a larger school system— were routinely denied. In 1980, Justice agreed to a student transfer action which resulted in a 7 percent change. He noted that "TEA has not rigidly applied the one percent figure, choosing instead to use it as a guideline, which is perfectly proper . . ."[41] However, he emphasized that the transfer action he was approving was unique and was not to be viewed as altering the thrust of the student transfer section in the original order.

The TEA Transportation Division, which was responsible for enforcing this section of the order, then used a 5 percent trigger. At the same time, it was relatively lax in scrutinizing whether or not transfers constituted white flight. The result was a complaint filed with the Office for Civil Rights (OCR) in 1984 involving five small East Texas school districts. OCR threatened to haul the agency back before Judge Justice unless more stringent monitoring of white flight occurred. TEA officials clamped down on student transfers, returning to the 1 percent figure.

However, detachment and annexation of territory from one district to another has been allowed to accomplish the same purpose. Thus, a detachment effort that promoted segregation in the Clarksville and Detroit school districts in East Texas was approved by the Texas commissioner of education in 1989 on the basis of an "understanding" predating Justice's order by which students could attend either district.[42] Earlier, the agency had disapproved a student transfer plan between the two districts because it increased segregation. Clarksville ISD chose not to contest the action in Justice's court, apparently out of fear that the Judge might issue a drastic remedy as he had in the Clarksville public housing case (see Chapter 14). TEA officials believe that the 1 percent trigger applying to student transfers does not apply to deannexation-annexation of territory from one district to another. Justice believes that it does. Future litigation may give him the chance to clarify the 1971 order on this point. But by the end of the decade, TEA and state officials had ceased to worry about what Justice might do or not do with regard to further enforcement of the 1971 order. They planned to appeal any decision he might issue and anticipated a victory before the conservative Fifth Circuit.

Justice's statewide desegregation order was an ambitious undertaking with limited payoff. When *United States v. Texas* was decided, only moderate segregation existed among the nearly 1,100 Texas school districts. Most had desegregated during the 1960s. For those districts which were still substantially segregated, the 5281 order added impetus to desegregation efforts by U.S. government agencies, particularly in East Texas, where school officials knew that foot-dragging would result in their appearance in Justice's court. A study of 5281 conducted by the Lyndon B. Johnson School of Public Affairs at the University of Texas at Austin in 1981 identified 35 to 40 school districts across the state which readjusted their campus student assignments in response to the 66 percent trigger in the order. The study noted that in 1970–1971, 12 percent of all districts encompassed by the order were moderately or severely segregated; by 1978–1979, the percentage had been halved. Similar progress in response to the court orders of other federal courts was evident in Texas metropolitan areas where segregation was much more pronounced.[43]

Still, the Texas public school system today is by no means integrated to the extent that whites consistently go to school together with minorities. A 1989 analysis of data collected by the Office for Civil Rights shows that while progress toward integration has been made since 1970, substantial racial isolation continues. In 1984, for example, 14.4 percent of the Texas public school population was black. Yet the typical black student attended a school that was 63.5 percent minority, down slightly from 69.3 percent in 1970. Mexican-American students, who in 1986 made up 32.5 percent of the Texas public school enrollment, typically attended schools that were 73.1 percent minority. In 1970 the percentage had been 68.9.[44] Thus, racial isolation has moderated somewhat for blacks but increased for Mexican-Americans. Much of the racial isolation, of course, relates to neighborhood residential patterns. One of the great public policy issues of our time centers on the extent to which further efforts at school integration should be made in the face of statistics like these— or, conversely, whether integration orders like 5281 should be terminated and school officials trusted not to revert to discriminatory practices in student transfers, school construction, school deannexation-annexation, and the myriad of other activities covered by *United States v. Texas.*[45]

Overall, the study of 5281 conducted by researchers at the Lyndon B. Johnson School of Public Affairs declares *United States v. Texas* a qualified success—"qualified by the fact that compliance has been more easily achieved with certain provisions of the order than with others."[46] For example, segregation in transportation routes throughout the affected districts has largely ended. The same is true for segregatory changes in the boundaries of school districts, for the transfer of school district real property, and, to a lesser extent, for discrimination in extracurricular activities. One of the reasons TEA was successful in these areas is that, by its nature, TEA routinely performs numerous auditing functions.

Without the administrative follow-through a special master could have provided, enforcement of the order was spotty across the state. According to Judge Justice, he received no support from fellow Texas federal judges. "I can't remember any single judge who helped me." In addition, metropolitan school districts where racial segregation was greatest were beyond the reach of the order.

Justice views the outcome of *United States v. Texas* with some disappointment. "I think it helped a great deal in stopping white flight in rural school districts, and to some extent in the metropolitan districts. But the ruling was not as effective as it could have been. The order that I entered, and that was affirmed by the Fifth Circuit, had the potential of effecting large-scale integration of the public school facilities of this state. What it lacked was someone to actuate it. I was perfectly willing to enforce it, but there was no one to take on the labor of pressing it. I tried my best. I brought in MALDEF and the NAACP, but in retrospect, that was a poor way to do it. When the Democrats finally did get back in power under Carter, Griffin Bell was the Attorney General, and his record on the Court of Appeals for the Fifth Circuit had not been particularly good in school matters. So there wasn't any push from the Department of Justice during that period. There really hasn't been any since Nixon became President. I think the Texas Education Agency got the idea that at least the judge that presided in the case was in earnest. But I was just one judge in East Texas, with no one to help in the enforcement of the order."

By the mid-1980s the tide on school desegregation in Texas had gone out, and Judge Justice knew it. "Except for the school testing case, I haven't had many dealings with *United States v. Texas* since the Gregory-Portland reversal.

The case has been at a standstill since then." Is the desegregation movement over in Texas? "I don't anticipate we'll have much more; we're in a state of retreat. I think the movement toward neighborhood super-schools is just one indication."

He adds, "It's kind of sad in a way. But as Judge Irving Goldberg of the Fifth Circuit has said, there are only proximate solutions in the law. I think he is absolutely right. *United States v. Texas* is drawing to a close."

CHAPTER 6

Juvenile Rights in Texas Reform Schools

Morales v. Turman is one of Judge Justice's most important decisions. Not only did it prompt fundamental change in the treatment of Texas juvenile offenders; it also has become a landmark in the juvenile justice field. *Morales* is regarded even by top officials of the Texas Youth Commission as a shining example of successful court-induced institutional reform.

The roots of *Morales* go back to a 1967 U.S. Supreme Court ruling and to the actions of a young Texas public interest lawyer. In 1967 the U.S. Supreme Court was confronted with a case involving a fifteen-year-old Arizona youth, Gerald Gault, who had been declared delinquent pursuant to a legal proceeding and committed to a state institution until he was twenty-one for making indecent statements on the telephone to a neighbor. No notice of his arrest had been given to his parents, nor were they informed of the specific charges filed with the court. The accuser was not present at Gault's first hearing, and no record was made. At a second hearing, conflicting testimony was given and a probation officer's referral report was filed with the court, but no copy was made available to the parents or to Gault. Once again, the accusor was not present and no record was made. The adjudication of Gerald Gault was not atypical since most of the rules of criminal procedure did not then apply to juvenile courts.

Do the benefits of the juvenile justice system in protecting children from being treated like adult criminals outweigh the necessity for providing them with basic procedural due process protections? A majority of the Supreme Court justices thought not and took the opportunity in *In re Gault* to dramatically extend the rights of juvenile offenders. That decision provided that in delinquency hearings juveniles are entitled to basic due process protections under the U.S. Constitution.[1] Specifically, the Court required notice of the charges, legal counsel, the privilege against self-incrimination, and the right to confront witnesses. The *Gault* requirements were seen not as a threat to the informal rehabilitative nature of the juvenile court system but rather as an assurance that fairness would be followed in adjudicatory hearings.

In re Gault had little initial impact on most of the over 250 juvenile courts in Texas. Though required under the ruling to provide due process in juvenile proceedings, they were not doing so. Attorney Steven Bercu found this out during his work for the El Paso Legal Assistance Society, a public interest legal services organization funded in part by the federal Office of Economic Opportunity. Much of his work involved juveniles. In his first two months with the legal aid organization, Bercu heard parent after parent who claimed to have "sent" his or her child to a state reform school operated by the Texas Youth Council (TYC) and now was trying to get the child back. Bercu knew that parents could not lawfully "send" their kids to TYC as if it were a summer camp, nor could they just go to the state school and "get them back." He thought it was a language problem, that he was misinterpreting the Spanish spoken by the parents.

However, in the course of investigating allegations of abuse at the detention center in El Paso, Bercu learned that the practice did in fact amount to little more than parents committing their children to the TYC. When conflicts arose at home, parents would take their kids to the detention center and leave them for a day or two. The kids were "shown how bad things could be" and then picked up by their parents. When conflict arose again, parents would take them in for a second lesson. The third time, the El Paso practice became a civil litigation procedure that included an agreed judgment: parents agreed to sending the kids away to a state institution, the judge signed the papers, and off the kids went. The children had no notice of the charges, no court appearance, no representation. According to Bercu, when he went to see State District Judge Edwin Berliner seeking an explanation, he was told to "get lost."

The El Paso practice was characteristic of practices across the state. It was estimated that as many as 30 percent of the boys and 70 percent of the girls in TYC institutions were there because their parents could not control them. Only a small percentage had committed crimes of violence.[2] In most cases, due process procedures during adjudication had been virtually nonexistent.

Tips by employees at the El Paso detention center and perusal of court records produced the names of twelve juveniles who had been declared delinquent without due process. While all were from El Paso, they were incarcerated in TYC institutions around the state. During the early 1970s, TYC operated six detention institutions, three for boys and three for girls, that housed over 2,500 inmates, two-thirds of whom were male.[3] The boys' schools included Mountain View State School, Gatesville State School, and Giddings State Home and School, which opened in October 1973. The girls' schools were Brownwood State Home and School, Crockett State School, and Gaines-ville State School. All were named after the towns in which they were located, except for Mountain View, the maximum-security facility for boys, which was in Gatesville.

Bercu sought a writ of habeas corpus in state court on behalf of the twelve youths to gain a legal proceeding to challenge their incarceration. At the same time, he obtained a discovery order enabling him to interview them to ascer-tain the circumstances under which they had been committed and to secure written authority to represent them.

One of the inmates was Alicia Morales. Her father had had her committed to the TYC for disobedience. According to Bercu, he was an alcoholic and had no income. Alicia was the oldest of eight children and, at fifteen, was the only person in the household to work. Her father required that she turn her earn-ings over to him; he in turn gave her about five dollars a week and spent the rest, mostly on alcohol. At some point, Alicia asked her father to increase her portion of the money. His response was to beat her and then to commit her to the TYC.

Sensing an important case, Bercu alerted the Youth Law Center in San Francisco, a public interest law office providing support to legal services law-yers involved in juvenile rights litigation. Bercu and William P. Hoffman, Jr., an attorney from the center, decided to conduct interviews first at the Gaines-ville State School, the maximum-security facility for girls located seventy miles north of Dallas, in part because it was within the jurisdiction of the U.S. District Court for the Eastern District of Texas. Federal cases for the Gaines-ville area are heard in the Sherman Division of the Eastern District, where Judge Justice was then the presiding judge. Bercu had worked on long-hair cases in West Texas and knew that Justice was "kindly disposed" to the hair-length issue. "I knew he was supposed to be a good guy, to have good instincts; he seemed to have the right idea about the long-hair cases," Bercu maintains. In the seventies, Bercu himself wore his hair long, down to the middle of his back, but pulled it back in a pony tail when in the courtroom. Lawyers at the Youth Law Center had also learned from contacts in Texas that every effort should be made to file the case in Justice's court.

Bercu and Hoffman ran into resistance when they showed up at the Gaines-ville school on January 27, 1971, to talk with their prospective clients. Thomas Riddle, the superintendent at Gainesville, told them that they could talk to the girls, but that a TYC official would have to sit in. Riddle and his superior, Dr. James A. Turman, who had been TYC executive director since 1957, were concerned about unethical solicitation of clients by attorneys. They were also concerned that the girls' parents might not know about the involvement of attorneys. What was perhaps more significant was that the media were beginning to probe TYC practices, and thus TYC officials were particularly sensitive to requests by outsiders to confer with inmates. Bercu and Hoffman argued that the presence of an observer would undermine the attorney-client relationship and the privilege against self-incrimination should the observer later testify in court. They told Riddle that the girls had a right to talk privately with their attorneys. Riddle called the attorney general's office. He and the attorneys had a three-way telephone conversation with Assistant Attorney General Roland Daniel Green, who advised Riddle not to let the girls talk privately with the attorneys.

Although not happy with this condition, Bercu and Hoffman talked with minors at Gainesville (and later at the Gatesville State School for Boys and the Brownwood State Home and School for Girls) in the presence of the school superintendent. They secured written authorizations to serve as the girls' attorneys. When they returned to Gainesville the following month to confer with their clients regarding the preparation of habeas corpus petitions to secure their release, they were again denied the opportunity of talking privately with the girls. Bercu at first tried to contact state legislators to get them to intercede on his behalf. Attorneys at the Youth Law Center urged Bercu and Hoffman to file the suit quickly, fearing that higher state authorities might persuade TYC officials to come to their senses and at least allow Bercu and Hoffman to see their clients. If that happened, the opportunity to file the case before Judge Justice might be lost.

Bercu and Hoffman sought an injunction in Justice's court against further denial by TYC officials of the right to confer privately with their clients. At the same time they filed a class action lawsuit in his court to enjoin Texas state juvenile judges from admitting minors to the TYC without according them due process rights. The hearing on the application for a preliminary injunction was set for February 16, 1971, in Beaumont.

The two young attorneys appeared in Justice's chambers in T-shirts and blue jeans. While they awaited the arrival of attorneys from the Office of the Attorney General, they talked with Judge Justice about the long-hair issue. When Green and Max Flushe from the attorney general's office arrived, they were anything but pleased to be there. Justice recalls that "Flushe in particular was absolutely incredulous that I would pay any attention to these lawyers, who were dressed in these odd costumes and had long hair and beards." After a full hearing, Justice granted the injunction against further state interference with the clients' right to confer privately with their attorneys either in person or through the mails.[4] The right to counsel, he wrote, encompasses the right to effective counsel, and the right to effective counsel includes the right to confer and correspond privately with counsel. He noted that a California case had held fifty years before that a juvenile confined in a state institution has a right to confer privately with counsel.

Interviewing the twelve juveniles from El Paso confirmed all of Bercu's suspicions. No legal basis existed for institutionalizing them. The twelve were eventually released to their parents in El Paso.

Events began to occur quickly in the case. In July 1971, Judge Justice sent a letter to all 2,500 TYC inmates informing them of the lawsuit and asking each to complete a short questionnaire "so that this Court will be in a better position to understand the situation." The questions centered on whether the inmates had had a court hearing and the services of an attorney before being sent to the TYC. Of the 2,294 who returned the questionnaire, over one-third had had a hearing but had not been represented by an attorney, while another 280 had had neither.

About fifty of the returned questionnaires also contained narrative comments about the abuses inflicted on the respondents by TYC staff members. These responses convinced plaintiffs' attorneys that in addition to a procedural rights case, they also had the makings of a major conditions-of-confinement case. Several months later Judge Justice granted their motion to conduct on-site interviews with all TYC inmates. This effort, which was strongly opposed by the state, was designed to produce the evidence and the names of witnesses to support such a case. Supported by a small grant from the American Civil Liberties Union, over a hundred volunteer attorneys and law students from the University of Texas and Southern Methodist University law schools descended upon TYC institutions in the winter of 1972. Bercu was also busy seeking release in state courts of those TYC inmates whose due process rights had been violated.[5]

It was increasingly evident that Texas had simply not been diligent in seeing that the *In re Gault* procedures were being followed throughout its juvenile court system. In December 1972, the parties agreed to a set of findings of fact in which the state admitted the wholesale denial of procedural due process in the adjudication of delinquent youth. The state also consented to a declaratory judgment order, which Justice signed, spelling out the due process rights to be accorded juveniles in all Texas juvenile courts. The new procedures went considerably beyond those set forth in *Gault*. For example, the state agreed to see that every child was provided with an attorney, at public expense if necessary. The state also agreed to a provision prohibiting parents or children from waiving their right to an attorney.[6] The agreement tracked many of the provisions contained in a bill defeated in the 1971 Texas legislative session. By providing rights to juvenile offenders, it made it harder for communities to use TYC as a dumping ground for their troubled youth.

According to the agreed order, Judge Justice would refrain from enforcing the new provisions for 180 days. Since the Texas Legislature was about to convene, this would provide sufficient time for it to make the changes itself by reconsidering the defeated bill and thus avoiding a court-imposed order. The order also required that a report be submitted to Justice within 60 days on how the defendants intended to provide for legal representation and due process protections for minor children coming before the Texas juvenile courts. Beginning in 120 days, the report had to contain the name of every child denied these rights.

With the added pressure from the court, the effort to revamp the adjudication of delinquent youth in Texas which had failed in the previous legislative session succeeded. The Texas Legislature enacted a sweeping revision of the family code incorporating the components of the order.[7] However, later on, some of the provisions were weakened through legislative amendment.[8] Since the parties did not protest the changes in his court, Judge Justice took no further action.

Justice's actions with regard to this phase of the *Morales* case have been praised by one commentator as "masterful." "Judge Justice had not released a single juvenile but had put into operation a procedure that released hundreds. Judge Justice did not force a confrontation with state officials and judges . . . , but he set into motion a method of operating that would yield proper adjudication or would result in subsequent sanctions."[9] It is important to note, however, that the state had agreed to past violations of the law and to the declaratory judgment order. The Judge minimizes his role in this phase of Texas juvenile correctional reform. "It was something that was submitted to me that was agreed to. I just read through the agreed order and it looked okay to me, so I signed it. If it had anything to do with defeated legislation, I was unaware of it." Nevertheless, his action added the authority of the federal court to an effort already underway to revise the adjudicatory system.

With the due process phase of the lawsuit coming to a successful conclusion, Bercu and Peter B. Sandmann, the senior staff attorney at the Youth Law Center, who succeeded William Hoffman as attorney of record in the case, embarked on a more ambitious mission. Based on the information they had collected during their interviews in the winter of 1972 about conditions inside TYC institutions, they amended their pleadings to shift the focus of the class action lawsuit to the treatment of incarcerated juveniles. The attorneys hoped that this case would establish an entitlement under the Constitution to a right to therapeutic treatment for incarcerated juveniles. If they were going to take on the state in this context, however, they could not go it alone. They sought assistance from both the U.S. Justice Department and a Washington, D.C., group called the Mental Health Law Project, a public interest law firm which specialized in the rights of institutionalized persons.

With the change in pleadings, Judge Justice realized the potential significance of the case. During a telephone conversation, he told David J. W. Vanderhoof, one of the Justice Department attorneys in the Texas school desegregation litigation, that he had what appeared to be a right-to-treatment case. "Vanderhoof jumped on this like a shark after live bait," Justice observes. As noted in an earlier chapter, the Judge has always desired to balance the considerable power the state can bring to bear in class action suits. For this reason and for the bright light he knew the Justice Department would shine on TYC activities through its broad investigative powers, he granted plaintiffs' attorneys' motion in May 1972 that the Justice Department be ordered to participate in the case as *amicus curiae* with the rights of a party. This meant that government lawyers would have the right to present evidence and cross-examine witnesses. Eventually, a team of five attorneys from the Civil Rights Division of the Justice Department was assigned to the litigation.

The Mental Health Law Project offered the plaintiffs both staffing and access to a host of experts in the juvenile justice field. With its ties to most of the big mental health organizations, the Project added considerable respectability to what the plaintiffs' attorneys were trying to do regarding improving conditions of confinement. Justice allowed them to participate as litigating *amici* through their mental-health-related clients such as the American Orthopsychiatric Association. "As far as I was concerned, the more light I could get on this case, the better, and they appeared to be a very responsible outfit from what I could see," he says.

Thus arrayed against the state were three sets of attorneys: two representing the original plaintiffs, five from the Justice Department, and two from the Mental Health Law Project. A defense witness on behalf of the Texas Youth Council would face a withering barrage of questioning during cross-examination. Representing the state was a team of four lawyers from the Texas Office of the Attorney General plus Robert F. Salter, staff attorney for the TYC, who provided liaison between the agency and state attorneys. Salter, a former state legislator from Gatesville, had joined TYC as in-house counsel in the spring of 1973. With so many attorneys in the courtroom, Justice found the trial difficult to conduct. "The respective sides were very hostile to each other," he notes. Several of the attorneys on the state team were also hostile toward Judge Justice.

Heading the state team was experienced trial attorney Larry York, who in a strange twist of fate would subsequently become a member of the Texas Youth Commission board in 1985 and its chairman in 1987 (the "council" was changed to "commission" in 1983). York had worked as a trial attorney for the prestigious Baker and Botts law firm in Houston and had agreed at Attorney General John Hill's invitation to join the attorney general's office as executive assistant. Within weeks, he became first assistant attorney general with orders to bring the ever-expanding and highly embarrassing *Morales* litigation under control. York regarded the Justice Department as an "even-handed" opponent in contrast to Bercu and Sandmann, who "were the bomb-thrower type." The Mental Health Law Project had, in his view, a definite agenda. "They were on the program of seeing what was wrong with our system and actively attacking it along with the plaintiffs." Patricia Wald, one of the Mental Health Law Project attorneys and later chief judge of the U.S. Court of Appeals for the District of Columbia Circuit, admits as much. "In all honesty, we were supposed to be, and I think we genuinely had set out to be, *amicus* in the sense of not taking sides. But you couldn't be a caring human being and not end up being on the side of the plaintiffs in that case. You might differ with them as to the exact relief, but it was pretty hard once you got into the institutions not to support their case."

The two attorneys from the mental health organization were experienced, and it showed. York recalls that he had almost succeeded in pretrial deliberations in maneuvering the case into a three-judge court, then a requirement when a state statute was challenged as unconstitutional. The purpose of the three-judge court was to lessen public resentment if a state statute were rendered unenforceable and to give these decisions speedy review by providing direct appeal to the U.S. Supreme Court. The three-judge court also curtailed the power of a single judge to overturn state laws on constitutional grounds. "We felt that we weren't going to get two other judges who were going to be as tough on us as Justice was going to be. I remember one of the Mental Health Law Project attorneys taking the plaintiffs' attorneys aside and saying, 'Wait a minute. You don't want to be doing that. They're trying to lead you into a situation where you're going to wind up getting two more judges on this case if you're not careful.'" The three-judge issue later became a matter of key importance in the appeal to the U.S. Court of Appeals for the Fifth Circuit.

York felt he was "paddling a little bit against the current" in Justice's court. "While Judge Justice is a very smart and very well motivated judge, I think this case would fall into an area in his continuum of different kinds of cases where you would expect him to have a bias toward the claims being made by the plaintiffs." Plaintiffs' attorney Peter Sandmann agrees. "I was surprised by his activism," he notes. "He was quite willing, even desirous, of doing what was right in this case." Given Justice's views about individual rights and the role of the federal court in protecting them, all the elements for activist judging were indeed present: alleged repressive government activity, a vulnerable and powerless minority, and little legal precedent to rely on. If the case should offer him the opportunity to issue a ground-breaking order, Judge Justice was prepared to do so.

At the same time, defense attorneys found the case difficult to defend. "The policies of the agency simply hadn't been examined much by anyone," York admits. "TYC had become insular, cut off from a lot of thinking that had gone on in more recent times in other parts of the country." The problems of the TYC were not unknown to Texas legislators, but efforts to reform the system had been blocked.[10] With little external accountability, TYC had become a law unto itself. Trial testimony would make it clear that despite its avowed statutory purpose to provide "a program of constructive training aimed at rehabilitation and reestablishment in society of children adjudged to be delinquent,"[11] the practice of the TYC in most of its institutions was punishment.

That the case would be difficult to defend became apparent as the trial began. For over a month during the summer of 1973, the plaintiffs and *amici* produced a steady parade of inmates and expert witnesses who offered dramatic testimony about the sordid conditions and practices within the TYC. Most of the parade of horrors focused on practices at the Mountain View maximum-security facility and the nearby sprawling Gatesville State School, both for boys, which together housed 60 percent of the juveniles in the TYC.

The evidence was dramatic. Juvenile witnesses described how new inmates at Mountain View were considered "fresh fish" and were "tested" by forms of physical and psychological abuse administered by staff or other boys. Though expert testimony indicated that labeling an adolescent a homosexual hinders the development of heterosexual identity, untrained staff at Mountain View placed youths they considered to have homosexual tendencies in special "punk" dorms, one for blacks and one for Anglos and Mexican-Americans. At the boys' institutions, use of force was encouraged and brutality a way of life. Inmates could be beaten for such innocent behavior as speaking Spanish.

The absence of system-wide TYC policies and rules had resulted in the development of a subculture unique to each institution in which rules were arbitrary and forms of punishment left to the discretion of the staff. At Gatesville, for example, losing a baseball game, wearing pants too low, or leaving a pack of cards out might subject an inmate to a "peel," a "tight," or "brogueing." A "peel" referred to forcing a boy to bend over, then striking him on the back with a fist or open hand. A "tight" was applied by forcing a boy to bend down, holding his own ankles and toes, then striking him on the buttocks with the handle or straw end of a broom. "Brogueing" referred to kicking a boy in the shins. Boys "on crumb" at Gatesville were punished by having to sit on a chair in the dormitory day room, facing the wall all day long, without acknowledging the presence of anyone. One youth, T.G., testified that an assignment to "R.D." meant working in a sewage or garbage ditch for hours at a time.

T.G.: It's got all the stuff from the kitchen. I don't know, but it's—you almost throw up. You go out there and you have to dig in it. It has been there for years, and we had to dig it up to about half way to our waist.

Bercu: When you're working in that ditch, when you finish working in that ditch, are you then allowed to go back and shower and clean up?

T.G.: No, sir, we finished at, I think 11:30, and we went into the dorm and washed our hands and face and then had to line up. Mr. Schultz [a TYC staff member] was the extra-duty man that worked us, and we had to line up toe to toe, heel to heel. There was five of us working on it, and we had to line up toe to toe and heel to heel and wait, and then we went in the lunchroom and ate, but we didn't shower, and we had it all over us.[12]

Later in the trial, Dwaine Place, superintendent of Gatesville, testified that working R.D. was therapeutic. "If this helps this child go back to his dormitory and behave a little better, we think it is therapeutic."[13]

Make-work assignments were common. When "picking," boys were lined up, then required to move forward in unison, striking the ground with heavy pickaxes. Nothing was ever planted in the picked ground. Boys "on shovel" would line up in a circle with shovels, run around the circle with a shovelful of dirt, then drop the dirt in another pile. Boys assigned grass-pulling would pull grass from the ground, bending at the waist, keeping their knees straight, without looking at or talking with others. Those who bent their knees were beaten. One incident of staff brutality related at the trial concerned a Mountain View inmate who bent his knees after three hours of grass-pulling. The youth, five feet, seven inches tall and weighing 130 pounds, was kicked in the back and punched in the mouth by a correctional officer, a man well over six feet tall and weighing nearly 300 pounds. When the same youth became tired again and started to stand up, he was kicked in the head. After repeated beatings, the youth ran to the superintendent's office. There he was confronted by another correctional officer, who lined him up against the wall and struck him repeatedly in the jaw and stomach, then kicked him when he fell down. The correctional officer ordered new clothes to be brought to replace the bloodied ones. The youth was forced to sign a false incident report, struck again, then sent back to grass-pulling. Later, he was placed in solitary confinement for running away from grass-pulling.

According to the testimony, the worst examples of abuse arose in the context of solitary confinement. At Mountain View, boys were placed in solitary confinement cells at the whim of correctional officers. The length of confinement averaged two weeks, but would vary, depending upon the officer and the offense. For example, throwing a bar of soap might result in confinement in a single cell for nine days; masturbation, twelve days; not doing exercises, twenty-three days; trying to slip letters out, twenty-five days. Each cell had a door with a small window, which was painted over, and a narrow slit for food trays. The sole furnishings consisted of a mattress and a bucket for body waste. The cell's light resembled an automobile headlight located in a wall near the door. The light was never turned off. Boys were not allowed to speak except to answer a staff member, could not sit on their mattresses during the day, attend school, have school books, or go to sleep before 10 P.M.

Beatings for youths in solitary confinement were frequent and often arbitrary. "Picking" for an hour and a half at a time with a fifteen-minute break was a common "make-work" assignment for boys in solitary. During the breaks, inmates were required to sit silently in a line with their heads between their legs, looking down. Boys who refused work detail were often tear-gassed in confined quarters where there was no escape. At Gainesville, girls assigned solitary confinement were not allowed to wear their own clothes but were forced to wear loose-fitting nightgowns. Expert witnesses found no therapeutic value in either solitary confinement or the practices associated with it.

The testimony of several of the experts was all the more credible because they had spent time living in two TYC institutions as "participant observers." Over defense objections, Justice accommodated the plaintiffs' request to place participant observers in the institutions, as a form of pretrial procedure. In his federal rules opinion, he wrote, "This request for discovery is perhaps extraordinary; yet this is an extraordinary case. Plaintiffs, all minor children, have alleged that the conditions of their confinement constitute violations of the First, Fifth, Sixth, Eighth, and Fourteenth Amendments. When important civil rights are in issue in complex litigation of widespread concern, a court must make every effort to enhance the fact-finding process available to counsel for both sides."[14]

One of the participant observers was Patricia Blakeney, a psychologist at the University of Texas Medical School in Galveston. She spent ten days living at the Gainesville State School for Girls in 1973 and testified at length about her experiences. Her overall impression was that Gainesville was an oppressive, impersonal environment offering little treatment or rehabilitation. "The girls are treated and seem to be just a mass, a unit of many girls, rather than each of them being individuals," she testified. "I heard phrases like 'Let 'em out,' 'Put 'em up,' which sounds as if you're herding cattle or you're manipulating objects, rather than doing something or giving directions to individual girls. The whole atmosphere was like that. It was something that was just depersonalizing." [15] Blakeney feared that had she remained in the institution any longer, she herself would have taken on the same apathetic and disinterested characteristics as the confined juveniles.

The testimony presented in open court did not come as a surprise to the Judge because he had himself toured TYC facilities the previous summer. At the suggestion of the plaintiffs and with the approval of the defendants, Justice toured the facilities in the company of Dr. Jerome Miller, the director of the Illinois Department of Children and Family Services. Miller had previously supervised the closing of large training schools in Massachusetts in favor of community-based facilities. He had long been involved with reform efforts in juvenile treatment and later would testify as an expert witness for the plaintiffs. Why would the state allow Justice to tour TYC facilities with an expert predisposed to the plaintiffs' case? Attorney York doubts that the state could have prevented it. Besides, "while Judge Justice might form some impression in that kind of trip that would turn out to be negative for us, how would he feel if he were on the bench and we'd refused to let him go? We could never get to the argument that 'if you could only see this with your own eyes, Judge, you'd know we're right.' Whatever sincerity would be gone if we'd said, 'Well, no, Judge, we don't want you to go see it.'"

Justice met Miller at the Dallas–Fort Worth airport and the two set out for Gatesville, forty miles west of Waco in the central part of the state. Justice recalls that "All the way down there he was giving me his experiences as a juvenile justice person. It was very interesting. And nearly everything that he told me came out in trial as evidence from other people, not just him."

The two spent the night at a motel. The next morning, they arose early and continued on to Mountain View State School, a prison-like edifice in Gatesville which housed the maximum-security unit for boys. Justice had drawn up an order requiring that he and Miller be admitted. He presented it to one of the guards at the gate, who took them to the superintendent. Justice remembers that the superintendent was "a rather weary looking old-timer," who appeared glad to see them. "Just go see anything you want to see; look around," the superintendent said. Miller had told Justice that the first thing to see was the maximum-security facility to get an understanding of the tone of the institution. This was where they headed.

Justice remembers what they saw vividly. "There we found these boys in cells by themselves. No contact with humanity at all. A little slot in the door where they'd push in their trays. No windows. They were just there by themselves all day long. I learned later that some of them had been in solitary as much as forty-five days. I talked to some of them, and they were fairly rational. I talked to the person, I think, that later was identified as Tweetybird at the trial. He was obviously irrational. He'd talk intelligently but drift off. I asked him about his background. He turned out to be the son of an insurance executive down in Galveston who'd apparently just given up on him. He told me he was fourteen or fifteen; he looked to me to be about twelve by his stature. It was a very unsettling experience. I'd never seen anything like that before. I'd been around prisons before; I'd been around jails all my life. But I'd never seen anything like that. These kids were so young."

According to trial testimony, Tweetybird was the name of a supposedly homosexual Mountain View inmate given to screaming fits. Testimony was produced indicating that the boy had been taken from his solitary confinement cell by a correctional officer for a "racking" in connection with some rule violation. "Racking" meant that an inmate was lined up against the wall with his hands in his pockets while a correctional officer punched him in the stomach. After "racking," Tweetybird's hands were bound behind his back and he was blindfolded. The officer twirled the boy around several times and commanded him to run to his cell, the order being accompanied by threats of another beating if he did not do so rapidly. In trying to follow the order, Tweetybird ran headlong into the corridor walls several times; finally, screaming and crying, he fell to the floor. The officer then placed his foot on Tweetybird's stomach and covered his face with a mop. Complaints by another correctional officer to a supervisor went unheeded.

Justice's tour proceeded through Mountain View. "Everything brought back to me the similarity between prisons and the military," he observes. "We saw these kids in formation running double time. And they were in very fresh uniforms. Everything looked spic and span; everything, even the cement, was very clean. All the inmates looked to be fit. I saw one thing that was interesting to me. They had a whole line, must have been fifty of them, out there in a field with pickaxes just digging away at the grass. Just gradually going forward in a line. That didn't mean much to me at the time, but afterward I found out that that was just some of the make-work activity going on there."

"We saw some of the dormitories. Observed that there were many more blacks there than I would have thought. All of the inmates had a very suppressed, distrustful attitude toward me. They'd never heard of me; to them I was just some old person, you know, that'd come off the street. They were not overly frank with me at all. I got the idea that it was a pretty heavy-handed place."

Miller and Justice also toured the Crockett State School for Girls. "It was a good bit more humane from what I could see," the Judge recalls. "A few of the girls there were in a form of isolation which was much less confining than the boys'. I got the idea that everything was very paternalistic. There wasn't much treatment going on." Crockett had been a black girls' institution and was headed by a black superintendent. Funding had always been a problem for

Crockett, unlike some of the other institutions located in districts with supportive local legislators. Largely for this reason, the plaintiffs did not base much of their case on conditions at Crockett. Nor did they attack conditions at Brownwood State Home and School for Girls, the most progressive of the six TYC institutions. The superintendent at Brownwood was Ronald (Ron) Jackson, who as an orphan had spent time in juvenile institutions and had become Turman's protégé. Jackson later succeeded Turman as TYC executive director.

The tour was an eye-opening experience, and it clearly affected the Judge—but no more so than others who had visited these facilities. Even Superintendent Jackson found Mountain View unsettling. "Mountain View was an evil place," he asserts. "You just had to walk inside to feel it. Nearly everyone I knew was uncomfortable going into Mountain View. Hell, I was one of the administrators in the system and they wouldn't even let me see some of the things going on there."

The six-week trial was not without incident. At one point, the plaintiffs' attorneys came to Justice requesting that their clients be housed elsewhere than in the Smith County jail. "Their allegation was that it was inhumane to let their clients languish in jail while the trial was in progress," Justice remembers. "They wanted to put them up in a motel here in town. And I said, 'Well, who's going to be responsible for them?' They said, 'We'll take care of them.' I asked the state, 'What's your attitude toward this request?' They said, 'We don't care; if they're going to take responsibility for them, we'll be willing to let them.'"

"I didn't like this idea at all. I told the plaintiffs' attorneys that I thought they were being very naïve in believing that their clients were going to conduct themselves properly in a motel. After all, they were juvenile delinquents. I told them, 'I think you're laying yourself in for a lot of misery.' They insisted. So against my better judgment I authorized it. Well, my better judgment was completely correct. Those kids really tore up the motel. The motel apparently had a good bit of trouble getting their money from the plaintiffs' attorneys."

Some TYC inmates regarded the experience of giving testimony as a great adventure. In an early stage of the litigation, two inmates, a seventeen-year-old boy and a sixteen-year-old girl, apparently fell in love at first sight while waiting to testify. The pair borrowed some change from Steve Bercu's mother, who was in the courtroom, purportedly to make a phone call. They walked out of the courtroom and never came back. They had several hours to get away before their disappearance was noticed. After a search of several days, they were picked up at their homes. Bercu from then on had the kids promise him that they would not run away until after they had testified.

Others gave testimony at considerable risk. Halfway through the trial, seven youths from the Mountain View maximum-security facility testified about beatings they had received from correctional officers. They told the court they were afraid they would be beaten again for what they had said on the stand. A young Beaumont boy who had testified that he had been beaten and sprayed with tear gas over a suicide attempt feared that if he were sent back, other boys would pick fights with him, jeopardizing his release. "I thought they were fully justified in their fears," Justice says. "What the state was running was penitentiaries, much on the scale of the Texas Department of Corrections." He issued an order that the youths be kept in a separate dormitory and supervised by the head caseworker, who was to report directly to the court. He also banned the use of corporal punishment on the youths. Kenneth Wooden, who sat through much of the trial and would later include a chapter on *Morales* in a book on juvenile detention, admired the courage of the youths who testified. "I began to appreciate the sacrifices these courageous children were making as day after day they sat in the witness chair and told it all to a strangely silent courtroom, knowing full well that when they left the proceedings, they would return to their keepers, who, in fact, were standing trial." [16]

Though the trial was one of high drama and intensity, there also were moments of humor. One such incident occurred—fortunately for the person involved—without the knowledge of Judge Justice. Despite a no-smoking rule, a lawyer for the state sat in the courtroom during a recess smoking a cigar. When Justice suddenly appeared and the proceedings began, the attorney quickly stuck the cigar in his pocket. Within seconds, the pocket began to catch on fire, and the attorney asked to be excused. "That was characteristic of the quality of our legal representation," a former TYC official comments. "Except for York, who was tops, the others were just bad news."

After the plaintiffs had completed four weeks of testimony, the defense presented one week of testimony and rested, much to the surprise of the other attorneys and to court personnel. Attorneys representing the Mental Health Law Project had been prepared for weeks of testimony and surmised that the short defense had something to do with rumors that James Turman, who had been TYC executive director for seventeen years, was about to resign. It was obvious from the trial that Turman did not know what was going on in his own institutions and had little knowledge of contemporary developments in juvenile corrections. He had tried to institute some reforms when first appointed but had been frustrated by the Texas Legislature. According to his successor, Ron Jackson, "Turman became isolated. He got in a position where he felt like nobody was doing it any better than we were. And I think his visits to the institutions were very superficial. He was the only one really monitoring the child care program in all of those institutions."

Jackson recalls that the trial had a devastating impact on Turman. "It just kept beating him down. He felt like people had really let him down." Jackson observes that in those days the general assumption was that TYC was doing what the people of Texas wanted. "They wanted a facility that created few problems, that was low cost, and that kept children in control. Texas has a reputation anyway of being kind of hard-assed." But times had changed. Rehabilitation and treatment had captured the attention of the juvenile correctional movement. For TYC personnel, the trial was a painful educational experience. Jackson frequently had his staff members at Brownwood sit in on the proceedings. "I made a decision that they really needed to watch this; it was an experience they just wouldn't have too many times. They'd come in for a day or two and watch, and of course go back thinking, 'My God, what's going on at our institutions?'"

The primary reason for the short defense was that the state had little to say. There were few experts who could be called upon to defend the harsh treatment of juveniles in TYC institutions. Turman had become so defensive and defiant that defense attorneys decided not to put him on the stand. Then, too, York points out that the state could not realistically put confined juveniles on the stand and have them testify what marvelous things the TYC was doing for them. Because the case was so difficult to defend, the attorneys for the state found themselves engaging in a second role of trying to influence the TYC to make their policies and practices more defensible. As York puts it, "At times, we were in the mode of suggesting advice and change, not because we wanted to run the agency, but because continuation of existing practices would mean continued legal problems."

When the trial concluded in August 1973, Justice almost immediately issued an emergency interim order sharply curtailing the use of force in TYC institutions as a violation of the Eighth Amendment's provision against cruel and unusual punishment.[17] According to the order, reasonable physical force could be used only in self-defense, defense of third persons, preventing escape, and preventing destruction of property. The threat to persons and property had to be imminent, and in the case of escape, force could not include striking and beating. Use of corporal punishment, mace, and tear gas was halted or severely limited.

The order also desegregated dormitories, prohibited make-work assignments, ended segregation of inmates for such reasons as suspected homosexual tendencies, established due process procedures and conditions for solitary and other forms of confinement, stipulated procedures for assignment of inmates to Mountain View, provided for an ombudsman at Mountain View to whom inmate complaints could be brought and who would report directly to the court, curtailed mail censorship, allowed inmates to speak in languages other than English, liberalized visitation rights, required twenty-four-hour nursing care, and required that prospective TYC employees be screened through psychological testing and psychiatric interviews to assure fitness to work with juveniles. The order further required that every employee of TYC sign a statement that the employee understood every provision in the order and that copies of the order be posted in all TYC facilities.

TYC Executive Director Turman was opposed to the order from the start, claiming that the staff could not operate the TYC without the use of force. Seemingly to prove his point, grievances over confinement conditions escalated into a full-scale riot at Gatesville almost immediately after the issuance of the order. The same scenario would repeat itself a decade later after Justice handed down his remedial order in the statewide prison case. The riots were given extensive newspaper coverage. Calling the uprising "probably 100 times worse than all the past disturbances together," Turman blamed Judge Justice for the rioting. He told reporters that he had a hard time reading the order. "This type of court order is difficult to read for a layman, and I speak as a layman." When questioned why it was hard to read, Turman told reporters, "It spells out in detail what force can be used. It's law and it's involved." He added that the order had been posted where inmates could read it, apparently implying that they had no trouble understanding that the order limited the authority of their keepers.[18]

While TYC officials blamed Judge Justice for their inability to control the situation, it was clear from media reports that Turman had allowed things to get out of control in order to embarrass the court. Jackson observes, "Whether Turman did it intentionally or not, I think those people were encouraged just to quit, to walk away from it and let the kids have control. The kids tore up the reception center at Gatesville. It spread after that." What Turman did not realize was that Judge Justice would not be affected in the least by adverse publicity. His standing in the eyes of the public or his peers has never deterred him from doing what he believes is right. As it turned out, Turman had overplayed his hand. There were calls for his resignation, which followed within a matter of days. TYC board chairman Robert Kneebone, who had been in the position eleven years, resigned as well after reformist board member Forrest Smith, a Dallas attorney, was elected chairman with the support of the third board member, Patsy Ayres of San Antonio.

There were also calls for Judge Justice to modify his order, something he saw no need to do. He recalls, "I learned about the rioting while I was at home. For some reason I had brought home a copy of my decision. I received a call from a state district judge down in Gatesville, complaining that there was a full-fledged riot out there and asserting that I should suspend my order. He said the governor and attorney general were there, and that they didn't know what to do. This was inconceivable to me. I said, 'You say the governor is there?' He said, 'Yes, sir.' I said, 'Well, let me speak to him.' So Governor Briscoe got on the line. And I said, 'Governor, I don't understand what the problem is.' He said, 'Well, the kids are out here doing all this rioting and I'm told that under your order there's nothing that can be done about it.'

"I said, 'This is inconceivable. Ask if somebody has a copy of that order.' I heard him say, 'Has anybody got a copy of that order?' And somebody gave him one. He said, 'Yes, I have a copy of it.' I told him to turn to a certain page and look at paragraph so-and-so. And I started reading from it. It gave the standard law of arrest, that if somebody is doing something that's in disobedience of the law, that you can corral him and put him in confinement, take whatever steps are necessary to control a riot. I said, 'In view of these provisions in my order, Governor, I simply don't understand why some kind of action isn't being taken.' He said, 'I don't either.' And from that point on, I never heard another word from Governor Briscoe. He was apparently convinced, just like I was, that there was something going on that was not kosher." Later, Governor Dolph Briscoe told the press that TYC officials had misinterpreted Justice's order and failed to apply the controls which the order permitted.[19]

Fifteen minutes later, Justice received a similar call from Attorney General John Hill. But Hill was not convinced that the order was sufficient. On September 13, Hill and TYC staff attorney Robert Salter met with Justice in the latter's Tyler chambers to discuss the order. Justice had C. Houston Abel, then assistant U.S. attorney, sit in on the meeting on behalf of the plaintiffs. Justice recalls that Hill began by discussing the riots and the inadequacy of the order to allow the staff to deal with them. "I was aggrieved by this, but I kept my temper. I turned to Salter. 'Mr. Salter,' I said, 'In this order I directed that its terms be read to the staff and explained to them. Was that done?' He said, 'No.' I was enraged, and I raked him over the coals very severely. Attorney General Hill just sat there, didn't say a word. He could tell that I was mad as the devil. I told Salter that if he did not do what the order required, I would hold him in contempt." Salter does not recall the conversation and maintains that he and TYC officials had bent over backward to implement whatever Justice required.

"When I got through dressing him over, I turned to Hill. And I said, 'Now I'm sorry that this riot has occurred, but the riot has occurred simply because the officials at the Texas Youth Council did not take advantage of the powers granted to them in this order, and I consider this whole thing to be their fault.'" Though he did not think it necessary, Justice said he would agree if requested to add the word "punitive" to the order to clarify for the staff that they could use whatever force was necessary to maintain order but they could not use force simply for punitive purposes. The change was never made.

Nearly a year later, Justice handed down his main decision in the case. The seventy-five-page memorandum opinion, which ran over two hundred typed pages in manuscript form and was the longest issued by Justice up to that point, incorporated the earlier emergency interim order and went considerably beyond it to detail the conditions under which juveniles were to be confined in TYC facilities.[20] Throughout, the strongly worded opinion drew extensively from trial testimony and the proposed findings of fact filed by all the parties, including the *amici,* to buttress its extensive conclusions. With an eye on the Fifth Circuit, Justice wanted to make sure that the egregious conditions existing within TYC institutions as revealed by trial testimony were clearly portrayed. "I wanted the Fifth Circuit to deal with the facts of that case, as I'd set them out, because I knew those facts were unquestionably supported by the record," he asserts. "There was no way that they could say that I had made clearly erroneous factual determinations." It took Justice and law clerks Marianne Wesson and Richard Mithoff a year, given the press of normal court business, to craft the opinion. The Judge recalls with a wince, "We didn't have word processors in those days. It was one helluva project."

The most interesting part of the 1974 memorandum opinion dealt with the right of incarcerated juveniles to treatment. The law pertaining to such a right was sparse, but both Wesson and Mithoff had had an interest in this area in law school and had done some research on the right to treatment of incarcerated juveniles while both served on the University of Texas Law Review staff. In addition, Wesson's interest in mental health law had been sharpened by her experience working at a mental hospital in Washington, D.C., prior to her last year of law school. Justice had talked at length with his friend Judge Frank M. Johnson, Jr., then a federal district court judge in Alabama, about the right to treatment. It was Johnson who described for Justice the rationale for such a right. Justice found the rationale particularly convincing in the case of incarcerated children and advanced it to support much of his order. He asserted that a state has an obligation to provide rehabilitative treatment in return for adjudging juveniles delinquent and confining them in state institutions under the relatively lax Fourteenth Amendment due process standards accorded juveniles as compared with adult criminals. In support of this proposition, he cited *Donaldson v. O'Connor,* a case which had just been decided by the Fifth Circuit involving the involuntary commitment of a person to a state mental hospital.[21]

Donaldson developed a two-part theory of a right to treatment for persons confined to mental hospitals, a theory based on the due process clause of the Fourteenth Amendment. The first part was that when the government abridges liberty, as by involuntary confinement in a state institution, it must have a permissible goal. In the case of juveniles, Justice wrote that the reason for confinement, according to Texas statutory law, was to bring about rehabilitation. Thus, "the juvenile must be given treatment lest the involuntary commitment amount to an arbitrary exercise of governmental power pro-scribed by the due process clause." [22] The second part of the theory was that the government has a *quid pro quo* obligation to justify confinement when the conventional limitations of the criminal process are lacking. The *quid pro quo* obligation here, Justice observed, was rehabilitation. While the Fifth Circuit had referenced a right to treatment for juvenile offenders in the *Donaldson* decision, only three cases were cited. One of them was Justice's earlier interim order against the use of force. A second was *Nelson v. Heyne,* a 1974 Seventh Circuit ruling, which directly held that incarcerated juveniles are entitled to a right to treatment under the Fourteenth Amendment. [23] Justice had used the lower court opinion in that case to support the right-to-treatment assertion in his earlier order. The meager precedent indicated that the right-to-treatment concept was emerging, with most of the case law developing at the very time Justice and his clerks were working on the memorandum decision.

Justice also found support for a right to treatment under the state statute providing that TYC must offer "a program of constructive training aimed at rehabilitation and reestablishment in society of children adjudged to be delin-quent." [24] "Certainly," he wrote, "the notion that the agents of the state should be permitted to exercise complete control over the lives of children by holding out the promise of treatment, and then brazenly to claim that they are under no obligation to provide such treatment, mocks the Constitution." [25]

Having found a right to treatment in the law, Justice proceeded to apply it to the facts in the TYC case. Over half of the memorandum opinion was devoted to describing existing conditions within TYC institutions and, in light of those conditions, setting forth requirements for the parties to follow to implement the constitutional right to treatment. The requirements were heavily based on the testimony of plaintiff expert witnesses. One who particu-larly impressed Judge Justice was Gisela Konopka, a professor of social work at the University of Minnesota. A refugee from Nazi Germany, Dr. Konopka had established an international reputation for her work with adolescents. She was one of the expert witnesses secured by the Mental Health Law Project. Her insight into adolescent behavior was apparent to those in the courtroom as she answered questions posed by attorney Wald. Repeatedly, Konopka testified that many of the staff members she had met at the Gainesville and Crockett schools meant well, but that the policy of institutionalization and lack of effective staff training prevented their carrying out the rehabilitative mission of the Texas Youth Council.

Konopka described in detail what the concept of treatment entailed and how existing practice fell short. One poignant example she described involved the denial of recognition and self-esteem for one particularly troubled girl at the Gainesville school. "There was a girl who was, by the way, described as exceedingly disturbed in her record, and who had been there for quite a while, and while she was in the Special Treatment Cottage, which is really a lockup, she had been discussing with one of the staff, or the staff discussed with her, that now she had to learn to behave, and I saw the contract that was written between her and the staff. Again, I don't have it verbally, but I have it, unfortunately engraved in my mind, which said something like, 'I will always be placed in the last room at the far end, so that I have on the one side of me no neighbor. Number two, I will always be the last to be called out to go to the toilet, to the school, and to everything else. I will be always walking with the house mother,' and things like that. This is a contract signed by staff and the girl and was shown to me with pride by the staff as a contract where the girl has input. I feel it was a contract, not only signed under duress, but a document again of a total diminishing of self-respect of a disturbed youngster." [26] Judge Justice listened intently to Dr. Konopka's comments. "A wonderful old woman," is how he remembers her. "I was particularly impressed with what she had to say."

TYC personnel and expert witnesses had agreed that the system then in use to assign inmates to various institutions and to develop a corrective program for them was woefully inadequate. Accordingly, Justice ruled that each child committed to the TYC was entitled to an individual treatment plan. He spelled out in minute detail how each juvenile was to be assessed to determine the components of the youth's treatment program. The qualifications of assessment personnel were also spelled out.

Though only 5 percent of TYC inmates were at their proper educational grade level and a sizable number were in need of special education, trial testimony had established that the TYC educational system was substandard. Based on the testimony of expert witnesses, Justice specified the type of testing to be used for educational assessment and for learning disabilities, as well as the required personnel necessary to conduct it. Bilingual education, which he would later order throughout Texas public schooling, was required. Each TYC inmate was to be provided an employability plan, based on extensive counseling regarding career options.

Justice asserted that in his opinion "the most striking characteristic of daily life in most TYC institutions is overwhelming monotony and regimentation." [27] The regimentation was so pronounced in boys' institutions that one expert witness testified he observed an entire dormitory of boys sitting torpidly before a broken television set.

TYC inmates were treated impersonally, often with contempt, and routinely subjected to many indignities. Boys, for example, sometimes had their heads shaved for failure to comb their hair or had their faces shaved with a pocketknife. Girls who wanted to use the restroom were required to call,

"Mama, can I go to the toilet?" At night, girls were not allowed to use the restrooms; a chamber pot was substituted. Charts showing the menstrual period of each girl were posted in the housemother's office at Gainesville and on the doors of the cottages where girls were confined at Crockett. Girls who were pregnant were given pills to trigger abortions. One of the most dramatic moments in the long trial occurred when a seventeen-year-old juvenile, T.B., testified about her miscarriage at the Gainesville State School for Girls. After taking the oath and glancing at her attorney, Steve Bercu, for support, she began her testimony. She explained that when she arrived at Gainesville, she was three months pregnant. Her sister had warned her about not taking anything that staff workers might give her. But on the evening of January 24, she did so, fearing that refusal would mean punishment.

On February 1, T.B. started bleeding badly. She informed the nurse, but no one came to see her; no treatment was prescribed. On the night of February 15, the rooms were locked as usual at 8:45 P.M. After gentle prodding by her attorney and by Judge Justice, she told a hushed courtroom what had happened that night.

T.B.: I was in my room at the time, but I was afraid to tell the nurse, because they told me if I told her, she would probably lock me up, you know, and I don't like to be locked up behind steel doors. I've got a very bad thing about them, and I was afraid to tell my house parent, so I used my—what you call it—my pot, covered it with a towel and took it to the bathroom.

Bercu: This "it" you're speaking about, is that the fetus, the baby?

T.B.: Uh-huh.

Bercu: Were you in any pain when you finally lost your baby?

T.B.: No, sir, I was just real weak, sick to my stomach.

Bercu: You were not able to tell anyone about this?

T.B.: I was afraid to. I was afraid it would get back to the nurse.

Judge Justice: Do I understand that you flushed this fetus down the commode?

T.B.: Yes, sir.[28]

Organized indoor activities at Gainesville were elementary in the extreme. One activity was "poor kitty." In this game, one girl crawled around on the floor and other girls patted her three times on the head and tried to say "poor kitty" without laughing. Other recreational activities included "hot potato" and "musical chairs." Socialization opportunities were limited.

Drawing upon expert testimony, Justice outlined the conditions under which juveniles could be confined in TYC institutions, leaving details to be worked out by the parties. Among the more notable requirements was the assignment of one person to each juvenile with responsibility for overseeing the implementation of that child's treatment plan. All persons with whom the youth associated, including houseparents, teachers, and medical personnel, were to be adequately trained to serve as members of a "treatment team." Inmates were entitled to privacy, freedom from unnecessary restraint, a coeducational living environment, and recreational opportunities. The right to treatment also required that inmates be provided with medical and psychiatric care, as well as with casework services and counseling by licensed practitioners.

From his experience in the statewide school-desegregation case, Justice recognized that remedial orders are not self-enforcing and that the plaintiffs cannot always be relied upon to bring violations to the attention of the court. Accordingly, he required the parties to develop a statewide monitoring program, headed by a monitor who would report directly to the court. Charles L. Derrick, who had been appointed ombudsman at the Mountain View facility under the August 1973 emergency interim order, was selected for this role. Prior to his appointment as ombudsman, Derrick had been chief of social services at Mountain View.

The most controversial part of the decision involved the ordered closing of Mountain View and Gatesville, along with a shift to community-based treatment facilities. Mountain View and Gatesville, the Judge observed, were beyond repair. Drawing on the testimony of Howard Ohmart, an expert witness in the field of penology, Justice wrote that the inhumane rituals and codes coupled with the brutal history of beatings, tear-gassing, and solitary confinement associated with both institutions were rooted within their very brick and mortar. Noting that Ohmart labeled Mountain View as worse than the notorious Angola Prison in Louisiana, Justice observed that "If ever confinement in an institution constituted a form of cruel and unusual punishment, Gatesville and Mountain View fully meet the applicable criteria." [29]

He observed that "an important incident of the right to treatment is the right of each individual to the least restrictive alternative treatment that is consistent with the purpose of his custody." [30] This being so, Justice found confinement of most TYC inmates in rural state institutions far from their homes counterproductive. He noted that the National Advisory Commission on Criminal Justice Standards and Goals had called for the closing of state institutions, concluding that institutionalization of juvenile offenders is more likely to foster delinquent and criminal behavior than to promote reform and reintegration into society. Contemplating the development of foster homes, supervised probation, group homes, halfway houses, outpatient clinics, and supervised home placement, Justice ordered that the TYC "must cease to institutionalize any juveniles except those who are found by a responsible professional assessment to be unsuited for any less restrictive, alternative form of rehabilitative treatment."[31] Those who were to be confined in state institutions were entitled to all of the court-ordered reforms previously noted, including staffing "in virtually a one-to-one ratio." The parties were directed to meet to develop the terms of a final remedial decree implementing the reforms spelled out in the memorandum opinion. If no compliance plan could be agreed upon, Justice himself would develop one.

The opinion was a remarkable demonstration of the powers of an activist federal district court, both in identifying rights and in determining remedies. The opinion was generally greeted favorably in the press insofar as the excesses of the TYC were concerned. Newspapers found the case good copy. But the court-mandated remedies, particularly the closing of the two institutions and the movement to community-based treatment facilities, were considered an unwarranted interference with the internal operations of a state agency and with state sovereignty. In an editorial entitled "Justice's Injustice," the conservative *Dallas Morning News* stated that Justice's "presumption boggles the mind." Claiming that his order "affronts the Constitution," the *News* questioned his authority to close a state institution. "Justice could, with equal philosophical ease, order the Legislature converted to a single house or the governorship made appointive." The editorial applauded the state's intention to appeal.[32]

The state initially sought a stay from the Fifth Circuit on the Judge's order, which required the parties to meet within thirty days to work out a compliance plan for implementing the extensive reforms. The stay was denied by both the appeals court and Supreme Court Justice Lewis F. Powell, Jr. The attempt to get a stay delayed negotiations for three months. The state also appealed Justice's decision rejecting the request for a three-judge court, as well as his reliance on a constitutional right to treatment. While this appeal was pending, the parties began deliberations on a compliance plan, but without much success. According to Jackson, who had replaced Turman following the Mountain View riots in September 1973, the plan put forward by the plaintiffs was unacceptable. "It was really a wild plan, calling for the immediate closure of Gatesville and Mountain View, the scaling down of other institutions, the placement of kids in foster care programs that were not in existence across the state—proposals that we just didn't feel comfortable with." Jackson also knew that the Texas Legislature would balk at supporting such a plan.

As it was, many members of the legislature were incensed with Justice's ruling. As the 1975 session geared up, several suggested that one of the community-based facilities be established on the vacant lot next to the Judge's house. In the 1977 session a bill to this effect was introduced by Representative Emmett Whitehead of Rusk. It passed the House but later died in the Senate. Though irritated by the move, Justice was not concerned. "Apparently it had never occurred to them that another federal judge would have immediately enjoined any such legislation even if it had passed because the state government cannot take action directed toward the punishment of a federal judge who decided against them," he says. "So I regarded the whole thing as being frivolous. But it occasioned a great deal of amusement, apparently, to those who were involved."

Indeed it did. The Texas Legislature has been known to be the scene of a good many shenanigans. The *Morales* decision provided an opportunity for several more. As the story goes, members of the House arranged to have someone purporting to be a U.S. marshal request permission to enter the chambers during the 1977 session. Permission was granted. The "marshal" walked over to Representative Whitehead and served him with papers supposedly signed by Judge Justice ordering him to appear in federal court to account for his actions. The prank caught Whitehead's attention, to say the least. Later several of his colleagues got him to sign in jest a hastily scribbled declaration which read, "Now comes Emmett W. Whitehead, state representative from District 15 who does now swear (does he swear!) that he will from this day forward cease and desist and quit cold from introducing any more Judge William Wayne Justice bills. He does not make any such promises about how he will vote on any such bill if it should be introduced by some other member. Honest Injun!"

Despite the lack of progress on writing a compliance plan, TYC officials had not been standing still.[33] The glaring deficiencies of juvenile corrections in Texas could no longer be ignored. Board chairman Forrest Smith was committed to reform. Within two years of his appointment as a board member in 1968, he had become disenchanted with TYC operations. "There simply were too many reports of abuses for me to continue to accept the administration's assertion that TYC was the third-best juvenile justice system in the United States," he says. The lawsuit added credence to his belief that abuses were not isolated incidents but pervasive throughout the system. Jackson too believed that reform was necessary. Between the time the lawsuit ended in the fall of 1973 and Justice's memorandum decision a year later, TYC had made most of its institutions coeducational and had eliminated the censoring of mail, allowed students to speak in Spanish, and provided due process procedures for confining inmates in secure facilities. Using federal funds, the TYC established a master planning committee in 1974 to begin moving toward community-based correctional programs.

But in-fighting among conservatives and liberals at the administrative and board levels, coupled with bureaucratic inertia, hampered progress. Though opposed to Justice's micromanagement of TYC, Smith had long supported juvenile correctional reforms, including the movement toward community-based programs. "I used the court order as an impetus for change in the juvenile justice system statewide," Smith points out. "It coincided with what I felt ought to be done." His eagerness for change alienated fellow board member Don Workman and Governor Dolph Briscoe, who was committed to keeping existing TYC institutions open—Gatesville and Mountain View had employed nine hundred people in 1971 and pumped nearly $6 million into the Gatesville economy in payroll alone—and who remained skeptical of community-based programs. Smith also had trouble working with TYC officials, including Ron Jackson, whom Smith had tagged as Turman's replacement. "I was perceived as the wild-eyed liberal from Dallas who wanted to do community-based programs," Smith admits. "When I lost the support of the governor, I also lost the support of Ron Jackson. I became chairman in name only." The extensive publicity given TYC activities during this period aggravated tensions. Even Jackson's tenure was not secure until January 1974, when the board finally voted unanimously to appoint him executive director.

Still, progress toward a fundamental change in TYC operation was evident. Under the pressure of the court order and with the support of the TYC board, the legislature appropriated $9 million in 1975 to support community-based programs, considerably less than TYC had requested but more than the governor wanted. Previously, all resources appropriated for the Texas Youth Council had been devoted to the operation of state institutions. One of the selling points to the legislators was that community-based programs were purported to be considerably cheaper. The legislature also approved the transfer of Mountain View to the Texas Department of Corrections, though the latter really did not want it, and expanded the TYC board to six members. Political problems arose again later that year when Briscoe appointed conservative Tyler Baptist minister William Shamburger, long an outspoken critic of Judge Justice, to replace Smith, whom the governor declined to reappoint. Patsy Ayres of San Antonio, who supported community programs, was elected chairperson. But later the board voted to trim back her powers and limit her tenure as chair. Politics continued to plague the TYC in 1976, when Briscoe, with support from some of the board members, impounded money appropriated for community assistance programs. The money was later released after Attorney General John Hill issued an opinion against the impoundment.

Meanwhile, Judge Justice refused to accept the state's attempts to secure dismissal of the suit on the basis of the changes they were in the process of making and ordered negotiations to continue toward working out a compliance plan. He had hoped to have a final order in place in time for the 1975 legislative session but was unable to do so. Looking back, Justice says that he recognized that the state felt "a sense of illegitimacy" in the order. "I despaired of there being any real progress in reaching any kind of agreement with the parties as to how the order was to be enforced." It was Justice's intention, however, to wait to issue his own remedial decree until the Fifth Circuit affirmed his memorandum opinion. He fully anticipated that the Fifth Circuit would affirm and was surprised when it did not in July 1976.[34]

The appeals court, composed of two Johnson appointees, Robert A. Ainsworth, Jr., and Lewis R. Morgan, and Nixon appointee Paul H. Roney, concluded that the practices under which the TYC was being operated were the equivalent of a statute with statewide applicability. This being so, Congress had established that such challenges must be heard by a three-judge panel. The court added, "Here, granting the relief sought would entail extensive alterations in virtually every phase of TYC operations. It is precisely this type of thoroughgoing disruption of a state's autonomous implementation of its own legislative and administrative policies that warrants the added deliberation and procedural protection provided by the three-judge court statute."[35] The case was remanded for a new trial. The reversal put an end to further negotiations between the parties.

In an editorial entitled "Judicial Coup d'Etat," the *Dallas Morning News* expressed the views of many when it applauded the Fifth Circuit's reversal. Decrying federal court involvement with state affairs, the *News* took pleasure in the rebuke to Justice. "For the moment, a single presumptuous jurist has been restrained from taking charge of the Texas Youth Council. If it is a small victory, it is nonetheless a victory to savor."[36]

For whatever reason, the Fifth Circuit had finessed Judge Justice's carefully designed strategy of having the facts set forth with such thoroughness that they could not be overlooked or rejected. Jutice doubted the ruling would stand up on appeal to the Supreme Court. "I had had a lengthy hearing about the question of the three-judge court at the beginning of the case," he points out. "I became convinced that there were no state rules that were applicable. All of the rules and regulations that I had to consider had to do with just particular institutions." His prophecy was correct. The plaintiffs appealed the ruling to the U.S. Supreme Court, which reversed it in a short *per curiam* decision (a decision issued "by the court," with no signed opinion) seven months later. It sent the case back to the Fifth Circuit for consideration of Justice's judgment on the merits.[37]

When the Fifth Circuit first reversed Justice's decision, TYC officials promptly dismissed the court monitor, Charles Derrick, who had become a thorn in their side. In truth, the role of monitor had never lived up to its potential. Justice had envisioned a statewide monitoring system for TYC. It was never established. Derrick's monitoring activities were limited to Mountain View. Since the order was not specific as to how the monitor should go about his tasks, Derrick elected to provide the court and the parties with reports of every complaint he received without comment. He knew that some of the complaints were fabrications but conducted no investigations because he believed that to be the function of TYC and/or the plaintiffs. The steady stream of reports, together with notes about TYC meetings which he was free to attend under the order, eventually undermined his position in the TYC. At one point, the Mountain View superintendent complained in a letter to Judge Justice, "He sends to you that which is given to him as is. Yet, the weight of his office, as outlined in your Order, lends face validity to his reports. . . . If this were not the case, then such references to his reports (many of which represent unsubstantiated allegations) would not be referred to so heavily by Plaintiffs in support of their claims that we are no different than our infamous predecessors." [38]

When Derrick was notified of his dismissal, he contacted Justice and told him the state was about to seize his records. Justice sent a U.S. marshal to impound them. Because of the Fifth Circuit reversal, the Judge was powerless to reinstate Derrick. But he regretted that his monitor had gotten caught in the cross fire. "He was a genuinely good man, and I regard what happened to him as a tragedy," Justice says. It was also a lesson for the Judge, who would discard use of a monitor in the *Ruiz* prison case in favor of an independent special master with extensive investigatory power.

When the case came back to the Fifth Circuit, the appeals court once again avoided following the path the Judge had laid out. Writing for the panel a second time, Circuit Judge Ainsworth concluded that sufficient time had lapsed to warrant a new trial. "Many of the objectionable practices in the Texas juvenile system may already have been ended. Further, these changes may indicate a new attitude on the part of the TYC that would eliminate the risk of further constitutional violations." [39] He added that consideration of additional evidence was especially warranted since Justice's order constituted "significant federal intrusion into a state's affairs." Justice believes the Fifth Circuit was "dead wrong" in ordering a new trial. "I think I was entitled to have that case decided on the record that was made."

In addition to remanding the case for additional hearings, the appeals panel confined Justice to the cruel and unusual punishment clause of the Eighth Amendment. Between the time Justice had issued his decision and the Fifth Circuit consideration of the matter, the U.S. Supreme Court had reversed the Fifth Circuit's ruling supporting a right to treatment in *Donaldson v. O'Con-*

nor. [40] Accordingly, the appeals court observed that the case law had not universally accepted a constitutional right to treatment even for the mentally ill. The court pointed out that "The argument for a right to treatment is even less strong as related to juvenile offenders." It noted that adult criminals are not entitled to a right to treatment and that, like adult criminals, many juveniles who are confined are dangerous. It hastened to add, however, that as a matter of social policy the rehabilitation of juveniles might be desirable.

Rejection of a right to treatment had the effect of limiting Justice's authority to sustain many of the reforms he had previously ordered. The appeals panel itself acknowledged that "the eighth amendment will not require the state to provide extensive vocational training, detailed personality assessments or coeducational facilities. The choice of providing these services properly remains with the State of Texas herein." [41]

The appeals panel further pointed out the problems associated with a detailed and specific remedial order in an area where the law is uncertain. It noted in a footnote, for example, that an order that guards cease beating prisoners will prevent cruel and unusual punishment. But a court cannot be sure that giving all juveniles the Weschler IQ test, adjusted for minority youths, will achieve rehabilitation. Such matters should be left to TYC personnel in light of new treatments and testing techniques. "The passage of time will render obsolete many of the requirements found in the District Court opinion."

The passage of time does indeed pose a problem for detailed remedial orders involving state institutions like the TYC when operational paradigms change. At the time of the lawsuit, the rehabilitative view was in ascendancy. Judge Justice was persuaded by expert testimony that the right to treatment in the least restrictive environment was the preferred approach. He himself readily admits to no specialized knowledge about juvenile corrections. "The only thing I know about juvenile justice and delinquency is what I heard in the six weeks trial." He also acknowledges that the science of juvenile corrections is soft. "It's a cycle, I think. They'll be really hard-nosed for a while, and then they realize that that doesn't work. And then they become more tolerant. But, of course, they still don't get the result they want. So they get impatient again and go back to the old feeling that 'we'll just slap them in there and forget about them.'"

Since becoming a federal circuit court judge, Patricia Wald, one of the Mental Health Law Project attorneys, has developed some reservations about the wisdom of prolonged judicial involvement in the operations of major state institutions through detailed remedial orders. "I think there's been disenchantment, some of which I share, as to how much a lawsuit can control the practices of another institution over a long period of time. I think courts can move into a situation that's logjammed or that really needs intervention, and make some quick relief. Except in extreme cases, I don't think they should hang on for two decades as a kind of overseer."

Judge Justice asserts that limited court involvement may not provoke a strong commitment to change unconstitutional practices. "*Morales* was one of the cases where the Fifth Circuit refused to recognize that if institutional authorities do not exhibit a willingness to conform to constitutional standards and actively oppose the efforts of the courts to impose constitutional conditions in their institution, detailed orders under those circumstances are necessary." In a 1980 speech delivered at the John F. Kennedy School of Government at Harvard University, he likened the action of the court to that of dealing with a mule: "Old hands in the mule business say that the best way to get a mule's attention is to hit it hard, right between the eyes, with a single-tree. Similarly, to get the attention of an intransigent governmental organization, a court must hit it right between the eyes with an attention-getting order—one that is detailed, that spells things out, that makes the agency cognizant of its constitutional duties and aware of the specific and precise steps it must take to satisfy those duties."

With the Fifth Circuit remand, Judge Justice's ability to oversee the operations of the TYC was significantly diminished. But he still retained authority to require the state to comply with the Eighth Amendment. He recalls, "The other parts of my docket were pressing heavily; the plaintiffs' attorneys were not showing a great deal of enthusiasm to retry the case; so it kind of stewed along on the docket for several years. During that period, I was dealing with the *Ruiz* case. I knew I was going to have to get back to it. Then lo and behold, one day Peter Sandmann announced to me that they had reached a settlement in the case. I was fairly incredulous."

Though TYC never considered Justice's 1974 order its blueprint for reform—Jackson says, "We ignored it"—both the trial and the order had had a catalytic effect in establishing momentum in the TYC to develop a first-class system. The Texas Legislature generally supported reform as well, with new legislation enacted each session. Though some, including former TYC board chairman Forrest Smith, had assumed that with judicial pressure off, little more would be done, the reform effort continued. New staff members, the court-appointed ombudsman, and new programs had ended most of the complaints about inhumane treatment. By 1976, halfway houses were operating in Austin, Corpus Christi, Dallas, and Houston, with more planned for the future. TYC was increasingly contracting with county juvenile probation departments to operate residential treatment centers. The resulting decline in institutional population largely eliminated the need for Gatesville, which was phased out.[42] By 1983, when the settlement was first proposed to Judge Justice, it was estimated that 70 percent of the reforms specified in his 1974 order had been implemented.

Not everyone, of course, approved the direction TYC was taking. TYC board member Don Workman told a newspaper reporter in 1983, "I'm not sure we haven't transferred the corporal punishment from the kids who go through the courts to the victims they prey on after escaping from an unstructured institution."[43] He recalled one boy, guilty of multiple rapes, who was paroled after three months in a state school. The boy raped a cheerleader soon after his release. "That girl will be affected for life, and I'm not sure we did the boy a favor, either. That court decision ordered us to get our numbers down—but did we do the best thing for that boy?" Workman maintained the reforms would have been less costly if they had been implemented gradually. He placed responsibility for the rapid pace of reform on Judge Justice, though Justice had remained in the background during most of this time. "There's a man appointed for life who doesn't answer to the taxpayers. We've made some radical changes and made them fast, but I don't think we've done a good job for the taxpayers over the last ten years."

After preparing for another trial between 1978 and 1981, the parties moved toward settlement. Peter Sandmann, lead counsel for the plaintiff class (Steve Bercu was no longer involved in the case), concluded that with the right to treatment no longer a viable legal argument, "the institutions had improved enough that we could not win another lawsuit." Both sides were also deterred by the costs of litigating another round in Justice's court. Democrats Mark White and Jim Mattox, who had been elected in 1982 as governor and attorney general respectively, wanted to settle a number of long-running cases, *Morales* among them. After lengthy negotiations, a settlement agreement incorporating most of the components of the 1974 remedial order was presented to the Judge on March 3, 1983.

At a hearing on April 15, an angry Judge Justice surprised both parties by rejecting the settlement from the bench as "unworkable, unfeasible, and simply not worthy of approval." He observed, "This is very important litigation, and I don't propose to see it go down the drain."[44] Part of his objection centered on the weak enforcement provision. The settlement was to be in the form of a contract between the parties, the enforcement of which would take place in a state court. This had the effect of removing the case from Justice's jurisdiction. Before the Judge would consent to giving it up, he wanted to assure himself that the interests of incarcerated juveniles would be safeguarded. He found the proposed settlement lacking in this regard. He was highly critical of attorney Sandmann for his role in negotiating the flawed agreement.

The parties quickly revised the agreement and resubmitted it to the court.

On June 28, Justice again rejected the amended agreement. In a written order, he questioned whether Peter Sandmann might have become overly trustful of the defendants, based on reforms made to date. Such trust, Justice wrote, "must be tempered, nonetheless, by the recognition that personnel will inevitably change, and that, just over a decade ago, many of the individuals who then comprised the officialdom of TYC, and at least one of the attorneys who represents them, unregenerately and callously endeavored to preserve and perpetuate debased, execrable institutions in which juveniles were tortured and terrorized."[45]

Judge Justice's careful study of the agreement convinced him that the agreed-upon committee to monitor TYC over a four-year period had little power and was seriously underfunded. The agreement required the committee to announce its annual inspections in advance. Announced visits, he observed, would give the TYC time to script and rehearse misleading presentations. Staff personnel were not required to answer committee members' questions. Successors to the original three committee members required approval by the defendants. Justice found the committee's $60,000 annual budget to be "a niggardly sum to accomplish its many contemplated purposes." He also noted that the agreement provided $295,000 in plaintiffs' attorney fees and, in a thinly veiled rebuke, observed that "the lengthy postponement of payment (over a decade in this instance) may severely tax the financial vitality of a law firm, and unwittingly color the judgment of otherwise circumspect counsel. Under those circumstances, robust representation may flag."[46]

Sandmann was shocked at the criticism he had received both at the April 15 hearing and in the memorandum opinion, and considers it unwarranted. "In retrospect, I think that Judge Justice didn't think we had prepared him enough to justify approving the settlement," he says. Sandmann questions why Justice never requested an evidentiary hearing to demonstrate support for the settlement if he thought it was important. "Basically," the attorney concludes, "we were kind of set up." He also points out that the $295,000 went to the Youth Law Center, not to him. "I think the Judge thought I was getting $295,000 out of that case."

The agreement did appear to favor the state. TYC Executive Director Ron Jackson acknowledges that this time around the agency was negotiating from a position of strength. "We'd gone into community-based programs, and we had some excellent due process procedures in place throughout the system. Many on the plaintiffs' side, including Sandmann, were pretty impressed with the changes that'd been made." He also points out that TYC bargaining power was enhanced by a tough negotiator in the person of attorney Richel Rivers, whom Jackson managed to retain to represent TYC after she had left the attorney general's office to enter private practice in 1980.

Jackson was not surprised that Justice refused to go along. "It was, I think, more than anything else, the money issue," he believes. "They couldn't adequately monitor the settlement agreement. And that was our strategy. We didn't want them monitoring. And he caught it immediately."

Justice was not about to rush into anything. He recalls, "I was being very careful about all this. I was very suspicious that things were not as represented to me. I didn't want all of my work to go for nothing." Rather than rely on the word of the parties, he decided to find out for himself. Over the objections of the parties, he appointed Linda Singer, an expert in the field of juvenile corrections, to make an independent study on behalf of the court. At the same time, he appointed Tyler attorney Otis Carroll, known locally as "The Big O," guardian *ad litem* for the class of incarcerated juveniles. When a class action is settled and the parties have agreed upon a fee for the plaintiffs' attorney, it is generally conceded that there is an apparent conflict of interest between the attorney and the class because it is feared the attorney is more interested in getting the fee than in seeing to the interests of the class. "I have always thought it to be unethical for a lawyer to settle on his fee in a class action case," Justice maintains. "I think it ought to be left to the court to set his fee. But that was the situation presented to me. So in accord with the *Manual for Complex Litigation,* I appointed another lawyer to represent the interests of the class."

Carroll was to act as an independent judge of any further proposed settlements on behalf of incarcerated juveniles. He notes an old saying in East Texas that the job of an *ad litem* attorney is to "sit at the counsel table, keep your mouth shut, and sign where the big attorneys tell you to." But Justice let both Singer and Carroll know that he expected a lot more than rubber stamps.

The Judge's decision to appoint Singer forced Sandmann and attorneys for the TYC to look again at the matter of verifying improvements in the system. At a hearing in July 1983, they proposed that outside observers make on-site inspections and report their findings to the court. Justice agreed to suspend appointment of Singer pending the report.

The parties continued to work on the agreement in the hopes of avoiding another trial. Carroll recalls that negotiations became tense toward the end. Both Sandmann and the state were tired of the case. As a former assistant U.S. attorney, Carroll had seen TYC lawyer Rivers argue on behalf of the state in the prison litigation and regarded her as "openly contemptuous" of Justice. At times he doubted that a settlement could ever be reached. So did Assistant Attorney General David Richards, representing the TYC in the negotiations. Richards, who as a civil rights attorney had successfully argued a number of voter discrimination cases before Justice, wondered if the Judge would ever be willing to release the case from his docket, the primary goal of the state. Toward the end of the negotiations, Carroll found himself conducting shuttle diplomacy as he moved from office to office in the courthouse working with the parties and Judge Justice to find common grounds of agreement.

One major area of controversy was the state's desire to include language allowing bad-faith damages to be filed against persons bringing lawsuits against the TYC. Justice flatly refused to condone any language which would have a chilling effect on the rights of TYC inmates to challenge TYC practices. Another was the continuing question of enforcement of the settlement. At one point, David Richards became so incensed with Justice that he threatened to call the airport and order the state plane's engines started. Ultimately, however, everyone connected with the lawsuit recognized that settlement was preferable to another trial. On April 16, 1984, Justice approved the second amended agreement proposed by the parties.

Justice recalls that at the settlement hearing, the outside expert witnesses selected by the parties "were almost lyrical in their praise of the settlement." Indeed, Sandmann had told the witnesses that in the interest of getting the case settled, he hoped they would mute criticism as much as they felt they could. Dean Fixsen, a psychologist and director of the off-campus program at Father Flanagan's Boys Home in Boystown, Nebraska, testified at length about the improvements he had seen in touring TYC facilities. Among those he described were the elimination of physical abuse and make-work assignments, the policy of having an individualized program plan for each inmate and placing each in the least restrictive environment appropriate to the plan, the development of a system of rules for student behavior and of due process procedures for discipline, the end to racial segregation and conversion to coeducation, the development of a grievance system, the implementation of a record-keeping system, the hiring of trained professional staff members, the redesign of the physical plant to afford youths privacy and personal security, and the development of a recreational system.

Fixsen noted that he had reviewed the standards set out by various child-welfare accrediting bodies and concluded that most of the TYC institutions were in compliance. He concluded, "I think they (TYC officials) deserve a round of applause, really, from all of us for the kinds of changes that they have made in their institutions over a long period of time." [47]

Daniel Creson, a psychiatrist at the University of Texas Medical Branch in Houston who had toured TYC facilities with plaintiffs' counsel prior to the beginning of the lawsuit and again during the settlement negotiations, seconded Fixsen's conclusions. He testified that the differences he found from his early tours were "really astounding." Both Fixsen and Creson, together with a third expert witness from New York, recommended that Justice approve the settlement.

Noting that his initial objections had been corrected, Judge Justice told a courtroom full of smiling attorneys that he would dismiss the action from his docket with the understanding that if the monitoring committee found it impossible to monitor or enforce the provisions of the agreement, the court would again intervene.[48] He concluded the hearing by complimenting both sides for their assiduous efforts to arrive at a settlement. "I am sincerely hopeful that this is the last that this court will ever see of *Morales v. Turman.* . . . It is obvious that the defendant Texas Youth Commission has made enormous strides since 1974 when this action came before this court, and I think they are to be commended for the wonderful changes that have been wrought in the system."[49] It had cost the state over $600,000 in plaintiffs' attorney fees, the time and expense of defending the agency, plus the cost of making the changes.[50]

Enormous strides had been made in reforming a state institution which the trial had revealed to be a throwback to an earlier age of repression and violence. Much of the credit must go to Ron Jackson, who accepted the challenge of reform despite the Fifth Circuit reversal. The stability of leadership he engendered in the fourteen years from the memorandum opinion in 1974 to the termination of the monitoring committee in 1988 provided a setting in which the reforms could take root. His tenure also resulted in the recruitment and training of a whole new cadre of TYC staff members. Interestingly, Judge Justice did not initially view Jackson as a supporter of reform. He recalls that "All during the trial, Jackson had this kind of gloomy, morose appearance on his face like he was disapproving of everything that was happening. I got the idea he was totally disapproving of my actions. But from what he's done since he's become director, it would seem that he was in entire sympathy with my order." The Texas Legislature deserves credit as well for providing support for the reform efforts despite initial reluctance. Once it freed itself from the paralysis of political infighting, the TYC Board of Directors also joined the movement toward reform.

But it is Judge Justice who deserves major credit for instigating a process of change which would have been unlikely to occur in the absence of his remedial order. Even after the Fifth Circuit remand, he prompted the parties to take the case seriously by keeping the door open to a retrial and by his close reading of the proposed settlement agreement. Allen F. Breed, former chairman of the National Institute of Corrections, who headed up the monitoring committee, considers *Morales* a sterling example of successful court-induced change. At a meeting of TYC officials and committee members in the Judge's chambers on November 19, 1987, the words of praise for what had been accomplished were effusive. In fact, the session had become a love-fest to such an extent that when it was over and the participants had left, the Judge laughingly held up his trouser legs and stepped gingerly around his secretary's office as though the floor were covered with manure.

It is important to note that Breed was talking about "court-*induced* change," not court-mandated change. The success of *Morales* was a result of the willingness of the TYC and the Texas Legislature to embrace much that was in the 1974 order as their own desire for the future. In *Morales* the Judge pointed the way, and the state agreed to follow. Had the TYC and the Texas Legislature been recalcitrant, it is unlikely that the Judge could have achieved compliance with his 1974 order, particularly since the Fifth Circuit undercut his ability to institute change when it threw out the right-to-treatment rationale.

How good has the TYC become? According to the monitoring team, Texas is not at the top of the list of states which have decentralized juvenile corrections, though it has made significant strides in this direction. However, insofar as quality of life in state institutions, coupled with a strong community-based program, is concerned, Texas ranks first. In fact, the monitoring team told Judge Justice at the November 1987 meeting that they frequently use Texas as a model to other states of how a successful nonpunitive juvenile correctional program can be established and run. The Judge commented wryly, "Back in 1972 I would never have believed that the Texas Youth Council might someday serve as a model for anyone."

It is less clear whether the TYC is more effective in rehabilitating juvenile offenders. Statistical data are sparse: 33 percent of TYC inmates will return to the TYC or be sent to Texas prisons within three years of their release. Methodological problems and population differences make pre-*Morales* comparisons risky. Even if meaningful comparisons were possible, Ron Jackson does not believe there would be much change. "I don't think you would see much change in recidivism or in educational achievement. If there is a change, you will see it in the quality of life in the sense that kids are not walking away from an institution feeling that they've been severely abused the whole time they were there."[51]

Part of the reason for the absence of significant change lies in the fact that the clients of TYC state institutions are increasingly the hard-core delinquents. The others are more apt to be processed through community-based programs. In light of changing clientele, it has been argued that the average length of stay—six months—is insufficient for effective behavior change in these youths. Jackson disagrees that a longer stay would produce better results. "The juvenile judges feel frustration with the return of these people to their court. Their desire is to get them out of the court and out of the community for a long period of time. You're asking an agency with limited resources which receives a hard-core delinquent of an average age of fifteen or sixteen to turn that kid's life around. It's not going to happen." Jackson believes that if intervention is to be effective, it must begin much earlier in the community through highly individualized—and expensive—treatment programs.

While the 1974 *Morales* order was a catalyst for overhaul of the Texas Youth Commission, its importance is far greater. The decision was the first from a federal court to set forth requirements for the treatment of juveniles in state institutions. National youth correctional associations such as the American Correctional Association and the National Advisory Council for Juvenile Justice promulgated standards for juvenile justice systems based on *Morales*. Dean Fixsen testified at the final settlement hearing that the decision also had a great impact on standards in the mental health and foster-care fields.

Despite a movement in recent years away from the rehabilitative paradigm which produced it, *Morales* remains the doctrinal decision for the treatment of juveniles incarcerated in state institutions. That this has occurred is even more remarkable for a decision that was initially reversed on appeal and later remanded for a new trial that was never held. When TYC attorney Robert Salter and his successor, Neil Nichols, attended a correctional conference in San Francisco not long after the Fifth Circuit reversal, they were asked repeatedly about the impact of *Morales* on the TYC from persons who considered it the seminal decision on juvenile treatment. Salter found it "simply amazing that the juvenile industry in the country could pick up the decision as though it were the last word from the highest judicial authority and carry it around the country so that juvenile correctional programs everywhere were affected by Judge Justice's 1974 order."

Amazing or not, the *Morales* decision has become a landmark that is likely to survive methodological changes within the juvenile correctional field. The reason lies in the basic humaneness which underlies it, a humaneness that Judge Justice believes the law should strive for. "I'll say this as a general proposition: I don't believe in being inhumane," Justice asserts. "Whether it's in institutions or outside of institutions, I just think it is counterproductive to be inhumane." That ethical principle underlies his decision in *Morales v. Turman* and goes a long way to explain its durability.

CHAPTER 7

The First Amendment

Since his days in Mrs. Tillman Owen's sixth-grade history class in the Athens Grammar School, William Wayne Justice has been a staunch supporter of the First Amendment freedoms of speech, press, religion, and assembly.[1] Mrs. Owen taught him that unless one hears all sides of an issue, one cannot ascertain what the truth is. That simple proposition made sense to Justice as a boy of eleven and has continued to make sense to him through the years.

The quintessential use of freedom of expression is to criticize government officials. In this context, Justice's position on the First Amendment is extreme. "In taking advantage of their rights under the First Amendment, persons can criticize public officials to the ultimate degree," he maintains. A corollary of wide-open, robust speech is that often the sensibilities of those on the receiving end are hurt. No one knows this better than Justice himself, for the Judge has probably been subjected to more public vilification than any other Texas public official. "I sometimes get very displeased with the inaccuracies that are so frequent in the news media," he admits, "but even though I get angry, I still maintain their right to say what they want to say—even when they're wrong."

Justice's reverence for the First Amendment is so great that even in jest he finds it difficult to talk about curtailing its freedoms. Some years ago, his clerks hosted a bookburning party. Circulars were mailed to guests, asking that they bring along a book to be burned. Houston attorney and professional humorist Kirk Purcell was master of ceremonies. Purcell held each book aloft, made some humorous comments about its sinful nature, and tossed it into a flaming fifty-gallon barrel. Justice was not amused. "I thought it was highly inappropriate." Purcell also admits to having second thoughts. But, contrary to some reports, the Judge did not walk away from the festivities—"except perhaps to get another beer."

Justice can recall no First Amendment cases he handled either as an attorney in private practice or as a U.S. attorney. But as a judge, he has had an opportunity to develop and apply his First Amendment jurisprudence in a number of decisions. Though the settings changed, Justice's support for First Amendment freedoms has remained consistently strong, as the representative cases discussed in this chapter reveal.

Freedom of Speech on the University Campus: *Duke v. North Texas State University*

While the U.S. Supreme Court had extended First Amendment rights to public school and college students and teachers by the early 1970s, the limits remained unclear.[2] Justice's first major First Amendment case involved a college instructor who was ousted during the tumultuous Vietnam protest era.

Elizabeth Anne Duke was a teaching assistant in the English Department at North Texas State University (now the University of North Texas) in Denton, about thirty-five miles north of Dallas and Fort Worth. She had been given a one-year teaching contract in 1967–1968 and again in 1969–1970. As with her two previous contracts, her one-year teaching contract for 1970–1971 was conditioned upon sufficient enrollment.

Following a stint in Chicago working with a ghetto ministry in the late 1960s, Duke had become involved in the student protest movement. She organized the "People's Community Center," an organizational center for anti-discrimination and antiwar activities, across from the North Texas State University campus. The community center also served as a home for itinerant student activists.

Duke's tribulations with the law began when she helped organize and publicize a rock concert to be held in a park on the university campus. On July 30, 1970, the day of the concert, Duke handed out leaflets announcing the concert to students attending a freshman campus orientation session. In addition to announcing the concert, the leaflets challenged students to question their status at the university. For example, students were challenged not to be a "sucker—paying high tuition while the fat cats get fatter." "Come to the park tonight at 7:30," the leaflets urged, "to dig on some music and to rap about where we are and what we can create."

At the concert, Duke made a speech on the general subject of oppression. She criticized university officials and policies. At one point, she stated that the "system" at the university "fucks over" students. A second rock concert was scheduled for August 3 but was halted by university officials because it had not met university requirements of being sponsored by a campus student organization. Before the public address system was turned off, Duke mounted the platform to assert that the real reason for the shutdown was the speech she had made on July 30.

On August 25 Duke was informed that her teaching assistantship had been canceled on the basis of written statements reporting her use of obscene language and conduct unbecoming an instructor in front of students and others on the university campus. Her appeal of this decision was directed to the President's Cabinet, a body composed of the acting president and three vice presidents, all but one of whom had played some role in the investigation of her activities. A campus American Association of University Professors (AAUP) committee urged that her appeal be taken to the University Tenure Committee rather than the Cabinet, because the latter did not normally hear such matters. The recommendation was denied. The AAUP committee then asked that faculty representatives be allowed to attend Duke's hearing, but that request, too, was denied.

The formal due process hearing was held on September 23. Both sides were represented by attorneys. Following the hearing, the Cabinet upheld Duke's dismissal. She appealed to the Board of Regents. Several days before the regents met, Acting President John L. Carter, Jr., sent each regent a personal and confidential letter enclosing a copy of a long harangue Duke had written against the university and the Board of Regents for stalling on her case, published in a local paper. The Board of Regents later affirmed the Cabinet's decision.

Duke took her case to federal district court. Cases from Denton are filed in the Sherman Division, and at the time, Justice was the sole judge assigned to that division. Justice was already familiar with Elizabeth Anne Duke, for while her appeal was being processed on the campus, the university had secured first a temporary restraining order and then a permanent injunction in state district court to keep her off school grounds. The university had acted in the face of a planned appearance by Duke at a campus rally to protest military activities in Southeast Asia. University policy prevented the appearance of outside speakers on campus unless sponsored by a campus student organization. Duke had no sponsorship. She challenged the authority of the state district court judge, Robert Scofield, to bar her. Touching only tangentially on the First Amendment issue in a complex and far-reaching decision, Justice ruled in Duke's favor.[3] Later, that decision was reversed by the U.S. Court of Appeals for the Fifth Circuit.

The appearance of the second *Duke* case on his docket gave Judge Justice the opportunity to apply the full force of the First Amendment to the facts of the case. Even though Duke did not have tenure or even a contract of employment, she did have an expectation of reemployment, he held, since her department chairman had told her that while her employment was conditional on enrollment, past experience had been that classes always filled up. This being so, Duke was entitled to a due process hearing. Justice concluded that the university had provided her with all the necessary due process requirements, except one. The President's Cabinet was not impartial. All but one of its members had been involved in some aspect of her case.

Because he did not believe Duke could obtain a fair hearing on the campus, Justice did not return the matter to university officials but instead reviewed the evidence himself. He concluded that the primary reason Duke had been dismissed was her criticism of university policies and her use of profane language. There was no evidence, he found, that her remarks had undermined her effectiveness or disrupted her working relationship with the university. As for the profanity, Justice observed that "Uncontradicted evidence introduced at the hearing before this court was to the effect that, to the younger generation, the compound verb 'fuck over' means 'oppress.' Thus, the use of the phrase was entirely consistent with the general tenor of plaintiff's remarks."[4] Though the university contended that Duke had also called the Board of Regents "a stupid bunch of motherfuckers," Justice found insufficient evidence to support the accusation.

Justice did not consider that Duke's use of profanity had compromised her performance as an instructor. "There was no showing that use of profanity by a teacher in front of students is likely by itself to cause the students to disrespect the teacher and thus to disrupt the school system. Moreover, there was no showing that use of profanity outside the classroom indicates that the teacher is of bad moral character or is unsuitable competently to discharge the important tasks the state places upon him to direct and shape the minds of the students entrusted to him."[5] Rather, all the evidence showed that Duke was a competent instructor.

The university claimed that the rally which Duke helped organize was in violation of a university policy requiring sponsorship by a student organization. Justice found, first, that Duke had tried to comply with university policy and, second, that the policy was invalid because it discriminated against ad hoc student groups which wished to use school facilities.

In weighing the free speech rights of Elizabeth Anne Duke and presumably others like her against the interest of the university in maintaining decorum on the campus and in the classroom, Justice had struck the balance decidedly in favor of the former. Like many jurists, he gave the First Amendment a preferred position in the balancing process. But both he and his clerk, Henry Skelton, realized their defense of the First Amendment on the college campus would be considered extreme by most standards, and they were not surprised when the Fifth Circuit reversed the decision.

The appeals court concluded in a two-to-one decision that there was insufficient evidence to show that the President's Cabinet lacked impartiality or had otherwise denied Duke due process of law. The majority found that Justice had been wrong in finding insufficient evidence. "As a past and prospective instructor, Mrs. Duke owed the University a minimal duty of loyalty and civility to refrain from extremely disrespectful and grossly offensive remarks aimed at the administrators of the University. By her breach of this duty, the interests of the University outweighed her claim for protection."[6] The majority also criticized Justice for reaching out to declare the university policy on use of campus facilities unconstitutional. Neither the plaintiffs nor the defendants had addressed the question.

Judge John C. Godbold wrote a thoughtful dissent in which he concluded that the unusual use of the President's Cabinet as a hearing body and the role of its members in investigating Duke's case indicated a lack of adherence to procedural due process. "[I]t simply will not do that the speaker whose words have flayed, and who has been penalized for what she has said, is to have her objections to the penalty, and her appeal therefrom, at the hands of the persons who are her victims, accusers, investigators, prosecutors, and the authority of the penalty as well. This is not judicial ivory towerism but common sense and everyday fairness in relationships between human beings."[7]

Justice's position in *Duke* harks back to the days after World War II when he so ardently supported another free speech advocate, Homer Price Rainey, for the governorship. Rainey had been dismissed from the presidency of the University of Texas for refusing to compromise academic freedom in connection with a ban by the Board of Regents of John Dos Passos' trilogy *U.S.A.* For Justice, the campus is uniquely a forum where free speech is necessary for the exchange of ideas and should reign supreme. "Anything that cuts back on freedom of speech worries me. I don't think that was what was intended by the people who wrote the Constitution and the Bill of Rights. If it were left to me, I would give practically unlimited free speech on the campus and in the community."

Since the *Duke* decision, the increasingly conservative U.S. Supreme Court has cut back on teacher and student rights first established during the Warren Court era. In 1983 the Court ruled that administrators control the campus mail system and can limit its use to official business.[8] That same year, the Court issued a ruling that expression in the workplace by public employees— including teachers and college professors—on matters of private concern such as one's job assignment or office morale is not entitled to any constitutional protection.[9] In 1986 the Court ruled that public school administrators have authority to discipline students who express themselves in lewd or profane terms.[10] In 1988 the justices upheld censorship of school-sponsored student newspapers so long as school officials have a legitimate pedagogical purpose and have not converted the newspaper into a public forum governed by the First Amendment. [11]

Justice finds these decisions troublesome. In a speech delivered on September 15, 1988, to the Dallas Civil Liberties Union, he examined the consequences of curtailing the First Amendment freedoms of public high school students. An indispensable part of the high school student's intellectual and social development, he asserted, is the "freedom to question, express, inquire, and criticize, which the founders of our republic regarded as the heart of democratic life." He accused the Supreme Court of equating the status of public school students with that of prisoners in ruling that school officials have broad censorship powers over school-sponsored student newspapers. He asserted that the "legitimate pedagogical purpose" the Supreme Court requires to justify censorship was derived from a prisoner rights case, *Turner v. Safley.* [12] In that case, the Court allowed prison officials to censor prisoner publications, provided they could assert a "legitimate penological purpose." "What future do we have a right to expect for our society," Justice asked rhetorically, "when students are treated, during the most critical years of their lives, virtually as inmates?" He added:

> Democracy imposes more demands on its citizens than any other form of government, because clear thinking is far more difficult than blind obedience. Without effective education—as opposed to imposed homogeneity, vacuous conformity, or fatuous trust in the wisdom of the powers-that-be—our republic becomes undistinguishable from the dreary totalitarian societies that civics classes warn our high school students about.

Using graphic terminology, Elizabeth Anne Duke spoke out on unpopular causes on a university campus. No doubt many of the students who listened to her were motivated to consider their own views. For Justice and for many others, this is the purpose of education in a free society.

The Right to Demonstrate in the Streets:
McGuire v. Roebuck

The candlelight march in Nacogdoches on May 13, 1970, was to be a peaceful demonstration in support of black and white brotherhood. The march began in Orton Hill, the black section of town. As it moved through the streets, its ranks quickly swelled. By the time the marchers emerged from Orton Hill and began to head downtown, some 250 demonstrators were walking five abreast, chanting slogans and singing civil rights songs.

As in many small communities in East Texas, desegregation had come slowly to Nacogdoches. Motion picture theaters had been integrated in 1969, the school system in 1970. The county jail was still segregated. Though nearly a quarter of the 22,500 residents were black, no black had ever been elected to either municipal or county office.

At Stephen F. Austin State University, a chapter of the National Black Students' Association was being established. Mickey McGuire, a nonstudent, had been recruited to organize the chapter and to promote racial awareness on the campus of ten thousand students. McGuire had been in trouble with the police as a youth, serving time in the Alabama state prison system for burglary and larceny. After his release from prison, he worked as an organizer for the black students' association. When McGuire arrived in Nacogdoches, M. C. Roebuck, chief of police, learned from the FBI about his background and made a point of watching him carefully. Roebuck had little affection for black militants or student activists. When a student who shadowed McGuire for Roebuck told the chief about one of McGuire's speeches, Roebuck was quoted as saying that he "could put an end to the nigger situation by putting a 30-30 bullet between [McGuire's] eyes." [13]

Roebuck knew that McGuire was not afraid to stir things up. Several weeks before the march, McGuire thrust himself into a police matter involving a black student at the university. The student had been arrested for forgery and passing bad checks. (She later pled guilty.) When told that the student's arrest was "none of his business," McGuire retorted, "I'll burn this damn town down around your neck." [14] That remark later triggered a criminal complaint against him.

Further exacerbating tensions in Nacogdoches and the university community was the dramatic shooting of several students at Kent State University in Ohio on May 4, 1970. The May 13 march was in part a response to that incident.

When the marchers reached the downtown area, local police swung into action. Following directions from headquarters, patrolman Smith Parmer sped to the head of the procession, where McGuire was in the lead. Parmer ordered the demonstrators to turn back. When they did not, he arrested McGuire and another black. They were placed in the patrol car and transported to city jail.

Up until McGuire was arrested, the march had been peaceful, consisting only of the chanting of slogans and the singing of civil rights songs. Parade marshals had kept the marchers on the sidewalk. But with McGuire's arrest, the marchers spilled out into the street; angry words were exchanged with the growing number of city, county, and state police. As the marchers were forced back to the Orton Hill area, several trash cans were overturned, bottles and rocks hurled at police, and plate glass windows broken. Black leaders worked to restrain the crowd from further violence. Without a clear sense of direction, the march eventually broke up.

McGuire was charged with five misdemeanor counts and with violating two city ordinances. One of the latter required that anyone planning a parade must obtain a permit from the city manager. It was this requirement that McGuire challenged in Justice's court.

McGuire v. Roebuck is typical of incidents accompanying desegregation in many southern communities. From bombings to employment discrimination, federal district court judges were called upon again and again to intervene. Judge Justice observes, "When people get to writing about the history of racial segregation and its ending in East Texas, some of the cases like *McGuire* are going to surface because they were where the boiling points occurred." His decision in *McGuire* demonstrates an unswerving commitment both to integration and to the First Amendment.

Since the law clerk who had been assigned to the case had left the court, Justice himself researched and wrote the opinion in *McGuire*. Citing *Shuttlesworth v. Birmingham,* a 1969 U.S. Supreme Court decision involving a similar civil rights demonstration, he had no trouble concluding that the parade permit requirement was an unconstitutional abridgment of freedom of speech.[15] The Court had held in *Shuttlesworth* that parade-permit ordinances are unconstitutional when unaccompanied by standards to limit the unbridled discretion of public officials. Justice wrote, "[B]ecause of its failure to set any standards whatsoever to guide the licensing authority, the ordinance is patently and flagrantly unconstitutional on its face."[16]

Judge Justice also cited the Supreme Court's celebrated *Terminiello v. Chicago* ruling involving an abrasive speaker who denounced various political and racial groups, as well as a crowd which had assembled outside the auditorium where he was speaking.[17] With Justice William O. Douglas writing the majority opinion, the Court reversed the speaker's conviction. Justice wanted to include some of Douglas' ringing commentary in support of free speech, but one of his law clerks talked him out of it as being injudicious. He regrets now that he did not include it. Douglas wrote in the *Terminiello* decision:

[A] function of free speech under our system of government is to invite dispute. It may indeed best serve its high purpose when it induces a condition of unrest, creates dissatisfaction with conditions as they are, or even stirs people to anger. Speech is often provocative and challenging. It may strike at prejudices and preconceptions and have profound unsettling effects as it presses for acceptance of an idea. That is why freedom of speech, though not absolute, is nevertheless protected against censorship or punishment, unless shown likely to produce a clear and present danger of a serious substantive evil that rises far above public inconvenience, annoyance, or unrest.[18]

This is vintage Douglas, and Justice, who reveres him, fully concurs.

The defendants argued that the issue of the parade ordinance was moot because the city commission had revised it. While Justice observed that the amended ordinance was not before the court, he nevertheless briefly reviewed its provisions in light of the mootness argument and found them also flawed.

In addition to declaring the parade ordinance unconstitutional and the actions of the police officers in arresting McGuire unwarranted, Justice observed that the city's failure either to prosecute McGuire on the parade ordinance violation or to drop the charges was nothing more than an attempt "to intimidate, threaten and coerce other blacks from exercising their constitutional rights to free speech and assembly."[19]

Justice had intended to grant broader relief than just declaring the permit requirement unconstitutional but "as I got into the state of the law, I realized there wasn't anything else I could grant to prevent them from reenacting a void ordinance." The attorney for the city, Charles F. Potter, had tried to convince Judge Justice that the city had made considerable progress toward integration and that the ordinance was constitutional. But he recognized that Justice "liked the plaintiff side of the bar" in this kind of case and that the whole incident had created considerable racial animosity in the community. "The blacks felt discriminated against," he acknowledges. "How can you attack a feeling that they have?"

Potter recognized that Justice had put considerable effort into the opinion. Potter advised city officials not to appeal the decision. "Had we appealed, his decision would almost certainly have been affirmed," he says. "The Fifth Circuit wasn't overruling any of these cases at the time." Potter acknowledges that Justice's decision may have been the right one. But he has doubts whether a similar decision would stand up on appeal today. Perhaps he is right. With the appointment of conservative judges during the Nixon and Reagan administrations, the Fifth Circuit is no longer a crusading court in racial discrimination and First Amendment matters as it was in the 1960s and early 1970s.

There is a postscript to the *McGuire* case. Some years later, following the swearing-in ceremony for several federal judges in Houston, Judge Justice was stopped by a black man. Justice did not recognize him immediately. The man identified himself as Mickey McGuire. Justice smiled with recognition, telling him, "You're the man who caused me quite a bit of trouble." McGuire bristled a bit at the remark. Justice had not recognized him in part because he was wearing a clerical collar.

The Right to Picket:
Nash v. Chandler

Police were extremely zealous in enforcing provisions of the Texas mass picketing act against striking employees of the Buddy Schoellkopf Products Company in Tyler in March 1979. The law provided that there were to be no more than two pickets within fifty feet of the entrance to a building or within fifty feet of other pickets. It also prohibited the use of "insulting, threatening, or obscene language" to inhibit nonstrikers and other persons from going to and from the premises.[20] The Texas picketing restrictions were part of the state's anti–collective bargaining statute. While the prohibitions on collective bargaining did not apply to Buddy Schoellkopf Products as a private employer, the picketing restrictions did.[21] The statute reflected the sentiment of the Texas Legislature and the majority of the Texas populace about labor relations and about picketing.

Beginning on March 15, the police began arresting third persons relieving one of the two pickets. They also arrested any picket who crossed the access road to the plant if the picket caused a car to slow down even momentarily, although the Tyler police chief had stipulated that arrests were to occur only if traffic was blocked for more than one minute. Pickets were arrested for calling out "scab" or uttering a profanity to nonstriking employees. Between March 15 and March 28, some ninety arrests were made on these grounds. Included among those arrested were two union attorneys who approached the picket line to consult with their clients. They were the only persons taken to jail in handcuffs. No actual force or significant threats of force by strikers occurred during the strike.

Labor strife is rare in Tyler. What triggered the Schoellkopf dispute was the certification by the National Labor Relations Board of a local of the United Rubber Workers (URW) to represent the mostly female workers at the plant. Schoellkopf Products manufactures marine safety equipment and down-filled hunting clothes. Collective bargaining began, following certification of the union, but little progress was evident. A strike was called for February 8, 1979, and picket lines were set. At first, the company sought to control the picketing in accordance with the statute through use of a security company, which placed three armed guards at the site. One guard apparently inflamed the female pickets by taunting them with threats of violence and with sexually explicit remarks. At times, the guards pointed their firearms at the pickets.

The tactics of the security guards prompted a number of male URW members from the nearby Kelly-Springfield Tire Company to join the picketing. With the additional pickets, the taunting and jeering between strikers and nonstrikers increased. Nonstriking employees were delayed in entering and leaving the building. Antennas on some of the nonstrikers' cars were broken. The president of the union local, John Nash, appeared on the picket line with a shotgun and was promptly arrested.

The company filed suit in state court in Tyler on March 14, seeking a temporary restraining order limiting picketing activities and requesting police to enforce the antipicketing statute. It was granted that same day. The next day, company officials met with representatives of the city, Chamber of Commerce, and chief of police to talk over enforcement of the Texas mass picketing statute at the plant. Later, Willie Hardy, chief of police, informed the union that the statute would be enforced.

Nash filed suit in Justice's court, alleging among other things that a conspiracy existed between the Schoellkopf Company and city officials to deprive union members of their constitutional right to engage in peaceful picketing, a right long recognized as protected by the First Amendment. Judge Justice was particularly displeased with the arresting of the union lawyers. "That caught my attention right at the beginning. I just couldn't conceive of it," he observes.

On April 4, following a three-day hearing, Justice concluded that the city and its police force had violated union members' rights. He granted a preliminary injunction against continuation of harassing police tactics, including arresting the union attorneys for seeking to consult with their clients. While circumstances suggested a conspiracy between the company and the city to break up the strike—Justice noted that representatives of both had held two meetings after the union was recognized and that the attorney for the company also represented the police chief—he concluded that the preponderance of the evidence did not support a conspiracy.

Subsequently, the strike ended and the union was decertified as the collective bargaining agent for the Schoellkopf employees. Union officials blamed the city. Some years later, Nash told reporters that "it's a sad situation that a city would join in concert with a private company to keep wages down. They were able to beat us."[22] There is no question that the temporary restraining order granted by the state court to enforce the Texas mass picketing statute had a dampening effect on the strike. By its terms, the statute limited the amount of pressure the union could bring on the employer in support of its bargaining demands.

But the lawsuit did not end. Through a series of motions, it evolved into a direct challenge by Nash and the union to the constitutionality of the mass picketing statute. Joining the city of Tyler and the police chief as defendants was the State of Texas. Specifically, the plaintiffs sought a declaration that the section of the statute limiting the number of pickets and their location, as well as the section prohibiting use of intimidating language, violated the First Amendment.

A trial was held in 1984. But Justice's decision striking down the two provisions of the state statute was not handed down until February 1986. The opinion went through three drafts with three different law clerks. When he could find the time, Justice himself did a good bit of the research. With the changing character of the Fifth Circuit, he wanted to make sure that his decision was particularly thorough and well supported.

He rejected the state's contention that prevention of violence justified a limitation of no more than two pickets within fifty feet of the entrance to a building or within fifty feet of other pickets. Finding the statute akin to laws struck down by the U.S. Supreme Court during the 1960s sit-in era, Justice wrote that the state certainly has a legitimate interest in preventing mob violence on a picket line, "but the state cannot validly argue that when more than two persons stand fifty feet from each other and from a company entrance, there is, perforce, a clear danger of violence." [23] The statute was thus an unconstitutional intrusion on protected rights of expression under the First Amendment. He noted the Fifth Circuit had disapproved a similar Louisiana ordinance in 1968. [24]

Given Justice's decision in *Duke v. North Texas State University,* it was no surprise that he also struck down the provision against intimidating language. Justice acknowledged that the U.S. Supreme Court has ruled that so-called "fighting words" may be regulated. [25] But in order for language to constitute "fighting words," it must be linked to an imminent breach of the peace. The Texas statute focused not on words likely to produce reactive violence but on words which intimidate others. He noted that the prohibition on "insulting, threatening, or obscene language" used "to interfere with, hinder, obstruct, or intimidate, or seek to" do the same with regard to persons entering or leaving premises would, under dictionary definitions, subject one to arrest who calls such a person a "clown," "nitwit," "meathead," "goon," or "turncoat." He noted that "If this statute were allowed to stand, local law enforcement officers conceivably could find such pejorative words as 'strikebreaker' or 'fink' to be in violation of section 2." [26] Because the intimidating-language section was subject to a variety of interpretations and because its scope encompassed protected expression, Justice declared it unconstitutional.

Justice knew that the matter was controversial in that state and federal courts had come to different conclusions with regard to the statute. The matter was resolved when a similar federal district court ruling from the Northern District was appealed to the Fifth Circuit. *Nash v. State* was a companion case but not the focus of the Fifth Circuit's ruling. In a broad-ranging opinion, the appeals court agreed with the federal courts that the numbers-distance provision "infringes too severely on constitutionally protected freedoms."[27] But, indicating that the statute was enacted with the presumption of compatibility with constitutional standards and thus could be interpreted in no other way than as limited to "fighting words," the appellate judges upheld the statute's intimidating-language provision.

The only direct consideration the appeals court gave to *Nash* involved the award of attorney fees. It affirmed the award of $167,607 in fees and $14,884 in expenses against defendants but remanded the issue of the state's share, ruling that Texas could not be held liable to the same extent as the others, because Texas had intervened only to defend the statute and had not itself been involved in unconstitutional action.[28]

Nash added weight to the rulings of other Texas federal courts striking down provisions of the Texas mass picketing act. Together, these cases set the stage for the Fifth Circuit ruling broadening the right of all individuals in Texas to engage in picketing as a constitutionally protected right.

The First Amendment in the Forest:
The Rainbow Family Case

Freedom-of-expression cases have never been close questions in Justice's court. He cannot recall ever ruling against the exercise of free speech. But in 1988, he was confronted with a strange case in which other important interests had to be considered as well.

The dispute arose when the Rainbow Family of the Living Light, a loosely organized network of 1960s-style individualists, decided to hold their summer gathering in the Angelina National Forest near Zavalla, Texas. Since 1972, members of the Rainbow Family have come by the thousands from across the country in old cars and battered vans, often painted in psychedelic colors, to a predetermined site in the national forests over the July 4 holiday with the stated intention of promoting peace and harmony. They hold seminars on topics such as solar energy, nuclear war, herbal medicine, and erotic massage. They listen to music and generally "do their own thing" in a communal setting. The highlight of the summer gathering is an hour-long July 4 meditation for world peace, ending in the singing of John Lennon's "Give Peace a Chance."

Having experienced problems with Rainbow Family gatherings in the past, the Forest Service sought an injunction against the 1988 gathering. It was rumored that advance scouts for the Rainbow Family sought the Texas site to demonstrate that they could meet anywhere, even in the backyard of U.S.

Forest Service Special Agent Billy Ball, a forty-seven-year-old former Dallas undercover agent, who had been charged with overseeing Rainbow Family summer gatherings. Ball did not think much of his charges. "Most of 'em, not all, their brains are baked anyway."[29]

The first that Justice heard of the Rainbow Family was in early May, when the U.S. attorney for the Eastern District filed suit on behalf of the U.S. Forest Service in the Lufkin Division, seeking a temporary restraining order to keep the Rainbow Family out of the piney woods of East Texas. The case had originally been assigned to Judge William M. Steger. But Steger, who had just taken senior status, exercised his option to decline to hear it. Thus, this odd case landed in Justice's courtroom.

In addition to the temporary restraining order, the government also requested an injunction against any Rainbow Family gathering unless pursuant to a special use permit. Judge Justice, who was hearing cases in Lufkin, assigned the matter to U.S. Magistrate J. Michael Bradford.

One of Bradford's initial tasks was to determine whether the Rainbow Family was sufficiently cohesive to constitute a defendant class of persons against whom the government could bring suit. The Family maintained that it had no organizational structure, that it was an informal group in which all decisions were made by consensus. Laird Lucas, one of Justice's law clerks, said, "It was like suing the Woodstock nation." The clash of two cultures was apparent in the Lufkin courtroom. Government attorneys found even asking simple questions was frustrating. Rainbow Family members identified themselves with names like Little White Owl and Water-Singing-on-the-Rocks, and with residences like "Planet Earth." Asked how they learned about the location of summer gatherings, defendants responded with such answers as "on the wind" or "when the spirit moved us." One of the defendants pulled out a large crystal, which he put on the defense table, telling Magistrate Bradford that it would help focus the energies in the courtroom.

Following a hearing, Bradford recommended that the government's request for a temporary restraining order be granted. Justice accepted the recommendation. After further hearings, Bradford recommended that the Rainbow Family could be sued as an entity and that they be required to apply for a special use permit.

On June 1, Justice issued a detailed and closely reasoned order accepting the former recommendation, but rejecting the latter on the grounds that the Forest Service's permit requirements abridged First Amendment rights.[30] This came as a surprise to the government attorneys, who had not anticipated that First Amendment rights would be a major issue. In another court, that might have been the case. But this was Justice's court, where any transgression of

First Amendment rights is likely to be regarded as a constitutional violation. In the order, Justice followed the reasoning of the U.S. District Court for Arizona, which two years before in an unpublished ruling had declared the permit rules invalid because they distinguished between expressive and other types of activities and because, based on the distinction, they provided different grounds for approving permits.[31] Justice also noted that the permit regulations were unconstitutionally vague, since they allowed Forest Service officials broad discretion in granting or denying permits. As in the *McGuire* parade-permit case, he based this conclusion on the U.S. Supreme Court decision in *Shuttlesworth v. Birmingham*. He also ruled that recent revisions to the rules had been invalidly adopted.

The government appealed the denial to the Fifth Circuit and filed an amended complaint in Justice's court, asking that the Rainbow Family gathering be barred in the interest of protecting the environment and in the interest of public health and safety. These concerns are not inconsequential. Even though expression may be involved, the camping of thousands in the national forests for an extended time is quite different from giving a speech in a public park.

In mid-June, the Judge held a four-day hearing in Tyler on the revised contentions. The dryness of the legal arguments was offset by the appearance of a coterie of Rainbow Family members. Justice remembers seeing hippies when he was attending a 1968 seminar for newly appointed judges in Berkeley, California. "These people looked like the same people I saw then, only twenty years older." For courtroom personnel and the media, the tie-dyed shirts, long hair and beards, love beads, and sandals provided a time-warp to the Age of Aquarius. About forty Family members conducted a ceremony outside the courthouse to focus the energy of the universe on their case. Before Justice would allow them into his courtroom, they had to leave the staffs they were carrying with the marshals and be appropriately attired. A marshal brought a rack of blue blazers held in reserve for those inappropriately attired, which, when donned, only partially obscured their unconventional dress.

One of the highlights of the hearing was the showing of two videotapes. The first was a training film prepared by the Forest Service on how to deal with the Rainbow Family. It showed campers at prior Rainbow Family summer gatherings dancing nude around a campfire, smoking pot, cooking in communal kitchens, and meditating in circles. It also showed traffic jams at forest entrances and trash remaining after the Family members departed. Forest Service rangers and health experts described a rash of drunk-driving charges and the outbreak of shigellosis, a contagious form of dysentery, following the 1987 summer gathering in North Carolina. Attributed to unhealthy camping conditions, this disease was spread through twenty-seven states by many of the thirteen thousand Rainbow Family members attending the gathering.

At first Justice wondered why the Rainbow Family attorney, longtime Tyler civil rights lawyer Larry Daves, did not object to the showing of the film as hearsay evidence. Daves did not do so because the defendants planned to show their own videotape. Predictably, it presented an entirely different perspective on the Rainbow Family. The montage of past gatherings showed, among other things, a children's parade and innocent group dancing and singing. The videotape also presented comments from two California Forest Service rangers on how well behaved the Rainbow Family members had been when over twenty thousand held a summer gathering there.

It was inevitable that Billy Ball, the law-and-order Forest Service special agent, and Judge Justice would clash at some point during the hearing. The clash occurred when Ball was testifying about how he believed the Rainbow Family intimidated public officials.

Ball: In my opinion, they operate off the theory of power of intimidation. Once a large group arrives on site, they're almost a situation where you cannot deal with them. In my opinion, they have intimidated federal, state, and local authorities, agencies. We've had testimony to that fact that they refuse to comply with the laws and rules and regulations in North Carolina and because of this attitude, agencies are unable to deal effectively with the Rainbow Family. The testimony provided yesterday indicated that they intimidated the state and federal authorities.

Justice: Well, I heard the testimony yesterday.

Ball: Okay.

Justice: So you don't have to repeat it for me.

Ball: All right. One other thing, Your Honor, I guess was a shock to me, having been in your court and other federal courts was the attitude and the demeanor within Magistrate Bradford's court of shouting out, carrying sticks, running in and out, which I know that you personally do not go with. I think they totally intimidated the federal courts.

Justice: That is about the most outrageous assertion I have ever heard from the witness stand and I reprimand you for making a statement like that. If Magistrate Bradford had seen fit to enforce those type of regulations, he certainly had the power to do so.

Ball: Yes, sir.

Justice: And I would reject entirely the concept that the federal courts have been intimidated in any way whatever.

Ball: Yes, sir.

Justice: Now, let's go on with something else more credible.[32]

Following the hearing, Justice and his clerks discussed the proper balancing of environmental concerns, public safety, and First Amendment rights. They could foresee the possibility of a major confrontation between the Rainbow Family and police, resulting in injury and even death. Aggravating the problem was the proximity of the Angelina National Forest to the major metropolitan areas of Dallas–Fort Worth, Austin, Shreveport, and Houston. Thousands of onlookers could be drawn to the event and might trigger a full-fledged riot. Indeed, Ball testified that he expected a great influx of outsiders, including runaways, drug dealers, and fugitives.

While the Judge and his clerks deliberated, the Rainbow Family litigation became a major news event. Even national publications including *Newsweek* and the *New York Times* sent reporters to cover the story. Residents of the tiny community of Zavalla, population 762, were repeatedly interviewed by reporters from the big city newspapers and radio and television stations. Residents of East Texas communities fussed and fretted over nudity, drug dealing, and trashing of the national forests. Typical was the comment from Lufkin resident James Stone, who told a *New York Times* reporter that "These people are no-good hippies and we should run them out of town."[33]

Governor William P. Clements said that, if necessary, he would call out the National Guard. U.S. Senator Phil Gramm made it known on numerous occasions that he would not tolerate any drug dealing in the national forest. He told the press that he had secured the loan of drug-sniffing dogs from the U.S. Customs Service to clamp down on illicit drugs. When it turned out that the use of drugs at the gathering was practically nonexistent, Gramm claimed it was because of his get-tough-with-drugs message.[34]

Ultimately, based on the facts presented, Justice downplayed possible harm to the environment in his June 23 memorandum opinion.[35] He acknowledged that environmental damage could result, but questioned the government's good faith in raising the argument. The government had asked that the summer gathering be put off until a formal environmental assessment could be conducted under the National Environmental Protection Act. Justice saw this as a ruse to keep an unpopular group out of the forest, since the government was both vague about when such a report could be completed and about having required similar reports in the past. Because of his prior experience in a hotly contested case involving clearcutting in the East Texas forests, he told his clerks that he doubted the Forest Service's sincerity.[36] Justice noted that no evidence had been presented showing environmental harm from previous gatherings. Indeed, Forest Service officials had testified that there had been no damage to the forest after Rainbow Family gatherings in California and North Carolina. Furthermore, the planned Rainbow gathering was to be held at sites bordering Sam Houston Reservoir, accessible by old logging roads. Thus, the campers would not be tearing up pristine forests.

But Justice did recognize that more was involved than free speech. Public health and safety could be endangered if the gathering were to be held unconditionally. In particular, the outbreak of shigellosis at the 1987 gathering convinced him of this. Consequently, under the law of public nuisance, he issued an order requiring the Rainbow Family to comply with health and sanitation provisions appropriate for an outdoor gathering of large numbers of persons before they could hold the summer gathering. Recalling his military and Texas National Guard experience, Justice secured army field service manuals dealing with sanitation from the local National Guard office and found they would suffice as standards for the Rainbow gathering.

He limited the number of persons assembling at any one gathering site to five thousand—a figure just short of triggering the Texas mass gathering statute that required a permit from a county judge. Before a site could be occupied, the United States Public Health Service had to inspect it and certify that minimum health and sanitation standards had been met. Justice chose the U.S. Health Service because he had little confidence in Texas health personnel. In order to avoid conflict between the Forest Service and the Rainbow Family, he ordered the U.S. Marshal for the Eastern District to control the flow of people into and out of campsites. Failure to comply with the terms of the injunction would result in closing of the sites. Unlawful behavior by Rainbow Family members occupying the sites was to be handled routinely under state and federal laws. Finally, Justice required the Rainbow Family to clean up the sites following the July 4 holiday.

The Judge was not troubled by the fact that he had become immersed in administrative detail often thought beyond the province of the court. For him, it represented a balancing of the interests involved. "I try to preserve constitutional values, but one has to have some idea of practicality," he maintains.

Accustomed to unconventional decisions emanating from Judge Justice's courtroom, Tylerites were neither surprised nor amused. Calling the Rainbow Family episode "unbelievable," the *Tyler Morning Telegraph* editorialized that though Shakespeare did not write a play called a "Farce of Fools," he did not have to because "the record of this procedure has done it for him."[37] The editorial called on the Fifth Circuit to nullify Justice's order. The advice was not heeded. The Fifth Circuit vacated its temporary stay on Justice's June 1 order and took no further action.

After all the hoopla, the July 4 Rainbow gathering was anticlimactic. The bitter legal battle, the hostility of local residents and the Forest Service, and the 100° heat of Texas summers had had their effect. Fewer than four thousand people showed up, only one site was used, and little lawlessness occurred. The most serious incident involved the running down of a Rainbow Family woman by two intoxicated local residents driving a jeep at high speed through the camp. The woman, named No Guns, was hospitalized in critical condition. Ironically, Forest Service Special Agent Billy Ball was the law officer who intercepted the pair.

For the Family, the gathering ended on a high note. Following a steady, cooling rain, a rainbow appeared over the 350 participants at the July 4 meditation ceremony. For Judge Justice, it was all in a day's work. Laird Lucas, one of the law clerks who worked on the decisions, worried about a disaster. "I was sure that the government was going to take a hard line and start arresting people. I foresaw the Lufkin high school football stadium filled with prisoners," he says. As he had so many times before, the Judge took a more stoic position. Fully aware of the recriminations that would be levied at his court if things did not work out, he told his clerks, "Don't worry about it. You give it your best. If it doesn't work out and you've done your best, you have nothing to reproach yourself on."

In the days following the 4th of July, the Rainbow Family matter faded into history. Apparently believing that his insistence on health and safety precautions vindicated their position, the Forest Service decided not to appeal Justice's ruling. Their reports indicated that the Rainbow Family had left the area cleaner than they found it. With the award of partial attorney fees to plaintiff's attorney Larry Daves, the case was closed. A year later, Justice was surprised to receive phone calls from Rainbow Family members who were having problems arranging a national gathering in Nevada. "They said their rights were being trampled upon, and they wanted me to enter an order," he laughs.

Freedom of Speech at a Hospital:
Albright v. Good Shepherd Hospital

Do individuals have the right to exercise free speech at a hospital? Before Judge Justice could examine this issue in *Albright v. Good Shepherd Hospital,* he had to decide whether or not the hospital in question was a public institution. Good Shepherd Hospital in Longview was operated by a private not-for-profit Texas organization under a lease from Gregg County, which had founded the hospital in 1934 and operated it for a time. If the hospital was determined to be private, then Gene Albright's constitutional claims would be irrelevant, since the rights to free speech and due process are held to apply only to the actions of government. Under these circumstances, the hospital could both terminate him for what he said and avoid providing procedural due process. The public-private issue is important in light of federal and state efforts to privatize many functions heretofore performed by state and municipal organizations, and could carry implications for several of Justice's decisions mandating reforms in the operation of state institutions.

The case arose when Gene Albright was terminated from his position as personnel director at the hospital on June 5, 1985. A second plaintiff, nurse supervisor Bettie J. Page, was also dismissed. Albright alleged that his termination was in retaliation for assisting black nurse supervisors with their grievances and for speaking out about violations of hospital policies. A week after his termination, Albright began handing out leaflets in an alleyway behind the hospital discussing the circumstances of his discharge. The alleyway separated the hospital from an employees' parking lot and provided access to the hospital emergency room. After Albright started distributing the leaflets, a hospital guard told him he was violating a hospital policy against distribution of literature by non-employees on hospital grounds. Albright was subsequently arrested when he did not stop leafleting and leave. In his complaint, Albright alleged that the hospital's no-solicitation policy was unconstitutional both on its face and as applied to him, and also that he was the victim of a false arrest.

The nature of the relationship of the private hospital to the county was critical to the success of Albright's lawsuit. After carefully reviewing both the status of the hospital and relevant case law, Justice concluded that the hospital was in effect a public institution and so advised the jury. This was so because, as he later wrote in his memorandum opinion, "Gregg County benefits directly from the private management of the hospital in several ways: revenues earned by the hospital, under the corporation's management, are used to pay county bond obligations; recent hospital improvements, paid for out of current hospital revenues, will become county property; and county residents, including indigents, are served by the hospital, fulfilling county obligations under state and federal law."[38] Justice found support for his conclusion in *Burton v. Wilmington Parking Authority,* a well-known 1961 U.S. Supreme Court decision involving racial discrimination by a private restaurant in a public parking facility, and a 1988 Fifth Circuit decision also involving the leasing of a county hospital.[39] Racial issues had been involved in each. Race was also a factor in the Good Shepherd case, given Albright's assistance to the black nurses with regard to their grievance filing. However, Justice did not stress the point in his memorandum opinion, a fact which may have made the decision vulnerable on appeal. The Judge sought to distinguish this case from an earlier Fifth Circuit decision, *Greco v. Orange Memorial Hospital*, which had reached the opposite conclusion in a nonracial context.[40]

Since the private corporation which operated the hospital was in effect an arm of the state, it was bound to observe constitutional mandates. Thus, Justice advised the jury that peaceful leafleting, such as the plaintiff's, was a form of expressive activity that is fully protected by the First Amendment. While the hospital was not a traditional public forum for a robust exchange of views, neither could it be completely closed to interpersonal communication. Citing legal precedents, Justice observed that "[T]he First Amendment demands that non-employees be able to communicate with hospital employees or visitors about matters of mutual concern, so long as the time, place, and manner of such communication occurs in non–patient care areas and hospital functions are not impaired. Hence, Good Shepherd Hospital's complete proscription of any solicitation is contrary to these requirements."

Not only was the hospital's no-solicitation policy constitutionally invalid; so was its application against Albright. Justice noted that Albright had specifically chosen the alleyway as the place to distribute his leaflets late at night so that there would be no disruption of hospital activities. The alleyway had traditionally been open to the public for both hospital and non-hospital business. There was no evidence that his presence had impeded the entry or exit of emergency or other vehicles. Nor had Albright come into contact with patients or their guests. For all of these reasons, Justice concluded that Albright had a constitutional right to distribute his leaflets in the alleyway. There was adequate evidence, he wrote, for the jury to find that the hospital had been motivated to suppress Albright's particular views when it had him arrested and thus violated his First Amendment rights.

Justice also instructed the jury that employee complaints about such matters as violations of safety regulations and racial discrimination laws are constitutionally protected, since they relate to matters of public concern. However, the jury subsequently found that while Albright had made the complaints, he was discharged for other reasons and thus the hospital was not liable. But the jury did find that Albright had not been accorded due process prior to his discharge and that the hospital had provided false information causing his arrest. Albright was awarded damages totaling $350,001—the $1 for the constitutional violations, the rest for actual and punitive damages.

The case was appealed to the U.S. Court of Appeals for the Fifth Circuit, where a conservative panel refused to accept Justice's assessment of the public character of the hospital.[41] Judges Edith H. Jones, William L. Garwood, and Jerry E. Smith, all Reagan appointees, based their analysis on the *Greco v.*

Orange Memorial Hospital decision Justice had sought to distinguish. They did not give much attention to the racial overtones in the Albright termination, perhaps because Judge Justice had not stressed them in his memorandum opinion. The hospital was not a state actor primarily because there was no direct oversight of hospital affairs by the county acting through a hospital board. Lacking such an intermediary, the county was not informed of, nor did it have a right to be informed of, Albright's dismissal.

The Fifth Circuit did not find either the lease agreement or the rent paid to the county sufficient to establish a symbiotic interrelationship between the county and the hospital. Since the hospital was not a public entity, Albright had no constitutional claims against it. This left only the claim of supplying false arrest information. The case was sent back for further proceedings relating only to it.

Justice's application of the First Amendment to Good Shepherd Hospital was thwarted by the rejection of his conclusion that Good Shepherd was a public institution. He was not surprised, since the question was close and the precedent not clear. He did take pleasure in noting that the appeals court had upheld his judgment regarding the second plaintiff in the case, Bettie J. Page.[42] But he was disturbed by the effort of conservative judges to limit the reach of one of the country's oldest civil rights laws, 42 United States Code Section 1983, giving access to federal court for persons whose U.S. constitutional or federal statutory rights have been violated by public officials. In a 1989 declaratory judgment ruling, Justice cited a U.S. Supreme Court ruling in support of his decision that prisons operated by private corporations are state actors under Section 1983 and thus must comply with the requirements of the *Ruiz v. Estelle* prison reform order.[43] Both an appeal to the Fifth Circuit and Justice's order were withdrawn when the parties settled the dispute, agreeing that the private prisons were public entities. The question is less clear in other situations. For example, are private educational institutions which educate students at public expense to be considered state actors under a voucher system where state money flows to parents and then to the schools? The Fifth Circuit *Good Shepherd* ruling may have relevance to situations like this in which the state provides public benefits through private vendors.

Judge Justice's First Amendment decisions clearly illustrate a view of the amendment as the first among Bill of Rights equals. Strongly believing that First Amendment freedoms differentiate American democracy from totalitarian regimes, Justice has steadfastly upheld the right of persons to exercise their First Amendment rights in settings ranging from a university campus to the public forest to the grounds of a hospital. While the decisions included in this chapter do not carry the weight of his rulings involving state institutions, each demonstrates an unswerving commitment to translate the terms of the First Amendment into operational principles applicable to the realities of daily living.

CHAPTER 8

Voter Discrimination

From his first days on the bench, Judge Justice expressed little hesitancy to intervene on behalf of the right to vote. Ratification of the Twenty-Sixth Amendment to the U.S. Constitution in 1971 enfranchised a new class of voters between the ages of eighteen and twenty-one and spawned a host of challenges to state voting laws. In one of the first decisions nationwide on the new amendment, Justice struck down a provision of the Texas Election Code requiring voters under the age of twenty-one to register only in their parents' home counties.[1] The case was decided on the pleadings—the paperwork submitted by opposing counsel—with the defendants concurring in the entry of the declaratory judgment. Senator Mike McKool (Democrat-Dallas), who sponsored the new Texas election law, applauded Justice's decision. He told reporters that Senate supporters of the bill had never wanted the provision because it discriminated against the young.[2]

A year later, in 1972, Justice struck down another provision of the state election code requiring that students wishing to vote in the community where they attended school had to affirm an intention to remain there after graduation, thus effectively curtailing student voting power in college communities.[3] Because the president of the Student Senate of the University of Texas at Austin was allowed to intervene as a plaintiff in the lawsuit, Justice's decision in *Whatley v. Clark* brought the Judge to the attention of state political leaders in Austin.

These early student voting rights disputes were neither very controversial nor difficult to decide. The law was straightforward. This would not be true for most of Justice's later voter discrimination decisions. He participated in a long-running lawsuit fundamentally altering the character of state legislative districts, ordered redistricting of a number of East Texas communities to benefit minorities, and was a member of a three-judge court striking down portions of the state legislature's congressional apportionment plan in the early 1980s. Justice's aggressive use of judicial power to democratize the political process thrust him center-stage into the political arena. He showed little reluctance to be there. "Our country is based upon a democracy, and if people can't vote and make their vote count, democracy fails," he observes. "I don't think courts have a choice not to intervene if the Constitution is going to be made effective."

State Legislative Reapportionment:
Graves v. Barnes

Until the 1960s, legislative apportionment was a matter left to legislators. Federal courts stayed out of the "political thicket" on the general premise that legislative redistricting was not compatible with judicial action. In a dramatic break with tradition, the U.S. Supreme Court ruled in *Baker v. Carr* in 1961 that the Fourteenth Amendment equal protection clause applies to legislative districting, thus inviting federal courts to intervene in disputes over gerrymandering.[4] In an equally dramatic ruling, the high court ruled three years later in *Reynolds v. Sims* that both houses of a state legislature must be apportioned on a population basis to satisfy the equal protection clause. Further, legislative districts in both houses must be constructed "as nearly of equal population as is practicable" so that the vote of one citizen is approximately equal to that of any other citizen.[5] In short, one person, one vote. While the *Reynolds* ruling mandated an equally weighted vote, the justices observed that mathematical exactness was not required or even possible. Thus, the Court did not lay down exact standards, opting to develop them on a case-by-case basis.

Prior to becoming a judge, Justice had limited experience with gerrymandering. About the only significant event was a case involving the incorporation of Malakoff into a municipality. Malakoff is a small community about seven miles from Athens. In the petition calling for an election, the boundary lines of the proposed municipality were set forth in an irregular pattern. All the people who supported incorporation were included; those opposed were not. The Commissioners Court of Henderson County, the local governing body, approved the petition and an election was set. The opponents hired Will Justice, Wayne's father, to challenge the petition. The senior Justice was successful in getting the election set aside. Several years later, the proponents of incorporation came to Will Justice and wanted to hire him to prepare a petition that was legally sufficient. "They had decided that they didn't want to have to deal with him again," his son laughs. Wayne's role was to help draw up the boundaries set forth in the second petition to conform with legal requirements. It was his first experience in political line-drawing.

In 1971, lawsuits challenging reapportionment of the Texas Legislature following the 1970 census were filed in each of Texas' four federal district courts. On November 2, a lawsuit challenging the Legislative Redistricting Board's plan for the Texas House of Representatives was filed in Justice's court with liberal State Senator Oscar H. Mauzy as plaintiff's attorney. The suit, *Regester v. Bullock,* alleged that the one-person—one-vote mandate had been violated and, further, that the use of multimember districts in many counties discriminated against minorities. Shortly before the lawsuit was filed, another lawsuit—*Graves v. Barnes*—was filed in the Southern District, challenging apportionment of senatorial districts in Harris County (Houston) on the grounds of racial discrimination. In part to deflect the thrust of *Regester* and *Graves,* similar lawsuits were subsequently filed in the Western District and in the Northern District. The political stakes in the outcome were high for the traditional all-white power structure and the emerging minority forces.

Since several parties were seeking an injunction against enforcement of the reapportionment plan, it would be necessary that three-judge courts be impaneled.[6] In the hopes of keeping his case before Judge Justice as the sole trial judge Mauzy had not requested an injunction but had sought only a declaratory judgment that the plan was unconstitutional. A single judge could issue such an order. Judge Adrian A. Spears, Chief Judge of the Western District of Texas, asked Chief Judge John R. Brown of the U.S. Court of Appeals for the Fifth Circuit to convene a three-judge court to hear the case he was presiding over. Brown requested that Chief Judge Joe E. Estes of the Northern District hold a pretrial conference with all the judges and the lawyers involved in the four lawsuits. Since Justice was handling the Eastern District lawsuit, he was notified of the conference and planned to attend.

However, while holding court in Marshall, Justice began experiencing severe muscle spasms in his stomach. At first he thought he might be having a heart attack. The pain became so intense that he recessed court. One of the lawyers involved in the case before him at the time, Scott Baldwin, gave him the name of a local internist. Justice's concern for judicial impartiality was so great in those first years on the bench that rather than have one of the lawyers drive him to the doctor's office, he insisted that all of them accompany him. "I didn't want one of them to have an advantage over the other," he asserts with a smile at the recollection of the car full of attorneys headed for the doctor's office.

The doctor was not sure of the cause of the illness. He advised Justice to rest in a back room. Later, Sue Justice arranged to have her husband transported by ambulance back to Tyler, where he was hospitalized. Though the illness was never positively diagnosed—inflammation of the pancreas was suspected—he was forced to spend several days in the hospital and missed the conference in Dallas. He sent Colin J. Carl, one of his law clerks, to represent him.

During the conference, Judge Estes announced that, in the interest of judicial economy, a three-judge district court would be appointed to hear the disputes. In accordance with the federal statute, the court would consist of one circuit court judge and two district court judges. The makeup of the panel was critical to the outcome. Three of the district court judges in whose courtrooms the suits had been filed agreed that Judge Brown should appoint other judges to take their places. No such waiver was forthcoming from Judge Justice. His recollection is that he did not execute a waiver since he was not in attendance at the conference. Nor was he later asked to sign one. For their part, Mauzy and David R. Richards, Mauzy's former law partner who had joined him in the lawsuit, insisted that they had a right to have their case tried singly before Judge Justice. Apparently in the face of these developments, Judge Estes advised Chief Judge Brown to appoint Judge Justice as one of the judges on the three-judge court and to have that court decide whether any of the lawsuits could be tried by a single judge. As it turned out, all four of the lawsuits were consolidated and heard by this court.

Brown subsequently appointed Justice to the three-judge panel. While not recalling the exact circumstances surrounding the appointment of the panel, Judge Brown maintains that it would not have been out of character for Justice to have insisted he be on it. Joining Justice would be Fifth Circuit Judge Irving L. Goldberg of Dallas and U.S. District Judge H. John Wood of El Paso. Goldberg, a liberal Democrat, was appointed to the bench by President Lyndon Johnson in 1966. Justice has long admired Goldberg as a jurist and scholar. Wood, a conservative Republican, was appointed to the bench by President Richard Nixon in 1970. He was assassinated on May 29, 1979. Though poles apart ideologically, Wood and Justice became friends during the long-running *Graves v. Barnes* lawsuit. "We got along fine," Justice says. "I grew to like Wood. I got to play tennis with him once or twice during the pendency of that case. He was an excellent tennis player. I grieve his passing." Of the three, Justice proved to be the most activist, consistently going the farthest to reshape the political map of Texas.

The case was transferred to the Austin Division of the Western District for trial. Justice was selected as the managing judge, since he was the only member of the panel who had presided over one of the original lawsuits. This assignment put him in charge of adjudicating pretrial procedures. The judges were under pressure of time, for the filing deadline for legislative candidates was February 7, only a few months away. On behalf of the panel of judges,

Justice held pretrial conferences in Austin on December 22 and 31, 1971. With more than two dozen lawyers involved in the case, agreement on facts and procedures was difficult. "Those were hard conferences," Justice recalls, "one of the worst experiences I have ever had on the bench. The parties were absolutely adamant about their positions. At first, they wouldn't stipulate to anything." This forced the Judge to take up each of the contested items in turn, seeking areas of agreement. "I finally got them to agree to stipulate to certain things, though it was a very time-consuming, tedious process." In order to get ready for trial after the New Year holiday, Justice ordered the attorneys to prepare final pretrial orders and submit them to him on Sunday, January 2. "I'm sorry this is a football weekend," he told them. "Judicial business comes first."[7] In addition to a courtroom full of litigants, the case attracted wide coverage from the media.

At the December 22 conference, Justice also named a University of Texas Law School professor to serve as special master to the court. Given their heavy case loads, the judges had unanimously agreed to Justice's suggestion that Professor George Schatzki be appointed to hear the challenges and make recommmendations to the court. Justice knew Schatzki well and respected his knowledge of the developing law in the reapportionment field. Schatzki was charged with drawing up his own redistricting plan if necessary. Criticism quickly mounted against Schatzki, who was a liberal Democrat and former law partner of Oscar Mauzy. (Because of illness, Mauzy had switched from being a lawyer to becoming a witness in *Regester v. Bullock*.) Schatzki was also vice president of the Texas Civil Liberties Union, which was aiding the plaintiffs. Following the filing of motions by Attorney General Crawford Martin and state Democratic Party Chairman Roy Orr challenging Schatzki's appointment, the panel unanimously agreed to his removal a week after his appointment. The judges themselves would hear the case.

Assisting the state in its defense was Leon Jaworski, president of the American Bar Association and later special prosecutor in the Nixon Watergate affair. Justice believes that the Texas political establishment selected Jaworski because they had little confidence in Attorney General Martin. Whatever his abilities as an attorney, Jaworski did not make a favorable impression on the Judge. Among other things, Jaworski made representations about his status in the case that apparently were not true. "He asserted to me, gratuitously, that he wasn't being paid, that he was there voluntarily," Justice says. "Well, I just simply did not credit that. My suspicions were afterwards justified because he submitted a hell of a big bill to the state, which they paid."

A week-long trial was held in Austin early in January. Circuit Judge Goldberg sat between Judges Justice and Wood. As the managing judge, Justice assumed that he would make the rulings from the bench regarding admissibility of the evidence. With Goldberg in the middle, the lawyers tended to look to him when filing objections. Justice chuckles, "Very often he would go ahead and rule. I didn't challenge him."

The trial was relatively informal, more in keeping with a hearing before an administrative agency than before a court of law. It was the first case of its type in Texas, so both lawyers and judges were feeling their way. "Very little attention was paid to the rules of evidence. Judge Goldberg was in favor of letting everything come in, and I wasn't opposed to the idea," Justice recalls. The plaintiffs took advantage of the opportunity by introducing masses of material into the record, including proposed reapportionment plans upon which the judges later heavily relied.

When the evidence was all in, Judges Goldberg and Justice concluded that the plaintiffs had a convincing case. Judge Wood concurred only in part. The three judges decided to pool their law clerks and let them sort through the issues and the proposed redistricting plans submitted by the parties in the process of working up a draft opinion. The clerks worked in Goldberg's chambers in the Federal Building in Dallas, where library facilities were extensive.

Because the judges and their clerks constructed much of the opinion as a joint effort and because combinations of the judges supported various sections of the opinion, it did not bear anyone's name but was listed as *per curiam*, meaning "by the court." Judge Goldberg has a distinct flair for ostentatious writing, and certain passages appear which can be attributed only to him. The lengthy opinion began with his play on words: "We are once again in the Texas sector of the political thicket of legislative redistricting and required to contour the condition of the individual trees as well as the physiography of the forest as we explore for 'crazy quilts,' 'groves,' contiguity, compactness, specie, motivation in planting, and other possible impedimenta to constitutionality in redistricting."[8]

As the two judges in the majority, Goldberg and Justice agreed that the apportionment of the Texas House of Representatives was unconstitutional. They began by noting that while the Supreme Court in *Reynolds* had not required mathematical exactness with respect to the apportionment of state legislatures, an examination of other decisions suggested that little variation would be permissible.[9] "The critical issue remains the same: Has the State justified any and all variances, however small, on the basis of consistent, rational State policy?"[10]

Applying this standard, Goldberg and Justice found that deviations among districts for the Texas House were not justified. Apportioning total population equally among the 150 districts would give each district a population of 74,645, based on 1970 census figures. The plan, developed by the five-member Legislative Redistricting Board when the legislature failed to act, showed as much as a 9.9 percent deviation from this figure between over- and under-represented districts. The two judges rejected the state's contention that commitment to a state constitutional provision against crossing county lines justified the variance. The Legislative Redistricting Board, the majority wrote, had not taken its responsibilities seriously in redrawing legislative districts. Indeed, it had never deliberated as a body but had acted as individuals. In an opinion in which he concurred with and dissented from parts of the *per curiam* judgment, Justice observed that depositions filed in the case indicated that Lieutenant Governor Ben Barnes had control of the redistricting process. The court was also bothered by the fact that the Texas House plan mandated single-member districting in Harris County (Houston), but multimember districts in all other heavily populated counties. "This irrationality, without reasoned justification, may be a separate and distinct ground for declaring the plan unconstitutional," the majority wrote.[11]

Having declared the state's reapportionment plan for the Texas House of Representatives unconstitutional, Goldberg and Justice left it to the legislature to correct, with the caveat that if the state failed to redistrict itself in such a manner as to eliminate interdistrict disparities by July 1, 1973, the judges would do it. Conservative Judge Wood dissented, expressing at the outset that while he disagreed with the Supreme Court's precedents allowing federal courts to intervene in apportionment cases, he would follow them where warranted. In this case, he found the state's efforts rational and the majority's conclusion unwarranted.

The other principal issue in *Graves v. Barnes*—one which was really at the heart of the case—involved the use of multimember districts in Dallas and Bexar (San Antonio) counties. While the plaintiffs had also challenged their use in other counties, there had been insufficient time to prepare the necessary evidence with regard to counties other than these two. Multimember districts have a number of features detrimental to minorities. First, representatives are elected at-large in such districts, and minority candidates are often unable to capture votes beyond their areas of concentration. Thus, their constituencies go unrepresented. Second, multimember districts require candidates to campaign district-wide, thus driving up the costs of campaigning. Evidence showed that in Dallas County, for example, a candidate for one of the eighteen at-large seats in the Dallas delegation to the Texas House of Representatives had to campaign to about 1,300,000 people, compared with 74,600 for a single-member district. Third, the court noted use of the majority requirement in Texas primary elections, a system virtually unheard of outside the South. Under this system, candidates must secure a majority of the votes cast in the election to be successful, whereas in most states only a plurality is required. The requirement tends to work to the disadvantage of minority candidates, who may secure a plurality of votes in the general election, only to lose when voters coalesce behind a white opponent in the runoff. Finally, the use of the "place" requirement requires each candidate to file for a particular place on the ballot, e.g., place one, place two, etc. The place has nothing to do with residence or geographic area, but does highlight the identity of candidates.

These features of the multimember district system constituted illegal discrimination, plaintiffs' attorneys argued, when viewed in the context of a history of government-sanctioned racial discrimination. In the case of Dallas County, only two blacks since Reconstruction had served in its delegation to the Texas House of Representatives. These two were the only ones ever slated by the white-dominated Dallas Committee for Responsible Government (DCRG). For all intents and purposes, the DCRG controlled the selection of candidates for the Democratic Party, which, in a one-party state, controlled the election outcome. The DCRG, the evidence showed, had a history of promoting segregation and conducting racist campaigns. "It was an 'everyone knows' situation," plaintiffs' attorney David Richards points out. "Everyone knew that the system was rotten. The question was, could we get the court to change it?" With respect to Dallas County, the answer was yes. Relying on the evidence, all three judges declared the multimember system unconstitutional under the Fourteenth Amendment equal protection clause.

Much the same situation existed with respect to the eleven House seats in the Bexar County delegation. Despite constituting half the county population, Mexican-Americans had not been able to penetrate the political process. Since 1880, only five Hispanics from Bexar County had served in the Texas Legislature. Describing the plight of Mexican-Americans resulting from both *de jure* (by law) and *de facto* (by circumstance) racial discrimination in Bexar County, the court concluded that "Mexican-Americans are frozen into permanent political minorities destined for constant defeat at the hands of the controlling political majorities." [12] Conversion to single-member districts would give Mexican-Americans representation in the Texas House, given their concentration in a well-defined section of San Antonio called the Barrio. Judge Goldberg concurred with the result in this section of the opinion but not with the reasoning behind it. Judge Wood wrote that he saw the need for an end to multimember districts in Dallas and Bexar counties "for the various reasons stated in the majority opinion." It is likely, however, that Judge Wood focused his attention primarily on advantages to the nascent Republican Party, which had concentrated strength in certain sections of Dallas and Bexar counties, rather than on benefits flowing to racial minorities.

Justice recalls summarizing the facts of discrimination for a state representative from Bexar County who was on the witness stand during the trial and then asking him what he had done to ameliorate the situation. "He couldn't think of a single thing." To illustrate that the existing political establishment was unresponsive to the needs of political minorities, Justice made a point of seeing that this testimony was noted in the opinion.

Attached to the court's opinion were maps indicating how new single-member districting plans were to be implemented in Dallas and Bexar counties. The Dallas plan was modeled on one submitted by State Senator Oscar Mauzy and the Bexar County plan based on one submitted by Ed Idar, Jr., of San Antonio, a lawyer for the Mexican American Legal Defense and Education Fund (MALDEF). Idar would later defend the state in the massive prison reform case, *Ruiz v. Estelle*. Justice's law clerk, Colin Carl, remembers how difficult it was to draw up the new Bexar County voting districts so that population would be equally balanced. Working over the maps in his Adolphus Hotel room in Dallas, where Judge Goldberg had his chambers, Carl was well aware of the awesome power the court was wielding. "I look back with amusement and amazement. Basically, whatever we adopted would be the plan until some other court said otherwise. We would be creating electoral districts and affecting political outcomes."

Judge Wood not only concurred with the multimember-district holding for Dallas and Bexar counties but also joined in rejecting a contention that the Bexar County redistricting scheme for the Texas Senate diluted the power of San Antonio Republicans (at the time, state senatorial districts throughout the state were single-member). The three judges found no constitutional preference "for a district shaped like a horseshoe as opposed to one shaped like a doughnut." [13] Justice found it amusing that the Republicans were trying to convince the court that the minority status of the Republican Party was similar to that of blacks and Mexican-Americans.

Wood joined Goldberg in rejecting a similar contention from black voters in Harris County (Houston) with regard to the Harris County single-member senatorial districts. Justice dissented from this portion of the opinion. He argued that the court should accept a plan which would redraw the Harris County senatorial districts so as to maximize black voting clout. In what appeared to critics to be an obvious tilt toward the labor-liberal-minority wing of the Democratic Party, Justice argued that the testimony showed that the single-member districts had been drawn so as to "fragment the inner city black votes." "Henceforth, they are likely to be represented, in two of the inner city districts, by Senators belonging to a faction of the Democratic Party which has been, in the past, inimical to the interests of blacks." [14] Justice accused the conservative Democrats of conscious partisan line-drawing in order to perpetuate their political success. But his favoring a configuration which had the political consequence of benefiting liberal Democrats undercut the force of his argument.

Reaction around the state varied, depending upon who gained and who lost under the ruling. Under a single-member districting plan for election to the house, Republicans and minorities were virtually guaranteed representation in both Dallas and Bexar counties. Conservative Democrats would see their strength eroded. There was no question that the political makeup of the Texas House of Representatives would be significantly altered. One writer in the *Dallas Morning News* termed the likely consequences "the biggest political upheaval in Texas since Reconstruction."[15] Another wrote in the *Austin American-Statesman* that, given the one-person–one-vote decisions of the U.S. Supreme Court, Texas lawmakers should not have been surprised with the panel's ruling or with the ruling of another three-judge federal court voiding the state's congressional redistricting plan. "If legislators had paid attention to what the courts said previously, they would not be in a position of bemoaning what some call judicial dictatorship."[16] Undoubtedly, a number of legislators had intended this very result, for, as Judge Justice observed on another occasion (Chapter 4), buck-passing to the courts enables legislators to shift the blame for painful decisions. Some legislators and political leaders hoped that the panel's decision would be reversed on appeal.

Judge Justice had studied the U.S. Supreme Court precedents carefully. "I had reached the conclusion that the likelihood was that Justice White would write the opinion. It was obvious to me that he paid a lot of attention to facts and figures. Consequently, I saw to it that all the facts and the figures were included. That was my contribution to that case." He insisted that his law clerks exhaustively present the facts in their portions of the draft opinion, and he himself spent a weekend drawing up the findings of fact supporting the need for single-member districting in Bexar County.

When the case was appealed to the U.S. Supreme Court under the name *White v. Regester* (Mark White was then secretary of state), Justice Byron White did indeed write the opinion.[17] On behalf of a six-person majority, he sided with Wood's view on the deviation issue, reversing Goldberg and Justice's decision. State reapportionment statutes, he wrote, are not subject to the same exact standards applicable to reappointment of congressional seats, and minor variations from mathematical exactness are allowed. While the total variation between two Texas House of Representative districts was 9.9 percent at the extremes, Justice White pointed out that the average deviation for all of the House districts was just 1.82 percent.

But the high court unanimously affirmed the three-judge court's conclusion regarding multimember districts in Dallas and Bexar counties, as well as its decision regarding the San Antonio Republicans and the Harris County blacks. Judge Justice had guessed right. Repeating many of the facts Justice had insisted be inserted in the three-judge opinion, Justice White deferred to the judgment of the district court. With respect to Bexar County, White wrote, "we are not inclined to overturn these findings, representing as they do a blend of history and an intensely local appraisal of the design and impact of the Bexar County multimember district in the light of past and present reality, political and otherwise." [18] Justice's strategy had worked, and he sought to use it to his advantage in later rulings.

Following the Supreme Court decision, the three-judge panel reconvened in 1973 to hear plaintiffs' challenges to multimember districting for the Texas House of Representatives in the nine districts that lack of time had prevented considering in the initial litigation. Once again, Goldberg and Justice found themselves on the same side and pooled their law clerks to work up a draft. Justice's clerks Marianne Wesson and Richard Mithoff went to Dallas to work on the case. Wesson was the first female law clerk assigned to *Graves*. Being the only woman, Wesson remembers that for awhile Judge Goldberg acknowledged her presence by adding "and girl" to his accustomed reference to his clerks as "boys." But as work on the case progressed, Wesson lost her distinction. She realized that when Goldberg called the clerks into his office by addressing them all as "boys," she had been promoted to "honorary boy."

In their January 28, 1974, decision in *Graves II*, Goldberg and Justice began by observing that the Supreme Court in *White* had "scythed much underbrush from the jungle to be penetrated in reapportionment cases." [19] While multimember districts were not per se unconstitutional, they would be declared unconstitutional if it could be shown that the political process was not equally open to participation by minority groups. The two-judge majority read *White* to give judges greater discretion to consider social and political factors in determining blockage of minority participation. "The Supreme Court," the majority exuberantly exclaimed, "has liberated us from any dichotomy of *de facto* and *de jure*. It is not necessary to establish that minority voters are being legally disenfranchised. We are permitted to explore the entire environment and to measure its political pollutants." [20] As the lengthy opinion in *Graves II* attests, they took up their task with a vengeance.

Judge Wood vigorously disagreed, accusing the majority of misinterpreting the Supreme Court's decision. Wood argued in his dissent that the high court had not altered an earlier ruling that state's intent to disenfranchise a minority group must be shown. [21] Lack of minority success at the polls or lack of attention to minority group interests by representatives elected at large, he argued, is not sufficient grounds to warrant striking down a multimember districting scheme.

With these polar positions on what the law required, it is not surprising that the judges drew different conclusions from the evidence regarding each of the contested counties. A case-in-point was Tarrant County (Fort Worth), the largest remaining multimember legislative district in the state with a population of 675,368. Eighty-two percent of the population was white, 12 percent black, and 6 percent Mexican-American, with the latter concentrated in a ghetto area.

Designated as District 32, the Tarrant County delegation to the Texas House of Representatives consisted of nine representatives, all elected at large. Goldberg and Justice noted a long history of racial and ethnic discrimination in the county. The community had resisted school desegregation. Busing pursuant to a court order continued to generate racial strife. By opposing the building of low- or moderate-priced housing in their areas, property owners and developers in wealthy neighborhoods had endeavored to keep minorities boxed into the ghetto. Goldberg and Justice concluded that "District 32 and its environs has been no oasis in Texas' 'colorful history of racial discrimination.'"[22]

Political control was exercised primarily by a labor-liberal coalition and by a loose association of business leaders, each of which agreed not to endorse candidates who opposed the other's favorites. Black candidates endorsed by the labor coalition were nevertheless doomed to failure because rank-and-file laborers refused to vote for blacks. To win elections, whites even used racially motivated smear tactics against their white opponents.

The outlook was so bleak for minorities, Justice and Goldberg found, that until 1968, no black had ever run for the legislature. From that time until the 1973 trial, three blacks had attempted to do so, none successfully. One black candidate, slated and endorsed by the labor-liberal coalition, had been told that he could not win and that he was being slated to attract black and Mexican-American votes for other slated candidates. Another black had refused to run television ads in an effort to disguise his race from the voters. Though both lost, they secured enormous majorities among ghetto voters. The pattern was similar for Mexican-Americans. No Mexican-American had ever been successful in securing a seat on the District 32 delegation.

Black and Mexican-American voters, the majority found, had become alienated from the political process as a result of their political impotence. "History and powerlessness create apathy and unresponsive representatives: unresponsiveness breeds more apathy, apathy more powerlessness and unresponsiveness. Not only those who do not learn from history, but also those who are trapped by history, are condemned to repeat it."[23]

Dissenting Judge John Wood viewed the evidence differently. He attributed minority candidates' lack of success at the polls to voters who did not follow the endorsements of the labor-liberal coalition. He noted that some black candidates had garnered as much as 47 percent of the vote in a county where minorities constituted only 18 percent of the population. While Wood agreed that minorities would be better represented if the county were divided into single-member districts, he observed that "no showing has been made . . . that the minority has not been allowed to register to vote, or vote, to choose a political party, and to participate in its affairs. No showing has been made that the minority has been excluded from slate-making and other candidate selection processes."[24] Supplanting the multimember-district scheme with single-member districts was unwarranted.

And so it went for each of the contested counties. When it was over, the court's majority had required single-member districting for all the counties except Hildalgo, where the plaintiffs had admitted that they could not marshal the necessary evidence to show discrimination. As in Dallas and Bexar counties in *Graves I,* local reaction varied, depending upon who benefited and who did not. In Tarrant County, Representative Gib Lewis told reporters that he was "amazed and bumfuzzled" by the court's action. "I think it was pretty obvious their minds were made up before they ever heard testimony," he said.[25] But the *Fort Worth Star-Telegram* supported the decision. "Not perfect," the paper commented in an editorial, "yet far from as bad as it could have been." The paper observed that complaining local legislators had "no one to blame but themselves and their colleagues with whom they could not reach agreement."[26]

The state appealed the case to the U.S. Supreme Court. But after the Supreme Court's decision in *White v. Regester* supporting single-member districting in Dallas and Bexar counties, the prospects for reversal were questionable. Meanwhile, the Texas Legislature decided to take control of its own political destiny and in 1975 enacted House Bill 1087, replacing multimember districts with single-member districts statewide. With this development, the high court sent the appeal back to the district court for reconsideration.[27]

House Bill 1087 was submitted to the U.S. Attorney General in accord with the 1965 Voting Rights Act, which requires states with a history of *de jure* segregation to obtain clearance for proposed voting changes from either the Attorney General or a three-judge district court in the District of Columbia. Shortly after the act's extension to Texas in 1975, Judge Justice had been the first judge to apply its pre-clearance provisions to a Texas statute in a hotly contested case involving the reregistration of state voters.[28] The Attorney General raised objections to the new single-member redistricting plans in three districts. Since the three were among those involved in the *Graves* litigation, the matter came yet a third time before the three-judge court. The parties prepared compromise plans for Jefferson and Nueces counties which Goldberg, Justice, and Wood subsequently approved. But the dispute over districting in Tarrant County went unresolved. A hearing was held in February 1976.

Goldberg and Justice once again presented a united front in *Graves III*.[29] The opinion began with a reference to the Greek god Sisyphus, who was doomed repeatedly to push a boulder to the top of a mountain, only to have it tumble down again. This was Justice's contribution. "I tried to imitate the style of Judge Goldberg, but not with much success," he admits. "Goldberg was aware of what I was trying to do, but I think he thought my efforts were rather feeble by his standards."

Reaffirming their holding in *Graves II* that single-member districting was constitutionally required for Tarrant County, the pair pondered the choice between two single-member plans presented to them, one by the plaintiffs and one by the state. Both provided for a primary district in which minority voters constituted a clear majority. After considering both, the judges accepted the state's plan for use in the 1976 election, since it would involve the least change in precinct lines. However, the court retained jurisdiction for possible further action after the election. Judge Wood concurred with the use of the defendant's districting plan, but dissented once again with regard to the need for a single-member districting plan for the county.

The single-member districting plan worked. From a district with a 65 percent minority population, a black was elected. For the first time in history, a member of a minority race was sent to the state legislature from Tarrant County. In two other districts with sizable minority populations (44 percent and 15 percent, respectively), whites won, but not without support from black voters.

The fourth and final installment of *Graves v. Barnes* occurred following the 1976 elections. Plaintiffs moved to replace the state's single-member districting plan for Tarrant County, which the court had accepted on an interim basis, with their plan. A two-day hearing was scheduled in September. In a decision which astounded Judge Wood, prompting him to write a strident dissent which minced no words in criticizing the majority, Goldberg and Wood accepted plaintiffs' argument.

The plaintiffs charged that the state's plan, which had been used in the 1976 elections, unconstitutionally diluted minority voting strength by establishing one single-member district with a 65 percent minority population and then scattering remaining minority voters among other districts. The plaintiffs also pointed out that representation among the districts had a 7.7 percent deviation factor. They presented a plan to reconfigure the single-member districts in Tarrant County to eliminate the alleged deficiencies.

While noting that both plans were constitutional, Goldberg and Justice concluded that there was no particular reason to favor the plan already in force, since it had not been formally adopted by the legislature but merely favored by legislative resolution. Since no deference to a state-adopted plan was required, the standards for a court-adopted plan had to be met. A court-adopted plan, the majority noted, had to approach mathematical exactitude. This being the case, the plaintiffs' plan was superior because it reduced deviations among legislative districts to 2 percent. "Our conclusion today is that the present scheme of districting in Tarrant County produces greater population disparities than necessary to effectuate any coherent and legitimate state policy."[30]

The reversal of positions was too much for Judge Wood. Accusing the majority of erratic and inconsistent vacillation, he branded the decision "another unconstitutional usurpation of the rights of the sovereign State of Texas."[31] In a lengthy dissent in which words like "shocking," "outrageous," and "incredible" are used with abandon, Wood pointed out that the plan the court had tentatively approved the year before had the support of local governmental bodies. Furthermore, it bore the imprimatur of the state and the U.S. Supreme Court itself, which had summarily affirmed the three-judge-court decision in *Graves III* in March 1976.[32] He accused the majority of "totally and absolutely" ignoring its duty to respect state reapportionment policy and prophesied that the change would result in confusion and disruption. He noted that the court itself had approved settlements in the other two contested districts with deviation factors of 10 (Nueces County) and 8.1 percent (Jefferson County).

Despite Wood's pointed dissent, Goldberg and Justice were supported by the U.S. Supreme Court, which summarily affirmed the *Graves IV* decision in 1978.[33] The long litigation had come to an end, except for the matter of attorney fees. Judge Justice's award of fees totaling nearly $1 million was substantially affirmed by the Fifth Circuit in 1983.[34]

The initial decision in *Graves v. Barnes* changed the political landscape in Texas. By forcing the Texas Legislature to abolish multimember districting for the Texas House of Representatives, *Graves* gave the state's black and Mexican-American populations, which now constitute nearly 40 percent of the state's population, access to the political process and contributed to the election of a small but growing number of minority members to state political office. Minority membership in the Texas Legislature increased 23.8 percent between 1973 and 1975.[35] By 1989, minorities constituted 25.8 percent of the Texas Senate and 21.3 percent of the Texas House.[36]

The decision also helped the Republicans emerge from minority status by giving them voting strength in districts where they were the dominant political party. The Republican composition of the Texas House rose steadily from 6 percent in 1971 to nearly 40 percent by 1989.[37] The fact that Texas has become a two-party state is in part attributable to *Graves*.

The decision also had national impact. In 1982 Congress incorporated the basic principles of *Graves*, as affirmed by the U.S. Supreme Court in its 1973 *White v. Regester* decision, into Section Two of the 1965 Voting Rights Act. Congress made the change after the Supreme Court backed away from its position in *White* that proof of discriminatory intent was not a prerequisite to establishing illegal discrimination—evidence of unequal participation in the political process would be sufficient. The change came in 1980 in *Mobile v. Bolden*, in which a majority of the justices seemed to opt for a showing of discriminatory intent, a much harder burden for plaintiffs.[38] This was the argument Judge John Wood had repeatedly made during the *Graves* litigation. The 1982 amendment, which is codified as 42 U.S.C. Section 1973(b), nullified the *Bolden* decision by stating:

> A violation of subsection (a) of this section [prohibiting voter discrimination] is established if, based on the totality of circumstances, it is shown that the political processes leading to nomination or election in the State or political subdivision are not equally open to participation by members of a class of citizens protected by subsection (a) of this section in that its members have less opportunity than other members of the electorate to participate in the political process and to elect representatives of their choice. The extent to which members of a protected class have been elected to office in the State or political subdivision is one circumstance which may be considered: Provided, That nothing in this section establishes a right to have members of a protected class elected in numbers equal to their proportion in the population.

By adding this section, Congress restored the so-called "results test," which the Supreme Court had approved in *White v. Regester*, and gave civil rights attorneys an important weapon against voter discrimination. Thus, the principles Judges Goldberg and Justice set forth in *Graves v. Barnes* have become an essential part of election law across the country.

In addition to a deep gratification in the results, Judge Justice enjoyed working on all the *Graves* decisions. "It involved one of my major interests. The political process has always been of fascination to me," he says. Ironically, the success in influencing the political process that eluded Wayne Justice as a political figure came with his elevation to the bench.

Redistricting in East Texas Communities

After the U.S. Supreme Court affirmed in *Graves* that federal judges could make a detailed appraisal of local conditions in assessing challenges to multi-member districts, Texas civil rights attorneys began to realize the potential to challenge at-large city, county, and school board election systems throughout the state. This was certainly true in East Texas, for Judge Justice had sent a clear message in *Graves* as to how he would deal with voter discrimination cases. Austin attorney David Richards said to Dan Weiser, a Dallas demographer he used in voter discrimination issues, "What the hell, why don't we just go over to East Texas and start changing things over there?" Up until this time, much of East Texas had escaped integration. Many communities even refused federal revenue-sharing funds, though the money was desperately needed, to keep from having to comply with antidiscrimination requirements. So Richards and Weiser began poring over census data, looking for every county in the Tyler Division with a more than 20 percent black population. Once they had identified the counties, they began searching out potential plaintiffs to file county reapportionment lawsuits in Justice's court.

The first case they filed was *Weaver v. Commissioners Court, Nacogdoches County,* in 1974. Historically, the precincts for electing officials to the Nacogdoches County Commissioners Court, the county governing body, had been divided so that the city of Nacogdoches composed one precinct and the rural areas composed the others. In 1969, as a consequence of litigation in state court, a new plan was adopted which divided the city into four parts and decreased somewhat the voter deviation among the precincts. However, substantial deviation still remained. No effort had been made since the 1970 census to correct the inequities. The parties to the 1974 lawsuit agreed that the population disparity between the precincts remained substantial.

At the time, blacks, comprising about 22 percent of the county and city populations, were substantially segregated into specific geographical areas in both. Richards argued that the existing precinct system fragmented the black vote in Nacogdoches by dividing the area of heavy black concentration into separate precincts. He also argued that the county commissioners had shown little interest in serving black needs: only 3 of the 103 persons on the county payroll were black. The county jail facilities were still segregated.

Richards remembers that Weiser, his expert witness in the case, was unconventionally groomed and dressed—long hair, beard, old clothes. Sitting in the front row of the courtroom were the conservative county commissioners, glowering at Judge Justice on the bench. As in prior segregation days, all the blacks sat in the back of the courtroom, occasionally calling out "Amen" to points made by their attorney. Richards recalls looking first at Justice on the bench and then around the courtroom as he began to question his hippie-appearing expert witness, and thinking, "Ye gods, these county commissioners must think that whatever they've read about the world going to hell in a handbasket is happening this day, right here, in Tyler, Texas!"

Arthur Weaver, the black activist who filed the suit, points out that segregation was such a way of life in East Texas that he had trouble at first in motivating blacks to join the cause for equality. The assassination of Martin Luther King, Jr., in 1968 was the turning point. That, and awareness that William Wayne Justice was prepared to support the quest for civil rights. Sitting in 1989 in the room of his house on Butt Street, which also served as an NAACP office, with its walls plastered with newspaper stories from the civil rights era, the black activist recalled hearing Wayne Justice talk about equal rights. "He said he hoped that one day he would see equal protection in education, voting rights, policy protection, and housing. I had never heard a white person talk that way before. When I heard him say that, I decided to follow through." Despite ugly and vicious repercussions from the white community in the form of harassment, cross-burning, and the like, Weaver became a perennial plaintiff in a number of cases filed by Richards and assumed the presidency of the Nacogdoches County NAACP chapter in 1974.

Justice had no difficulty finding the existing commissioners court election system unconstitutional as a violation of the Fourteenth Amendment equal protection clause, in large part because the county commissioners admitted that the system was flawed. Both parties proposed plans for remedying the defects. Justice opted for the plan developed by the plaintiffs, since it did not fragment the county's black population and significantly reduced the between-precinct population disparities in the county. Justice ordered it implemented immediately for the 1974 primary and general elections for county commissioners, and also ordered that defendants pay attorney fees in the amount of $1,400.[39]

This decision was a breakthrough for blacks. In 1974, a black was elected as county commissioner, the first black to hold such an office in the county, and purportedly in the state, in this century. *Weaver* paved the way for similar lawsuits in East Texas, since many of these counties had concentrations of black voters which, if located in a single election unit, would produce a black officeholder.

The city of Nacogdoches was the subject of another significant voter discrimination lawsuit brought by plaintiff Arthur Weaver. That case, *Weaver v. Muckleroy,* coincided with the parade-permit case *McGuire v. Roebuck,* discussed in Chapter 7. The tension and bitterness were apparent in the courtroom. Justice recalls that, as in all these cases, "the audience would physically segregate themselves in the courtroom and glare at each other in a state of high tension throughout the trial."

Weaver v. Muckleroy had its roots in the 1972 election for city office in Nacogdoches, whose population of some 22,500 residents was augmented much of the year by the 10,000 students attending Stephen F. Austin University. James D. Appling, a black student attending the university, and Lee Holbert, a white student, decided to run for city commissioner. Heretofore, these elections had been greeted mostly with apathy. But when Appling filed, the first black ever to do so, and a voter registration drive was started at the university, the election suddenly became a matter of intense community interest.

Appling and his supporters forged a coalition among black voters in Nacogdoches and students and professors at the university. The two incumbent commissioners who were running for reelection placed a large ad containing a picture of all the candidates in the city newspaper. It was obvious that Appling was the only black. Racial tensions were already at a high peak because of violence associated with the black protest parade which produced the litigation in *McGuire v. Roebuck*. Voters went to the polls in droves. The incumbent commissioners were reelected in the largest turnout in city history.

After the election, the five-member city commission scheduled a special election to approve amendments to the city charter. One of the amendments shifted the election for city commissioner from April to the third week in June, a time when most students would be away from the university. Another amendment also adopted a majority vote requirement and a place system. As previously noted, both have the effect of curtailing the election chances of black candidates.

The special election to approve the amendments was scheduled for July 15, 1972. As a result of a lawsuit filed on June 29 against R. G. Muckleroy, chairman of the city commission, and his fellow commissioners, a hearing was held on July 13 regarding the issuance of an injunction to halt the election.

Justice and his law clerk Henry Skelton gave the matter top priority. Reviewing the facts presented at the July 13 hearing, they concluded that the only reason the special election had been called for July 15 was to minimize the participation of university students. They began preparing a written order enjoining the holding of the election. Early in the afternoon of July 14, the day before the election, Judge Justice called Charles F. Potter, the attorney for the defendants, and told him that the order would be handed down by 5 P.M. so that Potter could seek a stay from the Fifth Circuit if

Justice should decide against him. No word was mentioned as to what the order would say.

Justice and Skelton continued to work feverishly on the order. About 4:30 P.M., Justice received a call from the Fifth Circuit in New Orleans informing him that the court had stayed his order. Justice was incredulous. He burst out, "How can you stay my order when I haven't even entered it yet?" Both he and Skelton were furious. But there was nothing to be done. The order granting the injunction was duly issued, even though it was "dead on arrival."[40] Charles Potter professes a hazy memory about the incident. But when asked how it could have happened, he tipped back in his chair, clapped his hands, and laughed.

The election was held, and the amendments were adopted. But then it was discovered that the election had been held in violation of the Texas Constitution. The amendments providing for majority and place requirements were resubmitted to the voters, who approved them in time for the April 1973 city elections. (The amendment advancing the holding of city elections to June was not resubmitted.) David Richards, who also represented the plaintiffs in this lawsuit, thought to himself, "I'm going to fix those bastards. I'm just going to convert this into a single-member districting case." The lawsuit was duly modified to charge that the at-large voting scheme for city elections unconstitutionally diluted the right of blacks to vote.

In a January 1975 order agreeing with the plaintiffs, Justice observed that blacks made up over one-fourth of the city population and were concentrated in one section of the town.[41] He noted that no black had ever been elected to the city commission or to county office until 1974, when, as a result of the Nacogdoches County Commissioners Court ruling he had issued, a black was elected to the county commission. Following his approach in *Graves v. Barnes*, Justice took judicial notice of the lack of responsiveness of city officials to the needs of black voters. He cited evidence that relations between the police department and the black community had not improved in the years following the parade incident which had resulted in *McGuire v. Roebuck*. He noted that aside from the virtually all-black garbage department, black employment by the city was negligible.

Justice also noted that a second black, Harvey Rayson, had run for city commissioner in the spring of 1973 and had secured a plurality of the votes cast. But because of the majority requirement, Rayson was forced into a runoff and lost. The campaign, Justice wrote, was rife with racism. He observed that the city commission scheduled the runoff election on the last day of final examinations at the university. "The court infers from the evidence," he concluded, "that the scheduling of the runoff on this date, over the protests of Rayson that it would result in disenfranchisement of resident student voters within the City of Nacogdoches, was an act intentionally designed by the defendants to frustrate Rayson's election chances, by insuring that there would be a minimal participation by students in the runoff election."

Justice mandated a single-member ward plan for city elections. Following further litigation, a plan was adopted whereby Nacogdoches was divided into four single-member city commissioner wards, with one commissioner to be elected on an at-large basis. As with the county commissioners court, a black was soon elected. The matter was not appealed on advice of attorney Charles Potter, who believed the city could not win, given the strong desegregative posture of the Fifth Circuit.

These local voter discrimination suits are typical of those that came before federal district court judges across the South during these years. Products of the communities in which they live, the judges were often not in sympathy with the mandates they had to enforce. Possible violent repercussions were also a deterrent. Such was not the case with Judge Justice, who welcomed the opportunity to eliminate voter discrimination and to open the way for those heretofore disenfranchised from the political process. In decision after decision, Justice mandated an end to voter discrimination in a region whose racism he knew all too well, even though for him personally it meant social isolation and opprobrium. Civil rights attorney Larry Daves, who was involved in many of these early and bitter discrimination cases, wonders how Justice stood it. "In those years, everyone feared for his life," Daves asserts. "There probably is no more courageous human being in East Texas than the Judge for simply staying there."

To the black community in East Texas, William Wayne Justice was godsent. "A legend in his time," says Arthur Weaver. "I do hope and believe that Judge Justice will be long, long remembered in the minds of blacks. When he's gone, there will be no more like him."

Congressional Redistricting:
Seamon v. Upham

Depressed economic conditions in the Snowbelt, coupled with the booming oil-driven economy in Texas, attracted a multitude of people to the state during the 1970s. Population grew 27.1 percent. Following the 1980 census, the Texas Legislature enacted Senate Bill 1, which apportioned Texas into twenty-seven single-member congressional districts, three more than under the old configuration. Following the governor's approval of the legislation on August

14, 1981, it was submitted to the U.S. Attorney General for clearance under the 1965 Voting Rights Act.

Before the Attorney General issued a decision, suit was filed in the Paris Division of the Eastern District of Texas challenging the legislation as an unconstitutional gerrymander which diluted minority voting strength. The case was clearly forum-shopped. Justice was the only judge in the Paris Division, and Leighton Cornett, who had worked with Justice during his tenure as U.S. attorney, was representing the plaintiff. Cornett played only a nominal role in the case; civil rights attorneys from other parts of the state were orchestrating the lawsuit. The Reverend A. M. Seamon was a black activist and resident of Paris, Texas. Seamon had appeared before Judge Justice before when he challenged the at-large election system for the Paris city council.[42] Cornett had also represented him in that lawsuit. In a decision graphically depicting nearly complete segregation of the races in the Old South community of Paris, Justice had ruled for Seamon, requiring single-member districting. Since the attorneys in the case had presented totally different descriptions of the black area of town, Justice himself walked the streets of Paris and came away appalled at the substandard conditions blacks endured and the extent of black-white separatism. He ordered the city to implement a seven-ward single-member system developed by the plaintiffs. He also ordered the city to pay the plaintiffs' attorney fees. The defendants instituted, then withdrew, an appeal to the Fifth Circuit. Later, Seamon also successfully challenged at-large election systems for the Paris junior college district and the Paris public school system in Justice's court.

In addition to Seamon, the Judge allowed numerous other plaintiffs to join the suit. One group alleged that they had been "packed" into one area of the state and "fenced" out of other areas in order to minimize their voting strength. Another group alleged that they had been fragmented among several districts for the same purpose. Sixteen congressional legislative districts were implicated. The legislation was challenged as a violation of the Fourteenth and Fifteenth amendments, as well as the Voting Rights Act (this was prior to the enactment of the 1982 amendment authorizing use of the "results test" employed in *Graves*).

Since the litigation involved the constitutionality of a state statute, Judge Justice notified Chief Judge John C. Godbold of the need for a three-judge district court. Godbold appointed Federal District Judge Robert M. Parker and Fifth Circuit Judge Sam D. Johnson to the panel, along with Justice. As the judge before whom the case originated, Justice served as managing judge, just as he had in *Graves v. Barnes*. Judge Parker is nearer to Justice's political views than any other judge in the Eastern District. Justice has known Johnson, a moderate Democrat, from his days in private practice. The two have remained friends through the years. All three judges were Democrats, thus giving the plaintiffs a favorable forum.

A three-day hearing was held in Austin in late November and early December 1981. As in *Graves,* the judges were lenient on rules of evidence, and a large amount of material was introduced. Shortly after the trial, Judge Justice told his clerk Fritz Byers, who was assigned the case, that he thought the plaintiffs had made a strong argument. For several hours, the Judge reviewed the issues and his thoughts on voting rights law with Byers and with Barbara Ellis, another law clerk who worked on parts of the case. He pointed out that any decision the panel reached would be appealed and that Justice Byron White would likely write the opinion for the Supreme Court. From his experience with *White v. Regester,* Justice believed that White would be heavily influenced by an appraisal of local conditions. Thus, he instructed his law clerks to become intimately familiar with the vast record of the case as it pertained to each locality involved in the litigation.

In January 1982, the three judges met in Judge Johnson's chambers in Austin to discuss the case. Each of the judges presented his views. All acknowledged that it was a difficult case, for the judges were being asked to review the state's purported efforts to benefit minorities. Justice by now had formed his own thoughts and considered the state's plan biased and skewed in such a manner as to dilute minority participation in the congressional political process. All three judges had come to this conclusion with regard to South Texas. But to Justice's great surprise, Judge Parker was in favor of affirming the rest of the state's plan. Justice was also surprised that Judge Johnson was prepared to accept only some of the plaintiff arguments. Because of their differences, each judge elected to work on his own opinion. During December 1981 and January 1982, Justice and his law clerks had to drop nearly everything else to work on the draft.

However, the judges held off taking any formal action, pending notification from the U.S. Attorney General's office. Because the latter was in no hurry to announce a position, the judges were forced to issue an order late in January postponing the filing deadlines in the affected districts. Finally, notice was sent that the Attorney General objected to two of the twenty-seven districts. The action rendered Senate Bill 1 unenforceable. In February, the judges issued a second order prohibiting the holding of any congressional elections in Texas until the court could devise a congressional redistricting plan for the 1982 primary and general elections. All parties had agreed that the court should develop an interim plan. A hearing was held in February to consider the extent of the court's jurisdiction in light of the Attorney General's decision and to receive additional evidence from the parties appropriate to the construction of a new plan.

Judge Johnson's opinion became the court's opinion, which was announced on February 27, 1982. It was clear that the judges were displeased with the inordinate delay in the U.S. Attorney General's office. In a footnote, Judge Johnson wrote, "The unseemly delay, inattention, and inactivity of the office of the Attorney General of the United States provided the State of Texas with anything but an expeditious mechanism for seeking approval of its congressional apportionment plan." [43] The court also was displeased with the Attorney General's superficial three-page letter of explanation.

Johnson did not rule on the constitutionality of Senate Bill 1, since it was rendered legally unenforceable by the Attorney General. Legal precedent, he wrote, requires the court to follow two guidelines: voter equality across districts and the absence of dilution of minority voting strength. With regard to the former, he accepted Senate Bill 1's division of the state into twenty-seven congressional districts, each within a few hundred of meeting the ideal target population of 526,977. With regard to dilution of minority voting strength, the judges redrew the two contiguous districts in South Texas which had been the focus of the Attorney General's objection. They rejected plaintiffs' contentions regarding dilution of minority voting strength in West Texas and Harris County, accepting the legislature's configuration for these areas.

But in the most controversial portion of the opinion, Johnson and Justice accepted the plaintiffs' arguments and redrew the Dallas County congressional districts. Senate Bill 1 had created one district in Dallas County where minorities were in the majority, thereby favoring the election of a minority representative. But this had reduced minority strength in an adjoining district, favoring the election there of a conservative candidate. Directly threatened were two white liberal Democrats, Representatives Jim Mattox and Martin Frost, both of whose districts prior to Senate Bill 1 were over one-quarter minority. Liberal Dallas County Democrats had opposed Senate Bill 1's line-drawing, arguing that the minorities had substantial "swing" influence in both districts and should not be packed into one district. But Dallas minority representatives and Governor William Clements had insisted upon it, with the announced intention of having one district "safe" for minorities. Behind all the professed concerns about minority interests, of course, were self-serving political considerations. This is what made the case so sensitive, for any decision the court made would also be regarded as politically motivated.

Noting that minority voters had strongly supported Frost and Mattox under the old districting plan in these districts and thus had significant access to the political process, the two-judge majority redrew the Dallas districts to avoid the retrogression that creation of a largely minority district would cause in the adjoining district.

In a lengthy concurring and dissenting opinion—Justice says Judge

Johnson "visibly flinched" when he saw the length of it—Justice took the occasion to set forth in detail his judicial philosophy regarding the role of the judiciary in voting rights disputes. By now, he had thought through his views on voter discrimination, and he endeavored to explain his jurisprudence carefully. Finding Johnson's professed deference to legislative action "puzzling," he argued for vigorous judicial scrutiny of legislative districting plans. Whatever plan the court might adopt, he wrote, must be free from any taint of arbitrariness or discrimination. While reapportionment is a legislative duty, the court must step forward to fill the void "left by the dereliction of the state legislature."[44]

Justice had been intrigued with plaintiffs' attorney David Richards' argument that under the Fourteenth Amendment equal protection clause judges ought to intensely scrutinize legislative line-drawing purportedly designed to benefit minorities, just as is done when invidious discrimination is alleged. This is a controversial assertion, for many civil rights proponents worry that thrusting judges deeply into the political process invites conservative jurists to strike down programs partial to minorities as being discrimination-in-reverse, as indeed the U.S. Supreme Court did in one controversial 1989 decision.[45] Even Richards felt uncomfortable asserting it. Parker and Johnson had rejected it out of hand when Justice brought it up at the January conference.

Justice remained convinced that the court should employ "intimate attention to particulars" because voting is a fundamental right and because racial classifications are involved. He pointed out that the Supreme Court had approved such a searching scrutiny in *White v. Regester*. "Deference to the legislature's choice, whether as to identification of relevant issues or regarding their final resolution, is inappropriate."[46] He cited Supreme Court and Fifth Circuit rulings supporting the view that a history of discrimination warrants a searching inquiry into legislative action. "In a situation in which the state has, in the past, overtly and consciously discriminated on the basis of race, later actions by the state must be closely scrutinized to insure that they do not bear the stamp of this prior discrimination, even if the actions are, nominally, racially neutral," he observed.[47]

Justice had experienced the parochialism and intransigence of the Texas Legislature before. He gave little credence to legislative claims of attempting to assist minority participation in the political process. "I was disgusted by the record that was presented to me," he says, looking back. "I thought the inference was clear that they set out to draw the lines in such a way as to dilute minority voting strength."

Judges should not accept professed assertions of benevolent line-drawing in voting rights cases, he wrote, but must probe to question real intentions. "The common awareness that explicit racist classifications will not survive judicial inspection may safely be assumed to have the effect of driving illicit motives into some darkened sanctuary of hidden purpose, from which they will emerge in the guise of some legitimate concernment."[48] The state presented computer-driven data to justify its treatment of minorities. But Justice found that use of the computer only facilitated legislative deviousness. "It was obvious to me," he says, "that they had used very sophisticated computer projections to draw that plan to deliberately dilute the voting strengths of the minorities."

Since the U.S. Supreme Court had ruled in its 1980 *Mobile v. Bolden* decision that intent to discriminate had to be shown (and Congress had not yet enacted its 1982 amendment restoring the "results" test used in *Graves*), Justice sought to glean intent from the circumstantial evidence of discriminatory effect, citing a long list of U.S. Supreme Court decisions involving the state. He pointed out that much of modern voting rights law had its origins in unconstitutional efforts by the Texas Legislature to discriminate against minorities. Among the decisions he cited were *Nixon v. Herndon* (1926), in which the Court held unconstitutional a Texas statute prohibiting blacks from voting in the Democratic primary;[49] *Nixon v. Condon* (1932), striking down a Texas statute permitting the executive committee of a political party to prescribe membership qualifications;[50] *Smith v. Allwright* (1944), holding that exclusion of nonwhites from participation in primary elections was unconstitutional;[51] *Terry v. Adams* (1953), holding that a pre-primary election conducted by a private association excluding nonwhites from membership is unconstitutional;[52] and *Terry v. United States* (1966), affirming a lower court decision striking down the poll tax.[53]

This history, he wrote, "stands as a disheartening testament to the perseverance and craft of the dominant political leaders, in their attempt to exclude minorities from participation in the process of self-government."[54] As evidence that voter discrimination continues in the state, he pointed out that since 1975, when Texas was brought under the terms of the Voting Rights Act, "the Department of Justice has lodged far more objections to governmental actions affecting voting rights in Texas than in any other covered state."[55] Voting practice in Texas, he asserted, "is replete with charges of vote fraud, ballot stuffing, ballot tampering, unpublicized re-location of polling places on the day of election, alterations in registration requirements and intimidation of voters."[56]

The result, he concluded, was that few minorities had been elected to political office. Since the Civil War, Texas had not elected a black or Mexican-American senator, nor had there been more than one black in the congressional delegation, nor more than two Hispanics. Blacks and Mexican-Americans were also significantly under-represented in the Texas Legislature. "A century of neglect, sometimes benign, frequently malign, has created a climate of alienation and apathy, mixed with deep-seated resentment in many of the minority communities of Texas."[57] It was a thorough and moving commentary.

Against this backdrop, the Judge reviewed the claims of the plaintiffs and the process resulting in the enactment of Senate Bill 1. Insofar as Dallas County was concerned, Justice questioned the validity of a petition signed by Dallas black voters in favor of a district safe for minorities. He noted that the legislature had not assessed minority voter sentiment in other sections of the state in this manner. While he acknowledged support among black community leaders for a safe district at the expense of influence in other districts, such support was not unanimous. He pointed out that all black legislators except one had voted against Senate Bill 1. He observed that Governor Clements' purported support for a district "safe" for minorities was self-serving, in that Dallas was Clements' home town, his desire was not based on any systematic study or legal advice, and he had not argued for safe districts in other parts of the state.[58]

Steve Bickerstaff, one of the state's attorneys, questions Justice's assessment. "I have trouble believing that a judge can evaluate within the context of a one- or two-day trial what was a very complicated, difficult, and lengthy legislative process." Bickerstaff points out that while a judge may accurately perceive what motivated a few legislators, the judge cannot ascertain the motives of the many others involved in the process. Bickerstaff had observed legislative deliberations over the minority district in Dallas County. "What struck me was the change in the position of many of the black community leaders who early on had favored retaining the existing congressional districts. This change of position, I think, affected a lot of the legislators who voted for the minority district." He adds, "I have no doubt that if you had taken a vote in Dallas as to which of those alternatives the black community wanted, it would have been the single minority district. Under such circumstances, a risk is that if the legislator disregards an outpouring at public hearings of apparent sentiment from a minority community and opts instead for a different option based on legal arguments about what is best for the community, the legislator may be accused of a racially patronizing attitude."

What more than anything else convinced Justice of the unconstitutionality of the Dallas reconfiguration was that it was highly questionable whether the new minority-dominant district really would elect a minority candidate. Under Senate Bill 1, the district was to be 46.5 percent black and 17.3 percent Hispanic. Justice noted that the white incumbent, Martin Frost, had previously attracted most of the minority vote. He observed that trial testimony had established that "blacks and Hispanics frequently find themselves at odds with one another in Dallas politics." [59] Further, minority voting participation was low. The result was that minorities had exchanged strong influence in two congressional districts for strong—but not necessarily controlling—influence in one. Consequently, Justice wrote, minority voting strength had been unconstitutionally diluted.

Dallas politicians and newspaper columnists accused Johnson and Justice of playing politics. But Justice heatedly denies that politics had anything to do with his or Johnson's decision. "Not one time did we ever discuss political factors. Not one time. That wasn't even mentioned. It would have been grossly improper had we done so."

Through a similar exhaustive analysis, Justice also found the plaintiffs' arguments convincing with regard to congressional districting in Harris County (Houston), South Texas, and West Texas.

In a short opinion, Judge Parker agreed with Justice and Johnson only with regard to the need to reconfigure the two South Texas counties which had been the focus of the Attorney General's disapproval. Parker refused to endorse the pair's redistricting of Dallas County. Like Johnson, Parker also refused to endorse Justice's conclusions with regard to the other claims in Harris County and West Texas. "Absent specific statutory or constitutional violations, any changes to S.B. 1 made in this Court's remedial plan on behalf of the minorities which brought this suit, are merely substitutions by this Court of its preferences for those of the legislature," he wrote. [60]

Republican Party officials quickly appealed the ruling to the U.S. Supreme Court, which in a unanimous *per curiam* ruling handed down on April 1, 1982, overturned the court's judgment with respect to Dallas County. [61] Since the Attorney General had not objected to the creation of the safe district for minorities in Dallas County and since only Judge Justice had ruled Senate Bill 1 unconstitutional in this regard, the three-judge court was without authority to make any changes. Judge Justice's lengthy exposition on voting rights law had been ignored. While the Supreme Court had not passed on Justice's views, it was apparent that neither Justice's fellow judges on the district court nor the U.S. Supreme Court justices favored the kind of intrusive judicial review of legislative redistricting decisions that Justice had advocated. [62] Yet his exegesis on voting rights law remains in the published volumes of district court decisions, a provocative argument on behalf of judicial activism to end voter discrimination.

When the reversal was announced, Justice wanted a copy of the opinion as quickly as possible. Fritz Byers had a friend who was then clerking for a Supreme Court justice. Byers contacted the law clerk, who arranged to have someone in the Supreme Court clerk's office read the opinion over the phone.

Justice had an old dictabelt recording machine. Byers held the microphone to the phone and produced a scratchy, nearly inaudible recording. To decipher the role the three-judge panel should play in making arrangements for the primary election, Justice listened intently to the recording. Because the May 1 filing date for the primary elections was only four weeks away, the Supreme Court had sent the case back for the trial court to determine whether its interim plan should remain in effect or whether the Senate Bill 1 configuration should be reinstated.

In a decision which infuriated Republicans and many blacks, Judges Johnson and Justice announced from the bench that the court's now discredited interim plan for Dallas County was to be followed in the primary election in the interest of avoiding confusion at the polls. The decision left those in the courtroom speechless. Plaintiffs' attorney David Richards was "absolutely thunderstruck." "The decision appeared to trouble Judge Parker, whose position had been vindicated by the Supreme Court," he adds. Later, Parker issued a dissenting opinion. Johnson and Justice later wrote a short opinion in which they explained that they had felt justified in taking up the Dallas issue in the first place because Senate Bill 1 had been rendered a nullity by the Attorney General's action. "Nevertheless, the Supreme Court has spoken," they wrote, with a certain amount of pique. "It now says, without delineating the applicable standards, that it is improper not to adopt a state's legally unenforceable plan unless the specific aspect of the state's proposal amounts to a constitutional or statutory violation."[63]

Dallas newspaper reporters and politicians had a field day. In an editorial entitled "What Arrogance!" the *Dallas Morning News* lambasted the action, observing that "a more modest duo than Justice and Johnson might have taken the hint and restored the legislative plan." "And federal judges wonder why, as a class, they arouse so much public obloquy," the *News* stated. "Maybe it's because growing numbers of Americans believe certain old-fashioned things, such as that we really do have a federal system, and that the Founding Fathers didn't mean for it to be run by unelected judges."[64] The criticism did not come as a surprise to the two judges. Both shrugged it off.

The following month, however, the Texas Legislature passed Senate Bill 480, which only slightly altered the court-ordered boundaries in the two disputed Dallas congressional districts. That plan was submitted to the Attorney General and later came before the district court in another installment of *Seamon v. Upham*. In the interim, the judges had to deal with a strange spin-off case.

After the general elections in November 1982, Representative Phil Gramm from Congressional District 6 changed his political affiliation from Democratic to Republican. He resigned his office and proposed to run again in the special election as a Republican. Plaintiffs, representing Democratic and minority interests, filed suit before Johnson, Justice, and Parker, arguing that the February 12, 1983, date set by Governor Clements for the special election deprived them of their rights under the Constitution and the Voting Rights Act. Justice laughs about the lawsuit. "That was the most evident case of forum shopping I ever saw in my life! They really reached out to get me in on a case." After a brief hearing in January 1983, the judges concluded that the matter had nothing to do with the original litigation and dismissed it. In his opinion for the court in *Seamon III,* Justice noted that Congressional District 6 "touches every federal judicial district of Texas except the Eastern District where the case is filed." [65]

After the state legislature substantially endorsed the court-ordered congressional redistricting plan for Dallas County, the case came back before the three-judge panel. But this time, Justice did not hear the dispute. Between the April 1982 decision in *Seamon II* regarding use of the court-approved interim plan in Dallas County and litigation in *Seamon IV* in the summer of 1983, circumstances arose which caused him to withdraw from the case.

Construction near Justice's Tyler home had altered the natural terrain so that water flowed onto his lot. After unsuccessful efforts to negotiate a resolution, he decided that he would have to go to court. "I was very fearful that I would not get an impartial jury panel here in Tyler." So he decided to hire an old established firm in Tyler to represent him in further negotiations with the contractor. He selected Charles Potter, who had tried the Nacogdoches parade permit and voting rights cases. Potter asked that another member of the firm, Leonard E. Davis, take responsibility for the matter. Justice, who knew Davis, a conservative Republican, and regarded him as a good lawyer and as a friend, agreed. It was Davis who had represented defendants in the first reversal Justice experienced in a criminal case. [66]

Davis negotiated a settlement with the contractor. But in the meantime the Texas Republican Party hired Davis as their general counsel. Speculation abounded that the choice was made to force Justice off the *Seamon* case, since having his personal attorney arguing before him would be a conflict of interest under judicial rules of ethics. Davis maintains that in his conversations with GOP State Chairman George Strake, no mention of the *Seamon* litigation was ever made. Whatever the motive behind the selection, in August 1983, prior to the hearing on the legislative plan for Dallas, Justice removed himself from the panel. [67] William Steger, a conservative Republican, was appointed in his place. The three-judge court went on to uphold the legislative plan—a virtual carbon copy of what Johnson and Justice had favored in *Seamon II,* with Steger dissenting on the basis that the absence of a safe district for blacks was discriminatory. Plaintiffs' attorneys joked about Steger's sudden "conversion" to the civil rights cause. The U.S. Supreme Court affirmed the decision in 1984.[68]

Seamon v. Upham did not have the impact of *Graves v. Barnes* on Texas political life. But it did give Justice the opportunity to express at length his views about the role of the federal court in contested issues of legislative reapportionment. His opinion followed years of hearing Texas voting discrimination cases and squarely presented the case for activist judicial involvement in the interest of democratizing the political process.

While the pace of voter discrimination litigation in Justice's court has slowed in recent years, the 1990 census may initiate another round. If so, plaintiffs' attorneys who get their cases into Justice's court know that they will get a thorough judicial review of the challenged scheme, regardless of legislative motives in enacting it.

CHAPTER 9

The Education of Undocumented Alien Children

Aliens who reside in the United States without authorization have often been victims of discrimination. But rarely have they sought redress in court for fear of being deported. Consequently, the law on their status has been sparse and unsettled. Such was the case with the entitlement of children of undocumented aliens to a free public education.[1]

When the Tyler Independent School District changed its tuition-free policy for these children, it set in motion a train of events which would culminate with a seminal U.S. Supreme Court decision. In *Doe v. Plyler,* Judge Justice was called upon to answer a difficult legal question, not design a complex remedial order. He knew he was entering upon new legal turf, and consequently his opinion was restrained and cautious.

In 1977 the Tyler Independent School District had noticed that its Mexican-American population, while small, was growing. Planning for enrollment, particularly in bilingual education, had become more difficult, given the transient nature of many of these students. The board was also aware that two years before, the state legislature in an effort to assist financially strapped school districts had amended the attendance law, Section 21.031 of the Texas Education Code, to exclude noncitizens from a tuition-free public education. Before the amendment, the attendance law made no distinction as to citizenship status. Indeed, a 1975 Texas Attorney General Opinion had concluded that Section 21.031 compelled the education of all alien children.[2]

Concerned about the financial consequences of an influx of undocumented alien children, the Tyler school board enacted a policy, effective with the start of the 1977 school year, that students who could not produce evidence of citizenship had to pay a $1,000 tuition fee. Since the average undocumented alien family in Texas then earned $4,000 a year, the tuition requirement effectively excluded these children from school. The prevailing view among members of the Tyler school board, and indeed Texans in general, was that state taxpayers should not have to foot the bill for the education of noncitizens.

At the time, Texas was the only state with such a law. Despite large Hispanic populations, California and New Mexico allowed undocumented alien children to attend their public schools tuition-free rather than face the consequences of a ghetto of ignorance. Looking back, John Hardy, the Tyler school district attorney, acknowledges that "it's hard not to be sympathetic when you have a cute little five-year-old who wants to go to school to learn how to color, write, and do the things like the other kids." Hardy concedes that the facts and certainly the sympathy were all in favor of the plaintiffs. Richard Arnett, the assistant attorney general who handled the case on appeal, labels the exclusion law "Texas at its worst."

While unwise and myopic, the legislation was not clearly unconstitutional. For his part, Hardy maintains that "legally speaking, I believe we were right to follow state law." He also points out that the federal government had failed to enforce its own policy on immigration, thus putting the onus on the state and school district to do something about illegal immigration and its consequences for social services. This argument was frequently made during the course of the litigation. However, one commentator has pointed out that Texas had time and again frustrated congressional attempts to establish a federal prohibition on the employment of undocumented aliens, the root cause of the problem.[3]

When the Tyler schoolhouse gates were closed to the children of undocumented aliens who could not pay tuition, several families contacted Mike McAndrew, a counselor and immigration specialist in Tyler. McAndrew tried without success to get the school district to reconsider its decision. The children involved in the litigation had been born in Mexico; none had documentation showing he or she resided legally in the United States. However, several of the families also had children who had been born in the United States. As citizens, these children could attend school on a tuition-free basis. They were not involved in the lawsuit. All but two of the undocumented children had attended the Tyler schools prior to the revocation of free tuition. The families had lived in Tyler from three to thirteen years. One family owned their own home; the others rented. At least one parent was employed. Three of the four families had purchased automobiles. In short, they had established roots in the community. McAndrew advised them to contact Larry Daves, a civil rights attorney in Tyler, who immediately applied to Judge Justice for a temporary injunction.

Daves knew that several similar cases had been filed in state court and that the plaintiffs had not been successful. The most notable case was *Hernandez v.*

Houston Independent School District. The plaintiffs had lost at the trial level but had appealed the decision to the Texas Court of Civil Appeals in Austin, where no decision had been reached.[4] Daves also knew that the law in this area was still evolving in federal court. While the U.S. Supreme Court had ruled that the Fourteenth Amendment prohibition against denial of equal protection of the laws applies to legally admitted aliens, the justices had yet to extend its protection to undocumented aliens. Daves concluded that it could be a ground-breaking case and immediately sought assistance. He contacted the Mexican American Legal Defense and Education Fund (MALDEF) in San Antonio. They referred him to Peter Roos in their San Francisco office. As it turned out, Roos and MALDEF were at that time conducting research on this very issue. Roos came to Tyler and assumed control of the case.

Roos and Daves filed their lawsuit on September 6, the day after Labor Day. As soon as Judge Justice saw the complaint, "I realized at once and I told my law clerks that this is one that's headed for the United States Supreme Court." His would be the first federal court to consider the sensitive matter. It would become one of the most divisive cases to reach the Supreme Court in recent legal history, raising questions not only about the status of an unpopular minority group but also about federal-state relations and the appropriate role of federal courts.

Justice scheduled an in-chambers conference with the parties to determine whether a temporary restraining order should be issued halting the enforcement of the school board policy until a hearing could be held on the merits. At the in-chambers conference, Roos and Daves requested that the Judge grant a protective order to keep the Immigration and Naturalization Service from deporting their clients solely because of involvement in the litigation. Justice refused to issue such an order. "I told Mr. Daves that I was sympathetic to his wishes but that I am a United States magistrate and if I learn of a violation of the law, it's my sworn duty to disclose it to the authorities."

Would the plaintiffs proceed on this basis? Daves talked the matter over with his clients in the courthouse parking lot. The men huddled together, then informed Daves through McAndrew, who served as their interpreter, that they wanted to proceed. Judge Justice fully realized and appreciated the risk the plaintiffs were taking. "I've always thought about how brave those aliens were," he says, recalling the early stages of the case. "Some of them had been here for a number of years, had houses, steady jobs, and had found a place for themselves in the community. And on behalf of their children, they decided to go ahead whatever the cost to themselves personally to pursue the lawsuit."

The Judge refused to grant the temporary restraining order because of insufficient evidence. He scheduled a formal preliminary hearing on the request for an injunction to take place several days later. Representatives from the

Justice Department and the U.S. Attorney for the Eastern District of Texas, as well as the Attorney General of the State of Texas, were to be included. According to Larry Daves, the Justice Department representative assured him that the plaintiffs would not be deported just because of their involvement in the lawsuit. However, there was no assurance that the Immigration and Naturalization Service (INS), which is a branch of the Justice Department, might not begin deportation proceedings if the plaintiffs' identities should come to their attention from another quarter.

The two plaintiffs' attorneys were still very much concerned about having an open hearing in the court on the preliminary injunction. In a celebrated case like this one, the resulting publicity could subject their clients to widespread harassment. Contrary to newspaper reports at the time, Justice did not schedule a closed hearing. However, to mitigate the possibility of adverse publicity, he scheduled the hearing to begin at 6 A.M. and arranged to have the plaintiffs enter through a side entrance reserved for court personnel. He was not trying to grant them asylum but was prepared to see that they had their day in court. At 6 A.M. the doors were open. If the newspaper reporters or a member of the general public had chosen to come in, they could have done so. But no one showed up except the parties to the case.

Appearing as families, the plaintiffs nearly filled the courtroom. Since many of them could not speak English, an interpreter was used. Judge Justice recalls that the Texas assistant attorney general who appeared was more than a little upset by the strange nature of the proceedings. "She had flown in the night before and had arrived at 1 or 2 A.M. They had lost her luggage, so she appeared at 6 A.M. in court in blue jeans. I could tell that she thought she was in a kind of zoo. She appeared to think that the contentions of the plaintiffs were ludicrous. And she apparently thought the idea of having the hearing at 6 A.M. was insane." From his vantage point on the bench, Justice was awed by the rapt attention of the parents of the children as the proceedings commenced. "They were so fascinated by that testimony. Since it was being interpreted, they could understand what was going on. I remember one of them in particular whose face was lit by the dawn of comprehension as the testimony proceeded."

The motion for a preliminary injunction against enforcement of the school board policy was granted on September 11, 1977, and the use of pseudonyms was approved. This meant that the children would be admitted to school and that their identities would be disguised both in the name of the case and in all documentary evidence. But the Judge was careful to advise the Justice Department representative that the order did not bind any officer of the United States who might desire to take action against the plaintiffs and their parents for violating the federal immigration law. Justice Department attorney Michael Wise told the Judge that the Immigration and Naturalization Service would not seek the identity of the plaintiffs in the interest of allowing the lawsuit to proceed. Justice responded that he would not interfere with enforcement of the laws.

Considerable controversy in Tyler and around the state greeted the announcement of the preliminary injunction. At first, the newspaper reports were confused about the involvement of the Immigration and Naturalization Service. It was generally assumed that Justice had issued a blanket protective order so that deportation could not occur under any circumstance. The Judge was furious to read in the newspapers that he was shielding the plaintiffs from deportation—something he had taken pains to avoid. In a September 14 article, *Dallas Morning News* reporter Carlton Stowers observed that the injunction "states that the identities of the illegal aliens named in the suit should not be revealed to protect them against deportation." Drawing from interviews, he noted that the restriction was engendering questions among Tylerites, questions "which no one seems to have an answer for." [5]

Justice recalls that an editor of the *Dallas Morning News* contacted him regarding a proposed congressional investigation of his action in the case. "I told him, 'I want you to understand right here at the beginning that I am the subject of a vicious libel. There hasn't been the slightest effort by a member of your staff or any other newspaper as far as I know to ascertain what went on at the hearing. If you will have the wit to send someone to review court records, you will discover that I made it plain in open court that the Justice Department is to be given this information. The only thing the protective order prohibits is the disclosure of their names to the general public.'" The stories were corrected. "But that was a week later and back about on page 5. I was aggravated, to say the least." [6]

A formal hearing began December 12, 1977, and lasted two days. A representative from the Civil Rights Division of the Justice Department was present as *amicus curiae* but did not present evidence and asked few questions. In his opening statement, Michael Wise indicated that the Justice Department was not aligned with either party. Later, he filed a post-trial brief supporting the plaintiffs.

The state's problems with immigration were apparent from the testimony. An increasing number of immigrants from Mexico were settling in border towns. While most were legally admitted, some were not. The result was overcrowding in the public schools and increased need for special services such as bilingual education. Since aliens usually are poor, it is generally assumed that they do not offset the additional cost by adding to the tax base. The state's response to this situation was the amendment of Section 21.031, excluding undocumented aliens from a tuition-free public education. But the legislation had little impact on the real cause of illegal immigration, the ready availability of jobs. Given strong pressure from employers, especially growers, neither the federal government nor the Texas Legislature had enacted legislation levying sanctions against employers who hired undocumented aliens.

The economies of excluding undocumented alien children from school were unclear and difficult to document. Several expert witnesses testified that undocumented aliens contribute much more through taxes than they utilize in social services. There was little reliable information on the numbers of children involved across the state. For Tyler, the figures were more definite. Superintendent James Plyler testified that twenty-four undocumented alien children had been enrolled in the Tyler school district prior to the enactment of the exclusionary board policy. For a school district of sixteen thousand students, the economies resulting from their exclusion were negligible. Yet the social costs were high. Dr. José Cárdenas, an expert witness for the plaintiffs, testified that exclusion from school locks the undocumented alien child into a life of poverty. Dr. Shane Davis, an expert witness for the defense, testified that the status of uneducated aliens was similar to that of exploited serfs.

Evidence was introduced that even though Texas law excluded illegally admitted aliens, the school finance law provided money on a per-pupil basis. Thus, despite the amendment of section 21.031, some school districts continued to enroll these children to obtain the additional money. In addition, the federal government underwrote many of the program costs of meeting their special needs. The fiscal problems, of course, were much greater in urban areas and in the southwestern section of the state. It was estimated that in Dallas nearly six thousand undocumented alien children would enroll if the exclusionary state law were struck down.

Following the conclusion of the hearing, Judge Justice took the matter under advisement. Initially, the work of researching the law and drafting the opinion was assigned to Ruth Epstein, one of the Judge's law clerks. But her tenure at the court concluded before the initial draft of the opinion was finished. The Judge completed the opinion himself. "It wasn't as good as I wanted it to be," he concedes.

To decide the case, Judge Justice had to consider the purpose of the equal protection clause of the Fourteenth Amendment to the U.S. Constitution. That clause states that no state "shall deny to any person within its jurisdiction the equal protection of the laws." Of course, laws often treat people unequally. For example, people must be a certain age in order to drive a car. Even when applied to the same class or group of people, laws are never passed with such mathematical exactitude that they treat each individual equally. Balancing the exigencies of legislating with the requirements of the equal protection clause, the U.S. Supreme Court traditionally has required that state legislation in the social and economic field be rationally related to a legitimate state purpose.[7] In effect, this means that few state laws are struck down, for a rational purpose can usually be found.

But more recently the justices have carved out an exception to the rational-basis requirement. Where fundamental constitutional rights or where certain "suspect classes" of persons are involved, the state must show a compelling reason for treating people differently.[8] The justices give state legislation or action in these cases what is called "strict scrutiny" or "heightened scrutiny" to determine whether there is a compelling state reason. It is rare that a state law is upheld under the compelling standard. The plaintiffs hoped to convince Judge Justice that this was a case where the state should be required to meet the higher standard.

The Supreme Court had ruled in another Texas case, *San Antonio Independent School District v. Rodriguez,* that education is not a fundamental right under the U.S. Constitution.[9] But the plaintiffs argued that that case had not resolved the question of whether an absolute deprivation of education might not be a constitutional violation. Thus, the exclusionary policy arguably deprived the undocumented aliens of a constitutional right. The plaintiffs also argued that while the Supreme Court had not ruled that undocumented aliens constitute a suspect class of persons under the equal protection clause, the Court had done so for legally admitted aliens.[10] Since the two are related subgroups, undocumented aliens should be considered a suspect class as well.

The defendants countered that undocumented aliens are not entitled to the protections of the equal protection clause because they are not in the country legally. Even if they are protected by the clause, the school district and the state have good reason to exclude undocumented aliens in order to conserve tax dollars for providing high-quality education for residents.

With little precedent to rely on, Judge Justice and his clerk, Ruth Epstein, wrestled with these issues. Are undocumented aliens included within the ambit of the equal protection clause? Since the language of the clause speaks in terms of "persons" and since the U.S. Supreme Court had earlier ruled that the companion due process clause of the Fourteenth Amendment applies to undocumented aliens, Justice concluded they are. He rejected defendants' argument that because the children were in the state illegally, they were not within the "jurisdiction" of the state.

But to say that undocumented aliens are entitled to the protections of the equal protection clause does not mean that they are entitled to exactly the *same* protections accorded native-born or naturalized citizens. The state argued that it had valid reasons to deny undocumented alien children a tuition-free public education. Still, if the Judge were to find that under *San Antonio* the absolute deprivation deprived them of a fundamental right, the state would be unlikely to advance a sufficiently compelling reason for doing so. Justice came close to finding support for such a right. But he did not base his ruling on this point. Nor did he explicitly find that the undocumented alien children constituted a suspect class under the equal protection clause, thus requiring the state to meet the higher standard of justification. After some initial posturing in both directions, the Judge concluded, "since it appears that defendants have not demonstrated a rational basis for the state law or the local school policy, it is not necessary to resolve finally [these] difficult conceptual problems."[11]

In retrospect, Judge Justice notes that when he issued the preliminary injunction, he was convinced that the state should be required to meet a compelling-purpose test. But when he and Epstein began to work on the memorandum opinion after the formal hearing, "we got a little skittish about it. We decided that maybe we could just find mere lack of rationality, and if we could, it might get by easier on appeal." Indeed, neither the Fifth Circuit nor the Supreme Court relied on the compelling-purpose test in affirming the decision.[12]

How could the state law and school board policy not be rational? The defendants argued that the policy of exclusion was compatible with the federal immigration scheme of discouraging illegal immigration. But Judge Justice found this unconvincing. The Texas Legislature had failed to pass bills prohibiting the employment of illegal aliens, the primary attraction for Mexican immigration. Since most illegal aliens do not bring their children with them, the Texas exclusionary policy was not aimed at deterring illegal immigration. Richard Arnett, who argued on behalf of the state before the U.S. Supreme Court, counters this assertion. "If someone knew that his kids would not be permitted to go to school, that they were going to be outcasts, then he's not going to bring them with him. It seems to me that it does make a tremendous difference."

Insofar as serious school overcrowding was concerned, the Judge noted that the bulk of the overcrowding resulted from the admission of legally admitted alien children. Thus, at best the legislation represented a piecemeal approach to cost-cutting. "Bent on cutting educational costs and unable constitutionally to exclude all such 'problem' children, the state has attempted to shave off a little around the edges, barring the undocumented alien children despite the fact that they are no different for educational purposes from a large proportion of legally resident alien children."[13] He observed that the reason the state chose this avenue may well have been that since the children of undocumented aliens had never been afforded judicial protection, little political uproar was likely to be raised on their behalf. Not only was such a state policy arbitrary, it was likely to be ineffective.

To the Judge, the state's position in the case was ironic. "Any spectator," he wrote, "might easily have mistaken it for a retrial of the *Rodriguez* case, with the State of Texas acting as *amicus curiae* for plaintiffs, emphasizing the plight of the property-poor border school districts under the state's educational financing scheme." In *San Antonio v. Rodriguez,* the state had argued that despite substantial disparities among school districts in educational funding, the state educational finance system was rational because it lessened the disparities from what they would have been without state intervention. In making this assertion, the state minimized the impact of educational funding on the quality of education in the poorer districts. The turnabout in *Doe* is what caught the Judge's attention.

Acknowledging that the state's school finance system had begun to "strain at the seams," he offered no solution other than to conclude that Section 21.031 was unconstitutional because it was arbitrary. He also ruled that the state was preempted by the federal government's control over immigration in enacting such legislation. Rather than being compatible with federal legislation, like California's law prohibiting the employment of illegal workers, Texas's law was incompatible with federal laws extending education benefits to undocumented children. Justice knew that this part of his ruling was weak, since the federal government has traditionally accorded great discretion to the states in handling their own immigration problems.

The unprecedented decision was greeted by considerable legal commentary, much of it critical.[14] Asserting that both Justice's equal protection and federal preemption analyses were flawed, one writer noted the incongruity in the fact that "provisions of Section 21.031 requiring payment of tuition by nonresidents of the state have been upheld as constitutional, thereby recognizing the state's legitimate interest in protecting and preserving the quality of education within its public school system, while provisions of the statute requiring a similar tuition fee for those illegally residing in the state are now declared unconstitutional."[15] The inconsistency, however, is illusory, since the payment-of-tuition requirement would apply to an undocumented alien child whose presence in the district was for the primary purpose of attending its schools, contrary to another provision of the statute. In the *Doe* case, the children resided in the Tyler district because their home was there.

Though Justice was not all that pleased with his opinion, the parties recognized that it was well reasoned and documented. And since it was the first federal ruling on the issue, a precedent had been established. Higher courts would study the matter very carefully. It would be tough to get the decision overruled.

From the plaintiffs' perspective, the case drew a favorable panel at the Fifth Circuit. The members were David W. Dyer, Henry A. Politz, and Frank M. Johnson. Dyer had been appointed by President Johnson, and Politz and

Johnson by President Carter. Judge Frank Johnson, a friend of Judge Justice with much the same judicial philosophy, wrote the opinion. In October 1980, the panel affirmed the trial court decision with regard to the lack of rationality under the equal protection clause but rejected the federal preemption holding. Like Justice, the appeals panel was reluctant to find either that education in this instance was a constitutional right or that illegal aliens constitute a suspect class under the Fourteenth Amendment equal protection clause.[16] However viewed, the state statute and the school board policy were both constitutionally infirm.

Despite the affirmance of Justice's decision by the Fifth Circuit, the defendants were determined to continue their appeal. "Having been blown out of the water in New Orleans before the Fifth Circuit, we had some hope at the Supreme Court level," says Tyler school board attorney John Hardy. Assistant Attorney General Richard Arnett, who represented the state, also was optimistic, though University of Texas law professor Charles Alan Wright told him that the state would likely lose. While preparing the memorandum opinion, Judge Justice and law clerk Epstein had spent time pondering how the U.S. Supreme Court would decide the case. They were fully convinced that the Court would hear it and would uphold the trial court decision. "We narrowed it down to Powell, who was going to be the swing vote," Justice recalls. They concluded that Justice Lewis F. Powell would vote to affirm based on his concerns for illegitimate children as expressed in another case.[17] And, as it turned out, they were right.

Meanwhile, political events had caused a change at the U.S. Justice Department. Now in the hands of the Reagan administration, the department reversed its position. During the Carter administration, it had filed briefs on the side of the plaintiffs, urging that the statute be declared unconstitutional as tainted by racism and designed to harm a vulnerable and unpopular group in an irrational and invidious manner. During the Reagan administration, it withdrew to the sidelines, explaining in its Supreme Court brief that it had no legal interest in the case. In announcing the change in September 1981, Solicitor General Rex E. Lee said, "This is an issue that is the state's interest, not the federal government's."[18] According to Justice Department sources, Governor William P. Clements had prevailed upon U.S. Attorney General William French Smith in asking that the department back off.[19] Until the reversal, the defendants had found the position of the Justice Department untenable in that the department was asserting that the state could best deal with illegal immigration by border patrolling and deportation, something the federal government was unwilling to do.

Oral argument before the U.S. Supreme Court clearly demonstrated the importance of the case. The gallery was packed. The justices all engaged in considerable questioning, interrupting the attorneys' prepared remarks repeatedly. Chief Justice Warren Burger allowed the oral argument to continue well beyond the allotted forty minutes for each side. Hardy remembers that the red light had come on at the lectern before the Supreme Court bench indicating that his time was up. But the justices would not let him leave. "I was getting questions from right and left." It appeared to Hardy that the justices were more interested in the situation in Tyler than in the whole state. Both Hardy and Arnett were the target of considerable pointed questioning from the more liberal members of the court. Arnett remembers that Justice Thurgood Marshall in particular "had his knives out and was coming after me." Arnett eventually concluded that Marshall was trying to disrupt his argument. So he gave Marshall only cursory answers. That strategy may have backfired. According to Hardy, at one point during Arnett's argument, Justice Marshall turned his chair completely around and faced the other way.

In a decision carrying major significance for the status of undocumented aliens, the Supreme Court decision upheld Judge Justice's original decision by a narrow five-to-four margin on June 15, 1982. The announcement came near the end of the Court term, a time usually reserved for important decisions. In the majority were Justice William Brennan, Jr., who wrote the opinion, and Justices Marshall, Harry Blackmun, Powell, and John Paul Stevens. It was a difficult case for the Court because if undocumented aliens should be entitled to a free public education, then why not to a myriad of other social benefits normally reserved for citizens?

The majority began by dismissing the state's contention that undocumented aliens were not "within the jurisdiction" of the state as required by the equal protection clause and thus not entitled to any state-conferred benefits. Noting that the equal protection clause speaks of "persons," the majority concluded that the clause "was intended to work nothing less than the abolition of all caste-based and invidious class-based legislation." [20] The equal protection clause extends to everyone—citizen or stranger—within a state's borders. For the first time, the high court ruled that undocumented aliens, both adults and children, are subject to its protections. But the justices were unwilling to grant special status to undocumented aliens as a suspect class, given their illegal entry into the country. Nor were the justices willing to declare education a fundamental right contrary to the holding in *San Antonio v. Rodriguez*. To limit the scope of their decision and at the same time accommodate the undocumented alien children, the majority simply acknowledged the importance of education to socialize these children to the ways of the United States and found the state had no substantial interest in excluding them. Justice Brennan observed that "It is difficult to understand precisely what the State hopes to achieve by promoting the creation and perpetuation of a subclass of illiterates within our boundaries, surely adding to the problems and costs of unemployment, welfare, and crime. It is thus clear that whatever savings might be achieved by denying these children an education, they are wholly insubstantial in light of the costs involved to these children, the State, and the Nation." [21]

Chief Justice Burger wrote for the dissent. Joining him were Justices Byron White, William H. Rehnquist, and Sandra Day O'Connor. He found credence in a point repeatedly raised by the attorneys for Texas. "By definition, illegal aliens have no right whatever to be here, and the State may reasonably, and constitutionally, elect not to provide them with governmental services at the expense of those who are lawfully in the State." [22]

It was clear that the dissenters did not think much of the Texas statute. "Were it our business to set the Nation's social policy, I would agree without hesitation that it is senseless for an enlightened society to deprive any children—including illegal aliens—of an elementary education," Burger admitted. [23] But he went on to argue that courts do not set social agendas; legislatures do. He accused the majority of stretching the Constitution to achieve their intended result. "Yet, by patching together bits and pieces of what might be termed quasi-suspect-class and quasi-fundamental-rights analysis, the Court spins out a theory custom-tailored to the facts of these cases." [24] The dissenters concluded that it was not irrational for the Texas Legislature "to conclude that it does not have the same responsibility to provide benefits for persons whose very presence in the State and this country is illegal as it does to provide for persons lawfully present." [25]

It was a major victory for Judge Justice. He was delighted. "I was convinced that I had made the legally correct decision, and I was elated that both the Fifth Circuit and the Supreme Court had affirmed my decision. But over and beyond that, I thought it would have been a terrible social tragedy for the children to have been denied an education." John Hardy was disappointed that the defendants had not prevailed, but he was pleased with the quality of oral argument before the high court. He had kept in contact with Judge Justice during the various stages of the case. When the decision was announced, he told the Judge that had it not been for the "final nails he put in the decision, I might have won a case before the Supreme Court."

Richard Arnett was also pleased to find four justices agreeing with his position. He took comfort in knowing that the state's appeal of the case had not come at the expense of the children. By virtue of the lower court injunctions, the illegal alien children had been attending school all along. He was also convinced that the legislature would have repealed the law regardless of the outcome. Arnett believes the only reason the legislature had not already repealed the statute was to avoid undercutting its position that the state should not be required to finance the education of undocumented alien children. "At that point we were trying to ransom the federal government to finance this education," he maintains.[26] Whether Texas would really have repealed the statute had the Court decided the other way is doubtful. A bill to this effect introduced into the 1981 session had never made it out of committee. Indeed, though it is null and void, the law excluding undocumented alien children from tuition-free education lingers on the statute books today.

The state was not successful in obtaining a substantial infusion of money from the federal government. But, then, the huge number of illegal alien children predicted to flood the state's schools never materialized. Using data collected by the Texas Education Agency in 1980 following court orders requiring the admission of undocumented children, the Intercultural Development Research Association in San Antonio concluded that only about 13,000 such students had enrolled.[27] It had been estimated that as many as 110,000 undocumented alien children were present in the state.

Since undocumented children display the same characteristics as legally admitted aliens, their impact upon curricular and instructional programs appears minimal. Indeed, it has been asserted that immigrant children who have previously attended school in their native country tend to outperform U.S.-born Mexican-American children in American schools. The extensive use of the children's native language in Mexican schools and the lack there of the negative expectations associated with Spanish-speaking populations in this country are said to account for the difference.[28] Of course, the continuing flow of illegal aliens into Texas has had serious impact on the border school districts, which were already underfunded. The continuing problems of the property-poor border districts were highlighted in a 1989 Texas Supreme Court decision striking down the Texas school finance system.[29]

By virtue of the U.S. Supreme Court decision, *Doe* established that the equal protection clause applied to undocumented aliens, both adults and children, and that all undocumented alien children in the United States have a right to attend public school on an equal basis with other children. While the law of equal protection had been broadened, it remained unclear what other social benefits undocumented aliens might be entitled to, since the Court sidestepped the issue. Back in Tyler, Judge Justice had reason to be pleased. In the face of discrimination by the state and inaction by the other branches of government, he had stepped in to protect the interests of a politically powerless and unpopular minority. His ruling had been upheld by the nation's highest court.

The *Doe* decision is Sue Justice's favorite. Intensely concerned with the welfare of the weakest and most vulnerable, she believes the decision has had the most social value of any her husband has handed down. Shortly after Justice issued his decision, a little bouquet of flowers arrived at the Justice home. The card contained two X's and one illegible signature. Sue called the florist who had prepared the bouquet. He told her that three Mexican laborers had put down two dollar bills and some change—all the money they had—and asked that the flowers be sent to Mrs. Justice. "That very meager bouquet of flowers went a long way to make up for all the suffering I've experienced," she says.

The celebration of victory in Justice's chambers over the Supreme Court's affirmance of his decision would be short. One month later came the devastating Fifth Circuit reversal in the bilingual education case.

CHAPTER 10

Bilingual Education

Judge Justice's 1981 ruling in *United States v. Texas (Bilingual)* created an uproar in the state and turmoil in the Texas attorney general's office. The decision, a sequel to the statewide school desegregation ruling, mandated that all 1,100 Texas public school districts instruct in their native tongue those Mexican-American and other students deficient in English, while at the same time teaching them English. Shocked by what they perceived to be the Judge's intrusion into the internal workings of the state educational system, state political leaders spared no effort in seeking a reversal. In short order, the state's trial attorney was removed from the case, a new attorney assigned, and an appeal strategy designed to undermine the legal basis for the ruling. In its reversal, the U.S. Court of Appeals was savage in its criticism of both the state's trial attorney and Judge Justice. Yet, as this chapter suggests, the bilingual decision was not a total loss for the court or the state of Texas.

Section G of the 1971 remedial order in *United States v. Texas,* the statewide school desegregation case, requested that the Texas Education Agency (TEA) conduct a study of the educational needs of minority children throughout the state, make recommendations as to how they could be met, and report back to the court. TEA dutifully filed the report; nothing further was required. The report was neither approved nor disapproved. In June 1975, the GI Forum and the League of United Latin American Citizens (LULAC), two groups which had been approved by Judge Justice in 1972 to enter the *United States v. Texas* lawsuit as representatives of persons of Mexican-American descent, filed a motion asking that the state implement a plan to provide English-deficient students with bilingual instruction and compensatory language programs.[1] The motion was introduced by Ed Idar, who later would switch sides and as an assistant attorney general represent the state in the prison reform case, *Ruiz v. Estelle*.

The two groups, known as "plaintiff-intervenors," asserted that the state was obligated to provide bilingual education under Section G. They claimed that Mexican-American students, like blacks, had been the victims of illegal statewide discrimination. Behind the filing of the motion were two powerful organizations, the Mexican American Legal Defense and Education Fund (MALDEF) and the Center for Law and Education at Harvard University. Both would assume major roles in the litigation. As representatives of the original plaintiffs in the school desegregation phase of *United States v. Texas,* the U.S. Justice Department also supported the request, though its ardor had cooled since the Republicans had taken over the White House from Lyndon Johnson in 1969.

The motion was in large part a response to a 1975 U.S. Supreme Court decision. In *Lau v. Nichols* the Court ruled that federal guidelines enforcing Title VI of the 1964 Civil Rights Act require school districts to eliminate language deficiencies where school board policies discriminate against minorities, even in the absence of an intent to do so.[2] The Court avoided deciding whether such discrimination is a violation of the equal protection clause of the U.S. Constitution. The decision gave a great boost to bilingual programs, which were then in vogue by virtue of a 1968 federal statute, Title VII of the Elementary and Secondary Education Act, known as the Bilingual Education Act.[3] The purpose of the federal legislation was to remedy the adverse effects of an English-only curriculum on non-English-speaking students. The plaintiff-intervenors based their motion on Title VI of the 1964 Civil Rights Act, the Equal Educational Opportunities Act (EEOA) of 1974, and the Fourteenth Amendment equal protection clause.

The State of Texas responded by asking that a three-judge court with direct appeal to the U.S. Supreme Court be convened to hear the case. At the time, Congress provided that a three-judge federal court must be convened to hear disputes involving the constitutionality of state statutes.[4] Having lost before Judge Justice in the original *United States v. Texas* statewide school desegregation case, the state wanted to take the matter out of his hands. But at a 1976 hearing on the three-judge-court issue, the plaintiff-intervenors sought to block this maneuver by dropping their constitutional claims, relying only on the federal statutory provisions. This had the effect of continuing the case before Judge Justice, but at the likely expense of a wide-ranging remedial order based on the Fourteenth Amendment. In June 1978, Judge Justice entered a formal order denying Texas' request for a three-judge court.

The plaintiff-intervenors' case was further weakened when the U.S. Supreme

Court ruled in 1978 that one of the statutes they were relying on, Title VI of the 1964 Civil Rights Act, required that discrimination must have been intentional.[5] It is much more difficult to prove discriminatory intent than merely to show that discrimination exists. With the dropping of the constitutional claims and with the new intent requirement on Title VI claims, the chances for another broad-based remedial order were lessened—or so it seemed.

The principal attorneys representing the Mexican-American plaintiffs were Peter Roos of MALDEF in San Francisco and Roger L. Rice of the Center for Law and Education, a federally funded public interest law group at Harvard University. Roos was already familiar with Judge Justice, having served as lead counsel for the undocumented alien children in *Doe v. Plyler*.

Plaintiff attorneys prepared a list of over 450 stipulations of fact establishing a legacy of *de jure* discrimination against Mexican-Americans in Texas. The stipulations were based on several sources, including a series of reports by the U.S. Commission on Civil Rights and an article appearing in the *Harvard Civil Rights–Civil Liberties Law Review* entitled "Project Report: De Jure Segregation of Chicanos in Texas Schools."[6] The plaintiffs also found support for the stipulations in federal bilingual education grant applications prepared by local school districts. Filed with the Texas Education Agency, these applications often sought to bolster the need for assistance by indicating past discrimination against the educational needs of Mexican-American students. If Rice could get the state to agree to the stipulations, then the difficult task of proving state-sanctioned discrimination against Mexican-Americans would not be necessary.

Representing the state in the case was Assistant Attorney General Susan J. Dasher. A young and aggressive attorney hired by Attorney General John Hill, Dasher had come to Texas from California, where she had clerked for the U.S. Court of Appeals for the Ninth Circuit and had been a deputy public defender.[7] Dasher's plan was to avoid contesting the issue of a history of state *de jure* segregation against Mexican-Americans in Texas, since she believed it to be common knowledge. "All we needed to show was that we had implemented a plan of bilingual education that was sufficient under his [1971] order," she maintains. At the time, she was involved in other major institutional litigation around the state. "I did not want to spend three months in Tyler doing something that had nothing to do with the litigation simply because it was a sexy thing to do." In a decision that would later come back to haunt her, Dasher agreed to most of the stipulations, which became Plaintiff-Intervenors' Exhibit 409.

Thus, the position the state would take in the litigation was aptly demonstrated by her opening statement before Judge Justice: "Your Honor, it's true that we have stipulated to large parts of this case. All of it tends to be historical. The State of Texas does not have a happy record over the past. What we hope to litigate today is where is bilingual education in the State of Texas today and where is it going to go for the next ten years . . ."[8] Dasher hoped to convince the court that the state had made significant strides to comply with the 1971 order and with the two federal statutes on which the lawsuit was based. It was an interesting strategy, but risky. If she failed to convince Judge Justice, then her acknowledging a legacy of discrimination in the state against Mexican-Americans invited the Judge to design an extensive remedy.

After completion of extensive pretrial discovery, the final pretrial order was filed on November 20, 1978, and an eight-day trial began on December 3, 1979, four years after the case began. Justice attributes the delay in part to his clogged case docket and in part to failure of plaintiffs' attorneys to push it faster.

The trial proceeded expeditiously because the parties were represented by effective counsel and because there was general agreement about a legacy of discrimination against Mexican-Americans in Texas. Judge Justice found the case intellectually stimulating and often questioned expert witnesses as they sought to explain the intricacies of pedagogy and social science research. On behalf of the plaintiff-intervenors, Peter Roos sought to assure that every Texas child who was in need of bilingual education received it. The state claimed that the cost of expanding bilingual programs through the twelfth grade would be astronomical. "They're talking about teaching every other subject in Spanish," Dasher told reporters.[9]

Dasher argued that the state had in good faith eliminated discrimination against Mexican-Americans in the public schools. In 1973 the Texas Legislature had enacted the Bilingual Education Act, which directed local school districts to determine the number of limited-English-speaking students in the district. Districts with twenty or more such students in any one grade were to offer bilingual education. There are two basic types of bilingual programs. A maintenance system establishes a permanent dual-track curriculum, one track for English-speaking students and one for non-English-speaking students. A compensatory system (also called a transitional system) instructs students in their native tongue while at the same time providing them with intensive training in English. The latter was the type mandated by the legislation. When students in a compensatory program master English, they are moved into the regular instructional program.

A bilingual program usually includes a cultural component to enhance the students' appreciation of their own culture and the culture of others. At the time of the lawsuit, experts testified that bilingual education was the preferred method of instruction. A 1975 U.S. Commission on Civil Rights report was cited which concluded that, "bilingual-bicultural education is the program of instruction which currently offers the best vehicle for large numbers of language minority students who experience language difficulty in our schools." [10]

The primary alternative to the bilingual approach is known as "English as a second language" (ESL). ESL essentially means immersing students in an intensive English language course while at the same time educating them in English through the regular curriculum. School districts prefer ESL, since it is significantly less expensive. This method was not strongly supported by either side at the trial because it was generally conceded that a student who knows little English will not perform well in an all-English curriculum. However, more attention was given to ESL on appeal. In oral argument before the Fifth Circuit, Richard Arnett, the attorney for the state who replaced Dasher, asserted that had the case been vigorously argued in the trial court, expert testimony would have been introduced challenging the bilingual approach.

The 1973 Texas Bilingual Education Act encompassed grades one through six, to be phased in a year at a time beginning with the 1974–1975 school year. Supplemental state aid was provided to assist local districts with this task. In 1975, the legislature amended the law by adding a bilingual component in kindergarten but eliminating it in grades four through six. Bilingual instruction was to be optional in grades four and five, with supplemental funding available from the state. No funding was available for bilingual education in grades six through twelve. School districts were to provide special English language development programs in grades one through twelve to students who were not in bilingual programs but had limited English-speaking ability. State Board of Education rules also detailed how students were to be identified for bilingual programs, what the components of the programs were to be, and procedures for moving students from bilingual education to the regular curriculum. At the time of the lawsuit, the state provided $25 to local districts for each child in a bilingual program, a figure the plaintiffs labeled as far too low to be of much value.

Between the end of the trial in December 1979 and the fall of 1980, little transpired in the case. But starting in August 1980, the Texas Office of the Attorney General embarked on a remarkable effort to undermine the significance of the stipulations agreed to by attorney Dasher. The effort began with a phone call from Richard Hall, the school district attorney in the hotly contested Gregory-Portland school desegregation case discussed in Chapter 5.

Smarting from Dasher's use of the same stipulations against his client in the Gregory-Portland case, which Judge Justice had decided on August 8, 1980, Hall contacted officials in Austin to alert them to what she had done. Word eventually reached the Office of the Attorney General. Officials in the office were incredulous that Dasher at one sweep had conceded a history of pervasive *de jure* discrimination by the state against Mexican-Americans. They worried about the use of the stipulations in other cases against the state. They were particularly concerned about how Justice might use the stipulations in his bilingual decision, which had not yet been issued. Attorney General Mark White, who intended to run for governor in 1982, realized that were the stipulations to go unchallenged, they could be devastating for his campaign. Civil rights cases are widely reported in the newspapers.

It was already occurring. The *Corpus Christi Caller-Times* in a copyrighted story appearing on September 13, 1980, revealed that the Texas attorney general's office had conceded discrimination by the Texas Education Agency against Mexican-Americans through the stipulations in the Gregory-Portland case.[11] An anonymous TEA official, using a mixed metaphor, was quoted as saying, "they sold the store down the river." In the article, Mark White disclaimed any knowledge about the stipulations and said he did not believe the Texas Education Agency had ever discriminated against Mexican-Americans. "They certainly haven't done it under any direction or advice of this office," he said. Likewise, Texas Education Commissioner Alton Bowen and David P. Ryan, then general counsel at the Texas Education Agency, disclaimed any knowledge of the bias admissions.

The story quickly spread across the state and was picked up by White's political opponents. The attorney general told his top lieutenants to get out from under the embarrassing stipulations. Richard Gray, who was then executive assistant attorney general, was given the responsibility, a tough assignment. According to Gray, Susan Dasher maintained that she had not agreed to the actual truth of the stipulations; she had only agreed, in the interest of shortening the trial, that certain people if called to the stand would testify that the stipulations were true. She was never to waver from this position. Taking her at her word, Gray had Dasher file a motion to this effect on September 15, 1980, with Judge Justice.

The Judge was incredulous. In a written order denying the motion, he reviewed the history of the stipulations.[12] He observed that on repeated occasions, Dasher had acknowledged their truth. Indeed, she had begun her opening statement at the trial by stating, "Your Honor, it's true that we have stipulated to large parts of this case." He noted that in the post-trial motions, the defendants again referred to the stipulations as true statements. They had not been conditioned in any way. Justice noted as well that Dasher had used the same stipulations against the school district in the Gregory-Portland case. While a judge does have the power to overturn stipulations to prevent "manifest injustice," he was not persuaded such a situation existed. The motion was denied without a hearing on December 31, 1980, just days before he would hand down his decision in the case. Looking back, the Judge says it was clear to him that the defendants, "having found their trial strategy to have backfired, were attempting to extricate themselves from the loss." The plaintiffs' attorneys were less charitable. "Unbelievably sleazy," is how Roger Rice characterizes the state's actions. "I thought it was a desperate move that reflected the fact that they had been beaten." The state's turnabout marked the beginning of rapid deterioration in working relationships between the parties.

How could Dasher have agreed to the stipulations in the first place without approval from her superiors? The attorney general's office is similar to a large corporate law firm with more than 150 attorneys arrayed in various divisions. Unlike a large law firm, though, it is viewed as a training ground for young attorneys and is subject to the budgetary whims of the legislature and the varying organizational styles of elected attorneys general. Absent special circumstances, top officials are not likely to be knowledgeable about the trial strategy of a single attorney. At the time, the civil rights division in the attorney general's office was understaffed and underbudgeted. Its attorneys were young and inexperienced. There was little time to worry about what somebody else was doing. Susan Dasher was generally acknowledged as an effective attorney and a "take-charge" person. She had successfully handled a number of important cases across the state. Though outnumbered by her opposition in the bilingual case, Dasher chose to go it alone. Her strategy was not developed by consensus in the attorney general's office.

The first effort to get out from under the stipulations had not worked. The Judge was adamant in his December 1980 order. Furthermore, his careful discussion of the history of the stipulations convinced Dasher's superiors in the attorney general's office that regardless of what she had intended, much of the case had indeed been stipulated away, leaving the state largely defenseless before Judge Justice. So the extrication effort escalated. In the meantime, the Judge issued his decision in the case.

The decision was handed down on January 12, 1981, over a year after the trial and on the eve of the legislative session. "It wasn't by accident that several of my decisions, including this one, occurred right on the eve of a legislative session," the Judge explains. "I wanted to give the legislature a chance to attempt reform. I wanted the matter to be fresh on their minds." He began by rejecting the plaintiffs' motion to have the court simply enforce Section G of the 1971 *United States v. Texas* order and require extensive bilingual instruction across the state. [13] Justice ruled that the 1971 school desegregation trial had simply not produced the requisite finding of fact to warrant ordering extensive bilingual education. There would have to be other grounds for doing so. He found them in the controversial stipulations. Insofar as the Judge was concerned, the stipulations "came as a pleasant surprise." He had expected a lengthy trial. But he wondered about the wisdom of the defendant's strategy.

"It seemed to me that the stipulations were rather far reaching, and if I was going to have to rely on them for my ruling, I wanted to make certain that they were properly a part of the record." Thus, the transcript of the trial reveals that Justice carefully questioned all attorneys as to whether they understood and accepted the stipulations. They responded in the affirmative.

Using the stipulations, Judge Justice found that statewide, pervasive discrimination against Mexican-Americans, though not mandated by state law, was equivalent to that practiced against blacks. For example, stipulation 706 stated, "Historically, Texas has failed to effectively educate Mexican-American students of limited English speaking ability." Stipulation 701 stated that discrimination against Mexican-Americans in Texas is "a historic fact." Stipulation 729 stated that by 1942 at least 122 Texas school districts in fifty-nine counties had segregated schools for Mexican-Americans. Though the state and local officials had justified the practice on the ground that these students spoke little English and needed to be educated separately, Justice found the discrimination intentional. "Both the language and cultural heritage of these children were uniformly treated with intolerance and disrespect." [14]

The stipulations showed that 44 percent of Mexican-American students suffered from severe reading retardation. More than 22 percent of Mexican-American first-graders were being retained in the first grade, compared with 7 percent of Anglo children. Nearly half dropped out of school before graduation. Only 16 percent attended college, compared with 50 percent for Anglo students. At the time of the trial, the unemployment rate for Mexican-Americans in Texas was nearly twice that of nonminorities. Those employed were often in low-level jobs.

In the face of such assertions of apparent fact—assertions to which the state had readily agreed—it is not surprising that Justice concluded, "The crippling educational deficiencies afflicting the main body of Mexican-Americans in Texas present an ongoing ethnic tragedy, catastrophic in degree and disturbing in its latency for civil unrest and economic dislocation." [15]

Even though the state itself had never by law discriminated against Mexican-Americans, the fact that local districts had done so with the apparent acquiescence of the state was enough. As in the Gregory-Portland segment of *United States v. Texas* discussed in Chapter 5, Justice referred to several U.S. Supreme Court rulings in support of the proposition that discrimination in a substantial portion of a school system creates a rebuttable presumption that the entire system is operating in violation of the Constitution. The fact that the state had agreed to the stipulations precluded their rebutting the presumption. "Accordingly," he wrote, "it is found that Mexican-Americans in Texas have been subjected to *de jure* discrimination by the defendants, the State of Texas and the Texas Education Agency, in violation of the Equal Protection

Clause of the Fourteenth Amendment." [16] The foundation for an extensive remedial order was in place.

Note that the Judge referred to the U.S. Constitution even though his earlier rejection of the three-judge court had been based on the plaintiffs' agreement to eliminate constitutional claims from the lawsuit and focus only on the more narrow federal statutes. The Fifth Circuit later observed, "having been abandoned by the plaintiffs in order to avoid a three-judge court, and having been read out of the case's front door by a formal order, these [constitutional] issues finessed the three-judge tribunal, found their way back into court by the window, were tried by a single judge, and form the primary and major basis of the court's opinion in the case." [17] Judge Justice later sought to show in a detailed analysis that the parties had reinjected constitutional issues into the case by the time of trial. [18] The Fifth Circuit judges found little support for this assertion. However, the panel did acknowledge that after the trial, the state defendants had allowed constitutional law to creep back into the case. The Fifth Circuit's characterization is poignant: "Having survived all . . . hazards and preserved the case free of constitutional questions, defendants steamed into harbor and tied up, only to sink at the slip." [19]

How had the defendants allowed constitutional issues to get back into the case, assuming they were not there all along? When the trial concluded, attorney Dasher left to try a case in Houston. According to Dasher, while she was away, much of the state's post-trial brief was prepared in the Texas Education Agency by nonlawyers. She maintains that she routinely signed the brief, unaware that it had reintroduced constitutional issues into the case. But indeed it did so. In a section entitled "Compensatory Education under the Fourteenth Amendment," the 114-page document explicitly discusses constitutional issues. The way was clear for a broad-based remedy anchored in the sweeping mandate of the Fourteenth Amendment equal protection clause and in the agreed-upon stipulations showing a history of *de jure* discrimination against Mexican-Americans in Texas.

Judge Justice ruled that the existing bilingual program was "wholly inadequate" to meet the state's obligations under the law. "Good intentions," he wrote, "are not enough. The measure of a remedy is its effectiveness, not its purpose." [20] Justice found the amended statute and implementing State Board of Education rules deficient in several respects. Included among them was the fact that the program was limited to elementary students in the lower grades. If a school district had fewer than twenty limited-English-proficient (LEP) students in any one grade, no bilingual instruction was required at all, thus shortchanging those who attended schools with few language-deficient students. Both the plaintiffs and the state agreed that large numbers of students who needed bilingual instruction were not being provided with it. Since the bilingual act did not apply to high school, no one was being served at this level. The state argued that while bilingual education for all those needing it would be preferable in a perfect world, budgetary constraints and a limited number of trained teachers necessitated a more modest approach. Justice found inadequate the alternative English language development program the state required of all LEP students who were not receiving bilingual education.

"All students should be administered a home language survey when they first enter the Texas public schools to ensure that no foreign language students are overlooked at this key stage," he wrote.[21] Exit criteria then in use for shifting bilingual students into the regular curriculum were set too low. A student could be transferred to the regular program upon achieving a score at the twenty-third percentile or higher in reading and language arts on an approved test of English-speaking ability. Expert testimony at the trial had been devastating. Dr. Robert Cervantes, assistant chief of the office of bilingual education for California, labeled the level "ludicrous," noting that students functioning at this level are "functionally illiterate."[22] Dr. John McFarlane, then dean of the College of Education at Texas Woman's University and former superintendent of several large Texas public school districts, including the Houston system, testified, "A person functioning at the 23rd percentile would be ineffective in our society in salesmanship, in merchandising, or in any other profession in seeking opportunities or, indeed, might be handicapped in his interpersonal relationship with others such as, for example, in seeking to participate in government affairs, to express himself to representatives or appear before the city council or county commissioners and so forth."[23]

Justice also found the Texas Education Agency to be deficient in monitoring school districts to see that they complied with the law—the same deficiency he had found with respect to school desegregation. Similar problems of lack of staffing and resources were also apparent. He concluded that because of the serious deficiencies, "meaningful relief for the victims of unlawful discrimination must be instituted by court decree."[24] Not only the Constitution but also federal statutes required as much. While he rejected the plaintiffs' claim under Title VI of the Civil Rights Act of 1964, he found that there had been a violation of section 1703(f) of the Equal Educational Opportunities Act (EEOA) of 1974. In part, that section prohibited a state from denying equal educational opportunity by failing "to take appropriate action to overcome language barriers that impede equal participation by its students in its instructional program." Under this section, unlike Title VI, no showing of discriminatory intent was necessary.[25] A discriminatory impact was sufficient to trigger a violation. Since Texas had not eliminated all of the language barriers to an equal education, the state was in violation of that section.

While bilingual education was not mandated by the federal law as the only way of eliminating language barriers, Judge Justice found that such a program "is uniquely suited to meet the needs of the state's Spanish-speaking students." For reasons indicated later, his tilt in the direction of bilingual education found disfavor with the Fifth Circuit. The Judge also found a violation of section 1703(b) of the Equal Educational Opportunities Act, which required affirmative action to eliminate the vestiges of prior illegal segregation.

A federal court, Justice wrote, has a clear duty "to frame a decree which will work immediately to eliminate the discriminatory effects of the past and to assure future compliance with the laws of the land." [26] As in his other decisions involving state institutions, Justice was not swayed by cost considerations. Nor was he swayed by TEA assertions that there were not enough bilingual teachers to undertake a broad program. TEA did not have a program to recruit and train them, he asserted.

Having laid the groundwork for a broad and comprehensive remedy, the Judge outlined the relief he envisioned: bilingual education must be provided to all Mexican-American students of limited English proficiency at all grade levels in the Texas public schools. He gave the state six years to phase in the required program. The program was to require a systematic survey of all students entering Texas public schools as to their predominant language. It would also require reliance on teacher observation. Students were not to be released into the regular curriculum until they proved capable of performing in all-English classes without significant impairment of their learning abilities or achievements. TEA was required to monitor local compliance by inspecting each school district in the state once every three years. Noncomplying districts were to receive appropriate warning and sanctions, including loss of accreditation and funding. Without such a broad remedy, "hundreds of thousands of Mexican-American children in Texas will remain educationally crippled for life, denied the equal opportunity which most Americans take for granted." [27]

Public reaction was swift and, aside from the state's Mexican-American population, negative. Attorney Dasher termed the rejection of her position "devastating." "As much as I love the man," she says, "I couldn't believe he did that to me. I really felt like I'd shot myself in the throat." Legislators, already reeling from Justice's multi-million-dollar prison reform decision issued a month before, were bitter and defiant. Senator Grant Jones, an Abilene Democrat and chairman of the Senate Finance Committee, labeled the ruling stupid and ridiculous, "something you'd expect from Justice." [28] Jones said the ruling would lead to U.S. separatism similar to that in Canada, where both French and English are spoken. Attorney Dasher, however, noting that Justice had not gone this far, told the press that at least the judge had not ordered a maintenance bilingual system which would do just that.

Governor Clements said he disagreed with the ruling "wholeheartedly." [29]

But Ruben Bonilla of Corpus Christi, national president of LULAC, said the ruling "clearly vindicates" those Mexican-American leaders who for years had labeled the state's education system "inadequate and discriminatory."[30] Editorial comment in the state's newspapers was overwhelmingly critical. The State Board of Education passed a resolution urging appeal of the bilingual education ruling, saying the state knows what is best for students. Indeed, that would become the rallying cry of the state's political leaders during the 1981 legislative session.

Ignoring the cries of protest, Judge Justice, in a now familiar pattern, required the parties to formulate a detailed plan conforming to his guidelines and submit it to the court by March 2, 1981. In the event they could not agree, the parties were to submit separate plans. The Judge himself would then formulate the decree in time for the 1981–1982 school year. Both the plaintiff intervenors and the Justice Department submitted plans detailing how Justice's decision would be implemented across all grade levels. The state asked for more time, asserting that the Judge had not given sufficient time for the legislative process to work. He was unmoved. No time extension would be granted. TEA Deputy Commissioner Thomas E. Anderson maintains that Justice was uniformly unsympathetic to the state throughout the litigation. "It became pretty obvious to me that we couldn't win in that court regardless of what the circumstances were."

Attorney General White asked the Judge to defer to a special bilingual task force established by legislative leaders and chaired by Willis Tate, president-emeritus of Southern Methodist University in Dallas. "Defendants are not idly standing by, blindly hoping for a solution to materialize magically," White said. "The legislative process represents the fundamental philosophy of the American constitutional form of government."[31] It should be given a chance to act, he asserted. Even if the legislature did not respond, the court could still order a new plan to begin by September 1. The plan the state eventually submitted rejected the Judge's request for a kindergarten-through-twelfth-grade bilingual program in favor of a more modest extension of existing legislation.

Justice is not a compromiser. Labeling what White had proposed as "lamentably short of addressing the defendants' unlawful conduct," he issued a remedial decree on April 17, 1981, detailing how bilingual education was to be phased in over a six-year period, beginning with the 1981–1982 school year.[32] The decree specified bilingual education from kindergarten through twelfth grade for every child who needed it. English as a second language (ESL) was not to be used as a substitute.

Once again, the newspapers reacted with disdain. In an April 23 editorial entitled "Impossible and Naïve," the *Dallas Morning News* charged the judge with "ignoring reality" in mandating a program without an adequate number of qualified teachers. Such a twelve-year program, the editorial argued, "places no burden on the student to become proficient in English." Critics feared that a bilingual program in the upper grades would result in high school graduates who could neither speak nor write English.

Meanwhile, efforts were under way in the attorney general's office to seek reversal of the bilingual decision. The conclusion had been reached that despite Susan Dasher's previous fine record as an attorney, she should not handle the bilingual appeal. She was removed from the civil rights division and assigned routine administrative law cases. By March 1981, the freeze-out strategy worked. Having been forced to undermine her own position over the use of the stipulations in the motion filed the previous September and shunted to handle routine cases, Dasher resigned.

Now rid of Dasher, the attorney general's office launched a frontal attack on Justice's decision. Leading the charge was Richard Arnett, a former assistant attorney general who had rejoined the office. Though at the time heavily involved in the undocumented alien case, he began working intensively on the bilingual case in June 1981, two months after the final remedial order had been issued and two months before school would begin. Arnett found the task arduous. The case record up to that time consumed four file cabinets.

He began by going through all of the materials associated with the case since its beginning in 1968. He quickly realized that the stipulations were devastating and had to be withdrawn—no easy task in that they had been knowingly entered into by the attorney for the state and had become a key part of the trial record. Not only had they hurt the state in the bilingual case, they were also so general that they were being used by attorneys in other civil rights cases. Arnett soon was assisted by another attorney. Having lost faith in the attorney general's office, the State Board of Education insisted that it have its own lawyer. William C. Bednar, Jr., a former member of the attorney general's staff and general counsel for the Texas Education Agency from 1976 to 1979, was selected.

Arnett and Bednar reviewed various strategies. Consideration was given to showing that Dasher had experienced mental problems which had undermined her competence. After some initial exploration in that direction, the idea was dropped. Consideration was then directed to getting Dasher to sign an affidavit that she had entered into the stipulations without consulting anyone. This she refused to do. She maintained that she had discussed them in detail with TEA officials, including David P. Ryan, TEA general counsel, and that they were fully aware of her trial strategy. However, in a July 1981 affidavit, Ryan said the stipulations were entered into without his knowledge or consent. Thomas Anderson, then executive assistant to the deputy commissioner for program administration and finance at the agency, said in an affidavit also prepared in July that while he had discussed the proposed stipulations with Dasher, neither he nor anyone else at the Texas Education Agency had authorized her to enter into them. Indeed, TEA had specifically disagreed with 250 of the stipulations. Dasher did agree to sign an affidavit stating that "the entering of the stipulations was not authorized by the policy-making officials of the Texas Education Agency or my superiors at the Attorney General's office nor was such authorization sought. I guess I convinced myself that there was sufficient truth in what I signed so that I wasn't lying about it," she says. But she would do no more.

Meanwhile, the legislature was at work on the bilingual bill. Attorney General White asked Arnett whether the legislation was necessary. Arnett replied in the affirmative. The legislation would help convince the Fifth Circuit that the judiciary should defer to the legislative process. The attorney general's office intensified its lobbying effort. The legislation passed late in the session and was signed by Governor Clements on June 12. It was modeled after the Tate Task Force's recommendation for mandatory bilingual education in the elementary grades, with ESL programs later on. When White telephoned the plaintiffs' attorneys to ask them to accede to the legislation, they declined. He bluntly told them the state would prevail before the Fifth Circuit in New Orleans. On July 6, Arnett presented Judge Justice with motions to overturn the court's decision and remedial decrees, backed up by the affidavits Dasher and TEA officials had signed. He recalls, "We hit the Judge hard and fast on those motions." Three basic arguments were advanced: attorney Dasher was not authorized to agree to the stipulations, the court had transgressed its authority by deciding constitutional issues which were not before it, and the court should stay its April 17 remedial order pending appeal to the Fifth Circuit because of the disruptive effect the order would have on the Texas public school system.

Arnett knew that he would not receive a very receptive audience in Tyler, but he had no choice if he was going to seek an appeal to the Fifth Circuit. His assessment was accurate. "I was outraged," Judge Justice recalls. "I was brought up to believe that if a lawyer says that he is going to do something, he'll do it. And here the State of Texas wanted to back out on the convenants that they had solemnly made in open court. I thought it was detestable."

Of course, Arnett was really making a record to take up on appeal. "My philosophy at that point was to hit him [Judge Justice] with the kitchen sink, to try to start building a 'they got screwed by their own lawyer' case to take to the Fifth Circuit." Justice was fully aware of this strategy, but it did not change his attitude toward the state's position. His reaction was swift and negative. Twenty-five days later he issued a closely reasoned forty-page order rejecting the motions.

He found meritless Arnett's contention that a stay should be issued based on hardship for the state and likelihood of reversal by the Fifth Circuit. As to the latter, the Judge proved to be a poor prophet when he wrote, "Although the Court of Appeals might conceivably disagree with this court as to the propriety of one or more specific elements of relief, there is little likelihood that the defendants will succeed in overturning the bulk of the decree." [33]

In rejecting the motions, the Judge had a new problem to deal with in the form of a Fifth Circuit ruling handed down after his initial decision in January 1981. The court ruled in *Castaneda v. Pickard* that Congress had not mandated any particular remedial program to eliminate language barriers in the public school curriculum when it enacted section 1703(f) of the Equal Educational Opportunities Act, one of the statutes upon which Justice had based his order. Rather, Congress "intended to leave state and local educational authorities a substantial amount of latitude in choosing the programs and techniques they would use." [34] Judge Justice sought to show that *Castaneda* had not undermined his insistence on bilingual education as a remedy. He pointed out that the evidence clearly established a statutory violation under requirements set forth in *Castaneda* and that the trial court possessed the requisite remedial powers to redress statutory violations. "It is simply too late for defendants to contend that they should be accorded the discretion to take measures of their own choosing in order to remedy their unlawful conduct." [35]

With all that had gone on before, Justice was in no mood to compromise. Had he done so, the humiliating reversal from the Fifth Circuit might not have occurred. He rejected the state's contention that its new 1981 Bilingual Education Act had mooted his decision. The act signed into law on June 12, 1981, overlapped the remedial order to a considerable extent. But, unlike the court's decree, he pointed out that it did not require bilingual education where there were fewer than twenty limited-English-proficient students in any one grade, did not require bilingual education after the elementary grades, did not specify eligibility criteria for receiving bilingual education, and granted the state two years to establish a plan for recruiting and training bilingual teachers.

With the new school year fast approaching, Arnett moved fast to get the April 17 remedial order stayed by the Fifth Circuit. Hurried phone calls resulted in the granting of a temporary stay on August 19. The stay was affirmed by a three-judge panel on August 21. Nearly a year later, on July 12, 1982, the Fifth Circuit reversed Judge Justice's ruling.

Judge Thomas Gibbs Gee, a Nixon appointee who had reversed Judge Justice in the Gregory-Portland ISD litigation the year before, again wrote for the panel composed of himself and Judges John R. Brown and William L. Garwood. Brown had been appointed by President Eisenhower in 1955 and Garwood by President Nixon in 1971. Gee's opinion was highly critical of both Susan Dasher and Judge Justice. He characterized the trial as one of "procedural oddities" and the trial court's jurisdiction as another manifestation of a "general undertaking to supervise broad aspects of Texas' educational system and policy."[36] He noted Dasher's trouble securing her license to practice law during the pendency of the litigation. Aided only by a part-time law student, she had had neither the experience nor the time to prepare the case for trial, he wrote. Considerable space was devoted to examining Dasher's strategy with regard to the stipulations. The appeals court found the stipulations extremely broad and vague, and entered into without the authorization of her clients. And it found that Dasher used them inconsistently. As Judge Gee characterized it, "the decision to run with the hare in this case and to course with the hounds in *Gregory-Portland* bore evanescent fruit for the state."[37]

Susan Dasher, who had successfully argued a number of important cases on behalf of the state prior to the bilingual litigation, maintains that she would have had a good chance of winning the case on appeal even with the damaging stipulations. As it was, the events leading up to the Fifth Circuit decision and her castigation by the appellant judges had taken their toll. "Let's put it this way; I didn't practice law for a year and a half afterwards," she says. "It was that hard on me. It has taken me a long time to get back feeling comfortable with anything that's fairly complicated. I'd never been involved with Texas politics before. I didn't know that you could get chewed up like that."

Not only did Dasher come in for considerable criticism, but Judge Justice observes that the three appellate judges "thought the trial court was pretty half-baked too." And so they did. The Judge, they concluded, abused his discretion in not conducting post-trial hearings on the disputed stipulations. "If the state's entire legislative process is to be superceded in such circumstances by the order of a single judge, it must be upon the basis of firmer matter than appears in this record."[38] For example, the Fifth Circuit concluded that the stipulations showed that at the high-water mark of Mexican-American segregation in Texas early in World War II, about 2 percent of Texas school districts had schools intended solely for Mexican-American students. The purpose of these schools, it concluded, was to totally immerse the Mexican-American students in the English language. "This, then, represents the worst of what is meant by segregation of such students as 'historic fact.'"[39]

Judge Justice's view of Texas history is different. "I think the history of *de jure* segregation against Mexican-Americans in Texas is so well known, so well proven, that to me these contentions are laughable." A recent study lends support to Justice's views. In *Anglos and Mexicans in the Making of Texas, 1836–1986,* David Montejano observes that 90 percent of South Texas schools were segregated in the 1930s. Since most of the Mexican-American population was concentrated in South Texas, this would account for the 2 percent statewide figure cited by Judge Gee. With regard to discrimination against Mexican-American children in public schooling generally, Montejano notes that "In the absence of a statutory [segregative] plan, the segregationist policy manifested itself in acts ranging from everyday administrative staff decisions to the informal opinions and formal decisions of school trustees."[40] Rather than finding any benevolent purpose in segregation, Montejano asserts that the widespread use of Mexican-Americans as cheap farm laborers had a direct bearing on the separate and subordinate status of their social institutions.

Later in the opinion, the Fifth Circuit did acknowledge that Justice had found there was adequate evidentiary support for a conclusion that the state's early bilingual programs were deficient under the Equal Educational Opportunities Act. But he had erred in not granting the state's motion to dismiss the case on the grounds of mootness in light of the 1981 legislation. The appeals court sent the case back for a hearing on the mootness issue. No further hearings have ever been held, though plaintiffs' attorneys gave some thought in the early 1980s to challenging the 1981 bilingual legislation as inadequate and discriminatory in the face of legislation strengthening the curriculum and mandating achievement testing in Texas public schools.

The appeals court also ordered Judge Justice to assess the effectiveness of the 1981 legislation in light of their *Castaneda* decision wherein educators are to decide the method by which English-language-deficient students are to be taught rather than being forced to use the bilingual approach. Justice was baffled about this aspect of the opinion. "That's what I'd been listening to, the testimony of world-renowned educators. The whole record was filled with their testimony." He acknowledges that other methods might be appropriate for some groups such as the Vietnamese and Cuban-Americans. But "all the evidence at the trial indicated that ESL [English as a second language] simply didn't work as well where Mexican-Americans are concerned." Justice was particularly impressed with the transitional component of bilingual instruction whereby the student is able to study basic subjects while learning sufficient English to function in the all-English curriculum. "Conducting the instruction in Spanish enabled the child to merge in comfortably without being handicapped by lack of knowledge of the basic subjects," he notes.

A trial judge is a captive of the experts in the sense that the judge must rely upon their testimony in weighing evidence and designing remedial orders. The testimony presented to Judge Justice was largely one-sided. The litigants generally agreed that compensatory bilingual education was the preferred method of teaching Mexican or Mexican-American students with limited English proficiency. Disagreement centered primarily on the extent to which it should be provided. Later studies, however, have questioned the validity of much of the research asserting the effectiveness of compensatory bilingual education.[41] One of the expert witnesses who testified before Judge Justice, Dr. Courtney Cazden of the Harvard Graduate School of Education, strongly supported compensatory bilingual education in her testimony, though she acknowledged that empirical research was limited.

> Judge Justice: You spoke at the very beginning of your testimony about the theory of bilingual education. Have these theories, so-called, been derived from empirical studies?
>
> Cazden: Theory is perhaps a little bit grandiose, but at least principles. These have been partly derived from empirical studies in educational settings.[42]

Shifting methodological paradigms pose a challenge to long-term, detailed orders of the type Justice employed in the bilingual case. With the passage of time, the components of the order may become dated. Justice points out, however, that the court is always open. If credible evidence is later presented that parts of an original order are no longer effective, it can be modified. "Changed circumstances demand changed relief," he asserts, pointing to the changes that are often made in long-term school desegregation orders as a prime example.

The appeals court also stripped Justice of his exclusive jurisdiction over bilingual cases involving individual school districts. Given what the court viewed as the absence of statewide segregation against Mexican-American students, each school district should have an opportunity to defend its practices regarding bilingual education. Without overriding reasons to the contrary, Judge Justice was directed to allow school districts to litigate such matters in their local federal courts. It was a none-too-subtle rap on the knuckles for judicial overreaching and carried grave implications for continued viability of the statewide school desegregation order itself (see Chapter 5).

The appeals court decision was a major reversal, and Justice was stung by it. He took little solace in the fact that the members of the appeals panel had all been appointed by Republican presidents. His critics rejoiced. "The appeals court has served both wisdom and justice in this ruling, and by the latter, we mean the quality and not the judge in East Texas," the *Dallas Morning News* crowed in a July 14 editorial. Said one Tyler businessman, "The shoe's on the other foot now. He should have been impeached a long time ago. I'm glad he got overturned on this one. He deserved it."[43]

Legal commentators took the opportunity to note the growing conservatism of the federal judiciary, along with greater reluctance to sanction detailed remedial orders of the type Judge Justice had imposed. University of Texas law professor Charles Alan Wright, a noted constitutional law authority, pointed out that Justice does not simply rule that a problem exists. Rather, he imposes "structural" injunctions mandating specific steps to be taken, thus leaving himself open to criticism that he goes too far.[44]

For the Judge, it is simply a matter of effective remedies. "I would not enter these detailed kinds of orders if I perceived that the persons I was dealing with were willingly going to implement my decisions. When you're faced with an obdurate, obstinate, and willful desire to circumvent the decision, you have to issue a detailed order because if you just put it in general terms, they'll disobey it, saying, 'Well, you didn't order me specifically to do that.'"

From the perspective of the Fifth Circuit reversal, the bilingual litigation was a major loss for Judge Justice. But from a broader perspective, it was not. Had his decision not mandated compensatory bilingual education throughout public education in Texas and had it not been handed down at the beginning of the 1981 legislative session, it is unlikely that the legislature would have significantly expanded the 1975 program as it did. The Fifth Circuit acknowledged as much, noting that Justice's effort "has had a useful effect, if one of no more than celerity, upon the state's arrangements."[45] Attorney General White, who was then the Democratic nominee for governor, overlooked this point when he told reporters that the Fifth Circuit ruling "indicates that given the opportunity, Texas lawmakers can take care of their own educational problems without unwarranted interference by the federal courts."[46] While it was the legislature which enacted the 1981 bilingual reforms, Judge Justice's decision provided the necessary impetus.

In an open letter to a "beleaguered judge," a Mexican-American engineer in San Antonio wrote prior to the Fifth Circuit reversal of the need to take the long view. "The courageous vision associated with your name in this instance will live long after the dust of history has suffocated your critics and blurred the scars of discrimination, irrespective of whether your order is upheld. It should suffice as a powerful word to the wise. However, as a native Texan, I have lived in its parochialism and thrived outside, and I do not deceive myself on the short-range outcome." He ended his letter, "Best wishes y que Dios te bendiga, William Wayne Justice, hombre valiente y visionario, and also a United States district judge."[47]

CHAPTER 11

Rights of the Accused

In his 1968 book, *The Limits of the Criminal Sanction,* Herbert L. Packer outlined two approaches to the criminal process within the United States: the crime control model and the due process model. For each, the goals and procedures of the criminal justice system are different. The crime control model considers the repression of criminal conduct as the most important function to be performed by the criminal process because a safe and secure society is essential to the meaningful exercise of individual rights. To achieve its goal, the crime control model, in the words of Packer, "requires that primary attention be paid to the efficiency with which the criminal process operates to screen suspects, determine guilt, and secure appropriate dispositions of persons convicted of crime."[1] Heavy reliance is placed on the efficacy of investigative and prosecutorial officials to reconstruct the facts in criminal events and to apprehend the perpetrators. Once apprehended, suspects are considered probably guilty, and the adjudicatory phase becomes relatively pro forma. Impediments to the initial fact-finding phase are minimized in the interest of efficiency.

While the due process model also considers the repression of criminal conduct an important social goal, it places greater weight on the need to eliminate mistakes in the process of bringing criminals to justice. This is so because the fact-finding phase is often unreliable and because the consequences for the convicted represent the greatest deprivation government can inflict on individual rights. Packer pointed out that "the aim of the process is at least as much to protect the factually innocent as it is to convict the factually guilty."[2] Thus, in order to curtail the possibility of error, the due process model emphasizes compliance with a set of procedures. The accused is considered legally innocent until guilt is proven through a process from which all procedural irregularities have been eliminated. "By opening up a procedural situation that permits the successful assertion of defenses having nothing to do with factual guilt," Packer observed, "[the due process model] vindicates the proposition that the factually guilty may nonetheless be legally innocent and should therefore be given a chance to qualify for that kind of treatment."[3] In short, some who are guilty may go free because the government violated the law in the process of enforcing it. When combined with the concept of equality—that the quality of legal services accused persons receive should not vary with the amount of money they have—this model exacts a high price for bringing criminals to justice and demands considerable judicial oversight to maintain its integrity.

Critics of the due process model charge that because it elevates procedure over result, the welfare of the victim and society is subordinated to the welfare of the accused. Yet anyone who is accused of a crime is apt to fight tenaciously for all the protections the law affords, as recent political scandals at the national level attest. It is often said that when it comes to criminal matters, a liberal is a conservative who has been arrested. One's involvement in the criminal law process—for example, as victim or accused—often has great bearing on one's position regarding which of these two approaches should prevail.

Early on, through his father's law practice, William Wayne Justice was introduced to the due process model. While 80 percent of the practice involved civil matters, it was the 20 percent devoted to criminal law that made the firm famous throughout East Texas and brought a steady stream of clients through the front door. It was standard practice for father and son to challenge the procedures by which their clients had been apprehended and charged. There was abundant opportunity, for peace officers in many small East Texas communities were not sophisticated in the niceties of criminal procedure. Searches, for example, were often conducted illegally. Texas law prohibited the use of illegally seized evidence at trial, and the Justices sought to assert that defense whenever possible.[4]

Wayne Justice switched sides when he became a prosecutor as U.S. attorney in 1961. During the seven years he served in that position, the Warren Supreme Court brought the due process model into prominence by handing down important rulings extending rights of the accused. In 1961 the Court held in *Mapp v. Ohio* that illegally seized evidence could not be used in a state trial.[5] In 1963, the Court ruled in *Gideon v. Wainwright* that the accused are entitled to court-appointed counsel in all serious criminal cases if they are too poor to afford private counsel.[6] A year later, in *Escobedo v. Illinois,* the Court held that the right to counsel must be accorded through all stages of focused investigations.[7] In 1966 the Court expanded the *Escobedo* precedent by deciding in *Miranda v. Arizona* that a confession could not be admitted as evidence unless the suspect had been explicitly informed of the constitutional rights to remain silent and to obtain legal counsel.[8] In 1967 the Court held in *Katz v. United States* that the right of privacy inherent in the Fourth Amendment requires the securing of a warrant before electronic surveillance can be conducted.[9]

Cries of protest from state and federal law enforcement personnel greeted each decision. Wayne Justice's voice was not among them. He did not find these rulings a hindrance to his work: "I approved of them entirely. It just seemed fair play to me," he observes. The 1966 *Miranda* ruling, the most controversial of the Warren Court criminal procedure decisions, is a case in point. *Miranda* requires the police to inform suspects facing arrest that they have a right to remain silent, that anything they say can be used against them in a court of law, that they have a right to an attorney, and that an attorney will be appointed if they cannot afford one. Upon his appointment as U.S. attorney, Justice was surprised to find that such warnings were not already routine among government agencies. "A person who doesn't think these warnings are necessary obviously has never had a child with no experience with the law arrested by police officers. It is terrifying to think what could happen to them if they are without counsel," he says, recalling an incident prior to *Miranda* involving the son of one of the secretaries in the U.S. attorney's office. The son had been arrested one evening for a felony offense. Because he had previously been in minor trouble with the law, the secretary and her husband decided to teach him a lesson by leaving him in jail overnight without the assistance of counsel. "When I heard about that, I thought to myself, God almighty, they are taking a tremendous risk." Indeed, the parents discovered the next morning that their son had signed a full confession. He was later convicted. Without the confession, Justice observes, the likelihood was that the local prosecutors could not have secured the conviction.

In private practice and as U.S. attorney, Justice had experienced many of the issues in criminal law that he would later face as a judge. By the time he took the bench, he was sophisticated in the criminal practice of law, both from the standpoint of the defendant and from that of the prosecution. With his adherence to the tenets of the due process model and his criminal law experience, it was to be expected that he would be more sensitive to and sympathetic toward the claims of the accused than many of his contemporaries on the bench. Some of his more notable and controversial decisions are presented in this chapter.

Fourth Amendment Search and Seizure

Many of Justice's criminal procedure decisions have involved habeas corpus petitions from incarcerated prisoners, asserting that their convictions were unjust and should be overturned. From his first days on the bench, Justice gave them more than *pro forma* attention, granting many. Michael P. O'Reilly, who clerked for the Judge during his first year on the bench, says that Justice told him and fellow clerk Wayne V. R. Smith that since prisoners who file *pro se* habeas corpus petitions do not have the services of a lawyer, "we as clerks were to be their lawyer. He told us to scrutinize the prisoner's claims carefully to determine if there was any legal validity to them." Prior to Justice's elevation to the bench, the fortune of habeas corpus petitions in the Eastern District had not been good. The result was that few were filed. "But after the Judge granted the first petition," Smith says, "he opened the floodgates. We were getting as many as two or three a week."

One of the first came from a prisoner who alleged that the taking of a blood sample from him constituted an illegal search and seizure in violation of his rights under the Fourth Amendment, which forbids unreasonable searches and seizures by government officials and requires the securing of a search or arrest warrant based on probable cause.[10] David Jessie Graves had been arrested in Plano, Texas, a Dallas bedroom community, on the charge of public drunkenness. Shortly before his arrest, an elderly deaf woman had been raped in her home near Plano. Her description of the assailant closely matched the appearance of Graves. Later, she picked him out of a police lineup and identified him at the trial. Blood was found on the bed where the rape had occurred. The Plano chief of police sought a blood sample from Graves to determine his blood group. No search warrant was obtained, though there was time to secure one. To obtain Graves' consent for the blood test, the chief of police told him that the purpose was to ascertain whether he had been intoxicated at the time of the arrest. Graves consented to the test on this basis. The blood grouping revealed that Graves' blood group, a rare type, matched that of the rapist. Since the blood group of the woman was a different type, proof of the matching blood group constituted significant evidence against Graves at his trial for rape. He was never brought to trial on the charge of public drunkenness.

When Justice first read through the record of the original trial, he concluded that no significant error had been committed. He was aware of an earlier U.S. Supreme Court ruling upholding the taking of blood without a warrant or consent from an arrested person in order to show that the person was driving a car while intoxicated.[11] No search warrant was deemed necessary in that case because medical detection would be impossible if time were taken to obtain one. But there was an element of deception involved in the *Graves* matter that was not present in the California case. Justice appointed longtime Tyler criminal lawyer Weldon Holcomb to represent Graves. As described in Chapter 3, Holcomb had succeeded in getting the U.S. Supreme Court to overturn one of the convictions Justice had helped secure as U.S. attorney.[12] At the hearing on the petition, Justice's experience as a criminal trial lawyer is evident in his close questioning of the police chief on the pivotal issue:

> Justice: And was it your object to determine whether or not this blood sample that you were proposing to have taken be checked to see whether or not it corresponded with the blood type that was on the pillow case and on the bedspread?
>
> Police chief: Yes, sir; I wanted to check it out.
>
> .   .   .   .
>
> Justice: . . . have you ever before or since had a blood test taken for a person who was charged with the offense of common drunkenness—common public drunkenness as distinguished from a D.W.I. charge—driving while intoxicated?
>
> Police chief: No, sir; I have not.
>
> Justice: Is that the only time that a test had ever been run in your—
>
> Police chief: (interrupting) First time in my career.
>
> Justice: All right.[13]

Later, during the final argument of Dunklin Sullivan, the assistant attorney general representing the state, Justice interrupted to ask whether Sullivan believed the misrepresentation comported with due process of law. "I don't know. It's a close question," Sullivan admitted.[14] Justice asked both attorneys to research the question and present their findings to the court.

With the benefit of the briefing and additional research he himself found time to do while holding court in Marshall, Justice concluded that Graves' Fourth Amendment rights had been violated because of the absence of a search warrant and the trickery used to gain his consent to the blood test. Concluding that "the performance of the blood grouping test without a search warrant, and the subsequent use of the results of the test as evidence at petitioner's trial, was illegal and in violation of his constitutional rights," Justice granted the writ releasing Graves from prison.[15] The Fifth Circuit affirmed the decision.[16] Whether Graves was guilty or not was irrelevant: the government had violated the law in the process of seeking to uphold it.

In the early 1970s, Judge Justice accepted invitations on two occasions from Chief Judge David L. Bazelon to sit by designation on the U.S. Court of

Appeals for the District of Columbia Circuit. During the few weeks he was there, he heard a number of cases involving rights of the accused. In one of the search and seizure cases where guilt was all but certain, he wrote a dissent in which he clearly expressed his adherence to the tenets of the due process model. *United States v. Diggs* involved contested convictions arising from a 1972 robbery of a Washington, D.C., bank.[17] The facts were relatively simple, but Justice found the underlying legal issues less so.

Before the robbery, two black men had been seen parking a white Cadillac with red leather door panels near the bank. Evidence at the trial indicated that the taller of the two robbers had a gun when he robbed the bank; was carrying an attaché case; and was wearing a dark raincoat, gloves, brown or tan trousers, and brown Hush Puppies shoes. The shorter robber, wearing a blue denim jacket and a black turtleneck pulled up around his face, was stationed in the lobby. The robbers made off with over $5,000, including $400 of bait money (marked bills). After they left the bank, they entered the get-away car, a green Chevrolet, driven by a third black man.

When word of the robbery reached the Washington office of the FBI, Special Agent Berry, who had been working on evidence linking Tyrone Diggs, his alleged accomplice Percy Floyd, and the white Cadillac to earlier crimes, immediately suspected them and drove to a location where he knew Diggs spent much of his time. On the way to the site, Berry and another agent learned over the police radio what the robbers were wearing and the identity of the get-away car they were driving. Berry concluded that the robbers would abandon the Chevrolet for another car. Shortly after the agents arrived at the site, the white Cadillac appeared, slowed, and stopped. The agents approached the Cadillac with drawn guns and asked the men to raise their hands. Inside the car, they spotted a rust-colored briefcase and noticed that one of the men, Garrett Keys, was wearing a black trenchcoat and that next to him was a short denim jacket. Their suspicions confirmed, the agents placed the three men— Diggs, Floyd, and Keys—under arrest. A search conducted incident to the arrest produced, among other things, the $5,000, including the bank's bait money.

Writing for himself and Judge Malcolm Wilkey, Senior Circuit Judge John A. Danaher, a New England conservative appointed to the bench by President Eisenhower, found there was ample probable cause for the arrest. He rejected all of appellant Diggs' contentions, including an assertion that the trial judge had acted improperly when he refused to allow appellant Floyd's lawyer to ask prospective jurors a question relating to their racial prejudice.

Judge Justice dissented. He reviewed the Warren Court's seminal 1968 ruling in *Terry v. Ohio* that street encounters between police officers and individuals can consist of simple conversation; investigatory stops, which require reasonable suspicion of criminal activity; or arrests, which require probable cause.[18] He acknowledged that the statement of the facts in the majority opinion was strongly indicative of the guilt of the appellants but observed that "very little of it was available to the special agents at the time they conducted their armed approach to appellants' automobile."[19] Citing discrepancies in the police radio reports about the appearance of the men, Justice concluded that the agents were acting on nothing more than a hunch. "There was no informer, no tip, and no description of the automobile or its occupants which matched Diggs as he drove up in the Cadillac," he wrote. "The site of the stop was approximately eight miles from the bank which had been robbed; a minimum of thirty-five minutes had elapsed since the robbery; and the occupants of the automobile were not engaging in any unusual activity. Moreover, since Diggs' car was coming to a stop, the exigencies appear to have been minimal." Accordingly, "the deficient nature of the information possessed by the special agents mandated further investigation by them before they undertook to seize appellants at gunpoint."

The values underlying the due process model are readily apparent in Justice's approach to the case. The Warren Court's *Terry* decision required probable cause to arrest the suspects. The requirement had not been met. Justice found the FBI agents overly eager in their desire to apprehend the guilty. In a key passage, he wrote, "I maintain that we must recognize that 'it is better . . . that the guilty sometimes go free' . . . than to adopt a constitutional standard which will make it probable that 'innocent citizens [will] be stopped, searched, and arrested at the whim of police officers who have only the slightest suspicion of improper conduct.'"[20] It is an assertion that fuels attacks by conservatives on federal judges who, they charge, are more concerned with the rights of criminals than the rights of their victims and the welfare of society. But by those who have felt the heavy hand of the police, the probable cause requirement is welcomed.

Judge Justice was also critical of the majority's decision that the trial judge had committed no error in not allowing Floyd's attorney to question prospective jurors about their racial prejudice. Over the years, Justice had become increasingly sensitive to the black-white issue in the courtroom, though this was not the case when he was practicing law in the 1940s and 1950s. Then, blacks were systematically excluded from jury duty. This created a problem for lawyers with black defendants. It was customary for attorneys to ask white jurors whether they had such prejudice against the Negro race as would keep them from rendering a fair and impartial verdict. If they answered in the affirmative, they were excused from jury service. "It was assumed you had prejudice," Justice observes. "The question was whether or not it was of such overriding concern to you that you wouldn't be able to give the defendant a fair trial." He adds, "Most of the time the lawyers didn't use the term 'Negro.' They'd say the 'nigger race.' 'Nigger' was frequently employed in the courtroom."

Justice saw his first black juror in a 1954 civil case. The woman had apparently been selected by mistake. "In those days when this occurred, the practice was that both sides by agreement would excuse the juror," he notes. When he saw the lone black among the potential jurors, Justice went over to the opposing counsel, who was from Dallas and told him that it was customary in Henderson County to excuse blacks from jury service. "He looked at me like I was trying to put something over on him. He said, 'That doesn't make any difference to me.' When he said that, I told him, 'Well, if it doesn't make any difference to you, it sure doesn't make any difference to me either.'" It turned out that the black woman had been a client of the Justice firm, and Justice knew she would be favorable to his side.

"I always had a bad conscience about the practice of excusing black jurors. Dad and I did the same thing everyone else did. We would have been regarded as 'nigger lovers' had we not conformed to the practice. And that was a very, very bad designation for a person in those days. I never did like what I was doing, but I didn't raise the red flag of rebellion against it. I conformed. It's embarrassing for me to have to say that, but that's the truth of the matter."

When the civil rights movement came to East Texas in the early 1960s, Justice was U.S. attorney, and while no crusader, he enforced the 1964 Civil Rights Act. Once assured the security of a lifetime appointment as federal judge in 1968, he welcomed every opportunity to strike a blow for integration. When confronted by the *Diggs* case, he understood what the lawyer representing the black defendant was trying to do in questioning potential jurors about their racial prejudice, and he sympathized with him. While he recognized that Diggs' lawyer had not followed up with a different question relating to the issue when the trial judge disallowed his initial question, Justice did not find this a bar. "It cannot be doubted that we are dealing with a right that is of utmost importance to the integrity of the jury system, for the opportunity to ascertain potential racial bias of veniremen is basic to the fundamental fairness of our system," he wrote.

Diggs was the first case that Justice heard as an appeals judge. The system of judicial decision-making was quite different from what he had experienced as a trial judge. On the morning the *Diggs* case was heard, the three-judge panel to which Justice had been assigned began hearing appeals at 10 A.M. and continued without recess until 1 P.M. Unlike proceedings at the district court level, there was no presentation of evidence. Rather, the judges, who had read legal briefs filed earlier by the attorneys, listened to the attorneys for the two sides deliver oral arguments of thirty minutes each. Occasionally, one of the judges interrupted the presentation to ask a question or make a comment. After the last case had been heard, Justice assumed the judges would break for lunch. But after shedding their judicial robes, Wilkey and Danaher ushered Justice into an adjoining room, where they began deliberations at the end of a long conference table.

As the presiding judge, Wilkey, a former U.S. attorney in Texas who had been appointed to the D.C. Circuit by President Nixon, began calling off the list of cases, starting with *Diggs*. "He turned to me after calling off that case and said, 'Judge Justice, how would you decide this case?' Well, I figured he wanted some discussion, so I talked for some five minutes about the intricacies involved. I was knowledgeable about Fourth Amendment law and the law of arrest, so I expounded on my thoughts. Finally, I ended up saying I would reverse the lower court." Both Wilkey and Danaher listened politely, but Justice could tell they were not moved by his presentation. Then Wilkey asked Danaher how he would decide the case. Danaher simply said he would affirm. Wilkey agreed and assigned the case to Danaher to write an opinion. Justice said, this being the case, he would likely write a dissent. The other two judges nodded and went to the next case. "By this time, I caught on," Justice says. "When the next case was called out, I simply announced my decision without explanation." And thus the trio of judges went through the list of cases they had heard.

"I got to thinking, God damn, this is summary," Justice recalls. But he discovered that this was only a preliminary look at the case. The judge who was assigned the opinion later circulated a draft to the other judges on the panel. At this point, comments and suggestions for changes would occasionally flow among the judges via the circulation of memoranda. The resulting deliberation sometimes resulted in a change of views. After Justice had read the draft of the majority opinion in the *Diggs* case, he followed through with his dissent. While the majority had no comment, he was later complimented by the chief judge of the circuit. In a dissent from refusal by the entire circuit to rehear the *Diggs* case, Chief Judge Bazelon noted, "Judge Justice's excellent dissent persuasively sets forth the reasons why the division's opinion is unsupportable on either the law or the facts."[21]

Justice found race again to be an underlying factor in a Texas Fourth Amendment case he decided several years later as federal district court judge in Texas. He and law clerk Lucas Guttentag found the case fascinating and wrote a decision which has occasionally been cited in later decisions by the U.S. Supreme Court. *United States v. Hall* involved a motion to suppress use of an illegal firearm in a criminal prosecution. The firearm, apparently a sawed-off shotgun, had been seized by deputies of the Anderson County Sheriff's Department and turned over to federal authorities. The department had received a tip that Alvin Hall had allegedly been counting some money at a table. The money was said to match the amount stolen from a Kentucky Fried Chicken restaurant. An arrest warrant was secured, and officers proceeded before dawn on December 14, 1977, to the home of Mrs. Ola Fay Pinson, where Hall was staying. Upon arresting Hall, the officers saw the shotgun lying on the couch in the living room and seized it pursuant to the "plain view" doctrine, which allows use of such evidence in a criminal prosecution.[22] After his arrest, Hall agreed to take a lie detector test regarding the robbery; none was ever administered and he was not questioned further about the robbery.

Justice had little difficulty finding the arrest warrant to have been issued "in utter disregard by both the Sheriff's Department and the magistrate for the requirements of the Fourth Amendment."[23] The police had simply asked the magistrate for an arrest warrant. No affidavits were presented to the magistrate indicating that probable cause existed for the warrant, as required by the amendment. Testimony revealed that it was customary for arrest warrants to be filled out by someone in the sheriff's department and presented to the magistrate for signature. The magistrate was not given the substance of the tip, or even told what premises had been robbed or where the robbery had occurred.

While an invalid warrant will not necessarily undermine an otherwise valid arrest, such was not the case in *Hall* because, in Justice's view, the tip was ambiguous and uncorroborated by independent observations of the police, as required by Supreme Court rulings. The informant had not linked Hall to the crime through incriminating statements Hall might have made. Nor did the informant say the money Hall was counting was the same money taken from the restaurant, though the sheriff's department believed it to match the amount of the stolen money, in both paper and coins. Justice wrote, "Otherwise innocent activity cannot form the basis for probable cause for an arrest simply because an informant denotes the activity as criminal or suspicious."

With the arrest unlawful, the government was left to prosecute Hall for possession of the shotgun which the police had seized when they entered the house to arrest him. But Hall objected that the seizure was illegal, since there had been no search warrant and since neither he nor Mrs. Pinson had consented to let the officers into the house. The officers disputed the latter assertion. From his long experience as an attorney in private practice in East Texas, Judge Justice could read between the lines. Hall and Mrs. Pinson were black. The two deputies who made the arrest were white. One was armed with a shotgun for "psychological reasons." They had approached the house in the darkness of the early morning hours, one to the back door and one to the front, and both started banging on the doors, announcing themselves as officers and demanding entry. "The totality of the circumstances," he wrote, "compels the conclusion that neither Mrs. Pinson nor the defendant voluntarily and validly consented to the deputies' entry into the house." Looking back on it, Judge Justice has no doubt that his assessment was accurate. "It was simply contrary to my experience that these black people would deny entry to the white officers under those circumstances," he points out. "It was just not the way things were done in East Texas." Thus, the shotgun could not be introduced into evidence, and the case against Hall collapsed.

Judge Justice's most important Fourth Amendment decision was a 1980 ruling involving the use of drug-detecting dogs in public schools. *Jones v. Latexo Independent School District* arose when school officials in Latexo, a small community in Houston County about fifty miles west of Lufkin, employed a private firm to help the district combat use of drugs in school in 1980. The firm used "Merko," a large German Shepherd, for this purpose. Merko was trained to detect the odor of marijuana and other narcotics.

On April 11, 1980, Merko and his handler appeared on campus. They moved from classroom to classroom while the students sat at their desks. Sniffing each child in turn, the dog walked up and down the aisles. If Merko alerted his handler to the odor of a target substance, the latter informed the superintendent. The dog later sniffed automobiles in the school parking lot. Based on the dog's reactions and subsequent search, six students were suspended from school.

Two of the six, brothers Scott and Michael Jones, were singled out by Merko during the class visits. They were removed from class and told to empty their pockets. A cigarette lighter was taken from Scott, a hair clip and bottle of nasal spray from Michael. The cars driven by the two students were also searched. Tag ends of marijuana cigarettes, known as "roaches," were found in both vehicles. A case suspected of carrying marijuana cigarettes was also found in one of the cars. Items identified as drug paraphernalia were found. The students denied using the confiscated items for drug purposes. They were given short suspensions from school and points for each day missed were deducted from their course grades. The Jones students through their mother sued the school district for violating their Fourth Amendment rights.

The use of drug-detecting dogs in the public schools was new to Judge Justice, and he was fascinated by the underlying issues it raised. James Sultan, the law clerk who worked on the case, recalls that "the practice of bringing these big dogs into the classroom to sniff little kids as a matter of routine with no semblance of probable cause or even a scintilla of evidence really took the Judge aback."

Justice began his sniffer dog opinion by applauding the school board's concern over drug abuse in the district. "Narcotics and other dangerous drugs have no place in our public schools," he wrote.[24] He acknowledged that school officials have broad authority to maintain order in the public schools. But school officials "would not be permitted to violate constitutional standards in attempting to enforce them." "If the dog's sniffing of the students and their property was an unreasonable search under the fourth amendment, a constitutional violation has occurred and the victims are entitled to redress."

The first question was whether the use of a sniffer dog constitutes a "search" within the meaning of the Fourth Amendment. Since there was then no ruling on this issue in the Fifth Circuit, the Judge was not bound by precedent and thus was free to develop his own rule of law.[25] He noted that under the plain view doctrine, people have no Fourth Amendment privacy right in that which they expose to the public. But how far does the doctrine go? Courts had upheld the use of a flashlight by police officers to view objects otherwise hidden from view, but not the use of electronic devices to listen in on telephone conversations. Was the use of a sniffer dog more like the flashlight or the electronic listening device? Judge Justice and law clerk Sultan concluded that Merko was more akin to the latter. Because Merko was able to detect odors outside the range of the human sense of smell, the dog did not enhance the perceptive abilities of school officials in the manner of a flashlight, but replaced them. "The dog's inspection was virtually equivalent to a physical entry into the students' pockets and personal possessions," Justice wrote.[26] Just as the use of a portable X-ray machine by police to discern what people are carrying in their pockets and purses as they walk along the street would be a search under the Fourth Amendment, the use of Merko's superhuman sense of smell to search inside student pockets and purses was also a search.

But deciding that the use of Merko was a search within the context of the Fourth Amendment did not end the matter, for the amendment permits government conducted or sanctioned searches which are reasonable. Justice concluded that the warrantless search was unreasonable and thus violative of the amendment. He noted that Merko was a large animal and had been trained as an attack dog. He noted testimony that the dog might physically touch a child during a search and had "slobbered" on one student. "Such a tool of surveillance could prove both intimidating and frightening, particularly to the children, some as young as kindergarten age, enrolled at Latexo." He downplayed the fact that the students had been forewarned of the presence of Merko, noting that "if the Government announced that all telephone lines would henceforth be tapped, it is apparent that, nevertheless, the public would not lose its expectation of privacy in using the telephones." Nor did he accept the analogy to passenger searches at airports. Unlike passengers, students are not free to avoid impending searches, since they are compelled under the mandatory school attendance law to be in school.

What particularly convinced him that the search was unreasonable was the lack of individualized suspicion. The sniffer dog was used indiscriminately to search all students. "Just as the police could not lawfully bring Merko into a restaurant, football stadium, or shopping center to sniff-search citizens indiscriminately for hidden drugs," he observed, "the school officials exceeded the bounds of reasonableness in using Merko to inspect virtually the entire Latexo student body without any facts to raise a reasonable suspicion regarding specific individuals." Since students had no access to their automobiles during school, the school had no legitimate interest in using Merko to sniff them as well. Because the evidence had thus been obtained by means of an unconstitutional search, it could not be used to justify the suspensions.

Most of Judge Justice's reasoning was upheld by the Fifth Circuit in a similar case arising in South Texas. In overturning the lower court's decision in *Horton v. Goose Creek Independent School District,* the appeals court spoke approvingly of Justice's conclusion that the use of sniffer dogs to search students in an indiscriminate fashion violates the Fourth Amendment, noting that "the result in *Jones* appears to be that favored by the commentators . . ."[27] But the court did not follow Justice's ruling with regard to the sniffing of lockers and cars. In that instance, the court observed, a Fourth Amendment search is not being conducted and the dogs may be used in this fashion if they are reliable at detecting drugs.

The *Jones* decision is significant not only for its careful reasoning in applying the Fourth Amendment to a situation unheard of when the amendment was adopted, but also because it was the first in the country to extend Fourth Amendment protection to students in the context of a sniffer dog search. Underlying the decision is the view that the public school is the training ground for democracy. In enforcing rules, school authorities must, like law enforcement personnel, observe the civil liberties of their constituents. For Justice, the tenets of the due process model are not limited to adults, but extend to schoolchildren as well. There are a good many educators who agree with him, but probably more who do not.

Due Process of Law

The Fifth Amendment to the U.S. Constitution states that no person is to be deprived of life, liberty, or property "without due process of law." The Fourteenth Amendment, which applies to the states, contains a similar provision. Ordinarily, due process of law is equated with adherence by law enforcement personnel to a set of predetermined procedures. But due process can also convey the substantive notion of fundamental fairness. Many judges are reluctant to consider the issue of fundamental fairness because the subjectivity of determining fairness inevitably invites them to second-guess the decisions of prosecutors and jurors. For Judge Justice, the very goal of the criminal process is to render fundamental fairness, and he has had no reluctance to consider allegations of its absence.

A case in point is *Roper v. Beto,* in which Justice was called upon to determine whether a convicted rapist had been accorded fundamental fairness. On October 26, 1962, a twenty-seven-year-old Tyler secretary arrived home after work. As she entered her apartment, a man grabbed her from behind. He ordered her to place over her eyes and mouth pieces of adhesive tape he had brought with him. She did so. He then bound her to the bed, removed her clothing, and raped her. After the attack, the assailant remained in the apartment. He spoke to the victim for some thirty minutes, removing the tape from her mouth at times to enable her to reply.

Jimmy Curtis Roper, who lived in the same apartment building as the victim, was later arrested and charged with the crime. The police told the secretary that they had made an arrest and brought her to the station house for a voice identification. Positioned a few feet outside an office in which Roper was being questioned, she identified the voice as that of her assailant. Roper was not aware that his conversation was being overheard. The following morning, he signed a full confession.

At the trial, the secretary testified to the voice identification. The confession was also introduced. Roper was found guilty and sentenced to seventy-five years in prison. After his confinement, he began a lengthy effort in state and federal court to overturn his conviction. In 1969 he sought to challenge the admissibility of the voice identification. After being rebuffed in state court, he filed a habeas corpus petition on this ground on January 27, 1970, in Judge Justice's court.

During the pendency of Roper's appeals, the U.S. Supreme Court had handed down its *Escobedo v. Illinois, Miranda v. Arizona,* and *United States v. Wade* decisions, expanding the right to counsel throughout the criminal investigation stage, including a lineup. But none of these decisions was applied retroactively. Thus, Roper, who had not been advised that he had a right to an attorney when the voice identification and confession had occurred, was not entitled to this protection. Instead, his conviction was to be reviewed in light of the more general standard of fundamental fairness. Justice had to determine whether the circumstances surrounding the voice identification were so unfair that its admission at trial denied Roper due process of law. Given his strong support for the Warren Court criminal procedure precedents, it is not surprising that Justice would view their protections as essential to achieving fundamental fairness.

From his review of the evidence under this standard, he concluded that the voice identification had to be excluded. The victim had been brought to the station house in an expectant frame of mind. "The police had *a* suspect whose voice they wanted her to identify. Such singling out necessarily suggested that *the* suspect was thought by the police to be the culprit." [28] He quoted from a 1969 U.S. Supreme Court decision in which a majority of the Justices held that repeated focusing of attention on one suspect so undermined the reliability of the eyewitness identification as to violate the suspect's right to fundamental fairness under the due process clause. [29] Justice Hugo Black had written a dissent in that case, in which he presented the classic criticism of the fundamental fairness approach used by the majority and by Judge Justice. "It has become fashionable to talk of the Court's power to hold governmental laws and practices unconstitutional whenever this Court believes them to be 'unfair,' contrary to basic standards of decency, implicit in ordered liberty, or offensive 'to those canons of decency and fairness which express the notions of justice of English-speaking peoples . . .' All of these different general and indefinable words or phrases are the fruit of the same, what I consider to be poisonous, tree, namely, the doctrine that this Court has power to make its own ideas of fairness, decency, and so forth, enforceable as though they were constitutional percepts. . . . This formula imposes no 'restraint' on judges beyond requiring them to follow their own best judgment as to what is wise, just, and best under the circumstances of a particular case." [30]

A criticism of Justice Black's view is that it curtails the ability of judges to assure that the law comports with evolving standards of decency through interpretation of such openended phrases as "due process of law" in the Fifth and Fourteenth amendments. For example, in attempting to ascertain the meaning of the ambiguous phrase "cruel and unusual punishments" in the Eighth Amendment, four members of the U.S. Supreme Court agreed in a 1958 case that the amendment "must draw its meaning from the evolving standards of decency that mark the progress of a maturing society." [31] It is a phrase Justice often repeats. To do otherwise, he notes, would be to lock the meaning of the Constitution into the anachronistic interpretations of the past, thus undermining its relevance to an advancing society. Advocates of judicial activism on behalf of individual rights assert that refusal to shoulder the difficult task of constitutional interpretation is an evasion of judicial responsibility.

Insofar as Roper was concerned, Judge Justice concluded that the voice identification procedure violated his due process rights and had to be excluded from the trial. Since the woman could not identify her assailant, the only other link between Roper and the crime was the confession. While the confession had supposedly been voluntary, Justice pointed out several inconsistent statements, along with the use of legalistic language, which cast doubt on its validity. He questioned whether the jury would have judged Roper guilty had it not been for the voice identification testimony. Thus, the introduction of the voice identification had not been harmless error but a denial of fundamental fairness under the Fourteenth Amendment due process clause. He granted the writ.

The Fifth Circuit reversed. Noting that objection to the voice identification was the latest in a series of unsuccessful efforts to overturn Roper's conviction, the appeals court downplayed the factors Justice had cited as casting doubt on its reliability. The victim had listened to her attacker talk for thirty-five minutes after the rape, had been brought to the police station three days later, and had been positive in her identification. The court noted testimony from the officer with her when the identification was made to the effect that "she about got sick—just couldn't hardly talk, got real nervous." [32] Nor did the appeals judges accept Justice's speculation about the credibility of the confession in the minds of the jury, labeling it "inconsequential and meaningless."

Justice largely blames himself for the reversal. "I should have found that there was a *probability* that the jury would not have found him guilty without the voice identification testimony rather than say the jury 'could have found him not guilty.' I thought it was extremely suspect. I don't doubt that they probably got the right man. Technically, however, I thought there was a violation of his due process rights." While the definitiveness of the appeals court ruling suggests that a change in wording might not have made any difference in the outcome, Justice did learn from this early case to set forth his conclusions forthrightly.

With the growing conservatism of the federal judiciary, the fundamental fairness component of due process has become harder to establish. This is particularly true in public education, where courts are now less likely to intervene in student discipline disputes, deferring to the judgment of school officials. As a trial judge, Judge Justice is bound by the precedents of higher courts. He follows them, though at times he finds it very difficult to do so. Such was the case in a 1987 decision denying relief to two parents who protested the corporal punishment of their children. The two children, five-year-old Crystal Cunningham and six-year-old Ashley Johnson, were given two swats on the buttocks with a wooden paddle by the school principal for snickering in the hall.

A short time later, they received an additional three swats from their teacher for snickering in the classroom.

Ashley Johnson's grandmother noticed black and blue marks on Ashley's buttocks when she bathed the child that night. Ashley told her grandmother what had happened. The child was taken to a doctor, who advised that she had been spanked too hard. Both Ashley and Crystal were then taken to the Jacksonville Police Department. Photographs were taken and a report made out. The next day, social workers at the Child Welfare Office took photographs and stated that the bruises clearly constituted child abuse. Crying and complaining that they did not wish to return to school, the two children were absent for several days. Subsequently, the parents filed a lawsuit in Justice's court, alleging that the corporal punishment had violated their children's substantive and procedural due process rights.

Justice and law clerk Tom Viles studied Supreme Court and Fifth Circuit precedents on corporal punishment, concluding reluctantly that their hands were tied.[33] No cause of action existed. The complaint was dismissed, a decision affirmed by the Fifth Circuit.[34] In a short opinion, Justice did note the moral conflict between Texas' prohibition of child abuse and its allowance of corporal punishment in the public schools.

Shortly after the newspapers reported that Justice's judgment had been affirmed by the Fifth Circuit, he was greeted at the barbershop by a muscular man in a T-shirt and crewcut. Justice assumed he was a school football coach. The man congratulated Justice on the affirmance of his decision. Justice quickly set the record straight. "I told him that I regarded the decision to be one of the worst I have ever made. If I hadn't been compelled by the Fifth Circuit's prior decisions, I would have held just the opposite. I thought it was outrageous conduct on the part of the school officials. He looked at me as if in surprise, and then nodded his head, apparently thinking, 'Well, this is what I should have expected.'"

Right to Counsel

The Sixth Amendment to the U.S. Constitution provides that in all criminal prosecutions, the accused shall "have the Assistance of Counsel for his defense." In its landmark *Gideon v. Wainwright* ruling in 1963, the U.S. Supreme Court held that this provision applies to the states through the Fourteenth Amendment, and therefore indigent defendants in felony prosecutions are entitled to state-appointed attorneys.[35] Up until this time, an attorney was provided only if the judge determined that one was necessary to accord fundamental fairness under the Fourteenth Amendment due process clause. Since the *Gideon* decision was applied retroactively, it sent a flood of prisoners into court seeking their release.

Among the habeas corpus petitions alleging denial of the right to counsel filed in Justice's court was one from Buck Haney, a prisoner in the Texas Department of Corrections. At Haney's arraignment in 1953, the state district court judge appointed attorney Edward T. McFarland to represent him. McFarland informed Haney of his right to trial by jury and told him that he did not have to plead guilty if he did not wish to. However, he did not tell him that if he pleaded not guilty, he was entitled to an attorney to represent him at trial. Haney then pleaded guilty to one count of robbery by assault and was sentenced to twenty-three years in prison. At the habeas corpus hearing, McFarland testified that prior to the *Gideon* decision, it was not uncommon for the defendant who chose to plead not guilty to a felony offense to assume the task of defending himself that same day or the next day. Counsel was not accorded unless the judge or the attorney who had previously advised the defendant felt an obligation. It was clear from the evidence that McFarland would have felt no particular obligation to defend Haney had he pleaded not guilty, a view then shared by most Texas attorneys and judges.

This was no surprise to Judge Justice. "Had I not been aware of the way things were being conducted in the pre-*Gideon* era in state court," he points out, "I would have not caught the particular error that I found there. I myself had been appointed only to advise the defendant of his rights. That order did not carry with it an obligation to represent the person at the trial of the case. You just told the defendant that he had a right to apply for suspended sentence, that's about what it amounted to." Since Haney had not been advised of a right to an attorney should he have pleaded not guilty, Justice granted his petition, but delayed issuing the order for thirty days to give the state the opportunity to initiate proceedings to retry the case or appeal. No action was taken, and Haney was released.[36]

A more complicated right-to-counsel issue that pitted the crime control model against the due process model was presented to Justice in 1975 in the form of a habeas corpus petition filed by Wesley Trahan, a black prisoner. Trahan had been charged, along with several other blacks, with repeatedly and brutally raping a young white girl in the Southeast Texas county of Liberty on December 31, 1968. The girl and her boyfriend were parked in a pickup, and after breaking into the pickup and robbing the couple, the youths initiated the attack. The heinous nature of the crime prompted the district attorney to seek the death penalty, even though Texas law precluded doing so for youths younger than seventeen. At the time of the crime, Trahan was sixteen. The death penalty motion filed in state court was withdrawn eight months later when Trahan agreed to plead guilty to the rape charge and accept a life sentence. Trahan later filed a habeas corpus petition in state district court, seeking his release. Following a hearing, the petition was denied, a decision affirmed by the Texas Court of Criminal Appeals, the highest state court with jurisdiction over criminal cases. Trahan then filed a habeas corpus petition in Judge Justice's court, alleging denial of the right to counsel, ineffective assistance of counsel, and an involuntary plea of guilty.

Did the racial context of the case prompt Justice to review the petition carefully? "Certainly," he responds without hesitation. "I had represented blacks as an attorney in private practice, and I knew the racial attitudes in the Eastern District of Texas. Anyone who was raised in East Texas and wasn't conscious of discrimination against blacks in the criminal law process would have been oblivious to reality." What caught his attention in reviewing the petition was the apparent use of the death penalty threat to elicit a confession. While Trahan's father had secured an attorney, C. C. Devine, to represent his son, the attorney was not present when Liberty County District Attorney W. G. Woods, Jr., met with Trahan in the county jail in August 1969. Woods apparently did not attempt to contact Devine. Woods testified that the agreement emerging from the conference was that Trahan would plead guilty to rape, the district attorney would recommend a life sentence, and the four related felony charges would not be prosecuted, provided that Trahan did not appeal his conviction for rape. Several days later, the agreement was ratified at the arraignment. Trahan's attorney again was not present, and the state district judge appointed another attorney, Wayne Carter, to represent him.

Based on testimony at the state court proceeding on the habeas petition and at a second habeas hearing in his court, Justice viewed with considerable suspicion the circumstances surrounding the confession and guilty plea. "Giving consideration to the district attorney's threats," he wrote, "it is hardly surprising that petitioner, a young black man, accused of raping a white girl in an East Texas community, was concerned and confused as to the possibility of his execution, despite his counsel's advice to the contrary, which had been given several months earlier."[37] Justice was also concerned that, contrary to American Bar Association standards, no effort had been made to contact Trahan's attorney, either prior to the meeting in the jail or at the arraignment. He also viewed with suspicion the fact that Carter, the newly appointed attorney, decided within thirty minutes of his appointment to permit his client to plead guilty to the maximum sentence available—life imprisonment.

Justice acknowledged that while he could not be certain District Attorney Woods had threatened Trahan at the county jail meeting with the death penalty if Trahan did not confess—Woods had testified that he had not, since he had received a birth certificate from Devine—"it is undisputed that no defense attorney was present to assure Trahan that any such threat would be meaningless." Further, despite assurances that the death penalty had not been a factor in the deliberations with Trahan, Woods did not withdraw the death penalty motion until after Carter was appointed on the day of the trial. Justice also questioned what benefit Trahan had received from his plea bargain, since the four felony charges were not dismissed but remained pending, thus assuring no reduction in his life sentence. Had Trahan pleaded not guilty and been tried on all the charges, he could have received no more than a life sentence. Throughout the habeas proceedings in state court, Woods had made it clear that he knew Trahan was guilty, and he occasionally asserted that on the basis of the photographs and other evidence, he felt fully justified in all his actions.

Noting that under U.S. Supreme Court rulings a criminal defendant is entitled to an attorney throughout all the critical stages of the criminal law process, Justice concluded that "when District Attorney Woods met with petitioner Trahan at the jail, in the absence of petitioner's attorney of record, and negotiated a plea agreement, the petitioner was denied the right to counsel at a critical stage of the proceedings." Justice did not consider it necessary to consider Trahan's contention that attorney Carter's performance was deficient or that the guilty plea at the arraignment was involuntary.

The decision was appealed to the Fifth Circuit, which reversed it and sent the matter back for further deliberations. The three-judge panel concluded that Justice had focused on the wrong component of the events leading to the guilty plea. Citing Supreme Court precedents, the appeals judges observed that Trahan's guilty plea in open court precluded raising independent claims pertaining to alleged prior violation of constitutional rights. "[S]ince Trahan pleaded guilty with at least some advice from court appointed counsel, any question with reference to his uncounselled meeting with the district attorney, two or three days previously, was not open to attack by federal habeas corpus."[38] Rather than having focused attention on the meeting with Wood, Justice should have considered the voluntariness of the guilty plea and the effectiveness of appointed attorney Carter. The case was sent back for such consideration.

Justice was surprised by the decision, particularly since Circuit Judge Irving L. Goldberg, his colleague from the landmark *Graves v. Barnes* legislative reapportionment case, concurred in the judgment. Dutifully, if reluctantly, applying the appeals court's rationale, Justice concluded following another hearing that Trahan was aware when he pleaded guilty that the death penalty could not be imposed and had acted rationally. Further, there was insufficient evidence to conclude that the prosecutor had gone too far when he met with

Trahan in the absence of Trahan's attorney or that appointed attorney Carter had rendered ineffective assistance to Trahan. The petition was denied. But Justice obviously was not pleased with the limitations imposed upon him by the Fifth Circuit. He expressed "continued dismay" at the prosecutor's participation in the uncounseled bargaining session and observed that "the circumstances attending the guilty plea of Wesley Trahan should be a source of no pride to members of the legal profession, and least of all to any of the participants." [39]

Judge Justice has often been a thorn in the side of judges of the U.S. Court of Appeals for the Fifth Circuit because he has been willing, even eager, to take on difficult cases and issue controversial rulings which are then appealed from his court into theirs. One apt illustration in the criminal procedure area is *In re Nash,* which threw the Fifth Circuit judges into considerable turmoil over the right to counsel. The case involved a young black man, Ira Nash, who was convicted of murdering a Tyler taxicab driver and sentenced to one hundred years in prison. Nash filed a habeas corpus petition, seeking to attack the introduction at his trial of two inculpatory statements he had made. The issue was deceptively simple: can a suspect continue to be questioned after he has invoked his right to counsel if the suspect then indicates he is willing to proceed with the interrogation in the absence of counsel?

Nash was arrested and taken into custody in March 1969. He was read his *Miranda* rights and questioned extensively. He consented to and was given a polygraph examination, then released. Two months later, he was again taken into custody and again read his rights. He was questioned for varying lengths of time on several occasions over the next several days. Between interrogations, he was confined and isolated in a small cell where a light remained steadily burning. Questioning began at 11:30 P.M. on May 30 and continued until 6 A.M. the next day. Deputy Sheriff Gene Carlson testified at the pretrial hearing that he had repeatedly asked Nash about the murder, the murder weapon, and certain items taken from the victim. At one point, he and Nash went to the latter's home to check out Nash's story that he had a watch and ring (apparently stolen from the taxicab driver) hidden under his house. Nothing was found, and the pair returned to the deputy's office for further questioning. Carlson testified that he continued to repeat his questions about the murder because he believed Nash was lying and that he mentioned a potential witness who would give a statement incriminating him. Carlson also testified that he may have told Nash that it would be better for him if he would "get his business done." [40]

The morning of June 2, 1969, Nash was brought to the office of F. R. Files, assistant district attorney for Smith County, for the purpose of making a confession. The conversation was tape recorded. Files read a lengthy statement regarding Nash's *Miranda* rights, and presented him with a written waiver for his signature. The following critical exchange occurred:

Nash: If, you know, if I want a lawyer present what do I do, just put down that I want him present?

Files: No, you just tell us about it. Anytime that we are talking and you decide that you need somebody else here and you just tell me about it and we will get one.

Nash: Well, I don't have the money to have one, but I would like to, you know, for one to be appointed to me.

Files: You want one to be appointed?

Nash: Yes, sir.

Files: I had hoped that we might want to talk about this but if you want a lawyer appointed, well then, we are going to have to stop right now.

Nash: I kinda want to talk about it. Kinda get it straight.

Files: I can talk about it with you and I would like to, but if you want a lawyer, well, I am going to have to quit talking, I can't talk to you. Now it is your life.

Nash: I would like to have a lawyer but I would rather talk to you.

Files: Well, what that says there is, it doesn't say that you don't ever want to have a lawyer, it says that you don't want to have a lawyer here, now. You got the right to have that lawyer here right now and I want you to know that. But if you want to have a lawyer here, well, I am not going to talk to you about it.

Nash: No, I would rather talk to you.

Files: You would rather talk to me? You do not want to have a lawyer here right now?

Nash: No, sir.

Files: Absolutely certain of that?

Nash: Yes, sir.

Files: Go ahead and sign that thing.[41]

Nash signed the form waiving his rights including the right to have a lawyer present at the session with Files. He then confessed to the crime. He waived his rights again the next day and made further incriminating statements.

Nash's attorneys argued that under the Supreme Court's *Miranda* decision, once Nash had requested a lawyer, he could not waive the right to counsel. Reviewing Fifth Circuit precedents, Justice found this assertion too restrictive. He concluded that after a suspect requests an attorney, the interrogation must cease. The suspect then can waive the right to counsel only if he has spoken with the requested attorney or sometime later initiates a conversation on his own accord. In *Nash,* neither had occurred. He noted that a psychiatrist had testified at Nash's trial that Nash was borderline mentally retarded and that his greatest disability was in verbal skills. The psychiatrist stated that a person with Nash's mental incapacity was highly susceptible to influence, especially from an authority figure. After listening to the tape of the interrogation, the psychiatrist opined that Files could have affected Nash's decision to discuss the case without waiting for an attorney. Justice thus concluded that "while he did not ignore Nash's request and begin interrogation nor blatantly coerce the petitioner to change his mind, Files' comments may well have influenced Nash to state that he would consent to discuss the case without the presence of a lawyer." Nash's attorney termed Files' continued questioning "inveigling." Since Nash had not effectively waived his right to counsel, it was constitutional error to have admitted the incriminating statements into evidence. Thus, the circumstances surrounding the confession convinced Judge Justice that Nash's rights had been violated.

The subsequent appeal of this decision to the Fifth Circuit had the effect of dropping a rock into a still pond. As they struggled with the issue, the members of that body ended up in a war of words, revealing different perspectives on the rights of the accused. The first panel of three judges split two to one in reversing Justice's decision and sending it back to him for further consideration. The two in the majority recognized that the case presented a novel issue, falling between a line of cases holding that there could be no subsequent waiver of the right to counsel without consultation with the requested attorney and other cases holding that after a suspect requests an attorney and the interrogation ceases, the suspect later can knowingly waive the right to counsel. In Nash's case, the interrogation had not ceased. The majority concluded, however, that the conversation after Nash requested an attorney was not evidence-seeking but rather an exploration of Nash's wishes. "It is apparent that Nash had inconsistent desires. He indicated that he wanted an attorney, but that he also wanted to go ahead and talk about the crime without waiting for an attorney to be appointed . . . His statement that he wanted to go ahead and talk was made without any prodding or questioning from Files what-soever."[42] Justice was wrong in automatically excluding the confession. The case was sent back to him for a consideration of whether Nash had knowingly waived the right to counsel.

In dissent, Judge Lewis R. Morgan argued that Justice's decision should have been affirmed. "The request [for counsel] followed quickly by waiver," he wrote, "at minimum suggests confusion on the part of the suspect. At worst, such action suggests questionable conduct on the part of the interrogators."

A request by one of the judges that the entire Fifth Circuit rehear the case was granted. This time, eight judges reversed Justice's order outright, with no remand. Five dissented. Writing for the eight, Judge Charles Clark implicitly followed many of the dictates of the crime control model in his opinion. He acknowledged that ordinarily, once a suspect requests an attorney, questioning must cease. But there are exceptions, one being when a suspect equivocates between the desire for an attorney and a desire to continue the interview. Such was the case with Nash. Assistant District Attorney Files, Clark observed, "is entitled to a presumption that he discharged his duties with regularity and in compliance with the Constitution."[43] Files was aware that Nash had orally confessed to the murder earlier, even though this confession had been excluded from trial (the dissenters suggested because it had been coerced). Thus, Files desired to make official through the tape recording what Nash had already said. "It would have been simple-minded for Files to have attempted to work some insidious stratagem during an interrogation he deliberately chose to preserve on magnetic tape." Reviewing the taped remarks, the majority con-cluded that "only by improperly assuming that Files was a devious trickster, who desired to subtly manipulate Nash, can the dialogue between Nash and Files be regarded as forestalling Nash's rights."

Four judges issued a lengthy dissent in which they expressed grave reserva-tions about the "equivocalness" exception and painstakingly reviewed the tape-recorded conversation to point out that Files had indeed engaged in the very trickery the majority concluded had not happened. If there had been any equivocation by Nash about his desire for an attorney, Judge John C. Godbold wrote for the dissent, it was because interrogator Files had produced it through his manipulative questioning. Nash had never effectively waived his right to counsel. Further, the dissenters found the presumption of regularity the ma-jority accorded law enforcement officials like Files misplaced and unwarranted. The fifth dissenter, Judge Alvin B. Rubin, wrote separately to say that the entire effort of rehearing the case was a waste of time. "The light we shed here is not worth the thirteen-judge candle."

Judge Justice watched these events unfold with some bemusement. But they did not change his view of the case. "I think the Fifth Circuit decision in that case was simply wrong. If I were confronted with the same set of facts today with the state of the law unchanged from those days, I would do the same thing again." In his mind, it is a simple matter of fairness.

In all of his decisions involving rights of the accused, Justice has exhibited strong support for the procedural requirements inherent in the due process model. As a former criminal trial lawyer, Justice was sensitive to the claims the prisoners were making. But he could not persuade the Fifth Circuit judges, who reversed most of his decisions. "I had a very poor record on habeases," he admits. "I had done a great deal of criminal practice in the state system, and I could see things in those records that the Fifth Circuit judges just couldn't see. Most of them had never practiced criminal law in Texas. They couldn't visualize what was happening. I had been in the courtroom, and I could read those records and think, my God, what have they done to this guy?" As is his custom, Justice would have his law clerks draft lengthy opinions for his review, setting forth the reasons for overturning the convictions and granting new trials. After awhile, his secretary, Marcelle Simmons, grew cynical. "She'd say, 'Well, this'll be back in about a year,'" the Judge says with a laugh. "And she was right for most of them." The reluctance of the Fifth Circuit to overturn convictions through the habeas corpus process discouraged Justice. After several years, he backed off and now rarely grants the writ.

Many accuse Justice of going too far to protect criminals. But it must be remembered that for seven years, Justice himself had been a prosecutor with a strong record of convictions. "I'm fully aware of the prosecutor's role. I don't think that anyone could say that I neglected my duties as a prosecutor. I think our record of convictions was good in contested cases. I fully understand the problems associated with prosecution and am not unsympathetic to them." Conversely, from his experience as a lawyer in private practice representing criminal defendants, he is also aware of prosecutorial abuse. "I think that being a prosecutor can certainly give you powers that can be exercised in a prejudicial way to the defendants."

His overriding concern for individual rights coupled with his experience as both a criminal lawyer and a prosecutor have resulted in concern that law enforcement personnel not trample upon hard-won rights in their zeal to bring criminals to justice. In a 1985 speech to the Criminal Law Institute, Justice warned against the consequences of U.S. Supreme Court decisions making it easier for governmental agencies to secure search warrants, introduce tainted evidence into trial, and overcome the constitutional proscription against self-incrimination. "It is truistic to say so," he told the attorneys, "but it is, nevertheless, reality, that the rights of criminals are the rights of lawyers, journalists, clergy, and businessmen, and, indeed, of all Americans; and if these rights are taken away from criminals, they are also taken away from every one of us."

In swearing in new attorneys to the U.S. attorney's office, Justice reads a statement from a 1934 U.S. Supreme Court decision which was read to him when he was sworn in as U.S. attorney:

> The United States Attorney is the representative not of an ordinary party to a controversy, but of a sovereignty whose obligation to govern impartially is as compelling as its obligation to govern at all; and whose interest, therefore, in a criminal prosecution is not that it shall win a case, but that justice shall be done. As such, he is in a peculiar and very definite sense the servant of the law, the twofold aim of which is that guilt shall not escape or innocence suffer. He may prosecute with earnestness and vigor—indeed, he should do so. But, while he may strike hard blows, he is not at liberty to strike foul ones. It is as much his duty to refrain from improper methods calculated to produce a wrongful conviction as it is to use every legitimate means to bring about a just one.[44]

Both as a federal trial judge and as an appellate judge sitting by invitation on the U.S. Court of Appeals for the District of Columbia Circuit, Justice has insisted that in enforcing the law, governmental officials must not violate it themselves.

CHAPTER 12

Employment

When Judge Justice ascended the bench in 1968, the employment relationship was essentially a matter between employer and employee. Employment matters were seldom litigated. Other than routine worker compensation cases, he and his father handled no employment cases in private practice in the 1940s and 1950s. When the landmark 1964 Civil Rights Act was enacted during Justice's tenure as U.S. attorney, school desegregation was the initial focus. Vigorous enforcement of the act in the employment context had yet to begin. For public employees, litigation over constitutional rights was still in its infancy.

But the rights of employees were beginning to expand, and with his liberal views about racial justice, First Amendment freedoms, and rights of the accused, Justice was ready to support them. The first opportunity came in the form of a 1969 decision supporting a black teacher whose contract had not been renewed by the Tatum Independent School District because he had gotten involved in political activities. Tatum is a small district about forty-five miles east of Tyler, and, as described in Chapter 5, had been involved in a desegregation lawsuit before Judge Justice the previous year. In order to prove his claim, the teacher, Billy Don Montgomery, brought a concealed tape recorder into a meeting with the school superintendent, Rex White. White made inculpatory statements on the tape, which was later played before the jury. Though the superintendent tried to show that there were other reasons to support the nonrenewal decision, cross-examination was devastating. At the close of testimony, Montgomery's attorneys moved for a directed verdict.

Justice granted the motion. Citing recent rulings from the U.S. Supreme Court and the Fifth Circuit, he noted that "simply because teachers are on the public payroll does not make them second-class citizens in regard to their constitutional rights." [1] He remembers *Montgomery v. White* as "an open-and-shut case if there ever was one." The decision, which Justice had published in the Federal Supplement, sent a message throughout East Texas that he was ready to support employee rights. Plaintiffs' attorneys responded by filing cases in his court. During his first years on the bench, he was the only judge in most of the divisions within the Eastern District, and thus plaintiffs' attorneys had ready access to him. In a few short years, his precedent-setting decisions caught the attention of employers in the region, and employment practices began to change.

In addition to revealing Justice's jurisprudence in the employment context, the decisions discussed in this chapter provide a social history of employment practices in East Texas, a region bearing many similarities to the Deep South.

Racial Discrimination

Without question, Judge Justice regards racial discrimination as the most egregious issue he has faced in employment cases. His distaste for racial bias in employment is long-standing. As a newly appointed U.S. attorney in the early 1960s, he confronted a subtle form of racism in his own office. He had employed a black secretary whose name had appeared on the civil service list, the first black to apply for a position. This was before enactment of the 1964 Civil Rights Act outlawed discrimination in a variety of public and private contexts. His selection prompted considerable reaction among the all-white office staff. Before the secretary came to work, Justice made it clear to his personnel that they were to treat the black employee equally, both on the job and during coffee and lunch breaks.

It was not long before sidewalk stares and comments in downtown Tyler caused the white secretaries to stop inviting their black coworker to accompany them on coffee breaks. At the same time, one of the white staff began making indirect offensive remarks directed to the black woman. For example, she would walk into a room where the black secretary was filing papers and sniff the air, commenting, "Something smells bad in here."

News of these developments eventually reached Justice. Enraged, he confronted the white secretary. "I invited Brooks Hardee, my first assistant, into the office to be a witness. I then called the white secretary in. I roundly condemned her conduct in about as forceful terms as I could use. I informed her that if there was any repetition of her conduct, I would consider it grounds for dismissal. She didn't say a word, but she saw that I was furious." The offensive comments stopped. To resolve the coffee break situation, Justice made arrangements for the office staff to have their coffee breaks in the building.

It is apparent that the restraints Justice had felt in speaking out about racial injustice when he was in private practice were absent when he became U.S.

attorney. He could express his true feelings about racial discrimination with relative impunity. But it was only when he became a federal judge with lifetime tenure that he began a crusade to eliminate it.

After Justice's appointment to the bench, the first challenges of employment discrimination arose in newly desegregated school districts. Later, racial discrimination lawsuits were filed against private employers throughout much of East Texas. Typical of the former is *Edwards v. Gladewater Independent School District,* involving a black teacher whose contract was not renewed because of her black accent and diction. Violet Edwards had been employed for many years in the small Gregg County school district, teaching students in black schools until the system voluntarily integrated in 1969 following four years under an unsuccessful "freedom of choice" plan. After she was not rehired in 1973, she filed a complaint with the Equal Employment Opportunity Commission (EEOC), arguing that the nonrenewal violated her rights under Title VII of the 1964 Civil Rights Act, which outlawed discrimination in employment. Later, she filed suit against the district.

Justice was not surprised that the *Edwards* case originated in Gregg County. "There was a lot of racial resentment in Gregg County at that time," he notes, "some of which still exists to this good day." Gregg County was the scene of the bus bombing incident involving the Longview school system described in Chapter 5.

Edwards testified that in the nineteen years she had worked in the district's all-black schools, her effectiveness had never been questioned. The principal in her integrated school testified that she was performing her duties as competently as white teachers. But he noted receiving a number of parent complaints. Several said that their children could not understand Edwards because of her black accent and diction. Others complained about Edwards' disciplinary measures and her proficiency as an instructor. She admitted having used a strap to administer corporal punishment but testified that she had stopped when told to do so. She also stated that while white teachers administered corporal punishment and had unruly students stand in the hall, she had been told not to do so because of her color.

Throughout the trial, the district sought to show that Violet Edwards was incompetent. Numerous instances were cited. The only black member of the school board testified that in his view Edwards' race had not been a factor in the nonrenewal. Other board members concurred. But Justice viewed the evidence differently. "The conclusion that race was, indeed, a factor in the defendant school system's decision not to rehire plaintiff is demonstrated by the administrators' reliance upon plaintiff's negro dialect as a reason for her contract not being renewed," he wrote. "It was apparent to the court that notwithstanding plaintiff's speech pattern, she could be easily understood. There was no evidence that plaintiff made grammatical errors rendering her speech difficult to understand."[2] He found further evidence of racial discrimination in the declining ratio of black to white teachers in the system, as well as in the instruction to Edwards not to use the same disciplinary measures used by white teachers.

While few would argue that teachers who have communication and discipline problems should be retained in the classroom, other measures aside from contract nonrenewal or termination were available. Indeed, the Gladewater district had a policy which required principals to attempt remediation where deficiencies existed. None had been used with Edwards. Justice's decision awarding reinstatement, back pay, and attorney fees was affirmed by the Fifth Circuit in a brief *per curiam* decision.[3] Civil rights attorney Larry Daves, who represented Violet Edwards, regards the case as typical of the problems encountered by black teachers "who came out of the old segregated schools and as a result carried with them much of the baggage of those schools, including some problems of grammar and style."

Probably the most blatant example of illegal racial discrimination in public employment to come before Judge Justice involved a black agricultural extension agent in rural Panola County in deep East Texas just west of the Louisiana border. The facts reveal the type of deep-seated racism so prevalent in the South in the 1960s and 1970s, some of which still lingers. When Harold Wells sought an agricultural extension service position in 1963, the Texas system was segregated. The Texas Agricultural Extension Service (TAES), a state agency established in 1915 and affiliated with Texas A&M University, was financed cooperatively by state, county, and federal funds. It served the white populace. A similar organization affiliated with all-black Prairie View A&M University served blacks. Wells was hired by the black extension service.

In 1964 Wells became the black county agent for Panola County. The county extension service was entirely segregated. The black office operated out of a local black school, while the white office was housed in the county courthouse. Unlike the black office, the white office enjoyed the services of a secretary and janitor paid by the county. In addition, though the white agent and the black agent performed the same services, the white agent was paid more.

Shortly after Wells became the black county agent, the black extension service was merged with the white extension service at Texas A&M, and field operations slowly were integrated. The title of all black county agents was changed to associate county agent, a position reserved primarily for blacks. The white county agents were given the additional title of county chairman.

At the time of trial in July 1976, only 2 of the 243 county chairmen in the state were black—ample evidence of the slow pace of integration. In Panola County, integration meant that Wells was moved to the county courthouse, where he continued to serve as associate agent until 1972. But the trappings of segregation continued: his office was across the hall from the white office, and he continued to be paid less than his white counterpart. In 1972, the white county agent resigned, and Wells applied for the job. But the Panola County Commissioners Court, the local governmental body, rejected his application, even though it was supported by TAES. A white man with qualifications similar to those of Wells was selected and given the same salary as the previous incumbent.

In 1973 when Wells' attempts to seek redress working through TAES and through county officials failed, he filed an employment discrimination charge against the commissioners court with EEOC. In response, the commissioners court promptly eliminated its share of the funding for the extension service, and the program was discontinued. Wells later was terminated by TAES. He filed suit against both the county commissioners court and TAES alleging racial discrimination on several grounds, including Title VII of the 1964 Civil Rights Act. Representing him was attorney Larry Daves.

Normally, employment discrimination claims require the plaintiff to establish a *prima facie* case of racial discrimination, with the burden then shifting to the defendant to establish some legitimate, nondiscriminatory reason for its action. If the defendant does so, then the plaintiff has an opportunity to show that the defendant's justification was, in fact, a pretext for racial discrimination or not worthy of belief.[4] Judge Justice did not have to perform a probing analysis to make these determinations in *Wells v. Hutchinson,* because racial discrimination was so rooted in the history of TAES and of Panola County. The county commissioners had made it clear that they would not select a black agent under any circumstances. The evidence revealed that in a conversation with a TAES district agent about salary disparities between black and white agents, Commissioner W. J. "Pig" Rich referred to Wells as a "nigger" because "that's what he is."[5] Justice found the decision to terminate county funding for the agricultural service to be in retaliation for Wells' claims of racial discrimination. Testimony revealed that one commissioner had told a citizen concerned about termination of funding that "With the nigger gone and when the uproar dies down we will have an extension agent."[6]

Justice recalls that his law clerk working on the case, Michael R. Smith, a graduate of Stanford Law School, "was open-mouthed" at some of the testimony. But it didn't come as any surprise to the Judge. "I was reared around people like that. It wasn't so surprising to me that references like 'nigger' would be made in public. I thought it was offensive, but not surprising."

While TAES had sought to intervene on behalf of agent Wells and had fought the termination of county funding, Justice held the state agency jointly liable with the county for the illegal discrimination. For years, TAES had discriminated against Wells and had terminated him after he asserted his right to equal treatment in Panola County. Justice ordered that Wells be appointed county agent in Panola County and awarded him back pay, attorney fees, and costs. Since the commissioners court had violated the Texas Open Meeting Law when it terminated TAES funding, the action was void. Justice ordered the county to reinstate the service and resume funding. Finally, he ordered "general prohibition against discrimination by the county in its treatment of Harold Wells, for so long as he continues to be a county employee."[7] Based on the difficulty of the litigation and noting that Daves "is probably the most experienced employment discrimination lawyer in East Texas," Justice doubled his attorney fees to nearly $21,000. The case was not appealed.

Justice submitted the opinion for inclusion in the published decisions of the federal district courts. "I thought it had some very valuable history in it, particularly as related to the state agricultural extension service, which had parallel offices, one white and one black. That's the main reason I had it published."

The *Edwards* and *Wells* cases are typical of the spin-off issues generated by the end to *de jure* segregation in southern states. With enactment of Title VII of the 1964 Civil Rights Act, racial discrimination in employment was an early and easy target. Title VII cases are tried before a judge; there is no jury. Since in a Title VII case an appellate court can overturn a lower court's findings of fact only if they are clearly erroneous, the decisions of federal district court judges usually have been upheld on appeal. For plaintiffs' attorneys, this means that assembling sufficient facts to convince the federal district court judge is all that is required. Given Justice's antipathy to discrimination in general and racial discrimination in particular, plaintiffs' attorneys have enjoyed a strong record of victories in his court, even when the question was close. Justice observes that "time after time I was confronted with discrimination cases which never should have happened." Faced with litigation before Judge Justice, many employers opted to settle.

Justice's ready willingness to grant class action status to individual plaintiffs also contributed to settlements. Class action status enables individual plaintiffs to represent employees throughout the organization. Although he has declined to grant class action in some cases where he has had doubts about the effectiveness of the attorney or where the requirements for class action status were lacking, he acknowledges that such instances have been rare. "I very seldom failed to allow the maintenance of a class action," he admits. Consequently, to avoid expensive litigation and compliance costs, many employers made out-of-court settlements. Through this method, women and minorities have been accorded job security and promotion rights, as well as equal pay, in a number of East Texas industries. Faced with aggressive plaintiffs' attorneys and a supportive judge, other employers instituted changes on their own. According to Daves, "it didn't take very long before we didn't have a whole lot of illegal discrimination charges coming in."

For judges with a different perspective, the outcome has been less certain. Daves, for example, has enjoyed little success before Judge William M. Steger, who was appointed to the bench by President Nixon and has a courtroom down the hall from Judge Justice. "I probably tried between 100 and 150 Title VII cases before Judge Steger and never won a one of them. Had those cases been tried before Judge Justice, I probably would have won somewhere between 30 and 50 percent." At the same time, Daves believes that he probably has had a better chance before juries in Steger's courtroom. "Because of Judge Justice's reputation, if jurors got a notion of where he stood on the case, I think many times they went the other way."

In several of his employment discrimination decisions, Justice eased the plaintiffs' burden to prove their claims. For example, in *Kinsey v. First Regional Securities,* a 1977 decision he wrote for a three-judge panel while serving by invitation on the U.S. Court of Appeals for the D.C. Circuit in the mid-1970s, he found erroneous the district court's exclusion of statistical data to buttress a claim of racial discrimination.[8] The case involved a black applicant with a strong educational background who was rejected for a securities sales position by Legg, Mason & Company, a Washington, D.C., investment firm. Kinsey sought to introduce statistical data showing a disproportionate number of qualified blacks in the geographic areas where the company recruited, compared with the sales personnel it employed. Justice's decision supporting use of the data has often been cited by other courts. "I couldn't imagine why the trial judge didn't allow that evidence. It seemed highly relevant to me," he observes.

Another decision easing the plaintiff's burden was rebuffed by the Fifth Circuit the same year as the *Kinsey* decision. *Turner v. Texas Instruments, Inc.* involved a black employee who was discharged when his supervisors believed that he violated the company's time-card policy by allowing a fellow employee to punch in for him after lunch. William Turner and three white employees had eaten together away from the plant. One of the other employees, who was white and physically handicapped, was not discharged for the same offense because supervisors believed he was unaware of the company's time-card policy. They did not believe Turner's claim that he too was unfamiliar with the policy. The evidence revealed that Turner had not attended an orientation session at which the rule was announced and had not been given a copy of the company's employee handbook. He denied giving another employee permission to clock in for him. Justice held that Turner had made a *prima facie* case of racial discrimination.[9] The Judge required Texas Instruments to show clear and convincing evidence that Turner had not been discharged because of his race. The supervisors' explanation did not measure up, especially since the company's equal opportunity employment officer testified that blacks were three times more likely than whites to be dismissed for time-card violations.

On appeal, the Fifth Circuit reversed.[10] Writing for the three-judge panel was Nixon appointee Thomas Gibbs Gee, who often reversed Justice's decisions. Though Gee acknowledged that the law on the employer's burden of proof was unclear in the Fifth Circuit, he rejected Justice's "clear and convincing" standard, the highest standard that can be imposed in a civil case. Rather, the less rigorous "preponderance of the evidence" standard should have been used. Judged in this way, there was no reason to disbelieve company supervisors. Gee rejected Justice's reliance on the disparate statistical data regarding time-card violations because the sample was too small to be statistically significant. Admittedly, Gee wrote, Turner may have been telling the truth when he said he had not known about the time-card policy. But "Title VII and section 1981 [a civil rights law prohibiting racial discrimination in the making of contracts] do not protect against unfair business decisions—only against decisions motivated by unlawful animus." The difference in perspective between Judge Gee and Judge Justice is readily apparent. In 1989 the U.S. Supreme Court endorsed Gee's view that "clear and convincing" evidence is an inappropriate standard in Title VII cases.[11]

"The Judge tried to move too fast in the *Turner* case," Larry Daves concludes. "This is the one area in employment law where he tried to move the law forward, and they wouldn't let him." Justice, however, disclaims any desire to advance the law. "I had no particular motive to redress the balance between employer and employee at the time. If I said that now, it would be an afterthought." The Fifth Circuit's *Turner* decision made it more difficult for civil rights attorneys to challenge the credibility of an employer's explanation for negative employment decisions which have a discriminatory effect.

Whatever his motives and intentions, Justice's willingness to entertain class action lawsuits, to give plaintiffs' attorneys broad access to employer records through the pretrial discovery process, and to ease the plaintiff's burden of proof made it easier for employees to sustain their lawsuits. Equalization of resources is also evident in the Judge's decisions involving state institutions in which he granted class action status to plaintiffs and allowed the U.S. Justice Department and other groups to intervene on the side of the plaintiffs. It is an orientation going back to his populist roots in Athens and reflects his father's antimajoritarian "little 'un against the big 'un" philosophy.

Sexual Harassment and Discrimination

Compared to other issues, sexual discrimination in employment has not been a major cause of action in Justice's court. One can only speculate as to why more of these cases have not been filed. Certainly, from the very beginning he has stood ready to remedy situations where sexual discrimination can be proven. This is clear from his decision in *Hodgson v. Behrens Drug Company,* a 1971 decision holding that the drug company violated provisions of the Equal Pay Act when it consistently paid women less than men for the same job.[12] He rejected the company's argument that the men were paid more because they were sales trainees. There was no discrete training program, and no women had ever been considered for sales training work. Furthermore, the company president had testified that when the sales program had been instituted, females were not considered suitable for traveling. The Fifth Circuit affirmed the bulk of the decision.[13] Similarly, in 1984 Justice ruled in *Martin v. W. K. M. Wellhead Systems, Inc.* that the employer violated Title VII of the 1964 Civil Rights Act as well as provisions of the National Labor Relations Act when it terminated an assertive female machine shop operator who advanced the causes of other employees and threatened to file a discrimination charge with the Equal Employment Opportunity Commission.[14] The woman also was passed over for a training assignment in favor of a junior male employee after her supervisor had allegedly said that a "machine shop is no fucking place for a woman." The decision was not appealed.

One of Justice's most difficult decisions involved a case of alleged sexual harassment with undertones of racial discrimination in a newly desegregated school district. "I agonized over that case as hard as any case I have ever had on my docket," he observes. *Strong v. Board of Education of the City of Lufkin* involved a black teacher, Harold Strong, who filed suit after his contract as vocational agriculture instructor at the Lufkin High School was not renewed. Strong had been employed by the district since 1959 and had taught in a segregated black school prior to being moved to the newly desegregated high school in 1970.

For fifteen years he had not been involved in any disciplinary action. But in May 1974, Ed Casburn, the high school principal, received reports of unwanted sexual advances by this black teacher toward white teachers, each of whom regarded his actions as offensive and improper.

Casburn and the school superintendent, Sam Slaydon, confronted Strong, who denied any improper behavior. Casburn asked each of the three teachers privately to dictate her version of what had occurred to his secretary, who would type up the statements for signature. Several days later on May 20, 1974, the superintendent requested Strong's resignation. When it was not forthcoming, Slaydon suspended Strong from his teaching position with pay and advised him that his contract would not be renewed. Strong continued to deny any improper behavior and asked for a copy of the statements. He was allowed to read them but not given a copy. Strong asked for and received a hearing before the school board. At the conclusion of the hearing, Strong's employment was terminated on the charge of "immoral approach to women faculty members on the staff of the Lufkin High School, continued harassment and conduct unbecoming a professional employee of this school district."

Strong filed suit alleging racial discrimination and asked for damages of $100,000. A four-day trial was held before Judge Justice in November 1975. Because of the racial context, Justice took special interest. "It was unquestioned in my mind that the Lufkin school board had collectively drawn a gasp of horror when they realized that they had a black schoolteacher who had the temerity to approach some of the white female teachers on their staff," he observes. "They simply couldn't countenance the idea of interracial romance." Thus, it was clear to him that racial animus might have been involved in the suspension decision. "I was adamant that racial prejudice was not going to play any part in that case. If it existed and it was the real motivating factor for the board's action, I was prepared to reinstate the black teacher."

Tyler attorney Tracy Crawford, who represented the school district, maintains the nonrenewal decision was difficult for the school district because Strong had been an effective and well-liked teacher. Colleagues told Crawford that given Justice's views about race relations, the district did not have a chance. Crawford avers that "we had to carry a very heavy burden throughout the case."

Testimony by the three teachers, coupled with that of a former teacher, eventually convinced Justice that unwanted sexual advances had indeed occurred. "Each of the four female school teachers," he wrote, "was acutely embarrassed and disconcerted by the unexpected, uninvited, unwelcome and insistent attentions of the plaintiff toward her. The court infers and finds that the plaintiff knew, or should have known, that his persistent actions *vis-à-vis* each of the female school teachers were unwanted by, and mortifying to her." [15]

He also noted that the school district had taken sanctions against white teachers who had engaged in similar actions in the past. Attorney Crawford had made a special effort to introduce this evidence into the record. "I thought it was very clever of Tracy Crawford to use this technique," Justice says. "It was pivotal to my decision."

Concerned about the right of privacy, Justice wrote that a person's private conduct will ordinarily not constitute good cause for termination. "However, if a teacher makes offensive overtures while on the job, or if his conduct is notorious, the reactions of other teachers and of the public with whom he comes in contact in the performance of his official functions may be taken into account." He cited a decision written by Chief Judge David L. Bazelon of the U.S. Court of Appeals for the D.C. Circuit to this effect.[16]

From the evidence, Justice concluded that "plaintiff was well aware that his conduct with relation to . . . the . . . female teachers was 'fundamentally wrong' in the context of his and their school activities." The decision was appealed to, then withdrawn from, the Fifth Circuit. Though he issued a relatively short opinion (for him), Justice agonized over it. "I spent more personal time with that case than many that were far more important."

Liberty and Property Rights in Public Employment

Shortly after Justice became a judge, the U.S. Supreme Court ruled in *Wisconsin v. Constantineau* that individuals have a liberty right under the Fourteenth Amendment to be free from government stigmatization of their reputations. This amendment provides in part that no state "shall deprive any person of life, liberty, or property, without due process of law." Writing for the Court, Justice William O. Douglas asserted in an oft-quoted phrase, "Where a person's good name, reputation, honor, or integrity is at stake because of what the government is doing to him, notice and an opportunity to be heard are essential."[17] The 1971 decision struck down the practice of posting the names of habitual drunkards in retail municipal liquor stores without first providing a hearing to them.

A year later, the Supreme Court ruled in *Board of Regents v. Roth* that in some situations, public employment becomes a Fourteenth Amendment property right which cannot be denied without providing due process. Property rights, Justice Potter Stewart wrote, "are created and their dimensions defined by existing rules or understandings that stem from an independent source such as state law—rules or understandings that secure certain benefits and that support claims of entitlement to those benefits."[18] Thus, the Court observed, a teacher tenure law creates a property right which cannot be taken away without complying with due process since the teacher has an expectation of continuing employment. But the Court observed in the companion case of *Perry v. Sindermann* that nontenured teachers do not have property rights beyond the duration of their contracts and thus are entitled to no constitutional due process unless they can show the existence of a *de facto* tenure system.[19]

These three rulings dramatically altered employment practices in the public sector by providing employees with constitutionally recognized liberty and property rights. But the implications of the decisions were not entirely clear. Under what circumstances would these rights be abridged? What would government employers be expected to do to satisfy constitutional requirements? The answers would be forthcoming from federal district court judges who would apply the rulings to specific situations. Four of Judge Justice's employment decisions helped define the dimensions of liberty and property rights in public employment in the Eastern District. Each demonstrates his ready willingness to apply, and even extend, the Supreme Court rulings. Of the four, two became important precedents beyond the Eastern District by virtue of affirmances by the U.S. Court of Appeals for the Fifth Circuit.

In the first case, Owen D. Roane, a superintendent in the Callisburg Independent School District, a small rural district about sixty miles north of Dallas, ran into trouble with his school board in 1971 when he opposed the site for new classrooms. At the time, Roane did not have a written contract but assumed that he, like his two predecessors, was employed for a two-year term. Board policy stated that after a one-year trial period, the superintendent would be employed from two to five years. Roane had served his initial one-year trial period, and his contract had been renewed on two occasions for unspecified periods.

To avoid the embarrassment of being fired, the superintendent resigned at the January 4, 1971, board meeting. However, it was his intention to have his resignation effective at the end of his supposed two-year contract—on June 30, 1972. To make this clear, Roane added the words "at the end of his present contract (June 30, 1972)" in red ink to the handwritten minutes of the board meeting. The minutes were later typed with this addendum and approved by the school board.

Thereafter, relations between Roane and the board further deteriorated. In May 1971, the school board voted to terminate the superintendent's employment on June 30, 1971. He received no pre-termination hearing. However, two weeks later, a hearing was provided at which the board gave a list of reasons purporting to justify its decision. Believing that he had been denied due process, he filed a lawsuit. Since Callisburg ISD is located within the Sherman Division of the Eastern District and Judge Justice was the only presiding judge in that division, the lawsuit appeared on the Judge's docket.

Following a hearing, Justice concluded that under the U.S. Supreme Court's *Perry v. Sindermann* decision, the school district had a *de facto* tenure program according Roane a two-year property right in his employment. Roane was thus entitled to due process before termination. Even assuming that the post-termination hearing had comported with due process, Justice found the list of reasons advanced by the board at the hearing to be merely makeweights for the board's action and not good cause to terminate the contract. "It was definitely a post-hoc rationalization, there was no question about that," he recalls. "None at all." The disagreement over placement of the new classrooms did not constitute adequate grounds for the dismissal. "Specifically, no finding was made by defendants that was supported by substantial evidence that plaintiff was not willing, despite any alleged expression of opinion on the classroom matter, 'to abide by the policies of the board of trustees' and 'to cooperate with the board of trustees' in carrying out its final decision," he wrote.[20] Lacking good cause, the board was required to pay Roane the balance of his salary, as well as his attorney fees.

What makes the decision noteworthy is Justice's close attention to the sufficiency of the evidence to support the termination. This concern with substantive due process—the fairness of the decision—is also evident in many of his decisions involving rights of the accused. It will not do for public employers to merely go through the motions of providing procedural due process. There must be adequate grounds to justify the cessation of a constitutionally recognized property right. Justice based this assertion on a phrase in the *Perry* decision to the effect that at the hearing the employee is to be informed of the grounds for the nonretention and given an opportunity to "challenge their sufficiency." Remembering Superintendent Roane as a well-educated person, one not inclined to thwart the wishes of a school board, he still finds it hard to believe that "they would fire a man of his quality on such flimsy evidence."

Frequently cited by courts across the country, the Fifth Circuit decision affirming all of Justice's decision except the attorney fees award has become a classic in the educational field.[21] The appeals court emphasized that property rights cannot be taken away without good cause, noting that "the possibility of arbitrary, undocumented action will not be tolerated when protected rights are at stake." Judge Justice was particularly pleased with the affirmance because "it made substantive due process something you could take into account." However, he did not consider his opinon sufficiently polished to submit for inclusion in the bound volumes of reported federal court decisions. "Besides," he observes, "I couldn't anticipate all the attention that case would later receive."

Several months after the *Roane* decision, Justice issued a decision involving a university instructor who had not been given tenure. Again, he expressed deep concern about the absence of due process and took it upon himself to specify exactly what procedures must be followed to accord both procedural and substantive due process. This time, the Fifth Circuit balked. The case arose when Mary Kaprelian, an assistant professor of modern dance at Texas Woman's University in Denton, thirty-five miles north of Dallas and Fort Worth, was told on July 8, 1971, that she would be terminated outright or given a terminal contract. Resignation was another option. She was then serving a one-year contract. The university vice president indicated that he had statements from various members of her department that she had engaged in unprofessional conduct and was disloyal to the university. But he did not explain further. Kaprelian refused to resign and contacted an attorney.

Her attorney, Michael J. Whitten, requested that nonrenewal of his client's contract be reviewed by an ad hoc faculty committee, as provided in university policies. But a day later, the university president advised Kaprelian that she would be reappointed for the 1971–1972 school year. This was to be a terminal appointment; when the term was up, the contract would not be renewed. Kaprelian accepted the reappointment but also announced that she would continue to pursue her cause. The president then notified Kaprelian that if she requested the appointment of an ad hoc faculty committee to review the decision not to grant her tenure, he would appoint one. University policies provided that a faculty member alleging violation of academic freedom could request appointment of such a committee. Based on its findings, the committee could recommend that a full hearing be given. If such a recommendation was not made, no further due process would be provided.

Attorney Whitten wrote the president that he had advised his client not to request the appointment of the committee until he could be sure that certain due process procedures would be provided. In particular, he protested the fact that Kaprelian could not have an attorney present and had not been advised of the grounds for the university's actions. Indicating that he was prepared to make the matter a *cause célèbre,* Whitten advised that it would be better for the matter to be settled within the university.

Kaprelian's lawsuit was filed in the Sherman Division before Judge Justice on October 15, 1971. But the case moved slowly on the docket. A year and a half later, the parties agreed that Judge Justice should issue a ruling based on the attorney briefs and the depositions taken of key witnesses. No hearing would be held. The documentary evidence revealed a not uncommon breakdown in communication between two strong-willed academicians—Kaprelian and her dean, Anne Duggan. Duggan maintained that Kaprelian had refused to comply with directives and had been the target of a number of student complaints. Further, she said that Kaprelian had made derogatory comments about the modern dance program. For her part, Kaprelian argued that Duggan had obstructed her efforts to improve the program and had pressured students to make derogatory comments about her. She asserted that as a result, her liberty right to a good reputation had been tarnished, thus foreclosing further employment opportunities.

It was clear that as an untenured employee hired only for the fixed length of her contract, Kaprelian had no property interest in continued employment beyond the expiration of the contract. But Judge Justice held that Kaprelian had established a right to a due process hearing because of her allegations that her nonrenewal was based on alleged unprofessional conduct and disloyalty. Potential damage to her reputation under the Supreme Court's *Wisconsin v. Constantineau* ruling required the university to provide her with a hearing so that she could try to clear her name and establish whether her First Amendment rights had been violated. Since she had not received a hearing at the university, Justice ordered that one be provided. While he noted that the law was unclear as to exactly what procedural requirements should be followed, he noted that Kaprelian was at least entitled to an attorney and to an impartial hearing tribunal. To make sure of the latter, he stipulated that each party was to appoint an equal number of persons "of academic expertise in plaintiff's field of study" to constitute the tribunal and these persons by majority vote were to select a single additional person to be chairman.[22]

The Fifth Circuit reversed the decision. Conservative jurist Thomas Gibbs Gee wrote the opinion. The appeals court found it startling that Judge Justice would assume Kaprelian could trigger a liberty interest merely by the allegations in her complaint. Gee wrote, "Courts do not decide disputed matters of fact, or even contested matters of law in which subsidiary factual findings are necessarily embedded, on their merits by consulting traversed pleadings. On remand the court should consult the evidence in the record."[23] If the record revealed either that Kaprelian was discharged for exercise of First Amendment rights or that the university had made stigmatizing charges in public, only then was she entitled to a hearing. Mere nonrenewal by itself or stigmatization done privately would not suffice. Further, if a due process hearing was required, Justice lacked the authority to formalize the process beyond what the Fifth Circuit had allowed in a 1970 decision.[24] The appeals court found fault with Justice's "reaching into the administrative process itself to determine the tribunal's composition." Such action was contrary to its 1972 ruling in *Duke v.*

North Texas State University, which reversed another of Justice's decisions, described in Chapter 7.

Judge Justice concedes that his *Kaprelian* decision was flawed. "I apparently misunderstood the law. In the first place, I didn't take to heart what had been said in the *Duke* case about deference to administrative bodies. Then, I was trying to impose the processes of labor arbitration into this field. The Fifth Circuit rejected that approach entirely. I was rather hard-headed, I confess. I should have realized after *Duke* that that wouldn't fly." He adds, "It was a comedy of errors on my part. Actually, Judge Gee's opinion is very scholarly. But I remain convinced that the remedy I imposed would have been a good solution."

The case was eventually dismissed when Mary Kaprelian decided not to pursue it further. In rejecting Justice's desire to broaden the application of due process in public employment and by identifying the limits of due process in the context of employees' constitutional right not to have their reputations stigmatized by governmental employees, the Fifth Circuit's *Kaprelian* decision became a significant precedent which is often cited by other courts. What is particularly noteworthy about Justice's rejected decision was his effort to incorporate conflict-channeling processes developed in collective bargaining into a constitutional requirement. By detailing the selection of the administrative hearing body, he sought to assure its impartiality so that the Fourteenth Amendment's command of due process of law could be achieved. That this worthy goal required considerable judicial gloss on the sparse wording of the Fourteenth Amendment's due process clause was not as troubling to him as to the appeals court judges. Nor was he concerned about the cost of compliance to public employers. His primary concern was assuring fair treatment to an outspoken and disfavored university professor.

The third decision involved a more direct liberty right infringement. John Dennis, a part-time principal and teacher at the Sadler and Southmayd Consolidated High School near Sherman, had worked under several consecutive one-year contracts which had been routinely renewed. However, after he quarreled with the school board president, who wanted to keep his son out of school to do farm work, and after he admonished the board of trustees for overturning the suspension of another student, Dennis' contract was not renewed. He requested a public hearing and the board agreed to provide one, even though none was required since Dennis had no property right in continued employment beyond the term of his single-year contract. The hearing became a donnybrook, with board members asserting that Dennis' contract was not being renewed because he had neglected his duties and was inefficient. Two board members asserted that he had "a drinking problem." Dennis denied all the allegations. A second hearing was held at which essentially the same events transpired. He subsequently secured employment in a neighboring district. Dennis filed suit in the Sherman Division, arguing that he had been denied due process.

Justice agreed. While the nonrenewal did not implicate a property right, Dennis did have a right to be free from public stigmatization of his reputation under the *Wisconsin v. Constantineau* precedent. When the board members accused him in public of having a drinking problem, they "knowingly, publicly, and gratuitously subject[ed] him to a badge of infamy."[25] Dennis was entitled to a name-clearing hearing under Fifth Circuit precedents, including the *Kaprelian* decision. Furthermore, citing an Eighth Circuit decision, Justice ordered that Dennis remain on the school district payroll until the hearing.[26]

This time the Fifth Circuit affirmed Justice's ruling that Dennis' reputational rights had been infringed.[27] The appeals court distinguished this case from a 1976 U.S. Supreme Court decision holding that stigmatization by and of itself does not implicate a Fourteenth Amendment liberty right.[28] As Justice had observed, the stigmatization of Dennis' reputation occurred when board members publicly accused him of having a drinking problem as partial reason for nonrenewal of his contract. But the court disagreed with Justice regarding the remedy. While Dennis had a right to a name-clearing hearing, he was not entitled to reinstatement or back pay. To Justice's surprise, the court simply ignored the Eighth Circuit case he had cited.

The *Dennis* decision has become a leading Fifth Circuit precedent on the deprivation of employee liberty rights in public employment and is often cited by other courts. Its significance lies in the articulation of a "stigma-plus" test: stigmatization of a public employee's reputation is actionable only in conjunction with nonrenewal, termination, or other denial of a benefit. Though he was partially reversed, Judge Justice takes pride in the *Dennis* decision and was able to apply it to later cases where damage awards were warranted.

By the early 1980s, employment law in the public sector had become complex and employers more sophisticated. Egregious employment decisions like those involving Billy Don Montgomery and Owen Roane were for the most part a thing of the past. For employers, attorneys, and judges, the facts in an employment dispute were often complicated, the issues intricate, and the prospects for a clean win diminished. Such was the case in the final decision discussed in this section, a case Justice later used as the basis for a 1985 speech to school administrators and attorneys on how public employers can stay out of federal court.

Patrick v. Board of Trustees of Mineola Independent School District arose when the contract of a junior high school principal in a small school district a few miles north of Tyler was not renewed. Jack Patrick, a twenty-year principal in the district, had become involved in a series of incidents, including a January 1982 altercation with a basketball coach over the latter's refusal to play Patrick's son in a game.[29] The coach testified that Patrick cursed him, threatened to kill him, and, to show that he meant business, scratched the paint on the coach's car. The coach reported the incident to B. R. Knight, the superintendent, and later filed criminal charges against Patrick. Patrick maintained that only a heated discussion had taken place. Although the superintendent had not heard Patrick's side of the story, could not corroborate all of the coach's allegations, and could not cite a board policy, he placed Patrick on probation. Later, he admitted that earlier incidents involving Patrick's inability to control his temper had figured in the decision.

Patrick employed an attorney to fight the decision. Some months later, the principal and his attorney appeared before the school board, but the board refused to discuss the issues. At about this time, Patrick was accused of becoming involved in two other incidents, one involved a hunting trip during which Patrick was accused of deliberately cutting another man on the thumb with a knife, and a second involving a heated argument with a high school principal over the suspension of Patrick's son from school.

Superintendent Knight had had enough of what he considered Patrick's combative behavior. In February 1982, he recommended nonrenewal of Patrick's term contract. Pursuant to a new Texas statute enacted in 1981 establishing procedures for contract nonrenewals, he sent a letter to Patrick informing him of this action and including a list of board policy provisions which Patrick had allegedly violated.[30] However, the list did not contain specific facts showing in what way the policies had been violated. Patrick hired another attorney to contest the proposed nonrenewal. The attorney requested a statement of the factual reasons, the witnesses who would testify at the school board hearing on the proposed nonrenewal, the nature of their testimony, and the basis for Patrick's being placed on probation. The school board president responded with a list of witnesses who might be called, but offered no additional information.

Agreeing only that he had trouble controlling his temper, Patrick lost at the school board hearing. He appealed the decision to the Texas Education Agency, which upheld the school board.[31] He then filed suit in Justice's court, seeking reinstatement and $1.3 million damages. He argued that he had been denied procedural due process because he had never received adequate notice of the charges against him and substantive due process because the board had been biased against him for his hiring an attorney.[32] Further, he argued that his First Amendment rights had been violated and that the school board was retaliating against him because he had alleged that members of the school board were guilty of nepotism and conflict of interest in the purchase of school supplies.

After a heated six-day trial which was thoroughly chronicled in area newspapers, the jury issued its verdict. It found that the school board had violated Patrick's right to procedural due process with the defective notice of the charges, that the board was biased, and that it had retaliated against Patrick for exercising First Amendment rights. But the panel also found that the board had good cause for not renewing the contract and had acted in good faith, thus blocking any punitive damages against individual board members. Patrick received three dollars in nominal damages, one for each violated constitutional right. Because he had prevailed on the constitutional issues, he was entitled to have half of his attorney fees, which totaled over $17,000, paid by the school district. But Judge Justice ruled that Patrick was not entitled to reinstatement or back pay.[33]

In his 1985 speech to school administrators in Dallas, Justice used a hypothetical situation based on the *Patrick* case to examine how the entire matter could have enjoyed "at most, a short, exciting life in federal court before losing on summary judgment." He noted how the school board had guaranteed Patrick's day in court by assuming a bellicose stance from the beginning, particularly with regard to not providing him with a detailed list of the charges, along with specific instances substantiating them, and a list of the witnesses and the nature of their testimony. "By simply quoting platitudinous proscriptions from [Patrick's] contract—as if the purpose of the notice was to establish good cause, not to insure fairness—the board denied [Patrick] the specific information which makes for an adequate notice." By its actions, the Judge pointed out, the board played into the principal's assertion that he was being terminated for illegitimate reasons, e.g., exercise of First Amendment rights.

From his experiences trying these cases, Justice had learned that employees threatened with contract nonrenewal or termination are convinced at the outset that the decision is wrong and seek an opportunity to tell their side of the story. When denied a fair opportunity to do so—as Patrick was—then "they are not seeking either procedural compliance or an unbiased tribunal—they seek *vengeance*. Often they are mistaken in their expectations. But the initial unfairness ignites in them a kind of holy fire which will not let them rest until they have had their day in court."

The point of his speech was that in the *Patrick* case, both sides lost. "In going into the legal process, both parties are mistaken in their beliefs that they will participate in a zero-sum game. I submit that, in fact, when an arguably legitimate desire to terminate a teacher is coupled with a lack of respect for that teacher's rights, litigation becomes a negative-sum activity that serves only to highlight the shortcomings of both parties."

Justice's position on contract nonrenewal and/or termination in the public sector is clear: employers who treat employees fairly, providing them with a detailed statement of the reasons for negative employment decisions and then according them both procedural and substantive due process, are less likely to lose in court. He has shown no hesitancy to impose these requirements as a matter of constitutional law. As he noted in his speech, the purpose is not to establish that employers have good reason to nonrenew or terminate contracts but rather to make sure that they treat employees fairly. The thrust of Justice's rulings has been to enhance public morality in the workplace by curtailing arbitrary personal decision-making. That this may increase costs and formalize the working relationship is, for him, irrelevant. While his expansive interpretation of constitutional requirements has not been supported consistently by the Fifth Circuit, his decisions have extended due process rights to public employees. Many East Texas employers have undoubtedly been motivated to afford a measure of due process to their employees if for no other reason than to avoid litigation in Justice's court.

In the employment context, there is no question that Justice used evolving federal statutes as a tool for social reform. Reform was Congress' intent in enacting the civil rights laws. The onus was placed on the federal district court judge to see that both public and private employers complied with legislative mandates. Thus Title VII has had more dramatic impact on employment practices than the U.S. Constitution, which applies only to the public sector and whose provisions have been circumscribed by higher courts. Accordingly, the impact of Justice's decisions on the behavior of employers has been more limited in deprivation-of-due-process cases like *Kaprelian* than in Title VII cases like *Wells*.

Given their interest in maximizing profits, private employers are often more sensitive to learning about and complying with legal mandates than public employers. In public employment, patronage promotes favoritism, and tight budgets provide little incentive to remove long-standing discriminatory practices such as unequal pay rates and promotion systems. As the *Wells* litigation so aptly demonstrates, government employers are also more likely to wait until a court requires changes than to invite voter retaliation by making them voluntarily. With Judge Justice, they did not have to wait very long.

Yet times change, and the impact of the growing body of case law is evident in the more sophisticated manner in which public employers make negative personnel decisions. A case in point is a 1989 decision involving the Longview Independent School District in Gregg County, the site of the bus-bombing incident described in Chapter 5. Despite a history of racial discrimination and evidence that racial discrimination and retaliation for the exercise of First Amendment rights had played a role in the nonrenewal of a black teacher's contract, the Longview school district was successful in convincing Judge Justice that its action was justified. He noted in his opinion that the school district had carefully evaluated the teacher, even to the point of having classroom evaluators scripting her word-for-word remarks with her students. The evaluations, he wrote, "form a compelling record of plaintiff's primary weaknesses . . . "[34] On the strength of the evidence, Justice concluded that the defendants had established that even in the absence of racial bias and retaliation, they would have decided not to renew the plaintiff's contract. It helped that the district had replaced the plaintiff with another black teacher.

The activities of a handful of activist civil rights attorneys coupled with an activist judge intent on vigorously enforcing the Constitution and civil rights laws to the fullest prompted considerable change in East Texas employment practices in the 1970s and 1980s. Of course, Judge Justice was not alone in breaking down the barriers of racial and sexual discrimination in both public and private employment and in enfranchising public employees with liberty and property rights. Other federal judges in the Eastern District and elsewhere in Texas have also vigorously enforced the law. But few have gone at it with the same consistent zeal as Wayne Justice, whose concern for nondiscrimination and fair treatment on the job coincided with the legal mandates he was charged to carry out. That his remedies have not been more extensive is attributable to the limitations imposed by Congress and federal appellate courts, rather than any lack of commitment on his part.

CHAPTER 13

Care of Mentally Retarded Persons

Always at or near the bottom among the states in per client funding, the Texas Department of Mental Health and Mental Retardation (TDMHMR) had long struggled to serve its mentally retarded residents, many of them medically fragile, through a centralized system of state institutions. As with the prison system and the state reform schools for juvenile offenders, the entrenched TDMHMR bureaucracy was slow to change. Critics labeled the Texas mental health and mental retardation system inefficient, ineffective, and frequently inhumane. It was an inviting target for reform-minded plaintiffs' attorneys.

On November 27, 1974, Dallas Legal Services Foundation, a federally funded public interest law firm, filed suit against officials of the department, alleging the unconstitutionality of conditions at two of the department's twelve schools for mentally retarded persons. The suit, *Lelsz v. Kavanagh,* was brought on behalf of parents of three mentally retarded residents. The suit made these charges: that John Lelsz, a twenty-two-year-old blind and brain-damaged resident of the Austin State School had been subjected to inhumane and inappropriate care since being confined and had contracted a number of illnesses because of the lack of sanitation, cleanliness, and hygiene; that Jean Gibson, a seventeen-year-old with Down's Syndrome, had been tied to her bed by the ankle and confined in a straitjacket, despite the fact that she was not violent or aggressive, and had received no treatment plan during her confinement in the Denton State School; and that thirty-seven-year-old Michael Huffman, who had the mental age of a four-year-old, had been so overmedicated that he remained in a stupor and had been abused and attacked by other residents at the Denton State School.

The thrust of the lawsuit was that the state institutions were little more than barren and dreary warehouses for mentally retarded persons where, rather than receiving treatment, the residents were being subjected to chronic abuse and neglect amid deplorable conditions. The plaintiffs asserted that the men-

tally retarded were entitled both to humane living conditions and to individualized treatment in the least restrictive environment possible. The suit maintained that many of the state school residents could be more effectively
"habilitated" in less restrictive community settings. The term "habilitated"
means providing the mentally retarded with the conditions necessary for them
to reach their maximum potential.[1]

The community-based treatment paradigm being asserted in *Lelsz* bore
remarkable resemblance to the arguments of plaintiffs in *Morales v. Turman,*
the conditions-of-confinement case involving juvenile offenders. Three months
before the *Lelsz* case was filed, Judge Justice had handed down a detailed
remedial order in *Morales* dramatically altering procedures in state juvenile
reform schools (see Chapter 6). The order was based in part on the right of
incarcerated juveniles to treatment.

A complicating factor in *Lelsz* was that many parents whose children were
confined in the state institutions strongly opposed the lawsuit. Some asserted
that it was a harassment lawsuit brought by a few parents angry with the
superintendent of the Denton State School. "It is a personal, vindictive suit,
and that's why I refused to back it," R. E. Threadgill told reporters.[2] Threadgill echoed the views of most parents when he asserted that monitoring of care
could be more easily conducted in a state institution. He worried what would
happen to his child if he, the parent, were to die. Several parents began
making plans to intervene in the case so that their views could be heard.

Plaintiffs' attorneys sought a favorable forum in which to file their lawsuit.
Since one of the targeted institutions, the Denton State School, was within the
Sherman Division of the U.S. District Court, Eastern District of Texas, the
suit was filed there. The only judge serving the Sherman Division in 1974 was
William Wayne Justice. Attorneys representing the residents of the state institutions for mentally retarded persons hoped that Judge Justice would extend the right to treatment recognized in *Morales* to their clients. But *Lelsz* was
a more complicated lawsuit, and Judge Justice did not have the same interest
in the case that he had in *Morales.* Then, too, the plaintiffs' attorneys did not
prosecute it initially with the same vigor as the *Morales* attorneys had.

For several years, the lawsuit lingered on Justice's docket. Other than the
filing of procedural motions, little activity was apparent until February 27,
1979, when the plaintiffs filed a thirty-six-page amended complaint. The new
complaint alleged violations of state and federal law touching every facet of life
in three of TDMHMR's thirteen state institutions for the mentally retarded—
those at Denton, Austin, and Fort Worth (the latter had opened in 1976)—
and called for their closure in favor of community-based treatment facilities.
But after the filing, the case once again stalled. Funding problems, a heavy
load of cases, and internal management problems precluded effective litiga-

tion. Though Justice was not at all averse to taking on such a complex case, he thought seriously of dismissing it for want of prosecution. He hesitated, however, because he knew the plaintiffs' attorneys were heavily involved in a federal court action against TDMHMR in the Northern District of Texas concerning conditions for the mentally ill and apparently did not have time to devote to *Lelsz*.

It was not until 1981, when Philadelphia lawyer David Ferleger became lead counsel, that the lawsuit assumed significant proportions and quickly got the attention of TDMHMR top officials. Born of Polish Jews who survived the Holocaust, Ferleger has made it his mission in life to conduct lawsuits on behalf of mentally ill and mentally retarded persons. In the landmark *Halderman v. Pennhurst State School* case in Pennsylvania, he had achieved a record as a crusading attorney for the rights of the mentally retarded. Begun in 1974, that litigation resulted in an expansive 1977 federal district court decision holding that mentally retarded persons have a federal constitutional and statutory right to be provided with minimally adequate treatment in the least restrictive environment possible.[3] The court ordered the Pennhurst State School, housing 1,200 profoundly retarded residents, closed and its residents transferred to community-based facilities. The U.S. Court of Appeals for the Third Circuit substantially affirmed the trial court's decision in 1979.[4] Much of the 1979 *Lelsz* amended complaint was taken from pleadings Ferleger had filed in the *Pennhurst* case.

Flush from his victory in Pennsylvania, Ferleger sought to duplicate his success on behalf of mentally retarded persons in Texas. He had initially been hired in 1979 as a consultant by the Association of Retarded Citizens of Texas (ARC/Texas), a group of parents who were strongly supportive of community care and who had become disillusioned with the progress the renamed North Central Texas Legal Services Foundation of Dallas was making in the lawsuit. Ferleger reviewed the files on the case and talked with Thomas E. Ashton, staff attorney in charge of *Lelsz*. Ashton told Ferleger that the organization could not or would not provide the resources to finance the lawsuit adequately. Ferleger concluded that *Lelsz* was going nowhere and told the parent group they should develop their own statewide strategy with regard to the litigation.

The ARC/Texas parents continued to bring pressure to bear on the legal services group to give them adequate representation. In the spring of 1981, they were successful. Ferleger was invited to take over the case as lead counsel. He would be paid a fee by North Central Texas Legal Services, to be repaid out of any attorney fees awarded by the court. A pertinacious attorney, Ferleger took up the cause of Texas mentally retarded citizens with a vengeance. After touring the three state schools later that year, he told reporters they were worse than warehouses. "At least in warehouses, things are kept neat and clean and safe."[5]

Ferleger called the court and talked with one of Justice's law clerks. He suggested a joint meeting with Judge Justice and the defendants to go over the status of the case and work out a litigation schedule. The law clerk told him that it was a good thing Ferleger had called, for the Judge was just about to dismiss the case from his docket. The clerk relayed Ferleger's request to Judge Justice, who responded that he did not desire a meeting. But Justice did indicate that he would be receptive to the filing of a motion for class certification. Having heard that Justice sometimes dropped hints to plaintiffs' attorneys involved in complex institutional litigation, Ferleger immediately filed the motion to get the case moving. It was the first of many motions he would churn up over the duration of the case. Critics have charged that Ferleger's interest in the case was as much in attorney fees as in the cause of his clients and that he is difficult to work with.[6] Indeed, deteriorating working relationships later prompted North Central Texas Legal Services to withdraw from the lawsuit.

The parties worked out an agreement on the composition of the class and expected Judge Justice to ratify it routinely at the July 1981 class-certification hearing. They were surprised to find themselves closely questioned regarding how the legal indices for class certification were being met. It was apparent that the Judge was not about to rubber-stamp what the lawyers had worked out. "I think that he really took very, very seriously his duty to be the guardian of class members' interests under Rule 23 of the Federal Rules of Civil Procedure," says Ferleger. "He was not going to rely just on the lawyers." Justice exercised the same caution in *Morales v. Turman,* rejecting the initial proposed settlement as not sufficiently protective of the class of juveniles confined or to be confined in Texas Youth Council facilities.

At the hearing Ferleger told the court that day-to-day lack of treatment, and not horror stories, was the real tragedy at the three state institutions. But there were horror stories. On the eve of the hearing, newspapers reported the deaths of two residents of the Fort Worth State School. Eighteen-year-old Mark Jones drowned in two inches of water in a bathtub. Preliminary investigations showed that he had left his room at 6 A.M. and turned on the water in the communal bathtub. An aide told him to return to bed. The aide had been on the job three weeks and had received three days of training. Fifteen minutes later, the aide heard water running and found Mark, who was profoundly retarded, dead. The father, Reese Jones, had been prepared to testify at the hearing that conditions were so deplorable that his son might die at any time. The other resident was found unconscious, slumped in his wheelchair.[7] Later, medical examiners reported that both residents had been undermedicated, possibly causing seizures that resulted in their deaths.[8]

Justice found *Lelsz* quickly becoming "the most depressing case I have ever been associated with" because of the nature of the clients and the conditions of their confinement. "It profoundly depressed me to hear testimony about them. With prisoners, you can see that maybe there's some hope for them. But there's so little hope for those people. It's just a question of keeping them as comfortable as you can and letting them progress as far as they can with their limited intellects."

On August 5, 1981, Justice certified the plaintiff class to include all residents of the three schools since 1974, when the case was first filed, and those on the waiting list (called "the register") for all thirteen schools. The class thus consisted of all 2,400 residents at these three institutions, representing 26 percent of the total population at the thirteen institutions. Because the class included those on the waiting list for placement in any of the schools, the size of the class quickly grew.

Meanwhile, the parents who disagreed with those behind the *Lelsz* lawsuit were busy trying to get into the case. A year and a half after the lawsuit had been filed, the parents of six residents of the schools sought to intervene, seeking its dismissal. In their motion, they argued that there was no right to habilitative care, much less habilitative care in the least restrictive environment, and that even if there were such a right, the state was providing it. Justice had little sympathy with this group. He concluded early on that they were concerned more with their own interests than those of their retarded children. On July 9, 1981, a day before the hearing on the class certification, he denied their motion, noting in a brief order that their position was adequately being represented by the defendants. However, he did point out that they could file an *amicus curiae* brief.

None was filed. Instead, the parents appealed to the U.S. Court of Appeals for the Fifth Circuit, but then withdrew their appeal. A new, more artfully drawn motion was filed on February 10, 1982, by the Parent Association for the Retarded of Texas (PART), a group of parents who opposed community-care facilities for their children. They had secured Washington, D.C., attorney Joel L. Klein, also a veteran of the *Pennhurst* litigation, to represent them. In *Pennhurst,* Klein had represented the Pennhurst Parent-Staff Association, which opposed the closing of Pennhurst State School. In its motion to intervene in *Lelsz,* PART asserted that it wanted the state schools to be brought into compliance with constitutional standards, but it opposed closing them in favor of community-based facilities.

Justice viewed this group with suspicion. He doubted that their position was significantly different from that of the state defendants. He concluded from the substance of the motion and from the names of those involved, that the intervention effort was a thinly disguised attempt to resuscitate the intervention he had already rejected. He summarily denied the motion. Law clerk Roger Parloff, who worked on this phase of the *Lelsz* litigation, admits to having doubts about the motivation of both Ferleger and Klein. "I had the unsettling feeling that these two ideologues were traveling about the country waging their philosophical battles almost without regard to the actual plaintiffs on whose behalf each nominally claimed to speak." [9]

PART filed an appeal with the Fifth Circuit, which requested that the Judge file a statement of reasons for his action. Justice was aware of the thin line he was walking, for it is generally recognized that all legally relevant interests should be represented in large-scale institutional litigation. The question was whether PART had a legally relevant interest. Justice asked Parloff to draft a detailed response to the Fifth Circuit request. Parloff believed that PART's position was more political than legal. The organization, he concluded, feared that TDMHMR might expand community-based treatment as a way of bringing its state schools into compliance with state and federal law. The parents were adamantly opposed to anything that would weaken the state schools or threaten their children's residence in them. But such a policy change would not necessarily violate the law. Parloff found considerable Fifth Circuit law involving the same concern of parents faced with school desegregation. In a number of cases, the Fifth Circuit had denied parent groups the right to intervene in such suits when the parents feared that school boards would be more conciliatory and reform-minded than the parents wanted them to be.

In the opinion, Justice acknowledged that his perfunctory rejection of the motion "reflected a pragmatic and, perhaps, hasty, judgment about wise allocation of time by a district judge who had before him 770 *other* pending civil actions." [10] He proceeded to set forth the reasons for his action, describing how PART's interests were already being represented. To the extent that PART agreed with the plaintiffs that conditions in the schools had to be brought into compliance with minimal legal and constitutional standards, its interests were being adequately represented by the plaintiffs. PART attorneys strongly disagreed. On the basis of the *Pennhurst* litigation, they asserted that Ferleger's real goal was to close state institutions and that he was giving mere lip service to their improvement. To the extent that PART advocated maintaining state institutions, Justice continued, its views were adequately represented by the state defendants. But PART attorneys argued that they sought more than maintenance of state institutions; they sought substantial upgrading. Justice was not persuaded. If PART had anything to add, it could do so through an *amicus curiae* brief. He noted that he had already granted two other organizations, Advocacy, Inc., and ARC/Texas, the right to file *amicus* briefs. The latter was the same organization that had brought Ferleger into the case. Both groups supported the plaintiffs. He had also appointed a university professor to conduct a study of habilitation and care at the three institutions.

Justice saved his strongest argument for the last. If PART was not the same group that had sought to intervene in 1976, why had the organization waited six years after the filing of the lawsuit? By 1982, the parties were deep into settlement negotiations. "Whatever progress has been made over the past three years would be jeopardized if the PART applicants, who fully appreciated this suit's potential impact upon them six years ago, were now allowed to intervene." [11] He again rejected the motion. And PART again appealed to the Fifth Circuit. This time, the panel of judges upheld Justice's ruling, but not without reservations. "We are wary, but for now are persuaded that the best course is to not interfere with the district court in its effort to manage this case. We will look again should, as it now appears, any settlement approval be contested." [12] It was a not-too-subtle hint to the Judge to allow PART to intervene at some point during the settlement phase.

By the early 1980s, TDMHMR had indeed become serious about negotiating a settlement. When Dallas Democrat Jim Mattox became Texas attorney general in 1983 and selected Austin civil rights attorney David R. Richards as his top assistant, pressure was brought on several state agencies to work out settlements to long-standing burdensome lawsuits. Among them were *Morales v. Turman, Ruiz v. Estelle,* and *Lelsz.* Officials in the attorney general's office had concluded that TDMHMR could not win the *Lelsz* lawsuit and feared another takeover of a state institution should the case come to trial. Pressure was applied to the TDMHMR board to seek an accord. Dr. Gary E. Miller, who had just been appointed TDMHMR commissioner, was reluctant to give up the fight. "Basically, my bias was against settlement because I had been aware of how settlement decrees can be the beginning of tremendous adversarial problems rather than their end." But the die had been cast, and Miller became a key negotiator. A settlement containing forty-five provisions was reached on April 15, 1983. The TDMHMR board approved it on May 10, three weeks before trial was to begin.

The settlement specifically recognized the right of mentally retarded persons to individualized services. These services, the agreement stated, "are best achieved in environments that approximate to the greatest possible extent those in which non-retarded people spend their lives, for example, ordinary homes and work places." [13] Section 8 committed the department to "provide each member of the plaintiff class with the least restrictive alternative living conditions possible consistent with the person's particular circumstances, including age, degree of retardation and handicapping conditions." Section 17 recognized that "The level of retardation and degree of disability of a member of the plaintiff class is not, in and of itself, a barrier to appropriate community placement." These provisions convinced PART attorneys that they had been right all along in fearing that the lawsuit was really aimed at closing state institutions. "We all thought the settlement was pretty bad," says PART attorney Paul M. Smith, who had joined Joel Klein on the case. "It was clear to us that the settlement was going to lead down the road to a substantial push of people into the community."

Despite the least restrictive provisions, no specific targets were set for community placement and no state institutions were slated for closing. All the agreement required was that the defendants "use their best efforts to overcome all obstacles and barriers" to development of community-based facilities. Similarly, there was little specificity in other areas, such as staff-client ratios. "The notion that we all had in negotiating the settlement was that the details would be put off until later," Ferleger says. In order to preserve as much management flexibility as possible, TDMHMR officials were unwilling to agree to specifics, and Ferleger saw it as in his best interest not to insist upon them lest PART file a successful appeal with the Fifth Circuit.

With the absence of specifics, conflicting interpretations of what the agreement required were apparent almost before the ink was dry. Ferleger told the press that "there's nothing in the settlement that says if they don't have the money, they don't have to do [community placement]. They have to do it, period." [14] However, Kent Johnson, director of legal services for TDMHMR, said that "Deinstitutionalization is not part of the settlement. It says we will continue to do what we have in the past, which is to continue to improve and expand our services in the community and in the [state] facilities." [15]

The settlement also contained numerous provisions upgrading conditions within state institutions. Residents were to be protected from physical and psychological abuse or neglect. The use of medication as punishment or as a substitute for habilitation was prohibited. Each resident was to be provided with a written individual service plan developed by an interdisciplinary team. Parents and, where possible, clients were to participate in the development of the plan. The settlement required TDMHMR to recruit and train qualified personnel to staff its facilities. Buildings were to be kept "safe, clean, free of bad odors, comfortably temperature-controlled and insect-free." A complaint system was spelled out. Finally, the settlement required the department to develop a comprehensive plan for implementing the terms of the agreement and report the status of implementation quarterly to the court.

A hearing on the proposed settlement was held in June, and all interested parties, including PART, presented testimony. Justice approved the settlement on July 19, 1983. In a lengthy order and memorandum opinion, he reviewed the settlement provisions in light of applicable legal standards. He recognized that "a case of this kind inevitably presents formidable legal questions concerning federalism—the limits to which a federal court may properly intervene in the affairs of a state institution."[16] Justice tried to show that the provisions of the settlement dealing with conditions of confinement were based on federal constitutional rights as recognized in a 1982 U.S. Supreme Court decision, *Youngberg v. Romeo.*[17] At the same time, he noted that had plaintiffs litigated the matter, relief could have been predicated upon explicit Texas statutes.[18] The discussion of the legal basis for the settlement would become of critical importance in a later Fifth Circuit decision regarding enforcement of the community-placement provision.

The absence of specificity in the agreement did not trouble the Judge, for he noted—erroneously, as it turned out—the general cooperative posture of the parties and assumed that progress would be made toward developing the required plan for its implementation. The parties would both benefit from settlement of the lawsuit, he observed, rather than spend "gargantuan" sums in litigation. The plaintiffs stood to gain in light of the dubious authority of the court to compel the state defendants to follow state law provisions. The defendants stood to gain by avoiding attorney fees, a finding of past liability, closure of state institutions, and the direct supervision of a special master.

PART had voiced strong opposition at the hearing to the community-placement provisions. After reviewing their concerns, Justice found that the contested provisions tracked state law, were supported by the defendants, and would not result in funds being siphoned off to support community treatment, thereby causing services at state institutions to deteriorate. He refused to accord parents a veto over their child's placement in a community facility. To do so, he wrote, "would be tantamount to acknowledging that parents are the 'true clients' of the institutions, a view that has been renounced as 'immoral' by the Court of Appeals for this Circuit."[19] He noted that under Texas law, parents were accorded the right to participate in an administrative hearing concerning placement of their child.

At the end of the July 19 memorandum opinion, Justice invited PART to become a party-intervenor. Aware of the Fifth Circuit's earlier nudge to let the association into the case, he found this a good time to extend the invitation. He recognized that the apprehensions of PART parents were real. "According formal intervention, it is hoped, will insure that each parent understands that he or she is armed with the means of enforcing the protective provisions of the [settlement] . . . and with the means of appealing the adverse orders of this court. The interests of the class will best be served by encouraging the vigilance of all interested parties and by maximizing their access to the court."[20] Justice had changed his mind about PART and its members. "I came to believe that those people were genuinely concerned about the welfare of their children," he acknowledges. "They just had a different philosophy than the other parents." Justice was impressed with the work of attorney Joel Klein on their behalf. "While I didn't adopt his arguments, he shed a lot of light on the case. I formed a high impression of him." While PART would be allowed to intervene, the settlement would still apply to the children of its members. In the fall of 1983, PART became a plaintiff-intervenor. At the same time, Justice granted intervention motions filed by Advocacy, Inc., and ARC/Texas.

While PART members were not happy with the settlement, their attorneys decided they could gain more by participating in the implementation process than by mounting a challenge to the Fifth Circuit. The parents were pleased that Justice had let them into the case. If implementation efforts proved not to their liking, they could file an appeal later on. Furthermore, the moderate tone of the settlement diminished the likelihood of a successful appeal at that juncture. Ferleger's strategy had worked.

In accordance with the settlement, Justice authorized the appointment of an expert consultant to monitor its implementation and ordered the state to pay $215,000 to establish a fund for this purpose. The state also had to pay $350,000 for plaintiffs' attorney fees. By agreement of the parties, on March 19, 1984, the Judge appointed Linda R. O'Neall as the expert consultant. She held a Ph.D. in sociology and operated a consulting service in Florida for community-based programs for the mentally retarded. A strong proponent of deinstitutionalization, she had served as a consultant to the Massachusetts and Florida mental health systems, and had helped place more than five thousand retarded Florida residents into community-based facilities. She had assisted in the design of four-bedroom community cluster homes and had helped overcome community opposition to them. Shortly after her appointment, she told a reporter that while Florida and Texas had similar rates of mental retardation, Texas had three times as many retarded people in state institutions. "What you have in Texas is a great propensity to institutionalize people," she said. [21] She added that once the institutions were built and staffed, they became part of the pattern of resistance to change.

Why did TDMHMR officials agree to the appointment of someone who opposed their management philosophy? "We had no choice," Commissioner Miller maintains. Although he considered all of Ferleger's candidates unacceptable, he accepted O'Neall, who had been ranked second on Ferleger's list and last on the department's list, as the least undesirable. According to Miller, TDMHMR had been advised by the attorney general's office that if it failed to reach an accommodation with Ferleger, Justice would very likely approve the appointment of someone even more hostile to the department's position. Justice maintains, however, that the employment of an expert consultant was pursuant to the settlement and entirely the parties' own doing. "I never considered whom to appoint or indeed even to have a consultant. Her appointment and the duties she was to perform were presented to me as an accomplished fact."

With the settlement approved and the expert consultant appointed, Justice assumed he had heard the last of a case he wasn't very much interested in to begin with. The settlement process in the *Ruiz* prison case was a matter of far greater concern, and his regular docket was burgeoning. But *Lelsz* was far from over.

Problems had surfaced almost immediately after approval of the settlement in July 1983. In February 1984, two severely retarded boys at the Fort Worth State School were lashed with a leather strap. Another was left in the shower too long and suffered blisters. In July, eight men at the Fort Worth School were discovered to have gonorrhea, raising concerns about homosexual activity. In August, the Denton State School had its Medicaid payments suspended for understaffing and lack of a resident training program. Health inspectors had found a retarded resident strapped to a board and lying on the floor unattended in a room with no observation window. O'Neall reviewed the inspection report and found that school officials had violated the terms of the settlement "paragraph by paragraph."[22] She also discovered that the state schools were underreporting incidences of client abuse. "They did not count it as a confirmed abuse unless the perpetrator was known," she said.[23] The procedure was changed to record cases even if the perpetrator was unknown. The Lubbock State School, not a party in the *Lelsz* lawsuit, also lost its Medicaid funding in August for what were termed "life-threatening" violations of state health and safety regulations.

Though he had anticipated that the settlement would not be self-executing, Ferleger rapidly lost patience with TDMHMR's foot-dragging. In March 1984 he filed a contempt motion over client abuse, staffing shortages, and safety deficiencies at the Fort Worth State School. On October 1, 1984, Justice ordered O'Neall's fee increased from $40,000 to nearly $180,000 so that she could carry out her responsibilities under the settlement. He took the occasion to note that TDMHMR's assignment of implementation responsibilities to a staff member with other full-time responsibilities "betrays at best a haphazard and indifferent attitude toward its obligations and at worst a complete failure to take those obligations seriously."[24]

Two days after Justice's order, Dr. Edward Skarnulis, deputy commissioner of mental retardation services, resigned. Skarnulis had recently joined the state agency and was recognized as a strong proponent of deinstitutionalization. But his relationship with Commissioner Miller, who found Skarnulis an ineffective administrator and poor communicator, rapidly deteriorated, and he was forced out. Skarnulis' departure added credence to what was regarded as a

policy of resistance by the agency. Meanwhile, by telling a committee overseeing the TDMHMR budget that legislative solutions are preferred to those
imposed by court order, O'Neall tried to prepare legislators for increased funding requests from department officials to comply with the terms of the settlement. "In court cases, you are forced to spend enormous sums of money on
things that are not productive," she said, pointing to Massachusetts' experience in trying to fulfill a court order to rehabilitate institutions as much as one
hundred years old.[25]

Noting that within the next six years the state would experience a 39 percent increase in mentally retarded persons needing state care, O'Neall put in a
strong word for community-based programs. She claimed the state could realize significant cost savings through community-based programs compared
with the $80 per day they were spending to keep a mentally retarded person in
a state institution. She also observed that many state schools were overloaded
with mildly or moderately retarded people who could be better cared for in
cheaper community facilities. While Commissioner Miller expressed reservations about the economies of community-based care, he told committee members that he had agreed to seek more money from the legislature when he
had consented both to the *Lelsz* settlement and to a settlement in *R.A.J. v.
Miller,* the companion case before U.S. District Court Judge Barefoot Sanders
in Dallas. *Miller* involved a 1974 class action suit over conditions at eight
TDMHMR hospitals for mentally ill persons.

Facing a significant shortfall in state revenue and not pleased with being
told what to do—certainly not by a monitor appointed by Judge Justice—the
legislators were skeptical. Dallas attorney Oswin Chrisman, chairman of the
committee, told TDMHMR officials, "I don't think we're locked into your
evaluation of the future," and urged the committee to seek an independent
evaluation of the department's budget.[26]

Miller maintains that he had to be very careful in how he asked for additional funding. "If the legislature ever thought I was using Judge Sanders or
Judge Justice as a vehicle to extort money by just letting the lawsuits happen,
that would have wiped me out." It was a difficult time for TDMHMR administrators. As Miller expressed it early in October 1984, "We are facing a hor-
rendous dilemma. We're between a rock and a hard place. If we don't ask for
everything we think is necessary, we're out of compliance with the courts. If we
do ask for it, we're out of compliance with the Legislature."[27] Seeming to prove
his point, plaintiffs filed another motion for contempt on October 26. The
Dallas Times Herald showed little sympathy toward either the department or
the legislature. It editorialized, "The Texas Legislature and the Texas Department of Mental Health and Mental Retardation have spent more time in recent years trying to avoid the issue than in designing a comprehensive system

of care for the state's mentally ill and retarded citizens. It is time to end the buck-passing and the hand-wringing and to act responsibly to provide adequate care for thousands of Texans in need of assistance." [28]

In light of the escalating reports about client abuse and faced with contempt motions, TDMHMR had to take some action to show a good-faith effort to implement the settlement. The agency was well aware of a potentially serious crowding problem with the expected increase in mentally retarded persons requiring state care. One legislator estimated that if the state built two state schools a year, it could not keep up. [29] Late in November 1984, the agency proposed to move hundreds of retarded residents to local facilities, diverting some funding from the state institutions for this purpose. It was a dramatic turnabout for the state agency and placed it in direct opposition to the increasingly vocal and powerful PART, whose president, Rix Rutland, told reporters, "The policy is flawed by this underlying philosophy and assumption that community services for all mentally retarded persons are somehow magically superior to the programs in the state schools." [30] He acknowledged that a "very few" in the state institutions might be better served in a community setting but "not very many."

Despite the heavy lobbying effort of parents opposed to community placement, the Board of Mental Health and Mental Retardation was committed both by state law and by the settlement to placing residents in community-based facilities. It approved the plan on December 7. But despite the new state plan, no releases were forthcoming. On January 8, 1985, a year and a half after the settlement had been approved, plaintiffs filed yet another motion for contempt, alleging failure of the department to establish a set of standards for community residential facilities.

Ferleger's primary interest in the case had always been to move residents out of the state schools and into community-based facilities. He concluded that Justice had much the same inclination. Indeed, the Judge had heard expert testimony in two prior cases—*Morales v. Turman* and *Ruiz v. Estelle*—about the drawbacks of large, impersonal state institutions. As a matter of personal belief, Justice favors small units as offering advantages over large units in several respects: ease of administration, greater accountability, and the means to devote more personnel to those in need. However, he doubted that de-institutionalization of TDMHMR could occur anytime soon, if ever. "My experience with *Morales* and *Ruiz* had led me to believe that community-based facilities are probably superior in most instances. But I realized that if that were ever to be instituted in the TDMHMR, it would have to be a long phase-in process. I always have in my mind what the legislative attitude is about things, and they would have to come to that kind of conclusion. And besides, there was some very active opposition to the closing of TDMHMR institutions by PART attorneys, and they made good arguments. There was something to be said on both sides."

On February 27, 1985, Ferleger, together with ARC/Texas and Advocacy, Inc., as plaintiff-intervenors, filed a joint motion to force TDMHMR to partially deinstitutionalize the Denton, Austin, and Fort Worth State Schools by placing in community facilities all residents of school age (twenty-one and under), all non–mentally retarded,[31] and other persons identified by an interdisciplinary team as being in need of community placement. The number came to over 713 persons, most of them in the school-age category. The purpose was to put as much pressure as possible on TDMHMR to implement a community placement program. The joint motion also requested that the expert consultant determine an unspecified number of persons on the waiting list to be provided community services and that the court so order. Matters had come to a head. Justice had no choice but to get back into the *Lelsz* case. Fortunately, he had a law clerk in the person of Susan Stefan, a Stanford Law School graduate, who had been assigned the case and took a personal interest in it. The Judge scheduled a five-day hearing in April on the contempt motion and several of the earlier motions.

The parties were able to resolve all issues on their own except for community placements. This became the primary focus of the hearing. In support of their joint motion, the plaintiffs and plaintiff-intervenors presented testimony from several witnesses. Two residents of the Austin State School expressed an urgent desire to live in the community. One resident who had cerebral palsy but was not retarded said he had made all the arrangements for his own apartment, only to be told by the superintendent of the Austin State School that it was not suitable. The former director of community services at the Brenham State School testified about the frustrations he had experienced in trying to place residents in the community. He told of efforts he had made to raise money for community placements and of becoming discouraged because of the obstacles he met. "I, quite frankly, was disappointed that there was no one else in my cheering section but me."[32] Several out-of-state administrators testified about the lack of privacy, the crowding, and the lack of trained staffing in Texas institutions and about the benefits of community-based placement. But all acknowledged that state institutions still had a role to play.

TDMHMR and PART objected to the joint motion on the grounds that it called for placement by category, rather than on the basis of individual determinations by a qualified team of experts. Such a quota system, the department maintained, flew in the face of the 1983 settlement. PART feared that mandatory placement of persons under the age of twenty-two would eviscerate the capacity of parents to participate in placement decisions. TDMHMR officials presented their own plan to place nine hundred residents (six hundred from the thirteen state institutions and three hundred from the waiting list) in the community over a two-year period. Jaylon Fincannon, deputy commissioner for mental retardation, acknowledged in his testimony that no great progress had been made to date in community placement but asserted that this was because the department had been involved in planning and trying to secure money from the legislature. He admitted that the figure of nine hundred was obtained by calculating the population reduction necessary to achieve an improved staff-client ratio in the state institutions.

The defendants were unable to say how many residents of the three schools involved in the *Lelsz* litigation would be included among the nine hundred. Commissioner Miller maintained that the department did not favor a "two-tiered" approach which would show favoritism to the *Lelsz* class. "The Department's position and the Board's policy is that we will treat all of our clients similarly situated in the same manner. . . ."[33] It was clear from Miller's testimony that while he supported the concept of community placement, he still valued the role of state institutions. He also valued the role of parents in placement decisions. One of PART's attorneys, Paul Smith, asked him about parent attitudes toward community placement. The interchange which followed revealed the fundamentally different views the parties to the lawsuit had about who were the proper clients of the state institutions.

Smith: Among state school parents, do you have a lot of parents coming in and urging you to allow their family members to get out into community programs?

Miller: Of state school members?

Smith: Parents.

Miller: Not very often. That's not a very common occurrence.

Smith: So it's not as if you have sort of fifty percent of the state school parents in there telling you, "Let my kid out. Let him be released from the state school," and fifty percent coming in and saying, "No, I want my kid kept in." Is that right?

Miller: Well, the overwhelming majority, while they may not say, "I want my kid kept in," they will express satisfaction with the care that their child is receiving, and they will also express perhaps some concern that something may happen to disrupt that.

Smith: The reality is that you have a real group of satisfied customers out there among the parents. Isn't that right?

Miller: Yes.

Ferleger: Your Honor, the term, customers, is a little confusing . . .

Judge Justice: Oh, I overrule your objection. I think I understand.

Ferleger: It's the clients in the state schools who are the customers, Your Honor.[34]

Judge Justice had listened to the conflicting testimony of expert witnesses for each side regarding placing mentally retarded persons in community facilities. Rather than defer to the judgment of the state agency as the PART attorneys hoped he would in light of the conflict, he turned to the court-appointed monitor for guidance. He asked Linda O'Neall to analyze the issues and the evidence relating to community placement. At the April 12 hearing, she recommended that over a sixteen-month period, more than 270 residents of the three state schools be placed in community homes. Given three weeks to review her testimony, the parties returned to the court on May 8 for purposes of cross-examination.

The testimony O'Neall gave on May 8 was one of the highlights of the hearing. For much of the day, she defended her proposal. She created a stir when she testified that while parents have a right to due process procedures if they object to a community placement for their child, they should not have veto power over the decision. "Having borne someone perhaps doesn't give one more knowledge than the person that cares for the child on a daily basis intimately."[35] PART attorney Smith asked if institutional placement might not be appropriate for some mentally retarded persons. She responded, "I think there are other kinds of placements that serve a client and a client's family better than a place that is 350 clients large."[36] An outcry arose from the courtroom audience, many of them PART members sporting yellow plastic flowers in their lapels. Justice called for order and threatened to clear the courtroom.

It had been a long and difficult hearing. The parties were antagonistic toward one another because the interests at stake were so divergent. PART attorney Paul Smith felt that throughout the hearing, Justice was not sympathetic toward parent concerns, and he was right. But at the same time, Smith maintains that Justice was fair. "For all you can say about how he was an activist intent on pushing the case in the other direction, he had a good judicial temperament. He was much nicer than a lot of judges to people who haven't had much experience in the courtroom. He kept the process clean and let it go forward. I have a lot of respect for him in that sense."

Justice handed down his decision in the form of a thirty-six-page order on June 6, 1985. He noted that it was beyond the power of the court to grant the joint motion with regard to community placement. Not only would it exceed the terms of the settlement by requiring wholesale placement-by-category, it probably would be unconstitutional as excessively intrusive.[37] However, the court did have the power to enforce the agreement. While the agreement was not specific with regard to community placement, it certainly envisioned such placement and reserved "unusually broad power to this court, not only to enforce the Resolution and Settlement, but to 'interpret, implement, and modify' its terms."[38] He noted that one reason the settlement did not contain target figures for community placement was because "defendants were so disorganized that they did not have the data on which to produce any figures. . . ." This assertion is questionable in light of the fact that, as noted earlier, the parties had expressly decided against inclusion of specificity in the agreement.

Justice quoted extensively from the deposition of Dr. Edward Skarnulis, the deputy commissioner for mental retardation who had resigned. Skarnulis testified that his boss, Dr. Miller, had either ignored his suggestions or actively thwarted his initiatives. Justice noted that Skarnulis' "entire deposition stands in stark contradiction to the stance taken by defendants at the hearing. . . ." From his review of the evidence, Justice concluded that "it is now abundantly clear that defendants have failed—and will continue to fail, without correction from the court—adequately to fulfill their responsibilities with regard to community placement of class members mandated by the Resolution and Settlement." He was unwilling to accept the department's assertions that residents of the three state schools involved in *Lelsz* would be "swept along" in the department's general statewide community placement plan. "It is possible that defendants' plan would have been acceptable if it at least planned for a certain number of class members to be placed. But for the Department, with no previous record of placing a significant number of class members, to ask the court to find that a plan with literally no guarantee that *any* class member will be placed is adequate protection for members of the class is asking too much."

Accordingly, Justice ordered the implementation of O'Neall's plan releasing 279 residents from the three schools to community programs within a sixteen-month period. If by this placement process a two-tiered system would be established, "they may so name it; it does not alter the court's obligation to the class." In addition, he ordered the development of an appeals process whereby parents could make their views known if they disapproved of the decision. But they were not to have veto power over a placement decision.

Assistant Attorney General Philip Durst had tried to get O'Neall to admit at the May 8 hearing that there had been problems with moving residents too fast into Florida communities. Judge Justice had shown impatience with this line of questioning, repeatedly asking the attorneys to move along. "It became apparent during the hearing," Durst says, "that whatever O'Neall said, he was going to do." Commissioner Miller agrees. "Judge Justice has a lot of power, and in this case, he chose to carry it out through one person. She was his eyes and ears. Whatever she offered him, he could not turn down because if he did, he undermined her credibility." Justice flatly rejects Durst's and Miller's assertions. "I would not have had a moment's hesitancy in overruling her thoughts about the matter if I thought she was wrong. I didn't think she was." He adds, "Linda O'Neall stated her conclusions in open court where she was subject to cross-examination. Moreover, the state had all the opportunity in the world to refute her, and they sought to do so. Of course, I listened to what Linda O'Neall had to say. But I also listened to the other side."

O'Neall maintains that from the beginning, her role was to provide information, chiefly in the form of data, to the court. "I was not an advocate," she says, adding, "I have worked with two federal judges in Texas, and I doubt I could have influenced either one to do something they weren't intending to do anyway."

In a July 1, 1987, letter to all TDMHMR employees entitled "Living under Lawsuits," Miller vented his frustration with having to contend with federal judges and court-appointed monitors. "The department is always the fall guy," he wrote. "If something goes wrong in our facilities, it is our fault; whatever progress is made is, of course, to the credit of the lawsuits and the court monitors. The court monitors can do no wrong; they do not have to account directly or indirectly to the people of Texas for the correctness of their conclusions about TDMHMR facilities or for the accuracy of their statements to the press." One of the reasons the lawsuits never ended, he asserted, was because they were lucrative business. "A lot of people make a lot of money as long as the lawsuits continue. There are attorneys' fees, expensive outside experts, and of course, the money that pays the salaries of the monitors and members of their organizations."

In *Lelsz* a major contributing factor to the longevity of the lawsuit which Miller did not cite was the ambiguity in the 1983 settlement agreement he had negotiated with Ferleger. Conflicting interpretations of settlement terms and the inordinate delay in negotiating an implementation plan resulted in additional trips to court. Judge Justice asserts that insofar as the court is concerned, "If there is anything a judge wants to do, it is to get rid of a lawsuit, particularly one of that magnitude. The quicker the better. The idea that we would institute a self-perpetuating group is ridiculous." The assertion can be turned around, the Judge points out. The reason the lawsuit continued was because entrenched bureaucrats sought to perpetuate their discredited practices.

Though his position had not been adopted, Ferleger was pleased with the order. He said that the state has always wanted to do as little as pos-

sible and now "the court's opinion makes it clear that that's not acceptable."[39] TDMHMR officials called the order unfair and incorrect. Coke Mills,
TDMHMR board chairman, said "If placement is good for 279 people in three
state schools, you ought not to discriminate against the rest of the system."[40]
Miller thought Justice was biased against the department from the start. "I
felt Justice had the need to believe those things that depicted the situation in
the mentally retarded system as being as terrible as possible so that he could
justify taking some drastic action. I think he was looking for an opportunity to
do something bold and dramatic, and look like someone who was taking a
terribly regressive system and struggling to reform it by knocking heads together." Justice responds, "That's the impression I formed of his system—
terribly regressive and inhumane—based on the evidence that was presented
to me. Anyone who had been in those facilities would, I believe, confirm what
I found, unless they deliberately closed their eyes." However, Miller points
out that Justice could have seen that the plaintiffs' litany of abuses was exag-
gerated had he visited the institutions himself, something he refused to do.

TDMHMR officials also pointed out that Justice's temporary appeals procedures for parents violated provisions of state law. The state filed a motion
asking Judge Justice to reconsider. He rejected it, and the state filed an appeal with the Fifth Circuit. Meanwhile, the political process was at work. On
June 7 Governor Mark White signed a bill providing for small, six-member,
family-oriented community-based living centers for mentally retarded persons
and preventing cities from using zoning laws to block the establishment of
community care homes in residential areas.

Justice continued to superintend the litigation, which was still generating
motions nearly every day, until November 11, 1985. In a sudden move which
caught all parties off guard, he then transferred the case to Judge Barefoot
Sanders in Dallas.

At the time, Justice was heavily burdened with *Ruiz v. Estelle,* the prison
case, and was hearing prisoner petitions from across the state pursuant to the
Fifth Circuit's decision in *Johnson v. McKaskle* (see Chapter 15, note 67). He
had over 1,100 civil actions on his docket, far more than the average for federal
judges in Texas. He had requested and received three additional law clerks to
help with the load. This gave him a total of five. Members of the Fifth Circuit
Judicial Council, an administrative body composed of all circuit judges on
active service and representative district court judges, expressed concern about
the pileup of these cases on Justice's docket, while others complained about his
having so many clerks and his oversight of so many institutional lawsuits.

Judge Thomas M. Reavley, the circuit judge serving as a liaison with the Eastern District, called Justice on behalf of the Circuit Council to talk to him about their concerns. Justice agreed that his case load, including the *Lelsz* case, had become overwhelming. "I was working literally seven days a week trying to keep up." The two agreed that it would be preferable for a state institution to have to deal with one, rather than two, federal judges. As already noted, Judge Sanders was then presiding over the companion case of *R.A.J. v. Miller*. Contrary to rumors at the time, no coercion was involved. Judge Reavley, who was closer to Judge Justice than anyone else on the Fifth Circuit, found Justice perfectly happy to transfer the case. "When Judge Reavley suggested transfer of *Lelsz* would be a good thing to do, I welcomed his suggestion," Justice says. But he adds, "I wouldn't have agreed to it if he had mentioned anyone other than Barefoot Sanders. From the way Sanders had been performing in the mental health case, I felt that he would likely do a good job."[41] Reavley called Sanders, who agreed to the transfer. Justice frankly was pleased finally to have the case off his docket. "My interest in that case was not profound," he maintains. "I handled it, but my heart wasn't in it." Despite invitations, Justice had declined to tour any of the state institutions as he had done in *Morales v. Turman*.

The move generated consternation among those involved with the case. Mary Keller, an assistant attorney general, told reporters that "We felt bewildered and we don't really know what this was all about." But she added, "Nobody is jumping for joy and saying, 'Whoopie, we're out from underneath this tyrant.'"[42] And rightly so, for Judge Sanders, a Democrat appointed by President Carter in 1979, would prove to be a stern taskmaster over the department.

Justice was no longer presiding over the case when, in January 1987, the Fifth Circuit reversed his 1985 order regarding community placement. Drawing upon the U.S. Supreme Court's decision in *Pennhurst II* (see note 4), the three-judge panel observed that a federal court is barred by the Eleventh Amendment from requiring state officials to obey state law.[43] Since the 1983 resolution and settlement provisions regarding treatment in the least restrictive environment possible had been based primarily on state, not federal, law, Justice was without jurisdiction to enter his order. In retrospect, law clerk Roger Parloff, who researched Justice's order approving the 1983 settlement, wishes that he had "come up with a cleverer, more explicit, and more durable federal hook" on which to base that portion of the opinion.[44]

The conservative-dominated appeals court rejected Ferleger's assertions that a constitutional right to community placement can be inferred from earlier Supreme Court decisions, in particular *Youngberg v. Romeo,* in which the Court recognized a constitutional right of mentally retarded persons to minimally adequate training.[45] The Fifth Circuit noted that the right related "not to the qualitative betterment of a retarded person's life, but only to the training necessary to afford him safety and freedom from bodily restraint."[46] The court further noted that the arguments in *Lelsz* dealt not with the substantive level of care being provided by the state, but rather with its locale. Since there was no constitutional basis for the settlement provisions regarding right to treatment in the least restrictive environment, "the district court's decree purporting to enforce them may not rest on that authority and is unauthorized."[47]

Nor did it make any difference that the action was in the form of enforcement of a consent decree. Writing for the majority, Edith Hollan Jones, a Reagan appointee, pointed out that the community placement issue was still a matter of state law and that the state had not waived its Eleventh Amendment immunity against being sued in federal court. A consent decree does not acquire a life of its own but must be read in conformity with applicable law. This being the case, Justice had no authority to enforce the consent decree by committing the state to a program of community placement. The court noted "the cruel irony" to which PART would be subjected if the agreement were construed to require community placements. PART had not been allowed to intervene during the litigation and negotiation of the settlement, objected to any language mandating community placements in the agreement, and assumed that no such mandate existed when the settlement was signed. PART's position had finally been vindicated. Since Justice was without authority to order community placements, he also could not establish an appeal process for parents. "Because the court could not award this relief, its concomitant wholesale revision of state procedures governing parents' participation in community placement decisions is unnecessary and therefore likewise unenforceable."[48]

Circuit Judge John Minor Wisdom, veteran liberal holdover from the rights-sensitive Fifth Circuit of the 1960s, dissented. He opted to remand the case for further hearings to determine if the minimal levels of care required by the Constitution for mentally retarded persons were being provided. He specially disagreed with the majority's sweeping use of the Eleventh Amendment to bar the litigation from the purview of the federal court. "The Eleventh Amendment enjoys no exalted position over the Fourteenth. If the plaintiffs have not had a full and fair hearing on their federal rights, they are entitled to one."[49]

The Fifth Circuit decision was upsetting and controversial because of its niggardly view of the authority of federal courts to enforce consent decrees. Justice could not understand the reversal. "To my way of thinking, it was a profound mistake on the part of the Fifth Circuit. Apparently, the judges just didn't want the courts to be interfering with state institutions." The decision alarmed him due to the possibility that the Fifth Circuit might use the same reasoning to undermine settlements reached in *Ruiz v. Estelle,* the prison reform case. At the time, that case had reached a critical stage, with a showdown imminent before a conservative Fifth Circuit panel over a contempt order he had issued in December 1986. As it turned out, the parties were able to reconcile their differences, and the matter was withdrawn from the Fifth Circuit's docket.

The plaintiffs' petition for rehearing by the full Fifth Circuit was denied by a seven-to-seven vote. Writing for the seven dissenters, Circuit Judge Thomas M. Reavley noted that the three-judge panel, not the parties, had separated out the "least restrictive alternative" provision of the agreement as based only on state law. Since the provision was based by consent of the parties on both state *and* federal law, the district court had the authority to enforce it. Reavley pointed out that "The panel disregards the possibility that community placement of some or all of the class members might be required to remedy the Fourteenth Amendment guarantees established in *Youngberg.*"[50] Further, a federal court has the inherent authority to require state officials to adopt far-reaching programs to remedy federal violations. He objected to plaintiffs' being denied their day in court on the federal claims.

Because Circuit Judge Wisdom had taken senior status and therefore was not actively assigned to the Fifth Circuit, he could not vote on the application for rehearing. But he stated that he agreed with the dissenters. Thus, of the fifteen circuit judges including Judge Wisdom, a majority differed with the three-judge panel. But this fact did not alter the outcome. The tie vote meant that the panel's decision would stand.

TDMHMR's position had been vindicated on a technicality by the appeals court action. In his July 1, 1987, letter to TDMHMR employees, "Living under Lawsuits," Commissioner Miller quoted from Circuit Judge Edith Jones' majority opinion and expressed a hope that "the lawsuits may eventually be resolved." Jaylon Fincannon, deputy commissioner for retardation, observes, "We wanted to move people with mental retardation who had been recommended for community placement but not necessarily people from the Fort Worth, Denton, and Austin state schools at the expense of the other individuals who could also benefit from the community program." However, since the Fifth Circuit decision was not handed down until after the sixteen-month deadline in Justice's order, the 279 *Lelsz* class members targeted by the order, along with hundreds of others, were moved without major incident into community facilities. Until late in the decade, the department steadily moved people from the thirteen state institutions into the community. In June 1985 when the order was handed down, there were 9,500 in state institutions. By early 1989, the figure had declined to about 7,200, with the placement of some 2,200 persons in community settings. But with the Fifth Circuit reversal on community placement, the pace slowed considerably, even though community placement is strongly supported by both parents and experts for quality of care and lifestyle.[51] Lack of funding, continued resistance within TDMHMR, and especially the opposition of PART are the primary reasons.

At the time of the announcement of the denial of a rehearing, the circuit judges in the majority did note in a brief *per curiam* decision that "we do not preclude the district court from enforcing the remaining portions of the consent decree if and when violations of those provisions are raised in the district court."[52] Judge Barefoot Sanders lost no time in doing so. On July 21, 1986, expressing exasperation at the state's noncompliance with the terms of the settlement, he upgraded Linda O'Neall's assignment from expert consultant to special master to develop a detailed implementation plan.[53] In August 1987, Sanders found the state in contempt for failure to live up to the 1983 settlement regarding the improvement of conditions in the state schools.[54] In his ninety-three-page opinion, Sanders cited case after case of shocking abuse and inadequate medical care leading to resident injury and death. He cited lack of money as the cause, noting that "By Defendant's own admission, Texas ranks 'fifty-first out of fifty' states in financial commitment to its mentally retarded citizens."[55] To head off ruinous fines, the state two months later reached a settlement.[56] The terms committed the state not only to a dramatic increase in funding, but also to having its institutions meet high accreditation standards set by the Accreditation Council on Developmental Deficiencies.

Justice knew that Judge Sanders would have trouble with the case, just as he had. "I have great sympathy for Judge Sanders. TDMHMR has no will to comply. If you don't have a will to comply, you've got problems." By 1985, Justice had grown tired of state intransigence. "I'm awfully glad he took that case off my hands." As in the statewide school desegregation and prison reform decisions, Justice had experienced strong resistance to change from the Texas Department of Mental Health and Mental Retardation. "Bureaucrats don't want to change things," Justice believes, "because they'll lose their jobs. No one likes to change their way of doing things."

By adding specificity to the portion of the 1983 settlement dealing with community placement, Justice's 1985 order got the department off dead center. Deputy Commissioner Fincannon credits the order with "requiring us at the central office to make the system move." Ferleger agrees. "The Judge's order prompted this amazing explosion of very good things for people with mental retardation." Commissioner Miller, who left the department in March 1988, is less charitable. "Justice's order produced a sense of panic and loss of control. It made people feel that the programs they were developing were not in the best interest of the clients but to meet some arbitrary quota." Miller argues that, given the TDMHMR's stated commitment toward moving to community-based care, Justice's community placement order was both intrusive and unwarranted, and only served to undermine effective administration of the department.

Unless one asserts that both Justice and Sanders were so strongly biased against the department that they simply ignored the evidence presented on its behalf, the years of litigation indicate that the illegalities were real. Conformity to court orders came slowly, the result of a reluctance to change, bureaucratic inertia, and legislative underfunding. Only when fines and imprisonment threatened did politicians and bureaucrats strive to comply. In the meantime, years passed, bad publicity about institutional conditions continued, and hundreds of thousands of dollars were spent in legal fees and associated costs that could have been better spent in complying with court-ordered mandates.[57]

While he may not have found the case as personally rewarding as the other state institutional lawsuits he had adjudicated, Justice did not hesitate to assert the authority of his court when the parties failed to implement their settlement. Ultimately rebuffed, he nevertheless achieved his goal of implementing the community placement portion of the settlement. Political factors, not economic or therapeutic, appear to stand in the way of further de-institutionalization of TDMHMR facilities for mentally retarded persons.

CHAPTER 14

Desegregating Public Housing

With the transfer of *Lelsz v. Kavanagh* to Judge Sanders, Judge Justice had more time to devote to an institutional reform case involving allegations of segregation in public housing. Heretofore, the Judge's major institutional law decisions had involved Texas institutions.[1] *Young v. Pierce* presented him with the opportunity to take on a $15 billion a year federal agency.

The seeds for *Young* were sown modestly enough when Lucille Young, a black mother with six children, and Virginia Wyatt, a black mother with five children, filed applications for public housing in Clarksville, Texas, in 1975 and 1978, respectively. A semirural town of 4,500 persons in the northeast corner of the state, Clarksville is steeped in the traditions of the Old South. A monument "In memory of our Confederate soldiers" stands in the town square. While *de jure* segregation in the community had ended years before, Clarksville public housing had remained rigidly segregated since the Housing Authority of Clarksville (HAC) had come into existence in 1961. Racist attitudes were particularly strong among the elderly.

Young was told that there were no vacancies in the two black housing projects, Cheathem Heights and Dryden. The Cheathem Heights structure was built in 1965, at the same time as the white project, College Heights. Dryden was added in 1972. Half of the fifty-two apartments in the two black projects had been designed for families and offered up to four bedrooms each. Tenants ranged from infants to a ninety-year-old. By contrast, the white project, College Heights, had been designed primarily for the elderly and handicapped, with handrails and ramps for wheelchairs. Only eight of the fifty-two units had more than one bedroom. The average age of the tenants was seventy-seven. The white site had paved streets, concrete curbs, gutters, and sidewalks. The black sites had unpaved streets, no drainage, and no sidewalks. The white and black units were about a mile apart, separated by State Highway 82, the unofficial dividing line between black and white communities in Clarksville.

Young and Wyatt were placed on the waiting list for Cheathem Heights and Dryden. They were not considered for the larger units in the white project when vacancies occurred. The mothers alerted attorneys at East Texas Legal Services, a public interest law group, to their plight. Subsequently, on March 14, 1980, lawyers Elizabeth Julian and Michael M. Daniel filed a complaint in the Paris Division of the Eastern District, charging that Young and Wyatt were not being considered for the few larger units in the white project. Instead, the units were being rented to white applicants who had not been on the waiting list as long as the plaintiffs. Later, the complaint was amended to include a similar complaint by Helen Ruth Jackson against the Housing Authority of Pittsburg, Texas. At the time the lawsuit was filed, Judge Justice was the only federal judge serving the Paris Division.

What was significant about the lawsuit was its inclusion of the U.S. Department of Housing and Urban Development (HUD) as a defendant. Julian and Daniel decided that merely suing the local housing authorities would be ineffective, since the authorities operated under the auspices of HUD and since only the federal agency had the resources to provide relief. "HUD," says Daniel, "clearly was the number one perpetrator." The attorneys sought a class action lawsuit against all 177 public housing projects in the thirty-six-county area of East Texas served by East Texas Legal Services. The class consisted of 5,466 black households residing in HUD-assisted segregated rental housing and nearly 30,000 other households eligible for such housing.

The first order of business was the question of HUD's involvement. HUD operated no public housing in East Texas, but three of its programs indirectly involved the agency in public housing. Under the first program HUD funded a local public housing authority which constructed and operated housing projects. Known as "traditional" low-rent public housing, this was the chief means of providing low-income housing until the mid-1960s. The Clarksville and Pittsburg projects were of this type. From the late 1960s to the mid-1970s, HUD's insured-assisted program subsidized mortgage insurance and interest in order to encourage private entities to construct low-income housing. HUD then provided supplemental rent payments. This second program is known as the "rent supplement" program. After the mid-1970s, HUD's so-called Section 8 new construction program provided assistance to families occupying apartments by making direct rental payments to landlords. All three programs were implicated in the lawsuit. Altogether, HUD had funding and oversight responsibility for some 90 percent of the 3.7 million federally subsidized apartments housing some 10 million people across the country. It was clear at the outset that the case could have major ramifications elsewhere. Consequently, the litigation was being closely watched by public housing officials.

The plaintiffs argued that HUD had knowingly acquiesced in the racially discriminatory housing practices of local housing authorities in East Texas. HUD countered that it was improperly implicated in the lawsuit. Following a hearing on the question, Judge Justice issued a lengthy decision on July 1, 1982, upholding the class action lawsuit against HUD.[2] He ruled that the plaintiffs had a valid cause of action under a section of Title VI of the Civil Rights Act of 1964 providing that "no person in the United States shall, on the ground of race, color, or national origin, be excluded from participation in, denied the benefits of, or be subjected to discrimination under any program or activity receiving federal financial assistance."[3] Justice asserted that both local housing authorities and HUD could be sued under this statute. He wrote, "To the extent a plaintiff asserts that the *federal agency* is violating the terms of the federal statute, by abdicating an affirmative duty to eliminate discrimination, then the action is properly brought against the agency. In such a circumstance, the agency is a partner in discrimination and may be held responsible for this complicity."[4]

He also ruled the lawsuit could be grounded in Title VIII of the Civil Rights Act of 1968, known as the Federal Fair Housing Act, whose provisions established the policy of the United States "to provide, within constitutional limits, for fair housing throughout the United States" and required the Secretary of Housing and Urban Development to administer programs "in a manner affirmatively to further the policies of this title."[5] "The scope of the Civil Rights Act of 1968," he wrote, "is majestic, and its enforcement provisions are commensurately broad."[6] He likewise accepted plaintiffs' contentions that HUD could be sued under the provisions of the venerable Civil Rights Act of 1866, providing that all persons have equal rights to make and enforce contracts and to lease real property,[7] as well as under the Fifth Amendment, which in effect extends the Fourteenth Amendment equal protection clause to apply to the federal government.

HUD argued that each housing program operated under the direction of the local housing authority without any meaningful participation by the federal department. HUD also asserted that the plaintiffs did not have standing to challenge HUD's conduct with respect to the projects in East Texas situated outside the plaintiffs' localities of Clarksville and Pittsburg. Justice rejected the contentions. "These arguments fundamentally miss the point of this civil action," he wrote. "Plaintiffs' claim is that HUD's failure to comply with the terms of its affirmative duties . . . violates their statutory rights. These rights are held in common by all residents of East Texas, regardless of the locality of their residence, and irrespective of the particular practices of the local housing authority."[8] He drew an analogy to the ending of discrimination in education: "The goal of this battle is to eliminate the vestiges of segregation, root and branch, from the system of public education. Of necessity, legal remedies have been aimed at trucklers to discrimination at all levels of the governmental hierarchy."

Justice had no difficulty ascertaining that the action could be maintainable as a class action. But he did sever the civil action against the Clarksville and Pittsburg housing authorities from the case against HUD.

Meanwhile, the three named plaintiffs continued to remain on the waiting list for public housing. A separate lawsuit, *Young v. Whiteman*, was instigated against the Clarksville Housing Authority when Young was about to be forced out of a rent-free home she was occupying, a dilapidated three-bedroom house with no hot water or gas utility service. The ceiling had collapsed in one room. Young could not afford another home, her only source of income being $248 a month from Aid to Families with Dependent Children (AFDC) and $387 in food stamps. Though HUD had confirmed the racist tenant assignment policy of the Housing Authority of Clarksville in 1981 and had negotiated an agreement to end it, the policy continued. No black had ever been offered a unit in the white unit and vice versa. The housing authority claimed that the races did not choose to mix. The lawsuit sought a reassignment of tenants occupying more space than they needed so that Young could be placed in a suitably sized apartment.

A brief hearing was held on October 5, 1983. The attorney for the housing authority, Pat C. Beadle, whom Justice had known "since day one" and with whom he had often argued politics, asserted that Young was not entitled to placement in public housing because she had not completed a valid application form. Her father had completed the form, but she had not signed it when the application was originally made. Plaintiff's attorney Elizabeth Julian argued that the housing authority was hiding behind a formality.

Two days later, Judge Justice issued his decision. He dismissed the defendant's argument regarding Young's eligibility for housing. "[P]laintiff filed this civil action in February 1980, and if defendants previously were unaware of such plaintiff's desire for housing—which does not appear credible to the court—, they were so notified by means of the lawsuit."[9] He attributed Young's not having been assigned an apartment to the housing authority's practice of allowing white tenants to occupy space greater than their need in order to keep blacks out of the white project, a practice known as "over-housing." "But for the purpose of maintaining racially segregated projects and the manipulation of the tenant selection and assignment process to that end, an appropriately sized unit would be available to plaintiff." He ordered that the units be integrated and that Young be assigned a suitably sized apartment. He requested that a mandatory tenant transfer plan be submitted to the court within five days. The plan was to result in a black-white makeup in each of the three housing units within 5 percent of 50 percent, the racial composition of the entire tenant population. All transfers were to be accomplished within twenty days of the court's approval of the plan. The defendants unsuccessfully sought a stay of his order from the Fifth Circuit.

Names were drawn out of a hat, and a list of tenants to be transferred was submitted to the court for Justice's approval. But problems surfaced almost immediately. Lucille Young was assigned a one-bedroom apartment, clearly too small for her six children and herself. Her attorneys filed a contempt motion, and a second short hearing was held on November 25, 1983. Judge Justice pointed out that Young had priority over tenants who had been given housing since the date of her application in 1979. Her needs had to be met. "Now, if that causes inconvenience to some one else, it will just have to be," Justice told the attorneys.[10] Michael Daniel, Young's attorney, told the court that the Housing Authority had each tenant in all three projects sign a sworn affidavit refusing to be transferred to another site contrary to the terms of their rental contracts. Defendants' attorney Pat Beadle asked how the housing authority should proceed when tenants refused to move. Justice's response was succinct: "I will be reluctantly compelled to hold them in contempt of court." He added, "I would hope that that won't be necessary." Three days later, he approved the tenant transfer plan. It was a decision which would focus the attention of the nation on the problem of segregated public housing.

Not feeling well at the time, Judge Justice was irritated by the intransigence of attorney Beadle and the Clarksville Housing Authority. "Looking back on it, if I had been feeling well, I might not have made the mistake of just telling them simply to integrate. I should have anticipated that it would be done clumsily unless I superintended the operation very carefully. I got impatient."

The apartment swap shattered the quiet community of Clarksville. News of elderly people packing up their meager belongings only a few days before Christmas in compliance with the court's sledgehammer blow for integration spilled over into neighboring communities, then across the state and the country. "It was raining the day the moves began," Justice recalls. "It was a really bad day, just ideal fodder for the TV cameras to come up there and show the poor pitiful old people being moved from place to place, and listen to their plaintive cries about how much they didn't want to move, didn't want to live with blacks. It was very, very poorly done. And it was my fault, because I should have foreseen just exactly what happened."

The white tenants forced to move to the black units were uniformly angry and defiant. Addie J. Griffin told a reporter, "Do you really want to know what I think? Dammit. That's what I think. And I used to try to be a Christian, but this hurts too much." [11] Griffin acknowledged that the move was hard on the blacks too. "They've got tears in their eyes just like I have." She and most of the other white residents were finding new homes rather than transfer to the black sites. When asked why he chose not to move to the black project, Frank Dale said, "Don't ask me a thing like that." [12]

The black tenants forced to move to the white project were likewise distressed. Lillie Mae Ricks, her father, husband, and three children were transferred from a four-bedroom apartment in the black complex to a three-bedroom apartment in the white complex. "I don't think they did us fair," she said. "To tell you the truth, I think it's crazy. We had two bathrooms in our old place and now we'll have to share one." The family kept pigs near its former apartment and used a vacant lot to store junked cars for salvage. "Now we have to give all that up," she said. [13]

Editorial comment was generally negative. Even the normally liberal *New York Times* voiced only muted support, noting that unless Washington pursued a more orderly and humane course toward desegregating public housing, more such heavy-handed orders might be handed down "to do it by the numbers." "Disrupting the lives of elderly, infirm people may produce housing integration, but it's hardly the most decent response to the problem. What's needed is an all-out Federal effort to desegregate public housing, using a wide array of carrots and sticks." [14]

Kyle Thompson, editorial page editor of the *Fort Worth Star Telegram,* bitterly attacked Justice, "the notorious dictator of nearly everything to nearly everybody in Texas," and suggested that he ought to be required to leave his "comfortable, middle-class home in Tyler and move into a public housing project on the north side of Clarksville." [15] But columnist Jim Schultze, writing in the *Dallas Times Herald,* offered a different view. He took issue with the often asserted argument that the white and black people of Clarksville had chosen to live separately and the federal government should not be telling them to do differently. "The truth, as anybody who has spent time in the small towns of East Texas knows, is that an appalling degree of segregation continues to exist there. One can argue that East Texas, passed over in a sense by the awakening that shook the Old South in the 1960s, continues to be an unattractive museum of the bad old days." [16] The two blacks on the Clarksville city council maintained that the projects should have been integrated years before. One of them, Mary Ricks, said, "Christian people say they want to go to heaven. But there are not going to be two heavens or two hells. There will be just one. If we're going to be together up there, we'd better learn to get along together down here." [17]

Justice was holding court in Sherman the day the moves began, and the news media quickly sought him out. He refused comment, citing a provision of the Code of Judicial Conduct for U.S. Judges. But this did not stop reporters from trying. Several days later Justice had a speaking engagement in Dallas and at the luncheon was startled to find blinding lights switched on and a microphone thrust into his face. Irritated, he explained that he could not comment on a pending case. Adverse mail once again poured into his Tyler office. He had made the issue of public housing segregation a nationwide concern.

The uproar also produced an unexpected result: Justice became the target of a murder plot. Newspapers revealed that because of the Clarksville decision, a white supremacist group called "The Order" planned to assassinate Justice for holding "anti-white" views. The plot was revealed during testimony in a Seattle trial of ten alleged members of the group on racketeering charges. Denver Parmenter testified that Order leader Robert Matthews kept a file about "leaders in our society who did things considered against the white race." [18] While the Judge made no comment to the press, he was upset by the story. What concerned him the most was that he had learned about the hit list from the newspapers. "When I saw that, I called in the local FBI agent and told him that I was disturbed I hadn't learned from them that I was on this list. He had a blank look, and I reached the conclusion that he hadn't known himself." Justice found that startling, since the government must have known about the hit list prior to the trial and apparently had not relayed the information to the local FBI office. "I made it plain to him that 'if you learn in the future that I'm on a hit list, I want to know about it.'"

Despite community upheaval, integration occurred, though initially most of the white residents opted for private housing. Plaintiff Young moved into a four-bedroom apartment in one of the black units. Plaintiff Wyatt obtained public housing under the Section 8 program. HUD records revealed that by 1988 the three Clarksville units were 33, 48, and 89 percent black. New friendships developed, as residents accepted integration as a way of life. [19] But the experience demonstrated that forced integration of public housing was at best a last resort.

The 1983 Clarksville decision became the focus of immediate attention at HUD central offices in Washington, D.C. The remedial order had required a far more drastic remedy than anything HUD had ever used or even contemplated. HUD feared that Justice might employ the same technique against other East Texas authorities in the larger action against HUD still pending in his court. At the same time, housing officials were aware that HUD standard compliance efforts had failed. A high-level HUD official who was dispatched to East Texas to survey housing conditions confirmed that housing patterns throughout the region were racially segregated and that many housing officials were either ignorant of or insensitive to civil rights requirements.[20] In some cases, housing officials were openly racist.

HUD organized a top-level task force to address discrimination within the region. One of its first actions was to end over-housing and under-housing of tenants to maintain segregation, primarily because HUD had the authority to force tenants to live in appropriately sized units and because the resulting shifts in tenant population would make a start toward desegregation. By the fall of 1985, some integration had taken place among East Texas housing authorities. But in a report prepared for a Congressional subcommittee, HUD officials admitted that "In none of the cases where HUD has found that compliance has been achieved has the housing authority achieved a racial balance comparable to that ordered by the District Court in the Clarksville case. The Department does not believe that removal of the effects of prior discrimination requires that result."[21]

Spurred by the Clarksville incident, the normally staid *Dallas Morning News* launched a nationwide investigation into public housing segregation. Following a fourteen-month visit to forty-seven cities, the *News* reporters documented pervasive discrimination in the nation's sixty thousand federally subsidized developments in an eight-part Pulitzer Prize–winning series in February 1985.[22] In one of the installments, the *News* reporters focused on thirteen East Texas towns. They found not only antipathy toward Judge Justice, but also nearly complete segregation and inferior facilities for blacks.[23] Justice was surprised to come across the series. "When I read those articles, it was as if I was reading something from the *New Republic* or the *Nation*. I couldn't conceive that the *Dallas Morning News* was the newspaper that was publishing all of this. Apparently they were in dead earnest about getting a Pulitzer Prize." The series came as a welcomed assist to the Judge, who once again was on the cutting edge of judicial activism. "That series made my task easier," he acknowledges. "They saturated the East Texas countryside with all the evils of the existing system and how it had to be dismantled in some fashion. Since that series of articles appeared, I have had very little heat from that case. I had anticipated a whole lot."

Meanwhile, the class action lawsuit against HUD was progressing through the discovery stage in preparation for trial. In 1985 both parties submitted motions for summary judgment on the issue of HUD liability. No hearing was required; the court's decision would be based on the mass of materials filed by the parties. Law clerk David Brown was given the task of sorting through the briefs, exhibits, and affidavits, and preparing a draft order for the Judge.

Since HUD had questioned Justice's decision certifying plaintiffs Young, Wyatt, and Jackson as appropriate representatives of a class of public housing applicants and tenants in East Texas, this matter was taken up first. HUD attorneys argued that contrary to a recent U.S. Supreme Court decision, the plaintiffs had been wrongly certified to challenge HUD's actions in all of its distinct housing programs and sites. The Supreme Court decision had partially invalidated so-called across-the-board class actions under Title VII, the federal statute prohibiting employment discrimination.[24] Under the across-the-board approach, an allegation of discrimination against an individual in one area of employment is considered indicative of a general policy of discrimination throughout the enterprise. This is what the Supreme Court decision had undercut. Justice rejected HUD's argument. Not only was employment practice not involved in the litigation, the argument was "largely semantic," since "HUD actually performs one function: it provides housing."[25] He affirmed his earlier decision that the plaintiffs were appropriate representatives for class-certification purposes.

HUD had produced 105 volumes of records from its regional offices in Fort Worth and Dallas, containing documents relating to the local housing authorities in the thirty-six counties implicated in the litigation. Law clerk Brown spent months synthesizing the material. "It was amazing to look at," he says. "Public housing tends to be segregated everywhere. But it was stark in East Texas. I saw a pattern again and again in the data for small towns: there would be two projects on either side of the tracks, one 100 percent white and one 100 percent black." The court had little trouble concluding that HUD's own records showed overwhelming segregation. Of the 219 separate housing sites, the data showed that more than 90 percent were either predominantly minority or predominantly white. Half were completely segregated.

HUD tried to argue that it had learned of the existence of segregation only through the lawsuit and that the segregation existed in spite of vigorous efforts to eradicate it. Plaintiffs countered that HUD not only had known about the segregation but had done little to eliminate it. Following a lengthy historical review, Justice concluded that the plaintiffs were correct. He cited examples from HUD's records illustrating the extent of the agency's awareness of the segregated housing system it had allowed to be established and operated in East Texas. He noted that HUD's typical response was to admonish the housing authority to follow HUD rules. "As long as the proper documents were adopted, and reports filed, HUD approved the [public housing authority's] actions."[26]

It was HUD's own records which were most damning. "The reports were all there staring them in the face," Justice asserts, reflecting on the litigation. "If they weren't aware of the segregation, it was because they willfully chose to ignore it." He found the government attorneys representing HUD accomplished, but apprehensive a good bit of the time. "I think they were in much the same position as a criminal defense lawyer with a guilty client. They couldn't discuss the facts very strongly, because the facts militated against them. So they kind of danced around the issues. I had sympathy for them, because as a lawyer, I've been in that position myself." He adds, "As a judge, I can remember lawyers who would get up on their hind legs and bellow out what they think through the force of their convictions. But there wasn't much these poor attorneys could talk about." He remembered feeling the same way about attorneys from the Texas Office of the Attorney General who were trying to defend the state in *United States v. Texas,* the statewide school desegregation case, though "the HUD attorneys were a lot better than the state's attorneys in that case."

HUD attorneys argued that in order to prevail under the Fifth Amendment cause of action, plaintiffs had to show not only that HUD had supported racial discrimination but that it had done so with discriminatory intent. Justice had no trouble finding it. "HUD's intent to discriminate is established by the combination of HUD's disingenuous assertions of ignorance, its actual knowledge of segregation, and its continuing financial support of each public housing site in the class counties."[27]

HUD maintained that the steps it had taken since the lawsuit was filed in 1980 rendered the controversy moot. Justice was not convinced. Action taken amounted to a review of public housing records and a requirement that housing authorities found in violation of HUD policies sign a voluntary compliance agreement and transfer tenants occupying space beyond their needs to appropriately sized units. As previously noted, this had resulted in the beginning of integration at various East Texas public housing sites. But Justice wanted more. He had had experience in the past with the professed assertions of a desire to do right by state institutional officials. He placed little faith in a similar assertion from the federal agency. "[HUD] alleges only that it has *begun* a process which *may* lead to desegregation. While these efforts may be relevant to the issue of appropriate remedy, it is clear that the effects of past discrimination still burden the plaintiff class. The action is not moot."[28] He upheld plaintiffs' motion that HUD was liable.

The decision shocked HUD and the public housing industry. It was the first time that a federal court had held HUD responsible for multicounty and multiprogram segregation, and the action opened up the possibility of similar lawsuits across the country. Despite their courtroom stance, HUD officials admitted they were having problems desegregating public housing programs. Deborah Dean, executive assistant to HUD Secretary Samuel Pierce, the named defendant in the case, told reporters, "This [desegregation efforts] is something that Secretary Pierce is personally angry about and absolutely committed to. This is a problem that is not just in East Texas, but all across the country."[29] She added, "We're glad somebody did something about it."[30] HUD announced plans to expand its investigation into racially discriminatory housing practices nationwide. Pierce himself was strangely silent. It was only later that the HUD waste and fraud scandals of the Reagan years revealed Dean to be much more than Pierce's executive assistant. She was running the agency.

East Texas housing officials expressed concern about overcoming the racist attitudes of older adults and about finding enough black and white tenants in their communities to integrate projects. They wondered whether Justice might seek to integrate privately owned apartment complexes whose tenants received rent subsidies under HUD's more recent rent subsidy program. Many of these complexes were completely segregated. Avery Friedman, a professor of housing law who specialized in fair-housing lawsuits, predicted a flood of individual civil suits seeking money damages based on Justice's ruling.[31] Robbie Hayes, director of the Texarkana Housing Authority, expressed the sentiments of East Texas public housing operators when she told reporters, "I'm teed off. This thing is going to really make a mess."[32]

Designing an appropriate remedy would be difficult. Plaintiffs' attorney Michael Daniel urged the Judge to establish racial quotas and to "move bodies" as he had in Clarksville.[33] HUD had no intention of supporting forced integration, claiming it was illegal. East Texas housing officials feared that forced integration would drive whites out of subsidized housing—the same "white flight" prevalent during school integration in the 1960s and 1970s. Since its research had confirmed what Justice found in *Young,* the *Dallas Morning News* was not as critical of his ruling as it had been of past decisions. But it too speculated about an appropriate remedy. "Why should federal bureaucrats tell free Americans, of any color whatever, where to live? Why can't they decide for themselves?" it editorialized.[34] The *News* suggested that HUD should try a voucher program whereby poor families receive housing money directly and spend it anyway they wish. (While such a program has much to commend it, the cause of integration would be lost unless the vouchers were conditioned so that they could be expended only on integrated housing.)

In response to plaintiffs' motion for injunctive relief, HUD submitted a proposed remedial plan for Justice's consideration in December 1985. The plan eschewed quotas in favor of voluntary compliance efforts. It described how a number of housing authorities had already moved to a more balanced black-white tenant population and listed actions HUD was prepared to take to help housing authorities and private providers integrate. Plaintiffs' attorney Daniel termed the proposal "woefully inadequate to deal with the massive constitutional violations" Justice had found. "HUD is saying in effect, 'Go out and maintain one-race sites—but with the right attitude.'"[35]

Justice too was concerned about the character of an effective remedy. The furor over the Clarksville integration experience had made him more cautious. "I was determined that there wasn't going to be anything more like what happened at Clarksville. From this point on, we were going to proceed in an orderly fashion, according to a plan, and under the supervision of the court." Given his heavy case load and preoccupation with the prison litigation, he worried about how he could superintend the implementation of a remedial plan. He decided he needed help to manage the case. He found it in the person of Francis E. McGovern, a law professor at the University of Alabama–Birmingham School of Law at Tuscaloosa whom he heard speak while attending a seminar on products liability at Yale. McGovern had practiced law in Houston during the 1970s and had served as special master in a class action asbestos lawsuit before Judge Robert M. Parker in the Marshall Division. He was thus no stranger to East Texas.

In his Yale speech, McGovern explained how product liability cases could be settled through negotiation. During his remarks, McGovern talked about the negotiations he had conducted in other fields. Justice was impressed as he listened to the speech. "I thought to myself, this person might be just the one I am looking for in my housing case." At a recess in the program, he asked McGovern if he would be interested in serving as special master in *Pierce*. McGovern expressed interest. On July 3, 1986, over HUD's objections, Justice entered an order appointing him special master. It was the first time that a federal judge had appointed a special master in a housing desegregation case. McGovern was charged with monitoring HUD's remedial efforts, determining additional ways to facilitate racial desegregation in HUD-assisted housing, and recommending action for the court to take. The costs of the special master were to be borne equally by the plaintiffs and defendants. Justice rejected HUD assertions that the doctrine of sovereign immunity prevented the government from assuming the costs of the special master. "The federal government cannot hide behind the immunity doctrine to avoid spending money for a remedy, no more than it can hide behind the Constitution to perpetuate the race discrimination that it has helped to create," he wrote.[36] Later, when it became apparent that the plaintiffs did not have sufficient funds to contribute, Justice changed the order to make HUD assume all expenses of the special master's office. He had no inhibition about doing so. "After all, they were responsible for making the appointment of the special master necessary."

In his July 3 order appointing McGovern, Justice also reviewed HUD's proposed remedial plan. He had hoped to wait to rule on the question until after the special master had had a chance to review it and advise the court. But HUD refused to desegregate further without a court order. Justice found the proposed remedial plan inadequate. "The freedom of choice plans adopted by local housing authorities after passage of the 1964 Civil Rights Act had no significant impact in desegregating projects. There is no reason to believe that the same policy will generate any more success twenty years later."[37] He entered a generally worded interim order enjoining HUD from committing further constitutional violations and directing it to "begin immediately to dismantle the system of racial segregation that exists in publicly funded housing in East Texas."[38]

Justice was neither surprised when HUD appealed to the Fifth Circuit, nor worried about a major reversal. "The facts were so stark that I didn't see how they could reverse me." Apparently, HUD officials came to the same realization, for in their appeal they did not contest liability with regard to oversight of the low-rent public housing programs administered by public housing authorities such as those in Clarksville and Pittsburg. HUD did challenge Justice's inclusion within the class action of the rent supplement and Section 8 programs involving mostly private housing providers. The Fifth Circuit did not have to rule on the issue, for plaintiffs' attorneys, having learned that two of the three judges on the appellate panel had been appointed by President Reagan, decided to seek a settlement.[39] On April 6, 1987, two days before oral argument, the parties resolved most of the contested issues.

By the terms of the settlement, the lawsuit was limited to traditional low-rent public housing owned by public housing authorities. At the same time, the agreement contained a provision stating that it did not "foreclose any argument opposing or supporting use of other HUD-assisted housing as a remedy" for public housing violations.[40] Plaintiffs' attorneys were sure that if they were able to make the argument, Judge Justice would accept it. In light of the settlement, the three-judge court sent both Justice's general interim injunction against continued racial segregation and his order appointing the special master back to him for revision.[41]

On remand, Justice noted in a March 1988 decision that the settlement "sharpen[ed] the description of the persons injured by HUD's purposeful conduct" by limiting the class to those involved in HUD's traditional subsidized housing owned by public housing authorities. But he added that "it does not limit the court's equitable powers to fashion relief that is reasonably tailored to remedy their injuries."[42] This meant that the rent supplement and Section 8 programs involving private housing providers could still be encompassed within the desegregation plan. "As a matter of law, HUD has both the power and the duty to prevent segregation in the operation of all three of the programs mentioned, not just the 'traditional' program." He found HUD's efforts to date unsatisfactory. He noted that resegregation had occurred in five public housing sites since the liability finding in 1985. In addition, four new sites and forty-six existing sites were either predominantly or completely one-race.

Accordingly, he issued an interim remedial order requiring that HUD implement an affirmative action tenant assignment plan for all the traditional low-rent projects.[43] The order incorporated proposals submitted by the plaintiffs, as well as the earlier HUD proposals advanced in December 1985. Its provisions required HUD to end segregatory practices in the thirty-six-county region covered by the lawsuit and directed all public housing authorities operating low-rent housing to adopt an affirmative action tenant selection plan. The plan specified that the pool of vacancies from which each applicant was to be assigned a unit had to encompass all the units operated by the public housing authority. The applicant at the top of the waiting list was to be offered a unit in a project site where the applicant's race was less than 75 percent of the applicant pool. If the assignment was refused, the applicant's name was placed at the bottom of the waiting list. The applicant would then not be offered another unit until either every other applicant eligible for the same size unit with the same or earlier application date had been offered an appropriate unit or six months had elapsed from the rejection of the offer, whichever was longer. The plan also gave class members the opportunity to transfer between housing programs operated by public housing authorities if such transfers would further desegregation.

Other provisions of the plan ended "over- and under-housing," required public housing authorities to submit racial occupancy data to HUD, and required the department to attempt to develop public housing so that the class members could be offered a desegregated housing opportunity.

To curtail "white flight" from the low-rent public projects to the two other HUD programs involving private housing providers, Justice specified what affirmative action activities they were to undertake.[44] At the same time, he was careful not to include forced integration components as he had in the Clarksville incident. "Affirmative placement into formerly black projects should not be allowed to work a hardship on white applicants. Moreover, voluntary integrative transfers should be encouraged by improving the quality of less desirable projects," he wrote in the companion memorandum opinion.[45] As it was, many housing officials predicted that all-white units would become all-black overnight, as whites left for alternative housing. Such predictions seem not to have been borne out.

With regard to the powers of the special master, Justice relied upon his experience with the special master in *Ruiz v. Estelle*, the prison reform case discussed in Chapter 15. He saw no conflict in McGovern's having the power both to investigate HUD's activities and to monitor the department's compliance with the new interim order. "The master is given investigative and monitoring responsibilities in the hope that the parties, together with the court acting through the master, can develop a final workable plan that will eliminate the widespread discrimination that has been found."[46] He did exempt from the master's powers the authority to collect information and view privileged HUD documents.

In his closing paragraphs, Justice recognized the complexity of desegregating public housing on a voluntary basis. The court, he acknowledged, "is dealing in the abstract, at least to some degree." He looked to the creative abilities of the parties and the special master to tailor the court's remedial requirements to the realities of public housing. It was clear from the order that forced integration as a remedy had retreated. Instead, the focus was on assisting both the victims of past segregation in East Texas and future minority applicants to secure an integrated housing opportunity without disrupting the lives of public housing residents.

Justice regrets that he was not able to devote more time to the case, especially in the early stages. "I had to relegate it to the sidelines because I've been preoccupied with other cases. I've given *Pierce* minimal attention compared with some of the others." Consequently, he had high expectations for the special master and was pleased when McGovern lived up to them. "McGovern's done miracles. I would not have dreamed that he would have been able to accomplish as much as he has. I can't praise him too highly." After his appointment, the amount of time the lawsuit demanded of the court dropped off dramatically, as McGovern sought to implement the remedial order and prepare the parties for close-out. His task has not been easy, for racist attitudes in many East Texas communities run deep.

The unfolding HUD scandal toward the end of the decade proved to be an unexpected source of assistance. Faced with a steady stream of negative publicity about influence-peddling by intimates of the Reagan administration, HUD officials, including Secretary of Housing Jack Kemp, were eager to cooperate with Special Master McGovern. An integrated public housing program in East Texas could serve as a model for other rural areas of the country. It could also improve the image of HUD as a progressive, client-oriented public agency. Thus, renewed efforts were made to work out a satisfactory integration plan to present to Judge Justice.

Even if it takes further action by Justice, public housing will eventually be substantially integrated in the thirty-six-county area involved in the lawsuit. Public housing authorities remember Clarksville and know that Justice will not hesitate to intervene if his order is not fulfilled. Daniel notes that places in East Texas where he was sure integration "would be a fight to the death" were not so "because they were afraid of the Judge and what he might do." [47] How much carryover from the *Pierce* ruling there will be to other parts of the state and the rest of the country is more questionable. This is particularly true of public housing in urban areas where the heavy concentration of minorities blurs the distinction between *de jure* and *de facto* segregation.

Judge Justice's *Young v. Whiteman* order briefly focused the attention of the nation on the problem of segregated housing and the difficulty of finding an appropriate remedy. His *Young v. Pierce* decision forced HUD to deal with the problem. The long-term significance of the latter decision depends on HUD's continuing commitment to integration, the effectiveness of the remedies outlined, and the willingness of an increasingly conservative federal judiciary to follow the precedent. Just as with school integration, the diminished commitment to affirmative action in American society makes housing desegregation increasingly more difficult to accomplish.

CHAPTER 15

Prison Reform

On the eve of the first day of trial in *Ruiz v. Estelle* on October 2, 1978, one of every ten prisoners in the nation was confined in a Texas prison. The Texas approach to law and order had resulted in the largest and, from some viewpoints, one of the best prison systems in the country.[1] Organized along strict paramilitary lines, the Texas Department of Corrections (TDC) had experienced little of the violence seen in the prisons of other states. Rates of homicide, suicide, rioting, and officially recorded assaults were low as compared with other prison systems. Escapes were rare. Prison gangs were unknown. In most states a person was safer on the streets than in prison. In Texas the reverse seemed true.[2] TDC was also efficient. The staff-to-inmate ratio was the lowest in the country. The prisoners produced most of their own food and marketed a significant quantity of prison-made goods. For most of the two preceding decades, TDC had enjoyed the lowest per-prisoner costs in the nation. In short, TDC appeared to be a model prison system.

But below the surface, decay was evident. Litigation filed by inmates in the late 1960s and the early 1970s alleged a pattern of abuse by correctional officers and inmates. Beginning in 1972 as one of the early prisoners' rights disputes, *Ruiz* quickly developed into the most comprehensive prison reform case in legal history. Judge Justice's 1980 memorandum opinion and the remedial order that followed had a profound impact on TDC operations and the underlying correctional philosophy. His decision also provoked an unprecedented counterattack by the state. As in earlier decisions, Justice was accused of abusing his judicial powers.

It was not until late in 1987 that the details of the case were made public, vindicating the plaintiffs and the court. In a book about TDC operations during this period, former TDC general counsel Steve J. Martin and University of Texas sociology professor Sheldon Ekland-Olson describe how TDC's resistance to change, coupled with lack of external accountability, enabled the agency to conceal shocking prisoner abuse.[3] After months of "outright defiance" of Justice's orders and "openly hostile rhetoric" intended to denigrate the Judge, TDC conceded that it had routinely abused prisoners through the use of inmate-guards known as building tenders.[4] That admission, coupled with a series of other revelations, the authors conclude, destroyed TDC's credibility.

This chapter adds another dimension to the *Ruiz* story by looking at this seminal case from the standpoint of the judge presiding over it.

Origins of
Ruiz v. Estelle

As the son of one of the most prominent criminal defense attorneys in East Texas and later as a practicing attorney himself, William Wayne Justice had been around jails and prisons most of his life. Before ascending the bench, he had no particular views about prisoners' rights. "I took it as a matter of course that prisoners would possibly be oppressed. But I really wasn't particularly concerned about it."

What triggered his initial interest was the growing number of petitions prisoners filed in his court alleging violations of inmate civil rights based on prison conditions and treatment. At the time, two of the TDC's prisons were located within the Eastern District of Texas: the Coffield Unit in Tennessee Colony and the Eastham Unit in Lovelady. For the claims from these units which might have some merit, the regular hearing process did not yield a fair result in Judge Justice's view. Prisoners would appear, take the oath, and tell their stories. In a halting and inarticulate fashion, they would explain the nature of their complaints. Then a Texas assistant attorney general would cross-examine them and present witnesses to refute their assertions. The prisoners were so unversed in legal procedure that they could not summon witnesses in their own behalf, effectively cross-examine witnesses against them, or otherwise present their cases.

After several of these hearings, Justice's concern began to mount. "I wasn't satisfied because what the prisoners were saying about getting beaten up and about inferior medical care and that kind of thing had the ring of truth about it, even though these persons are supposed to be, by their nature, very untruthful. Besides that, it was all so one-sided. It was disturbing to me that all of the power lay on one side and all of the weakness on the other. I regarded it as a breakdown of the adversary system." At first, he attempted to cross-examine the state's witnesses from the bench. But lack of knowledge of the circumstances and charges of bias from the state made this strategy less than fruitful.

What did result was a massive influx of prisoner petitions, as word about his interest in prison conditions spread.

Justice's concern about the plight of TDC inmates prompted him to prepare a speech to be delivered at a Practicing Law Institute seminar on prisoners' rights at Southern Methodist University in Dallas in 1972. At the end of a detailed discussion on the evolution of prisoners' rights, Justice concluded with this revealing, if provocative, statement:

> Should prisons not aim to protect the public and to deter and rehabilitate the criminal without abandoning the civilized ideal that we treat our fellow men, even those who have deviated from society's norm, with some dignity and compassion? Much of the literature of other disciplines . . . indicates that prisons should give way to other alternatives. Ideally, of course, these other disciplines are better suited to tackling this fundamental issue. Yet the federal judiciary convenes to decide the hard cases as well as the routine; we would do less than our constitutional duty were we to refrain from a task that . . . nevertheless demands our attention.[5]

This speech served notice that Justice believed in basic rights for prisoners, and that courts should be willing to deal with the problem.

At the seminar, Justice heard a speech on prisoners' rights by William Bennett Turner, a San Francisco lawyer for the NAACP Legal Defense and Education Fund. The presentation made an impact on Justice, who observes, "After hearing Turner, I decided that I'd have a little test case to see what a first-class lawyer could do with the state's contentions and what he could develop in favor of the inmates, because I wanted to find out if there was any substance to what they [the prisoners] were saying." A native of Fort Worth and a graduate of Harvard Law School, Turner had established a reputation as one of the nation's preeminent prisoners' rights lawyers and had already been involved in litigation involving the TDC.[6]

Some time later, Justice had his two law clerks review the hundreds of prisoner petitions and categorize them by type of complaint. Four major categories of alleged abuses were discovered: brutality by staff and other inmates, inadequate medical care, lack of due process, and overcrowding. "I told them to find me a typical letter for each of the complaints," Justice recalls. "One of them was a complaint from David Ruiz. That's how he and the others became the original named plaintiffs. I consolidated their cases for trial, one with all of these various representative plaintiffs. It wasn't a class action, just a consolidated trial. I wanted to hear something about the quality of medical care, the overcrowding, the lack of due process, and the staff brutality. I wanted to hear about the building tenders, which was something new to me." The consolidation effort also served the interest of judicial economy, for the Judge would be able to address a number of matters in one case without having to hear each one separately.

David Ruiz was serving a twenty-five-year term for armed robbery when he filed his suit on June 29, 1972. Ruiz was one of the early activist "jailhouse lawyers" or "writ-writers" who would do much to challenge abuses in the Texas Department of Corrections. He alleged in his hand-printed fifteen-page petition that he was being confined under unconstitutional conditions at the maximum-security Eastham Unit. In his rambling account, he alleged, among other things, harassment by TDC officials and staff for his legal activities, inadequate medical care, and unlawful solitary confinement. He told of repeated self-mutilation in an effort to escape the conditions of his confinement.

Judge Justice consolidated Ruiz's petition with seven others on April 12, 1974. It was the first of several steps occurring in rapid-fire order which would convert the suit into a major prison reform case. While federal law at that time did not allow Justice to order counsel to represent plaintiffs, it did allow him to request an attorney to do so, and if the attorney agreed, to issue an order to this effect. Justice sought out William Bennett Turner to represent the petitioners. Turner, who was on a mountain-climbing holiday in Katmandu, Nepal, sent word that he would be interested in the case and would contact the Judge upon his return. In the interim, Turner's associate, Stanley Bass, would handle the litigation. Justice was pleased that Turner and the NAACP Legal Defense Fund would take on the task of representing the plaintiffs because the Judge had been unable to interest local attorneys in handling prisoner cases in the past. "Bass and Turner wouldn't be like the attorneys around here worrying about time away from the office and all those missed fees," he says. Tall, dark, and good looking, Turner had a quiet, determined manner that radiated competency. The prisoners now had a courtroom advocate who was among the best in the business.

Though Turner's expenses would be paid by the Legal Defense Fund, he did not have the resources to conduct a thorough investigation of TDC conditions. Judge Justice had anticipated this problem, and when the petitions were consolidated, he ordered the U.S. Department of Justice to appear as *amicus curiae* and issued instructions commanding the department "to investigate fully the facts alleged in the prisoners' complaints, to participate in such civil action with the full rights of a party thereto, and to advise this court at all stages of the proceedings as to any action deemed appropriate."[7] Justice Department officials, then involved in a racial discrimination suit involving the TDC, were aware of problems within the prison system.[8] Gail Littlefield, who served as co-counsel for the Justice Department in *Ruiz*, was pleased when ordered into the litigation. "It was very frustrating to be hearing a number of complaints from inmates about serious issues which seemed to have a real basis and not be in a forum where we could do anything about them."

In taking this step, Judge Justice drew upon the experiences of Federal Judge Frank M. Johnson. "I had been talking over the period of several years with my friend Frank Johnson, who handled a prison case over there in Alabama. He told me that he had requested the United States to act as *amicus curiae* in his case, to investigate the complaints of the prisoners and present evidence if it wanted to. I asked him for a copy of his order. I wrote a letter asking if the United States would be willing to participate as an *amicus,* and they said they would. I entered an order requesting them to do so for the record. The Department of Justice began sending the FBI into these prison units. They apparently were fascinated by what they found."

Indeed they were. Six months later the Justice Department filed a motion to intervene as a full-fledged plaintiff in the case and to add as defendants the Texas Board of Corrections. The Justice Department also sought to broaden the claims against the TDC beyond those made by the individual petitioners. Judge Justice held a hearing and allowed the Justice Department to enter the suit, bringing the full weight of its investigators and attorneys to bear on the side of the prisoners. He knew from his experience as U.S. attorney that federal investigators would be particularly thorough. He also granted the plaintiffs' motion to convert the case into a class action lawsuit. This meant that the prisoner-plaintiffs were now suing on behalf of all fifteen thousand prisoners confined in the TDC. Their claims for monetary damages, which would have required a jury trial, were severed from the case, allowing the remaining lawsuit to be heard before Judge Justice without a jury. Thus, Justice had placed himself in a position to make major changes in TDC operations if he deemed them warranted.

TDC officials and the Texas Office of the Attorney General, which represents the Texas Department of Corrections in litigation, objected strenuously to all of these developments. On January 17, 1975, TDC Director W. J. Estelle, Jr., ordered unit wardens to prohibit interviews of prison employees by Justice Department officials on grounds that they would jeopardize the security of inmates, personnel, and prison facilities. Two weeks later officials in the Texas attorney general's office filed a motion to remove the Justice Department from the case. Judge Justice denied the motion.

The state then petitioned the U.S. Court of Appeals for the Fifth Circuit for an order reversing Justice's decision, alleging that he had abused his judicial discretion and that involving the Justice Department would result in burdensome and expensive pretrial preparation. The maneuver, one of dozens in a pattern of resistance by the state during the *Ruiz* suit, was unsuccessful.[9] The

U.S. Supreme Court refused to hear the issue, though three justices dissented—one short of the four necessary to grant a hearing. Speaking for the three, Justice William H. Rehnquist asserted in a particularly pointed dissent that Judge Justice had gone too far in the absence of clear authority in allowing the Justice Department to intervene against the state, thus raising serious questions regarding federal-state relations.[10]

Unquestionably, in his effort to learn more about prison conditions, Justice had actively used his judicial powers to establish the potential for a major institutional lawsuit. Conservative jurists would have been reluctant to use their judicial powers in this fashion, particularly since only two of the TDC prisons are located in East Texas. Justice hesitated only briefly. "I considered that fact," he acknowledges, "but I felt that I was justified in granting the class action status because apparently the same problems were endemic to the whole system." In a presentation on March 21, 1990, at the Stanford University School of Law, Justice justified his actions as necessary to assure that the prisoners could have their day in court. "The right to be heard, whether one's conditions be exalted or lowly, is one which it is the duty of courts to vindicate," he told the students. "It was to vindicate that right, and to get at the truth about conditions of some of the lowliest offscourings of our society, that I helped bring *Ruiz v. Estelle* to birth."[11]

While Justice had established the potential for a major case, whether or not it would become one was up to the plaintiff and plaintiff-intervenor lawyers. Turner and the Justice Department attorneys were experienced; it did not take them long to see the potential significance of the case. If they could marshal facts that showed a constitutional violation, Justice's 1972 speech on prisoner rights indicated that he was ready to take action.

Prison Management in Texas

From 1962 to the beginning of the *Ruiz* litigation, the Texas Department of Corrections was under the administration of Dr. George Beto, an ordained Lutheran minister and former president of two small religious colleges, one in Illinois and one in Texas. Tall and powerfully built, Beto had the look and self-assurance of a leader. Before becoming TDC director, he had served on the Illinois Board of Parole and also on the TDC Board of Corrections. During the Beto administration, the TDC became an exemplar of the so-called "control" model of corrections, a rigidly authoritarian approach to prison administration introduced by Beto's predecessor, O. B. Ellis. Beto's blunt, no-nonsense style appealed to the TDC staff and to hard-nosed Texas politicians. He quickly assumed control of TDC and sought to expand and refine the system instituted by Ellis. During these years, TDC was small enough to accommodate Beto's hands-on management style. He became known as "Walking George" for his frequent tours throughout the prison system.

Under the control model, TDC ran most units as maximum-security institutions. The correctional philosophy behind this highly regimented and structured prison system was to provide an orderly environment in which prisoners could be forced to act in socially acceptable ways. Beto believed that a prison environment emphasizing work, discipline, and education, in that order, will be most conducive to changing prisoner behavior. Interviewed in his office at Sam Houston State University in 1988, Beto talked openly about his approach to prison management. "Most of these people have no record of sustained employment. I think they ought to work an eight-hour day. The working day should approximate that of the free world in the areas of quality control and quantity of production. Secondly, the prison should provide a disciplined environment in the hope that you may habituate prisoners to taking a bath every day, eating good food instead of junk food, saying 'yes, sir,' and 'no, sir,' to dress appropriately—if they're going out to get a job, they're not going to walk in dressed like a clown and be disrespectful to their prospective employer. The third item is education. It can be empirically proven that you can provide much more education in a much shorter time in prison than you can outside the prison. You don't have any truancy. You don't have any discipline problems. If the survival of a democratic society is dependent on an informed electorate, the state has a compelling interest to educate prisoners."

In accord with these views, Beto expanded prison industrial and agricultural programs and organized the Windham School to provide basic literacy and vocational training to inmates who had not completed high school. He continued the practice, long part of Texas prisons, of using specially selected inmates called building tenders as janitors and informers. With the advent of serious overcrowding in the early 1970s, the building tenders also played a much more important, and highly irregular, role. As one recent study of the TDC notes, the TDC building tender system came to represent "perhaps the most extensive and institutionalized system of inmate guards in American corrections." [12] Beto considers this characterization as "hyperbole at best" and, in any case, untrue during his tenure as director, which ended with his retirement in 1972. But evidence would later show that much of the hands-on control in the prisons was exercised by building tenders, some of whom were kind, others cruel and sadistic. Not only did the building tender system provide the means of maintaining control over a rapidly expanding prison population at low cost, it also kept would-be gang leaders on the side of the prison staff—but at a high price, as subsequent events were to reveal.

Under the control model, prisoners were never allowed to forget their crimes. The model was based on the assumption that prisoners are inferiors without the usual rights of citizens. Beto, for example, never shook the hand of a prisoner because a prisoner was not to be regarded as an equal in any sense. When the prisoner was released, Beto would offer his hand. As one commentator notes, under the control model, "the prisons were to be run as benevolent, paternalistic despotisms in the interests of orderly, humane, and just treatment of convicted criminals." [13] Although this was the ideal, in reality, the absence of external accountability and internal controls allowed tyrants in the system to operate just as freely as any benevolent dictator. Indeed, trial testimony was to reveal that some TDC wardens maintained control through unnecessarily brutal force.

Beto's hand-picked successor, W. J. Estelle, Jr., who took office in 1972, sought to continue the Beto management system with the same ostensibly impressive results in terms of inmate control and prison efficiency. TDC officials liked to boast that the system was one of the best in the nation.

Any institution that asserts total control over those confined within it is likely to be highly resistant to challenge and to change. So it was with the TDC. Prisoners' rights litigation was not new to the TDC when David Ruiz filed his petition in Justice's court in 1972. The TDC had experienced an increase in such litigation since the U.S. Supreme Court had ruled in 1964 that prisoners could challenge the conditions of their confinement in federal court. [14] At first, prisoner complaints were dismissed as the whinings of lying convicts, and the protests of a few "do-gooder" prison reformers were ignored. In the face of a growing number of challenges, an effort was made within the TDC to suppress the "jailhouse lawyers." These inmates sought either their release through filing writs of habeas corpus challenging the legality of their confinement (hence the term "writ-writers") or relief from allegedly unconstitutional conditions of confinement. Prisoners like Ruiz who brought suit against prison officials were isolated from the general prison population, harassed by prison officials, and disciplined by building tenders. The retaliation only stimulated their efforts. Litigation quickly became a way of life in the TDC. [15]

At the same time that prisoners began challenging the conditions of their confinement in court, members of the Texas Legislature became more interested in the internal affairs of the TDC. In 1973 the legislature passed a resolution introduced by State Senator A. R. "Babe" Schwartz establishing the Joint Committee on Prison Reform, made up of a House-Senate joint committee and a citizens' advisory committee. In December 1974 the committee published a report harshly critical of state criminal justice practices and made hundreds of recommendations covering every facet of prison life. The report observed that "the criminal justice system creaks along attempting to solve complex problems with archaic structures, conflicting philosophies, fragmented organization and insufficient resources. The wonder is not that it functions so badly, but that it functions at all."[16] While little in the report was acted upon at the time, virtually all of the recommendations resurfaced in the *Ruiz* suit and in the remedial orders that followed it.

Crowding began to plague the TDC shortly after Estelle took over in 1972. Prison population grew from 15,000 when the case was filed in 1972 to 25,000 when trial began in 1978. It was growing much more rapidly than state population, which increased by 19 percent between 1968 and 1978, while the prison population more than doubled in the same years.[17] The rapid growth reflected a get-tough-with-crime attitude in the state. By the mid-1970s Texas was sending felons to prison at a rate of 143.7 per 100,000 population, compared to the national rate of 86.9. Moreover, the time inmates spent in prison was increasing. In 1973 the average maximum sentence was eight years and five months. By 1979 it had risen to ten years and seven months. Reflecting Texas' tough sentencing and conservative parole practices, the average time actually served increased from one year and four months to two years and five months.[18] Since there was little increase in appropriations for prisons, conditions worsened. Increasingly, TDC was forced to house two, three, and sometimes more inmates in cells built for one.

During Beto's administration, he and the Board of Corrections worked to defeat legislation promoted by local law enforcement groups to ship more convicted persons off to the TDC. "I tried to keep the population down by keeping legislation from being passed that would enhance penalties and keep them in prison longer," he maintains.[19] However, after Beto left the directorship in 1972, these proposals were enacted. As a result of the policy of sending most lawbreakers to state prison, the majority of Texas prisoners were and continue to be nonviolent offenders. Other prison models recommend housing nonviolent offenders in local jails or processing them through less expensive community-based probation programs.

Overcrowding has a devastating effect on prisons. The classification system which assigns prisoners to appropriate facilities and programs breaks down. First-time offenders are mixed in with hardened criminals. Programs tailored to the needs of a segment of the prison population are overrun by those whose needs are different. All parts of the prison—cells, dormitories, recreational areas—become significantly harder to control. Staffing shortages develop. Prisoners are unable to engage in industrial and agricultural activities because there is no one to supervise them. Instead, they learn how to survive in an increasingly lawless and violent world. They learn how to become more effective criminals. All of these undesirable effects of overcrowding multiplied in the Texas prison system during the pendency of the *Ruiz* litigation.

Under Estelle, who declined to be interviewed for this book, the celebrated control model so carefully nurtured by George Beto began to break down, mostly because of the pressure of numbers. TDC officials remained reactive and defensive in the face of lawsuits, overcrowding, and calls for change. This bunker mentality only exacerbated tension and conflict.

The Trial of
Ruiz v. Estelle

When the case began to take on major significance, the TDC, which was to concede that overcrowding was not desirable but never conceded it was a constitutional violation, dug in for battle. Justice recalls the arduous process of moving the case toward trial. "About like an iceberg moving, the parties started their discovery efforts. It went on for several years. The state was dragging its heels. You just couldn't move the state. Everything had to be done by court order."

Ed Idar, Jr., the Mexican-American attorney who early on inherited the case from other attorneys in the Texas Office of the Attorney General, denies that the state was being obstructionist. Though he played a steadily diminishing role in the case after the trial ended in 1979 and had retired from state service when interviewed in his Austin home in 1988, the memory of *Ruiz* remained vivid in Idar's mind. It was apparent that he believed a great wrong had been perpetrated in Justice's courtroom. His eyes flashed with anger as he accused the Judge of unremitting bias toward the plaintiffs and hostility toward the TDC. He said that he had concluded from the start that the state could not win in Justice's court. He had not forgotten that the Judge had called him in 1972 when Idar was an attorney with the Mexican-American Legal Defense and Education Fund (MALDEF) and asked the fund to intervene as a plaintiff against the state in the school desegregation case, *United States v. Texas*. Idar was fully confident that "the Judge was going to do to the TDC what he had done to the Texas Youth Council in *Morales v. Turman*." Thus the state from the beginning had to prepare for an appeal to the Fifth Circuit and possibly the U.S. Supreme Court. "What we needed to do every step of the way was to protect our record the best way we possibly could," he maintains.

Early on, concern arose over the welfare of the prisoners who had brought the lawsuit. Justice issued five orders protecting Ruiz and his co-plaintiffs while their allegations were being investigated. The Fifth Circuit, denying a TDC appeal seeking relief from one of these orders, noted in a brief *per curiam* opinion in April 1977 that there was evidence that Ruiz and the others had been subjected to "threats, intimidation, coercion, punishment, and discrimination, all in the face of protective orders to the contrary by the district court and our long-standing rule that the right of a prisoner to have access to the courts to complain of conditions of his confinement shall not be abridged." [20] Idar attributes the failure of the appeal to the inexperience and heavy case load of the young assistant attorney general assigned the case.

After several years of delays triggered by procedural matters, Justice drew the line. "Finally, I said, 'Halt. This is enough.' I set the case down for trial." Trial began on October 2, 1978, six years after the case was filed, in Houston. TDC lawyers had requested that the case be shifted there because a large number of inmate witnesses were to be called and Houston's jail facilities were larger than those in Tyler. The TDC lawyers also hoped to replace Judge Justice with a more sympathetic jurist in the Southern District. To the state's surprise, Justice granted the state's motion.

But any solace the state and TDC felt was short-lived. "It was true that we weren't going to be able to house prisoners here in Tyler," Justice observes. "It was a logistical impossibility. I thought about having the prisoner witnesses transferred to the Coffield Unit and placed under some kind of restrictions there that would protect them. But the more I thought about it, the less I believed that they would receive any protection. So I finally decided I'd just transfer the case down to Houston. I got hold of Reynaldo Garza, who was the chief judge down there at the time. I knew Garza quite well. I told him I was getting ready to transfer the case but that I couldn't in good conscience transfer a case of this magnitude without making an offer to follow it. I told him that if he felt any injustice would be done to his judges, I was perfectly willing to follow the case and try it. He accepted my offer with great joy. When I transferred the case, he assigned it to me."

Attorneys for the state were anything but pleased. "They thought, apparently, that they were going to get rid of me as the judge," Justice says with a smile. The state protested Garza's action and asked for a hearing on Justice's impartiality. Garza rejected the state's motion with the pointed observation that he did not need to be lectured by the Texas attorney general's office on what his power, duties, and responsibilities as chief judge were.

The trial occupied 159 often-acrimonious days over the next twelve months, during which the courtroom was filled with attorneys. As with the *Morales v. Turman* litigation, Judge Justice found the case difficult to try. The relationship between the Judge and Idar, who headed the state's legal team, quickly degenerated. "I kind of liked Ed up until then," Justice says, "but at that trial he was utterly intransigent. He sought to delay the trial in every way that it was possible to do. He was damned-near contemptuous throughout the trial, and very frequently accused me of acting unfairly." The Judge was unhappy, Idar believes, "because we were giving him so much trouble. I think he had expected us just to fold over as they did in the *Morales* case."

Idar's lengthy cross-examinations particularly bothered the Judge. "His idea of cross-examination was to ask the witness about every single thing that he had testified to on direct examination. Well, all that does is to reinforce the testimony of what the witness testified to in the first instance." Other than prolonging the trial, Justice could not fathom the strategy in this approach. William Bennett Turner believes Idar's questioning style was self-defeating. "Our case got better the more the state brought out. We learned things on cross-examination that even we didn't know."

Idar maintains that lengthy cross-examination of many witnesses was necessary because state attorneys had not been given adequate time to prepare for trial. Richel Rivers, Idar's co-counsel, believes Justice's propensity to allow all testimony into the record, even that which was hearsay, prolonged the trial. The Judge acknowledges that "there is some merit to her comments." But he adds, "I was trying to get away from the idea that I was being arbitrary. I have always been taught from my earliest days on the bench that in a non-jury case you don't necessarily rule on the admissibility of the testimony. You go ahead and let it in because there's a presumption that the judge is going to disregard anything that is inadmissible." He adds, "What amazed me was the fact that the state left most of the prisoners' testimony unchallenged." A Fifth Circuit judge, who requested anonymity, is critical of Justice's passive stance with regard to admissibility of evidence. "If another judge had presided in that case, the length of the trial would likely have been a fraction of what it was."

The work of Justice Department investigators paid off in a comprehensive and highly detailed presentation of evidence by the federal government. For example, to demonstrate the abuses of overcrowding, the Justice Department placed a full-scale model of a 5-by-9-foot cell in the courtroom. Most of the TDC cells were of this size. Then five volunteers (including Justice's law clerk Lucas Guttentag) were sandwiched into the forty-five square feet to illustrate TDC's crowding practices. Justice Department attorneys found that, unlike their experience in other prison cases, they had no difficulty getting former TDC inmates to come to Houston from all over the country to give testimony. All but one of the forty ex-convicts subpoenaed appeared at the trial. The one exception called to explain why he could not do so. It was evident that the former inmates had a story they wanted to tell.

On December 1, 1978, two months after the trial had started, proceedings were halted for three months while the state went to the Fifth Circuit over Justice's decision to transfer the case back to Tyler after most of the prisoner witnesses had testified. "I had been using Judge Woodrow Seals' courtroom, which he'd very kindly set aside for me. I felt very badly that I was keeping him out of his courtroom. So, I just decided that since we didn't have adequate courtroom facilities in Houston, I would transfer the case back up to Tyler, using my courtroom, but letting it continue as a Southern District case." The Fifth Circuit reversed this ruling, sending the case back to Houston. The remainder of the trial was conducted in the courtroom otherwise used by the Fifth Circuit on the few occasions it sits in Houston.

During the many months he spent in Houston, Justice resided at the Holiday Inn at Memorial Plaza. "I'd start off on Monday morning and recess at about 3:30 in the afternoon on Friday, so that all of us could go home," he said. "Traffic was a nightmare. Most of the time I'd come home on weekends." The courtroom trial was exceedingly stressful for the Judge and his staff, particularly his courtroom reporter, Dorothy Daugherty, who dutifully transcribed the lengthy trial. To unwind, he regularly lifted weights and jogged five miles daily in a park across from the Holiday Inn. While the Judge was trying the *Ruiz* case, his regular docket was at a standstill, so that he faced a huge backlog of cases when the trial finally ended. Several years later, in a speech to the John F. Kennedy School of Government at Harvard University on August 7, 1980, he observed that "I would as soon have a live rattlesnake thrust at me as a lawsuit dealing with constitutional claims against an administrative organization."

Neither during the discovery phase of the lawsuit nor during trial did Judge Justice repeat his *Morales* experience by visiting a prison. George Beto maintains that judges are likely to make more tutored decisions in institutional litigation when they visit the institutions themselves rather than relying exclusively on the testimony of experts. In retrospect, Justice agrees that a visit might have been a good thing to do, but he had deep reservations at the time. "A visit on my part would have been regarded with a great deal of hostility. The TDC was totally repugnant to everything I was doing." He conceived of all kinds of embarrassing events that could occur and decided that a visit could well prove counterproductive.

On September 20, 1979, the parties rested. Some 349 witnesses had been called, most of them prisoners, corrections experts, and TDC staff. The trial, as the Judge noted later in the conclusion of his memorandum decision, "lasted longer than any prison case—and perhaps any civil rights case—in the history of American jurisprudence."[21]

Numerous law clerks were involved in the *Ruiz* litigation over the years. The initial work of drafting the opinion in accordance with Justice's directives fell to Ann Maclaine, a graduate of the University of Michigan Law School. She was the first of additional clerks assigned to Justice to assist with *Ruiz*. Later, Robert McDuff worked on the draft. Justice took great care in writing his opinion, for he knew it would have major impact on the operation of the Texas prison system and would serve as a precedent in other prison cases. Many months were required to review and condense the voluminous trial record, research the law on complex issues, and evaluate the constitutional dimensions of arguments presented in the case. All the while, Judge Justice tended to his regular case docket in Tyler.

Justice's memorandum opinion, which ran an astounding 249 double-spaced pages with 219 footnotes, was handed down on December 12, 1980, nearly a year and a half after the trial had concluded. The Judge was holding court in Paris, Texas, when the massive document was released. McDuff recalls that at dinner that night, the Judge "was the most relaxed and happiest I had ever seen him." A heavy weight had been lifted from his shoulders.

The Judge's Decision

For the most part, the memorandum opinion did not set forth new legal doctrine. Rather, its uniqueness among prison decisions lay in its comprehensiveness. Nearly every facet of TDC's operations was affected.

The opinion began by generally reviewing the characteristics of the TDC prison population, explaining the procedural history of the litigation, and outlining the structure of the opinion.[22] The Judge then set forth detailed findings of facts. As in earlier decisions, he sought to establish an irrefutable factual basis upon which to anchor his remedial order. One cannot read the opinion without being struck by the amount of brute force required to maintain the control model of corrections as it had been employed in the TDC and by the many abuses it engendered.

"It is impossible," the Judge wrote, "for a written opinion to convey the pernicious conditions and the pain and degradation which ordinary inmates suffer within TDC prison walls—the gruesome experiences of youthful first offenders forcibly raped; the cruel and justifiable fears of inmates, wondering when they will be called upon to defend themselves against the next violent assault; the sheer misery, the discomfort, the wholesale loss of privacy for prisoners housed with one, two, or three others in a forty-five-square-foot cell or suffocatingly packed together in a crowded dormitory; the psychological suffering and wretched physical stress which must be endured by those sick or injured who cannot obtain adequate medical care; the sense of abject helplessness felt by inmates arbitrarily sent to solitary confinement or administrative segregation without proper opportunity to defend themselves or to argue their causes; the bitter frustration of inmates prevented from petitioning the courts and other governmental authorities for relief from perceived injustices."[23]

Such injustices, he declared, were routine for Texas prison inmates. Nevertheless, Justice wrote in a passage echoing his 1972 speech at Southern Methodist University, "these iniquitous . . . circumstances are prohibited by the great constitutional principles that no human being, regardless of how disfavored by society, shall be subjected to cruel and unusual punishment or be deprived of the due process of the law within the United States of America. Regrettably, state officials have not upheld their responsibility to enforce these principles." [24]

Beginning with overcrowding, Justice categorized the dozens of constitutional and state law violations in six broad groups. Highlights of his opinion follow.

Overcrowding

By admission of its own officials, the Texas Department of Corrections had been overcrowded since at least March 1977. By 1979, crowding had reached crisis proportions. Estelle testified during the trial that a thousand of the system's twenty-six thousand prisoners were sleeping on the floor. Cells and dormitories held roughly twice their design capacity, resulting in TDC's violating the minimum standard of every professional association that addressed housing of inmates. Inmates were in constant presence of one another and slept knowing they might be assaulted at any time.

Justice found TDC's contention that new construction would solve crowding problems "extremely suspect." Estelle testified that it was TDC's "hope and intention" to get all inmates off the floors by April 1, 1980. But December 1979 population figures showed a more rapid expansion than prison officials had projected.

"All told, the evidence makes it clear that TDC's construction plans—geared as they are toward huge maximum-security facilities which take years to build—promise little hope in the foreseeable future of significant relief from the overcrowding which permeates Texas prisons," the Judge wrote. [25] Despite his strong support for keeping inmates in prisons, Estelle admitted during cross-examination that he had told legislative committees 40 percent of the TDC population would not have to be confined in the TDC if community-based correctional facilities were available. He also admitted telling legislators that continuing the policy of placing prisoners in state facilities would likely bankrupt the penal justice system. [26] According to Estelle's testimony and the testimony of others, parole and probation costs were then about one-seventh the cost of maintaining a prisoner in a state prison.

Justice concluded that overcrowding in the TDC amounted to cruel and unusual punishment under the Eighth Amendment.

Absence of Security and Supervision

Inmates lived in constant fear of physical assault, Justice concluded, blaming inadequate numbers of security officers, most poorly trained. Nationwide, the average guard/prisoner ratio was 1 guard for every 5 inmates, but in the summer of 1979 there was 1 uniformed TDC guard for every 12.45 inmates, a ratio Justice called "one of the most unfavorable, if not the worst, . . . in the nation."[27] Estelle himself characterized the 1 : 12 ratio as "extremely dangerous."

Most TDC guards spent their time supervising inmates at work and managing and controlling inmate movements into, from, and within units. Few guards were available to supervise the three-tiered cellblocks and dormitories. Though TDC adamantly denied it, trial evidence revealed that to a large extent Texas prisons were ruled by the prisoners, with the expected results. "[A]ggressive and predatory inmates are free to do as they wish in the living areas, and their victims can be threatened, extorted, beaten, or raped, in the absence of protection from civilian personnel," Justice wrote.[28]

As staffing shortages became more acute, the use of prisoner-guards in the form of building tenders increased. Justice recalls that when he first learned of the low guard-to-inmate ratio, he speculated that the only way the TDC could maintain control was through the use of some type of prisoner-control system, even though state law specifically prohibited it.[29] In 1974, according to statistics presented at trial, some 800 building tenders worked in the Texas prison system, 4.7 percent of the total prison population of 17,000. By May 1979, there were 2,265 building tenders, 9 percent of TDC's 25,000 prisoners.

Building tenders often carried weapons. At the Eastham Unit, some of them were equipped with hunting knives, trace chains, pipes, and baseball bats. Methods of maintaining control were often brutal. Justice cited the testimony of a former building tender who, in exchange for favors by prison officials, sought to intimidate a troublesome writ-writer by slitting his throat. The building tender was never disciplined for the act because a TDC captain characterized the throat-cutting as self-mutilation. In another instance, building tenders forced an inmate to engage in homosexual acts by attaching the ends of an extension cord first to a wet electric blanket wrapped around the inmate and then directly to the inmate's body. Prisoner-guards were able to peddle their influence, extort money or goods from other inmates, and promote prostitution and usury. Justice found that responsibility for building-tender abuses stretched all the way up the TDC chain of command, which "directly and indirectly permitted its abuses to be visited on the inmates of Texas prisons."[30]

Abuse by guards was also routine. Justice cited numerous instances in the opinion. One involved a psychologically disturbed and ill inmate who was forced to "stand on the wall"—meaning to face the wall with nose and feet touching it—for several days. For part of the time, he was handcuffed to the back gate of the unit. He was also handcuffed to machinery in the field. After a few days of this treatment, the inmate died. Inmates were often trampled by the horses used to herd them to and from the fields. Savage beatings for rule violations were common. Justice observed that "[I]nmates must live in fear not only of their fellow inmates, but of their keepers as well."[31]

As with overcrowding, Justice held that the absence of effective security and supervision, together with the abuses it engendered, violated the Eighth Amendment's proscription against cruel and unusual punishment.

Inmate Health Care

Health care provided inmates was found to be so woefully inadequate as to violate the Eighth Amendment. Justice cited the 1974 Joint Commission on Prison Reform report, which concluded that TDC needed nineteen full-time physicians to serve the seventeen thousand prisoners it then held. During most of 1974, the Judge noted, TDC employed only one physician. During the trial, fewer than thirteen physicians were available for the system's twenty-six thousand inmates. Four or five of these were permanently assigned to Huntsville Unit Hospital, the main TDC medical unit.

To compensate for the shortage of qualified professional medical staff, TDC hired medical assistants, a few of whom were licensed as vocational nurses, but most of whom had little medical training or experience and would be regarded as orderlies in a regular hospital. They nonetheless routinely performed procedures that should have been performed only by a physician or nurse. For example, they made almost all initial screening decisions, determined whether an inmate was to receive any treatment, conducted sick call, diagnosed illnesses, prescribed and dispensed medication, and supervised inmates in solitary confinement.

Inmate "nurses" made up the backbone of the TDC health care system. Lacking even the training or supervision of medical assistants, they routinely performed medical procedures for which they were unqualified, including intravenous injections, Pap tests, prescription of medication, suturing lacerations, taking X-rays, conducting eye exams, lancing boils, and setting broken bones. The state attempted to show that the inmate nurses generally performed well, but Justice found that the evidence "showed that inmate nurses often make mistakes which increase their patients' pain and suffering," citing a number of instances in which inmate nurses had botched treatment efforts, such as removing stitches or inserting catheters, causing extreme pain and hemorrhaging.[32]

Unit infirmaries were filled beyond capacity. Everything from beds to equipment was in short supply. The lack of a reliable emergency transportation system resulted in inordinate delays in getting patients to hospitals. In one instance, a Wynne Unit inmate with metal splinters embedded in his eyes waited seven hours without pain medication before being taken to a hospital. The Huntsville Unit Hospital had long before lost accreditation by the Texas Hospital Association and was operating in violation of state licensing requirements.

Constitutional deficiencies also pervaded TDC's mental health care system. Some schizophrenic or psychotic inmates had spent up to five years in segregated status without treatment. Mentally retarded inmates, who made up an estimated 10 to 15 percent of the TDC population, were expected to live up to the standards of other prisoners or be punished. A disproportionate number had been repeatedly sentenced to solitary confinement. "Several TDC officials agreed that prison is not an appropriate setting for mentally retarded persons," Justice noted. "Regardless of this consensus, TDC has taken no steps to obtain alternative care for such inmates. Rather, they are simply lost in the system, where their usual lot is abuse, exploitation, and frequent punishment."[33]

Prisoner Discipline and Due Process

In 1974 the Supreme Court had ruled in *Wolff v. McDonnell* that prisoners facing serious sanctions such as loss of good time in disciplinary hearings are entitled to a number of due process protections.[34] Among them are twenty-four hours' advance written notice of hearings on alleged violations, a written statement by investigators listing evidence and the reasons for the disciplinary action if found guilty, and the right of inmates to call witnesses and present documentary evidence in their defense when it would not be unduly hazardous to institutional safety or correctional goals. TDC had adopted procedures ostensibly to comply with the *Wolff* requirements, but Justice found that on close inspection many TDC practices "unquestionably violate both the letter and spirit of *Wolff*," as well as TDC's own stated policies.[35] In 1975 he had issued a preliminary injunction based on findings that TDC had routinely violated the *Wolff* guidelines, but by the time of the trial, it was apparent to him that the injunction had had little effect.

Any rule violation could land a prisoner in solitary confinement. Despite a TDC rule that provided that solitary confinement should be used sparingly, Justice found that it was widely and frequently used throughout the prison system. In solitary confinement, prisoners were confined twenty-four hours a day to cells typically illuminated only by a light bulb. They received showers three times a week, were served a diet that expert opinion said was nutritionally inadequate, and were permitted nothing in their cells but a Bible. However, while Justice viewed solitary confinement as degrading and ineffective, he concluded that under existing legal precedent, it did not constitute cruel and unusual punishment.

But even though the conditions of solitary confinement were not unconstitutional, the TDC rule that allowed "recalcitrant" inmates to be returned to solitary after a brief respite clearly violated the Fourteenth Amendment due process requirements specified in *Wolff*. "Contrary to TDC directives, solitary confinement is imposed frequently and often arbitrarily," Justice wrote. It is "commonly wreaked upon inmates in disfavor with TDC officials, including those who have pursued their constitutional rights by filing lawsuits against TDC."[36] Administrative segregation—confinement to one's cell in a separate part of the prison for various lengths of time—had also been arbitrarily used, often to punish writ-writers.

Prisoners' Access to Courts

Justice was particularly incensed with TDC obstruction of prisoners' access to the courts, a fundamental constitutional right. Ruiz and his fellow plaintiffs had battled general harassment, limitations on time to work on legal matters, restrictions on communication about legal questions, difficult procedures to notarize court papers, and intrusions on opportunities for talking with lawyers. Judge Justice concluded that none of the impediments to legal assistance served any purpose other than to discourage inmates from seeking legal aid.

Many writ-writers had been moved for long periods of time to administrative segregation, where they spent months or years "for no discernable security reasons," Justice noted. There they became the targets of arbitrary application of TDC's vague disciplinary rules, being punished for infractions such as "threatening an officer" (orally contemplating a suit) or "disrespectful attitude" (mentioning a possible investigation by an attorney).[37]

TDC officials regularly imposed unnecessary hardships on inmates who attempted to communicate with their attorneys. No private conversations were allowed in TDC's inadequate interview facilities; documents could not be passed between lawyers and inmates without a guard checking (and reading) them; attorneys had difficulty scheduling interviews and occasionally interviews were forbidden altogether; and attorneys were not permitted to interview prisoners in administrative segregation. "This type and degree of intransigence is inexcusable," Justice wrote, finding that the state could offer no justification for TDC's long history of impediments to court access, legal research, and communication with counsel.[38]

Fire and Work Safety, Sanitation, and Hygiene

Violations of state law in prison fire safety, work safety, sanitation, and hygiene were evident. The number of fire exits in TDC prison units was inadequate.

The system's plumbing was filled with cross-connections which could allow wastewater to infiltrate the fresh water supply. Several unit kitchens would have been closed by public health authorities if they had been inspected by standards used for the general public.

TDC officials had maintained that prison operations were not specifically included in state sanitation and work safety regulations. But Justice asked how the state could be responsible for protecting public health and safety, and at the same time be excluded from the same responsibility when it came to prison inmates. "Indeed the fact that inmates have no choice but to eat the food provided them, and to work and live in prison facilities, suggests that the inmates may be in greater need of such protection than members of the outside populace," Justice wrote, "for the latter have the power to boycott an unclean eating place or to leave an unsafe work facility." [39]

In sum, illegality pervaded the Texas Department of Corrections. And while the violations existed independently, each was exacerbated by the others. The effects of overcrowding, as well as the shortage of security officers, made the problems of security and supervision worse. Overcrowding and inadequate medical staff and facilities made health care worse. Chances for redress of the many wrongs infecting TDC were made worse by the building tender system and the many institutional barriers to courts, attorneys, and public officials. The aggregate effects of these violations, Justice ruled, "undeniably contravene the Constitution." [40]

Toward the end of the massive opinion, Justice asserted that many of the Texas Department of Corrections' problems were the result of an antiquated theory of prison management which put emphasis on large institutions located in rural areas built for efficient movement of prisoners and agricultural and industrial self-sufficiency. He found especially compelling the testimony of penological experts that an effective and humane prison operation required that the warden be personally acquainted with the staff, officers, and inmates. Only in this way, the experts testified, could the kind of brutality which characterized TDC be eliminated. TDC's "telephone pole" design epitomized a prison management philosophy which emphasized centralization, mass movement, and control. [41] The modern prisons favored by most prison planners and by Justice were designed according to a modular or "pod" concept. In these prisons small groups of prisoners lived, ate, worked, and studied together. The wardens knew the prisoners, and guards, not building tenders, supervised them.

The defendants argued that the plaintiffs were misusing the Constitution to challenge the Texas philosophy of prison management. Justice conceded that it was not ordinarily the province of the courts to decide between competing theories of prison management. Yet courts could not shirk their duty to protect constitutional rights. Although the Constitution does not mandate comfortable prisons, Justice wrote, it does require that they be operated in conformance with constitutional requirements. He doubted that TDC practice could be remedied without a change in management structure and philosophy. Harking back to the arguments he had used in ordering the Texas Youth Council to close Mountain View and Gatesville to protect the rights of incarcerated juveniles, Justice wrote that existing prisons would have to be reorganized into much smaller units, and future Texas prisons would have to be smaller and located closer to urban areas.

Both parties were given a month in which to propose a joint remedial plan to solve the TDC's many constitutional defects or six weeks in which to present separate proposals based on Justice's memorandum opinion.

The Remedial Order

The lawyers for the state had lost decisively. Democratic Attorney General Mark White, who was to struggle with *Ruiz* two years later as governor, said in his initial reaction that the decision would cost the state "many, many millions of dollars." White told the *Houston Post* that the state always had been open to settlement of the suit, but he criticized Justice for demanding nothing short of "complete surrender."[42] Director Estelle repeatedly impugned Justice's opinion to the press. He accused Justice of blatant bias and questioned his competency as a judge, at one point labeling the Judge's writing style as showing a "crass, gross, almost incredible lack of literary skills."[43] By this time Justice had grown accustomed to adverse reaction to his decisions and was not surprised by the lambasting he took in the press. Nevertheless, he was particularly upset by Estelle's comments. "He'd go around making speeches to the effect that this opinion read like a dime-store novel, making light of my literary style. That chagrined me, I'll confess."

William Bennett Turner, the plaintiffs' lead attorney, was elated by Justice's ruling, but disappointed that the Judge had delayed ordering the needed reforms. "The court is being extremely generous to the state, in light of the findings of unconstitutionality, in letting them continue for even a day with business as usual," Turner told the *Houston Post*.[44]

The settlement deadlines came and went with little movement toward resolving the major issues that divided the state and the plaintiffs. Both sides submitted proposed remedial plans. Justice later said he had found the state's submission "very disappointing." The parties did reach agreement on certain matters pertaining to health care, special-needs prisoners, solitary confinement, use of chemical agents, work safety and hygiene, and administrative segregation. And in March 1981 Justice approved the first of several consent decrees on these issues. But the thorniest issues of overcrowding, security and supervision, court access, and prison management, size, and location remained.

In April 1981 Justice issued his final remedial decree. Martin and Ekland-Olson maintain that Justice had learned from the earlier *Morales* litigation not to delay the issuance of a final remedial order setting forth explicitly what the state had to do to remedy the wrongs identified in the memorandum opinion (see Chapter 6). "The remedial orders issued in *Ruiz* would be more timely, precise, and enforceable. Justice had learned his lessons well." [45]

According to the Judge, it wasn't so much his experience with *Morales* which prompted him to act expeditiously as his experience with the state during the *Ruiz* trial. He had no confidence that the parties would make progress on their own. "The whole situation demanded action," he maintains. He did learn from *Morales* not to delay until the Fifth Circuit acted on an appeal of his decision. "I learned that you go ahead regardless of what you think the Fifth Circuit might do." He was fully confident that the major portions of his decree would be upheld by the Fifth Circuit.

The April 20, 1981, order reflected most of what the plaintiffs had submitted in their proposed plan and was more comprehensive and specific than any other prison order ever issued by a federal court. Like Justice's earlier memorandum opinion, the remedial order covered every facet of prison life, detailing what TDC had to do to comply with the Constitution. Justice ordered TDC to reduce overcrowding immediately by stopping any delay in the award or restoration of "good time" and parole, and at the same time to expand its work and prisoner furlough programs. He set ceilings on the number of prisoners the system could house. The number of prisoners per cell was to be reduced gradually to one. TDC also was to expand the space per prisoner confined to a dormitory to sixty square feet.

The Judge ordered that more guards be hired so that one guard would be in place for every six prisoners by November 1982. Besides requiring more guards, Justice specified that they be deployed in a way to increase safety, with at least one officer to each tier of every cellblock and in each dormitory.

TDC officials were ordered to bring prisoner disciplinary procedures into compliance with the Supreme Court's *Wolff* guidelines. Justice prohibited enforcement of vague rules such as those prohibiting "disrespectful attitudes and actions" and issued detailed instructions for improved prisoner access to courts, counsel, and public officials. He ordered Huntsville Unit Hospital downgraded to an infirmary and required TDC to comply with the Life Safety

Code of the National Fire Protection Association. In addition, TDC was required to follow seven state health and safety laws and to file a plan for regular health inspections of all TDC facilities with the court.

One part of the order struck at the philosophical and organizational heart of the control model of corrections. Justice required state officials to submit a plan for the reorganization and decentralization of prison management of all existing units housing more than 500 prisoners, ensuring, among other things, that they would be divided into subunits of 500 or fewer inmates. TDC officials were given six months to accomplish the reorganization. Justice also barred the TDC from building any new prison unit for more than 500 prisoners, or building in a way that required one warden to supervise more than 500 inmates. In addition, he required that all new prisons be built within fifty miles of a metropolitan area of at least 200,000 population, unless state officials could show that adequate numbers of qualified staff members could be hired for facilities located farther away.

Unlike other measures in the remedial order, neither the requirement that TDC reorganize existing prisons into smaller units nor the provision requiring that new units be located near metropolitan areas—both advocated by Justice Department lawyers—was supported by legal precedent. In these two respects, the order was charting a new direction in corrections and was a target for reversal on appeal. But both provisions had been supported by expert testimony. Justice recalls that "Virtually every expert said that these huge institutions were unmanageable and that they should be broken down into smaller units—some said as small as units of 250 prisoners. Their theory was, and I thought it was a good one, that a warden has to be intimately familiar with what is going on in his institution; otherwise he can't properly administer it. So they said an institution should not be so big that the warden would be unable to know every one of his subordinates and preferably every one of his prisoners." Locating prisons near major metropolitan areas was similarly recommended by the experts because doing so would increase the recruiting of competent professional and paraprofessional employees. One of Justice's law clerks, Robert McDuff, warned him that this part of the order was a potential candidate for reversal on appeal, but the Judge left it in anyway since he was trying to achieve an equitable remedy. "I felt justified by the evidence to issue those two particular orders," he maintains.

The comprehensive order stunned state officials. "It would be difficult to describe how this could get any worse," Attorney General White said at a news conference in Austin. He told reporters that he agreed that the state had an obligation to move as quickly as possible to reduce crowding, but added, "the court has suggested we do that by letting people go free, and I don't think the people of this state are prepared to let people go free until they are prepared to return to a law-abiding status in society."[46] The attorney general added that the Constitution did not guarantee "private rooms for prisoners," and estimated that the order could cost up to $4 billion.

Republican Governor William P. Clements said in a statement he was convinced that "our department of corrections is one of the finest in the country and I am confident that we will prevail in the higher courts." Clements added, "The judge ignored our attempts to reach a reasonable compromise, but that should come as no surprise."[47]

Outraged letters from the general public began pouring across editors' desks. Typical was this letter from a *Houston Post* reader: "Please print in *The Post* a copy of the U.S. Constitution," wrote Bruce Ellis of Stafford. "Obviously Judge Justice has not read it. Otherwise, he would know that the federal government has specific limits to its power, and that constitutional amendment, not a judge's ruling, is required to grant it more power."[48]

Freshman U.S. Representative Ken Riley (Republican–Corpus Christi) introduced a resolution asking Congress to impeach Justice for burdening taxpayers with the responsibility of paying for prison reforms and for deliberately weakening the state's powers. "I think somebody needs to get his attention," Riley told reporters.[49] The resolution got nowhere.

For several years after the detailed remedial order was issued, the TDC was wracked by change and controversy, the state legislature was beset with declining oil-generated revenues and spiraling prison costs, the Office of the Texas Attorney General focused every effort on extricating the TDC from the remedial order, and Judge Justice steadfastly continued to oversee implementation of his order. Many of these events have been described elsewhere.[50] Three are discussed here: the effort to remove the special master, the Fifth Circuit's partial reversal of Justice's order, and the catalytic role of Justice's 1986 contempt order toward final resolution of the case.

Challenging the Special Master

The most important lesson Judge Justice had learned from *Morales v. Turman* was that a stronger mechanism than the court-appointed monitor used in that case would be needed to actively oversee the implementation of the 1981 order. By the time of *Ruiz,* judges faced with enforcing detailed remedial orders involving complex organizations such as school districts and prisons had begun employing special masters. While their duties vary, special masters generally conduct investigations, hold hearings, make findings of fact, and

suggest recommendations to the court regarding implementation of a remedial order. If the judge learns that the order is not being effectively implemented, additional remedies or sanctions may be applied.

Justice likens special masters to bankruptcy trustees, who under the general
direction of the courts, have long been involved in the reorganization of major
industries. "I don't see any essential difference between a court handling a
bankrupt business organization, which is a very complex matter, and handling
a state institution which is constitutionally bankrupt," he says.

Before issuing the remedial order in 1981, Judge Justice told the parties to
submit up to five names of candidates for special master. Justice had done some
thinking about the matter himself. "I thought it would be better to get somebody from out of state, since I knew a resident of the state would be subjected
to a lot of political pressure." Justice traveled to Washington, D.C., where he
talked over the role of the special master with officials at the Federal Judicial
Center, a think-tank for the federal judiciary, and with Allen F. Breed, director of the National Institute of Corrections. Breed was later to serve as the
chairman of the monitoring committee in *Morales v. Turman* (see Chapter 6).
Breed named several individuals who could serve as special master. The first
one he mentioned was Vincent M. Nathan, who had achieved national recognition for his work as special master in several important prison reform cases.
Nathan was a transplanted Texan, a former professor at the University of
Toledo, and a veteran of several prison reform oversight assignments. Justice
recalls, "I didn't ask Breed who his choice was. But it became clearer the more
I talked with him that he thought Vincent Nathan was the leading candidate."
Nathan's name was one of two submitted by the plaintiffs and the first name on
the list submitted by the Justice Department.

When Nathan came to Texas, Justice told him that the case was complex. "I
told him that I was inundated with my docket, that anybody I appointed was
going to have to do it virtually on his own." Justice also told Nathan that he
would authorize the appointment of assistants. Nathan, who had never met
the Judge, brought with him a draft document outlining the duties and responsibilities of the special master, as well as a budget. Justice was pleased
with the budget, but rejected Nathan's concept of a committee of correctional
experts to oversee implementation of the order. Justice wanted the special
master to maintain an office in Texas and to have a significant on-site presence
in Texas prisons. He told Nathan that it was his impression from the trial that
the state was likely to be very resistant to change. Nathan says Justice "expressed pessimism" as to whether TDC would ever be willing or able to comply but expressed determination to stay with the case regardless.

When he handed down his remedial decree in April 1981, Justice also
appointed Nathan as special master. Nathan was initially received well by

Attorney General Mark White and the TDC, but state attorney Ed Idar was hostile from the beginning and remained so. As Nathan's staff began to monitor prison activities, relations with White and the TDC began to sour. The first several years after the order were marked by resistance and hostility on the part of the state.

The seeds for the falling out between Nathan and the TDC were sown when he appointed one of his four monitors to gather compliance data on the phase-out of building tenders. After three months of data gathering, monitor David Arnold submitted his detailed report to Nathan on October 16, 1981. A short time later it was released to the news media. Though Justice had ordered an end to the building tender system, a system TDC officials repeatedly claimed did not exist, Arnold found abundant evidence that the system not only continued to exist but played a major role in prisoner supervision and discipline. His report was greeted with immediate denial by the TDC. However, it triggered an internal investigation by TDC staff attorneys that ultimately verified much of Arnold's findings.

Sharing the news with the building tender report was prison violence, which had surfaced for the first time in the fall of 1981. Newspapers were filled with stories about stabbings, beatings, and rioting. Attorney General White alleged that since Nathan's appointment, prison disturbances had increased from one every nineteen months to one every nineteen days. Both White and Governor Clements laid the blame on the Office of the Special Master. "The activities of the special master and his staff," White charged, "are clearly the cause of inmate disturbances at TDC."[51] TDC officials were irate that the Office of the Special Master would not turn over the names of building tenders who possessed weapons. That decision, Nathan maintains, was a deliberate one. The special master feared that if his staff did turn over the names of inmates possessing weapons given them by prison administrators, they would immediately be the subject of such retaliation by prison administrators and fellow building tenders "that we couldn't guarantee that they would stay alive." Justice told Nathan that names had to be turned over to the TDC. "We couldn't be in the position of trying to hide the names of the lawbreakers," he points out.

On January 25, 1982, the state filed a strident motion in Justice's court to discharge Nathan for "gross misconduct." The Office of the Special Master, it was asserted in the motion, was undermining discipline and fostering unrest by spreading rumors, establishing a clandestine courier system, and scheming with inmates to thwart prison discipline. Fritz Byers, the law clerk working on *Ruiz* at the time, describes the motion as a press release, and, indeed, it was widely reported in the media. "The tone of the motion made clear that at least part of its purpose was use in the department's public relations campaign against the special master and Judge Justice's order," Byers observes. Attorney

Ed Idar, who claims authorship of most of it, denies that it was anything other than a serious effort to contest the special mastership.

The attack on the special master launched White's campaign for the Democratic gubernatorial nomination. It was tailor-made for the occasion: opposition to meddling in Texas' well-run prison system by a liberal federal judge and his out-of-state special master. White became the Democratic nominee and went on to defeat Governor Clements in the extremely bitter 1982 campaign. Both candidates, who dislike each other intensely, sought to make political hay out of the prison issue, attributing most of the blame for prison troubles to Judge Justice. Unfortunately, the injection of politics into the prison issue seriously hindered efforts to seek resolution and added significantly to costs in time and money.

Nathan rejected the accusation against him as baseless. In Nathan's view, Estelle and the TDC were making the same fatal mistake that Beto had made with regard to the writ-writers: "By fighting the litigation, they guaranteed that they would lose control of the prison system." However, the state firmly believed that Justice's order was illegitimate and would be overturned on appeal, as had happened with the Texas Youth Council case and would shortly happen with the bilingual spin-off of the school desegregation case. Hence there was no pressure to accept what the order required and work to change the prison system accordingly.

Judge Justice had already scheduled a hearing on the building tender issue for March 15, 1982. He and law clerk Byers talked over the best way to deal with the motion to discharge the special master. Byers recalls that the Judge's primary concern was that the TDC might be intentionally disobeying his order prohibiting use of the building tender system, a prohibition he fully expected the Fifth Circuit to uphold. Possible illegalities involving the special master's office were of secondary importance. Accordingly, Justice consolidated the hearing on the special master discharge motion with the building tender hearing, allowing testimony on the building tender issue to go first. One commentator labeled this a "masterful move" because it "gave Nathan a decided tactical advantage, since [monitor] Arnold's observations [about the building tender system], if proven, would irreparably damage the state's credibility." [52] Indeed, the state objected to the consolidated hearing for this reason, but to no avail.

Justice disclaims any Machiavellian intention in scheduling the consolidated hearing. It was simply a practical way of sorting out conflicting assertions. "I recognized that it was possible that this was just some diversionary tactic on the part of the state. On the other hand, there might be something to it. How was I to know? The best way to figure it out would first be to see whether or not the special master had indeed found these abuses. If he had, that would cast into considerable doubt the state's motives in bringing the suit to remove him. On the other hand, if the special master had failed to make any kind of a case of violation of the order, then it would become much more credible that he was guilty of some of the things he was being accused of."

Steve Martin, then TDC general counsel, recalls the "feeding frenzy" the state's lawyers experienced in putting together the case to get rid of Nathan. They were so taken up with their cause that they never suspected Justice might put off the special master issue until he had heard evidence concerning the building tender system. When Justice scheduled the motions, "it brought all of us back to reality and to the fact that our problem was a very real one," Martin acknowledges.

At the hearing, a steady parade of former building tenders testified about possession of illegal weapons, use of force against prisoners, and deals struck with prison officials. With accounts of the graphic testimony appearing in the newspapers, top state leaders became convinced that TDC was not what Estelle portrayed it to be and that a change in strategy was in order. Veteran state senator Ray Farabee (Democrat–Wichita Falls) called Nathan at home during the recess in the hearings and told him the state would like to consider settlement of the building tender issue. Farabee, who had become a major actor in prison matters by virtue of his senate committee assignments, concluded early on that it was in the state's best interest to communicate with Nathan because Nathan would be an independent source of information about what was going on inside the prisons. Farabee had become progressively more distressed at the deterioration of relations with Nathan and was impatient and disappointed with Estelle's intransigence. Matters had gotten out of control. Nathan insisted that before he would even talk with state officials, the state would have to drop the motion seeking his discharge. Several days later, attorney Richard E. Gray, executive assistant to Attorney General White, notified the court that the state was withdrawing the discharge motion. He asked for a two-week recess so that the parties could work out an agreement over the building tender system.

For the first time, Judge Justice began to view the state differently. "Gray," Justice maintains, "was the first of the state's attorneys that I had any confidence in." The Judge told the parties in open court that he hoped the withdrawal of the motion would prove to be a turning point in the long litigation. "The defendant's application for withdrawal, it should be noted, terminates at least temporarily an unseemly campaign of vilification against the Special Master as well as the court. Hopefully, today's action by the defendants will provide more than a temporary respite from this behavior, thus changing the tone of this litigation. This development gives me some encouragement that the parties will begin to communicate in a meaningful and professional manner with each other and with the Special Master. While the history of this case prevents me from being overtaken by optimism, I nonetheless regard the withdrawal of the motion seeking dissolution of the mastership as promising." [53]

Not all were pleased. Ed Idar, who had argued the case as lead counsel before Justice and still was nominally involved, was thoroughly disgusted. "I could see that the Judge and the special master were going to run TDC from there on out. I told Gray that White and the others were buying a pig in a poke."

The confidence Judge Justice had placed in Vincent Nathan was fully justified during the ensuing two weeks when Nathan was able to get the parties to resolve the most volatile issue in the litigation. Armed with proposals advanced by the parties, Nathan and staff members David Arnold and Jacqueline Boney developed a negotiation process which ultimately succeeded. Each role-played one of the three parties in the lawsuit—TDC, Justice Department, and plaintiffs—and hammered out a proposed settlement. They presented their product to the parties. The simulation exercise worked. "We put together a document that formed the basis for the final settlement [of the building tender issue]," Nathan says.

The building tender agreement resulted in the dismantling of the old system and the formulation of strict guidelines on future use of inmates in support service work. Judge Justice approved the agreement on June 1, 1982. It was, in the words of William Bennett Turner, "by far the most important settlement in the case." Nathan gives much credit to Attorney General Mark White and his staff, who, stung by the deceit of TDC officials, pushed the state into settling.

The Fifth Circuit Partially Reverses

The U.S. Court of Appeals for the Fifth Circuit was no stranger to the *Ruiz* litigation by 1982. The case had been before it in one form or another six times before on largely procedural issues. In 1982, however, it confronted a direct appeal regarding Justice's findings of a constitutional violation and his remedial order. It was the Fifth Circuit's first opportunity to rule on the substantive merits of the case.

During the appeal, Governor Clements had made a concerted effort to get the Justice Department out of the case, using his ties to the Reagan administration. But he was unsuccessful. "I came to the conclusion that the Justice Department really was on the side of the plaintiffs," Clements observes. William Bradford Reynolds, chief of the Justice Department's Civil Rights Division, argued against the state during the appeal of Judge Justice's decision before the Fifth Circuit. Turner admits to having doubts about the Justice Department's position at this stage of the litigation. "I was afraid that Reynolds was going to stand up and give away the store."[54] But he did not.

The state made a concerted effort to convince the appeals court that Justice's order should be overturned. This time, the appeal would not be entrusted to attorneys in the attorney general's office. Instead, using TDC funds and with the concurrence of Governor Clements, the TDC board hired the well-known Houston law firm of Fulbright and Jaworski, whose senior partner, Leon Jaworski, had served as special prosecutor during the Watergate hearings. In addition to working on the appeal, Fulbright and Jaworski attorneys, who had no working knowledge of the case, also represented the TDC before Judge Justice and the special master, and handled the motion to discharge Nathan. Justice recognized that part of the game plan was to overwhelm the trial court. "In those days," he recalls, "they were still trying to harass the court. The Jaworski firm was filing motions every day. Fortunately, I had Fritz Byers as a law clerk at that time. He was very interested in the case and kept right on top of it. Every time they'd file a motion, he'd draft a response. They finally saw that they weren't going to run me out of the case."

After four and one-half months of work, the firm produced a 124-page brief to file with the Fifth Circuit and charged the state $600,000 in attorneys' fees for the effort.[55] The brief, which was highly critical of Judge Justice's handling of the case, took full advantage of a ruling handed down by the U.S. Supreme Court after Justice had issued his remedial order. In *Rhodes v. Chapman* the Court ruled that confining two inmates to one cell, without more, was not cruel and unusual punishment.[56] The Constitution does not mandate "comfortable prisons," the Court observed.[57] The justices also pointed out that federal judges draw their power from the Constitution, not from their own ideas about how best to operate a prison. Writing for the majority, Justice Lewis F. Powell warned courts not to assume that state legislators and officials are insensitive to constitutional requirements or to "how best to achieve the goals of the penal function in the criminal justice system."[58] It was just such insensitivity and biased decision-making, the state asserted, that had motivated Justice in the *Ruiz* case.

The state tried to convince the Fifth Circuit that Justice had made many errors in conducting the trial and was so partial to the plaintiffs that the TDC had not had a fair hearing. The appeals panel, composed of Chief Judge Charles Clark, Alvin B. Rubin, and Albert Tate, Jr., was not persuaded. In the decision, handed down on June 23, 1982, the panel noted, "Neither any one episode pointed out in the briefs nor the weight of all of them cumulatively demonstrates that the trial judge was unfair. . . . [T]he district judge never became personally embroiled in the proceedings and he presided over them patiently and fairly."[59] Justice's record of impeccable courtroom management remained unsullied.

Justice was never in doubt on this aspect of the appeal. "I thought that upon examination, the wild accusations that were being made by the Houston firm would not stand up. I didn't really worry about it." He admits, however, coming close to losing his temper during the trial. "I formed the conclusion early on that they were trying to goad me into making ill-advised remarks. Their strategy was to make me become very severe with them, so that they could afterwards point out to the Fifth Circuit that I lacked impartiality. And they very nearly succeeded because I became utterly disenchanted with the way that they were conducting their case." William Bennett Turner observes that Justice was "patient to a fault. Both by nature and by canny judicial sense, he wanted to make sure that all sides had their full day in court." Richard Gray, who represented the state in the latter stages of *Ruiz,* concurs. "I never have seen anything but complete professionalism from the Judge."

While the appeals panel accepted all of Justice's findings of fact and agreed with him that the totality of conditions within the TDC constituted cruel and unusual punishment and that TDC practices denied inmates due process of law, it agreed with the state that the Judge's remedial orders had intruded too deeply into the management of the TDC. A federal judge's discretion in fashioning remedies is not absolute, Rubin wrote, and should be targeted only at the elimination of unconstitutional conditions by the least "intrusive remedy that will still be effective." Justice's decree "administers a massive curative dose when it is not yet demonstrated that a lesser therapeutic measure would not suffice."[60] It was a message to be repeated throughout the opinion, underscoring the concern about the involvement of federal judges in day-to-day institutional decision-making.

The appeals court noted that Justice, not having the Supreme Court's *Rhodes* decision to guide him, had failed to consider the cost of remedial measures and the possibility of achieving constitutional conditions without requiring single-celling. Meeting Justice's one-prisoner, one-cell requirement, the circuit panel held, would cost the state at least $300 million and take three to four years.

But the appeals panel did not close the door entirely to the overcrowding remedy. If provision of additional guards and other measures required by Justice's order did not within a year remedy the problems stemming from overcrowding sufficiently to comport with the Eighth Amendment, the plaintiffs would be entitled to further relief. "This 'wait and see' approach ensures that the intrusion into state processes will be no greater than that required to achieve compliance with the Constitution," said the Fifth Circuit.[61] Justice believes the appellate judges were naïve to assume that a year would make a difference. "They assumed, I think, that I could wave a magic wand and see to it that all of the reforms that they did uphold would be done in a year. I knew better than that. I'd dealt with institutions before. It was going to take years."

The Fifth Circuit also determined that Justice had overstepped his authority in ordering TDC to use good time, parole, and furlough programs to reduce overcrowding. "Directing state officials to achieve specific results should suffice," the panel wrote. "[H]ow they will achieve those results must be left to them unless and until it can be demonstrated judicial intervention is necessary." The appeals court found Justice's order breaking existing prison units into smaller ones and requiring that new prison units house no more than five hundred inmates and be built within a fifty-mile radius of a metropolitan area to be an unnecessary intrusion. "Palaces may be erected in the wilderness," Rubin asserted.[62] Since this part of the order had no precedent, Justice was not surprised that the appeals panel rejected it.

Harshly criticizing Justice for attaching the state claims to the *Ruiz* action in the first place, the appeals court struck down the ordered compliance with state work safety and health codes. Justice acknowledges that the law in this area was changing and that the Fifth Circuit was following the trend. "In light of what the Supreme Court has done since then, they were right because the Supreme Court has cut back on the ability of a federal judge to enforce state standards on the state," Justice observes.[63] But the Judge still believes there is some merit in the argument that it is a violation of equal protection to apply state health and safety standards everywhere except prisons.

Despite these and other setbacks, the plaintiffs nevertheless won on important issues. The appeals panel affirmed Justice's order on prisoner due process issues, court access, disciplinary hearings, and exercise for prisoners confined in administrative segregation. The appellate judges found that violations of prisoners' rights "occurred so frequently and were so pervasive that they reflected a pattern of misconduct."[64]

Opponents of the *Ruiz* litigation were elated by the Fifth Circuit's ruling. Attorney Richard Gray termed it "a clean win for the state."[65] An editorial in the *Dallas Morning News,* long critical of the plaintiffs and of Justice, took a more moderate position, saying the best news was the appellate court's deletion of the single-cell requirement, which gave taxpayers breathing room. But more important, the *News* said, "Texas officials themselves have regained control of the destiny of the prison system." "It is an important victory," the *News* continued, "but not one that relieves the state of the responsibility of making improvements."[66]

Although the Fifth Circuit had put a dent in the 1981 remedial order, the underlying legal conclusion that TDC was operating unconstitutional prisons had been upheld. Furthermore, the appeals court indicated that the plaintiffs could return to court if the TDC did not take important steps to resolve over-crowding and tangential issues. Thus, contrary to exuberant cries of victory from the state, the pressure of reform remained and would be an important stimulant to settlement of many issues by the parties.[67]

The Settlement Process, the 1986 Contempt Citation, and the In-Chambers Meetings with Governor Clements

Continuing pressure on the state stemming from the Fifth Circuit ruling coupled with the process toward negotiated agreements started by the 1981 health care settlement and the resolution of the building tender issue in the spring of 1982 led to settlement of numerous matters during the remainder of the decade. Judge Justice considers this the most important phase of the *Ruiz* litigation. "There are a number of things that I didn't order that the state agreed to do in the form of stipulations and consent agreements," he points out. Special Master Vincent Nathan, who took the leading role in the settle-ment process, maintains that what was brilliant about Justice's April 1981 order was that "the Judge did not specify the means by which to get to objec-tives but only the objectives." Once the legitimacy of most of the order was established by the court of appeals and by revelations like the existence of the building tender system, Nathan observes, "then the steps developed by the parties to implement the order were very innovative, very creative, and pro-vided the necessary operational detail wisely omitted from the court's order."

For example, the Judge had ordered that TDC establish a fair internal disciplinary system for inmates. The parties responded by agreeing to a counsel-substitute program in which inmates are represented by non-uniformed staff who are their advocates at disciplinary hearings. Other detailed agreements were made regarding occupational health and safety, access of prisoners to the courts, discipline rules, overcrowding, use of force by prison guards, and ad-ministrative segregation. Administrative segregation consists of specially built cellblocks where violent prisoners and known or suspected gang mem-bers can be isolated. In some instances such as fire safety and guard training, the negotiated settlements restored some of the provisions eliminated from Justice's remedial order by the Fifth Circuit. One of the settlements Judge Justice considers particularly important is the prisoner classification plan de-signed to place prisoners into various categories, separating violent from non-violent inmates and first-time offenders from hardened criminals. Developed by the parties in 1983, the plan was conditionally approved by Justice on January 3, 1985. Justice claims that the TDC had no classification system worthy of the name at the time of the lawsuit. "They'd throw these eighteen-year-old boys right off the farm into cells with three-time losers. The first thing that would happen is the hardened prisoners would beat them up, rape them, take their commissary from them."

Despite steady progress toward settling outstanding issues, problems continued to arise. Prison control problems surfaced in 1983, as building tenders were phased out before sufficient numbers of guards had been trained and assigned to units. Ever since the state had agreed to terminate the use of building tenders in 1982, Justice had been warning the defendants about the threat of a power vacuum which prisoners and prisoner gangs would be only too eager to fill. He did so again in a March 15, 1984, order, calling particular attention to a report prepared by two experts.[68] But prison violence escalated in 1984 with the deaths of twenty-five prisoners. It was even worse in 1985, when twenty-seven prisoners were killed. During the entire ten-year tenure of George Beto, there had been only seventeen homicides. Only by periodically isolating all inmates in their cells to confiscate weapons and break up gangs in 1986 were TDC officials able to regain control. Justice remains shocked at TDC's inertia. He says angrily that "lives could have been saved" if prison authorities had acted promptly. It is a "scandal and a disgrace," he asserts, that the experts' report on potential prison violence was ignored by TDC officials. "They just couldn't even conceive of doing things differently from the way they had been done in the past."

On the issue of overcrowding, a wide-ranging settlement agreement was approved by the court in July 1985. The agreement set forth population ceilings in each TDC unit, established a depopulation table to gradually reduce crowding, prescribed conditions for new construction, and specified single-celling for certain classes of prisoners. Yet prison overcrowding remained a problem. Governor White won points with the voters in September 1986 when he attempted to house an overflow of prisoners on a temporary basis in other facilities, including the Fort Wolters National Guard Armory in Mineral Wells, rather than accelerate their release. The overcrowding settlement had established the maximum size of the prison population at 95 percent of capacity. Provisions in the state's Prison Management Act enacted in 1983 detailed the procedures for lowering prison population when the prison population rose above 94 percent.[69] White said that releasing prisoners early would result in more parole violations and serious crime.[70] The plaintiffs objected to White's proposal, and Judge Justice issued an injunction prohibiting the move.

Denunciations from across the state greeted the decision. Critics charged that Justice was putting prisoner welfare ahead of public safety. White said he could not understand that what was good enough for soldiers was not good enough for prisoners. The problem was that the alternative housing arrangements violated the agreement the parties themselves had made regarding over-crowding only the year before. Justice's decision was affirmed by the Fifth Circuit.[71]

Overcrowding problems continued. Days before the legislature convened in January 1987, the Texas Board of Corrections voted to turn away convicts for the first time since 1982, as prison population hovered around 95 percent of capacity. On January 16, TDC closed its doors. It was to do so again more than twenty times between January and August, a period when the system spas-modically opened for a day or two and then shut again as it reached the 95 percent population limit.

For the most part, Judge Justice had shown considerable patience when faced with failure by the state to comply with his order and the settlements in the case. Former TDC general counsel Steve Martin observes that Justice "gave the state every opportunity to remedy matters without sanctions."[72] Martin adds, "he has been criticized countless times for heavy-handedness when in fact he has displayed the patience of Job." But by the mid-1980s, his patience was wearing thin.

With the settlement negotiation phase winding down, William Bennett Turner and his partner, Donna Brorby, who had been working on the case since the trial, devoted more attention to reviewing how previous orders actually were being enforced within the TDC. They were not happy with what they learned. Matters came to a head on January 8, 1986, when they asked that the state be found in contempt for failing to meet its obligations. Attorneys for the parties were able to work out a resolution to the problem, only to have it blocked in an election-year move by Governor White, who, among other things, objected to a provision allowing prisoners to purchase television sets. White was running against former Republican Governor Clements, who had been defeated in 1982. Both were exploiting the prison issue in their cam-paigns, just as they had four years before.

In their motion, Turner and Brorby alleged that TDC was failing to provide enough cells for dangerous, mentally ill, or vulnerable inmates; that it con-tinued to mix prisoners of different backgrounds and crimes despite the new classification system; that deadlines for construction of recreation yards and gymnasiums had been missed; that TDC failed to provide proper food, daily showers, and recreation for inmates in administrative segregation; that it failed to hire enough doctors, nurses, physical therapists, and psychiatrists to treat prisoners; that it failed to provide security guards for many housing areas; and that it restricted handicapped inmates' access to educational, rehabilitative, and work programs. They asked for daily fines for each of the deficiencies.

Scott McCown, who had taken over from Richard Gray as lead counsel for the state, realized that a contempt citation was inevitable. Turner had sent him a draft of the contempt motion in September 1985. McCown went over every item with the Board of Corrections and Lane McCotter, who had taken over as TDC director. But McCown made little headway. While he had not given up hope of a settlement, he began preparing for trial. He also had doubts about the settlement process. Every time a settlement was agreed to and TDC failed to perform, the result was a more comprehensive settlement. From his perspective, TDC was in a no-win situation.

A seven-day contempt hearing was held in July 1986. On December 31, Justice issued his decision. He agreed with Turner and Brorby on all points. "In numerous cases, TDC unquestionably has not reached compliance with particular orders," the Judge wrote in the ninety-six-page memorandum opinion issued with his contempt order. "It is also glaringly apparent that TDC made no efforts whatsoever to comply with the orders in question for long periods of time, and that in other instances attempts to observe them were extremely tentative. In sum, it is unmistakable that, on the whole, TDC has been habitually and inexcusably dilatory in fulfilling its obligations in respect to the relevant orders."[73]

McCown does not dispute that procedurally he had gotten a fair trial. But he questions whether Justice was able to weigh the evidence fairly. "His perspective about the TDC had become so rigid that the case was over before it began. An open-minded judge who took a fair view of the evidence would have decided about half the issues in TDC's favor and half in favor of the plaintiffs," he maintains. McCown asserts that "Judge Justice has no appreciation of how difficult it is to do things in the real world and how long it takes to get things done." One of Justice's former law clerks who worked on the case disputes the account. "Look at how much progress the state made after the contempt order was issued," the former clerk points out.

To get the state's attention and to ensure compliance, Justice threatened fines of up to $800,000 a day for continued noncompliance. But the fines were put off until April 1, 1987. This would give the Texas Legislature, which would convene in January, and newly elected Governor Clements time to take quick action. Clements had defeated White in a second particularly bitter campaign. Justice's contempt order and threatened fines were extremely risky ventures, for the state's certain appeal would be filed in an appeals court increasingly dominated by conservatives.

Though the state was awash in red ink, Judge Justice fully intended to secure the money to pay the fines. Following precedent established by a federal judge in Mississippi, Justice intended to add the state auditor and state treasurer as defendants in the litigation.[74] If necessary, he would order the state auditor to issue a warrant in the amount required upon any available funds and then order the treasurer to honor it. Such an action would throw the state into turmoil and pillory the court. But Justice was clearly angry.

It looked as though another head-to-head clash was in the offing. But after Clements was elected, the state's posture suddenly changed. In an interview with the *Dallas Times Herald* before taking office, Clements said he was sincere in his campaign promise to settle the prison issue. He told the *Herald,* "I'm optimistic that we can have a meeting of minds and, yes, we can solve this problem once and for all." [75] Clements planned to ask the legislature for a transfer of money to the TDC to help head off the fines and to seek a permanent solution to the prison funding problem. He also announced his intention to confer before his inauguration with Judge Justice about resolving outstanding issues in the case. The state meanwhile appealed the contempt citation and order to the Fifth Circuit.

Clements and Justice met on January 9, 1987, in the federal courthouse in Tyler. Also in attendance were all the key *Ruiz* players, including the lawyers, top TDC officials, Special Master Vincent Nathan, and Attorney General Jim Mattox. Following coffee served on Sue Justice's fine china in the Judge's study, the formal meeting in the Judge's chambers began. It lasted forty minutes. Claiming he had been misled by other state officials, Clements acknowledged having had no working knowledge of the case during his first term as governor. Despite the Fifth Circuit appeal, he said he was glad the Judge had entered the contempt order and that the state would strive to settle outstanding issues. He also indicated that he and Attorney General Jim Mattox, a Democrat, enjoyed a good working relationship, unlike his relationship with Attorney General Mark White. Clements also divorced himself from what he termed past "calculated acts of procrastination." For his part, Mattox said that the state would make every effort to comply with the contempt order by the April 1 deadline.

Judge Justice responded briefly, indicating that he was impressed with what the governor was saying and that he too hoped that the case, which "has been a millstone around my neck since the early '70s," could be resolved quickly. He declined to speak further, citing the restraints imposed by his position as judge. Both Nathan and Turner voiced approval of the meeting, Nathan going so far as to term it a watershed in the history of the case. After the meeting in the Judge's chambers, the parties, including the governor and attorney general, adjourned to the jury room for negotiations on a settlement. Rather than have them take the hall route to the jury room, Judge Justice led them through the court library and the courtroom itself as a subtle reminder that they were in the chambers of a federal judge.

Justice was greatly surprised by Clements' talk about settling outstanding issues. "I am utterly unable to account for the transformation of Governor William P. Clements in his attitude toward this case," he maintains. "He said on national TV that I'm a 'goofball,' or something to that effect. Then he came here, sitting right over there in that chair, and told me that I was completely right in the case, that he had been lied to. He was glad that I entered that contempt order; that it just brought things to a head. And he said he was going to see that it was completely lived up to. I don't know what happened to cause this dramatic about-face."

Clements says that when proceedings began on Turner's contempt motion, it became clear to him that the state was not living up to its agreements. "It was just absurd to have this dichotomy between the State of Texas and Judge Justice when in fact the lawsuit was over." Though he regarded many of the consent agreements and stipulations as "ill conceived," Clements concluded that it would be fruitless to try to back out of them or to challenge them before the Fifth Circuit. "It's a done deal. This is what I told Judge Justice. The sooner that we get about our business and comply, the sooner that we are going to ease our pain."

Clements acknowledges that some of the settlements between the parties date to his previous administration. But he places the blame solely at the feet of Democrat Mark White, who was serving as attorney general at the time. "I did not know what Mark White was doing. Neither did the TDC Board of Corrections." Clements claims that as attorney general, and later as governor, White was making agreements outside the normal circuit of communications within state government. "I couldn't depend upon a thing he'd tell me."

Mark White has a different view. "Not a single settlement during my tenure as attorney general was ever reached without first asking if the prison board could accomplish it and what objections they had to it," he says. The problem, White maintains, was that the prison board did not want to be told what to do. "I told Clements and the prison board that the problem we had in the prison suit was not bad lawyers, but bad facts." White pointed to prison overcrowding as a prime example. Clements undercut the state's position in the lawsuit, he asserts, by vetoing new prison construction at the very time state attorneys were arguing before Justice that Texas was doing everything it could to expand prison capacity. "Clements wasn't trying to solve the problem but rather was trying to damage me politically." At one point, White told Clements that if the governor "would get the guy who is sleeping on the floor of a cell off the floor, we'll win the lawsuit." Clements wanted to know where to put him. "Put him in a tent, for all I care," White says he responded. Clements soon thereafter used tents to reduce overcrowding. "Clements," says

White, "should have known as governor that the prison system was not being well operated and was over capacity. Those were major issues in the case. He never went into the prisons to see what was going on."

White maintains that it was he who was outside the communications loop until he became governor in January 1983. Even then, he asserts, he was saddled with appointees Clements had made to the prison board. However, he distances himself from the settlements negotiated during his gubernatorial administration. "They bear Mattox's signature, not mine. If Clements didn't like those settlements, maybe he should talk with Mattox."

Clements acknowledges that his 1982 attack on Special Master Vincent Nathan was ill advised. "That was part of the misinformation I was receiving from the TDC staff as well as White." And he maintains that despite his disappointment at the time, the Justice Department was right when it refused to back off from the case during the Fifth Circuit appeal. "We in Texas were in fact doing things that we ought not to have been doing, and in a large measure, the issues in the lawsuit and the corrections we needed to make were long, long overdue." This much White agrees with. "If Judge Justice hadn't been there to have these abuses illuminated, then they probably still would be continuing in Texas prisons," White admits. "I praise him for what he has done." Considering that both political leaders had bitterly and personally attacked Judge Justice throughout the long lawsuit and had prolonged the conflict by politicizing the issue, their expressions of commendation are all the more remarkable.

Oral argument before the Fifth Circuit on the contempt order was held on March 17. State attorneys had spent considerable time preparing and were confident that they would prevail at least to some extent, for they believed Justice had awarded the plaintiffs more than he should have. Furthermore, the wording of Justice's contempt order made him appear inflexible and uncompromising. They hoped that at least two of the three-member Fifth Circuit panel would see it that way. And they were very nearly right.

The three-judge panel included conservatives Edith Hollan Jones and Thomas Gibbs Gee and moderate Thomas M. Reavley. Jones and Gee, both of whom had voted to overturn Justice's decisions in other cases, are regarded as having little respect for his activist approach to judicial decision-making. While there was a general feeling following oral argument that the two conservatives on the appeals court were supportive of the state's position, no one could be sure. As McCown saw it, even if the Fifth Circuit did decide in the state's favor, the case would be sent back to Justice's court for further hearings. It was possible, but not likely, that the Fifth Circuit would take the opportunity to dismantle *Ruiz*. There was even some doubt whether the Fifth Circuit had jurisdiction over the dispute, since Justice had not levied any fines at that juncture and several days before oral argument had set a date for a compliance hearing. Thus, to avoid an uncertain outcome in the Fifth Circuit and also to avoid the crushing fines Justice had ordered, the state made a concerted effort to work out a resolution to the contempt order. In the meantime, Justice himself began to appear more accommodating, as he accepted the state's invitation and toured the Beto I Unit in Tennessee Colony and the Eastham Unit in Lovelady—the first time he had been in a prison during the entire case. It appeared that all participants were working toward resolving the dispute.

Testimony at the compliance hearing before Judge Justice on March 31, 1987, indicated that the parties had made significant progress since the contempt citation had been filed over a year before. Turner said he had won pretty much everything he wanted for his side. "We've got about as close to compliance on the seven issues raised in our motion as it's possible to do." He added that he thought the state probably would escape the threatened fines, thanks in large part to some "dazzling footwork . . . motivated solely by a court order with dollar signs attached to it." [76] McCown also was confident that the state had proved nearly full compliance. An emergency appropriation of $20.4 million from the legislature had helped finance the state's efforts. The optimism was justified. Less than a month later, citing "remarkable progress" made by the state in complying with the contempt order, Justice waived the fines. The parties filed a joint motion to withdraw the appeal to the Fifth Circuit, and, after a puzzling fifty-day delay, it was granted.

On April 8, 1988, Vincent Nathan submitted a plan to the court for phaseout of the special master's office. A week later, Governor Clements and Attorney General Mattox, together with key figures in the litigation, made a second pilgrimage to Justice's chambers. As before, the group gathered in the Judge's study for coffee before the formal meeting. Conversation was spirited and good-natured. A few jokes were bandied about. A camera materialized, and Clements, Mattox, and Justice posed for photographs. Later, in the formal meeting in the Judge's chambers, Clements requested that the plaintiffs and the court give the state some leeway in coping with the problem of overcrowding, which continues unabated in Texas as elsewhere. [77] Turner was adamant against making any concessions. Justice spoke little, other than to point out as he had in the first session that he could not comment other than through the formal motion process. After further discussion about drug intervention programs, the parties adjourned for further negotiation in the jury room.

Despite the formality of the two in-chambers meetings, the key players in *Ruiz* were sitting together in one room, sharing coffee and engaging in conversation. It could not help but have a mollifying effect. During the next two years, steps were made toward a final settlement, though a new issue surfaced in 1990 as increasing numbers of convicted criminals began to back up in county jails while awaiting transfer to overcrowded prisons. County jail over-crowding threatened to add a new chapter to *Ruiz* as TDC and the *Ruiz* judge were drawn into the litigation.[78] Still, the steady pace toward winding down federal involvement in TDC operations continued. In March 1990 Judge Justice issued an order phasing out the Office of the Special Master after nine years of operation.

An Assessment of
Ruiz v. Estelle

Ruiz is a seminal case both for Judge Justice and for the Texas Department of Corrections. It has had a major impact on the way TDC is run and on the day-to-day life of the prisoners. Its significance also extends to other states where similar prison lawsuits are pending or contemplated. Justice used his federal judicial remedial powers to the fullest. He incurred the wrath of many in the legal and political community and certainly a good portion of the Texas popu-lace. Justice was a visible target. "He was an easy scapegoat," former Lieuten-ant Governor William P. Hobby observes. "The best kind of scapegoat for anything is one you can't do anything about." Hobby points out that Justice's order was one of four forces which converged to force legislative action. The others were the decline in state revenue, the exploding TDC population, and the rapid rise in prison costs.

The costs to the state of fighting *Ruiz v. Estelle* were staggering. In addition to its own attorney and defense costs, the state through August 1988 had to pay $3.9 million to the lawyers and firms representing the plaintiffs, and $4.9 million to defray the costs of the special master's office.[79] Under the federal Civil Rights Attorneys Fees Award Act, the losing defendants in a civil rights case must pay the attorneys' fees and costs of the plaintiffs. The state budgeted another $1.1 million for such costs in the *Ruiz* case in 1989. The decision to employ the Houston law firm of Fulbright and Jaworski was an expensive gamble, designed to defeat *Ruiz* and leave TDC basically unchanged. The gamble failed. Justice was not run off the case, the special master was not removed, and the Fifth Circuit did not reverse the remedial order outright. The firm collected $1.2 million from the state.

Largely as a result of the vast increase in state appropriations necessitated by the remedial order and the settlement agreements, the annual cost to maintain a prisoner in the TDC rose from $2,679 in 1979 when the trial began to over $12,500 in 1988.[80] Yet these costs are low compared with costs in other prison systems. For example, in 1988 the annual per-prisoner cost was $22,597 in California, which now has the largest prison system in the country (Texas is now third, after New York).[81] The total appropriations for the Texas Department of Corrections (operating and capital) increased from $104 million in 1979 to $722 million in 1989.[82] A major portion of the increase is for expanding prison capacity to handle overcrowding and for additional personnel costs, chiefly resulting from the end of the building tender system. The TDC prison staff never appreciated the fact that Judge Justice was their best advocate for increased legislative funding.

While costs were rising, TDC was experiencing organizational upheaval. After years of stable leadership under Ellis, Beto, and Estelle, there was rapid turnover in the directorship. Between October 1983, when Estelle resigned under fire, and 1988, the prison system had four directors. Each had his own style of administration. They have ranged from the high-profile leadership of transplanted Californian Raymond Procunier (1984–1985), who sought to get TDC into compliance with the court order as rapidly as possible and wiped out most of the legacy of Estelle in the process, to the military-oriented administration of O. Lane McCotter (1985–1987), to the accountant and budget professional James Lynaugh (1987–   ). Certainly the fact that the TDC directorship had become a lightning rod for controversy and had been caught up in state politics was a major factor in the turnover. But so, too, was the fact that the TDC has become a difficult organization to administer. Beto asserts that more than the remedial order, the consent agreements handicapped effective administration. The prison system became muscle-bound by layers of bureaucracy, he maintains. Others disagree. William Bennett Turner points out that prison directors in other states manage to administer prisons which must comply with equally detailed legal requirements. Still, no one would deny that the Texas prison system is far more complex to operate today than before *Ruiz*.

The fact that James Lynaugh, a relatively colorless career bureaucrat, replaced McCotter as TDC director in 1987 when Clements became governor demonstrates how changed TDC had become from the days of high-profile, charismatic leadership. Before he became director of the TDC in 1987, Lynaugh was finance director for the prison system and had spent nearly twenty years as an accountant in the state comptroller's office.

Changing leadership at the top coupled with pressure to change old ways of doing things placed considerable stress on prison staff. Almost overnight, prison guards found severe limits on their ability to use force to control inmates. They lost building tenders as auxiliary guards and informants, experienced increasing verbal and physical abuse from prisoners, labored under a mushrooming growth of bureaucratic paperwork, and watched power flow from the prison units to system headquarters. At the same time, a vast platoon of new and inexperienced guards was hired to replace building tenders—the prison guard staff more than tripled from 2,500 in 1979 to 9,000 by 1985.

Organizational restructuring, according to researchers Ben M. Crouch and James W. Marquart, "undermined the traditional officer subculture," resulting in low morale and a perceived loss of status.[83]

Ruiz also resulted in a restructuring of inmate society, as building tenders were phased out and strong-willed prisoners took their place. For the first time, prison gangs emerged, but their membership has never encompassed more than a tiny fraction of the inmate population. For a time, disorder replaced what had been a highly ordered inmate society. Trafficking in illicit drugs and alcohol became a major problem. Interracial conflict escalated as heretofore suppressed black and Hispanic prisoners began to assert themselves. Cellblocks became noisy, cluttered, and dirty.[84]

The demoralization of the staff and the upheaval within the inmate population largely account for the explosion of prisoner violence in 1984–1985. In these years Judge Justice was often blamed for ruining what was once a fine prison system, and calls were often heard to return to the old ways of running the prisons.[85] But the pessimistic assessments were premature and ultimately erroneous. It took time for the prison system to assimilate the new procedures required by the court orders. The increasing use of technology in prison control and the vastly expanded use of administrative segregation restored order to the prisons by 1986.

Perceptions to the contrary, TDC remains a rigidly authoritarian prison system where prisoners' rights extend little beyond the minimum the law requires. Even George Beto, looking at the prison system in 1988, observes that the prison is under tight control, too tight in his estimation. He describes helping a state district judge who was visiting Huntsville, the site of the TDC central administration and the famous prison unit known as the Walls, locate a prisoner he had sentenced. Beto was informed that the judge would have to wait awhile because the prisoner would have to be brought to him in chains. "I don't recall in my administration that we put anybody in chains," he says.

To what extent has *Ruiz* improved the Texas Department of Corrections? If the criterion is the recidivism rate, *Ruiz* has had little or no impact. As with *Morales v. Turman* and the state facilities for juvenile delinquents, reliable recidivism data are not available. But it is generally believed that recidivism rates are about the same as they were prior to the reform orders. The benefits of *Ruiz* are more likely to be found in prison environment and administration than in changing prisoner behavior—a matter about which little is known.

First and foremost, the Texas Department of Corrections is now operating prisons that conform to constitutional requirements. The suffocating overcrowding has abated and the shocking abuses by guards and by violent inmates and building tenders appear to be a thing of the past. The TDC is a safer and more humane system, thanks in large part to the settlement agreements worked out by the parties. After 1985, guard morale and pride began to improve.[86] A 1987 survey reveals that most prisoners believe Justice's reform orders have made the prison a better place for the average inmate, though many people would argue that this is an inappropriate objective for a prison. The prisoners surveyed also believe the prison to be a much less dangerous place compared to the late 1970s and early 1980s.[87] It should not be forgotten that most prisoners are eventually released back into society, where the experiences of incarceration will influence their future behavior.

The *Ruiz* orders have made the prison system accountable to external agencies. The closed environment that enabled TDC to become a law unto itself prior to initiation of the lawsuit no longer exists. To make sure that it does not happen again, the Texas Legislature overhauled the state's criminal justice system in 1989 with enactment of House Bill 2335. The Legislative Criminal Justice Board was established as a legislative agency charged with monitoring criminal justice matters and making sure that legal mandates are carried out. Board members are required to attend meetings of the Texas Board of Criminal Justice, which was established to oversee the newly constituted Texas Department of Criminal Justice (TDCJ), composed of the divisions of community justice assistance, institutions, and pardons and paroles. The Texas Board of Corrections and the Texas Department of Corrections became the TDCJ institutional division on September 1, 1989. The TDC of Beto and Estelle's days had ceased to exist.

Despite the reforms, Texas prisons are not operated in total conformity with the *Ruiz* orders. Abuses still occur. As in any large, labor-intensive bureaucracy with diverse goals and an unclear technology of how to achieve them, considerable slippage is present in the system. Special Master Vincent Nathan admits that subtle retaliation by guards and other inmates against prisoners, particularly those who are highly offensive or contentious, is hard to control. "I can't promise the Judge that a guy like David Ruiz is never going to be the subject of retaliation," he says.[88]

Crouch and Marquart assert that a kind of "uneasy peace" has settled over the prisons.[89] And just as was true before the reform orders, unrelenting growth in prison population threatens to undo what progress has been made. Attorney Turner claims that if he had to choose between doing time in the pre-*Ruiz* prison system or today, he would choose today, "but it is a close question" because relentless growth threatens to undo the reforms.

The economic implications of *Ruiz* have had an enormous impact on Texas corrections. The cost of complying with *Ruiz*-initiated reforms together with the cost of building more prisons to relieve overcrowding has forced even archconservative legislators to take a serious look at alternatives. Programs such as electronic surveillance and intensively supervised community-based probation which includes restitution to victims and/or mandated community service are now appearing in prison reform measures enacted by the Texas Legislature, leaving prisons for violent offenders who pose a real threat to society.[90] In 1989 the Texas Legislature approved some $50 million for alternative prison programs as part of a massive expansion and reform of the state prison system.

In a speech delivered to the American Correctional Association in San Antonio on August 20, 1984, Judge Justice observed that "Each criminal environment is discrete, possessing its own unique characteristics, and requiring a suitable response to the given set of circumstances. The utilization of only one response, that is, incarceration, makes about as much sense as treating all medical conditions with one medicine or with one procedure." *Ruiz* has already begun to prompt fundamental change in the Texas criminal justice system, just as *Morales v. Turman* fundamentally altered the Texas juvenile justice system.

For Judge Justice, *Ruiz v. Estelle* is a major professional achievement. The decision is regarded by many as the most successful prison reform case in the country and will have a major impact on correctional policy in Texas and elsewhere for years to come.

CHAPTER 16

A Measure of Human Dignity

Judicial decision-making is in part value-based. The debate centers on which values should prevail. Justice explored the issue in a 1989 law review article discussing the relationship between judicial activism and natural law.[1] He began by noting that throughout constitutional history, natural law—defined as an expression of the point of intersection between law and morals—has played an important role in constitutional interpretation. He noted how the natural law concepts of life, liberty, and estate were enshrined in the Declaration of Independence; how Supreme Court Justice Joseph P. Bradley in 1873 invoked natural law as a justification for denying a woman the right to practice law; and how Abraham Lincoln used the same concept to support the principle that slavery was morally wrong. Justice observed that after the Civil War, conservative activists on the Supreme Court drew from natural law the protection of private property owners against state regulation of industrial abuses, and, later, liberal activists used natural law to secure personal freedoms such as the right to privacy.

"For the most part," he wrote, "the language of natural law provides the basis for interpreting the enumerated rights in the Constitution and their concomitant moral concepts, specifically, free speech, free press, and free exercise of religion in the first amendment; the ban against cruel and unusual punishment in the eighth amendment; the equal protection of the laws in the fourteenth amendment; the due process regarding deprivations of life, liberty, and property in the fifth and fourteenth amendments."[2]

But Justice recognized that natural law cannot be all things to all people. He noted that the Court's value-laden 1973 decision in *Roe v. Wade* stood for the principle that a woman's right to choose an abortion is so fundamental that society cannot permit it to be infringed legislatively. The Court's 1905 opinion in *Lochner v. New York* was borne on the same reasoning, he observed, with the substitution of the right to contract. The *Lochner* decision has since become the archetypal example of abuse of judicial power because the justices gave constitutional recognition to a right which is not listed in the document but which coincided with their economic beliefs. "[A]ssuming the posture of natural rights advocates, can we find a principled way of approving *Brown v. Board of Education of Topeka* [striking down school segregation] while disapproving *Lochner* [striking down a maximum hour law for bakery employees]?" he asked. "If the two cannot be distinguished on principle by natural rights advocates, we must concede a flaw in the methodology."[3]

The intent of the Constitution's framers provides little guidance, Justice asserted. Citing a 1985 *Harvard Law Review* article on the writing of the Constitution, he noted that nothing in the document, its history, or the early history of the Supreme Court suggests that the framers intended anything other than that the words had their own intrinsic meaning. If interpretation is called for, it is for judges to decide what the meaning is, regardless of what the authors may have intended.[4] And to determine the meaning, judges must consider values outside the written document. In making this assertion, Justice is at odds with jurists who assert that judges should not stray beyond the specific words of the framers, even if refusal to do so leaves the Constitution silent on such matters as a right to marry, to procreate, to raise a family, to privacy, and to one-person—one-vote—rights which the Supreme Court has accorded constitutional status.[5] Rights not specifically delineated in the document, these theorists posit, should be left to legislatures to recognize and shape. Acceptance of this view would make many rights considered fundamental in modern society dependent upon the whim of legislative bodies and would subordinate minority interests to the will of the majority.

While Justice clearly opted in the article for an activist judiciary, he accused neoconservative activists on the U.S. Supreme Court who seek to reassert the constitutional status of property rights and economic interests of suffering from the same misconception as their predecessors who wrote liberty of contract into the Constitution in *Lochner v. New York*. "They both ignore the most basic concern of rights decision making, the protection of human dignity."[6]

Protecting human dignity, Justice asserted, provides the transcendant moral perspective to guide the application of principles set forth in the Bill of Rights to the realities of modern life. Conservative activists can claim no compelling moral argument merely by asserting that the Constitution accords absolute dominion over one's property, he noted. Likewise, liberal activists can be criticized for neglecting important economic interests which, from the human dignity perspective, arguably deserve elevation to the status of fundamental rights. While rights of expression, association, education, academic freedom, privacy of the home, and personal autonomy have been constitutionally protected, "why, it may be asked, have such rights as the right to a job, to food, or to housing *not* been included?" [7]

The quest for protecting and enhancing human dignity has guided much of Justice's judicial decision-making. It is a value he believes underlies the writing of the Bill of Rights. Accordingly, he has expansively interpreted its provisions to protect individual rights and improve the conditions of persons confined in state institutions. His decisions involving the latter have had a deep impact on programmatic and funding priorities of Texas state government and have generated accusations of abuse of judicial power. There is no question that Justice's involvement represents a departure from traditional notions of the role of a judge. Harvard Law Professor Abram Chayes, who wrote a definitive law review article on public law litigation in 1976, described the changed role of a judge faced with adjudicating an institutional law case. "[A] judicial decree establishing an ongoing affirmative regime of conduct is *pro tanto* a legislative act. But in actively shaping and monitoring the decree, mediating between the parties, developing his own sources of expertise and information, the trial judge has passed beyond even the role of legislator and has become a policy planner and manager." [8]

Justice's extensive involvement in the operations of Texas prisons provides an apt illustration of Chayes' characterization. Former Texas Lieutenant Governor William P. Hobby argues that "there is a line between interpreting the law, which is a judicial function, and making the law, which is not. Upon occasion, Judge Justice has crossed it." Hobby cites Justice's proposed fines in the 1986 *Ruiz v. Estelle* contempt order as an example. "When you have one level of government talking about confiscating taxpayers' money, that's wrong. That's over the line of legitimate judicial power."

There are indeed legitimate concerns about the consequences of judicial involvement in institutional life, however justified. Federal judges, who are appointed for life, are not accountable to the state legislature or to the people. Judicial involvement saps the vitality of administrators by curtailing their independence. Legislators learn that it is politically preferable for judges who are not accountable to the voters to order reforms than for politicians to initiate them themselves. Overextension of the judicial role undermines respect for judges and for courts. Long-term remedial orders lock into place methodological paradigms extant at the time the orders were issued. Once issued, an order is hard to change. When Justice mandated extensive operational changes in the state's institutions for juvenile offenders in his 1974 *Morales v. Turman* order, due process and rehabilitation dominated thinking in the juvenile justice field. Ten years later, determinant sentencing and punishment held sway. Could the Texas Youth Commission today establish Marine-type boot camps at its state schools and still be in accord with the *Morales* settlement?

Offsetting the criticisms are important benefits. Texas' propensity to carry out its social responsibilities through large impersonal institutions, the legislature's refusal to fund the institutions adequately, and the weak oversight character of the Texas agency form of government all contributed to an environment in which illegal and inhumane practices flourished. The facts Justice so meticulously set forth in his opinions make it nearly impossible to deny that these conditions existed. Unless one believes that government-sanctioned segregation is permissible, that undocumented alien children have no entitlement to a free public education, or that juvenile offenders, mentally retarded persons, and prisoners have no right to humane conditions, reform was in order. Given the political powerlessness of these minorities, a force outside state government was required to effectuate a remedy. Former veteran state legislator Ray Farabee observes, "There are only so many dollars. If there is no pressure, human services and corrections tend to get the short end of the stick. More than any other federal judge, Justice has been their advocate, and vastly more appropriations have flowed in their direction as a result."

A major difficulty with Justice's use of human dignity as a transcendant value is that the concept is not precise. Wholly disparate courses of action can be justified by its assertion. Thus, for example, advancing human dignity can arguably be used to justify recognizing the right of individuals to make contracts free of governmental interference, for liberty of contract is endemic to the free enterprise system. Likewise, human dignity can justify a right to privacy encompassing both the right to an abortion and the right to engage in homosexual activity. Its meaning varies over time and with the decision-maker. Yet human dignity, though imperfectly understood, represents a common-sense, practical approach to assuring that the legal system serves a socially desirable goal.

At a symposium held in 1976 at the Aspen Institute for Humanistic Studies in Aspen, Colorado, Justice asserted that the judiciary has a responsibility to assure some measure of human dignity to those who are powerless to act on their own behalf when the legislative and administrative branches of government fail to live up to their social responsibilities. Chief Justice Warren Burger, who had joined the symposium, immediately pronounced Justice's position unconstitutional. The legislature, he maintained, has a right not to act. Does our two-hundred-year-old Constitution prevent the federal judiciary from correcting the abuses of public institutional life and advancing human liberties? Or is Justice truer to the founders' intentions in asserting that the judiciary must assume an activist role in furthering individual rights and promoting social justice in a changing society, using the principles set forth in the Constitution as a starting place? The question admits of no easy answer.

Justice wants to be remembered "as a very careful judge in the sense that

I was trying to follow the law." He adds, "I hope that I can be regarded as a professional willing to do whatever I felt the law required me to do, right and justice considered." The second statement is closer to the mark, for William Wayne Justice will never be considered a mainstream federal judge who merely followed the law. His rights-oriented style of judicial activism has made him unique on the federal bench, just as a similar jurisprudence made William O. Douglas stand out on the U.S. Supreme Court. No one can dispute the fact that Justice's bold and creative use of judicial power to effectuate a just remedy in the cases coming before him has dramatically changed Texas and has had a spillover effect beyond its borders. In the span of a decade, he advanced the cause of school integration across the state, provided the catalyst for dramatic reform of the state's juvenile reform schools, opened the schoolhouse doors to undocumented alien children, prodded the legislature to expand bilingual instruction, improved conditions for the state's institutionalized mentally retarded persons, and transformed the state prison system. In the process, he articulated a jurisprudence at once controversial and thought-provoking. While considerable concern and criticism continue about his ready willingness to interpret the Constitution and his judicial remedial powers broadly, few doubt his courage or sincerity.

Rather than a pioneer or crusader, Justice is best viewed as a courageous and fiercely independent jurist with a deep sense of right and wrong. When the cases came before him, he sought to employ the law to render compassion and justice, regardless of the consequences for him or his court. He has not been averse to pushing the law beyond existing precedents to promote individual rights and to render a measure of human dignity for those most disfavored in society. He has been true to his name: he has sought to secure justice in an often unjust society.

APPENDIX

List of Law Clerks

Wayne V. R. Smith
July 1968–June 1970
University of Texas School of Law

Michael P. O'Reilly
July 1, 1968–June 28, 1969
University of Texas School of Law

Robert F. Stein, Jr.
June 28, 1969–July 3, 1971
University of Texas School of Law

Colin J. Carl
June 15, 1970–March 3, 1972
University of Texas School of Law

Henry T. Skelton
July 5, 1971–May 18, 1973
University of Texas School of Law

Richard W. Mithoff
March 19, 1972–June 30, 1974
University of Texas School of Law

Marianne Wesson
July 23, 1973–June 27, 1975
University of Texas School of Law

Jack T. Friedman
August 5, 1974–June 30, 1976
University of Texas School of Law

John Heard
August 5, 1975–July 30, 1976
University of Texas School of Law

Mary Ellen Endres
July 1, 1976–July 31, 1976
St. Mary's University School of Law

Kathlyn A. (Kay) Knobloch
August 3, 1976–July 29, 1977
University of Texas School of Law

Mark Glasser
August 3, 1976–June 19, 1978
University of Texas School of Law

Ruth Epstein
August 1, 1977–August 4, 1978
Harvard Law School

Lucas Guttentag
July 12, 1978–June 1, 1979
Harvard Law School

Toni Palter
August 14, 1978–August 10, 1979
University of Texas School of Law

Steve Fury
June 4, 1979–June 24, 1980
Harvard Law School

Ann Maclaine
June 4, 1979–December 19, 1980
University of Michigan Law School

Michael R. Smith
August 3, 1979–August 15, 1980
Stanford Law School

Robert McDuff
June 24, 1980–June 26, 1981
Harvard Law School

James L. Sultan
August 18, 1980–August 21, 1981
Harvard Law School

Fritz Byers
June 29, 1981–July 16, 1982
Harvard Law School

Barbara Ellis
August 24, 1981–August 20, 1982
Yale Law School

Jennifer Harbury
May 24, 1982–August 1, 1983
Harvard Law School

Roger Parloff
August 23, 1982–August 12, 1983
Yale Law School

Martha Davis
June 27, 1983–June 29, 1984
Baylor Law School

Mark Englehart
November 14, 1983–August 30, 1985
Harvard Law School

Mark F. Walter
May 25, 1984–May 31, 1985
Brooklyn Law School

David D. Brown
June 25, 1984–May 24, 1985
Harvard Law School

Susan Stefan
August 27, 1984–September 20, 1985
Stanford Law School

Denise Wintenberger
September 10, 1984–August 16, 1985
Brooklyn Law School

Amy Johnson
June 10, 1985–May 30, 1986
Harvard Law School

Martin Minsky
August 19, 1985–April 4, 1986
Brooklyn Law School

Virginia L. Looney
August 26, 1985–August 22, 1986
University of Georgia School of Law

Jackee Cox
September 20, 1985–May 24, 1986
University of Texas School of Law

Juanita Hernández
September 16, 1985–September 5,
1986
Harvard Law School

Audrey Selden
June 16, 1986–September 18, 1987
Harvard Law School

Daniel Gunther
August 25, 1986–March 18, 1988
Stanford Law School

David Weiser
September 8, 1986–September 4, 1987
Yale Law School

Thomas C. Viles
September 7, 1987–September 2, 1988
New York University School of Law

Laird Lucas
September 21, 1987–September 21,
1988
Yale Law School

Carol Clifford
September 9, 1988–August 29, 1989
New York University School of Law

Lynn E. Blais
September 21, 1988–September 14,
1989
Harvard Law School

James E. Tourtelott
August 30, 1989–September 12, 1990
Yale Law School

James A. Wooten
October 16, 1989–August 29, 1990
Yale Law School

Susan A. Huber
August 29, 1990–September 1991
Boalt Hall School of Law, University of
California at Berkeley

David H. Herrington
September 12, 1990–September 1991
University of Texas School of Law

Timothy J. Moran
September 1991–
Harvard Law School

Michael C. Subit
September 1991–
Stanford Law School

Notes

Interviews from which direct quotations and specifically attributed references have been taken are listed at the beginning of the notes for each chapter. Other interviews are not listed. Given their great number, quotations from interviews with Judge Justice are also not referenced. All persons who are quoted directly, including Judge Justice, have signed authorization forms permitting use of the quoted material.

In the case of lengthy judicial decisions, excerpts are referenced to the pages on which they appear. For short decisions, only the initial excerpt is referenced.

In the interest of readability, the formal style of referencing legal materials has been slightly modified.

1. The Early Years

References from interviews: Matt Dawson, February 24, 1989; Ellen Justice, October 27, 1988; John Neal Justice, January 13, 1989; Sue Justice, April 1, 1988; William H. Kugle, September 30, 1986; Donald Lamb, November 16, 1989; Elvin Lamb, November 14, 1989; J. Mike Rowan, August 26, 1987; Marcelle Simmons, April 10, 1987.

1. Peter Larson, "His Honor William Wayne Justice," *Dallas Times Herald*, November 13, 1983.

2. Letter from Ed Blythe, November 6, 1989.

3. Letter from Lelia May Garner, November 6, 1989.

4. Letter from Helen Carroll Bever, October 27, 1988.

5. The most controversial episode involving Rowan's employment in a case before Judge Justice occurred in connection with an employment discrimination lawsuit filed against the Texas Power and Light Company. The case is discussed in Chapter 8, note 67.

6. Paul Moore, "Pamphlet Is Introduced as Evidence," *Corsicana Daily Sun*, March 6, 1956.

2. Political Activity: Outside the Mainstream

References from interviews: Farris Block, March 27, 1990; Creekmore Fath, August 31, 1988; Sue Justice, April 25, 1990; Willis D. Moore, August 15, 1988; Frank C. Oltorf, January 12, 1988.

1. In *The Establishment in Texas Politics* (Westport, Conn.: Greenwood Press, 1979), pp. 36–38, George Norris Green discusses the role of former governor Jim (Pa) Ferguson in arranging extra votes to put O'Daniel in the lead. Johnson considered, then rejected an investigation, since the results might be as unfavorable to Johnson as to O'Daniel.

2. Donna A. Barnes, *Farmers in Rebellion* (Austin: University of Texas Press, 1984), p. 5.

3. "Justice" (KERA-TV, Public Broadcasting System, Dallas), aired January 1986.

4. Green, *The Establishment in Texas Politics,* pp. 17–20.

5. *Smith v. Allwright,* 321 U.S. 649 (1944).

6. Green, *The Establishment in Texas Politics,* p. 95.

7. David Maraniss, "Justice, Texas Style," *Washington Post,* February 28, 1987.

8. Yarborough disagrees that the prospects for winning were that dim. He maintains that after his campaign kickoff in Athens, Shivers and Lyndon Johnson forged a temporary alliance to keep him from winning by arranging for the Shivers delegation rather than the liberal-loyalist Maury Maverick contingent to be seated at the Democratic National Convention in Chicago (this event is described later in the chapter). Had Shivers not been seated, Yarborough believes he could have won the primary as the loyalist Democrat. "Friends in East Texas, where our strength was greatest, phoned me that the courthouse crowd (meaning the oldtimers, there being no air conditioning, who whittled and played checkers and dominoes around the courthouse) were saying that "if Shivers ain't got enough sense to be seated, he ain't got enough sense to be Governor." Though Yarborough could not afford expensive polling, he had learned toward the end of the campaign that the Shivers forces were showing him with 45 percent of the vote. When Shivers was seated, the percentage dropped. "If the press had not concealed the facts from the people, and showed how he violated his pledge to the Democratic Party at the National Convention, I think my 45 percent would have held, and gone possibly higher," he maintains. "Shivers' actual seating saved him." Letter from Ralph Yarborough, May 21, 1990.

9. Letter from Ralph Yarborough, April 30, 1990.

10. The events are described by James Reston, Jr., in *The Lone Star: The Life of John Conally* (New York: Harper & Row, 1989), pp. 170–181.

11. Robert Caro, *Means of Ascent* (New York: Alfred Knopf, 1990), p. 15.

12. Letter from Ralph Yarborough, April 30, 1990.

13. "Democratic Reporter," Democrats of Texas Clubs, March 1980.

14. Charles W. Stephenson, "The Democrats of Texas and Texas Liberalism, 1944–1960: A Study in Political Frustration" (MA thesis, Southwest Texas State University, 1967), pp. 122–128.

3. U.S. Attorney: The Road to the Bench

References from interviews: Leighton Cornett, October 13, 1987; John Glass, Jr., July 19, 1990; Richard Brooks Hardee, August 26, 1987; Sue Justice, April 1, 1988; Lloyd W. Perkins, May 31, 1990; Carl Roth, July 21, 1988; Robert J. Stevens, July 13, 1988; William Louis White, April 11, 1990; Halbert O. Woodward, April 17, 1990; Ralph Yarborough, April 29 and June 6, 1986.

    1. Letter from Ralph Yarborough, December 29, 1989.

    2. Tunnell was criminal district attorney in Van Zandt County and was prosecuting a young man by the name of Johnson for bigamy in 1952. The Justice law firm represented Johnson and had secured several continuances in accordance with Will Justice's general philosophy that time is the best defense in a criminal case. But after several had been granted, the Justices knew that they had to get serious about a trial. As it turned out, the day the case was set for trial, the Justices were also scheduled to be in court in Gregg County. Will Justice wrote a letter to the judge in the Johnson case, A. A. Dawson, informing him of the conflict and requesting another postponement. No reply was received. Justice then wrote out a formal motion for continuance and asked E. E. Cornelius, Jr., a young lawyer in town who happened to be going to Canton, where the case was to be tried the next day, to file the motion for him. The senior Justice assured him that it was a routine matter.

    Cornelius dutifully presented the motion to Judge Dawson on the morning of January 30, 1952. But to Cornelius' great shock and surprise, Dawson rejected it and started the trial. Cornelius knew nothing of the case and took no action. Dawson did not appoint him or anyone else to represent Johnson. With a vigorous prosecution by Tunnell and no contrary evidence, the jury found Johnson guilty. He was sentenced to four years in the penitentiary. When the Justices returned from Grett County that evening, they found an angry Cornelius waiting for them. Will Justice immediately appealed the decision to the Texas Court of Criminal Appeals, which overturned the verdict and sent the case back for another trial so that Johnson could be afforded counsel. *Johnson v. State,* 251 S.W.2d (739 (Tex. Crim. App. 1952).

    Tunnell again vigorously prosecuted the case. Johnson was found guilty a second time. Wayne Justice sought to overturn the judgment but was rebuffed by the Texas Court of Criminal Appeals, which found sufficient evidence to support the verdict: *Johnson v. State,* 258 S.W.2d 829 (Tex. Crim. App. 1952). Justice acknowledges that the case was strong against Johnson and that Tunnell was an effective prosecutor. "Joe had a good case, and he put it to us hard at the second trial. The jury gave Johnson two years instead of four as they had at the first trial. That's how I got to know Joe Tunnell. He was a competent lawyer, let me tell you."

    3. David F. Prindle, *Petroleum Politics and the Texas Railroad Commission* (Austin: University of Texas Press, 1981), p. 84.

    4. *Tyler Morning Telegraph,* September 4, 1963.

    5. *Duncan v. United States,* 357 F.2d 195 (4th Cir. 1966). In his appeal, Duncan maintained that while suspicion regarding his involvement in the actual robbery might have been established, his guilt had not been. He claimed that he was drunk that night and that Berry gave him a portion of the loot in order to keep him quiet.

The court of appeals concluded that the jury had ample evidence to reject this hypothesis. Why would Berry pay money to Duncan to keep him quiet if they were friends and had gone to Mount Enterprise together to cash traveler's checks, the appellate judges wondered. Furthermore, Berry refused to say unequivocally that Duncan had not joined him in the burglary. The evidence "is clear, strong and convincing that appellant was in possession of a good portion of the stolen property immediatley after the burglary and that Berry divided 'the take' with appellant" (p. 196). The trial court had been correct in rejecting Duncan's motion for acquittal.

6. Mary Jane Maddox, "Letter Used in Testimony," *Marshall News Messenger,* November 10, 1965.

7. *United States v. Wade,* 87 S.Ct. 1926 (1967), p. 1937. The majority rejected the self-incrimination claim. While Wade may have participated in the lineup against his will, his mere presence there and his being compelled to speak the phrase "Put the money in the bag" were not "testimonial within the scope of the privilege."

8. *Hawkins v. United States,* 417 F.2d 1271 (5th Cir. 1969).

9. Letter from Phillip B. Baldwin, April 24, 1990.

10. A full account is contained in Riley Kennedy, "Justice Sworn In as Federal Judge," *Tyler Courier-Times-Telegraph,* June 30, 1968.

11. Ibid.

4. Life as a Judge

References from interviews: Steve Bickerstaff, May 25, 1989; David Brown, November 15, 1988; Howell Cobb, November 9, 1990; Jack T. Friedman, April 28, 1988; John C. Hardy, April 9, 1987; Amy Johnson, May 20, 1986; Ellen Justice, October 27, 1988; Sue Justice, April 1 and April 25, 1988; William H. Kugle, September 30, 1986; Robert McDuff, November 18, 1988; Robert M. Parker, April 26, 1990; Roger Parloff, November 16, 1989; Thomas M. Reavley, October 30, 1989; David R. Richards, January 5, 1989; Woodrow Seals, November 17, 1989; Wayne V. R. Smith, April 29, 1988; William M. Steger, July 24, 1989; Robert F. Stein, October 27, 1987; Ralph Yarborough, April 29, 1986.

1. *McCuin v. Texas Power and Light Co.,* 714 F.2d 1255 (5th Cir. 1983), p. 1261. Reviewing the options available in our legal system to attorneys in selecting the courts in which to file their lawsuits, the Fifth Circuit observed, "The existence of these choices not only permits but indeed invites counsel in an adversary system, seeking to serve his client's interests, to select the forum that he considers most receptive to his cause. The motive of the suitor in making this choice is ordinarily of no moment: a court may be selected because its docket moves rapidly, its discovery procedures are liberal, its jurors are generous, the rules of law applied are more favorable, or the judge who presides in that forum is thought more likely to rule in the litigant's favor." *McCuin* involved a challenge to Justice's brother-in-law's becoming an attorney in an employment discrimination case, resulting in Justice's removing himself from the case as presiding judge. The circumstances surrounding the litigation and the Fifth Circuit's ruling in *McCuin* are discussed in Chapter 8, note 67.

2. *Taylor v. Campbell,* Dkt. No. TY-79-332-CA (July 2, 1981).

3. "The Honorable William Wayne Justice Dedication," *Annual Survey of Ameri-*

can Law, March 1986, p. xx. In citing Justice as the Outstanding Federal Trial Judge four years before, the Association of Trial Lawyers of America noted his decision in *Hill v. United States* Civil Action No. P-79-8-CA (E.D. Tex. August 21, 1981), dismissing plaintiff's claim under the Federal Tort Claims Act on the basis of a lack of jurisdiction, while at the same time explaining how the complaint could be amended to remedy the defect, and allowing time for the amendment. *Hill* involved a serviceman who sought compensation for injuuries he asserted arose from his compulsory participation in an experimental atomic bomb blast in Nevada in 1955. Justice dismissed the case based on the fact that the FTCA does not encompass injuries sustained incident to military service. But he noted that if the plaintiff were to assert that the failure to warn of the potential dangers of exposure to radiation or to provide medical care after plaintiff's discharge caused a distinct injury, jurisdiction under FTCA might be established. Plaintiff was given ten days to amend his complaint.

4. Under the federal Civil Rights Attorney Fees Award Act, 42 U.S.C. Section 1988, prevailing plaintiffs in civil rights cases are entitled to have their attorney fees paid by the defendants. The act is intended to encourage compliance with civil rights laws. Fees can be awarded to defendants under the statute only if the court finds that the plaintiff's lawsuit was frivolous, unreasonable, or without foundation.

5. The phrase "polysemantic neologism" refers to a word or expression of recent origin which is often disapproved and which is susceptible to a variety of definitions. He noted that "the most striking of several proffered definitions—many of which were by way of simile or hyperbole—was that a nerd is a person who is dominated by his pet rock. Other definitions were: a socially maladroit person; a dolt; a 'bozo'—one who always spills his soup in a restaurant (as opposed to a 'nebbish,' who always gets the soup spilled on him)." *Martin v. W.K.M. Wellhead Services,* Civil Action No. TY-80-378-CA (E.D. Tex. April 4, 1984).

6. *Nash v. State of Texas,* 632 F.Supp. 951 (E.D. Tex. 1986). *Nash* is discussed in Chapter 7.

7. Letter from Kathlyn A. Knobloch, June 5, 1986.

8. At the time Justice became chief judge, the law provided that the district judge senior in service and under seventy years of age shall become chief judge when a vacancy occurs (28 U.S.C. Section 136). The statute was amended in 1982 to provide that the judge must be sixty-four or under and senior in service when a vacancy occurs. Because of the change, Judge William M. Steger, who was next in seniority but over the age limit, could not become chief judge.

9. Paul Burka, "The Real Governor of Texas," *Texas Monthly,* June 1978, p. 115.

10. *Lansdale v. Tyler Junior College,* 318 F.Supp. 529 (E.D. Tex. 1970), p. 533.

11. Ibid., 470 F.2d 659 (5th Cir. 1972). The Fifth Circuit, which heard the case *en banc* (all the judges participating), affirmed by a nine-to-six split. Seven separate opinions were filed, indicating how divisive the issue was among the judges. Interestingly, in a hair-length case that same year involving students in elementary and secondary schools, the same court ruled against the students: *Karr v. Schmidt,* 460 F.2d 609 (5th Cir. 1972). The fact that a community college and older students were involved influenced a sufficient number of judges to distinguish the *Lansdale* case from the *Karr* decision. Students who live within the jurisdiction of the Fifth Circuit thus

appear to gain a new constitutional right of personal grooming when they graduate from high school. Note: At the time of these decisions, the Fifth Circuit's jurisdiction extended to six southern states and the Canal Zone. In 1981, Congress split the jurisdiction between the Fifth Circuit (Texas, Louisiana, and Mississippi) and the newly created Eleventh Circuit (Alabama, Georgia, Florida, and the Canal Zone).

12. Laura Richardson and Jo Clifton, "William Wayne Justice: An Interview," *Texas Observer*, January 20, 1978, p. 5.

13. "Tyler's Plan Given Support," *Tyler Morning Telegraph*, February 28, 1969.

14. In *Green v. County School Board*, 391 U.S. 430 (1968), the U.S. Supreme Court ruled against the use of freedom-of-choice plans which did not result in integrated schools. In both *Green* and *Alexander v. Holmes County Board of Education*, 396 U.S. 19 (1969), the Court concluded that the obligation of every school board was to terminate dual school systems "at once" and operate only unitary schools. Like the Supreme Court, the U.S. Court of Appeals for the Fifth Circuit had refused to countenance nondiscriminatory geographical zoning and voluntary freedom-of-choice policies which did not create a unitary system. Justice cited a number of Fifth Circuit decisions to this effect in his Tyler desegregation order.

15. *United States v. Tyler Independent School District*, Civil Action No. 5176 (E.D. Tex. July 27, 1970).

16. David Maraniss, "Justice, Texas Style," *Washington Post*, February 28, 1987.

17. *Dunn v. Tyler Independent School District*, 327 F.Supp. 528 (E.D. Tex. 1971). On appeal, the U.S. Court of Appeals for the Fifth Circuit in a two-to-one decision partially reversed Judge Justice's decision: 460 F.2d 137 (1972), *reh. and reh. en banc denied*. The majority concluded that Justice was wrong in holding that before a suspension could occur, there must be a specific rule pertaining to the misconduct. He was also found wrong in concluding that the Tyler regulation against boycotts and walkouts was unconstitutionally vague. The majority did uphold his decision with respect to the lack of due process for suspensions lasting longer than three days. Though reversal was in order, the appeals court allowed Justice's original decision to stand in light of the passage of time and the mootness of the dispute. Judge Richard Rives in a spirited dissent argued that Justice's decision should have been upheld on all counts in light of his closeness to the scene and the soundness of his decision. The reversal served as vindication for many in Tyler who had asserted all along that Justice had abused his authority by undertaking to second-guess school administrators.

18. Order, July 8, 1971.

19. Burka, "The Real Governor of Texas," p. 190.

20. Ibid.

21. A particularly poignant account of the tribulations four judges on the U.S. Court of Appeals for the Fifth Circuit and their families experienced in desegregating the South in the late 1950s and 1960s is contained in Jack Bass, *Unlikely Heroes* (New York: Simon and Schuster, 1981). The four, Elbert Tuttle, John Minor Wisdom, Richard Rives, and John R. Brown—all Republicans except Rives—were subjected to the same social ostracism and vituperation that Justice encountered in Tyler. Along with the four, the Bass book also includes as unlikely heroes Federal District Court Judges Frank M. Johnson, Jr., and J. Skelly Wright. Johnson later provided valuable insight to William Wayne Justice with regard to lawsuits over conditions of confine-

ment in Texas public institutions. Both Johnson and Wright were later elevated to court of appeals judgeships.

The *Brown v. Board of Education* story itself is chronicled in Richard Kluger's celebrated book, *Simple Justice* (New York: Alfred A. Knopf, 1976).

22. Frank Klimko and Evan Moore, "Czar of Texas," *Houston Chronicle,* January 1, 1987.

23. Richardson and Clifton, "William Wayne Justice: An Interview," p. 4.

24. William H. Rehnquist, "The Notion of a Living Constitution," *Texas Law Review* 54 (1976): 693. A shortened version of this article together with the one written by Judge Justice was included in a collection of essays on the judiciary: Mark W. Cannon and David M. O'Brien, eds., *Views from the Bench* (Chatham, N.J.: Chatham House Publishers, 1985).

25. William Wayne Justice, "A Relativistic Constitution," *University of Colorado Law Review* 52 (1980): 19.

26. *Dred Scott v. Sanford,* 60 U.S. (19 How.) 393 (1857).

27. *Lochner v. New York,* 198 U.S. 45 (1905).

28. Justice made this same point in a 1986 speech to the Rose City Chapter of Phi Delta Kappa, in Tyler. The speech was later reprinted in a leading educational journal under the title "Teaching the Bill of Rights": *Phi Delta Kappan* 68, no. 2 (October 1986): 154–157. Justice stressed the need for teachers to teach dispassionately the components of Bill of Rights and their history "to counter the ubiquitous and often distorted perceptions of these rights fostered by television and other mass media" (p. 156).

29. "Justice" (KERA-TV, Public Broadcasting System, Dallas), aired January 1986.

30. *United States v. Carolene Products Co.,* 304 U.S. 144 (1938).

31. *Trop v. Dulles,* 356 U.S. 86 (1958).

32. To cite but one interesting example, in 1970 he was faced with an extradition hearing involving Tex Watson, one of the members of Charles Manson's clan charged with complicity in the Sharon Tate murder case in California. Watson had been reared in Collin County. Considerable adverse publicity had been released about the case. Watson's attorneys, Boyd and Boyd of McKinney, argued that their client could not get a fair trial in California. Justice noted that the precedents did not provide him with the flexibility of doing otherwise than upholding extradition. The order denying the writ of *habeas corpus* is attached to the affirmance by the U.S. Court of Appeals for the Fifth Circuit. *Watson v. Montgomery,* 431 F.2d 1083 (1970), *per curiam.*

33. Richardson and Clifton, "William Wayne Justice: An Interview."

34. *Watson v. Thompson,* 321 F.Supp. 394 (1971), pp. 401–402.

35. *Griswold v. Connecticut,* 381 U.S. 479 (1965).

36. Charles L. Black, Jr., "The Unfinished Business of the Warren Court," *Washington Law Review* 46 (1970): 3–45; quote from p. 32.

37. *Pierce v. Hill Military Academy,* 268 U.S. 510 (1925).

38. A thorough discussion of the "intent of the framers" is offered in H. Jefferson Powell, "The Original Understanding of Original Intent," *Harvard Law Review* 98, no. 5 (March 1985): 885–948.

39. *Karr v. Schmidt,* 460 F.2d 609 (5th Cir. 1972). (See note 11 above.)

40. Speech delivered at the University of Texas School of Law, March 25, 1988, as part of the 20th Annual W. Page Keeton Law Week program.

41. *Texas House Journal,* Regular Session 69th Legislature (1985) 1: 19.

42. *Oldham v. Smith County,* TY-81-362-CA. The case was dismissed on April 19, 1984.

43. The Judge has always taken pride in the fact that it was ten years before he was reversed in a criminal case by the Fifth Circuit. The reversal came in a case involving the conviction of a defendant for shipping allegedly stolen cattle in interstate commerce. The Fifth Circuit held that there was insufficient evidence to support the verdict and sent the case back to the trial court for a judgment of acquittal: *United States v. Hines,* 563 F.2d 737 (1977). The judge who wrote the opinion in the two-to-one decision was Byron Skelton, an old political associate of Justice's from Temple, Texas, who was appointed to the U.S. Court of Customs and Patent Appeals by President Johnson. Skelton was sitting by designation. Justice still believes the defendant was guilty.

That it was a decade before a reversal sounds more impressive than it actually is, for Justice heard relatively few criminal cases during these years. Criminal cases have accounted for, on the average, between 5 and 10 percent of the docket. During some years, pending criminal cases numbered fewer than thirty. An expert on criminal law when he took the bench, Justice admits that by the mid-1970s when his docket became inundated he depended on his clerks to keep him abreast of legal developments in this field.

5. Statewide School Desegregation

References from interviews: Robert Alexius, April 15, 1987; Richard Arnett, January 23, 1987; William C. Bednar, Jr., January 22, 1987; Alexandra P. Buek, November 18, 1988; Colin J. Carl, October 20, 1987; Gilbert Conoley, May 16, 1987; Susan J. Dasher, January 22, 1987; William H. Kugle, September 30, 1986; Richard Mithoff, June 3, 1988; Ralph Yarborough, April 29, 1986.

1. "Justice" (KERA-TV, Public Broadcasting System, Dallas), aired January 1986.

2. *United States v. Tatum Independent School District,* 306 F.Supp. 285 (E.D. Tex. 1969).

3. *United States v. Texas,* 321 F.Supp. 1043 (E.D. Tex. 1970), pp. 1050–1051.

4. Ibid., 330 F.Supp. 235 (E.D. Tex. 1971), p. 250.

5. The full order from which this excerpt comes was attached as an appendix to the later Fifth Circuit opinion affirming most of Justice's decision: *United States v. Texas,* 447 F.2d 441 (5th Cir. 1971), p. 443. Justice's supplemental decision issued in April 1971, is styled *United States v. Texas,* 330 F.Supp. 235 (E.D. Tex. 1971).

6. Richard Morehouse, "'Massive Busing' Wasn't Ordered," *Dallas Morning News,* May 6, 1981.

7. *Dallas Morning News,* May 14, 1971.

8. *United States v. Texas,* 447 F.2d 441 (5th Cir. 1971).

9. *United States v. Edgar,* 404 U.S. 1206 (1971), pp. 1207–1208. The full

Court subsequently refused to hear the case: *Edgar v. United States* 404 U.S. 1016 (1982).

10. *Swann v. Charlotte-Mecklenburg Board of Education,* 402 U.S. 1 (1971).

11. *United States v. Texas,* 342 F.Supp. 24 (E.D. Tex. 1971), p. 29.

12. As quoted by Paul Burka, "The Real Governor of Texas," *Texas Monthly,* June 1978, p. 196.

13. *United States v. Texas,* 466 F.2d 518 (5th Cir. 1972), *per curiam.*

14. *School Desegregation in Texas: The Implementation of U.S. v. Texas* (Policy Research Report Number 51, Lyndon B. Johnson School of Public Affairs, University of Texas at Austin, 1982), p. 18.

15. *Hayes v. United States,* 444 F.2d 472 (5th Cir. 1971), cert. denied, 404 U.S. 882 (1971). Hayes and McMaster later unsuccessfully sought to challenge their sentences while confined to prison: *Hayes v. United States,* 464 F.2d 1252 (5th Cir. 1972).

16. *School Desegregation in Texas,* pp. 22–24, 35.

17. *Gillespie et al. v. Highland Park Independent School District,* No. 72-6487-H/I (162nd Judicial District, 1972).

18. Letter from Arlen D. Bynum, October 4, 1988.

19. *United States v. Texas,* 356 F.Supp. 469 (E.D. Tex. 1972). The defendants did not appeal Judge Justice's order, but they did appeal his award of attorney fees to the plaintiffs. In rejecting that appeal, the Fifth Circuit observed that "the appellants, with notice, left the 'plainly illuminated path,' which means that the finding of the District Court that they acted in obstinate noncompliance with the law cannot be said to have been clearly erroneous." 495 F.2d 1250 (5th Cir. 1974), *per curiam,* p. 1252.

20. *United States v. Texas (Gregory-Portland Independent School District Intervention),* 498 F.Supp. 1356 (E.D. Tex. 1980), p. 1374.

21. Ibid., p. 1362.

22. Ibid., pp. 1366–1367.

23. Ibid., p. 1366. When *United States v. Texas* was decided in 1971, a showing of intent to discriminate was not a requirement either under the Fourteenth Amendment equal protection clause or under Title VI of the 1964 Civil Rights Act, the primary school desegregation law. Thus, a federal court could order desegregation measures upon a showing of disproportionate impact on a minority group. But by the mid-1970s several U.S. Supreme Court decisions indicated that intent to discriminate in addition to racially disproportionate impact had to be shown under both the equal protection clause and Title VI: *Washington v. Davis,* 426 U.S. 229 (1976); *University of California Board of Regents v. Bakke,* 438 U.S. 265 (1978). In the absence of pervasive segregatory laws and policies, determining segregative intent is often difficult, and the Supreme Court continues to struggle to enunciate clear rules of evidence. See, for example, the conflicting views among the U.S. Supreme Court justices in *Columbus Board of Education v. Penick,* 443 U.S. 449 (1979), decided by a 5 to 4 vote. The problem is particularly vexing in the North where statewide de jure segregation against blacks never occurred and in most parts of the country where segregatory laws have been absent for nonblack ethnic minorities, such as Mexican-Americans.

24. *United States v. Texas (Gregory-Portland Independent School District Intervention),* 498 F.Supp. 1356 (1980), p. 1373.

25. *Portland News,* August 21, 1980.

26. *United States Gregory-Portland Independent School District,* 654 F.2d 989 (5th Cir. 1982), p. 996.

27. Ibid., p. 999.

28. Ibid., p. 1005.

29. *Price v. Denison Independent School District,* Civil Action No. 1565 (E.D. Tex. 1981), p. 33.

30. "Justice" (KERA-TV).

31. The creation of these "super-schools" has met with court approval: *Tasby v. Wright,* 630 F.Supp. 597 (N.D. Tex. 1986). While Judge Barefoot Sanders did not minimize the importance of crosstown busing, he noted that it must have a significant purpose. "In the Court's opinion, it is pointless to bus minority students from the minority neighborhoods of West Dallas to attend predominantly minority schools in North Dallas; such transportation does not serve a desegregative purpose" (p. 603).

32. Since the 1970s, research has consistently shown that school integration has no significant impact on the achievement levels of whites, but does produce gains in achievement levels among minorities. The achievement levels of minorities in integrated schools surpass those of minorities attending largely one-race schools. See, for example, Robert L. Crain and Rita E. Mahard, "Minority Achievement: Policy Implications of Research," in *Effective School Desegregation,* ed. W. Hawley (Beverly Hills, Calif.: Sage Publications, 1982). Further, recent attitudinal research shows that those who are bused are much less likely to regard the experience negatively than when busing was first implemented: William Snider, "Opposition to Busing Declines, Poll Finds," *Education Week,* January 21, 1987, p. 6. However, a 1987 report issued by the U.S. Education Department entitled "The Carrot or the Stick in School-Desegregation Policy" reveals data showing that voluntary measures such as magnet schools are more likely to produce interracial mixing over the long run than mandatory busing. According to the study, the latter is more likely to result in white flight, thus increasing segregation.

33. Increasingly, members of the black community are expressing frustration with the results of school desegregation. They question why minorities have to bear the brunt of desegregation through the closing of black schools, disproportionate busing of black children, and desegregation plans drawn up by whites. Though support for school integration remains strong among blacks, support for black separatism has surfaced, particularly in urban school districts. Voucher programs for low-income black students and all-black enrichment schools are two manifestations. For a discussion of discontent in the black community, see Lynn Olson, "Black Community Is Frustrated over Lack of Results from Desegregation," *Education Week,* October 17, 1990.

34. *United States v. Texas,* 628 F.Supp. 304 (E.D. Tex. 1985), p. 316.

35. Terrence Stutz, "State to Appeal Skills Test Ruling," *Dallas Morning News,* August 29, 1985.

36. Richard S. Dunham, "Justice Department Backs Texas on Teacher Testing," *Dallas Times Herald,* October 8, 1985.

37. *United States v. LULAC,* 793 F.2d 636 (5th Cir. 1986). With regard to jurisdiction, the Fifth Circuit fully upheld the right of intervenors representing Mexican-

American and black elementary and secondary school students to challenge violations of the 5281 order. However, the fourteen college students involved in the case were another matter. While there was some question whether these same organizations could represent the college students, the Fifth Circuit did not rule on the question since appellants had not objected. Judge Justice had also allowed the college students to intervene on their own behalf. The Fifth Circuit found some procedural flaws in the manner in which this was done but agreed that at this stage of the proceedings, judicial economy justified recognizing the students' claims. However, the panel noted, "Our decision is not to be viewed as sanction for this type of intervention which, by resting on a slender legal reed, enables a litigant to select the cause in which, and the judge to whom, it will present its case. The primary focus of the 1971 school desegregation order is on primary and secondary schools. It is at least open to question whether this fifteen-year-old litigation should have been expanded to encompass the separate and distinct claims of college students who desire to become teachers" (pp. 644–645).

38. See note 23 above.

39. *United States v. LULAC,* p. 639.

40. Ibid., p. 643.

41. *United States v. Texas (Hightower Intervention),* Civil Action No. 5281 (E.D. Tex. September 8, 1980).

42. *Townes v. Clarksville Independent School District,* Dkt. No. 082-R6-1287 (Tex. Comm'r of Educ. July 26, 1989).

43. *School Desegregation in Texas.* To determine changes in desegregation over time, researchers at the Lyndon B. Johnson School of Public Affairs used a common research tool called the "index of dissimilarity." The index of dissimilarity employs a scale to compare the racial composition of the school district as a whole with the racial composition of each of its campuses. An index of 0 indicates a perfect match, i.e., complete integration. An index of 1 indicates complete racial isolation, in effect, a dual school system. But note the distortion evident in a district that is 95 percent black and has schools that also are 95 percent black. With a 0 rating, the school presumably would be considered completely integrated. The same would be true for a district with a 40 percent black enrollment distributed evenly across its schools. Hence, the dissimilarity index must be used with caution, particularly in central cities, where minority enrollments are apt to be high. As used in the literature on desegregation, 0 to .20 indicates districts which are relatively well integrated, .20 to .40 indicates moderate segregation, .40 to .60 indicates serious segregation, and .60 to 1.0 indicates pronounced racial isolation.

Because most school districts in Texas have only one high school and one junior high school, the researchers computed the index of dissimilarity for all school districts having at least two elementary schools for 1970–1971 and 1978–1979. There were over 500 districts in this category. They found that the median index for these districts was .10 in 1970–1971 and .07 in 1978–1979. The percentage of districts at .40 and above had declined from 17 to 9 in the same period. When the 43 districts under separate court order were compared with those under Judge Justice's order, the median index of the former was .59 in 1970–1971 and .39 in 1978–1979. The percentage of those in this group at .40 and above were 66 and 48 for the same time periods.

The data thus indicate that for the group as a whole, the degree of segregation was much greater in those school districts under separate court order than for those under the *United States v. Texas* order. The most segregated districts were located in metropolitan areas. Court-imposed desegregation clearly brought about increased integration for school districts in both categories.

44. *Status of School Desegregation, 1968–1986: A Report of the Council of Urban Boards of Education and the National School Desegregation Project at the University of Chicago* (Alexandria, Va., 1989).

45. In January 1991, the U.S. Supreme Court handed down a decision in the most important school desegregation case since the mid-1970s. By a 5 to 3 vote in *Board of Education of Oklahoma City v. Dowell,* 111 S.Ct. 630, the Court concluded in a cautiously worded opinion that once all the vestiges of *de jure* segregation have been eliminated, federal court supervision may end, even if one-race schools re-emerge. The question the trial court should ask, wrote Chief Justice William Rehnquist for the majority, is "whether the board had complied in good faith with the desegregation decree since it was entered, and whether the vestiges of past discrimination had been eliminated to the extent practicable" (p. 638). In making this determination, the court must consider "every facet of school operations," ranging from student assignment to faculty hiring, facilities, and extracurricular activities. Justice Thurgood Marshall wrote a dissenting opinion in which he argued that continued existence of one-race schools should preclude the end of court-ordered supervision. The decision will likely affect the continued viability of Judge Justice's order in *United States v. Texas* as state officials seek an opportunity to show that the conditions outlined in *Dowell* for declaring Texas school districts unitary have been met and thus court oversight is no longer necessary. That task may be complicated by the fact that the order covers so many school districts.

46. *School Desegregation in Texas,* pp. 53–54.

6. Juvenile Rights in Texas Reform Schools

References from interviews: Steve Bercu, October 20, 1987; Otis Carroll, July 13, 1988; Charles L. Derrick, January 28, 1988; Ron Jackson, January 29, 1988; David R. Richards, January 5, 1989; Robert F. Salter, January 28, 1988; Peter B. Sandmann, April 27, 1988; Forrest Smith, November 19, 1990; Patricia Wald, June 19, 1987; Larry York, June 23, 1987.

1. *In re Gault,* 387 U.S. 1 (1967). The due process clause of the Fourteenth Amendment states, "nor shall any State deprive any person of life, liberty, or property, without due process of law."

2. Statistics for 1972 revealed that 60 percent of the boys admitted to TYC institutions were there for crimes of stealing, 19 percent for disobedience and immoral conduct, 16 percent for other reasons, and only 9 percent for crimes of violence. For the girls, 68 percent were admitted for disobedience and immoral conduct, 15 percent for stealing, 13 percent for other offenses, and only 4 percent for crimes of violence. In 1973 the Texas Legislature tightened up the definitions of delinquent conduct when it

enacted a sweeping new juvenile law: Tex. Fam. Code Ann. Section 51.01 *et seq.* (Vernon 1982 Supp.); *cf.* Tex. Rev. Civ. Stat. Ann. Art. 2338-1 (Vernon 1971), *repealed* (1973).

3. The inmate population as of 1972 was 43 percent Anglo, 32 percent black, and 25 percent Mexican-American. The staff, however, was largely Anglo.) The median confinement in TYC institutions was about one year. Some were confined as long as three years.

4. *Morales v. Turman,* 326 F.Supp. 667 (E.D. Tex. 1971).

5. E.g., *Lockamy v. State,* 488 S.W.2d 954 (Tex. Civ. App., Austin, 1972). This ruling directed the lower court to order the release of over 500 TYC inmates who had been denied procedural due process during their adjudication.

6. Other provisions required that before a confession, guilty plea, or agreed entry of judgment, can be accepted, a juvenile must be given the warnings included in the U.S. Supreme Court's controversial *Miranda v. Arizona* ruling for criminal confessions: the suspect has the right to remain silent, anything the suspect says can be used against him or her in a court of law, the suspect has a right to an attorney, and an attorney will be appointed if he or she cannot afford one. In addition to full notice and a hearing in open court, the state agreed to provide juveniles with an opportunity to confront and cross-examine adverse witnesses, to present evidence, to have a trial by jury, and to be given a transcript of the proceedings, and an explanation of the right to appeal. These procedures were required even though under the juvenile justice system, children are not considered criminals and adjudicatory hearings are civil, not criminal, in nature.

Justice included both the 1972 agreed findings of fact and the order in two lengthy introductory footnotes in his 1974 memorandum opinion: *Morales v. Turman,* 383 F.Supp. 53 (E.D. Tex. 1974) (footnotes 11 and 12). "They hadn't been published anywhere," he says, "and I thought it would just be a good thing to let the record reflect that these agreements had been made."

7. Tex. Fam. Code Ann. Section 51.01 *et seq.* (Vernon 1982 Supp.).

8. For example, in 1975 the legislature amended Section 51.09(b) of the Family Code to allow waiver of rights, including the right to an attorney, during questioning. Waiver can occur only under certain conditions set forth in this section of the code.

9. Michael J. Churgin, "Mandated Change in Texas: The Federal District Court and the Legislature," in *Neither Angels nor Thieves: Studies in Deinstitutionalization of Status Offenders* (Washington, D.C.: National Academy Press, 1982).

10. Recommendations for reform legislation based on a 1969 legislative investigative report had gotten nowhere. Committee members believed Turman was responsible. Tom Barry and Wayne Jackson, "Senator Says TYC Reform Politics Victim," *Austin American-Statesman,* December 6, 1973.

11. Tex. Rev. Civ. Stat. Ann. Art. 5143d (Vernon 1971).

12. Record of proceedings, July 10, 1973, pp. 1529–1530.

13. Record of proceedings, August 8, 1973, p. 5758.

14. *Morales v. Turman,* 59 F.R.D. 157 (E.D. Tex. 1972), p. 159.

15. Record of proceedings, July 6, 1973, pp. 947–948.

16. Kenneth Wooden, *Weeping in the Playtime of Others* (New York: McGraw-Hill, 1976), p. 6. Wooden's chapter on *Morales* includes excerpts from some of the shocking testimony presented at the 1973 trial.

17. *Morales v. Turman,* 364 F.Supp. 166 (E.D. Tex. 1973). The Eighth Amendment states, "Excessive bail shall not be required, nor excessive fines imposed, nor cruel and unusual punishments inflicted."

18. George Kuempel, "30 Boys on Loose after Gatesville School Violence," *Houston Chronicle,* September 13, 1973. Many of the inmates, however, blamed conditions within TYC for triggering the rioting.

19. *Dallas Morning News,* September 22, 1973.

20. *Morales v. Turman,* 383 F.Supp. 53 (E.D. Tex. 1974).

21. *Donaldson v. O'Connor,* 493 F.2d 507 (5th Cir. 1974).

22. *Morales v. Turman,* 383 F.Supp. 53 (E.D. Tex. 1974), p. 71.

23. *Nelson v. Heyne,* 491 F.2d 352 (7th Cir. 1974).

24. Tex. Civ. Stat. Ann. Art. 5143d (Vernon 1971). This statute was repealed in 1979. The current operations of the Texas Youth Commission are detailed in Tex. Human Resources Code Section 61.001, *et seq.* (Vernon 1980). The commitment to rehabilitate and re-enter delinquent youth into society remains. See Section 61.002.

25. *Morales v. Turman,* 383 F.Supp. 53 (E.D. Tex. 1974), pp. 118–119.

26. Record of proceedings, July 18, 1973, pp. 2161–2162.

27. *Morales v. Turman,* 383 F.Supp. 53, p. 95.

28. Record of proceedings, July 11, 1973, pp. 1914–1915.

29. *Morales v. Turman,* 383 F.Supp. 53, p. 122.

30. Ibid., p. 124.

31. Ibid., p. 125.

32. *Dallas Morning News,* September 6, 1974.

33. For a detailed description of these events, see Churgin, "Mandated Change in Texas," pp. 885–893.

34. *Morales v. Turman,* 535 F.2d 864 (5th Cir. 1976).

35. Ibid., p. 873.

36. *Dallas Morning News,* July 23, 1976.

37. *Morales v. Turman,* 97 S.Ct. 1189 (1977), *per curiam.* Congress had enacted a law that required a three-judge court for issuing injunctions against enforcement of any state statute when the constitutionality of such statute is challenged: 28 U.S.C. Section 2281. "Enforcement" included an order made by an administrative board or commission when acting under the statute. Justice had concluded that the plaintiffs were not challenging any state statute in *Morales,* including the statute establishing the TYC. Indeed, they had relied on the latter to support their argument for a right to treatment. Nor were they challenging any rules and regulations made by the TYC pursuant to the enabling statute, because TYC had none. Each institution was largely left to its own discretion in developing operating procedures. Justice wrote in his 1974 memorandum opinion that "almost *any* action, however arbitrary, by an employee short of physical abuse of a child is probably *consistent* with TYC 'policy,' because that 'policy' is so vague as to be non-existent" (emphasis in original). The Supreme Court's unanimous decision noted that the Fifth Circuit had "transformed the jurisdictional inquiry from a threshold question to one depending upon the shifting proof during litigation, injecting intolerable uncertainty and potential delay into important litigation." The three-judge-court statute was not intended to apply to "generalized, unwritten practices of administration." Though repealed in 1976, the

three-judge-court statute could have been applied to cases such as *Morales* which were still being litigated at the time of repeal.

38. As contained in Churgin, "Mandated Change in Texas," p. 892.

39. *Morales v. Turman*, 562 F.2d 993 (5th Cir. 1977), p. 996.

40. The Supreme Court unanimously vacated the Fifth Circuit judgment in *Donaldson* a year after Justice issued his memorandum decision in *Morales* and sent the case back to the circuit court for additional consideration, concluding that the case could be decided without ruling on the difficult issue of a constitutional right to treatment. The Justices specifically pointed out in a footnote that the vacating of the Fifth Circuit decision "deprives that court's opinion of precedential effect, leaving this Court's opinion and judgment as the sole law of the case" (fn. 12): *O'Connor v. Donaldson*, 95 S.Ct. 2486 (1975). All the high court chose to decide was that a nondangerous person who can survive safely in freedom alone or with the assistance of family and friends cannot be constitutionally confined by the state.

41. *Morales v. Turman*, 562 F.2d 993 (5th Cir. 1977), p. 999.

42. The population of Gatesville, built for 2,000, was down to 427 inmates when Justice issued his 1974 memorandum opinion. Mountain View's population was only 56. It had a capacity of 480. In addition to the 1973 interim order, which limited those who could be sent to these institutions, a number of teenagers were removed from TYC jurisdiction as a result of the enactment of a new juvenile code in 1973 and the passage of legislation establishing eighteen as the age of majority the same year. The new juvenile code eliminated two categories of delinquent behavior that could have resulted in commitment to TYC: "One who habitually so deports himself as to injure or endanger the morals or health of himself or others" and "one who habitually associates with vicious or immoral persons." The code also prevented the commitment of children in need of supervision (CHINS) to TYC facilities, though later this provision was relaxed. CHINS are those children who engage in status offenses such as truancy or running away from home. More recently, the state has returned to a policy of prohibiting the commitment of these children to TYC institutions: Tex. Fam. Code Ann. Section 51.03(a) and 54.04(d) (Vernon 1986). The age-of-majority legislation was applied retroactively and resulted in the release of a number of youths. Though local legislators tried to hold onto these two institutions despite the court order, economic and political realities dictated that they be closed.

43. Peter Larson, "Youth Corrections Suit Nearing End," *Dallas Times Herald*, March 14, 1983.

44. Peter Larson, "Judge Rejects Youth Council Settlement," *Dallas Times Herald*, April 16, 1983.

45. *Morales v. Turman*, 569 F.Supp. 332 (E.D. Tex. 1983), p. 334. The attorney Justice was referring to was Robert Salter.

46. Ibid., p. 337.

47. Record of proceedings, April 16, 1984, pp. 34–35.

48. Other than this exception, enforcement of the settlement was to be a matter for the state district court in Travis County, the site of the state capital. The state had as one of its prime objectives the removal of the case from Justice's docket. To this end, the state attorneys proposed that complaints regarding enforcement at a particular TYC institution should be processed through the local state district court. Both the

plaintiffs' representatives and Judge Justice questioned the diligence of locally elected judges in seeing that the agreement would be enforced. The issue was resolved by lodging this responsibility in the Travis County District Court, which has broad experience in governmental matters. Plaintiffs' attorney Peter Sandmann says he had hoped to leave open an avenue of redress in federal court and was disappointed when Justice accepted the defendants' position on enforcement. Sandmann maintains that Justice's action deprived the plaintiff class of an important sanction against future backsliding by the TYC. Judge Justice doesn't recall that Sandmann ever raised any objections about it at the time.

49. Record of proceedings, April 16, 1984, pp. 78–79.

50. The Fifth Circuit later overturned Justice's decision granting attorney fees and costs in the amount of over $340,000 to the Mental Health Law Project on the grounds that the Project never intervened as a party in the lawsuit but rendered services on a voluntary basis. Thus, it was not entitled to attorney fees either on common law or statutory grounds: *Morales v. Turman,* 820 F.2d 728 (5th Cir. 1987).

51. Annual reports prior to 1976 give detailed statistics concerning the committing offense, length of stay, age, race, parents' marital and employment status, and the juvenile's schooling status. Reports following 1976 focus more on TYC policy and procedure. Annual reports, or sometimes quarterly reports, give fewer statistics and have eliminated information about parents. This trend, including pictures of new facilities and smiling faces, reflects the change in TYC since *Morales.*

The inability to obtain convincing data about success rates fuels philosophical pendulum swings within the correctional field. When *Morales* was initially decided, rehabilitation was "in." More recently, the pendulum has swung more toward "just deserts"—the belief that juvenile delinquents should be punished for their antisocial acts. Texas has not escaped the swing. In 1987 the legislature passed a determinate sentencing bill. The TYC is characterized by indeterminate sentencing, in which a child is sent to the TYC for an unknown length of time. The length of stay depends on the program the child is placed in and his or her behavior while in it. House Bill 682 permits a juvenile court to give a child aged ten to seventeen a determinate sentence for as long as thirty years for the commission of murder, capital murder, aggravated kidnapping, aggravated sexual assault, deadly assault on a law enforcement officer, or criminal attempt to commit capital murder. The sentence is served in TYC until the child's eighteenth birthday. TYC may petition the juvenile court to parole a child with a determinate sentence at any time, but if the sentence is not completely served by age eighteen and the child has not been paroled by that time, he or she is taken back to the juvenile court to be paroled or transferred to a Texas prison. Upon transfer to the Texas Department of Corrections, the time spent in TYC is counted as if spent in TDC. When finally released, the young adult remains an adjudicated delinquent, never acquiring the convicted felon label. With its high cost and its questionable constitutionality, the future and effect of determinate sentencing remain uncertain.

7. The First Amendment

References from interviews: Ben G. Levy, December 10, 1990; Laird Lucas, July 13, 1988; Charles F. Potter, October 26, 1988.

1. The First Amendment provides that "Congress shall make no law respecting an establishment of religion, or prohibiting the free exercise thereof; or abridging the freedom of speech, or of the press; or the right of the people peaceably to assemble, and petition the Government for the redress of grievances." The Fourteenth Amendment applies the same prohibition to the states. Despite being located in the Bible Belt, Justice has not presided over any major religion cases. Thus, this chapter will focus exclusively on the freedom-of-expression provisions of the First Amendment.

2. In 1969 the U.S. Supreme Court extended First Amendment protection in *Tinker v. Des Moines School District,* 393 U.S. 503, to public high school students who wore black armbands to school to protest the Vietnam War. *Tinker* was a seminal First Amendment decision, for the Court explicitly stated that neither students nor teachers "shed their constitutional rights to freedom of speech or expression at the schoolhouse gate." The Court noted, however, that student expression loses its protection if material disruption or substantial invasion of the rights of others results. A year earlier, the Supreme Court had ruled unanimously that a public school teacher has the right to express views as a citizen on matters of public concern such as a school bond election so long as the teacher's performance or working relationships are not undermined: *Pickering v. Board of Education,* 391 U.S. 563. The expression in that case had occurred off campus.

3. *Duke v. State of Texas,* 327 F.Supp. 1218 (E.D. Tex. 1971). Judge Justice based his decision in part on the fact that Scofield had held an *ex parte* hearing (a hearing in which only one side in the dispute is represented) on the temporary restraining order despite the fact that Duke and David Haylon, a fellow activist also barred from the campus, lived directly across from the campus security office. Officials had made no effort to contact the pair. Further, Justice ruled that the injunction was unconstitutionally overbroad in imposing "a blanket prohibition against plaintiffs Haylon and Duke from going onto the university campus" (p. 1231). Citing extensive case law, he also struck down a section of state law giving university officials the power to bar persons "having no *legitimate* business" from the campus and to eject "any *undesirable* person" from their property (emphasis in opinion). Vernon's Ann. Civ. Stat. Art. 2651a, Section 9. Because of the ambiguous terminology, the statute, Justice wrote, could be used to penalize constitutional exercise of First Amendment rights. Similar language in the university's policies was likewise ruled unconstitutional. Justice's constitutional scythe also swept away parts of the North Texas State University's outside speaker regulations, thus undercutting the university's grounds for seeking the restraining order.

Having viewed a videotape of the rally during the trial, Justice could find no justification to warrant barring Duke and Haylon. "[T]he circumstances of this rally, far from seriously portending violence, bespeak a considerable lack of enthusiasm from most of those present," he wrote. The only incident which caused any flurry of activity "was the action of the Sheriff of Denton County and a Deputy Sheriff in serving Mrs. Duke with the temporary restraining order" (p. 1231).

Justice also had some harsh words for Judge Scofield. "The failure and refusal of the State district judge to rule on the constitutional issues, which were squarely presented to him, presents an abuse of judicial discretion of such magnitude as to amount to a denial of the most fundamental element of the Due Process Clause—the right to a full and fair hearing—and to a denial of the equal protection of the laws" (pp. 1231–1232).

The state questioned whether Justice even had jurisdiction to hear the case. In his opinion, the Judge included a lengthy and detailed judicial exegesis on the relationship between the civil rights statute relied upon by the plaintiffs, 42 U.S.C. Section 1983, and a federal law restraining federal courts from issuing injunctions in state court matters, 28 U.S.C. Section 2283. He concluded that the former was an express exception to the latter, thus justifying his blocking the state court's action. Looking back, Justice says that he never doubted that he had jurisdiction. "I was dismayed by the assertion of the state district judge that he wasn't going to pass on the constitutional issues. I thought that that in and of itself justified the federal court's entering the field."

The Fifth Circuit did not agree. The three-judge panel did not issue a decision immediately, waiting for the U.S. Supreme Court to rule in a related case, *Mitchum v. Foster*, 407 U.S. 225 (1972). The high court's ruling appeared to support Justice's position, for the high court held that the civil rights statute was an express exception to the anti-injunction act. But the appeals panel concluded that the time was not ripe for Justice's intervention because the plaintiffs had not exhausted their remedies under state law. "Thus, the federal court here intruded itself into the processes of state litigation at a time when an adequate appellate remedy was available in the state courts. Such intrusion was improper as disruptive to the delicate balance between federal and state courts implicit in traditional concepts of comity and federalism. As representative of the dominant partner in the necessary interplay between two sovereigns, federal courts must be especially sensitive to this balance and assiduous in its preservation. These goals were disregarded in this case." 477 F.2d 244 (5th Cir. 1973), p. 252.

The ruling was clearly a rebuff to Justice's activism as a federal district court judge. Since he did not have jurisdiction in the first place, all the points he had raised in his decision were moot. But at least one judge on the Fifth Circuit panel was sensitive to the First Amendment issues which had been raised. In his specially concurring opinion, Judge Irving R. Goldberg noted, "I have no doubt . . . that First Amendment expressional freedoms were unquestionably frozen here. I also have no doubt that a federal remedy would have been appropriate had plaintiffs shown that a thaw could not have been obtained in state court" (p. 255).

Since the rebuff in *Duke* (known as *Duke I*), Justice has been very careful about matters of jurisdiction. "I started being very careful about that," he observes, "and I've learned that there are a lot of remedies in the state court system that are available. I've made it my business to learn."

4. *Duke v. North Texas State University*, 338 F.Supp. 990 (E.D. Tex. 1971), p. 996. This decision is known as *Duke II*.

5. Ibid., p. 997. In 1986, the Fifth Circuit upheld the dismissal of a teacher who used profanity in the classroom: *Martin v. Parrish*, 805 F.2d 583.

6. *Duke v. North Texas State University*, 469 F.2d 829 (5th Cir. 1973), p. 840.

7. Ibid., p. 843.

8. *Perry Education Association v. Perry Local Educators' Association*, 460 U.S. 37 (1983).

9. *Connick v. Myers,* 461 U.S. 138 (1983). In a case involving three police officers who criticized the chief of police, Justice had ruled to the contrary three years before: *Clary v. Irvin,* 501 F.Supp. 706 (E.D. Tex. 1980). After the police officers spoke informally with city council members about employment conditions within the police department, they were terminated. Justice ordered them reinstated, claiming that "just as there is a right to, and a legitimate need for, criticism of government from within its own ranks in such metropolitan areas as Washington, D.C., and Austin, Texas, so is there the same liberty, license, and necessity in the municipalities lying within the Piney Woods of East Texas" (p. 711).

10. *Bethel School District v. Fraser,* 106 S.Ct. 3159 (1986).

11. *Hazelwood School District v. Kuhlmeier,* 108 S.Ct. 562 (1988).

12. *Turner v. Safley,* 107 S.Ct. 2254 (1987). The student censorship case is *Hazelwood School District v. Kuhlmeier,* cited in note 11.

13. *McGuire v. Roebuck,* 347 F.Supp. 1111 (E.D. Tex. 1972), p. 1114, footnote 5.

14. Ibid., footnote 7.

15. *Shuttlesworth v. Birmingham,* 394 U.S. 147 (1969).

16. *McGuire v. Roebuck,* p. 1120.

17. *Terminiello v. Chicago,* 337 U.S. 1 (1949).

18. Ibid., p. 4.

19. *McGuire v. Roebuck,* p. 1125.

20. Section 1 of the law provided in part that "It shall be unlawful for any person, singly or in concert with others, to engage in picketing or any form of picketing activity that shall constitute mass picketing as herein defined. 'Mass picketing,' as that term is used herein, shall mean any form of picketing in which: 1. There are more than two (2) pickets at any time within either fifty (50) feet of any entrance to the premises being picketed, or within fifty (50) feet of any other picket or pickets."

Section 2 of the statute provided that "It shall be unlawful for any person, singly or in concert with others, by use of insulting, threatening or obscene language, to interfere with, hinder, obstruct, or intimidate, or seek to interfere with, hinder, obstruct, or intimidate, another in the exercise of his lawful right to work, or to enter upon the performance of any lawful vocation, or from freely entering or leaving any premises." Tex. Rev. Civ. Stat. Ann. Art. 5154d (Vernon 1971).

While the picketing provisions were part of the Texas anti–collective bargaining statute, they were not expressly limited to labor-related picketing. Given both the general language of the statute and a U.S. Supreme Court decision holding that an antipicketing statute distinguishing among types of picketing is unconstitutional, *Police Department of Chicago v. Mosley,* 408 U.S. 92 (1972), Judge Justice interpreted the provision to apply to all picketing occurring in Texas.

21. As a private employer, Schoellkopf Products was subject to the terms of the federal National Labor Relations Act, which permits collective bargaining in the private sector.

22. Kent Wall, "Tyler Union Chief Ready for Round 2 in Picketing," *Tyler Morning Telegraph,* February 27, 1986.

23. *Nash v. State of Texas,* 632 F.Supp. 951 (E.D. Tex. 1986), p. 970. A state court of appeals considered the numbers-distance provision in 1987 and upheld its

constitutionality. The two judges in the majority noted Justice's decision to the contrary, indicating "we strongly disagree": *Olvera v. State,* 725 S.W.2d 400 (Tex. Ct. App., Houston, 1987), p. 404. The court observed that the state's interest in preventing violence and maintaining free passageway in public areas "justifies some First Amendment infringement" (p. 405). However, Judge Ben G. Levy dissented, agreeing explicitly with Judge Justice and with two other federal district court rulings that the numbers-distance provision was invalid. The different values placed by the respective judges on workers' rights and First Amendment freedoms is evident.

Unlike federal judges, Texas judges are elected. If they stray too far from the prevailing view of the electorate, they risk retaliation by the local bar associations and at the polls. Levy was later defeated in a reelection bid, a fact he attributes in part to his position in the *Olvera* decision.

24. *Davis v. François,* 395 F.2d 730 (5th Cir. 1968).

25. *Chaplinsky v. New Hampshire,* 315 U.S. 568 (1942).

26. *Nash v. State of Texas,* 632 F.Supp. 951 (E.D. Tex. 1986), p. 980. He distinguished a Fifth Circuit ruling which had upheld a similar federal statute by noting in part that the federal statute applied only in the context of foreign embassies or officials and to persons who "wilfully . . . intimidate . . ." The Texas statute applied anywhere and did not contain the term "wilful": *CISPES v. F.B.I.,* 770 F.2d 468 (5th Cir. 1985).

27. *Howard Gault Co. v. Texas Rural Legal Aid, Inc.,* 848 F.2d 544 (5th Cir. 1988), p. 561.

28. *Nash v. Chandler,* 848 F.2d 567 (5th Cir. 1988), *Reh. denied,* 859 F.2d 1210.

29. As quoted in *Newsweek,* June 27, 1988.

30. *United States v. Rainbow Family,* 695 F.Supp. 294 (E.D. Tex. 1988).

31. *United States v. Israel,* No. CR-86-027-TUC-RMB (D. Ariz., 1986).

32. Record of proceedings, June 15, 1988, pp. 338–340.

33. Lisa Belkin, "2-Way Shock as Hippie Meets Texan," *New York Times,* July 5, 1988.

34. Heber Taylor, "Gramm Wanted to Curb Rainbows' Lawlessness," *Lufkin Daily News,* July 7, 1988.

35. *United States v. Rainbow Family,* 695 F.Supp. 314 (E.D. Tex. 1988).

36. *Texas Committee on Natural Resources v. Bergland,* 433 F.Supp. 1235 (E.D. Tex. 1977), *rev'd,* 573 F.2d 201 (5th Cir.), *cert. denied,* 439 U.S. 966 (1978). In a lengthy and detailed analysis, Justice ruled that the government's environmental impact study regarding the environmental effects of clearcutting was insufficient and a violation of the National Environmental Protection Act (NEPA). Clearcutting is generally opposed by environmental groups, who assert that it destroys the natural beauty of the forests, hurts animal and plant life, and encourages disease. They favor mixing pine and hardwood trees, then selectively cutting only mature trees, a more expensive process opposed by the Forest Service. The opposition of the Forest Service convinced Justice that it viewed NEPA as a hindrance to its work. Thus, when the Forest Service suddenly became very concerned about the environment in the Rainbow Family litigation, Justice was skeptical. The facts demonstrated that protection of the environment was not the service's major concern.

Following reversal of the *Bergland* ruling by the Fifth Circuit, the plaintiffs refiled under the Endangered Species Act, alleging that clearcutting threatens the Red-cockaded Woodpecker with extinction by 1995. This time the case came before Judge Robert M. Parker. Parker issued an injunction in June 1987 forbidding clearcutting near the woodpeckers' present or former habitats: *Sierra Club v. Lyng,* 694 F.Supp. 1260 (E.D. Tex. 1988). His order coincided with the Rainbow Family litigation. One of the sites where some of the Rainbow Family had gathered in May was within the protected area. Judge Justice told Parker that if the issue arose, he would sever that part of the action and transfer it to him. But the Forest Service never pursued it, further demonstrating to Judge Justice that it did not regard environmental concerns as of major importance.

37. *Tyler Morning Telegraph,* June 20, 1988.

38. *Albright v. Good Shepherd Hospital,* Civil Action No. TY-85-453-CA (E.D. Tex. May 24, 1988), p. 9.

39. *Burton v. Wilmington Parking Authority,* 365 U.S. 715 (1961). The Fifth Circuit decision, which would play a significant role in the appeal, was *Jatoi v. Hurst-Euless-Bedford Hospital Authority,* 807 F.2d 1214 (5th Cir.) *modified on other grounds and reh. en banc denied,* 819 F.2d 545 (5th Cir. 1987), *cert. denied sub nom. Harris Methodist H-E-B Board of Trustees v. Jatoi,* 108 S.Ct. 709 (1988).

40. *Greco v. Orange Memorial Hospital,* 513 F.2d 873 (5th Cir.), *cert. denied,* 423 U.S. 1000 (1975).

41. *Albright v. Longview Police Department,* 884 F.2d 835 (5th Cir. 1989).

42. Page alleged that her termination from her position as a nurse supervisor at the hospital had been racially motivated. She also alleged retaliation for filing a worker's compensation claim, a claim the jury upheld, awarding her $120,000 actual and $40,000 punitive damages. Judge Justice upheld her racial discrimination claim, ordering her reinstatement and awarding her over $20,000 in back pay. Justice had been particularly impressed with Page's testimony. "I considered her one of the most competent individuals I have ever come in contact with. She seemed to be a completely devoted nurse. I think that fact even communicated itself to the Fifth Circuit. She had been ill treated; there wasn't any question at all about that. Some people can just project their goodness; she was one of those persons."

43. *Ruiz v. Lynaugh,* Civil Action No. H-78-987-CA (E.D. Tex. July 19, 1989). The issue in that case was whether facilities operated by Wackenhut Services, Inc., and Corrections Corporation of America under contract with the Texas Department of Corrections were subject to the terms of the *Ruiz v. Estelle* prison reform order and subsequent negotiated settlements (see Chapter 15). Justice cited the U.S. Supreme Court ruling in *West v. Atkins,* 108 S.Ct. 2250 (1988), in support of his decision that the two corporations were acting under color of state law. In *West* the high court held that a part-time doctor rendering medical services to prisoners under contract with the state department of corrections was acting as a public official. In his opinion, Justice noted, "The provision of an *entire* prison facility by a private entity compels inclusion, under the principles of *West,* of private operators under the court's Section 1983 jurisdiction" (p. 9).

8. Voter Discrimination

References from interviews: Steve Bickerstaff, May 25, 1989; John R. Brown, December 14, 1990; Colin J. Carl, October 20, 1987; Larry Daves, October 1, 1989; Leonard E. Davis, February 14, 1990; Charles F. Potter, October 26, 1988; David R. Richards, January 5, 1989; Arthur Weaver, September 21, 1989; Marianne Wesson, July 14, 1989.

1. *Ownby v. Dies,* 337 F.Supp. 38 (E.D. Tex. 1971).
2. Terry Kliewer, "Judge Strikes Residence Rule," *Dallas Morning News,* September 29, 1971.
3. *Whatley v. Clark,* Civil Action No. 5474 (E.D. Tex. 1971), *aff'd,* 482 F.2d 1230 (5th Cir. 1973).
4. *Baker v. Carr,* 369 U.S. 186 (1961).
5. *Reynolds v. Sims,* 377 U.S. 533 (1964), p. 577.
6. A provision of 28 U.S.C. Section 2281 required the convening of a three-judge court in cases involving a request for an interlocutory or permanent injunction against enforcement of a state statute on grounds of unconstitutionality. The provision was repealed in 1976. A district court composed of three judges is now required when an action is filed challenging the apportionment of state legislative or congressional districts on constitutional grounds: 28 U.S.C. Section 2284. When a federal district court judge requests that the chief judge of the circuit establish a three-judge court, the latter is to appoint two additional judges, one of whom must be a circuit court judge.
7. George Kuempel, "Plaintiffs Get the Ball in Redistricting Case," *Austin American-Statesman,* January 1, 1972.
8. *Graves v. Barnes,* 343 F.Supp. 704 (W.D. Tex. 1972), p. 708.
9. A key case the majority cited in support of this position was *Kirkpatrick v. Preisler,* 394 U.S. 526 (1969), a congressional redistricting case. Goldberg and Justice recognized that the Supreme Court had distinguished between congressional and state legislative representation, requiring less stringent standards for the latter, but believed—erroneously, as it turned out—that the Court had retreated from this differentiation.
10. *Graves v. Barnes,* p. 713.
11. Ibid., p. 717.
12. Ibid., p. 732.
13. Ibid., p. 734.
14. Ibid., p. 747.
15. Sam Kinch, Jr., "Court Orders 1-Man Redistricting for Dallas," *Dallas Morning News,* January 29, 1972.
16. Robert Heard, "Legislature Earns Worst Marks Yet," *Austin American-Statesman,* January 30, 1972.
17. *White v. Regester,* 412 U.S. 755 (1973).
18. Ibid., p. 769.
19. *Graves v. Barnes,* 378 F.Supp. 640 (W.D. Tex. 1974), p. 642. This decision is known as *Graves II.*
20. Ibid., p. 643.

21. Wood relied primarily on the Supreme Court's decision in *Whitcomb v. Chavis,* 403 U.S. 124 (1971), which involved an unsuccessful challenge by ghetto blacks to a multimember districting scheme in Marion County, Indiana. The blacks had sought to show that their lack of proportionate representation on the Marion County delegation stemmed from invidious discrimination. The Supreme Court majority concluded that it stemmed from lack of success at the polls, rather than from any state policy to restrict voting rights contrary to the Constitution. Goldberg and Justice sought to distinguish *Graves* from *Whitcomb* by noting that the same history of *de jure* discrimination against minorities had not been present in Marion County, Indiana, as in Texas.

22. *Graves v. Barnes,* 378 F.Supp. 640 (W.D. Tex. 1974), p. 645.

23. Ibid., p. 647.

24. Ibid., p. 671.

25. "Tarrant Reps Vary on District Ruling," *Fort Worth Star-Telegram,* January 29, 1974.

26. *Fort Worth Star-Telegram,* January 31, 1974.

27. *White v. Regester,* 422 U.S. 935 (1975).

28. *Flowers v. Wiley,* Civil Action No. S-75-103-CA (E.D. Tex. November 3, 1975). The case was brought by MALDEF and the Texas Civil Liberties Union on behalf of all black citizens of Texas who were then registered to vote. Filed in Sherman, where Justice was the only presiding judge, the complaint alleged that the voter reregistration procedures of S.B. 300 would cause confusion among black voters and would result in their disenfranchisement. The statute directed county tax assessors to mail a notice to each registered voter, as of November 5, 1975, stating that the voter's current registration would expire on March 1, 1976, and that the voter must complete an application for new registration and return it by January 31, 1976, in order to remain registered to vote. Those who did not reregister were to be purged from the voter registration list.

On behalf of the plaintiffs, attorney David Richards asked Justice to issue an order prohibiting implementation of the reregistration procedures until the U.S. Attorney General had passed on the provisions of the statute pursuant to the Voting Rights Act. Over strenuous objections by the state, Justice did so on November 3. The state defendants immediately sought a stay of Justice's order and obtained it the next day from Fifth Circuit Judge Thomas Gibbs Gee. Both Justice and Richards were furious. Richards called Gee, telling him that Gee had heard only one side of the story. Gee invited him to his chambers and, after listening to Richards, amended the stay to halt further mailings of registration materials. Subsequently, a three-judge court composed of Judges Gee, Justice, and William M. Steger reinstated Justice's temporary restraining order pending a hearing on the merits. In December the U.S. Attorney General notified Secretary of State Mark White that the purge provisions of S.B. 300 were disapproved. All other provisions of the statute were upheld.

Following the Attorney General's action, the three-judge court precluded voter reregistration unless the notice to be mailed out included a statement in both English and Spanish that reregistration was voluntary.

29. *Graves v. Barnes,* 408 F.Supp. 1050 (W.D. Tex. 1976). This decision is known as *Graves III.*

30. *Graves v. Barnes,* 446 F.Supp. 560 (W.D. Tex. 1977), p. 571. This decision is known as *Graves IV.*

31. Ibid., p. 573.

32. *Escalante v. Briscoe,* 424 U.S. 937 (1976) (companion case).

33. *Briscoe v. Escalante,* 435 U.S. 901 (1978).

34. *Graves v. Barnes,* 700 F.2d 220 (5th Cir. 1983).

35. Richard H. Kraemer and Charlean Newell, *Texas Politics* (St. Paul: West Publishing Co., 1979), p. 162.

36. Ibid., 4th ed. (1989), p. 191.

37. *Texas Almanac* (Dallas: A. H. Belo Publishing Co., 1973 and 1989).

38. *Mobile v. Bolden,* 466 U.S. 55 (1980).

39. *Weaver v. Commissioners Court, Nacogdoches County,* No. TY-73-CA-209 (E.D. Tex. March 15, 1974).

40. *Weaver v. Muckleroy,* Civil Action No. 5524 (E.D. Tex. July 14, 1972).

41. Ibid., (E.D. Tex. January 27, 1975).

42. *Seamon v. Brunette,* No. P-75-3-CA (E.D. Tex. March 15, 1976).

43. *Seamon v. Upham,* 536 F.Supp. 931 (E.D. Tex. 1982), p. 937 (footnote 3).

44. Ibid., p. 961.

45. In a 1989 employment discrimination case, the U.S. Supreme Court endorsed a searching Fourteenth Amendment equal protection inquiry regardless of whether invidious or benign discrimination is present. All racial classifications are inherently suspect. Writing for the six-justice majority in *City of Richmond v. Croson,* 109 S.Ct. 706, Justice Sandra Day O'Connor pointed out that "Absent searching judicial inquiry into the justification for such race-based measures, there is simply no way of determining what classifications are 'benign' or 'remedial' and what classifications are in fact motivated by illegitimate notions of racial inferiority or simply racial politics. Indeed, the purpose of strict scrutiny is to 'smoke out' illegitimate uses of race by assuring that the legislative body is pursuing a goal important enough to warrant use of a highly suspect tool" (p. 721). The case involved a so-called "set-aside" program whereby 30 percent of the public works contracts negotiated by the City of Richmond, Virginia, were reserved for minority firms.

The difference between conservatives like Justice O'Connor and liberals like Judge Justice is that the latter are deferential to legislative action which actually benefits minorities, even when the white majority is disadvantaged, in the interest of erasing the scars of past racial discrimination. In the *Richmond* case, O'Connor was highly critical of such deference, observing that it "effectively assures that race will always be relevant in American life, and that the 'ultimate goal of eliminating entirely from governmental decision-making such irrelevant factors as a human being's race' will never be achieved" (p. 722). The set-aside program was declared unconstitutional.

46. *Seamon v. Upham,* 536 F.Supp. 931, p. 971.

47. Ibid., p. 974.

48. Ibid., p. 971.

49. *Nixon v. Herndon,* 273 U.S. 536 (1926).

50. *Nixon v. Condon,* 286 U.S. 73 (1932).

51. *Smith v. Allwright,* 321 U.S. 649 (1944).

52. *Terry v. Adams,* 345 U.S. 461 (1953).

53. *Terry v. United States,* 384 U.S. 155 (1966). One of the Fifth Circuit decisions Justice cited was *Robinson v. Commissioners Court,* 505 F.2d 674 (5th Cir. 1974), which upheld Justice's lower court ruling that a 1969 reapportionment plan adopted by the commissioners court in Anderson County was an unconstitutional racial gerrymander. The commissioners court was the governing body of the county. The plan formed a wedge through a substantial section of the black community in Palestine, the largest city in the county, by means of an S-shaped curve dividing blacks into three different precincts. Prior to the gerrymander, all the blacks in Palestine were included in one precinct. At the time, blacks comprised a quarter of the Palestine population. About half of the blacks in the county lived in Palestine. As a result of the gerrymander, the first black precinct chairman to serve in Anderson County was defeated. One of the boundary lines of the wedge ran in front of the chairman's home, placing him in a precinct with a white majority.

Noting a history of unresponsiveness to black community interests, Justice ruled that the commissioners had intended to dilute the vote of the black community and ordered replacement of the plan with one proposed by the plaintiffs. That plan contained no significant population variance among precincts and restored the black community to its single precinct. In upholding Justice's ruling, Judge Irving Goldberg for the three-judge panel expressed "profound disappointment in the irresponsibility" of the commissioners court: 505 F.2d 674 (5th Cir. 1974), p. 676. In their respective opinions, both Justice and Goldberg drew support from the U.S. Supreme Court *White v. Regester* multimember districting decision with regard to the court's role in assessing local factors to determine voter discrimination.

54. *Seamon v. Upham,* 536 F.Supp. 931, p. 988.

55. Ibid., p. 989.

56. Ibid., p. 990.

57. Ibid., p. 993.

58. Clements had fought against giving a deposition, arguing that his position as governor provided him with executive privilege. He also feared that having to give a deposition in the case would result in his being compelled to testify in a multitude of cases involving the state. In a November 14, 1981, editorial, the *Dallas Times Herald* supported his position, asserting that "the redistricting plan in question should be assessed by the courts entirely on its own merits, not on any political motives that may have inspired it" and that the whole idea of the deposition was a "fishing expedition." Judge Justice, acting for himself and Judge Johnson, ordered Clements to give testimony. Judge Parker dissented. Clements appealed the order to the Fifth Circuit. Following an adverse decision, he submitted to the deposition.

59. *Seamon v. Upham,* 536 F.Supp. 931 (E.D. Tex. 1982), p. 1001.

60. Ibid., p. 1029.

61. *Upham v. Seamon,* 456 U.S. 37 (1982).

62. Note that under the 1982 amendment to the 1965 Voting Rights Act, Congress has authorized such a searching standard of review. The basis is statutory, not constitutional. The amendment was enacted after the *Seamon* case had been litigated.

63. *Seamon v. Upham,* 536 F.Supp. 1030 (E.D. Tex. 1982), pp. 1033–1034. This decision is known as *Seamon II.*

64. *Dallas Morning News,* April 7, 1982.

65. *Seamon v. Upham*, 563 F.Supp. 396 (E.D. Tex. 1983), p. 398. This decision is known as *Seamon III*.

66. *United States v. Hines*, 563 F.2d 737 (1977). See Chapter 4, note 43.

67. About this same time, Justice was forced to remove himself from another case when his brother-in-law, Mike Rowan, was hired to represent the defendant. As noted in Chapter 1, Justice and Rowan have not been close. The case involved an employment discrimination suit brought by Tyler civil rights attorney Larry Daves against Texas Power and Light Company. On November 17, 1981, the defendant added Mike Rowan as one of its attorneys, and Daves moved to have him disqualified. Judge Justice believes the power company selected Rowan in retaliation for the Judge's entry-of-discovery motions requiring the power company to reveal considerable information about its internal practices. At the time, there were no rules dictating to whom Justice should assign the case. Passing over fellow Judge William Steger in Tyler, Justice assigned the matter to Judge Robert M. Parker, who was then sitting in the Beaumont Division of the Eastern District.

Texas Power and Light maintained that it had had Rowan on retainer for other matters for years and countered that Daves had purposely filed his case in the Sherman Division to secure Justice as the judge. In his harshly worded opinion, Judge Parker noted that under 28 U.S.C. Section 455, the amended judicial disqualification statute, Judge Justice could not preside over a case where his brother-in-law represented the defendant. He asserted that the defendant had intentionally created the problem, observing that the case had been pending for six years before the company sought to employ Rowan. He noted that Rowan had no reputation for expertise in class action lawsuits or employment discrimination law and virtually none in litigation. "His primary qualification as a trial lawyer arose with the enactment of amended section 455, and consists of his ability, up until now, to assist litigants in removing themselves from Judge Justice's purview." *McCuin v. Texas Power and Light Co.*, 538 F.Supp. 311 (E.D. Tex. 1982), p. 314. Parker observed that the strategy was being used for the same purpose in other lawsuits before Judge Justice. "The practice is fast becoming epidemic," he wrote, hinting that the matter might be appropriately referred to the State Bar for disciplinary action. Labeling the practice "a sham," Parker granted Daves' motion to disqualify Rowan from the case, denied Rowan any fee in the case, and returned the case to Justice for further proceedings.

Texas Power and Light appealed to the Fifth Circuit. Noting an absence of a policy in the Eastern District on the matter, the appeals court indicated that Justice should not have taken any action in the matter at all—even to reassign it to another judge—when the issue arose: *McCuin v. Texas Power and Light Co.*, 714 F.2d 1255 (5th Cir. 1983). The reassignment should have fallen to the next senior judge in active service. Justice agrees: "I should not have bucked the case to Parker or anyone else." In its decision, the Fifth Circuit set forth in some detail the law in this area, concluding that while forum-shopping is sanctioned by the judicial system, an attorney's being chosen solely to disqualify the judge is not. "The general rule of law is clear: a lawyer may not enter a case for the primary purpose of forcing the presiding judge's recusal" (p. 1265). The judges noted that their decision did not preclude possible disciplinary action against Rowan.

On remand, Judge Steger, as the next senior judge in active service in the Eastern

District, assigned the matter to himself. He found no evidence to warrant removing Rowan, rejecting Daves' assertions that inferences could readily be made from the course of events, and let the case proceed with Rowan as one of the attorneys. The case was eventually settled. The entire matter did nothing to further good relations between Justice and Rowan, and, for a time, strained relations between Steger and Justice as well. But the ploy of attempting to use Rowan to force Justice off cases—a ploy first started by an Austin school district attorney—stopped.

68. *Strake v. Seamon,* 105 S.Ct. 63 (1984).

9. The Education of Undocumented Alien Children

References from interviews: Richard Arnett, January 23, 1987; John Hardy, April 9, 1987.

1. At the time of the lawsuit, an alien's unauthorized presence in the United States was not a crime under the Immigration and Nationality Act of 1952, and an individual who was apprehended was usually subject to deportation rather than criminal sanctions: 8 U.S.C. Section 1251 (a)(2) (1976). Thus, the term "undocumented alien" is used, rather than "illegal alien."

2. Tex. Att'y Gen. Op. No. H-586 (1975).

3. Elizabeth Hull, "Undocumented Alien Children and Free Public Education: An Analysis of *Plyler v. Doe,*" *University of Pittsburg Law Review* 44 (1983): 409–432. Hull observed that "By virtue of the so-called Texas Proviso, the United States remains one of the few industrialized countries in the world that refuses to penalize employers who knowingly hire undocumented workers" (p. 425). The section referred to is 8 U.S.C. Section 1324(a), which concerned the bringing in and harboring of undocumented aliens. It included this provision: "Provided, however, that for the purposes of this section, employment (including the usual and normal practices incident to employment) shall not be deemed to constitute harboring." The exemption was eliminated in 1986. A new section was added, 1324a, making employment of undocumented aliens a crime subject to fine and imprisonment.

4. The appeals court decision affirming the trial court decision was handed down after Judge Justice had issued his temporary injunction in the *Doe* case. The appellate judges briefly discussed Justice's findings of fact and conclusions of law in a footnote, noting that they were not the final judgment in the case and had no precedential value: 558 S.W.2d 121 (Tex. Civ. App., Austin, 1977). In its opinion, the appeals court observed, "The fact that a child leaves his country and covertly enters the state without complying with the immigration laws, should not somehow create a state responsibility to provide him with a free education" (p. 124). How a child could "covertly enter the state" to attend school was not explained. The Texas Supreme Court refused to hear this case, noting no reversible error.

5. Carlton Stowers, "Alien Issue Triggers Uneasiness in Tyler," *Dallas Morning News,* September 14, 1977.

6. Actually, it was two days later. Dan Watson, "Aliens Get No Protection from Court in School Suit," *Dallas Morning News,* September 16, 1977.

7. *Dandridge v. Williams,* 397 U.S. 484 (1970).

8. *Shapiro v. Thompson,* 394 U.S. 618 (1969).

9. *San Antonio Independent School District v. Rodriguez,* 411 U.S. 1 (1973).

10. *Graham v. Richardson,* 403 U.S. 365 (1971).

11. *Doe v. Plyler,* 458 F.Supp. 569 (E.D. Tex. 1978), p. 585. In discussing the suspect-class issue, Justice referred to the U.S. Supreme Court's ruling in *Griffin v. Illinois,* 351 U.S. 12 (1958), where the Court required states to provide trial transcripts to indigent prisoners when such a transcript is necessary for an effective appeal. The ruling was based on both the due process and the equal protection clauses of the Fourteenth Amendment. In the *San Antonio* ruling, the high court noted that in order for legislation to be invalidated based on wealth discrimination under its precedents, it has to be shown that there has been an absolute deprivation because of poverty and, as a result, those affected cannot enjoy the state-proffered benefit. The undocumented alien children arguably fell into this category, particularly where their impecunity prevented them from paying the necessary tuition to attend public school. Justice also referred to a Supreme Court ruling where the justices seemed to be particularly solicitous of children, *Weber v. Aetna Casualty and Surety Company,* 406 U.S. 164 (1972). In *Weber,* the Court ruled that Louisiana cannot discriminate against unacknowledged dependent illegitimate children by preventing them from recovering for the death of their father under the state's worker compensation laws on an equal footing with dependent legitimate children.

12. In a similar case two years later, another Texas federal judge was less hesitant to rule that there is a constitutional right of access to public education and that denial of that right to undocumented alien children based on their indigency discriminates against a suspect class. In *In re Alien Children Education Litigation,* 501 F.Supp. 544 (S.D. Tex. 1980), Judge Woodrow Seals, who was also appointed to the bench by President Johnson, concluded that the state must show a compelling reason to discriminate. The reasons advanced by the state were not viewed as compelling, and Judge Seals struck down Section 21.031 as an unconstitutional denial of equal protection of the laws. He distinguished his case from *Doe v. Plyler,* noting that Judge Justice was primarily concerned with the Tyler policy and less with the state statute. After the trial, Justice had refused to grant the state's motion to introduce additional evidence, since he intended to order relief only against the Tyler Independent School District.

The action before Judge Seals squarely addressed the issue of statewide application of Section 21.031 and reflected the consolidation of several lawsuits filed in Texas' federal district courts pursuant to a decision of the Judicial Panel on Multidistrict Litigation. After affirming *Doe v. Plyler,* the Fifth Circuit summarily affirmed Judge Seals' decision in February 1981. *In re Alien Children* was consolidated with *Doe v. Plyler* for hearing before the U.S. Supreme Court.

13. *Doe v. Plyler,* 458 F.Supp. 569 (E.D. Tex. 1978), p. 589.

14. See Elizabeth Hull, "Undocumented Aliens and the Equal Protection Clause: An Analysis of *Doe v. Plyler,*" *Brooklyn Law Review* 48, no. 1 (Fall 1981): 43–74; Case Note, *Texas International Law Journal* 14 (Spring 1979): 289–316; Case Note, *Vanderbilt Journal of Transnational Law* 12 (Summer 1979): 789–793; Case Note, *St. Mary's Law Journal* 11 (1979): 549–569. Hull's article was the most supportive.

15. Case Note, *St. Mary's Law Journal* 11 (1979): 549–569, p. 566. Subsection d

of the statute providing that students who reside in the district for the primary purpose of attending school must pay tuition was upheld by the U.S. Supreme Court one year after it affirmed Judge Justice's *Doe* decision: *Martinez v. Bynum*, 461 U.S. 321 (1983).

16. The Fifth Circuit noted at one point, "However much we are impressed with the importance of basic education to a child's development, we find no solid constitutional precedent for determining that some kind of access to basic education is a fundamental interest sufficient to invoke strict scrutiny." But in the next sentence, the panel observed, "Nevertheless, in light of the Court's *Rodriguez* opinion, we decline to find that complete denial of free education to some children is not a denial of a fundamental right": *Doe v. Plyler*, 628 F.2d 448 (5th Cir. 1980), p. 457.

17. See *Weber v. Aetna Casualty and Surety Company*, discussed in note 11 above.

18. Ann McDaniel, "Justice Department Pulling Out of Alien Case," *Dallas Times Herald,* September 9, 1981.

19. Ibid. See also Stuart Taylor, "United States Retreats from Its Challenge to Texas Law on Alien Schooling," *New York Times,* September 9, 1981.

20. *Plyler v. Doe,* 457 U.S. 202 (1982), p. 213.

21. Ibid., p. 230.

22. Ibid., p. 250.

23. Ibid., p. 242.

24. Ibid., p. 244.

25. Ibid., p. 250.

26. While the lawsuit was pending before the Supreme Court, Attorney General Mark White had written an editorial in the *New York Times* in which he asserted that it was the "height of hypocrisy" for Congress to refuse to finance the education of undocumented children who were here in the first place because the federal government was unable or unwilling to enforce its immigration laws. *New York Times,* November 25, 1981.

27. José A. Cárdenas and Albert Cortez, "The Impact of *Doe v. Plyler* upon Texas Public Schools," *Journal of Law and Education* 15, no. 1 (Winter 1986): 1–17.

28. Ibid., p. 14.

29. *Edgewood Independent School District v. Kirby,* 777 S.W.2d 391 (Tex. 1989).

10. Bilingual Education

References from interviews: Thomas E. Anderson, June 23, 1987; Richard Arnett, January 23, 1987; Susan J. Dasher, January 22, 1987; Richard E. Gray, April 15, 1987; Roger L. Rice, November 14, 1988.

1. The acronym LEP, meaning "limited English proficiency," is usually used to denote this group of students. "Limited English proficiency" encompasses speaking, reading, writing, and understanding the language.

2. *Lau v. Nichols,* 414 U.S. 563 (1975).

3. 20 U.S.C. Section 3221 *et seq.* (1982).

4. The three-judge-court statute, 28 U.S.C. Section 2281, provided that plaintiffs seeking an injunction against a state statute as being unconstitutional must have

their case heard and determined by a court consisting of three federal judges. The statute was repealed in 1976. However, because this action had commenced prior to this date, the three-judge court remained a viable option.

5. *Regents of the University of California v. Bakke,* 438 U.S. 265 (1978). Though the Court did not overrule *Lau v. Nichols,* it did undercut the application of Title VI to situations where there is no showing of discriminatory intent.

6. *Harvard Civil Rights—Civil Liberties Law Review* 7 (Winter, 1972): 307–391. The authors, Jorge C. Rangel and Carlos M. Alcala, were two Harvard Law School students interning at the Center for Law and Education at Harvard. In preparation for the article, they spent one summer at the San Antonio office of MALDEF studying the extent of *de jure* segregation against Mexican-Americans in Texas public schools. Their research convinced them that MALDEF and the Center should join forces against the state, and they actively encouraged the two organizations to do so.

7. An interesting side issue which would later surface in the Fifth Circuit's reversal involved Dasher's extensive personal litigation to secure a license to practice law in Texas. Because she had graduated from San Francisco Law School, which was not on the list of law schools approved by the Texas Supreme Court, she was not eligible to take the Texas bar exam, even though she was already licensed to practice in California. She filed suit on July 19, 1978, in the U.S. District Court for the Western District of Texas. The district court allowed her to take the examination, which she passed, and then ordered her admitted to the practice of law. Several years later, the U.S. Court of Appeals for the Fifth Circuit reversed the lower court, first on technical jurisdictional grounds, then in a subsequent decision, on the merits: *Dasher v. Supreme Court of Texas,* 650 F.2d 711 (5th Cir. 1981), supplemented, 658 F.2d 1045. Until the order of the district court was reversed, she continued to practice law in Texas. Dasher also had a fall-back position. The legislature had amended the attorney licensing law in 1979 to ease the process by which persons like Dasher who are licensed in other states can be admitted to the state bar. Thus, contrary to accusations made later in the newspapers, Susan Dasher was a licensed attorney during the litigation of the bilingual case.

8. Record of proceedings, December 3, 1979, p. 21.

9. Ann Arnold, "State Bilingual Education Issue Back in Court," *Dallas Times Herald,* December 2, 1979.

10. "A Better Chance to Learn," U.S. Commission on Civil Rights, 1975. As quoted in *United States v. Texas (Bilingual),* 506 F.Supp. 405 (E.D. Tex. 1981), p. 420.

11. Jesse Treviño, "State Attorney Admits Bias in Schools," *Corpus Christi Caller-Times,* September 13, 1980.

12. The order was subsequently included as an appendix to a later order, which was published: *United States v. Texas (Bilingual),* 523 F.Supp. 703 (E.D. Tex. 1981).

13. Ibid., 506 F.Supp. 405 (E.D. Tex. 1981).

14. Ibid., p. 412.

15. Ibid., p. 416.

16. Ibid., p. 414.

17. Ibid., 680 F.2d 356 (5th Cir. 1982), p. 359.

18. Ibid., 523 F.Supp. 703 (E.D. Tex. 1981), pp. 717–720.

19. Ibid., 680 F.2d 356, p. 361.

20. Ibid., 506 F.Supp. 405 (E.D. Tex. 1981), p. 434.

21. Ibid., p. 424.

22. Record of proceedings, December 6, 1979, p. 560.

23. Ibid., December 5, 1979, p. 357.

24. *United States v. Texas (Bilingual)*, 506 F.Supp. 405 (E.D. Tex. 1981), p. 428.

25. Title VI prohibits discrimination in any program receiving federal funds. By virtue of U.S. Supreme Court rulings in *Washington v. Davis*, 426 U.S. 229 (1976), and *Regents of the University of California v. Bakke*, 438 U.S. 265 (1978), Title VI had been held to require a showing of discriminatory intent to trigger a violation. Since Texas had taken steps through its 1973 and 1975 bilingual legislation to rectify past inequities, the requisite showing of discriminatory intent was lacking.

26. *United States v. Texas (Bilingual)*, 506 F.Supp. 405, p. 435.

27. Ibid., p. 441.

28. George Kuempel, "Clements, Other State Leaders Find Fault with Justice's Order," *Dallas Morning News*, January 13, 1981.

29. Ibid.

30. Ibid.

31. Saralee Tiede, "White Files Plan Rejecting Judge's Bilingual Demands," *Dallas Times Herald*, March 27, 1981.

32. Order, April 17, 1981.

33. *United States v. Texas (Bilingual)*, 523 F.Supp. 703, p. 735.

34. *Castaneda v. Pickard*, 648 F.2d 989 (5th Cir. 1981).

35. *United States v. Texas (Bilingual)*, 523 F.Supp. 703, pp. 737–738.

36. Ibid., 680 F.2d 356, p. 358.

37. Ibid., p. 364.

38. Ibid., p. 370.

39. Ibid., p. 369.

40. David Montejano. *Anglos and Mexicans in the Making of Texas, 1836–1986* (Austin: University of Texas Press, 1987), pp. 160, 192.

41. See, for example, Christine H. Rossell and J. Michael Ross, "The Social Science Evidence on Bilingual Education," *Journal of Law and Education* 15, no. 4 (Fall 1986): 385–419. The authors found that compensatory bilingual education has been the most frequently used approach but that there is "no consistent research support for transitional bilingual education as a superior instructional practice for improving the English language achievement of limited-English-proficient children" (p. 398). They concluded that "despite general acceptance by courts that submersion or doing nothing has failed, it fares no worse than transitional bilingual education" (p. 413). Compare the more supportive findings of Ann C. Willig, "A Meta-Analysis of Selected Studies on the Effectiveness of Bilingual Education," *Review of Educational Research* 55, no. 3 (Fall 1985): 269–317. Though Willig found evidence to support the bilingual approach, she was critical of the overall quality of the research studies she examined. Shifting paradigms also affect social science research. Government and other decision-makers are known to choose those researchers who have a certain outlook on the subject to be studied. Consequently, truly "objective" social science evidence is nearly impos-

sible to obtain. For more on the social science objectivity gap, see Henry M. Levin, "Education, Life Chances, and the Courts: The Role of Social Science Research," *Law and Contemporary Problems* 39 (Spring 1975): 217–240.

42. Record of proceedings, December 3, 1979, p. 187. Rossell and Ross make much of the fact that in a letter to them, Cazden acknowledged the lack of reliable research support for her testimony ("The Social Science Evidence on Bilingual Education," p. 391). However, in correspondence with me, Cazden detailed the portions of her testimony supported by empirical research, citing the studies upon which the statements were made (letter, February 8, 1989).

43. John C. Henry, "'Dictator' Justice Quietly Faces Attacks on Activist Rulings," *Austin American-Statesman*, July 25, 1982.

44. Patti Kilday, "Justice Reined In," *Dallas Times Herald*, July 14, 1982.

45. *United States v. Texas (Bilingual)*, 680 F.2d 356, p. 370.

46. Clara Tuma, "Bilingual Education Order Reversed," *Houston Post*, July 13, 1982.

47. José Olivares, "An Open Letter to a Beleaguered Judge," *San Antonio Express-News*, July 12, 1981.

11. Rights of the Accused

References from interviews: Michael P. O'Reilly, November 9, 1989; Wayne V. R. Smith, April 29, 1988; James L. Sultan, November 15, 1988.

1. Herbert L. Packer, *The Limits of the Criminal Sanction* (Stanford: Stanford University Press, 1968), p. 158. Chapter 8 of the book describes the two models in considerable detail. Only the highlights are presented here.

2. Ibid., p. 165.

3. Ibid., p. 167.

4. Enacted in 1925, the statute stipulated that "No evidence obtained by an officer or other person in violation of any provisions of the Constitution or laws of the State of Texas, or of the Constitution of the United States of America, shall be admitted in evidence against the accused in the trial of any criminal case." Tex. Code Crim. Proc. Ann. Art. 727a (Vernon, 1925). The successor statute is found at Tex. Code. Crim. Proc. Ann. Art. 38.23 (Vernon, 1949).

5. *Mapp v. Ohio*, 361 U.S. 643 (1961). *Mapp* overruled *Wolf v. Colorado*, 338 U.S. 25 (1949).

6. *Gideon v. Wainwright*, 372 U.S. 335 (1963).

7. *Escobedo v. Illinois*, 378 U.S. 478 (1964).

8. *Miranda v. Arizona*, 384 U.S. 436 (1966).

9. *Katz v. United States*, 389 U.S. 347 (1967).

10. The Fourth Amendment reads, "The right of the people to be secure in their persons, houses, papers, and effects, against unreasonable searches and seizures shall not be violated, and no Warrants shall issue, but upon probable cause, supported by Oath or affirmation, and particularly describing the place to be searched, and the persons or things to be seized." The Fourteenth Amendment applies the provisions of the Fourth Amendment to the states.

11. *Schmerber v. California*, 384 U.S. 757 (1966).

12. *United States v. Wade*, 87 S.Ct. 1926 (1967). The Supreme Court held that a suspect is entitled to legal counsel prior to being placed in a police lineup.

13. Record of proceedings, April 21, 1969, p. 51.

14. Ibid., p. 75.

15. *Graves v. Beto*, Civil Action No. 4948 (E.D. Tex. June 30, 1969).

16. Ibid., 424 F.2d 524 (5th Cir. 1970), *reh. denied.*

17. *United States v. Diggs*, 522 F.2d 1310 (D.C. Cir. 1975).

18. *Terry v. Ohio*, 392 U.S. 1 (1968).

19. *United States v. Diggs*, 522 F.2d 1310, p. 1324.

20. Ibid., p. 1330.

21. *United States v. Floyd*, 525 F.2d 1299 (D.C. Cir. 1976), pp. 1299–1300. The U.S. Supreme Court refused to hear the case: 429 U.S. 952 (1976).

22. *Harris v. United States*, 390 U.S. 234 (1968). In *Harris*, the Supreme Court in a short *per curiam* decision reaffirmed earlier rulings to the effect that "It has long been settled that objects falling in the plain view of an officer who has a right to be in a position to have that view, are subject to seizure and may be introduced in evidence" (p. 236).

23. *United States v. Hall*, 468 F.Supp. 123 (E.D. Tex. 1979), p. 126. See the terms of the Fourth Amendment in note 10 above.

24. *Jones v. Latexo Independent School District*, 499 F.Supp. 223 (E.D. Tex. 1980), p. 230.

25. The only other federal court that had ruled on the issue was in Indiana, and thus Judge Justice was not bound to follow its ruling. The judge in that case had ruled that the warrantless use of dogs to ferret out drugs in a public high school when only internal disciplinary measures are to be employed does not violate student privacy rights because such use is not a "search" within the purview of the Fourth Amendment: *Doe v. Renfrow*, 475 F.Supp. 1012 (N.D. Ind. 1979). The appeals court later affirmed this part of the lower court ruling: 631 F.2d 91 (7th Cir. 1980), *per curiam, petition for hearing denied*, 635 F.2d 582, *cert. denied*, 451 U.S. 1022 (1981).

26. Justice noted that the judge in the *Doe v. Renfrow* case discussed in the reference above had mistakenly viewed the dog as enhancing the powers of school officials to detect drugs rather than replacing them with its own heightened investigatory powers. He observed that *Doe* had been justifiably criticized by legal writers.

27. *Horton v. Goose Creek Independent School District*, 690 F.2d 470 (5th Cir. 1982), p. 475.

28. *Roper v. Beto*, 318 F.Supp. 662 (E.D. Tex. 1970), p. 665.

29. *Foster v. California*, 394 U.S. 440 (1969).

30. Ibid., pp. 449–450.

31. *Trop v. Dulles*, 356 U.S. 86 (1958), p. 101.

32. *Roper v. Beto*, 454 F.2d 499 (5th Cir. 1970), p. 503; *cert. denied*, 406 U.S. 948 (1972).

33. The U.S. Supreme Court held in *Ingraham v. Wright*, 430 U.S. 651 (1977) that corporal punishment of schoolchildren does not violate the Eighth Amendment provision against cruel and unusual punishment. Nor is procedural due process prior to its imposition necessary under the Fourteenth Amendment, since parents who believe it has been abused may pursue civil and criminal remedies under state law. The

Fifth Circuit concluded in a 1984 decision that corporal punishment is not a deprivation of fundamental fairness under the Fourteenth Amendment due process clause unless "it is arbitrary, capricious, or wholly unrelated to the legitimate state goal of maintaining an atmosphere conducive to learning." *Woodard v. Los Fresnos Independent School District,* 732 F.2d 1243 (5th Cir. 1984), p. 1246. Justice and Viles concluded that that condition had not been fulfilled in their case, since the Fifth Circuit the year before had rejected a substantive due process claim involving a six-year-old child whom a teacher allegedly struck on the head with a coffee cup for engaging in horseplay in the halls. Two stitches were required to close the wound. *Coleman v. Franklin Parish School Board,* 702 F.2d 74 (5th Cir. 1983).

34. *Cunningham v. Beavers,* Civil Action No. TY-87-332-CA (E.D. Tex. February 29, 1988), *aff'd, Cunningham v. Beavers,* 858 F.2d 269 (5th Cir. 1988), *cert. denied,* 109 S.Ct. 1343 (1989).

35. *Gideon v. Wainwright,* 372 U.S. 335 (1963).

36. *Haney v. Beto,* 308 F.Supp. 262 (E.D. Tex. 1970).

37. *Trahan v. Estelle,* Civil Action No. TY-73-CA-240 (E.D. Tex. May 29, 1975), p. 5.

38. Ibid., 544 F.2d 1305 (5th Cir. 1977), p. 1309.

39. Ibid., Civil Action No. TY-73-CA-240 (E.D. Tex. June 2, 1978), pp. 4–5.

40. *In re Nash,* Civil Action No. 73-CA-224 (E.D. Tex. October 1, 1975), p. 3.

41. Ibid., p. 4.

42. *Nash v. Estelle,* 560 F.2d 652 (5th Cir. 1977), p. 658.

43. Ibid., 597 F.2d 513 (5th Cir. 1979), p. 518.

44. *Berger v. United States,* 295 U.S. 78 (1934), p. 88.

12. Employment

References from interviews: Tracy Crawford, October 24, 1989; Larry Daves, October 1, 1989.

1. *Montgomery v. White,* 320 F.Supp. 303 (E.D. Tex. 1969), p. 304. The U.S. Supreme Court ruling he cited was *Pickering v. Board of Education,* 391 U.S. 563 (1969), holding that a public school teacher has a constitutional right to speak out on matters of public concern and cannot be dismissed for doing so unless the exercise of the right interferes with school operation or undermines the teacher's effectiveness. The Fifth Circuit ruling was *Pred v. Board of Public Education,* 415 F.2d 851 (1969), holding that community college teachers stated a cause of action under the First Amendment in alleging that their contracts were not renewed because of their activities in a teacher association. Justice's "second-class citizens" statement was taken from this decision.

2. *Edwards v. Gladewater Independent School District,* Civil Action No. TY-75-205-CA (November 16, 1976), pp. 8–9.

3. Ibid., 572 F.2d 496 (5th Cir. 1978).

4. This proof process was established by the U.S. Supreme Court in *McDonnell Douglas Corp. v. Green,* 411 U.S. 792 (1973) with regard to private, non–class action challenges under Title VII of the 1964 Civil Rights Act.

5. *Wells v. Hutchinson,* 499 F.Supp. 174 (E.D. Tex. 1980), pp. 194, 197.

6. Ibid., pp. 194, 198.

7. Ibid., p. 208.

8. *Kinsey v. First Regional Securities, Inc.*, 557 F.2d 830 (D.C. Circuit, 1977).

9. *Turner v. Texas Instruments, Inc.*, Civil Action No. S-73-89-CA (E.D. Tex. May 20, 1975).

10. *Turner v. Texas Instruments, Inc.*, 555 F.2d 1251 (5th Cir. 1977).

11. *Price Waterhouse v. Hopkins*, 109 S.Ct. 1775 (1989).

12. *Hodgson v. Behrens Drug Company*, Civil Action No. 5238 (E.D. Tex. October 29, 1971).

13. *Hodgson v. Behrens Drug Company*, 475 F.2d 1041 (5th Cir. 1973).

14. *Martin v. W. K. M. Wellhead Systems, Inc.*, Civil Action No. TY-80-378-CA (E.D. Tex. April 4, 1984).

15. *Strong v. Board of Education of City of Lufkin*, Civil Action No. TY-74-190-CA (E.D. Tex. December 29, 1976).

16. *Norton v. Macy*, 417 F.2d 1161 (D.C. Cir. 1969). Justice took his "overtures while on the job" assertion directly from the Bazelon opinion. See p. 1165.

17. *Wisconsin v. Constantineau*, 400 U.S. 433 (1971), p. 437.

18. *Board of Regents v. Roth*, 408 U.S. 564 (1972), p. 577.

19. *Perry v. Sindermann*, 408 U.S. 593 (1972).

20. *Roane v. Callisburg Independent School District*, Civil Action No. 2032 (E.D. Tex. September 25, 1973), pp. 10–11.

21. *Roane v. Callisburg Independent School District*, 511 F.2d 633 (5th Cir. 1975). The Fifth Circuit concluded that under existing precedents, the case did not justify the award of attorney fees. A year later, Congress enacted the Civil Rights Attorney's Fees Awards Act, which provides that the prevailing party in a civil rights action is entitled to have attorney fees paid: 42 U.S.C. Section 1988. Thus, had the statute been in existence, Roane would have won on this issue as well.

22. *Kaprelian v. Texas Woman's University*, Civil Action No. 2016 (E.D. Tex. December 12, 1973).

23. Ibid., 509 F.2d 133 (5th Cir. 1975), p. 138.

24. *Ferguson v. Thomas*, 430 F.2d 852 (5th Cir. 1970). In *Ferguson* the appeals court outlined the components of due process required when a property right is implicated:

1. Be advised of the cause or causes of the termination in sufficient detail to fairly enable the teacher to show any error that may exist.

2. Be advised of the names and the nature of the testimony of witnesses against the teacher.

3. At a reasonable time after such advice, be given a meaningful opportunity to be heard in one's own defense.

4. Be given an opportunity for a hearing before a tribunal that both possesses some academic expertise and has an apparent impartiality toward the charges.

25. *Dennis v. S&S Consolidated Rural High School District*, No. S-75-6-CA (E.D. Tex. May 4, 1976), p. 10.

26. *Wellner v. Minnesota State Junior College Board*, 487 F.2d 153 (8th Cir. 1973). The appeals court in *Wellner* affirmed a district court's decision ordering that a college

coach whose contract was not renewed be given the salary he would have received had he been reappointed until such time as he was lawfully discharged. The court overturned the lower court's decision that the coach also be reinstated.

27. *Dennis v. S&S Consolidated Rural High School District,* 577 F.2d 338 (5th Cir. 1978).

28. *Paul v. Davis,* 424 U.S. 693 (1976).

29. Since the trial proceedings were never transcribed, this factual account is based on findings of fact established by the Texas Commissioner of Education during an earlier appeal, documents filed in the case before Judge Justice, and newspaper stories.

30. Tex. Educ. Code Ann. Section 21.204(c) (Vernon Supp. 1982).

31. The Texas Commissioner of Education issued two decisions on the case. The first rejected Patrick's claim of entitlement to a trial *de novo* before the commissioner, holding that under the statute, the commissioner was limited for most purposes to a review of the record established at the hearing before the local school board: Docket No. 111-R1a-382 (November 11, 1982). The second decision reviewed the merits of the decision. The commissioner concluded that the notice Patrick received had been deficient but that Patrick had failed to show how he was harmed by the deficiency. He concluded that the evidence introduced at the local hearing showed a continuing pattern of physical violence and threats of violence. Thus, there was substantial evidence to support the contract nonrenewal as required by the statute: Docket No. 111-R1a-382 (July 18, 1983).

32. In 1989, the U.S. Court of Appeals for the Fifth Circuit curtailed challenging issues of alleged due process violations under the Texas Term Contract Nonrenewal Act in federal court as Patrick had done by holding that the act does not create Fourteenth Amendment property rights. Thus, federal courts no longer have jurisdiction over these claims: *English v. Hairston,* 888 F.2d 1069 (5th Cir. 1989).

33. *Patrick v. Board of Trustees of Mineola Independent School District,* Civil Action No. TY-82-376-CA (E.D. Tex. September 13, 1984). The basis for the denial of reinstatement and back pay was a 1977 U.S. Supreme Court ruling holding that after a public employee has established that the exercise of a protected right played a substantial role in a nonrenewal or termination decision, then the burden of justification shifts to the employer to show that there were other reasons unrelated to the exercise of the right to support its decision: *Mount Healthy School District v. Doyle,* 429 U.S. 274.

34. *Johnson v. Longview Independent School District,* Civil Action No. TY-87-481-CA (E.D. Tex. November 1, 1989).

13. Care of Mentally Retarded Persons

References from interviews: Philip Durst, March 2, 1989; David Ferleger, February 14, 1989; Jaylon Fincannon, January 6, 1989; Gary E. Miller, April 12, 1989; Linda R. O'Neall, October 12, 1989; Paul M. Smith, June 22, 1989.

1. One federal court defined habilitation as a "term of art which refers to the education, training, and care which will enable a retarded person to reach his or her maximum potential." *Halderman v. Pennhurst State School,* 610 F.Supp. 1221 (D.C. Pa. 1985), p. 1223. The term was later defined in the *Lelsz* litigation to mean "that

education, training, and care required by each plaintiff class member to improve and develop the person's level of social and intellectual functioning, designed to maximize skills and development and to enhance ability to cope with the environment, and provided in the setting that is least restrictive of the person's liberty." Resolution and Settlement, May 12, 1983.

2. Julia Wallace, "Families Fight Battle against State Institutions," *Dallas Times Herald,* July 19, 1981.

3. *Halderman v. Pennhurst State School,* 446 F.Supp. 1295 (D.C. Pa. 1977).

4. *Pennhurst State School v. Halderman,* 612 F.2d 84 (3rd Cir. 1979), *en banc.* While the court affirmed the district court's remedial order, it did not order the Pennhurst State School closed, observing that some residents could not be served in a residential setting. It also sidestepped the controversial constitutional issue regarding a right to treatment in the least restrictive environment. The majority held instead that such a right was conveyed by the Developmentally Disabled Assistance and Bill of Rights Act, 42 U.S.C. Section 6000 *et seq.,* a law which the district court had not considered. The case was appealed to the U.S. Supreme Court. Writing for the majority, Justice Rehnquist rejected the contention that the federal statute conveyed a right to treatment in the least restrictive environment: 451 U.S. 1 (1980). The case was sent back to the appeals court to determine whether there were other bases for the right under federal or Pennsylvania law.

The appeals court concluded that Pennsylvania state law supported a right to treatment in the least restrictive environment but did not reach the federal issues: 673 F.2d 647 (3rd Cir. 1982). The case was appealed once again to the U.S. Supreme Court. In *Pennhurst II,* a five-person majority concluded that federal courts are barred by the Eleventh Amendment from ordering state officials to comply with state law, even when exercising pendent jurisdiction (when a case involves both federal and state claims): 465 U.S. 89 (1983). The Eleventh Amendment provides, "The Judicial power of the United States shall not be construed to extend to any suit in law or equity, commenced or prosecuted against one of the United States by Citizens of another State, or by Citizens or Subjects of any Foreign State." The Supreme Court has construed the amendment to prohibit federal courts from hearing suits against a state by citizens of that state as well. The case was once again remanded to the court of appeals to determine if the district court had a basis under the U.S. Constitution or under Section 504 of the Rehabilitation Act of 1973, 29 U.S.C. Section 794, for its decision.

The question was never addressed, for while the suit was pending before the appeals court, the parties entered into settlement negotiations. In 1985, the district court approved a settlement which resulted in the closure of the Pennhurst State School and the relocation of most of its residents to community-based facilities. It also spelled out their entitlement to individually developed habilitation plans, as well as quality care. In its opinion, the district court noted that the litigation had consumed over ten years, with 2,192 docket entries, some 500 court orders, 28 published opinions, and three arguments before the U.S. Supreme Court. It concluded, "This settlement is more than just a termination of litigation; it is the beginning of a new era for retarded persons. It is a confirmation that all parties to the litigation are now in complete agreement that the retarded citizens of this Commonwealth have a right to care, education, and training in the community. It is a recognition by the Commonwealth and its Counties that retarded persons are not subjects to be warehoused in institutions, but that they are individuals, the great majority of whom have a potential to become productive members of society." 610 F.Supp. 1221 (D.C. Pa. 1985), pp. 1233–1234.

5. Wallace, "Families Fight Battle against State Institutions."

6. Denise Gamino, "Holocaust Inspires Lawyer for the Retarded," *Austin American-Statesman,* August 16, 1987.

7. Julia Wallace, "Father Blames Son's Death on Institution," *Dallas Times Herald,* July 10, 1981.

8. Wallace, "Families Fight Battle against State Institutions." Ferleger later won a $237,000 damage award in settlement of a civil rights damage claim over the drowning of Mark Jones.

9. Letter from Roger Parloff, June 6, 1989.

10. *Lelsz v. Kavanagh,* 98 F.R.D. 11 (E.D. Tex. 1982), p. 14.

11. Ibid., p. 25.

12. *Lelsz v. Kavanagh,* 710 F.2d 1040 (5th Cir. 1983), p. 1048.

13. Resolution and Settlement, April 15, 1983. This provision was drafted by Miller. Miller says that he wrote a good portion of the final draft and that he and Ferleger "agreed on most everything."

14. Pamela Lyon, "State to Improve Services for Mentally Retarded," *Dallas Times Herald,* May 11, 1983.

15. Ibid.

16. Memorandum Opinion and Order, July 19, 1983, p. 16.

17. *Youngberg v. Romeo,* 457 U.S. 307 (1982).

18. See especially the Texas Mentally Retarded Persons Act, Tex. Rev. Civ. Stat. Ann. Art. 5547-300, *et seq.* (Vernon 1982 Supp).

19. Memorandum Opinion and Order, July 19, 1983, p. 32.

20. Ibid., pp. 42–43.

21. Peter Larson, "New Inspector Battles for State's Retarded," *Dallas Times Herald,* October 7, 1984.

22. Ibid.

23. Ibid.

24. Order, October 1, 1984, p. 14.

25. Richard Fish, "State Urged to Reform Schools for Retarded," *Dallas Morning News,* October 6, 1984.

26. Ibid.

27. Virginia Ellis, "Mental Health Care Burden Will Intensify, State Warned," *Dallas Times Herald,* October 6, 1984.

28. *Dallas Times Herald,* December 7, 1984.

29. Ellis, "Mental Health Care Burden Will Intensify."

30. Virginia Ellis, "Move Retarded to Community, State Proposes," *Dallas Times Herald,* November 28, 1984.

31. These were people who, prior to the beginning of comprehensive testing in 1973, had been classified as mentally retarded because of their behavior. Fewer than thirty were still confined in the institutions in 1985.

32. Record of proceedings, April 9, 1985, p. 340.

33. Ibid., April 12, p. 1282.
34. Ibid., pp. 1306–1307.
35. Ibid., May 8, p. 30.
36. Ibid., p. 112.
37. Citing the cases of *Parham v. J.R.*, 442 U.S. 584 (1972) and *Youngberg v. Romeo*, 457 U.S. 307 (1982), Justice observed that the U.S. Supreme Court had disapproved judges substituting their own judgment for that of medical professionals in the fields of mental illness and mental retardation.
38. Order, June 5, 1985.
39. Denise Gamino, "State Ordered to Put 279 Mentally Retarded in Homes," *Austin American-Statesman*, June 6, 1985.
40. Ibid.
41. On rare occasions, the Fifth Circuit has ordered the transfer of a case from Justice's docket. One which was especially humiliating was *Fredonia Broadcasting Corp., Inc., v. RCA Corp.*, 569 F.2d 251 (1978), a breach-of-contract case. What concerned the appeals court was Justice's refusal to recuse himself when one of his former law clerks, Robert Stein, was one of the attorneys involved in the early stages of the lawsuit. Justice had concluded that recusal would not be necessary since Stein had withdrawn from the case when the objection was raised. The Fifth Circuit disagreed. Noting that the law clerk, by virtue of his position, "is obviously privy to his judge's thoughts in a way that the parties cannot be," the court concluded that allowing the proceeding to continue tainted the appearance of impartiality. The appeals court ordered retrial of the case before another judge. Justice was chagrined by the action. "I did not like it one bit that I would be reversed on something like that, especially since at the time I was a member of the Judicial Ethics Committee. After that case, I have been extraordinarily diligent to avoid the appearance of impropriety."
42. Virginia Ellis and Robert M. Feinstein, "Judge Shifts Major Case on Retarded," *Dallas Times Herald*, December 6, 1985.
43. *Lelsz v. Kavanagh*, 807 F.2d 1234 (5th Cir. 1987).
44. Letter from Roger Parloff, June 6, 1989.
45. The Supreme Court recognized in *Youngberg v. Romeo*, 457 U.S. 307 (1982), that the mentally retarded who are involuntarily committed to a state institution have a Fourteenth Amendment right to safe conditions, to freedom from bodily restraint, and to minimally adequate training. The Court emphasized with regard to the latter that "courts must show deference to the judgment exercised by a qualified professional" (p. 322). In *Parham v. J.R.*, 442 U.S. 584 (1979), the Court ruled that while children have no independent constitutional right to challenge the decision of their parents to have them committed to a mental hospital, they are entitled to "some kind of inquiry" by a neutral fact finder such as a physician prior to commitment to assure that state statutory requirements are met (p. 606). In neither decision did the Court explicitly address the issue of treatment in the least restrictive environment, and the Fifth Circuit refused to interpret the rulings to encompass it.
46. *Lelsz v. Kavanagh*, 807 F.2d 1234 (5th Cir. 1987), p. 1250.
47. Ibid., p. 1251.
48. Ibid., p. 1255.
49. Ibid., p. 1256.

50. Ibid., 815 F.2d 1034, p. 1036.

51. A 1987 University of Texas study commissioned by TDMHMR to determine parent or guardian satisfaction with community placement showed overwhelming positive responses. Overall satisfaction with community placement was reported by 92.2 percent of the respondents, compared with 84.3 percent satisfaction for state school residency: Lee Williamson and Catherine M. Ford, *Consumer Satisfaction with Community Placement of Mentally Retarded Clients in the State of Texas: A Preliminary Report* (Austin: University of Texas at Austin, February 27, 1987). Similar results were reported regarding community placement in Pennsylvania following phaseout of the Pennhurst State School and Hospital beginning in 1977. In the Pennhurst study, those making the most rapid progress toward independence in community placements were people with the most severe impairments. The researchers found progress toward independence was ten times greater among community residents than among a matched group of people still at Pennhurst. Initial family opposition reversed itself. See James W. Conroy and Valerie J. Bradley, *The Pennhurst Longitudinal Study* (Philadelphia: Developmental Disabilities Center, Temple University, 1985).

52. *Lelsz v. Kavanagh,* 815 F.2d 1034 (5th Cir. 1987), p. 1035.

53. Ibid., 112 F.R.D. 367 (N.D. Tex. 1986).

54. Ibid., 673 F.Supp. 828 (N.D. Tex. 1987).

55. Ibid., p. 832.

56. The implementation agreement was attached to Judge Sanders' memorandum opinion and order cited in note 54.

57. Through 1988, Texas paid $654,910 in plaintiffs' attorney fees and expenses, and $1,233,466 to defray the cost of the special master's office. Letter from Neal Kelly, Claim Division, Texas Comptroller of Public Accounts, March 15, 1989.

14. Desegregating Public Housing

References from interviews: David D. Brown, November 15, 1988; Michael M. Daniel, April 18, 1989.

1. A notable exception is an interesting decision impacting the health care field and the Department of Health, Education, and Welfare (HEW). The case involved the planning and coordination of health resources to the poor in a nineteen-county area in the north central region of Texas by an agency operating under the auspices of HEW. In accord with provisions in the National Health Planning and Resources Development Act of 1974, 42 U.S.C. Section 300k *et seq.,* HEW officials in 1976 had recognized the Texas Area Five group as the official agency to oversee the provision of health services to the poor in that region of the state. Funding was initiated shortly thereafter. Texas ACORN, a public interest legal group concerned with the interests of low-to-moderate income groups, filed suit, contending that the governing body of the Texas Area Five agency seriously underrepresented poor people.

In a decision which potentially affected health delivery systems for the poor nationwide, Judge Justice agreed with the plaintiffs. He noted that at the time of the lawsuit, only three of the forty-one consumer members of the Texas health systems agency governing board and only two of the thirteen consumer members of the executive committee had annual family incomes below $10,000. He granted plaintiffs' motion for summary judgment and ordered the agency to increase representation of low-income groups so that poor people would constitute approximately half of the board and the executive committee: *Texas ACORN v. Texas Area Five Health Systems Agency,* Civil Action No. S-76-102-CA (E.D. Tex. March 1, 1977).

In reversing Justice's decision, the Fifth Circuit noted that the case raised questions "striking at the heart of this nation's health planning policy and health resources development." *Texas ACORN v. Tex. Area 5 Health Systems Agency,* 559 F.2d 1019 (5th Cir. 1977). For the three-judge panel, Judge Homer Thornberry wrote that Justice had misread the statute and federal regulations. There was no specific requirement that only those with low incomes could represent the poor. He criticized Justice's failure to hold an evidentiary hearing "where, as here, the litigation involves issues of major public importance." "This litigation involves . . . judicial intrusion into the administrative realm. The result here will set precedent for the plight of all HSA's [health systems agencies] and could have a major effect on the national health plan. Courts must make certain that conclusions in cases involving important public questions rest on definite factual foundations. The conclusions in the instant case do not" (p. 1026). The appeals court sent the matter back to Justice, with orders to determine whether the HEW Secretary's decision to recognize the Texas Area Five agency as it was composed was arbitrary, capricious, or an abuse of discretion.

Justice was not pleased. "That was simply not a good decision on the part of the Fifth Circuit. It was unjust. The equities in that case seemed so abundantly plain." In 1979, a congressional conference committee noted that poor people did appear to be underrepresented on health systems boards and prompted HEW to issue corrective regulations: 1979 *U.S. Code Cong. & Admin. News,* p. 1431. HEW did so in 1982, requiring that agency boards include representatives from racial or linguistic population groups, income groups, women, persons over sixty-five, and the handicapped. In order to be considered a representative, the individual had to either be a member of the specific group or have been selected by it: 42 C.F.R. Section 122.109 (1982). Following these changes, the case was settled.

2. *Young v. Pierce,* 544 F.Supp. 1010 (E.D. Tex. 1982).

3. 42 U.S.C. Section 2000d.

4. *Young v. Pierce,* 544 F.Supp. 1010, p. 1015.

5. 42 U.S.C. Sections 3601 and 3608(d)(5).

6. *Young v. Pierce,* 544 F.Supp. 1010, p. 1017.

7. 42 U.S.C. Sections 1981 and 1982.

8. *Young v. Pierce,* 544 F.Supp. 1010, p. 1023.

9. *Young v. Whiteman,* Civil Action No. P-82-37-CA (E.D. Tex. October 11, 1983), p. 2.

10. Record of proceedings, November 25, 1983, p. 15.

11. Steve Blow, "Unsettling Move," *Dallas Morning News,* December 8, 1983.

12. Janet Elliott, "Desegregation in Two Projects Going Smoothly," *Houston Post,* December 15, 1983.

13. "Desegregation Order under Fire," *Houston Post,* December 18, 1983.

14. "Housing Message from Texas," *New York Times,* December 16, 1983.

15. Kyle Thompson, "Home Sweet Home," *Fort Worth Star Telegram,* January 15, 1984.

16. Jim Schultze, "Judge Justice Offers Encouragement for East Texas Blacks," *Dallas Times Herald,* December 19, 1983.

17. Bob Meckel, "Project Residents Mad at Race-Mixing Order," *Houston Post,* December 9, 1983.

18. "Neo-Nazi: Texas Judge in Group's Death File," *Dallas Times Herald,* September 17, 1985.

19. See, for example, Rob Meckel, "Residents Adjust to Integration," *Houston Post,* April 3, 1988.

20. This report of HUD reactions to the Clarksville decision is contained as Appendix 3 to a November 1985 HUD report entitled "Subsidized Housing and Race," which was submitted to a subcommittee of the House Banking Committee. The report was generated after the publication of the *Dallas Morning News* series on segregated public housing, which is discussed in a subsequent paragraph.

21. Ibid., p. 15.

22. Craig Flournoy and George Rodrigue, "Subsidized Housing in America," *Dallas Morning News,* February 11–17, 1985. Justice's Clarksville ruling, together with the newspaper series, spurred U.S. Representative Henry B. González of San Antonio, chairman of the House Subcommittee on Housing and Community Development, to order a committee investigation of housing discrimination. At the same time, the U.S. Commission on Civil Rights also ordered an investigation. See *Issues in Housing Discrimination: A Consultation/Hearing of the U.S. Commission on Civil Rights,* vols. I and II (Washington, D.C., November 12–13, 1985).

23. Flournoy and Rodrigue, "Subsidized Housing in America," February 12, 1985.

24. *General Telephone Co. v. Falcon,* 457 U.S. 147 (1981).

25. *Young v. Pierce,* 628 F.Supp. 1037 (E.D. Tex. 1985), p. 1042.

26. Ibid., p. 1051.

27. Ibid., p. 1056.

28. Ibid., p. 1060.

29. Peter Larson, "Judge: HUD Promotes East Texas Housing Bias," *Dallas Times Herald,* August 1, 1985.

30. Craig Flournoy, "Judge Finds Bias in East Texas Public Housing," *Dallas Morning News,* August 1, 1985.

31. Craig Flournoy, "Attorney to Seek Quick Integration of East Texas Projects," *Dallas Morning News,* August 2, 1985.

32. Ibid.

33. Ibid.

34. *Dallas Morning News,* August 2, 1985.

35. George Rodrigue, "HUD Offers Plan to End Bias in East Texas Public Housing," *Dallas Morning News,* December 28, 1985.

36. *Young v. Pierce,* 640 F.Supp. 1476 (E.D. Tex. 1986), p. 1495.

37. Ibid., p. 1482–1483.

38. Ibid., p. 1483.

39. The three appellate judges were Carolyn Randall, William L. Garwood, and W. Eugene Davis. Randall was appointed by President Carter; Garwood and Davis were Reagan appointees.

40. *Young v. Pierce,* 822 F.2d 1368 (5th Cir. 1987), p. 1373. Plaintiffs' attorneys noted that the U.S. Supreme Court itself had approved such a broad-based approach to remedy housing discrimination in Chicago. For a unanimous Court in *Hills v. Gautreaux,* 425 U.S. 284 (1976), Justice Potter Stewart distinguished a school desegregation ruling where a metropolitan remedy had been disfavored because the suburban school districts surrounding Detroit had not engaged in segregative conduct, though the Detroit school district had: *Milliken v. Bradley,* 418 U.S. 717 (1974). In contrast with the suburban school districts in *Milliken,* HUD was found in the *Hills* ruling to have violated constitutional and statutory prohibitions against racial discrimination in selecting housing sites in the Chicago housing market, a market not confined just to the city. The Court upheld a remedial decree which used HUD's new Section 8 housing program as a desegregative tool, even though the program itself had not been implicated in the segregative action. For a discussion on how integration efforts in Chicago have involved private housing providers in the suburbs since the *Hills* decision, see William E. Schmidt, "Some Chicagoans Are Moved out of Projects into a Future," *New York Times,* February 3, 1989. See also Flournoy and Rodrigue, "Subsidized Housing in America," February 18, 1985.

41. *Young v. Pierce,* 822 F.2d 1368 (5th Cir. 1987). In a companion ruling, the appeals court also remanded Justice's interim award of $465,204 in plaintiffs' attorney fees and $10,202.80 in expenses for reconsideration in light of the settlement: *Young v. Pierce,* 822 F.2d 1376 (5th Cir. 1987).

42. *Young v. Pierce,* 685 F.Supp. 975 (E.D. Tex. 1988), p. 977. Justice cited the Supreme Court's ruling in *Hills v. Gautreaux,* 425 U.S. 284 (1976), in support of this assertion.

43. *Young v. Pierce,* 685 F.Supp. 986 (E.D. Tex. 1988).

44. HUD was required to notify class members periodically of all HUD-assisted low-income housing projects and programs in their areas, including rent-supplement and Section 8 housing. Private providers of public housing under HUD's rent-supplement and Section 8 programs were required to broaden their affirmative-action plans to recruit class members and to give them a priority equal to the special priorities such as need for emergency housing already in place at such sites. These providers were also required to supply information regarding the racial composition of residents and those on the waiting list. HUD was required to designate personnel to assist class members to locate housing in non–racially impacted areas and to respond to complaints. HUD was also required to determine the effect of Section 8 rent levels in the class action counties on desegregation.

Another provision required HUD to give priority to public housing authorities in the provision of funds to end the physical disparities between white and black units. In addition, HUD was required to furnish plaintiffs, the court, and the special master with periodic compliance reports and with detailed information about housing resources and opportunities in the thirty-six-county area.

45. *Young v. Pierce,* 685 F.Supp. 975, p. 982.

46. Ibid., p. 983. The responsibilities, powers, and duties of the special master

were detailed in a brief companion order: *Young v. Pierce,* 685 F.Supp. 984 (E.D. Tex. 1988).

47. At the same time, Daniel maintains that there are pockets of resistance in East Texas. "Vidor and Bridge City, which are notorious Klan cities, were all-white the last time we met with the Department of Housing and Urban Development," he told a reporter in 1988. "They're never going to be desegregated. They'll never let blacks in." The housing director responsible for Vidor denied that the Klan was still active, but admitted, "I don't think Vidor is ready for black families." Rob Michel, "Residents Adjust to Integration," *Houston Post,* April 3, 1988.

15. Prison Reform

References from interviews: George Beto, February 25, 1988, and letter of August 24, 1989; Fritz Byers, August 18, 1988; William P. Clements, Jr., July 18, 1988; Ray Farabee, June 13, 1989; Richard E. Gray, April 15, 1987; William P. Hobby, Jr., September 18, 1989; Ed Idar, August 30, 1988; Gail Littlefield, November 17, 1988; F. Scott McCown, January 6, 1989; Robert McDuff, November 18, 1988; Steve J. Martin, March 2, 1989; Vincent M. Nathan, August 10, 1988; Richel Rivers, August 31, 1988; William Bennett Turner, April 27, 1988; Mark F. Walter, November 16, 1988; Mark White, September 12, 1988.

1. John J. DiIulio, Jr., *Governing Prisons: A Comparative Study of Correctional Management* (New York: Free Press, 1987). The thrust of DiIulio's book is that the quality of prison life depends upon the quality of prison management. DiIulio opts for a system which places primary emphasis on order as a necessary precondition to rehabilitative activities. He presents detailed case studies of the Texas, Michigan, and California prison systems. DiIulio toured Texas prisons and interviewed both prison personnel and inmates. His praise of the control model represented by the Texas system and for former TDC Director Dr. George Beto, who did more than anyone else to establish it, is extensive. DiIulio recognizes the abuses and credits Judge Justice for eliminating them.

2. Ibid., p. 53.

3. Steve J. Martin and Sheldon Ekland-Olson, *Texas Prisons: The Walls Came Tumbling Down* (Austin: Texas Monthly Press, 1987). This book provides a much harsher view of Texas prison affairs than the DiIulio volume. DiIulio did not have the same intimate knowledge of TDC affairs that Martin had as a TDC staff attorney.

4. Ibid., p. 176.

5. Speech delivered at the Practicing Law Institute seminar, Southern Methodist University, Dallas, 1972. Subsequently published in *Texas Law Review* 51 (1973): 720.

6. Turner and another civil rights lawyer, Frances Jalet, represented two prisoners, Ronald Novak and Fred Cruz, in a late 1960s lawsuit involving prisoner-to-prisoner legal assistance and conditions in solitary confinement (inmates assigned to solitary were fed a bread-and-water diet). When Beto banned Jalet from the prison system and retaliated against the writ-writers in 1971, Turner was one of the attorneys representing them in several cases. See note 15 below for more information about these cases.

7. *Ruiz v. Estelle,* Civil Action No. 5523 (E.D. Tex. 1974). Order of April 12, 1974.

8. *Lamar v. Coffield,* Civil Action No. 72-H-1393, Consent Decree (S.D. Tex. 1977).

9. *In re W. J. Estelle, Jr.,* 516 F.2d 480 (5th Cir. 1975).

10. *Estelle v. Justice,* 426 U.S. 925 (1976). Judge Justice notes that several sessions later, "Congress cut Justice Rehnquist off at the pass" when it enacted legislation authorizing the Justice Department to institute civil suits against a state or political subdivision of a state when there is reasonable cause to believe that confined persons are being denied their rights under the U.S. Constitution or federal laws: Civil Rights of Institutionalized Persons Act, 42 U.S.C. Section 1997 *et seq.* (1980). For prisoners, only constitutional rights violations are actionable: 42 U.S.C. Section 1997(a). Ed Idar, Jr., the lead counsel for the state, regards the need for congressional action as vindication of the state's position that the Justice Department was without authority to intervene as a plaintiff in the lawsuit.

11. This speech has been published: William Wayne Justice, "The Origins of *Ruiz v. Estelle,*" *Stanford Law Review* 43, no. 1 (November 1990).

12. Ben M. Crouch and James W. Marquart, *An Appeal to Justice: Litigated Reform of Texas Prisons* (Austin: University of Texas Press, 1989), p. 84. The history and nature of the building tender system is described in detail in Chapter 4 of this volume.

13. DiIulio, *Governing Prisons,* p. 177.

14. *Cooper v. Pate,* 378 U.S. 546 (1964).

15. Early on, the prisoners began experiencing some success in federal courts other than Justice's. In 1971 prisoners Ronald Novak and Fred Cruz, represented by prisoner rights lawyers Frances Jalet and William Bennett Turner, successfully challenged a TDC rule prohibiting prisoners from assisting one another in legal matters: *Novak v. Beto,* 453 F.2d 661 (5th Cir. 1971). When the *Novak* decision was not effectively implemented, a second lawsuit, which eventually forced compliance, was started in 1972: *Corpus and Sellars v. Estelle,* 409 F.Supp. 1090, *aff'd* 551 F.2d 68 (5th Cir. 1977). In 1972 the U.S. Supreme Court in a *per curiam* decision reversed a Fifth Circuit ruling and upheld the right of Fred Cruz, one of the early writ-writers and a Buddhist, to use the prison chapel in the same manner as prisoners of other faiths: *Cruz v. Beto I,* 405 U.S. 319 (1972).

The successes prompted the TDC—or inmates acting in its stead—to counterattack in a suit against attorney Jalet alleging that she was fomenting revolutionary ideals and encouraging violence in TDC: *Dreyer v. Jalet,* 349 F.Supp. 452 (S.D. Tex. 1972). During the six-week trial, the court heard ample evidence that TDC prisoners were subject to shocking repression and harassment, but there was little evidence that a conspiracy existed between the writ-writers and their lawyers to subvert the prison system. The court threw out the suit, and the Fifth Circuit affirmed in a brief *per curiam* opinion: 479 F.2d 1044.

Beto barred Jalet from the TDC in September 1971. Together with a dozen of her writ-writer clients, she filed suit against Beto alleging that he had unlawfully barred her from seeing her clients and that in isolating the inmate activists, he had deprived them of privileges enjoyed by the general prison population. A federal district court in the Southern District found Beto's actions unlawful and assessed more than $10,000 in money damages against him. The Fifth Circuit upheld the lower court decision: *Cruz v. Beto II,* 603 F.2d 1178 (5th Cir. 1979).

These and other early prisoner rights cases are discussed in some detail in Martin and Ekland-Olson, *Texas Prisons,* Chapter 2.

16. Final Report of the Joint Committee on Prison Reform, 63rd Legislature, December 1974.

17. Crouch and Marquart, *An Appeal to Justice,* p. 120.

18. Ibid. Another factor was opposition from top political leaders to early release via the parole process. By 1980 Governor Clements was routinely vetoing 30 percent of the parole recommendations he received: ibid., p. 134.

19. Beto believes that only hardened, dangerous criminals should be confined in prisons. All others should be handled through alternative correctional programs at the community level.

20. *Ruiz v. Estelle,* 550 F.2d 238 (5th Cir. 1977), *per curiam,* p. 239. The details surrounding the issuing of these protective orders are described in Martin and Ekland-Olson, *Texas Prisons,* pp. 98–104.

21. *Ruiz v. Estelle,* 503 F.Supp. 1265 (S.D. Tex. 1980), p. 1391.

22. Ibid. The characteristics of the TDC prison population are revealing and are central to considering the purpose of prisons and conditions of confinement (see pp. 1274–1275). On the eve of trial in 1978, 96 percent of the prisoners were male. Crime is thus preponderantly a male activity. Forty-three percent were black, 39 percent white, and 19 percent of Hispanic ancestry. The fact that a substantial majority are members of minority groups supports the view that social and economic conditions are major factors in creating a propensity for criminal behavior. It might also be indicative of latent racism in the criminal justice system. Over 60 percent were from the Dallas–Fort Worth, Houston, and San Antonio urban communities. Increasing urbanization in the state thus contributes to the problem of prison overcrowding. The mean age of TDC inmates was 29.58, with 41 percent twenty-five years of age or younger. More than 60 percent of new admissions in 1978 were first-time offenders.

The average maximum sentence of all inmates was 23.54 years. Some 20 percent of the inmates were incarcerated for violent crimes, 65 percent for crimes of property, and 15 percent for other offenses. The high percentage of inmates confined for crimes of property helps account for the perpetual crowding problem. Many states are moving toward community-based corrections for these inmates.

The mean IQ for TDC inmates in 1978 was 93.92. Expert witnesses testified that 10 to 15 percent of the inmates were mentally retarded. Five percent of the inmates were considered acutely mentally ill, and as many as 65 percent were considered mentally or emotionally disturbed. Thirty percent had histories of serious alcohol abuse; a similar percentage had records of drug abuse and dependency.

Fifteen percent of the prisoners were illiterate. Eighty-five percent were high school dropouts. Of these, 50 percent had less than a fifth-grade education. The average reading ability of a TDC inmate was approximately at the sixth-grade level. Most experts agree that the vast majority of lawbreakers are never apprehended. Those who are caught tend to be, in the words of George Beto, "the poor, the stupid, and the inept."

23. *Ruiz v. Estelle,* p. 1391.

24. Ibid.

25. Ibid., p. 1281. The "law-and-order" philosophy prevalent in the TDC and in Texas generally stood in the way of alternatives to incarceration, even if they might be less expensive. Testimony at the trial showed that TDC had made little headway in implementing a Texas statute mandating a work-release program which would have both reduced crowding and saved money: Tex. Rev. Civ. Stat. Ann. Art. 6166x-3 (Vernon 1988).

26. Record of proceedings, August 28, 1979, pp. 128–131.

27. *Ruiz v. Estelle,* p. 1290.

28. Ibid., p. 1292.

29. Tex. Rev. Civ. Stat. Ann. Art. 6184K-1 (Vernon's Supp. 1980). Section 1 provided that "An inmate in the custody of the Texas Department of Corrections or in any jail in this state may not act in a supervisory or administrative capacity over other inmates." Section 2 stated, "An inmate in the custody of the Texas Department of Corrections or in any jail in this state may not administer disciplinary action over another inmate." George Beto maintains that this law did not preclude the use of building tenders for nondisciplinary and nonsupervisory purposes. "In those cell-blocks, some convict is going to rise to a position of authority. To oversimplify, either you pick them or they pick them. I wanted to pick them." The primary purpose of the building tenders during his years as TDC director, Beto asserts, was to serve as informants. But testimony in early litigation against the TDC suggests otherwise (see note 15 above). By the time of the *Ruiz* trial, the abuses of the building tender system were clearly evident. As one proponent of the control model concludes, "In the BT system, the control model contained the seeds of its own destruction. . . . The BT system had given rise to horrible abuses of inmates by their specially anointed peers and had permitted, even encouraged, the victimization of inmates by staff" (DiIulio, *Governing Prisons,* pp. 208–209).

30. *Ruiz v. Estelle,* 503 F.Supp. 1265 (S.D. Tex. 1980), p. 1298.

31. Ibid., p. 1299. For a detailed examination of the TDC guard system and how it operated prior to *Ruiz,* see Chapter 3 in Crouch and Marquart, *An Appeal to Justice.* Both of the authors had served as TDC prison guards.

32. *Ruiz v. Estelle,* 503 F.Supp. 1265, p. 1312, note 96.

33. Ibid., p. 1345.

34. *Wolff v. McDonnell,* 418 U.S. 539 (1974).

35. *Ruiz v. Estelle,* 503 F.Supp. 1265, p. 1351.

36. Ibid., p. 1363.

37. Ibid., p. 1369.

38. Ibid., p. 1370.

39. Ibid., p. 1382.

40. Ibid., p. 1384.

41. Ibid., p. 1386.

42. Felton West and Richard Vara, "White Says Decision Likely to Cost State Millions," *Houston Post,* December 13, 1980.

43. See, for example, "Prison Director Lambasts Judge Justice's Partiality, Literary Skills," *San Antonio Express,* February 21, 1982.

44. West and Vara, "White Says Decision Likely to Cost State Millions."

45. Martin and Ekland-Olson, *Texas Prisons,* p. 178. The order is included as an appendix to a later Fifth Circuit opinion: *Ruiz v. Estelle,* 666 F.2d 854 (5th Cir. 1982).

46. Richard Vara, "Texas Told to Cut Prison Population or Reject Inmates," *Houston Post,* April 21, 1981.

47. Ibid.

48. *Houston Post,* January 29, 1981.

49. Ibid., February 11, 1981.

50. Martin and Ekland-Olson, *Texas Prisons,* offer a detailed discussion of the major events in the case through 1987 from the legal and political perspective. Crouch and Marquart, *An Appeal to Justice,* cover much the same ground but with emphasis on the sociological impact of the events on life within the prisons.

51. "Prison vs. Court in Texas," *Newsweek,* February 22, 1982, p. 27.

52. Martin and Ekland-Olson, *Texas Prisons,* p. 201.

53. Record of proceedings, March 29, 1982, pp. 6–7.

54. Toward the later stages of the litigation, the Justice Department played less and less of a role in the critically important settlement process and in working with Turner to enforce the court's orders. At one point, Turner sought to remove the government from the case, arguing that the Reagan administration was siding with the state and no longer acting as plaintiff-intervenor. After keeping the motion under advisement for some time, Justice denied it.

55. Martin and Ekland-Olson, *Texas Prisons,* p. 187. Martin and Ekland-Olson estimate that during the three years the Fulbright and Jaworski firm, along with other outside attorneys, worked on the case, the cost to the state was over $2 million in legal fees (see p. 186). Justice Department attorney Gail Littlefield recalls that the state strongly resisted discovery of the amounts paid to the Fulbright and Jaworski firm (letter, February 15, 1989).

56. *Rhodes v. Chapman,* 452 U.S. 337 (1981).

57. Ibid., p. 349.

58. Ibid., p. 352.

59. *Ruiz v. Estelle,* 679 F.2d 1115 (5th Cir. 1982), p. 1132.

60. Ibid., p. 1145.

61. Ibid., p. 1148.

62. Ibid.

63. See the discussion of *Lelsz v. Kavanagh* in Chapter 14.

64. *Ruiz v. Estelle,* 679 F.2d 1115, p. 1154.

65. Stan Jones, "Court Guts Portions of Prison Order," *Fort Worth Star-Telegram,* June 23, 1982.

66. "Prison Case: State Can Do It," *Dallas Morning News,* June 25, 1982.

67. In a related development, a different panel of Fifth Circuit judges ruled two years later that in the interest of consistent application of the *Ruiz* order, all allegations of prisoner rights violations anywhere in the TDC were to be channeled through Justice's court. In addition to concern about consistency, the action constituted a mild rebuke to Justice's undertaking to reform the Texas Department of Corrections. "Being able to see prison litigation that implicates the terms of its decree may . . . indicate to the *Ruiz* court that its decree should be modified to be more or less inclusive," wrote Chief Judge Clark for himself and Judges Henry A. Politz and Sam D.

Johnson. *Johnson v. McKaskle,* 727 F.2d 498 (5th Cir. 1984), p. 501. Justice was determined to master his new, unwanted responsibilities, though he acknowledges that "it placed a crushing burden on this court. For a couple of years there, I was running as fast as I could."

To assist him with the addition of over a thousand cases to his already burgeoning caseload, he requested three additional law clerks. The Fifth Circuit approved the request. The Judge and his clerks worked out a system for deciding how prison complaints were to be processed. Many were referred back to the courts from which they originated for hearings and recommendations for disposition by magistrates. But since neither the magistrates nor other district court judges were familiar with the complex *Ruiz* order, they had trouble following it. As Justice explains, "The orders that I entered had the prospect of making many prisoners' cases quite a lengthy procedure. And if the magistrates did everything that I required of them to do, it had the effect of tripling their workload. They were crying for relief." Additionally, as former law clerk Mark Walter observes, "It got touchy when the case would be referred back to the initiating judge with instructions from Judge Justice."

A year and a half later, the Fifth Circuit panel withdrew its previous mandate and allowed prisoner rights cases to be heard in the district courts where the disputes arose: *Johnson v. McKaskle,* No. 82-2472 (5th Cir., Dec. 5, 1985) (unreported). Attached to the brief *per curiam* order were guidelines established by the Fifth Circuit Judicial Council, an administrative body, for handling cases subject to the orders entered by Judge Justice. Included was one provision affirming Justice's continuing jurisdiction over *Ruiz v. Estelle* (then known as *Ruiz v. McCotter,* since Estelle had left the Texas Department of Corrections).

68. The report prepared by Dr. F. Warren Benton and Don Stoughton, had been attached as an appendix to the *Nineteenth Monitor's Report of Factual Observations to the Special Master—Report on Section I,C of the Amended Decree (Use of Force).* It stated, "It is a difficult and precarious business to manage and operate any prison or prison system, and it is going to be doubly so for the State of Texas during this transition period and for the foreseeable future. Maintaining the capacity to control and manage the prisoners will require numerous changes in operational practice, and perhaps in law. This process will need the support of elected officials and other policy makers. If these things do not occur and prisoners realize they have nothing to fear and nothing to lose, TDC institutions will become unmanageable and very dangerous" (p. 4 of the report).

69. Tex. Rev. Civ. Stat. Ann. Art. 6184o (Vernon 1988). The statute requires the director to inform the governor whenever the prison population exceeds 94 percent of capacity as defined by the Texas Board of Corrections. (The TDC's definition of "capacity" is consistent with that agreed to in the overcrowding stipulation.) If the population exceeds 95 percent, the law specifies the steps to be taken to secure early releases by awarding good time and advancing parole eligibility.

70. In his order denying the move, Justice noted that the best available evidence was to the contrary: Order, September 19, 1986.

71. *Ruiz v. Lynaugh,* 811 F.2d 856 (5th Cir. 1987), *per curiam.*

72. Correspondence with Steve Martin, March 8, 1989. Martin cites as an example a February 1983 show-cause contempt hearing over failure of Wynne Unit administrators to implement an administrative segregation plan. At the hearing,

evidence was introduced showing that a building tender who had been the subject of considerable testimony at trial regarding abuses of the building tender system was still operating as a building tender and living in an open cell at Eastham—some six months after settlement of the building tender issue. Rather than issue an order or threaten any further sanctions, Justice asked Martin and attorney Richard Gray to look into the matter and take whatever steps were necessary to insure that the inmate would not act as a building tender.

73. Order, December 31, 1986, p. 72.

74. The Mississippi judge was Chief Judge William C. Keady of the U.S. District Court for the Northern District of Mississippi, who had acted in the face of state intransigence in implementing his order in a prison case. Keady's unpublished order was affirmed in *Gates v. Collier,* 616 F.2d 1268 (5th Cir. 1980).

75. Raul Reyes, "Clements Eager to Discuss Prison Reform with Justice," *Dallas Times Herald,* January 8, 1987.

76. Jim Phillips, "Fear of Fines on Prisons Less after Hearings," *Austin American-Statesman,* April 15, 1987.

77. The explosive growth of the prison population in Texas reflects a national trend. The prison population since 1970 has doubled despite a stabilized crime rate. Peter Applebome, "With Inmates at Record High, Sentence Policy Is Reassessed," *New York Times,* April 25, 1988.

78. Serious overcrowding with all of its attendant problems of safety and sanitation in the Harris County Jail in Houston prompted Chief Judge James DeAnda of the Southern District to issue an order late in 1988 requiring TDC to accept prisoners awaiting transfer to TDC units: *Alberti v. Klevenhagen,* Civil Action No. H-72-1094 (S.D. Tex. November 8, 1988). The *Alberti* case is a long-standing class action lawsuit against the sheriff of Harris County and others over conditions in the jail. When TDC refused to accede to Judge DeAnda's order, the *Alberti* defendants sought a writ of mandamus from the Fifth Circuit to compel TDC to do so. TDC officials argued that if they were to accept the prisoners, they would be violating the *Ruiz* order and settlements. The Fifth Circuit agreed that "mandamus should issue requiring the transfer, to the judge presiding over the *Ruiz* case, of so much of the *remedy* portion of the *Alberti* third-party action against our individual petitioners . . . as seeks to enjoin them to receive or take prisoners into TDC confinement (or to otherwise take action in the operation or management of TDC-operated confinement facilities)." *In re William P. Clements,* No. 89-2706 (5th Cir. August 11, 1989). By its action, the Fifth Circuit forced cooperation between Judges Justice and DeAnda, and their respective special masters, in working out an equitable solution to overcrowding in the Harris County Jail, which accounts for a quarter of all inmates sent to TDC.

79. Correspondence from the Claims Division of the Texas Comptroller of Public Accounts, August 9, 1988. The Justice Department's costs were borne by the federal government.

80. These figures were obtained from correspondence with Larry Farnsworth, TDC Coordinator of Research, September 12, 1988, and from a telephone conversation with Neal Kelly, Claims Division, Office of the State Comptroller of Public Accounts, on November 28, 1988. The figures do not include money appropriated for capital expenditures.

81. This figure is obtained from statistics contained in *The Corrections Yearbook* (South Salem, N.Y.: Criminal Justice Institute, 1988).

82. Of this amount, $213 million was for additional capacity including new construction and was appropriated for the 1988–1989 biennium.

83. Crouch and Marquart, *An Appeal to Justice*, p. 179. Chapter 6 of this volume explores in some detail the impact of *Ruiz* on the TDC prison staff. In addition to survey data, the authors include numerous excerpts from interviews they conducted, mostly at the Eastham maximum security unit.

84. Ibid. Crouch and Marquart explore the impact of *Ruiz* on the prison population in Chapter 7. Their discussion is based both on inmate interviews and on a 1987 survey of a random sample of 460 inmates in eight TDC units, most of them housing violent multiple recidivists. They also conducted inmate interviews.

85. See, for example, Dick J. Reavis, "How They Ruined Our Prisons," *Texas Monthly,* May 1985.

86. Crouch and Marquart, *An Appeal to Justice*, p. 183.

87. Ibid., p. 232.

88. David Ruiz was transferred to federal prison in 1979 because of fears for his safety in the TDC. But in the spring of 1988, Judge Justice approved his transfer back to the Texas prison system. Ruiz had requested the transfer so that he could be closer to his family in Austin and could work on his Texas appeal. Ruiz is serving a life term for armed robbery and twenty-five years for aggravated perjury, and will not be eligible for parole until 2004. He received the life term for the September 1984 robbery of three men and a woman in Austin, following his parole on a earlier charge. His criminal trial lawyer told reporters at the time of his transfer that "David Ruiz, I'm afraid, will never get out of prison alive. I think they will murder him in prison" (as quoted in Douglas Freelander, "Inmate Comes Back to Texas despite Danger," *Dallas Times Herald,* May 27, 1988). While in federal prison in Terre Haute, Indiana, Ruiz was knifed as part of a contract put out on him and a fellow inmate.

89. Crouch and Marquart, *An Appeal to Justice*, p. 235.

90. According to one commentator, most states spend an average of $65 a day on housing an inmate. Electronic bracelets which monitor a prisoner at home cost $8 a day, while parole supervision costs 99 cents a day. Jonathan Turley, "Our Prison Profiteers," *New York Times,* August 3, 1990.

16. A Measure of Human Dignity

References from interviews: Ray Farabee, June 13, 1989; William P. Hobby, Jr., September 18, 1989.

1. William Wayne Justice, "The New Awakening: Judicial Activism in a Conservative Age," *Southwestern Law Review* 43, no. 2 (October 1989): 657–676.

2. Ibid., p. 658.

3. Ibid., p. 665.

4. Ibid., p. 671. The article he referred to was H. Jefferson Powell, "The Original Understanding of Original Intent," *Harvard Law Review* 98, no. 5 (March 1985): 885–948.

5. For a provocative advancement of the strict-constructionist viewpoint, see Robert Bork, *The Tempting of America* (New York: Free Press, 1990). Bork takes direct aim at both conservative and liberal activists, though most of his criticism is leveled at the latter, whom he accuses of doing nothing more than reading their own liberal moral values into the Constitution.

6. Justice, "The New Awakening," p. 674.

7. Ibid., p. 675.

8. Abram Chayes, "The Role of the Judge in Public Law Litigation," *Harvard Law Review* 89, no. 7 (May 1976): 1302.

Case Index

Index of Names and Topics